Windows 7 and Vista Guide to Scripting, Automation, and Command Line Tools

Brian Knittel

800 East 96th Street
Indianapolis, IN 46240 USA

D1509670

Windows 7 and Vista: Guide to Scripting, Automation, and Command Line Tools

ISBN-13: 978-0-7897-3728-1
ISBN-10: 0-7897-3728-0

Library of Congress Cataloging-in-Publication data is on file.

Printed in the United States of America

First Printing: December 2010

Trademarks

All terms mentioned in this book that are known to be trademarks or service marks have been appropriately capitalized. Que Publishing cannot attest to the accuracy of this information. Use of a term in this book should not be regarded as affecting the validity of any trademark or service mark.

Warning and Disclaimer

Every effort has been made to make this book as complete and as accurate as possible, but no warranty or fitness is implied. The information provided is on an "as is" basis. The author and the publisher shall have neither liability nor responsibility to any person or entity with respect to any loss or damages arising from the information contained in this book.

Bulk Sales

Que Publishing offers excellent discounts on this book when ordered in quantity for bulk purchases or special sales. For more information, please contact

U.S. Corporate and Government Sales
1-800-382-3419
corpsales@pearsontechgroup.com

For sales outside of the United States, please contact

International Sales
international@pearson.com

Associate Publisher
Greg Wiegand

Acquisitions Editor
Rick Kughen

Development Editor
Todd Brakke

Managing Editor
Sandra Schroeder

Project Editor
Mandie Frank

Copy Editor
Megan Wade

Indexer
Tim Wright

Proofreader
Jovana Shirley

Technical Editor
Ron Barrett

Publishing Coordinator
Cindy Teeters

Designer
Anne Jones

Compositor
Studio Galou, LLC

Contents at a Glance

Table of Contents

About the Author

Brian Knittel has been a software developer for more than 30 years. After doing graduate work in electrical engineering applied to nuclear medicine and magnetic resonance imaging technologies, he began a career as an independent consultant. An eclectic mix of clients has led to long-term projects in medical documentation; workflow management; real-time industrial system control; and, most importantly, over 25 years of real-world experience with MS-DOS, Windows, and computer networking in the business world. Brian has coauthored Que's *Windows 7 In Depth*; *Upgrading and Repairing Microsoft Windows*; and bestselling books in the *Special Edition Using* series covering Windows Vista, Windows XP Professional and Home Edition, and Windows 2000 Professional.

Brian lives in Oakland, California. He spends his free time restoring antique computers (for example, www.ibm1130.org) and trying to perfect his wood-fired pizza recipes.

Dedication

To the teachers and staff of San Rafael High School, who gave me an education for which I am still grateful every day, more than 30 years later.

Acknowledgments

I had a conversation with Que Executive Editor Rick Kughen several years ago about the nifty but unglamorous tools and programs that are provided with Windows, the tools we somehow never have room to write about in those thick *In Depth* and *Special Edition Using* tomes. Perhaps I caught him at a weak and confused moment, for he suggested that I ought to write a book about them and that Que ought to publish it. That led to *Windows XP Under the Hood* and now this revised and enhanced second-edition titled *Windows 7 and Vista Guide to Scripting, Automation, and Command Line Tools*. I bring this up because this was and is quite an honor. It's not every day that a publisher says, in essence, "If you're excited about this, we are too." So, to start with, I thank Rick Kughen for his confidence in me and in this project, and for his unflagging support, patience, encouragement, guidance, and lots more patience. All that, and the guy is kind, funny, and one heck of a fisherman to boot.

It's an honor to work with a highly respected publisher like Que. Thanks to Associate Publisher Greg Wiegand and the rest of the outstanding Que team during this arduous project. This book would not have made any sense at all, or at least, it would not make whatever sense it does make without Todd Brakke's hand in developing and editing it. I am grateful for his organizational guidance and enthusiasm for the material. Also, many, many thanks to Megan Wade for amazing attention to detail in copy editing. Don't let those job descriptions fool you—at Que at least, titles such as "development editor" and "copy editor" don't begin to describe the breadth of the contributions that each team member makes to each book.

I'd also like to acknowledge the support of our technical editor Ron Barrett, who meticulously tried every sample program and example. Then, there is an entire army of people who labor largely unseen and unthanked—the people who do the real work. I'd like to thank the editorial, indexing, layout, art, proofing, and other production staff at Que. And finally, thanks to Mandie Frank for managing the whole project through its erratic course.

We Want to Hear from You!

As the reader of this book, *you* are our most important critic and commentator. We value your opinion and want to know what we're doing right, what we could do better, what areas you'd like to see us publish in, and any other words of wisdom you're willing to pass our way.

As an associate publisher for Que Publishing, I welcome your comments. You can email or write me directly to let me know what you did or didn't like about this book—as well as what we can do to make our books better.

Please note that I cannot help you with technical problems related to the topic of this book. We do have a User Services group, however, where I will forward specific technical questions related to the book.

When you write, please be sure to include this book's title and author as well as your name, email address, and phone number. I will carefully review your comments and share them with the author and editors who worked on the book.

Email: feedback@quepublishing.com

Mail: Greg Wiegand
            Associate Publisher
            Que Publishing
            800 East 96th Street
            Indianapolis, IN 46240 USA

Reader Services

Visit our website and register this book at informit.com/title/9780789737281 for convenient access to any updates, downloads, or errata that might be available for this book.

Introduction

Although this book has a brand new title, it is really an updated and revised second edition to *Windows XP: Under The Hood*. The first edition's automotive-themed title came about because of a certain nostalgia that I felt and I know many people share: Don't you long for the good-old days when you could pop the hood of your car and recognize what was underneath? When you could take a wrench and fix just about anything yourself? Cars aren't like that anymore; they've gotten so complex and intimidating that it's hard to imagine digging into one now.

Many of us have come to feel the same way about Windows. Windows has grown into a huge operating system with thousands of complex parts masked behind a slick but seemingly impenetrable graphical user interface (GUI).

This book is an attempt to reclaim those days when we could dig into our machines with confidence and satisfaction. Windows comes with powerful tools and interfaces that let you take control of every detail, if you're willing to roll up your sleeves and dive in.

Whether you're a Windows system administrator or a "power user" who's always on the lookout for more effective ways to use your computer, you're probably familiar with batch files, scripts, and command-line programs. Although they might seem unglamorous, they've been around longer than the PC itself, and sooner or later everyone who uses a computer for serious work runs into them. They might seem like something out of the past, but they've continued to evolve along with Windows. The automation tools provided with Windows are incredibly powerful and useful.

For most people, though, they remain mysterious and are seldom used. I wrote this book to help dispel the mystery. I have five aims in mind:

- To teach how to use the batch file and scripting languages provided with Windows.

- To show how to use command-line utilities and scripting objects as everyday tools.

- To provide an introduction to and reference for the hundreds of command-line programs and scripting objects provided with Windows.

- To provide an introduction to Windows PowerShell, Microsoft's newest command-line automation tool.

- To show you, above all, how you can *learn* to use these tools. No one book is going to solve all your Windows problems. This book teaches you how all these tools work and how to organize your scripting efforts, so you can go beyond canned solutions and create your own.

Although several books on the market are devoted to Windows Script Host, Windows PowerShell, Windows automation tools, and one or two cover Windows command-line utilities, this is the only book I know that combines all four in one volume.

In this book, I explicitly cover Windows 7, Vista, and XP. You can also use the techniques I show you with Windows Server operating systems and Windows 2000 Professional, if you still have that floating around.

Why Learn About This Stuff?

In the age of the GUI, you might wonder why you should spend time learning about scripts, batch files, and command-line programs. Aren't they part of the past, something we can leave behind with a big sigh of relief?

Well, obviously, I don't think so, or I wouldn't have spent months and months slaving away over a hot keyboard, in the dark, just for you. And in case guilt alone isn't enough to make you buy this book, I have some actual good reasons for you.

To begin, here are some important points about scripts and batch files:

- They let you make quick work of repetitive tasks. When you have a large number of files or items to process, or when you perform the same tasks day after day, automation can save you an amazing amount of time. Sure, you can point-and-click your way through running a file through several different programs or adding a user to your network, but when you have to do this job a few hundred times, the graphical approach is a nightmare.

- They encapsulate knowledge and serve as a form of documentation because they record in precise terms how to perform a job. If you write a script or batch file to perform some management function, years from now it can remind you or your successors what the job entails. This makes good business sense.

- They let you use the "insides" of application programs, such as Word and Excel, as tools to write your own programs.

- They let you write procedures that can manipulate files and settings not only on your own computer, but on others in your organization, over your network. Whether you have dozens or thousands of computers to manage, scripting functions can "push" changes to computers without requiring you to physically visit each one.

- They let you write procedures to "reset" a computer's environment to a standard, known configuration. Logon scripts, especially, can set up printers, mapped network drives, and Control Panel settings the same way every time a user logs on, thus eliminating support headaches and user confusion.

If that's the case for learning about scripting and batch files, then how about command-line utilities? Hear ye:

- Many Windows administration, maintenance, and repair functions don't appear anywhere in the Windows GUI. They're found in command-line programs only.

- Sometimes it's faster to type a few letters than to poke around the screen with a mouse!

- Because most command-line utilities are designed to act on data or text files in some particular useful way, you can often use command-line programs as building blocks to perform complex tasks such as sorting, extracting, and formatting information. Instead of writing a custom program, you sometimes use a series of command-line programs to get the job done with little effort. Think of command-line programs as the scissors and staplers on your computer desktop.

Although the Windows GUI has all the flash and gets all the attention, you can see that these behind-the-scenes tools are the real "meat" of the Windows operating system.

How This Book Is Organized

Although this book advances logically from beginning to end, it's written so you can jump in at any location, get the information you need quickly, and get out. You don't have to read it from start to finish, nor do you need to work through complex tutorials. (Even if you're familiar with the material, though, you should at least skim through the references because the batch file language and Windows Script Host program have evolved considerably over the years.)

This book is broken into four major parts. Here's the skinny on each one:

- Part I, "Scripting with Windows Script Host," covers the Windows Script Host tool, introduces the VBScript programming language, discusses the use of objects, and describes the process of writing and debugging scripts. It also provides a detailed reference for many of the scripting objects provided with Windows.

- Part II, "The Command-Line Environment," describes the Windows command language used to write batch files. The batch language has been enhanced considerably since its origin in MS-DOS, and it has become a much more useful way to automate the manipulation of files and directories. Part II also discusses the command-line environment, MS-DOS emulation, and the ways to alter the command environment through administrative tools. Finally, there is a guided tour of the 20 or so most important command-line programs provided with Windows, covering text file management, networking utilities, GUI shortcuts, and more.

- Part III, "Introduction to Windows PowerShell," introduces Windows PowerShell, Microsoft's newest and most peculiar command-line scripting environment. PowerShell is a powerful, and somewhat unusual, programming language. You can use it to perform general-purpose computing, to munch on files and all sorts of data, and to manage Windows workstations, servers and applications. You'll definitely find it worth investigating.

- Finally, Part IV, "Appendices," gives you concise references and indexes to the tools discussed in this book. Where appropriate, items include page references to the sections of the book where you can find information that is more detailed. There is also an index of sample scripts and batch files you can use as a starting point for your own projects. You can download these scripts and files from www.helpwin7.com/scripting. There you can also download some additional bonus appendixes we love but couldn't fit into this printed edition.

Within these sections, each chapter follows a common pattern. An introduction explains a particular type of tool or programming scheme, a reference section describes the tool in exhausting detail, and finally, a discussion shows how to use the tool to apply to real-world programs. I chose this structure because I want this book to serve both as a tutorial for readers who are new to these techniques and as a reference for readers who are familiar with the techniques, but just need a quick refresher.

I also want the material to be somewhat challenging. The early chapters on Windows Script Host and objects take more of a "tutorial" approach, but then the pace picks up. I hope I leave you with some questions unanswered and a few puzzles unsolved; because in your own pursuit of the answers, you learn more than you ever could from reading any book.

Conventions Used in This Book

To help you get the most from this book, special conventions and elements are used throughout.

Text Conventions

Various text conventions in this book identify terms and other special objects. These special conventions include the following:

Convention	Meaning
Italic	New terms or phrases when initially defined.
`Monospace`	Information that appears in code or onscreen or information you type.
Command sequences	All Windows book publishers struggle with how to represent command sequences when menus and dialog boxes are involved. In this book, we separate commands using a comma. Yeah, we know it's confusing, but this is traditionally how Que does it, and traditions die hard. For example, the instruction "choose Edit, Cut" means that you should open the Edit menu and choose Cut.
Key combinations	Key combinations are represented with a plus sign. For example, if the text calls for you to press Ctrl+Alt+Delete, you would press the Ctrl, Alt, and Delete keys at the same time.

In this book's reference lists, which describe the syntax and use of programming statements and objects, the following conventions are used:

Convention	Meaning
`boldface()`	Text and symbols in boldface are to be typed literally.
`italic`	Italics indicate names and values to be replaced by your own data.
`[options]`	Square brackets indicate optional items that are not required. The brackets are not to be typed in.
`{choice A	choice B}`	Curly brackets and the vertical bar (|) indicate items from which you make a choice of one alternative.
`item [, item...]`	Ellipses (...) indicate items that might be repeated as many times as desired.

Special Elements

Throughout this book, you find reference lists, patterns, tips, notes, cautions, cross-references, and sidebars. These items stand out from the rest of the text so you know they're of special interest.

Reference Lists

Reference Lists

Describe the syntax and usage of programming statements, object properties and methods, and command-line programs.

Patterns

Pattern

Patterns show how to solve a particular programming problem in a way that you can use in many situations. They provide a general-purpose way of going about some computing task.

Tips

Tip

Tips give you down-and-dirty advice on getting things done the quickest, safest, or most reliable way. Tips give you the expert's advantage.

Notes

Note

Notes are visual "heads-up" elements. Sometimes they just give you background information on a topic, but more often they point out special circumstances and potential pitfalls in some Windows features.

Cautions

Caution

Pay attention to cautions! They could save you precious hours in lost work.

Cross-References

Cross-references point you to other locations in this book (or other books in the Que family) that provide supplemental or supporting information. Cross-references appear as follows:

➜ For more information on Hollerith cards, see Chapter 1, "Windows Script Host," p. 9

Sidebars

> **Sidebar**
>
> Sidebars provide information that is ancillary to the topic being discussed. Read this information if you want to learn more details about an application or task.

1

Windows Script Host

IN THIS CHAPTER

- Start here to learn the mechanics of writing and running script files.

- This chapter is an overview of scripting, scripting languages, and the commands used to run scripts.

- After you've started writing scripts, return to this chapter for a refresher on the Script Debugger.

- The last section tells where to go on the Internet to get scripting questions answered and to get more information.

What Is a Windows Script?

The short answer to this question might be "a program written in an interpreted language with access to OS components through the COM object model". Although accurate, it's not a useful answer to anyone but a computer scientist. I think scripting is important for everyone to know about, so let's try again, in English this time.

The "Script" Part

To explain what a script is and why you would want to know how to write one, spend a moment thinking about the word *script* in its original, literary sense. A theatrical script is a *plan*, a series of instructions for presenting a play. All the necessary words are along with directions that tell the actors where to move and what to do along the way. The script presents the plan and relies on capable actors to do the actual work. The script propels those actors to perform familiar real-life actions, over and over again, as many times as the play is performed…and *you* get to just sit there and watch.

In the software sense, you can probably guess that scripts are a type of computer program, but the word *script* emphasizes the points I noted earlier:

- They're written in more or less plain English.
- They take advantage of capable actors to do the hard work. Scripts just tell the actors what do to.
- They perform real-life tasks for you, and you can just sit there and watch.

Scripting isn't a new concept. Programs and operating systems, from AutoCAD to z/OS, have included scripting features for decades. Windows Script Host (WSH) first appeared in Windows 95 Service Release 2, although even now few people know about it. And, as you'll see in the upcoming chapters, it gives you access to a variety of actors (software components and programs) to process data, manage your computer, and otherwise get your job done more efficiently.

The "Windows" Part

WSH lets you write scripts that manipulate files, process data, change operating system settings, install and uninstall software, send email, and so on. It does this by giving you access to other programs—many of which are provided with Windows and others that you can add on later—that do the actual work. These are the actors in our theatrical model. It's a very powerful concept because the scripting software itself only needs to tell other programs what it wants done and doesn't have to know the details of doing the job. This means the range of things your scripts can do isn't limited by what the scripting language has built in—Windows scripting is *extensible*.

In Microsoft's jargon, these outside software components are packaged as *objects*. Objects are self-contained program modules that perform tasks for other programs through a set of well-defined programming links. Objects are usually meant to represent some real-world object or concept, such as a file, spreadsheet, or computer user's account, and the programming links provide a way for other programs—scripts, for instance—to get information about and to manipulate the thing the object represents.

It's a concept that takes a little getting used to, and Chapter 3, "Scripting and Objects," is devoted to the topic. For now, I'll just say WSH comes with object components that give you access to files and folders, the email system, the networking system, Windows services and device drivers, Active Directory, and many other parts of Windows.

Here's a concrete example: Suppose as part of my job people send me Word documents that have to be distributed to several people in the organization—vacation requests, let's say. The documents come in by email at various times all day, and I save the attached documents in a folder. Every afternoon at 5p.m., I have to send an email to the company supervisors with that day's requests included as attachments.

I could do this job by hand every day, but I could also write a script to do it. With a single click, a script can take advantage of built-in Windows objects to perform the following tasks:

- Get a list of all the files in the "to be sent" folder.
- Construct an email message and address it to the list of supervisors.
- Attach each of the files to the email and then send it.
- Move the request files to a "taken care of" folder.

Wouldn't it be nice to do this job with just one click and get out the door at 5:00 p.m. instead of 5:10 p.m. every day?

You're not limited to the object components provided with Windows. Many software companies sell add-on components that provide a variety of services to scripts and Windows programs—from networking to graphics display to database access.

In addition, scripts can make use of many application programs such as Microsoft Word and Excel. In the jargon, they *expose* objects that represent their documents, worksheets, and so on. If you've written Word or Excel macros, you've already taken advantage of this capability. Windows scripts can manipulate these objects, too. For example, a script could do all the following tasks:

- Use Word to format a report listing all the files on a computer.
- Create an Excel chart showing how much disk space each network user has used.
- Create and maintain a database listing all computers and their network settings.

These are just a few examples. Finally, you can create your own add-on objects if you can write programs in C, C++, Visual Basic, or any number of other programming languages.

The "Host" Part

The "Host" part of WSH refers to the fact that Microsoft has split its scripting system into two parts: one (the script *host*) takes care of managing the script's component objects, and the other (the script *engine*) interprets the actual script language itself. This division of labor makes it possible to use any of several programming languages to write a script. You have several to choose from, based on your personal preferences.

In other words, WSH serves as an intermediary between a language engine (a software component that interprets the language you've chosen for your script) and the components or objects that do the actual work, as shown in Figure 1.1.

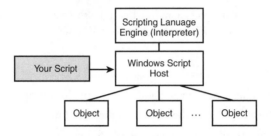

Figure 1.1   WSH acts as the intermediary between a
scripting language engine and objects.

For example, the following sample script written in the VBScript language obtains the
computer user's logon name and displays it:

```
set wnet = CreateObject("WScript.Network")
uname = wnet.UserName
MsgBox "Your user name is " & uname
```

In this example, VBScript and WSH don't actually do the job of finding the logon
name. Instead, they use the WScript.Network object, which can provide information
about and make changes to the Windows Networking environment. This is illustrated
graphically in Figure 1.2.

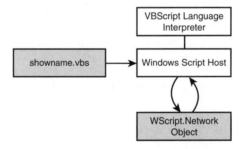

Figure 1.2   A script can use the WScript.Network object
to obtain the current user's logon name.

The point of this is that WSH provides a simple, efficient way for you to take advantage of hundreds of software modules provided with Windows and other add-on
applications.

Just as you can add to the collection of component objects provided with Windows,
you can add interpreters for other programming languages beyond to the two that
Microsoft provides. I discuss this later in the chapter.

How Is This Different from Writing Batch Files?

If you've been working with PCs since the nearly prehistoric, pre-Windows days, you might be familiar with batch files. Batch files are scripts, too; they let you script a series of programs to run, let you scan and process files, and serve as a sort of primitive programming language. Batch files are still useful today. I discuss them in detail in Chapter 11, "Batch Files for Fun and Profit." Here, however, I want to make the case for scripting.

The major limitation of batch files is that they can only start up programs and don't give you a way of interacting with them. Batch files work at the level of whole programs and files. This might be fine for some tasks. In general, though, batch files *don't* give you the ability to use objects and to manipulate text and numbers, nor do they give you as powerful a programming language as VBScript or JScript. In short, scripting is a more modern and powerful approach to Windows automation.

Scripting Languages

Scripts themselves are text files that you can edit with a simple text editor such as Notepad. In the text files are instructions written in a scripting language. You can choose from several languages, depending on your preferences. I describe the options in this section.

Windows 7, Windows Vista, Windows XP, and Windows 2000 come with two script language interpreters: VBScript and JScript. You can do pretty much anything you want to do with either one of these. Other powerful scripting languages are available, though, and you are free to add them to WSH. In this section, I list the most common scripting languages currently available.

Scripting Languages versus Compiled Languages

You could write a program to do the same job as any script with a standard compiled programming language such as C++. What's the difference between an interpreted language such as VBScript and a compiled language?

Interpreted languages are stored on the computer in plain-text form and have to be examined line-by-line every time they're run for the computer to determine what it is being told to do. Compiled programs are analyzed just once and are converted into hardware "machine instructions" that the processor can digest directly. As a result, compiled programs run faster. However, interpreted languages don't require the conversion step, and this saves some time when you're in the process of writing and refining them. Interpreted languages also tend to be easier to learn and use, and they can be modified as your needs change.

For the important but relatively small processing jobs we discuss in this book, the complications of using a compiled language outweigh any speed benefit.

VBScript

The *VB* in VBScript stands for Visual Basic, a programming language that has evolved far from its origins at Dartmouth University in 1964. More than 45 years later, Basic is still a good "beginners'" programming language, and in Microsoft's hands, it has become a capable modern language.

VBScript is one of several versions of Visual Basic Microsoft has developed. VBScript is the dialect used in WSH, and it can also be used in web browsers and servers. Visual Basic for Applications (VBA) is used as the scripting or macro language for Microsoft desktop products such as Word and Excel. Programmers use the full Visual Basic development product to build standalone Windows programs. Its latest incarnation is VB.NET, which can be used to develop desktop and web applications using Microsoft's.NET Framework technology.

VBScript is probably the easiest scripting language to learn, and because it's also used to write macros (scripts) inside Microsoft Word, Excel, and several other widely used applications, it's probably the best first language to learn. Any experience you might have writing either macros or scripts translates easily to the other.

JScript

JScript is a programming language modeled after Netscape's JavaScript language. (Microsoft made its own variant match its former archrival's capabilities but made it slightly different to keep things interesting and incompatible.) The language is designed as a way of building programming capabilities into web pages. Have you ever seen web pages whose menus or pictures change when you move your mouse around? That's most likely done through the use of JScript or JavaScript because it's the scripting language most web browsers support.

Note

JavaScript and JScript are not Java. JavaScript is a completely separate language that bears some superficial similarities to Java, but it's not the whole proverbial ball of wax. As mentioned, JScript is a variety of JavaScript, so it's not Java either.

JScript can be used for Windows scripting, and it can be the language of choice for people who are already comfortable using it due to their experience in programming scripted web pages and server-side scripts.

As I mentioned, interpreters for both VBScript and JScript are provided as part of the WSH package installed on all versions of Windows since Windows 2000. Other languages can be obtained from third parties or from Microsoft's Windows Resource Kits. I list some of these in the next sections.

Perl

Perl was developed in 1987 by developers in the Unix community. From the start, Perl was an "open" language—its writing, debugging, and subsequent development were carried out by the public for free. It's a popular, powerful language that's especially well suited for manipulating text. It has extensive string-handling and pattern-matching capabilities as well as all the other features of a major programming language.

Perl is also cryptic and dense—Perl programs can be difficult even for experienced programmers to read and understand. (It's what we jokingly call a *write-only language*.) Still, the Linux community has embraced and advanced Perl, and huge repositories of free Perl scripts are available on the Internet. Chances are, whatever you want to do, there's a Perl script already out there that does it.

ActiveState Corporation, which bills itself as "the leading provider of Open Source–based programming products and services for cross-platform development," has packaged Perl as a "Windows Script Host-able" language, and it's available for free download at www.activestate.com. The ActiveState product is a fully capable, Windows-integrated version of Perl, and it's a must-have for any Perl enthusiast.

Python

Python is a popular scripting/programming language that originated at the National Research Institute for Mathematics and Computer Science (CWI) in Amsterdam. It's a portable object-oriented language, much less cryptic than Perl, and has made big inroads in the Linux community.

A free WSH plug-in is available at www.activestate.com.

Open Object REXX

REXX originated in 1979 as a scripting language for IBM mainframes. Since then, IBM has made versions available for IBM Linux, AIX, OS/2, and Windows as well as its mainframe operating systems. Open Object REXX is its latest Windows incarnation. It was originally a formal IBM product, but IBM has released it under an Open Source arrangement. Visit www.oorexx.org for details.

Ruby

Ruby is a relatively new language that originated in Japan. It's currently more popular in Europe and Japan than in the United States, but it's picking up steam. A port of Ruby to the WSH environment is available at http://arton.hp.infoseek.co.jp. You might also search the Web for "ActiveScriptRuby."

Note

If you have a preferred scripting language that's not listed here, check to see whether a WSH-enabled version is available. If you find one, please let me know. Just visit www.helpwin7.com/scripting and leave me a message.

Choosing a Language

In this book, I focus on VBScript because it's the most common and the most "vanilla" of the scripting languages.

If you use many Microsoft products, VBScript is definitely the most important language to learn because it's used inside Word, Excel, Access and many other Microsoft products as the built-in macro language. Unix and Linux enthusiasts rightly sing the praises of Perl and Python, but if you're going to learn just one language, and you work with Microsoft applications, I recommend learning VBScript.

To that end, the next chapter covers VBScript and provides a brief tutorial. Unfortunately, it would take many more pages than we can spare for this book to teach any of the other languages. If you know and love any of the other available scripting languages, I encourage you to use them. In Chapter 3, I show you how to access Windows objects in several alternative languages. You should then be able to translate the examples I give in the remainder of the book to your language of choice.

Note

I use VBScript exclusively in the sample scripts in Chapters 4–9.

I considered teaching both VBScript and JScript and providing sample scripts in multiple languages. However, I decided against this. With the VBScript-only approach, I can provide a greater variety of sample scripts than I could if I had to repeat each one in several languages. I also think that VBScript is the better choice as a first scripting language due to its applicability in many other Microsoft applications.

For readers who already know another scripting language, I realize I'm making your job a little more difficult. If you already have enough experience to have a preferred language, however, I think the greater variety and depth of the VBScript examples in this book will make the translation work worthwhile.

A Simple Script

So, enough with the philosophy and overview! It's time to show you a practical example of what I've been talking about. Here is a script that examines all the files in a given directory (folder) and displays the total size of all the files in bytes:

```
1          ' script0101.vbs
2          ' total up space used in a given directory
```

```
3    dir = "C:\"
4
5    set Fsys = CreateObject("Scripting.FileSystemObject")
6    totsize = 0
7    for each file in Fsys.GetFolder(dir).Files
8        totsize = totsize + file.size
9    next
10   wscript.echo "The total size of the files in" , dir, "is" , totsize, "bytes"
```

In this example, the script is set up to tally all the files in the root directory of the hard drive (C:\). What I've shown here is the contents of a file I named script0101.vbs.

I should point out that the preceding printed listing contains a number in front of each of the 10 lines of text, so I can refer to them in the discussion that follows. These numbers aren't in the script file itself. If you type the script in yourself, omit these numbers.

Note

You don't need to type it yourself. I've made all the named and numbered sample scripts shown in this book available for download from www.helpwin7.com/scripting. Follow the link tto download the sample script ZIP file. The download page has instructions and tips on installing and running the sample scripts.

Now, if I double-click this file in Windows Explorer on my computer, the dialog box shown in Figure 1.3 appears. (If you've downloaded the sample script files, you can try it on your computer.)

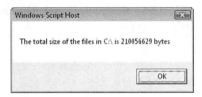

Figure 1.3   Result displayed when the sample script file is double-clicked.

Note

Double-clicking the file on your computer might not work. For security reasons, some people or companies configure their Windows computers not to run VBS scripts with just a double-click. If this happens to you, don't worry; just read on.

To see how this dialog box appeared, let's take a look at the contents of the script file, line-by-line. If you're not familiar with VB or programming in general, don't worry (yet). We cover the programming details in Chapter 2, "VBScript Tutorial."

Lines 1 and 2 are comments. In VBScript, anything after a single quote character (') is ignored. Comments mean nothing to Windows. Their job is to help you and other people understand what the script does. It's a good idea to add comments to all your scripts, describing what they do and how they do it. In longer scripts, you can describe things in detail. In this script, it's enough to say briefly what the script does. Notice that this script starts with a comment that gives the name of the script file itself. I've done that so you can find it among the set of sample scripts you can download.

Line 3 sets the name of the folder whose contents need to be counted.

Line 4 is blank. It's good programming style to use blank lines to give visual separation between parts of a program or script. Although the WSH doesn't care either way, it's easier for you and other people to read and understand a program when separate steps in the program are broken apart by whitespace (that is, blank lines).

Line 5 lets us use a programming component (object) called `Scripting.FileSystemObject` that enables the script to poke into the contents of drives and folders and lets us get information about the files inside. VBScript doesn't have this capability built in to the language itself, but the `FileSystemObject` object does, and we can use it in our program.

Line 6 sets up the counter (a *variable*, as it's known by programmers) we use to collect the total size of all the files. It starts at zero, and we add the size of each file to this.

Lines 7 and 9 form a *loop* that processes any program lines inside the loop once for each file in the chosen directory. Notice that I've indented the text inside the loop. VBScript doesn't care whether these extra indenting spaces are there—it's just a way of making the beginning and ending of the loop easier for a human reader to see, and this helps us to understand the program.

Line 8 does the real work: It adds the size of each file in the Windows directory to the variable named `totsize`. When the loop has done this for each file, we have the total size of all the files in the directory.

In VBScript, the equals sign (=) as used here doesn't mean "these two things are identical," as it does in algebra. The program line tells VBScript to take the number in variable `totsize`; add to it the value `file.size`, which is the size of the file in question; and put the result into variable `totsize`. (If computer keyboards had more symbols available, VBScript would probably have been designed so we wrote it this way: `totsize <= totsize + file.size`.)

Line 10 displays the results in plain English. By default, the `echo` command displays text in a pop-up box.

This is a pretty simple script. It's not too useful, but it does illustrate several important points about Windows scripting:

- Script languages have advanced programming features that the batch file language lacks, such as variables and loops. (This isn't completely true—batch files can have rudimentary variables and loops, but *rudimentary* is the key word).

- Scripts can take advantage of objects to extend the language with additional capabilities.

- Scripts can interact with the operating system (for example, by examining information about the files in a folder) and can interact with humans (for example, by displaying results in formatted text).

- Scripts can be made more understandable by using whitespace to make the structure of the program easy to discern.

- Script files can and should contain comments that describe and document what the scripts do and how they work. Comments help make script files an important form of documentation by recording in writing how particular jobs get done.

Types of Script Files

Script files are plain, basic text files, the kind you can edit with Notepad. Inside are program statements, written out in the syntax that the scripting language you're using can understand.

To let Windows know which language your script uses, you must use a consistent filenaming scheme when naming your script files. The most important part is the *extension* or *file type*. For example, in `myscript.vbs` the extension is `.vbs`. You have to use this extension if you're writing VBScript. By default, Windows Explorer doesn't display the extension when it lists filenames—it might just list `myscript` as a VBScript Script File.

> **Tip**
>
> I think that having Windows Explorer hide extensions is a bad idea. To make extensions visible, open any Explorer window (for example, My Computer or My Documents). On Windows 7 and Vista, press and release the Alt key so the menu appears. Click Tools, Folder Options. Select the View tab. In the Advanced Settings list, locate Hide Extensions For Known File Types and uncheck it. Then, click OK.

In the course of working with scripts, you might run into files with various extensions. The most common ones are listed in Table 1.1.

Table 1.1   **Script File Extensions**

Extension	File Type
.js	JScript script
.jse	JScript Encoded script
.pls	Perl script
.vbe	VBScript Encoded script
.vbs	VBScript script
.wsc	Windows Script Component
.wsf	Windows Script File (XML format)
.wsh	WSH settings

Note

If you used an early version of WSH and created files with the .ws extension, you need to rename them to .wsf in WSH version 5 and higher.

If you use PerlScript, be careful if you install RealAudio's Real Player. It tries to hijack the .pls file extension away from PerlScript. If this happens, first disable the Audio Playlist media type in Real Player. Then, on Windows 7 and Vista, open Control Panel, click Programs, Make a File Type Always Open in a Specific Program, and check the association for .pls files in that window. If it's not Microsoft Console Based Script Host, click Change Program and locate \windows\system32\cscript.exe. On Windows XP, open Windows Explorer, click Tools, Folder Options, File Types. Find PLS File in the list and check the association there.

Other scripting languages use specific extensions as well; the document for each language indicates which is conventionally used.

Some of the file types listed in Table 1.1 might be unfamiliar, so I discuss them in more detail in the following subsections. Feel free to skim or skip over this information if you're just getting started with scripting; not all these details will be of immediate use to you.

JSE and VBE: Encoded Scripts

Some scripts are written by commercial software developers and licensed for a fee. These developers have an interest in protecting their efforts from casual copying and piracy. Other scripts are written by system administrators who'd rather keep the details of the corporate operations away from prying eyes and tinkerers. To help these authors, some scripting languages provide encoding tools that compress and encrypt the script files so they're no longer easily readable.

Microsoft provides a downloadable tool to encode VBScript and JScript files. It converts VBScript .vb files into encoded .vbe files, and JScript .js files into encoded .jse files. You can download the utility from www.microsoft.com. Search for "Script Encoder" and click the Download Details result.

> **Caution**
>
> The Script Encoder makes it difficult, but *not* impossible, for others to read the contents of a script. The determined hacker could still decode the file. Do not put passwords or other confidential information in a script, even if it's encoded.

Windows Script Files (WSF)

To help maintain and write complex sets of scripts, Microsoft developed a file format that allows several separate scripts to be stored in one text file and even lets you use several languages in one script. The new file format is called a Windows Script File (WSF), and the extension used is .wsf.

It's easier to show than explain, so I show it first:

```
<package>
   <job id="script1">
      <script language="VBScript">
         WScript.Echo "This is script 1!"
      </script>
   </job>

   <job id="script2">
      <script language="JScript">
         WScript.Echo("This is script 2!");
      </script>
   </job>

   <job id="script3">
      <script language="VBScript" src="c:\scriptlib\anotherfile.vbs" />
   </job>
</package>
```

WSFs are still plain-text files, but they're structured with text markup called *tags*. This might look familiar to you if you've ever done web design because this looks a lot like Hypertext Markup Language (HTML), which is used to create web pages. However, this markup is called Extensible Markup Language (XML), and its required structure is very strict. XML is used to indicate where the beginning and end of the pieces of a script go. XML isn't a script programming language itself.

In this example, you can see that three separate script fragments exist in this file, delimited by <package>, <job>, and <script> tags.

Each separate script, which would otherwise have to be in a separate .vbs or .js file, is placed between <job> and </job> tags. The ID attribute gives a name to each. This can seem confusing, but the purpose is to let you put many scripts in one file, so you have only one file to copy and keep up-to-date. You can choose the desired script by its job name when you run the script file—I describe this later in the chapter under "Wscript and Cscript Command Options."

What makes WSF files interesting is that you can combine different language script components in the same file, and even in the same job, by surrounding the bits of program with <script> and </script> tags. These tags specify in which language the bit of program is written. Notice in the example that the first job is written in VBScript, whereas the second is written in JScript. You can use other languages as well, if you have them installed.

The third job demonstrates another special feature of WSF files: the capability to pull in parts of the script from other files. In the example, script3's program is pulled in from the file c:\scriptlib\anotherfile.vbs. Notice that this <script> tag ends with /> instead of the usual >. This is a special indicator, required by the XML language, and indicates that there is no matching </script> end tag. The <script> tag comes in two forms. It can surround some program text, as shown here:

```
<script language="VBscript">
     VBScript programming goes here
     There might be lots of it
</script>
```

It can also indicate that the script program is to be pulled in from somewhere else:

```
<script language="Vbscript" src="path or URL" />
```

In the second form of the <script> tag, the src entry tells WSH where to find the material to read in. This can be in the form of a full file and path or even a URL, in which case the material is obtained from an Internet location. This feature makes it possible to store commonly used bits of script programming once, where it can be used by many scripts. In Chapter 2, where we discuss VBScript programming with subroutines and functions, I have more to say on this topic.

Finally, the <package> tag surrounds the entire file. If more than one separate job exists in the file, the file must start with <package> and end with </package>, as shown in the example. If there's just one job, <package> and </package> can be omitted.

Note

There's quite a bit more to the WSF file format. I discuss it in more detail in Appendix G, "Creating Your Own Scriptable Objects," that you can download from www.helpwin7.com/scripting.

Windows Script Components (WSC)

A Windows Script (WSC) Component file is another type of script file with XML structure markup added to it. Component files let you develop your own programming "objects" to be used by scripts and other programs. I discuss components in Appendix G.

WSH Settings

If you right-click the icon for a script file and then select Properties, Windows displays a special Script tab on the Properties page that's unique to that script, as shown in Figure 1.4.

Figure 1.4   The Properties page for a script file contains a Script tab.

Here, you can specify how long the script is allowed to run before the system considers it "dead," and you can inhibit the Microsoft copyright notice that's usually printed when scripts are run in command-line mode. If you change the default settings on this Properties page, Windows stores the information in a file with the same root name as the script file, but with the extension .wsh. WSH files have no other content or function than to hold these settings.

These options can also be set on the command line when you run the script, but I'm getting ahead of myself. Let's get back to basics and see how to create a new script file from scratch.

Creating Your First Script File

As I mentioned earlier in this chapter, you can create script files with any text editing program that can deal with plain-text files. The Notepad accessory that comes with Windows can do this, so let's use it to type in a script file on your computer. I walk you through the steps in this section. (Later, I suggest that you get a better script editing program, but for this example, Notepad is fine).

Making and Securing a Script Folder

To start, let's make a folder just to hold scripts. If you keep your scripts in one place, you can find and modify them more easily, and as we see later in this chapter, use them in a Command Prompt window more easily. Follow these steps:

1. Click Start, [All] Programs, Accessories, Command Prompt.

   (For the remainder of this book, I write "Open a Command Prompt window.")

2. Type the following three commands, pressing Enter after each one:

   ```
   c:
   mkdir \scripts
   cd \scripts
   ```

Now, anyone else who uses your computer can see and use the scripts in this folder. However, you definitely do not want other users to be able to *modify* your scripts; otherwise, they can make your script do something undesired, such as to make their account a Computer Administrator. The next time you ran your script, it would do their bidding using *your* account's privileges. You might never even know this happened, so you *have* to make sure that only you can modify your scripts.

> **Note**
>
> This is the unfortunate nitty-gritty part that you just have to do to make Windows secure against not just hackers, but accidents and casual interference. Take solace in knowing that you have to do this just one time.

To secure your `scripts` folder on Windows 7, Vista and XP Professional, follow these steps. If you have Windows XP Home Edition, you can perform these steps only if you boot your computer in Safe Mode. (You might not feel that it's worth the trouble in this case). Do the following:

1. Click Start, [My] Computer.

2. Under Computer, under Folders, click Local Disk (C:).

3. In the right pane, locate your `scripts` folder. Right-click it and select Properties.

4. Select the Security tab.

5. Under Group Or User Names, click Authenticated Users, Users and Everyone, in turn, for any of these names that appear. After selecting each one, look at the bottom part and see whether Write or Modify is checked. They shouldn't be. If they aren't checked for *any* of these accounts, skip to step 9.

   However, if either Modify or Write is checked for even one of these names, click the Advanced button and proceed to step 6.

6. On Windows 7, click Change Permissions. On Vista, click Edit. Uncheck Include Inheritable Permissions From This Object's Parent, and in the resulting dialog box, click Copy.

7. Repeat the following three steps for each of the names Users, Authenticated Users, and Everyone, if they appear:

   a. In the Name column, select Users, and click Edit.

   b. Make sure that the Apply To item (near the top) is set to This Folder, Subfolders and Files. Change it if necessary.

   c. Make sure that only four boxes are checked: Traverse Folder/Execute File, List Folder/Read Data, Read Attributes, and Read Extended Attributes. Uncheck any other box, and then click OK.

   Repeat these three steps for the following other names, if they are listed: Authenticated Users, and then Everyone.

8. Click OK.

9. You should be at the original Scripts Properties dialog box. On Vista and Windows 7 click the Edit button.

10. Click Add, then Advanced, and then click Find Now. Locate your own account under Search Results, double-click it, and then click OK.

11. Your account should now appear in the list of Group Or User Names. In the bottom part, check Full Control, if Windows lets you; otherwise, Modify is good enough.

12. Click OK, and you're finished.

Now, you have a permanent, secured folder set up to hold scripts.

In the future, you can return to this folder by following these steps:

1. Open a Command Prompt window.

2. Type the following two commands:

   ```
   c:
   cd \scripts
   ```

Later, I show you how to put this folder into your computer's PATH list, so you can run the script by typing its name in any Command Prompt window. Now, though, let's create a first script.

Creating a Script

After you have a Command Prompt window opened up to your script folder, type the following command:

```
notepad firstscript.vbs
```

This opens Notepad. Type the following command, exactly as printed here:

```
wscript.echo "This is output from my first script"
```

Click File, Save, and then close Notepad. Now, type the following command into the Command Prompt window:

```
wscript firstscript.vbs
```

This should pop up a small window with the text This is output from my first script. What you did is to tell Windows to run the wscript WSH processing program on the script file firstscript.vbs, and the script told Windows to display the message.

Click OK to close the message window. You've now created and run your own script.

To create new scripts in the future, you can use these same steps:

- Open a Command Prompt window.
- If you want to put the script into your general-purpose script folder, type the c: and cd \scripts commands. (You can create scripts in other drives and folders, if you want; just type a different drive letter or folder path.)
- Type **notepad** followed by the name of the script.

Tip

Whenever you create a new script file, open a Command Prompt window and type the word **notepad** followed by the name of the file you want to create, for example:

```
notepad newscript.vbs
```

You can also specify a path, if you want the file to be placed in a specific folder, for example:

```
notepad c:\scripts\newscript.vbs
```

When Notepad asks if you'd like to create a new file, click Yes.

If you started Notepad without typing the filename on the command line, when you saved your new script using File, Save As, the script is saved with the name newscript.vbs.txt and you'd have to rename it. Putting the filename on the command line avoids this problem.

You can also use your \scripts folder to hold scripts you acquire from others or downloaded from the Internet.

Script Editing Tools

In this book, I show you how to use the standard Windows Notepad accessory to create and edit scripts and other batch files. Notepad can certainly do the job, and I used nothing but Notepad myself for years, but after I tried the following tools, and saw how incredibly useful they are, I had to smack my own head—what was I thinking? A good script editing tool can save you enough time and trouble to pay for itself in a single day. There are several good editing programs out there, a few of which are listed here. Whether you're just getting started with scripts or you're a seasoned pro, I strongly urge you to invest in one (or more) of the following tools:

Table 1.2   **Third-Party Script Editing Tools**

Program	Description
VBSEdit	VBSEdit is not just a text editor. It also lets you interactively step through (debug) your scripts and lets you view the contents of variables as you go. It also provides an Object Browser, which we discuss in Chapter 3. Additional features include syntax coloring and an "autocomplete" feature that can save you a lot of typing. Free to try and $59 to fully unlock from www.vbsedit.com. Give it a try, and I promise you'll never use Notepad again.
AdminScriptEditor	Like VBSEdit, AdminScriptEditor includes syntax coloring, autocomplete, and an interactive debugger. Beyond that, it adds wizards to help write complex Windows Management Instrumentation and Active Directory scripts, and it provides add-on objects that let you create interactive forms and programs. It also has Windows PowerShell support. $100 from www.adminscripteditor.com.
PrimalScript	Purveyors of a nifty script-editing program called PrimalScript. It too definitely beats using Notepad, but at $179, from www.sapien.com, it's not for the casual user.
UltraEdit	Ultraedit isn't specifically a script editing tool, but it's worth mentioning. If you need to do any serious editing of text files and text data, UltraEdit is well worth $59.99. It has a huge list of features. Although it can't help you debug scripts, it can sort, search, convert, slice, and dice text any way you might need. When editing script files, it automatically highlights and colors program and script keywords and syntax elements. From www.ultraedit.com.

How Windows Runs Scripts

In the examples in the previous sections, I mentioned that you can run a script by double-clicking its file in Windows Explorer or by typing a command in a Command Prompt window. In this section, I discuss this in detail.

Wscript and Cscript

WSH comes in two flavors: a windowed version named Wscript and a command-line version named Cscript. Either version can run any script. The difference between the two is that the windowed version (wscript) displays text output messages with a pop-up dialog box, whereas the command-line version (Cscript) displays text through the normal "standard output" mechanism common to command-line programs.

To see what I mean, follow these steps:

1. Open a Command Prompt window.
2. If you didn't create `firstscript.vbs` by following the steps I gave earlier in the chapter under "Creating Your First Script," do so now. If you did, return to the `\scripts` folder by typing
   ```
   c:
   cd \scripts
   ```
3. Type the command `wscript firstscript.vbs` and press Enter. Click OK to close the window.
4. Type the command `cscript firstscript.vbs` and press Enter. This time, the message appears in the Command Prompt window.

You should see the results shown in Figure 1.5.

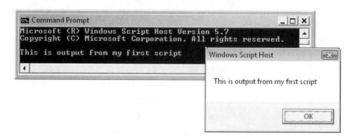

Figure 1.5   Output of a sample script run by `wscript` (top) and `cscript` (bottom).

Wscript is best suited for scripts that do their work quietly and display very little information to the user—scripts that, for example, just display error messages and maybe an "I'm finished" message, like our scripting example did earlier in this chapter.

The advantage of using a pop-up message is that the script processing stops while the message is displayed, and it waits until you've read the message and closed the dialog box.

Cscript is the command-line (or character or console mode) version of WSH. Cscript displays results in a command prompt window, which mimics the old DOS command-line environment. It's best suited for scripts that produce lots of output, such as directory listings, and for scripts whose output you'd like to capture into a file.

The advantage of using Cscript for scripts that display lots of output—or whose output you want to process with other programs—is that you can redirect the output to a file using the standard command-line technique. The following command runs the sample script file `script0101.vbs` and saves the output in a file named `results.txt`:

```
cscript script0101.vbs >results.txt
```

You can view the results by typing:

```
notepad results.txt
```

Note

This is a good way to view the output of a script that generates a lot of text because it would otherwise scroll by in the command prompt window in a blur.

You can use either script processor according to your preferences. In the next section, I show you the various ways to run scripts.

Ways to Run a Script

As you know, Windows usually offers several ways to accomplish the same thing through clicking, double-clicking, right-clicking, or dragging things around. This is certainly true for running scripts. There are six ways to start the processing of a script file, as listed in Table 1.3.

Table 1.3   **Ways of Running a Script File**

Action	Runs Under
Double-click the file in Explorer, a Find Files window, or the Desktop. (On Windows Vista, a security warning might pop up; click Open to run the script. We talk more about this later.)	Default host
Right-click the file and select Open.	Wscript
Right-click the file and select Open with Command Prompt.	Cscript

continues

Table 1.3 **Continued**

Action	Runs Under
Type the name of the script file at a command prompt, in the Windows 7/Vista Start menu's search box, in the Run dialog box, or in a shortcut.★	Default host
Enter **cscript** or **wscript** followed by the script filename at a command prompt, in the Start, Run dialog box, or in a shortcut.★★	Specified host
Drag one or more files and drop them onto the script file's icon in Explorer or on the Desktop.	Default host

★*In Windows 7, Vista, XP, NT, and 2000, you don't need to type the script file's extension (*.vbs, *.pl, or whatever). You can simply type the file's base name. If you are still using Windows 95, 98, or Me, you must include the extension with the filename.*

★★*You must always include the script's extension when you're explicitly running Wscript or Cscript by name.*

Tip

You should try each of these methods at your computer now, using the firstscript.vbs sample script I had you type earlier in this chapter.

You notice that the right-click "wscript" and "cscript" methods choose a specific host—either Wscript or Cscript. The other three methods use the *default host*, which is a setting you can alter. Initially, Windows uses wscript as the default host. If you want, you can change the default host by typing one of these commands into a command prompt window:

- wscript //H:wscript ← Sets the default host to wscript
- wscript //H:cscript ← Sets the default host to cscript

In general, during the development of new scripts, the command-line version (cscript) is probably the most useful because you probably want to have your script print debugging remarks to help you understand what it's doing. Remember that even after setting cscript as the default, you can always force the issue with individual scripts; you can run the script with the right-click method or type the cscript or wscript command explicitly.

Note

In the remainder of this chapter, I describe the more arcane details of how WSH is started and how to communicate with it. If you're new to scripting and programming, you might want to skim the remainder of this chapter now so you know what's covered and continue with the tutorial in Chapter 2. The following material is fairly advanced and might make more sense after you've gotten some more experience with VBScript.

Passing Information to Scripts

The command line used to start up Wscript or Cscript can come from a shortcut; from the Start, Run dialog box; or from your own fingers typing away at the command prompt. If the script is self-contained (that is, has all the information it needs to perform its job), you can simply enter the script's filename.

However, it's often useful to write a script in a more generic way and to specify some information at the time you run the script. Our sample script earlier in the chapter provides a good example: The name of the folder whose files are to be sized is built in to the script. It would be much more useful if we could tell it which folder to examine when we ran it; this way, we could use the same script to count any folder's files.

One way to do this is to have the script prompt (or *ask*) the user to type in any desired information. We discuss how this is done in Chapter 2.

Another technique is to specify such information on the command line when you run the script. In computer jargon, bits of information passed to a procedure such as a script file are called *arguments*. In the following command line, `myscript.vbs` and `c:\windows` are two arguments being given to the program wscript:

```
wscript myscript.vbs c:\windows
```

In a wscript command line, arguments starting with two slashes (//) control the action of wscript itself and the first filename argument is the name of the script to run. Any *other* arguments are passed along to the script file for *it* to interpret as it sees fit. There is no predetermined meaning to arguments; it's up to the script's programmer to determine whether they are to be used and how they affect the script. In one script, the extra command-line arguments might be used to indicate the names of folders to delete. In another, they might enable or disable functions that the script performs.

Each scripting language has its own way of getting argument information passed through its command line. If you're familiar with writing DOS batch files, you might remember that wherever "%1" appears in a batch file, it is replaced with the first command-line argument. WSH makes the command-line arguments available through the use of a feature called the `WScript` object, which I discuss in detail in Chapter 3. In VBScript, the first argument typed on the command line after the script's name is `WScript.Arguments(0)`. The second is `WScript.Arguments(1)`, and so on. For example, the statement

```
dir = WScript.Arguments(0)
```

assigns the first argument to the variable dir.

Note

This use of `WScript` in `WScript.echo` and `WScript.Arguments`, by the way, is always `WScript`, regardless of whether you're running the script with wscript or cscript. Here, `WScript` refers to the name of an object provided by the script host, and it is named `WScript`, regardless of which version is running. Yes, it's confusing.

We could rewrite the original sample script to take advantage of this, as follows:

```
' script0102.vbs
' total up space used in the directory named on the command line
dir = WScript.Arguments(0)

set Fsys = CreateObject("Scripting.FileSystemObject")
totsize = 0
for each file in Fsys.GetFolder(dir).Files
    totsize = totsize + file.size
next
wscript.echo "The total size of the files in" , dir, "is" , totsize
```

Note that the only difference between this script and the earlier version is the way that that the variable dir is set up in the third line of the script.

Now, we can type these commands at the command prompt to count the files in the Temp and Windows directories, respectively:

```
Script0102 c:\temp
```

```
Script0102 c:\windows
```

Trouble arises when we try to count a folder whose name has spaces in it. For example, I might type

```
Script0102 c:\Program Files\Internet Explorer
```

Windows considers the spaces in this long pathname to indicate that we're specifying three separate arguments:

- WScript.Arguments(0) = c:\Program
- WScript.Arguments(1) = Files\Internet
- WScript.Arguments(2) = Explorer

The solution is to put quotes ("") around the misbehaving text, so Windows knows to treat it as one long item:

```
Script0102 "c:\Program Files\Internet Explorer"
```

Using command-line arguments in your own scripts helps you create more general-purpose, useful tools. In the examples later in this book, I show you several examples of this.

Saving the Results from Scripts

If you want a script to record information, rather than just have it appear on your screen, you have two choices.

First, you can use Cscript and have your script program display its results in the command prompt window. You saw how this looks earlier in the chapter in Figure 1.5.

You can save this output to a file with *output redirection*. If you add *>somefile* to any command-line program, its output is saved in the file named *somefile*. You can then print this file, process it with some other program, view it with Notepad, and so on. Here's an example:

```
cscript script0102.vbs c:\windows >wincount.txt
```

This runs one of our sample scripts and saves the results in the file named wincount.txt. You can then view results using Notepad with this command:

```
notepad wincount.txt
```

If you want to view the output in the Command Prompt window, but too much output goes by to read at once, you can use the more command, using the *pipe* (|) mechanism:

```
cscript script0102.vbs c:\windows | more
```

In this case, | tells Windows to send the output of your script to the program more, which is a program built in to Windows that displays output one full screen at a time. Pressing the spacebar advances you from one screen to the next.

The second way of saving information that a script has produced is to have the script program create a file directly using program commands in the script. We discuss this in Chapter 4, "File and Registry Access."

Wscript and Cscript Command Options

After the earlier discussion about command-line arguments, it shouldn't be a surprise that you can control the behavior of cscript and wscript through arguments on the command line. Indeed, you can add several special arguments to the wscript or cscript command line to change its behavior.

Cscript usually prints a message every time it starts, before printing any output from your script. For example, if I type

```
cscript script0102.vbs c:\windows
```

the result looks something like this:

```
Microsoft (R) Windows Script Host Version 5.7
Copyright (C) Microsoft Corporation. All rights reserved.

The total size of the files in c:\windows is 10512614
```

One change I can make is to add //Nologo to the command line, being careful to use forward slashes rather than backslashes, like this:

```
cscript //Nologo script0102.vbs c:\windows
```

This causes the output to display as follows:

```
The total size of the files in c:\windows is 10512614
```

This is much nicer. WSH recognizes several special optional arguments, each preceded by `//` to notify the host that the argument is for its use rather than something to be given to the script. The complete list of command-line options is shown in Table 1.4. After the table, I show you a couple of commands you can type right now that will make your scripting life easier.

Table 1.4   **Command-Line Options for** `wscript` **and** `cscript`

Option	Effect
`//H:host`	Sets *host* to be the default script from now on. Enter `wscript` or `cscript` in place of *host*.
`//S`	Saves the current settings as the default settings for this user. Any of the other options listed in this table used along with `//S` will "stick" for all future runs of WSH, until you change the default settings again.
`//B`	Uses "batch" mode and suppresses any script errors and input prompts from displaying. Normally, errors in your script program cause the script to stop with an error message. `//B` makes it try to carry on regardless.
`//D`	Enables Active Debugging. When this option is used, if the script encounters an error and you've installed Windows Script Debugger (or another Microsoft visual debugging tool, such as Visual Studio), the debugger takes over and indicates the source of the error.
`//E:engine`	Uses the named language *engine* to process the script. Normally, WSH guesses the correct engine from the script file name: VBScript for `.vbs` files, JScript for `.js` files, and so on. Use this option only if you're using unusual filename extensions or an unusual language that WSH can't guess.
`//I`	Uses Interactive mode, which is the opposite of the batch mode discussed earlier. Because `//I` is the default setting, you need to use this option only if you previously changed the default using `//S //B`.
`//Job:jobname`	Runs the script job named *jobname* from within a .WSF file. WSF files were discussed earlier in the chapter.
`//Logo`	Displays the WSH copyright and version information. (This is the default unless you use `//Nologo` or change the setting permanently with `//S //Nologo`.)

Option	Effect
//Nologo	Suppresses printout of the copyright and version.
//T:*nn*	Sets the maximum time the script is permitted to run to *nn* seconds. For example, //T:5 means that the script will be stopped if it takes more than 5 seconds to run. This is useful if your script might "stick" or try to run forever when something goes wrong.
//X	Executes the script in the debugger. I discuss this option later in the section "Debugging Scripts."
//U	Used with cscript only. Tells cscript to write Unicode data instead of ASCII data to the output. You probably never need to use this option.

Tip

There's no need to memorize this list. At the command prompt, you can type **cscript /?** or **wscript /?** and the program displays the list of valid options. Most Windows programs do this if you put /? on the command line.

Right now, I recommend you take advantage of these options to make WSH a little easier to use.

First, turn off the version text that cscript prints every time you run it—the stuff that looks like this:

```
Microsoft (R) Windows Script Host Version 5.7
Copyright (C) Microsoft Corporation. All rights reserved.
```

To get rid of this, open a command prompt window and type

```
cscript //nologo //s
```

The //nologo runs cscript without that version text, and //s makes the setting permanent.

Then, if you want to work primarily with cscript, and if you want just type a script's name on the command line and have it run with cscript by default, type this command:

cscript //h:cscript

If you want some more information about cscript and wscript command-line options, read on; otherwise, you can skip ahead to the next section.

Let's look at some examples of using the other options. I discussed the //S and //H options. The other options usually change WSH's behavior only when they're used on a given command line. Here's an example:

```
cscript somescript.vbs //T:5 //B some arguments for the script
```

This tells cscript to run script `somescript.vbs` for a maximum of 5 seconds and not to stop even if there are errors. The other arguments are passed along to the script.

The `//S` option, though, makes the other options stick permanently, just as the `//H` is permanent. If I want to turn off the copyright and version printout that appears every time on a permanent basis, this command does the trick:

```
cscript //Nologo //S
```

The `//S` argument makes the `//Nologo` option stick.

Note

Capitalization doesn't matter when using these options. For example, `//T:5` and `//t:5` have the same effect.

For Registry Wonks Only...

If you're a Windows Registry guru, you might want to know where WSH setup information is stored. The `//S` switch saves preference values in the Registry under `HKEY_CURRENT_USER\Software\Microsoft\Windows Script Host\Settings`.

The default engine (`//H`) option changes the default value of keys `HKEY_CURRENT_USER\Software\Classes\`*xxx*`\Shell` where *xxx* stands for JSFile, VBSFile, WSHFile, and other script file types. The default value is set to `open` or `open2`, corresponding to the verbs listed under `HKEY_CLASSES_ROOT\`*xxx*`\Shell`.

The actual script interpreters (engines) are DLLs registered under `HKEY_CLASSES_ROOT\CLSID` under the `CLSID` associated with the script engine entries (for example, `HKEY_CLASSES_ROOT\VBScript`). The script engine file type and engine `CLSID` keys are marked with a subkey named `OLEScript`.

The `//E` switch sets the engine associations by changing the `Command` key under `HKEY_CLASSES_ROOT\`*xxx*`\Shell\Open` for each associated script file type. The list of registered script file types is under `HKEY_LOCAL_MACHINE\Software\Microsoft\Windows Scripting Host\Script Extensions`. (Notice the `ing` there). This setting requires Administrator privileges, but not elevated privileges, to change.

Running Your Own Scripts

As you develop scripts you use regularly, you can make them easy to locate and run if you know some tricks of the trade. I show you these tricks in this section.

Adding Scripts to the Path

As I mentioned previously, as you write general-purpose scripts, it's a good idea to put them into a single folder. To create a script folder, see the instructions given earlier under "Making and Securing a Script Folder."

You can then put your script folder into Windows' PATH list, which is a list of folders Windows searches when you type a name into the command prompt window, in the Run box on Windows XP, and the search box on Vista's start menu. If you add your script folder to the PATH, you can run a script anytime, from any folder, just by typing its name.

In the following instructions, I assume that your script folder is `c:\scripts`. You could also create your script folder inside your personal profile folder, `c:\Users\youraccount\scripts`, for example. If you use a different location, substitute that folder name for `c:\scripts` in the following instructions.

You put the folder into the PATH list for users on your computer or just your own user account, according your preference.

> **Note**
>
> After you make these changes, close any command prompt windows you have open. The change only affects *new* command prompt windows.

Windows 7 and Vista, Scripts Available to All Users

To add your script folder to the PATH for *all* users on Windows 7 and Vista, follow these steps:

1. Click Start, right-click Computer, and select Properties.
2. Click Advanced System Settings, and confirm the User Account Control prompt.
3. Click the Environment Variables button.
4. Locate the PATH entry in the *lower* part of the dialog box and double-click it.
5. Click in the Variable Value field. Press the End key, type a semicolon (;), and then type `c:\scripts` after the semicolon.
6. Click OK to close the dialog boxes.

Windows 7 and Vista, Scripts Available Just to You

To add your script folder to the PATH for just your user account, follow these steps:

1. Click Start, Control Panel, User Accounts and Family Safety, User Accounts.
2. At the bottom of the Tasks list, select Change My Environment Variables.

3. In the *upper* part of the dialog box, if there is an existing PATH entry, double-click it. Click in the Variable Value field, press the End key, type a semicolon (;), and type `c:\scripts` after the semicolon.

   Otherwise, if there is no PATH entry in the *upper* list, click New, type **PATH** as the Variable Name, and type `c:\scripts` into the Variable Value field.

4. Click OK to close the dialog boxes.

Windows XP, Scripts Available to All Users

To add your script folder to the PATH for *all* users on XP, follow these steps:

1. Log on as a Computer Administrator.
2. Click Start, right-click My Computer, and select Properties.
3. Select the Advanced tab, and click Environment Variables.
4. Locate the PATH entry in the *lower* part of the dialog box and double-click it.
5. Click in the Variable Value field. Press the End key, type a semicolon (;), and type `c:\scripts` after the semicolon.
6. Click OK to close the dialog boxes.

Windows XP, Scripts Available Just to You

To add your script folder to the PATH for just your user account on XP, follow these steps:

1. Click Start, right-click My Computer, and select Properties.
2. Select the Advanced tab, and click Environment Variables.
3. In the *upper* part of the dialog box, if there is an existing PATH entry, double-click it. Click in the Variable Value field, press the End key, type a semicolon (;), and type `c:\scripts` after the semicolon.

   Otherwise, if there is no PATH entry in the *upper* list, click New, type **PATH** as the Variable Name, and type `c:\scripts` into the Variable Value field.

4. Click OK to close the dialog boxes.

After you've set up the PATH list, all you have to do is type the name of any of your script files into the command prompt window or the Run or Search boxes, and Windows will find the script. To try it, open a new command prompt window, type **firstscript**, and press Enter. Your sample script should run.

Running Scripts with a Shortcut Icon

If you have a script you use regularly and run with wscript, I suggest you make a shortcut to the script file.

Tip

If you use your scripts on a local area network, I recommend that you store your commonly used scripts in a shared network folder. This way, you can create shortcuts on any networked computer. When you create the shortcut, enter the script's Universal Naming Convention (UNC) pathname—for example, `\\bali\scripts\myscript.vbs`. Or you can use Browse to locate the shared file under My Network Places. It's also handy to copy the shortcuts themselves to a shared folder. Then, you can just drag these shortcuts to any networked computer without having to re-create them.

Making a Script Shortcut

You can put a shortcut to a frequently used script on the Desktop, in a folder, on your Start menu, or on the Quick Launch bar. This is usually useful only with scripts run with wscript or scripts that produce no output, however. If you use a shortcut with cscript (command-line version), as soon as the script finishes, its window closes and you don't have a chance to read the results.

To make a shortcut to a script file, follow these steps:

1. Right-click the Desktop and select New, Shortcut.
2. Click Browse and locate your script file. Click OK.
3. Move the cursor to the beginning of the Location box and add `wscript` before the path and filename. Be sure to add a space after `wscript`. Click Next.
4. Change the description from `wscript.exe` to something reasonable that describes the script's function, such as Count File Sizes. Click Finish.

You can then drag this shortcut anywhere you want, including into your Start menu, Quick Launch bar, or elsewhere. Double-clicking the shortcut runs the script with a minimum of fuss.

Tip

You can drag one or more files and drop them onto a script shortcut. This runs the script with the full pathname of each file passed to the script as an argument. You can use this with scripts that send emails, print, or perform other file-related tasks.

Running Scripts from Batch Files

Finally, you can also run scripts from batch files. This sounds strange, but it can be convenient. Batch files are useful when you need to string several programs together in succession, and there's no reason that a script file can't be one of those programs. Windows network administrators might also want to run scripts from batch files as part of a logon script, which I discuss in Chapter 9, "Deploying Scripts for Computer and Network Management."

You can use either wscript or cscript to run a script in a batch file. Both versions can communicate success/failure information back to the batch file through the errorlevel environment variable, as shown in the following example:

```
badscript.vbs:
    Wscript.echo "Oops, I've run into a problem."
    WScript.Quit(1)

runbad.bat:
    @echo off
    wscript badscript.vbs
    echo Wscript returned %errorlevel%
    if errorlevel 1 echo The script reported an error!
```

Note

You might run into articles on the Web claiming that Wscript doesn't set errorlevel, but that information is obsolete. Versions of Wscript and Cscript since Windows 2000 do properly set the errorlevel value.

Running Scripts Automatically

You can instruct Windows to run scripts automatically when you log on, log off, at scheduled intervals, or based on other system events. For information on automatic scripting, see Chapter 9.

Security Concerns

Because Windows has a default file-type association between the filename extensions used by scripts (for example, .vbs and .js) and WSH, when you ask Windows to "start" or "open" a VBS file, it knows it's a script and runs it.

This makes using scripts easy, but it can also be a security risk, and there are two reasons you might want to change the default behavior:

- Because scripts can be written to erase files and perform serious operating system changes, you might consider it too dangerous to make it this easy to run scripts on your computer.

- Hackers have exploited the willingness of Windows to run scripts by writing virus and worm scripts and sending them as email attachments. If a mail recipient opens the attachment and Windows is set to automatically run VBS files with WSH, the virus starts and does its damage.

Because you can always run scripts by explicitly typing the wscript or cscript command and because you can explicitly put the word wscript or cscript before the script file name in the Target part of any shortcut, it's safe to disable the Windows association between scripts files and WSH, and you don't lose any significant functionality.

If you want to do this on Windows 7 or Vista, here's how:

1. Click Start, Control Panel. Click the green Programs title; then, under Default Programs, select Make A File Type Always Open In A Specific Program.
2. Locate `.vbs` in the list. Select it, and then click Change Program.
3. Click Browse, and then type **`\windows\system32\notepad.exe`**.
4. Click Open, and then click OK.
5. Repeat this for the `.vbe`, `.js`, `.jse`, and `.wsh` file types.

On XP, follow these steps:

1. Open Windows Explorer, and select Tools, Folder Options.
2. Select the File Types tab.
3. Locate VBS in the list under Extensions and select it.
4. Click the Advanced button, and under Actions, select Open.
5. Click Edit. Write down the existing setting (which looks like `C:\WINDOWS\System32\WScript.exe "%1" %*`), and change the entry to the following:

   `notepad "%1"`
6. Click OK to close both dialog boxes.
7. Locate JS in the Extensions list and repeat steps 4 and 5. Afterward, you notice that your changes automatically apply to JSE and WSF files.

Now, you can't right-click or double-click a script file icon to start it. Instead, you have to perform one of the following actions:

- Create shortcuts with `wscript` or `cscript` in the Target line, as discussed earlier in the chapter. (After you create a shortcut to a script file, right-click it, select Properties, put the cursor before the filename in the Target field, and type **`wscript`** followed by a space.)
- Run scripts from the Command Prompt or Start, Run window by typing **`wscript`** or **`cscript`**, followed by the script filename.

This isn't a strong security measure: If a malicious script manages to get started despite these changes, it can still do whatever it wants. Some people have gone so far as to delete `cscript.exe` and `wscript.exe` from their computers, or at least rename them, for this reason.

Trust Policy and Script Signing

For Windows 7, Vista, and XP users on a Windows Domain network (that is, a network that is controlled by Windows Server), there is another more powerful way to prevent unauthorized scripts from running. Through the network's Group Policy feature, Windows can be instructed only to run scripts found in specified directories and/or to disallow scripts that don't contain a valid *signature*, which is an encrypted data block that guarantees the script file has come from an authorized, trusted source. A network administrator must grant this authorization, called *Trust Policy control.*

Note

If a network manager enables the Trust Policy feature, you might not be able to write and run your own scripts! If you run into problems running scripts, contact your network administrator.

I discuss script security, Trust Policy, and script signing in more detail in Chapter 9.

Debugging Scripts

Just writing a program can be hard enough, but getting it to work correctly can try the patience of a saint. Thankfully, Windows scripting comes with a graphical debugger that lets you see what's happening inside your script program as it runs. If you've written and debugged macros in Word, Excel, Access, or other Microsoft applications, you've probably already encountered the visual debugger. If not, here's a short tour.

If a script encounters a glaring programming error (for example, a misplaced comma or an unrecognized word), WSH reports the error. For example, here's a script with a serious error:

```
        ' bad.vbs - a script in need of debugging
for counter = 1 to 3
    wscript.echo "Counter is now", counter
next

badcommand

wscript.echo "Got past the bad command"
```

VBScript does not recognize the word `badcommand`. What happens when you try to run this script depends on which host you've used.

Cscript prints an error message describing the problem and indicates which line in the file contains the error, like so:

```
Counter is now 1
Counter is now 2
Counter is now 3
D:\scripts\01\bad.vbs(7, 1) Microsoft VBScript runtime error:
   Type mismatch: 'badcommand'
```

Wscript, the graphical version, stops and displays a dialog box informing you of the error, as shown in Figure 1.6.

Figure 1.6   WScript displays a dialog box when it encounters a programming error.

In either case, the error message tells you that WSH is having some sort of problem with line 7 in your script file and, in many cases, this leads you close enough to the problem that you can see and fix it.

Tip

When you're editing and debugging scripts, it helps if you have a text editor that can move the cursor directly to the specific line number mentioned in a script error message. Notepad can do this, if you know this trick: Click the Format menu and uncheck Word Wrap. Now, you can jump to a specific line number by pressing Ctrl+G. Type the line number and press Enter.

If your script doesn't behave as you expect, and yet there aren't any glaring typographical errors—at least none that your scripting language can detect—you have to do a bit of detective work.

In some cases, it's helpful to insert commands to display the contents of your program's variables and intermediate results to see that they make sense. In the `bad.vbs` script we're working with in this section, for example, I've had the program display the contents of variable `counter` as the loop takes its turns. Sometimes this kind of output, called *tracing*, is helpful. You can always remove extra `echo` or other output commands when you know your script is working correctly.

This technique works, but it's so 1960s. We're not in the punched card era anymore, are we? If your script doesn't behave as expected or if you're in the first stages of writing it and want to watch what is happening inside to assure yourself that it's working, there's a much more modern tool you can use to peer inside as the program runs. It's called the Script Debugger. The only catch is that you have to download it because it's not supplied with Windows. If you're going to be developing scripts, visit www.microsoft.com, search for Windows Script Debugger Download, select Script

Debugger for Windows NT 4.0 and Later; then download and install the program. (On XP, you need to be logged on as a Computer Administrator user to install the download.)

Note

If you have Microsoft Visual Studio, .NET Studio, or InterDev installed, or have another "Active" debugger installed, do *not* download the Windows Script Debugger yet—you might already have a more powerful debugger in place. To check, create a small script named test.vbs. It can contain just one statement, such as x = 3. Then, type this command: **cscript //D //X test.vbs** and press Enter. If a debugging window (or dialog that lets you select a debugger) appears, you're ready to go, and you should use your existing debugger. If no debugger or dialog appears, then go ahead and download the Microsoft Script Debugger and continue with the rest of this section.

After Script Debugger is installed, you can use //X on the command line to start a script using the debugger. Now, the command

```
cscript //X d:\scripts\01\bad.vbs
```

causes the debugger to appear, as shown in Figure 1.7.

Figure 1.7   The Windows Script Debugger
displays the contents of your script as it runs.

As the script runs, a yellow pointer shows the next script statement that is to be processed. In Figure 1.7, because I've just started the script, the pointer is on the first actual script command after the comment and blank line.

Now, you can walk your script through its paces one step at a time, or you can let it run ahead to a desired point and make it stop. Although you can use the debugger's menus to do this, you find it much easier to use if you learn the keyboard shortcuts. The most important shortcut keys are shown in Table 1.5.

Table 1.5 **Windows Script Debugger Function Keys**

Key	Action
F8	Steps the script ahead one statement at a time. If the script calls a script subroutine or function, the debugger "steps into" the subprogram and stop at its first line.
Shift+F8	Similar to F8 but "steps over" any subroutines or functions.
F9	Click the cursor in any of the script's program lines and press F9 to set or clear a *breakpoint* in the line. A breakpoint stops the program in its tracks when the program reaches the marked line. This is useful if you want to see what happens at a certain point in the program and don't want to tediously step to that point one line at a time; set a breakpoint and press F5.
F5	Lets the program run ahead full speed until it ends, encounters a serious error, or encounters a breakpoint.
Ctrl+Shift+F8	If the program is inside a script subroutine or function, the script runs until the routine returns and then stops.

Viewing and Altering Variables

Besides letting you step through your script, the debugger also lets you view and modify the contents of variables inside the script. This is the debugger's most valuable feature. Click View, Command Window to display the command window, as shown in Figure 1.8.

The Command window lets you do three things to help you debug your program:

- You can display the value of any variable by typing a question mark followed by the variable name and the Enter key. In Figure 1.8, I requested the value of variable num, and the debugger displayed 1.

- You can alter the value of a variable by typing an assignment statement, as shown in Figure 1.8, where I changed the value of num from 1 to 4. You can use this capability to work around an error when your script has made a mistake and you'd like to continue debugging. Although you can't fix the program itself while the debugger is running, you get a bit more information out of your debugging session by correcting the variables and continuing.

- You can call any subroutine, function, or object method or property by typing an appropriate program statement. Use ? to call and display function values—for example ? mid("ABC",2). To call subroutines, type the subroutine name and any arguments. In Figure 1.8, I call subroutine shownumber with argument num = 15.

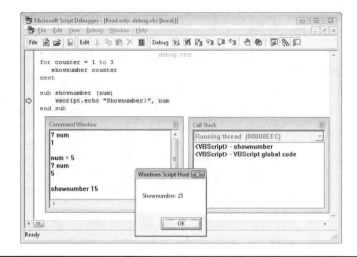

Figure 1.8   The Command window lets you view and alter variables
and execute program statements manually. The Call Stack window shows the
order in which subroutines and functions have been called.

Viewing the Call Stack

The Call Stack window, also shown in Figure 1.8, is another tool that helps you monitor the inner workings of a script. To display it, select View, Call Stack. This window lists the names of any subroutines or functions that are currently in use. It lists the current routine on top, followed by the name of the routine that called it, and so on down to the main script program.

Viewing the call stack is helpful when debugging scripts that call many subroutines or that use recursion, which is a programming technique I discuss in Chapter 4. You can double-click any of the entries in the Call Stack window, and the debugger will display the location in your script where a subroutine call is in progress.

Although this is a useful tool for ensuring a script runs through all the steps you think it should, if you're used to the full-featured debuggers found in other Microsoft products, you find this one lacks three important features:

- You can't select a "next statement to run" to change the script's order of processing statements (for example, to skip over a problem area).
- If the script encounters a serious error, it displays an error message in the usual fashion and stops. You can't work around the problem in the debugger.
- You can't edit the script and tell the debugger to restart. You must exit the debugger and start it up again.

Ah, well, what do you expect for free? It's still a useful tool to have on hand when you want to know how your script is behaving inside.

> **Tip**
>
> If you put debugging output commands in your script to display the values of variables, when you've gotten the script working, comment these statements out rather than delete them. This way, you can easily restore them if you need to debug again later.
>
> If you have a copy of Microsoft Word or Excel installed, you can develop scripts using the built-in Visual Basic for Applications environment. You can get there from the menu bar by clicking Tools, Macros, Visual Basic Editor. You don't have access to the WScript object here, but you can develop other aspects of your script in this more powerful debugging and testing environment.

> **Tip**
>
> Most scripting languages provide a special command that activates the debugger and halts the script when it is encountered. In VBScript, this is the stop statement. In JScript, it's debugger;. These act like breakpoints, except they're built directly in to your script and are especially handy when you're debugging WSC scripts used to create scriptable objects, which I discuss in Appendix G, which you can download from www.helpwin7.com/scripting.

Where to Get More Information

There is a wealth of information about scripting on the Web. In particular, for any particular scripting job you have in mind, you can probably find a script already written that does most or all of what you need.

With this mind, you might want to check out the sites listed in Table 1.6.

Table 1.6   **Web Resources for Windows Script Host**

Website or Newsgroup	Description
technet.microsoft.com/scriptcenter	The definitive source of information for WSH is the Microsoft Technet Script Center. It includes detailed documentation, tutorials, and examples.

continues

Table 1.6   **Continued**

Website or Newsgroup	Description
www.helpwin7.com/scripting	Download site for the sample scripts printed in this book.
www.microsoft.public.scripting.wsh	You should also check this site for post-printing corrections and tips.
www.microsoft.public.scripting.vbscript	Public newsgroups hosted by Microsoft. A great place to scout for scripting ideas and to post any questions you have. Although you probably don't get feedback or tech support from Microsoft employees here, the community of visitors seems to do a good job of answering questions and giving advice.

If you find other particularly useful scripting resources, let me know by dropping me a line through the guestbook at www.helpwin7.com/scripting.

2

VBScript Tutorial

IN THIS CHAPTER

- This chapter introduces the VBScript programming language.

- You should have some familiarity with the basics of programming. If you have previous programming experience of any sort, you can pick up VBScript.

- If you're new to programming, don't worry if you don't understand a topic. Study the examples, pick up what you can, and keep reading. In time, it will make sense.

- If you already know another scripting language, you don't have to use VBScript, but you should be familiar with it so you can follow the examples in this book.

Introduction to VBScript

VBScript is the free version of Microsoft's Visual Basic programming language provided with Windows Script Host (WSH). It's virtually identical to Visual Basic for Applications, which is built in to many Microsoft applications for use as a scripting and "macro" language. Despite being somewhat stripped down from the full-price Visual Basic language, VBScript is fully capable of performing calculations, working with filenames and dates, and manipulating external objects. Although it can't display the complex dialog boxes, windows, and menus of a full-featured Windows application, it's powerful to serve the purpose of helping you manage your computer and automate day-to-day tasks. Although you could use many other languages to write scripts, VBScript is an excellent choice because you can transfer your experience in writing macros and programs for Word and Excel to Windows scripts and vice versa.

In this chapter, I introduce you to VBScript and show you its most important features. I assume you have at least some familiarity with computer programming. Programming concepts change little from one language to another, so if you have experience with *any* computer language, even if it was a one-day Word macro workshop or a class on

FORTRAN using punched cards back in the 1970s, I think you'll pick up VBScript pretty quickly. Pay special attention to the illustrations called *patterns*. These are programming building blocks you will find yourself using repeatedly.

> **Note**
>
> After reading this chapter, you should visit the Microsoft TechNet website at www.microsoft.com/ technet/ scriptcenter. This is *the* official scripting resource site. It has the most current VBScript language reference online, which you can browse by following the VBScript Language Reference at the left side of the page. It has articles, tutorials, sample scripts, and add-ons that you can download. You can also download the full VBScript reference from www.microsoft.com/downloads by searching for "Windows Script Documentation." Get the download that includes a version number like 5.6 in its title. This delivers a help file that you can save to your desktop and review at your leisure. I highly recommend doing this!
>
> (But don't bother with the download titled "Comprehensive JScript and VBScript Reference." Despite the promising name, it's meant to be used only from within an obsolete version of Microsoft FrontPage.)

The program examples in this chapter are brief because they're designed to illustrate the basic commands and functions in VBScript. Meatier examples follow in subsequent chapters.

> → I encourage you to test the scripts as written and also to modify them yourself just to see what happens. For instructions on downloading and using the sample scripts, see www.helpwin7.com/ scripting.

The first VBScript topics I cover are variables and constants.

Variables

Variables hold the data you want to process. The data could be dates, times, numbers, or a series of arbitrary characters (commonly called a *string*). Strings are the most common type of data you'll work with because your scripts will usually manipulate filenames, people's names, the contents of files, and other such information.

Variables are stored in the computer's memory and are accessed by a *name*. You refer to a variable by name to see or change its value. To assign a value to a variable, you use the = sign.

For example, consider the following lines of VBScript code:

```
FullName = "Sue Smith"
Age = 40
```

When VBScript encounters these statements, it stores the string value `"Sue Smith"` in a variable called `FullName` and the integer value `40` in the variable `Age`.

Note

Although I don't really discuss this in detail until Chapter 3, "Scripting and Objects," variables can also contain *objects*, which are blocks of data managed by software add-ons to VBScript. Objects are what give VBScript its real power because they let you take advantage of the capabilities of other system programs to perform complex tasks, such as sending email messages, writing files, and installing printers on the computer.

Several restrictions are placed on the names you can use for variables:

- Names must begin with an alphabetic character and can contain only letters, numbers, and the underscore (_) character.
- They cannot contain an embedded space, period, or other punctuation character. For example, `big house` and `House.Big` are invalid.
- They must not exceed 255 characters in length.

(And just to be clear, these restrictions apply only to variable names, not to the information that variables can hold).

Information can be placed into variables directly by your program (as in the `Age = 40` example), it can be read in from files, or it can be derived or computed from other variables.

In most other programming languages, you have to define a variable's data type before using it—be it string, integer, object, date, or whatever. However, VBScript works the variable type out for itself, making life much simpler for the programmer as a result. In VBScript, all variables are of one fundamental data type called a *variant*. VBScript converts data from one type to another as needed. For example, if you attempt to join a variable containing a string to a variable containing a number, VBScript converts the number to its text representation and then joins the two strings together. If you add a number to a date, VBScript adds this number of days to the date, and so on.

Constants

In computer terminology, numbers and values that are typed into a program literally can be called, not surprisingly, *literals*, but they are most often called *constants*. The number 40 in the previous example is a constant. It's called a numeric constant because its value is…a number. VBScript lets you type in four types of constant values: Numeric, String, Date, and Boolean. Here's a rundown of all four types:

- Numeric constant values are entered using digits and, optionally, a decimal point and/or a plus (+) or minus (-) sign indicator. Examples are `40`, `-20`, and `3.14159`. Don't insert commas in large numbers; for example, `1,234` is not allowed. Write 1234 instead.

- String constants are entered as text characters surrounded by quotation marks (`""`). Examples are `"ABC"` and `"Now is the time"`. If you want to put a quotation mark inside the string, double it up. For example, `"ABC""DEF"` has the value ABC"DEF.

- Date values are entered using the format Windows uses for your chosen locale (country), surrounded by pound signs. In the United States, you could use `#1/3/2002#` to specify January 3, 2002. In most of the rest of the world, this represents March 1, 2002. (VBScript uses the Locale setting you've made in the Windows Control Panel under Regional and Language Options to decide how to interpret this kind of date constant.)

  You can also use long date formats. For example, `#January 3, 2001#` and `#3 January, 2001#` are equally acceptable. If you don't mind typing things like this, it's better to use a long date format because it's not subject to the regional ambiguity of the short format. Also note that if you specify a year with two digits, VBScript interprets 00 through 29 as 2000 through 2029, and 30 through 99 as 1930 through 1999. It's best to spell out years fully, so it's clear to both you and VBScript what year you mean.

- Time constants should be based on a 24-hour clock or should include text to indicate whether it is A.M. or P.M., as in `#22:30:10#` or `#10:30:10 PM#`.

- You can also combine the date and time into one constant, as in `#January 3, 2001 22:30:10#`.

- Boolean values can be entered as the words `True` and `False`.

Named Constants

Sometimes you write scripts with literal values that play an important role. For example, in a script that deletes all temporary files more than 30 days old, the number 30 has to appear somewhere in your script, perhaps in several places. It might look something like this:

```
for each file in folder
    if AgeOf(file) > 30 then file.Delete
next
```

Now, there's nothing magical about the number 30, and you might want to write your script in such a way that you can change this threshold later without having to look for every occurrence of "30" in the script file. You could put the number 30 in a variable that you would use throughout the script:

```
MaximumAge = 30
```

⋮

```
for each file in folder
    if AgeOf(file) > MaximumAge then file.Delete
next
```

The advantage of this is that you can set MaximumAge once at the beginning of the script and use the variable in as many places as necessary. If you want to change the value, you only need to edit the first statement. Additionally, named values make the script easier to understand; they provide context that the numeric values don't.

However, variables are designed to, well, vary, and this particular value isn't intended to change while the script runs. Like most programming languages, VBScript lets you define *named constants* that solve the literal value versus variable dilemma.

In VBScript, the statement

```
const MaximumAge = 30
```

defines a value named MaximumAge, which you can use by name throughout the rest of your script and which has the value 30. The word *const* means that the value can't be changed by the program as it runs. Named constants can be defined for any of the value types we discussed earlier: dates, times, numbers, and strings.

When you use a named constant in your scripts, you signal to anyone reading the script that the value is important and fixed, and you get the benefit of defining it in one place while using it in many places. It's best to define all the constants you use in your script at the beginning of the script file so you can easily find them.

> **Note**
>
> The word *constant* is often used to describe both literals, such as 30, and named constants, like MaximumAge. It's a bit misleading, but you see this in Microsoft's VBScript documentation and in the error messages VBScript produces.

When your script starts, several constants are already defined by VBScript. For example, the constants vbMonday, vbTuesday, and so on represent the days of the week; you can use them when working with dates and times. I discuss some of the predefined constants in this chapter, and there's a complete summary of them in the online VBScript references I mentioned at the beginning of this chapter.

Now that we've covered how to specify variables and values, we can discuss how to manipulate them with operators and expressions.

Operators and Expressions

VBScript variables can be manipulated with *operators* to perform mathematical or character-string operations. For example, the + operator adds numeric variables. To compute Sue Smith's age next year, you could use this VBScript command:

```
age = age+1
```

This means, take the variable age, add 1 to it, and store the result back in variable age.

When used with variables containing string values, the + operator *concatenates* the strings (joins them end to end). For example,

```
firstname = "Sue"
lastname = "Smith"
fullname = firstname + " " + lastname
```

concatenates `"Sue"`, a blank space (designated by the quotation marks), and `"Smith"`, and then stores the result (Sue Smith) in the variable `fullname`.

In the previous example, I could also have written this:

```
fullname = firstname & " " & lastname
```

VBScript lets you use the & character as an equivalent way to join strings. With strings, & and + do the exact same thing, but as a matter of good programming style, & makes it clearer to someone reading your program that strings are being added rather than numbers. Also, & has the added advantage that it can be used with variables and expressions of any type.

Operators are grouped into three categories:

- **Arithmetic operators**—These include +, -, * (multiply), and / (divide).
- **Comparison operators**—For example, > (is greater than) and <= (is less than or equal to).
- **Logical operators**—For example, AND, OR, and NOT.

The comparison and logical operators produce neither a numeric nor string result, but rather a *Boolean* value (either True or False). These operators are frequently used to direct the flow of control in a program, as in this example:

```
if Age > 40 then
    write "You're not getting older, you're getting wiser"
end if
```

A combination of values and operators is called an *expression*. Here are some examples of expressions:

Expression	Value of Expression
3+3	The number 6
2 < 20	The Boolean value True
"A" & "B"	The string "AB"
Date() + 1	Tomorrow's date

Each of the operators in each category has a *precedence*, or priority, that determines the order in which the parts of the expression are calculated. The order of precedence within calculations *does* matter. For example, the value of the expression 1+3*3 is 10, not 12. Following the conventions used by mathematicians, multiplication has a higher precedence than addition. VBScript computes 3*3 first, and then adds the result to 1.

(Remember this discussion from high school algebra class?) You can use parentheses to force VBScript to evaluate expressions differently. For example, `(1+3)*3` does produce 12. Expressions in parentheses are computed first.

Sometimes expressions contain operators from more than one category. For example, the following comparison contains both an arithmetic and a comparison operator:

```
if A+B > C then ...
```

In these situations, arithmetic operators are evaluated first, comparison operators are evaluated next, and logical operators `like`, `and`, and `or` are evaluated last. Comparison operators all have equal precedence; that is, they are evaluated in the left-to-right order in which they appear.

Tables 2.1–2.3 list all the VBScript operators.

Table 2.1   **Arithmetic Operators from Highest to Lowest Precedence**

Operator	Meaning	Example	Result
-	Unary negation	-5	-5
^	Exponentiation	2^5	32
*	Multiplication	2*3	6
/	Division	9/2	4.5
\	Integer division	9\2	4
Mod	Modulus (integer remainder)	9 mod 2	1
+	Addition	3+5	8
-	Subtraction	8-5	3
&	String concatenation	"abc" & "de"	"abcde"

The + operator also concatenates strings, but as I mentioned, it's best to get in the habit of using + for numbers and & for strings. Using & makes it clearer to someone reading your program that strings rather than numbers are being manipulated.

Table 2.2   **Comparison Operators**

Operator	Meaning	Example	Result
=	Equal to	3 = 4	False
<>	Not equal to	3 <> 4	True
<	Less than	3 < 4	True
>	Greater than	3 > 4	False
<=	Less than or equal to	3 <= 4	True
>=	Greater than or equal to	3 >= 4	False
is	Object equivalence	obj1 is obj2	False

The comparison operators are used mostly to let a script choose different actions, depending on the circumstances the script encounters. For example, a script can choose to delete a file if it's more than 24 hours old:

```
file_hours = DateDiff('h', file.DateLastModified, Now())
if file_hours > 24 then
    file.Delete
end if
```

The first line determines how many hours have elapsed since the file in question was created or modified. Then, the comparison `file_hours > 24` is `True` if `file_hours` is more than 24.

Table 2.3   **Logical Operators From Highest to Lowest Precedence**

Operator	Meaning	Example	Result
not	Negation	not (3 = 4)	True
and	Conjunction	(3 = 4) and (3 < 4)	False
or	Disjunction	(3 = 4) or (3 < 4)	True
xor	Exclusion (different)	true x or true	False
eqv	Equivalence (same)	false eqv false	True
imp	Implication (same value or second value True)	false imp true	True

The logical operators are used to combine individual comparisons to address more complex situations, such as "If the file is more than 3 days old *or* the file is named anything.`TMP`, then delete the file."

> **Note**
>
> Advanced programmers: The logical operators can be used with both Boolean and numeric values. They perform bitwise operations on numeric values and logical operations on Boolean values.

If this is new territory, don't worry about all these operators right now. (In fact, neither I nor anyone at Microsoft knows what `imp` is good for.) I use the more important ones in the examples throughout this chapter. For now, remember that operators exist for every basic mathematical function, and you can refer to these tables when you find the need.

Automatic Conversion

As mentioned earlier, when you combine variables or constant values of different types in one expression, VBScript tries to convert the values to appropriate types. Although it doesn't make sense to multiply a date by a number (what's 2 times August 4?), the addition and subtraction operators work in a surprisingly sensible way, as shown in Table 2.4.

Table 2.4 **Automatic Conversions for Add and Subtract**

Operation	Result
Number + or - String	If the string represents a number, it is converted to a number and the result is a number. Otherwise, the program stops with an error message
Date/time + or - Number	Date. The whole (integer) part of the number is added to the date as a number of days. Any fractional part of the number is added as a time offset, as a fraction of a day (1 second = 0.0000115741; 12 hours = 0.5).
Date + or - String	If the string represents a number, it is converted to a number and the result is a date. Otherwise, an error occurs.
Anything & Anything	Values of any type are converted to strings, and the strings are concatenated.

Flow Control

It's all well and good that you can assign values to variables and perform calculations, but the real power of programming is in the capability to perform operations over and over and to take different actions when conditions require. That's where flow control comes in. Instead of executing each and every line of a program in order from top to bottom, *conditional statements* let you specify how the program is to respond to various situations it might encounter. With *looping statements*, you can execute certain statements repeatedly. Looping statements record not only how to handle a repetitive task, but also how to know when to start and stop the task.

Note

In this chapter and in Microsoft's documentation, you see VBScript commands capitalized some times but not others. The case doesn't matter; VBScript is *not* case sensitive. For example, the commands

```
IF A = 3 THEN
if A = 3 Then
If a = 3 then
```

are all the same to VBScript. Microsoft's convention is to capitalize the words of VBScript statements, but I think this looks strange and it's too much of a bother, so I'm not going to capitalize most VBScript words in this chapter.

It is helpful to capitalize certain letters in long names, such as `CreateTextFile`, just to make them easier to read, so I do tend to capitalize the names of functions, objects, methods, and properties, as you see in this chapter. Remember, the case doesn't matter one bit to VBScript. It just makes the scripts easier for humans to read.

The **If...Then** Statement

The `If...Then` statement examines what is called a *condition*, and if the condition is true, it executes one or more VBScript statements.

Consider this example:

```
                                        ' Example File script0201.vbs
if Hour(Time()) < 12 then
    MsgBox "It's morning, rise and shine!"
end if
```

A condition is an expression that can be examined and found to be either true or false. In the preceding example, the condition is `Hour(Time()) < 12`. Now, in VBScript, `Time()` represents the current time of day, and `Hour(Time())` represents the current hour of the day—a number from 0 to 23. From midnight until just before noon, this number is less than 12, so the condition `Hour(Time()) < 12` is true, and the script displays the "It's morning" message. From noon on, the hour is 12 or greater, so the message is not displayed. Figure 2.1 shows what I saw when I ran this script one morning.

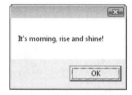

Figure 2.1 The "It's Morning" message is displayed when the hour of the day is less than 12.

`If…Then` statements can control your script's behavior based on any kind of condition that can be written as a combination of VBScript variables, operators, and functions that results in a Boolean (true/false) value.

The `If…Then` statement has several variations that help you manage more complex situations. First, when there is only one command you want to use if the condition is true, you can put the entire statement on one line:

```
if Hour(Time()) < 12 then MsgBox "It's morning, rise and shine!"
```

If you need to use more than one statement when the expression is true, you must use the `If…End If` version. The word `Then` at the end of the line starts a group of commands that are executed when the condition is true, and `End If` marks the end of the statements. Here's an example:

```
if Hour(Time()) < 12 then
    MsgBox "Good Morning!"
    runreport "Today's Activities"
    DeleteTemporaryFiles
end if
```

In this example, if the script is run before noon, the `if` statement runs the three statements between `if` and `end if`.

If you want to perform some commands if the condition is true, but other commands if the condition is false, you can use the `If…Then…Else` version of the command:

```
if condition then
    vbscript commands to perform
    when condition is true
else
    vbscript commands to perform
    when condition is false
end if
```

Only one set of commands or the other is performed when the script is run. Here's an example:

```
                                    ' Example File script0202.vbs
if Hour(Time()) < 12 then
    MsgBox "Good morning"
else
    MsgBox "Good day"
end if
```

If there is one command in the `Else` section, you can put the command on the same line as `else` and omit the `end if`. Here are the four possible arrangements:

```
if condition then
    statements

    . . .
else
    statements
```

```
    . . .
end if #

if condition then
    statements
    . . .
else statement

if condition then statement else    ' note that else must go at the end of the line
    statements
    . . .
end if

if condition then statement else statement
```

Finally, sometimes you find that one `Else` isn't enough. Another variation of the `If` command uses an `ElseIf` statement. With `ElseIf`, you test multiple conditions with one long statement:

```
if condition then
    vbscript commands go here
elseif othercondition then
    other vbscript commands here
elseif yetanothercondition then
    yet more commands
else
     last set of commands
end if
```

Again, only one of the sets of VBScript commands is performed—the commands belonging to the first *condition* that is true. If none of the conditions turn out to be true, the optional final `Else` statement is used.

If you use `ElseIf`, you cannot use the all-in-one-line format.

Note that `If` statements can also be nested one inside the other for more complex situations, as shown here:

```
if filetype = ".EXE" then
    if filename = "WINWORD" then
        MsgBox "The file is the WINWORD.EXE program"
    else
        MsgBox "The file is some other program"
    end if
else
    MsgBox "This is some other type of file"
end if
```

Here, the "inner" `If` statement is executed only if the variable `filetype` is set to `".EXE"`.

> **Tip**
> When you use nested `If` statements, debugging and understanding the script is much easier if you indent the contents of each successive `If` statement as I did in the preceding example. VBScript doesn't care, but it helps you and other people read the script.

The `Select Case` Statement

Suppose I have different commands I want to run depending on the day of the week. You know from the preceding section that I could use a series of `If` and `ElseIf` statements to run one section of VBScript code depending on the day of the week. For example, I can assign to variable `DayNumber` a numeric value (using the constants `vbMonday`, `vbTuesday`, and so on) corresponding to the day of the week. Then, I can use a long `If` statement to handle each possibility:

```
DayNumber = Weekday(Date())
if DayNumber = vbMonday then
    MsgBox "It's Monday, Football Night on TV "
elseif DayNumber = vbTuesday then
    MsgBox "Tuesday, Music lessons"
elseif DayNumber = vbWednesday then
    MsgBox "Wednesday, Go see a movie"
elseif DayNumber = vbThursday then
    : (and so on)
end if
```

However, there's an easier way. When you need to perform a set of commands based on which one of several specific values a single variable or expression can have, the `Select Case` statement is more appropriate. Here's an example:

```
                                    ' Example File script0203.vbs
DayNumber = Weekday(Date())
select case DayNumber
    case vbMonday:    MsgBox "It's Monday, Football Night on TV"
    case vbTuesday:   MsgBox "Tuesday, Music lessons"
    case vbWednesday: MsgBox "Wednesday, Go see a movie"
    case vbThursday:  MsgBox "Thursday, fishing!"
    case vbFriday:    MsgBox "Friday, Party Time!"
    case else:        MsgBox "Relax, it's the weekend!"
end select
```

When the `Select Case` statement is run, VBScript looks at the value of `DayNumber` and runs just those commands after the one matching `Case` entry. You can put more than one command line after `Case` entries, complex statements including `If...Then`, and other flow-of-control constructions. You can also specify a `Case Else` entry to serve as a catchall, which is used when the value of the `Select Case` expression doesn't match any of the listed values. In the example, `Case Else` takes care of Saturday and Sunday.

Tip

The Weekday function actually returns numbers 1–7 to indicate the days Sunday through Saturday. I can never remember whether 1 means Sunday or Monday or what. Luckily, VBScript includes predefined constants named vbSunday, vbMonday, vbTuesday, and so on, which you can use instead of the numbers. I discussed constants at the beginning of this chapter.

Although it's powerful and elegant, Select Case can't handle every multiple-choice situation. It's limited to problems where the decision that controls the choice depends on matching a single specific value, such as Daynumber = vbWednesday or Username = "Administrator".

If your decision depends on a range of values, if you can't easily list all the values that have to be matched, or if more than one variable is involved in making the decision, you have to use the If…Then technique.

Here are some other points about the Select Case statement:

- Statements can follow case *value*: on the same line or on a separate line. VBScript permits you to write

    ```
    case value: statement
    ```

  or
    ```
    case value:
        statement
    ```

  I typically use the all-on-one-line format when all or most of the cases are followed by just one statement, as in the days of the week example I gave earlier. When the statements after the cases are more complex, I start the statements on a new line and indent them past the word case.

- If one set of statements can handle several values, you can specify these values after the word case. For example, you can type case 1, 2, 3: followed by VBScript statements.

- If more than one case statement lists the same value, VBScript does *not* generate an error message. The statements after the first matching case are executed, and any other matches are ignored.

- You can use a variable or expression as the case value. Here's an example:
    ```
    somevalue = 3
    select case variable
        case somevalue:
            statements
        case 1, 2:
            statements
        case else
            statements
    end select
    ```

If the value of `variable` is 3, the first `case`'s statements are executed. If the variable can take on values that are listed as other cases, remember that only the first match is used.

The `Do While` Loop

Many times you want to write a script where you don't know in advance how many items you have to process or how many times some action needs to be repeated. Looping statements let you handle these sorts of tasks. As a trivial example, the task of folding socks might be described in English this way:

```
as long as there are still socks in the laundry basket,
    remove a pair of socks from the basket
    fold them up
    place them in the sock drawer
repeat the steps
```

In VBScript, we have the `Do While` statement to repeat a block of code over and over. In VBScript, the laundry-folding task might look like this:

```
do while NumberOfSocksLeft >= 2
    MatchUpSocks
    FoldSocks
    PutSocksAway
    NumberOfSocksLeft = NumberOfSocksLeft - 2
loop
```

Here, the `Do While` part tells VBScript whether it's appropriate to run the statements following it and `Loop` sends VBScript back to test the condition and try again. `Do While` statements can be nested inside each other, if necessary. Each `Loop` applies to the nearest `Do While` before it:

```
do while condition
    statements
    do while othercondition
        more statements
    loop
    still more stuff perhaps
loop
```

As you can see, indenting the program statements inside each `Do While` statement helps make this easy to read and follow.

There are actually five versions of the `Do While` loop, each subtly different:

```
do while condition
    statements
loop

do until condition
    statements
loop
```

```
do
    statements
loop while condition

do
    statements
loop until condition

do
    statements
    if condition then exit do
    statements
loop
```

With the first version, VBScript evaluates the Boolean *condition*. If its value is `True`, VBScript executes the *statement* or *statements* inside the loop and goes back to repeat the test. It executes the set of statements repeatedly every time it finds that *condition* is still `True`.

The second version loops again each time it finds that *condition* is `False`—that is, until *condition* becomes `True`. You could also write

```
do while not (condition)
    statements
loop
```

and get the exact same result. Why have both versions? Sometimes you want to write "while there are more socks in the laundry basket," and sometimes you want to write "until the laundry basket is empty." The `While` and `Until` versions are provided so you can use whichever one makes more intuitive sense to you.

Notice, though, that in these first two versions, if the `While` or `Until` test fails before the first go-round, the statements inside are never executed. In the second two versions, notice that the test is at the *end* of the loop, so the statements inside are always executed *at least* once.

The last version shows how you can end the loop from the *inside*. The `exit do` statement tells VBScript to stop running through the loop immediately; the script picks up with the next statement after the end of the loop. In this fifth version, the loop always executes at least once, and the only test for when to stop is somewhere in the middle. You can actually use `exit do` in any of the five variations of `Do While`. I discuss `exit do` more in the next section.

Every time you write a script using a `Do While`, you should stop for a moment and think which is the most appropriate version. How do you know which to use? There's no single answer. You have to think it through for each particular script you write. In general, you have two patterns from which to choose:

Pattern

When you want to perform a task as many times as necessary, as long as there is more work to be done, put the test at the beginning, as shown here:

```
do while (condition that tells if there is work to do)
    statements
loop
```

When you want to perform a task at least once and stop only when something happens *during* the task, put the test at the end, as shown here:

```
do
    statements
while (condition that tells if there is more work to do)
```

Choose between the While and Until versions by trying both and seeing which seems to make more intuitive sense when you say the statement out loud.

Terminating a Loop with Exit Do

Sometimes it's desirable to get out of a Do While or other such loop based on results found in the middle of the statements inside, rather than at the beginning or end. In this case, the Exit Do statement can be used to immediately jump out of a loop to the next command after the loop line.

For example, suppose you expect to process five files, named FILE1.DAT, FILE2.DAT, and so on. If you find that a given file doesn't exist, you might want to stop processing altogether and not continue looking for higher-numbered files. The following shows how you might write this in a script:

```
set fso = CreateObject("Scripting.FileSystemObject")
num = 1
do while num <= 5                               ' process files 1 to 5:
    filename = "C:\TEMP\FILE" & num & ".DAT"    ' construct filename
    if not fso.FileExists(filename) then        ' see file exists
        exit do                                 ' it doesn't, so terminate early
    end if
    Process filename                            ' call subroutine "process"
    num = num + 1                               ' go on to next file
loop
```

In this example, the first time through the loop, we set variable filename to FILE1.DAT. Each turn through increments the variable num by one. We test to ensure that the file whose name is stored in the variable filename really exists. If the file does not exist, Exit Do takes the program out of the loop before it attempts to process a missing file.

There's no reason we have to limit the `Do While` loop to a fixed number of turns. If we omit the "do" test entirely, it runs forever. We could rewrite the previous script to process as many files as can be found, from 1 to whatever:

```
                                       ' Example File script0204.vbs
set fso = CreateObject("Scripting.FileSystemObject")
num = 1
do                              ' process as many files as found
    filename = "C:\TEMP\FILE" & num & ".DAT"   ' construct filename
    if not fso.FileExists(filename) then     ' see file exists
        exit do                              ' no, terminate early
    end if
    Process filename                         ' call subroutine "process"
    num = num + 1                            ' go on to next file
loop
```

Here, without a `While` or `Until` clause, the loop runs indefinitely (it's what programmers call an *infinite loop*), until `Exit Do` ends it. This means that you have to be careful that `Exit Do` eventually does get executed; otherwise, your script will churn through the loop forever (or until your patience runs out and you cancel it by typing Ctrl+C).

The `Exit Do` statement works in any of the four variations of `Do While` and `Do Until` statements.

Counting with the For...Next Statement

When a loop needs to run through a set number of iterations, the `For...Next` statement is usually a better choice than the `Do While` statement. The first example I used for `Exit Do` can be rewritten as a `For` loop like this:

```
                                       ' Example File script0205.vbs
set fso = CreateObject("Scripting.FileSystemObject")
for num = 1 to 5                         ' process files 1 to 5:
    filename = "C:\TEMP\FILE" & num & ".DAT"   ' construct filename
    if not fso.FileExists(filename) then     ' see file exists
        exit for                             ' no, terminate early
    end if
    Process filename                         ' call subroutine "process"
next
```

The `For` loop sets a variable (num, in this example) to the first value (here, 1) and processes the statements inside. It then increments the variable and repeats the statements until the variable is larger than the number after `To` (here, 5). This loop thus processes the statements with num = 1, 2, 3, 4, and 5.

In the example, I also used the `Exit For` statement, which works exactly like `Exit Do`, except that it breaks out of a `For` loop rather than a `Do` loop. (Makes sense, doesn't it?!) The `Exit For` statement makes VBScript continue processing the script with the line after `Next`.

The For statement can be written in either of two ways:

```
for counter = startvalue to endvalue
```

or

```
for counter = startvalue to endvalue step stepvalue
```

Here, *counter* is the variable to be used; *startvalue* is the value that the variable is to take the first time through the loop; *endvalue* is the largest value the variable is to take; and *stepvalue*, if specified, is the value by which to increment *counter* each time through. The *stepvalue* can be negative if you want your loop to count backward, as in this rendition of a well-known, irritating song:

```
                                             ' Example File script0206.vbs
for number_of_bottles = 100 to 0 step -1
    wscript.echo number_of_bottles & " bottles of beer on the wall!"
next
```

▶ **Note**

This example demonstrates the power of looping commands. Without the For loop, you would have to type each verse

```
        wscript.echo "100 bottles of beer on the wall!"
        wscript.echo "99 bottles of beer on the wall!"
        wscript.echo "98 bottles of beer on the wall!"
```

and on and on. If you use the For loop, you can take care of the whole thing with just three lines.

If the Step clause is left out, the *counter* variable is incremented by one each time.

▶ **Note**

There's no reason the *step* value has to be an integer. You can step by fractional values as well if, for some reason, you need to do such a thing. When the variable surpasses the upper limit, by any amount, the loop stops.

Processing Collections and Arrays with For...Each

Some special-purpose VBScript functions can return a variable type called a *collection*. A collection is a list of filenames, usernames, or other data contained in a single variable. For example, a directory-searching function might return a collection of filenames when you ask for all files named *.DOC. Because you probably want to print, view, or manipulate these files, you need a way of accessing the individual items in the collection.

The For…Each loop runs through the loop once for each item in a collection. Here's an example:

```
                                       ' Example File script0207.vbs
set fso = CreateObject("Scripting.FileSystemObject")
set tempfiles = fso.GetFolder("C:\TEMP").Files

filelist = ""
for each file in tempfiles
    filelist = filelist & ", " & file.name
next

MsgBox "The temp files are:" & filelist
```

In this example, the variable `tempfiles` is set to a collection of all the files found in folder `C:\TEMP`. The For…Each loop creates a variable named `file`, and each time through the loop it makes variable `file` refer to the next object in the collection. The loop runs once for each file. If the collection is empty—that is, if no files are included in folder `C:\TEMP`—then the loop doesn't run at all. You also can use the For…Each statement with array variables, executing the contents of the loop once for each element of an array, as shown in this example:

```
dim names[10]
⋮
for each nm in names
    ⋮
next
```

The VBScript statements inside this loop are executed 10 times, with variable `nm` taking 1 each of the 10 values stored in `names` in turn.

→ To learn more about arrays, see "Arrays," **p. 89**, later in this chapter.

You can use any variable name you want after `for each`; I chose names `file` and `nm` in the examples because they seemed appropriate. You can use any valid variable name you want.

VBScript Functions

Functions are special blocks of VBScript's program code that can be activated (or *called*) by name. A function can be given data to operate on, and it always returns a value to the part of the script that called it. The technical term for a value passed to a function is an *argument*.

For example, the built-in `UCase` function takes a string variable, a constant, or an expression as its argument and returns a string with all the letters set to uppercase. Now, check out this example:

```
str1 = "my file.dat"
str2 = Ucase(str1)
```

In this script, the variable `str2` calls the `UCase` function, which converts the value of `str1` to all uppercase and then assigns that value, `"MY FILE.DAT"`, into variable `str2`. The original variable, `str1`, is left untouched.

We cover many examples of functions in the coming chapters. If this doesn't make sense now, the examples will make it clearer as we go.

Calling Functions and Subroutines

In the example I gave earlier, I showed how functions are called by specifying their arguments in parentheses. For example, I might call the `MsgBox` function this way:

```
selectedbutton = MsgBox("Do you want to continue?", vbYesNo)
```

The function `MsgBox` displays a text message in a pop-up dialog box and returns a value indicating which button the script's user clicked.

In VBScript, if you don't care about and don't intend to use the value returned by a function, you can omit the parentheses. In this case, you're treating the function as a *subroutine*, which is a fancy name for a function that does something useful but doesn't return an answer to the program that called it.

The following example illustrates this idea with the function `MsgBox`. I might use `MsgBox` to display a useful message, but I don't care which button the user clicked. Because I am not going to use the value `MsgBox` returns, I can call it using the subroutine form without parentheses:

```
MsgBox "The script has finished", vbOK
```

In the rest of this chapter, I show functions used both ways. Remember that parentheses are always used when you're using the value returned by the function and are omitted when you're not.

By the way, in VBScript, parentheses can also be omitted when a function doesn't take any arguments. You might see functions called this way in Microsoft's VBScript documentation. The built-in function `Now()`, which returns the current date and time, is an example. Both lines in this script do the same thing:

```
wscript.echo "The date and time are:", Now()
```

```
wscript.echo "The date and time are:", Now
```

The second line is actually calling function `Now` and printing the returned value. I find this confusing; you can't tell from looking whether `Now` is a variable or a function.

Tip

To help avoid confusing variables with functions, I recommend that you always use parentheses when calling functions.

Documentation and Syntax

About 100 predefined functions are available in VBScript, provided for your convenience as a programmer. These functions manipulate strings, perform complex math functions (such as square roots), and calculate dates and times.

All these functions are listed in the summary at the end of this chapter, and they are completely explained in the VBScript documentation at Microsoft's website (technet.microsoft.com/scriptcenter). To give you an introduction to the type of functions and their applications, I go through some of them in this chapter. But first, I should explain what you see in the online documentation.

The VBScript documentation shows the *syntax* (that is, the required formatting and wording) for each function and statement in the language. For example, the syntax for the `MsgBox` function looks like this:

```
MsgBox(prompt[, buttons][, title][, helpfile, context])
```

The parentheses tell you that `MsgBox` is a function. The list inside the parentheses shows that `MsgBox` can take five arguments. The square brackets ([and]) around some of the arguments aren't meant to be taken literally; that is, you don't type them. Instead, they indicate that the arguments are optional. Anything shown inside [and] can be omitted.

The documentation's explanation of each argument tells you what the argument signifies, what values are permitted, and what value is assumed if you don't supply one. The assumed-if-missing value is called the *default value*.

In the case of `MsgBox`, you can see that *prompt* is the only required argument. All the other arguments are shown surrounded by left and right brackets, so the rest are optional. The simplest use of `MsgBox` can look like this:

```
x = MsgBox("This is a message to display on the screen")
```

However, you could also use `MsgBox` with three arguments, like this:

```
x = MsgBox("This is a message to display", vbOK, "This is the title")
```

If you want to specify some of the arguments without specifying the ones in between, you can use commas with nothing between them. For example, you could write

```
x = MsgBox("This is a message to display", , "This is the title")
```

to specify the *prompt* and *title* arguments without specifying *buttons*. In this case, the `MsgBox` program uses the default value for *buttons*.

Finally, notice that the *helpfile* and *context* arguments are surrounded by a single set of brackets, which indicates that you can use both or neither.

Don't worry too much about these details right now. I gave these examples mainly to show how the documentation works.

String-Manipulation Functions

Most of the work you probably want to do with VBScript involves working with strings such as filenames and usernames, so it's helpful that VBScript has a rich complement of built-in functions to work with strings.

Searching for Strings with InStr() and InStrRev()

I've found that the most common task I perform when working with strings is to determine whether a string contains some other string. For example, if your script is to scan through the contents of a directory looking for DAT files, it needs a way of finding out whether the string ".DAT" occurs in any given filename.

The InStr function does this job. The expression

```
InStr(filename, ".DAT")
```

has the value 0 if .DAT can't be found in the string filename. The value is equivalent to the character position where .DAT starts, if it does occur. Here's an example:

```
filename = "TEST.DAT"
pos = InStr(filename, ".DAT")
```

In this case, pos is set to 5 because .DAT occurs starting at the fifth character in filename. If .DAT didn't occur in filename, pos would be set to 0. Here's how a program might take advantage of this:

```
if InStr(filename, ".DAT") > 0 then
    msgbox filename & " is a .DAT file!"
end if
```

Keep in mind that InStr is case sensitive. For example, it would say that ".DAT" can't be found in the string "somefile.dat". So, when filename might contain both upper- and lowercase characters, the correct way to write the test is as follows:

```
if InStr(Ucase(filename), ".DAT") > 0 then
```

The UCase function returns a string identical to the string it's passed, except that lowercase characters are turned to uppercase. Then, InStr looks for the uppercase .DAT.

Tip

Case is a constant concern when dealing with strings. To a computer, *a* and *A* are different letters. Always think through the consequences of having upper- and lowercase characters in the data you're working with. You should usually convert all user input and filenames to upper- or lowercase before performing tests on them—or be careful to account for case when testing.

If the first argument to InStr is a numeric value, it's interpreted as the starting character for the search. In this case, you have to pass three arguments to InStr. The following expression returns the value 4:

```
InStr(2, "ABCABC", "AB")
```

AB occurs at positions 1 and 4 in the string "ABCABC", but you told InStr to start looking at position 2. Therefore, the first occurrence is skipped.

Function InStrRev() is similar to InStr(), except that it searches starting from the right end of the string. The following line returns 4 because it finds the rightmost "AB":

```
InStrRev("ABCABC", "AB")
```

Extracting Parts of Strings with Left(), Right(), and Mid()

VBScript has several functions to pull pieces out of strings based on the starting position and length of the desired piece, as shown here:

Function	Returns
Left(*string, length*)	The leftmost *length* characters from *string*
Right(*string, length*)	The rightmost *length* characters from *string*
Mid(*string,start*)	That part of *string* from character position *start* onward
Mid(*string,start,length*)	*length* characters of *string* from position *start*

The following are a few examples:

Expression	Returns
Left("ABCDEF", 3)	"ABC"
Right("ABCDEF", 3)	"DEF"
Mid("ABCDEF", 3)	"CDEF"
Mid("ABCDEF", 3, 2)	"CD"

In real life, you will use these functions with variables, not fixed strings such as "ABC". For example, to find the base name of a filename without its file type or extension, you could use this VBScript code:

```
filename = "My file.DAT"          ' set name of file
dot = InStrRev(filename, ".")     ' find the rightmost . in the name
basename = Left(filename, dot-1)  ' the base name is everything BEFORE the .
```

This code sets dot to the position of the period that starts the file type part of the file-name. We use InStrRev to find it because files can have more than one period—for example, file.doc.txt is a perfectly valid filename—so if there is more than one period in the name, we want to be sure to locate the *last* one. Then, the script sets basename to that part of the filename up to, but not including, the period. In this example, basename would be set to My file. (If you find this at all confusing, you might want to work this out with paper and pencil to see that it's true.)

But what happens if filename doesn't have a period in its name? We have a problem: dot would be set to zero, and VBScript stops with an error message when you tried to set basename to the leftmost –1 characters! Good programming practice requires that you handle this situation as follows:

Pattern

To extract the base name from a filename with an extension, use a series of VBScript commands, like this:

```
                                        ' Example File script0208.vbs
filename = "test.file"              ' set name of file

dot = InStrRev(filename, ".")       ' find the rightmost . in the name
if dot = 0 then
    basename = filename             ' there is no . so pick up the entire name
else
    basename = Left(filename, dot-1) ' the base name is everything BEFORE the .
end if

MsgBox "The base name is " & basename
```

It would be a good exercise to run this improved script with filename = "xxx" and filename = "xxx.yyy.zzz" to see that it works no matter how many periods the name contains.

Other String Operations

The following are some more string manipulation functions you find handy:

Function	Returns
Len(*string*)	The length of *string* in characters
Lcase(*string*)	The same *string* but with all alphabetic characters in lowercase
Ucase(*string*)	*string* with all alphabetic characters in uppercase
Trim(*string*)	*string* with leading and trailing spaces removed
Ltrim(*string*)	*string* with leading spaces removed
Rtrim(*string*)	*string* with trailing spaces removed

Here are a few examples:

Expression	Returns
Len("ABC")	3
Lcase("My Documents")	"my documents"
Ucase("My Documents")	"MY DOCUMENTS"
Trim(" ABC ")	"ABC"
Ltrim(" ABC ")	"ABC "
Rtrim(" ABC ")	" ABC"

Converting Between Strings and Other Types

VBScript has a set of functions that lets you convert strings to other data formats. Most of these functions can take an argument of *any* type and converts it to one specific type. The most useful of the functions are listed here:

Function	Returns
cstr(*value*)	A string representation of *value*. Use to turn a numeric or date-time value to a text string. For example, cstr(47) returns the string 47.
clng(*value*)	A long (32-bit) integer. Use to turn a string representation of a number into a numeric value. For example, clng("47") returns the integer 47.
cdbl(*value*)	A double-precision floating point value. Use to convert a string representation of a number into a floating point value. For example, cdbl("1.23") returns 1.23.
cdate(*value*)	A date-time value. Use to convert a text string representation of a date or date-time into a date-time value. For example, cdate ("10-Jan-2011 11:30 AM") returns the corresponding date-time value.
chr(*value*)	Returns a one-character string containg the character corresponding to the integer ASCII *value*.
asc(*string*)	Returns the ASCII value of the first character in the *string*.

There are other several other conversion functions. You can see the full list in Microsoft's VBScript reference material under the heading Functions.

Date and Time Functions

As you would expect, because computers frequently refer to the date and time, VBScript has a number of built-in functions to make working with dates and times easy.

Reading the Clock with `Date()`, `Time()`, and `Now()`

The `Date()` and `Time()` functions return the current calendar date and local clock time, respectively, as determined by the operating system. For example, to display the current date and time in a message box, you can use the following code:

```
                                    ' Example File script0209.vbs
MsgBox "The current date is " & Date() & " and the time is " & Time()
```

The `Now()` function returns the current time and date combined.

> **Note**
>
> Using & to join strings with functions that return dates might seem strange, but this is a neat feature of VBScript. Because it knows that the & symbol always operates on strings, it knows to convert the date and time values to their string representations.

Dates and times are actually stored as numbers. The date is stored as an integer number of days since January 1, 0099, and times are stored as decimal fractions of a day (1 second equals 0.0000115741). You don't need to worry about *how* this is done, but it's helpful to know because you can manipulate dates using the arithmetic + operator. For example, the following line assigns today's date plus one day to the variable *tomorrow*:

```
tomorrow = date()+1
```

It's better, though, to use special built-in date and time calculation functions provided in VBScript, which I discuss next.

Computing a Future Date with `DateAdd`

Using the `DateAdd` function, you can add a specified interval to a given date, time, or combined date/time. The syntax of the function is as follows:

```
DateAdd(interval, number, date)
```

You use the *date* argument to set the initial date. The *interval* argument is the interval type, such as month, day, or year, and the *number* argument is the number of intervals to add. Table 2.5 shows a list of interval types. They must be passed to the `DateAdd` function as a string in quotation marks.

Table 2.5 **Interval Types for the `DateAdd()` Function**

Interval	Description
YYYY	Years
Q	Quarters
M	Months
W	Weeks

continues

Table 2.5   **Continued**

Interval	Description
D	Days
H	Hours
N	Minutes
S	Seconds

The following are some examples:

Expression	Returns
`DateAdd("M", 2, Date())`	Today's date plus two months
`DateAdd("H", -1, Time())`	The current time minus one hour

The `DateDiff()` Function

The `DateDiff()` function calculates the interval between two dates. The syntax is as follows:

```
DateDif(interval, date1, date2)
```

The *interval* argument describes the format of the result you want returned. Refer to Table 2.5 for these values.

For example, `DateDiff("D", "9/9/1999", "1/2/2001")` returns the number of days between September 9, 1999 and January 2, 2001.

This function is especially useful in scripts involving the age of files. For example, you might want to delete a given file if it's older than three hours. If variable `timestamp` holds the last-modified date and time of a file, the following test determines whether the file should be deleted:

```
if DateDiff("H", timestamp, time()) > 3 then
```

Other Date Functions

The following are a few more date and time functions you should be aware of:

Function	Returns
`Day(date)`	The day of the month of the given *date* from 1 to 31.
`Weekday(date)`	The day of the week of the given *date* as a number from 1 to 7, where 1 equals Sunday, 2 equals Monday, and so on.
`Month(date)`	The month of the given *date*, where 1 equals January and so on.

WeekdayName(*date*)	The day of the week of *date* as a string.
MonthName(*date*)	The name of the month in which *date* falls.
Hour(*time*)	The hour (0 to 23) of the given *time*.
Minute(*time*)	The minute (0 to 59) of the given *time*.
Second(*time*)	The second (0 to 59) of the given *time*.
Date(*time*)	With an argument, Date returns just the date part of a date/time value, effectively, midnight of the specified date. (Without an argument, Date returns today's date).
Time(*time*)	With an argument, Time returns just the time part of a date/time value. (Without an argument, Time returns the current time).

VBScript has the predefined constants vbSunday, vbMonday, and so on that you can use to test the values returned by Weekday in If statements and others. vbMonday makes more sense than the number 2 to someone unfamiliar with this function.

The following are some examples of what VBScript returns when the expression is run at 3:10:37 p.m. on Tuesday, January 11, 2000:

Expression	**Returns**
Day(now())	11
Weekday(now())	3 (for Tuesday)
Month(now())	1 (for January)
WeekdayName(Weekday(now()))	"Tuesday"
MonthName(Month(now()))	"January"
Hour(now())	15
Minute(now())	10
Second(now())	37

Date Tricks

Here are some tricks I often use to calculate the first and last days of a given month. You might find these handy to use when you want to write a script that, for example, needs to locate all files created during the previous month.

The tricks are based on the fact that for any date value dt, dt - Day(dt) gives you the last day of the previous month. For example, if dt is the first day of any month, dt - 1 gives you the previous day, which is the last day of the previous month. The same thing happens for the second of the month: dt - 2 is again the last day of the previous month. This holds true for any date at all; no matter how many days are in the month.

If you can find the last day of the previous month, you can then calculate other month start and end dates. Here's an example:

```
                                              ' Example File dates.vbs
prev_m_last  = Date() - Day(Date())           ' last day of previous month
prev_m_first = prev_m_last - Day(prev_m_last) + 1   ' then move up to first of prev month

this_m_first = Date() - Day(Date()) + 1       ' first day of this month

this_m_last  = this_m_first+40                 ' move solidly into next month
this_m_last  = this_m_last - Day(this_m_last)  ' then back up to end of this month

next_m_first = Date() - Day(Date()) + 40       ' move solidly into next month
next_m_first = next_m_first - Day(next_m_first) + 1 ' then back up to first of next month

next_m_last = next_m_first + 40                ' move solidly into following month
next_m_last = next_m_last - Day(next_m_last)   ' back up to end of next month
```

(The downloadable version of this script includes `wscript.echo` commands to display the results—give it a shot!)

What makes these tricks especially useful is that you don't need to know how many days are in any of the months. The calculation just doesn't need to know. However, you do have to be careful about one thing. The dates calculated by these expressions, if interpreted as date/times, are effectively midnight on the given date. If you want to use them, say, to select files created in a given date range, you have to be careful. This test

```
    if file_time >= prev_m_first and file_time <= prev_m_last then
```

misses most files created on the last day of the month because `prev_m_last` actually represents midnight of that last day, 23 hours, 59 minutes and 59 seconds short of the real end of the month. For a file created at, say, 3 p.m. on the last day, `file_time` is greater than `prev_m_last`, and the `if` test does not pick up this file.

To correctly pick up all dates in the range, you can test this way:

```
    if file_time >= prev_m_first and file_time < (prev_m_last+1) then
```

It's a subtle but important change! This version of the `if` statement checks for files created *before midnight of the day after* the end of the desired range, so it correctly selects a file created any time on that last day.

Alternately, you can force VBScript to examine just the date part of the file's timestamp:

```
    if Date(file_time) >= prev_m_first or Date(file_time) <= prev_m_last then
```

This works too, by stripping off the "time" part of `file_time`'s value.

Interacting with the User

VBScript is not designed for writing programs with complex user interfaces, but it can display simple messages and receive simple input strings from the user with its `MsgBox` and `InputBox` functions.

> **Note**
>
> Scripts can also read and write files and interact through the Command Prompt window using the `TextFile` object, which I discuss in Chapter 4, "File and Registry Access." In this chapter, I only discuss the basic VBScript input and output methods.

The `MsgBox()` Function

In its most basic form, `MsgBox` displays a text message to the user. For example, the following code produces the output shown in Figure 2.2:

```
                                                    ' Example File script0210.vbs
MsgBox "This message was displayed by VBScript at " & time()
```

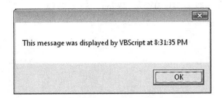

Figure 2.2   A basic message box displaying a string to the script user.

You can also use `MsgBox` to ask simple yes/no questions of the script's user. To do so, you use the advanced form of the `MsgBox` function, with the following syntax:

```
MsgBox(prompt [, buttons] [, title])
```

The three arguments are as follows:

- *prompt* specifies the text to display.
- *buttons* specifies which buttons to offer to the user.
- *title* is a text title displayed at the top of the resulting dialog box.

You can omit the *buttons* and *title* arguments; in their absence, VBScript displays an OK button and the title "VBScript." The value for *buttons* needs to be one of those listed in Table 2.6. You can use the constant name or the numeric value.

Table 2.6 *Buttons* **Options for the** *MsgBox()* **Function**

Constant Name	Value	Displays
VbOKOnly	0	OK button
VbOKCancel	1	OK and Cancel buttons
VbAbortRetryIgnore	2	Abort, Retry, and Ignore buttons
VbYesNoCancel	3	Yes, No, and Cancel buttons
VbYesNo	4	Yes and No buttons
VbRetryCancel	5	Retry and Cancel buttons

For example, you can tell the user that a required file wasn't found and ask whether to proceed by using this code:

```
choice = MsgBox("The preferences file is missing, should I proceed?", vbYesNo)
```

MsgBox returns either the value vbYes or vbNo, depending on the button clicked. The possible return values for MsgBox are listed in Table 2.7. The value indicates which of the buttons the user has selected.

Table 2.7 **Return Values from the** *MsgBox()* **Function**

Constant Name	Value
VbOK	1
VbCancel	2
VbAbort	3
vbRetry	4
vbIgnore	5
VbYes	6
VbNo	7

You can ask VBScript to display an icon along with the message by adding another value to the *buttons* argument, using one of the values listed in Table 2.8.

Table 2.8 **Icon Values to Use with the** *MsgBox()* **Function**

Constant Name	Value	Displays
VBCritical	16	Critical Message icon
VBQuestion	32	Question icon
Constant Name	Value	Displays
VbExclamation	48	Exclamation icon
VBInformation	64	Information icon

The following code displays a message with an Information icon:

```
                                        ' Example File script0211.vbs
x = 33
MsgBox "The value of variable x is " & x, vbOKOnly + vbInformation,_
    "Debugging Info"
```

The results are shown in Figure 2.3. The vbInformation option also causes Windows to play a special Information sound; you have to run the sample script to hear it for yourself.

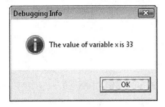

Figure 2.3   A *MsgBox* with a title and an icon.

Sometimes you want MsgBox to display some interesting message but don't care which button the user clicks or which value MsgBox returns. In this case, omit the parentheses from the MsgBox call. I discussed this point earlier in the chapter in the section "Calling Functions and Subroutines."

Tip

You can use MsgBox to display the contents of variables and values inside your program to help debug it. For example, if you assign the variable

```
    debug = True
```

at the top of your program, you can add debugging aids like this throughout the program:

```
    if debug then MsgBox "The value of variable x is " & x
```

When you get your program working correctly, you can disable all the debugging messages by changing the first line of the program to the following:

```
    debug = False
```

These are especially helpful when you use the WSH debugger, as described at the end of Chapter 1, "Windows Script Host." The debugger shows you which statements of your script are being run, and the MsgBox statements can show you the contents of important variables.

The `MsgBox` function displays a dialog box that stays up until the user clicks a button. Don't use it in a script that needs to run unattended! Your script will never finish because it will be waiting for a user who isn't watching.

If you want to display information without stopping the script, you can use the `Wscript.Echo` statement, as I discuss in the next section.

The `InputBox()` Function

VBScript lets you ask your users for a simple text string by using the `InputBox` function, as in this example:

```
                                        ' Example File script0212.vbs
UserName = InputBox("Please enter your first name")
MsgBox "Hello, " & UserName
```

This script displays the input-type dialog box shown in Figure 2.4.

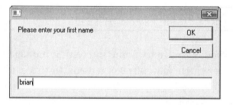

Figure 2.4   The *InputBox()* function as seen by the user.

The function returns whatever the user types. In the preceding example, this is stored in the variable `UserName`.

As with `MsgBox`, you can add arguments to the `InputBox` function to get better control of its appearance. You can use several options, only three of which are really interesting:

```
InputBox(prompt, title, default)
```

Here, *prompt* is the message to display above the input field, *title* is the title to display at the top of the dialog box, and *default* places a specific character string into the editing field when it first appears; the user can then accept or change this value.

A practical use of `InputBox` is to select a folder for the script to process, as in this example:

```
fldr = InputBox("Enter folder to be cleaned up", "Cleanup Script", "C:\TEMP")
```

Because VBScript is so flexible about the types of data stored in its variables, if your user types 23, the value returned by InputBox can be treated as a number or string. Here's a handy script to calculate square roots (something I'm sure you need to do several times a day):

```
do
    num = InputBox("Enter a number", "Square Root Calculator", "0")
    if num < 0 then
        MsgBox "You can't take the square root of a negative number like " & _
            num, VbOKOnly+VbExclamation
    elseif num = 0 then
        exit do          ' entering 0 ends the program
    else
        MsgBox "The square root of " & num & " is " & sqr(num), VbOKOnly
    end if
loop
```

This script fails with an error message if the user types something nonnumeric, such as "XYZ." It's always best to check a user's input for correctness so that the program either tells the user when something is wrong or at least behaves sensibly if it is. Here's how:

Pattern

When prompting a user for numeric or date input, use the IsNumeric() or IsDate() function to confirm that the value entered is legitimate, as shown here:

```
                                            ' Example File script0213.vbs
do
    num = InputBox("Enter a number", "Square Root Calculator", "0")
    if not IsNumeric(num) then
        MsgBox "You call that a number?"
    elseif num < 0 then
        MsgBox "You can't take the square root of a negative number like " & num, _
            VbOKOnly+VbExclamation
    elseif num = 0 then
        exit do           ' entering 0 ends the program
    else
        MsgBox "The square root of " & num & " is " & sqr(num), VbOKOnly
    end if
loop
```

InputBox displays a Cancel button. If the user clicks the Cancel button instead of OK, InputBox returns the empty string (""). You can detect this with a statement such as the following:

```
str = InputBox("Please enter your name:")
if len(str) = 0 then ...
```

Then you can respond appropriately by exiting the script, ending a loop, and so on. In the square root calculator, it turns out that the empty string satisfies the IsNumeric test and evaluates as 0, so the calculator responds correctly to Cancel without explicitly checking for the empty string.

Printing Simple Text Messages with Wscript.Echo

When you're debugging a particularly obstinate script, at some point you probably want to see what's held in your script's variables while the program runs. However, if you need to print debugging output inside a loop or you have dozens of variables to display and you try to use MsgBox for this job, you quickly get tired of clicking OK over and over. There's a better way: The Wscript.Echo command can display text *without* stopping your program.

The Wscript.Echo command is useful in scripts even when you're not debugging—sometimes you like a script to display text information on your screen. Later in the book, I show you scripts that display lists of folder contents, user accounts, network shares, and other information in Chapters 4 and beyond.

The command is simple:

```
wscript.echo expression
```

This prints the value of any expression of any type: Date, Numeric, Text, or Boolean. You can list any number of expressions, separated by commas, as in

```
wscript.echo expression, expression, expression
```

and VBScript displays each of them, separated by a single blank space.

Note

Wscript.Echo is only helpful when you run your script with the cscript command. If you run your script with Wscript, WSH displays all the Wscript.Echo text with pop-up dialog boxes, just like MsgBox.

For example, the script

```
username="Mary Smith"
lastlogondate=#03/04/2002#
wscript.echo username & "'s last logon was", lastlogondate
```

displays the text

```
Mary Smith's last logon was 3/4/2002
```

Note that I added 's to the username string using the string concatenation operator &. (I'm picky about this sort of thing. I like computer output to use proper English.)

As you saw earlier, VBScript is flexible joining strings with **&** and lets you join any variable type with a string—it converts a Boolean, Date, or Numeric variable or expression to a string and then joins the resulting strings. You can use this to add a period to the date at the end of the sentence, like so:

```
username="Mary Smith"
lastlogondate=#03/04/2002#
wscript.echo username & "'s last logon was", lastlogondate & "."
```

This prints, properly punctuated, as follows:

```
Mary Smith's last logon was 3/4/2002.
```

A Touchy Subject

Because I've taken a bit of a diversion into the topic of formatting messages, let me add one more thing. How often do you see a computer print a sloppy message like this?

```
1 files deleted.
```

This drives me *crazy*. There's no reason for it because it's easy to format this type of message in proper English (or whatever language you want to use).

Pattern

When counting in English, use the singular if the count is 1; otherwise, use the plural. This rule works for any number from 0 up. Here's an example:

```
                                              ' Example File script0214.vbs
for nfiles = 0 to 3
    if nfiles = 1 then plural = "" else plural = "s"
    wscript.echo nfiles, "file" & plural, "processed"
next
```

You don't have to go to this trouble for a one-time, quick-and-dirty program, but if your program is going to be used by others, it's worth paying attention to language in this way. As an exercise, I'll leave it to you to modify the sample script `script0206.vbs` so it prints "1 bottle" rather than "1 bottles" at the end of the song.

Advanced VBScript Topics

I want to cover some important topics here for more advanced programmers to help you get going in the right direction. Don't worry if these topics don't make sense now; they're applicable only to the most complex VBScript programs.

Error Handling

It's a given that scripts and other programs eventually encounter problem situations: a file isn't where it is expected to be, or a user types invalid input, or… well, the list is endless. You can make your script able to survive these problems by using a VBScript feature called *error handling*. Normally, if a VBScript statement or object encounters a problem, WSH displays an error message and your script simply stops running in the middle of whatever it was trying to do. Error handling lets you tell VBScript to *ignore* errors and keep on running. This requires you to take over the job for checking for errors yourself.

The statement `on error resume next` tells VBScript to continue running the script if any statement encounters an error. While this is in effect, you can check the built-in value `err.number` to see if an error has occurred; it's non-zero if it has. If an error did occur, the value `err.description` is a string that explains what went wrong. You can restore the normal halt-on-error behavior with the statement `on error goto 0`.

Generally, you usually want to let VBScript catch and halt on errors because most script errors are due to genuine bugs, and you want to hear about them so you can fix them. Use error handling only to protect a statement that you know is likely to fail due to circumstances beyond your control. Here is the general pattern to use:

Pattern

To protect a statement that is likely to fail, use the following VBScript construct:

```
⋮
on error resume next                      ' don't halt on error
statement(s) that might run into trouble  ' take action that may result in error
failed = err.number <> 0                  ' remember if failure occurred
err_cause = err.description               ' store error description (if any)
on error resume next                      ' restore normal halt-on-error
if failed then                            ' take action if error occurred, for
example
    msgbox "The following problem occurred: " & err_cause
    ⋮
end if
⋮
```

This script sequence sets variable `failed` to `True` if an error occurred. (You must record this result before `on error resume next` because any `on error` statement resets the information.)

In general, you want the protected part to be as short as possible because if one statement fails, the ones that follow it probably don't work either. If an error is detected, you can perform any reasonable action: work around the problem, attempt to fix it, try again, or whatever is appropriate.

You see this pattern used in many of the sample scripts in this book.

Note

The on error setting is very localized. If you change it in the main script body, it has an effect only in the main script body, not in any functions or subroutines you call. If you change the on error setting inside a function or subroutine procedure, it affects only that procedure.

Procedures: Functions and Subroutines

Procedures are the building blocks of large VBScript programs. A procedure is a separate section of code in your program that performs a particular task. The two types of procedures are functions and subroutines.

You have already learned about many of the built-in functions in VBScript, but you can create your own, too. You can also create subroutines, which are like functions but don't return a value.

The great power in procedures is that after you have written them once in your code, you can call them as often as you want. You can concentrate on *how* to perform a particular task just once when you write a function so that later you can simply *use* the function without worrying about the details.

Functions

To create a function, use the Function and End Function statements. Put any functions and subroutines *after* the main body of your script. (Although VBScript runs any statements in between or after your functions and subroutines as part of the "main program," scattering the code around the file this way can be extremely confusing for anyone reading your script.)

For example, the following simple function accepts one argument and returns the value of the argument plus 2:

```
function addtwo (value)
    addtwo = value+2
end function
```

The (value) part tells VBScript that the function expects one argument and is to hold the value in a variable named value. This variable is *local* to the function; if your script also uses a variable named value, it is *not* altered when function addtwo is called. Instead, addtwo has its own, temporary variable named value that exists only while addtwo is working.

The following is an example of how this function might be used elsewhere in the script:

```
a = addtwo(3)
```

When VBScript encounters the expression addtwo(3), it begins to run through the statements of the function, and the variable value holds the argument 3. The value to be returned by the function is set when the program assigns a value to addtwo (that is, to the variable with the name of the function itself). As you might guess, the end result is that ultimately the script assigns the value 5 to variable a.

In this way, you can extend the built-in functions of VBScript with your own. When you choose names for the argument variables, such as value in the example, you should choose meaningful names that explain what type of information is expected. For example, when a function is to be given a filename, I often name the argument fname, just out of habit. In my scripts, a variable or argument named fname always holds a filename.

The following function takes a filename, removes its extension (its file type), and adds the extension .OLD. You might use this function in a program that is going to update a file. If you want to create a backup copy of the file before changing the original, you can use this function to determine the desired name for the backup file, given the original file's name:

```
                                            ' Example File script0215.vbs
function backup_file_name (fname)
    idot = InStrRev(fname, ".")
    if idot > 0 then
        backup_file_name = left(fname, idot-1)+".OLD"
    else
        backup_file_name = fname+".OLD"
    end if
end function
```

Here's how the function works: The Instr function searches its first argument (fname, in this case) for the rightmost occurrence of the second argument (in this case, just a period character). It returns the value 0 if the second string is not found; otherwise, it returns the position within the first string at which it was found—1, 2, and so on. So, here, idot is set to 0 if no period appears in the filename argument fname, or it is set to a number greater than zero if a period does appear. (You might remember that we used this technique earlier in the chapter, in example script0208.vbs.)

The remainder of the function computes the backup filename. If the period is found, the function constructs the new filename from the first characters of the old name, up to but not including the period, and adds .OLD. If no period is found in the old name, the function tacks on .OLD anyway. Put into use, the following statements set variable file1 to MY.OLD and file2 to SOMEFILE.OLD:

```
file1 = backup_file_name("MY.DATA")
file2 = backup_file_name("SOMEFILE")
```

Subroutines

Subroutines are like functions, except they don't return values. They are used to do some specific job that the remainder of your script can then take advantage of. For example, the following subroutine takes as its argument the name of a file. It prompts the user to specify whether the file can be deleted; if the user clicks OK, it deletes the file:

```
                                          '  Example File maybedel.vbs
sub maybe_delete (fname)
    if msgbox("Should I delete file " & fname & "?", vbYesNo) = vbYes then
        set fso = CreateObject("Scripting.FileSystemObject")
        fso.DeleteFile(fname)
    end if
end sub
```

This subroutine uses the built-in function MsgBox to ask the script's user whether the file can be deleted. It displays a dialog box with two buttons: Yes and No. If the user clicks Yes, the program uses a FileSystemObject to actually delete the file. (I cover FileSystemObject in Chapter 4.)

With this subroutine at the end of your script file, you could use statements like this in your program:

```
maybe_delete filename
maybe_delete "OLD.DATA"
```

You can see how this lets you concentrate on the task at hand (deleting certain files) as you write the script, knowing that the details of *how* to delete files are taken care of in the subroutine.

Arrays

VBScript supports array variables. Arrays are variables that hold more than one distinct value. An array is a bit like an apartment building, where each apartment has a separate occupant. Just as the units in an apartment building are numbered, the individual values in an array are identified by a number called an *index*. Arrays are used when a script has to manage a varying number of items (say, usernames or filenames).

Whereas you can create an ordinary variable in VBScript simply by assigning a value to it, you must tell VBScript that a variable is to be an array before you first use it. Arrays are declared using a dim (which stands for *dimension*) statement, which tells VBScript the largest index value you intend to use. Array indexes start at zero, so the statement

```
dim var(10)
```

actually creates an 11-element array, with values var(0), var(1), ... and var(10). After it's declared, you can assign values to the elements of the array like this:

```
var(0) = "First value"
var(1) = "Second value"
var(2) = "Third value"
```

The big advantage of using arrays is that they let you write programs that are independent of the number of items you need to process. Using the looping statements that we discussed earlier in the chapter, you can run through the items in an array and a process each one in turn. Here's an example:

```
' set up an array with three items
dim var(3)
var(0) = "First value"
var(1) = "Second value"
var(2) = "Third value"
nitems = 3

' run through all items in the array using For Each

for each value in var
   wscript.echo value
next

' run through the items using indexing

for i = 0 to nitems-1
   wscript.echo var(i)
next
```

In this example, I first created an array with three elements and stored information into each one. You don't need to use all the elements; you can make arrays larger than you need if you don't know in advance how many items you put into them.

The example prints the contents of the array twice. The first time, it uses the For Each loop, which assigns the values in the array to a variable, each in turn. The For Each loop is the easiest to write, but it's not useful unless you want to process every one of the array's elements.

The second loop runs through the array by indexing each value in turn. This loop is a bit more complex to write because array indexes start with 0 and you have to take this into account when deciding where to stop. To visit every element, the indexes must run from 0 to the number of items minus 1. This example has three items, so we need the For loop to run through values 0, 1 and 2. Yes, this is awkward, but it's just the way arrays work in languages such as C and VBScript, and it's the basis of a common pattern.

This is a trivial example, but it shows how arrays can make short work of dealing with a large number of items. In this example, I'm only printing the array values, but the script could do much more. When you use arrays, you only need to write instructions to handle the general case for one item (for example, var(i)), and the loop takes care of repeating the work with every item you need to process.

> **Pattern**
> To visit the elements of a VBScript array where the number of actually used elements might be less than the dimension of the array, use a For loop. If the number of items used is *nitems*, use this loop statement:

```
for i = 0 to (nitems-1)
    work with array element(i)…
next
```

If necessary, arrays can be set up so that their size can be changed as the program runs. The array must first be declared without any dimensions, like this:

```
dim varname()
```

Then, before its first use and anytime thereafter, the array's dimensions can be set or reset with the ReDim statement, like this:

```
ReDim [preserve] varname(subscripts) [, ...]
```

The preserve keyword, if present, causes VBScript to preserve the existing data in arrays being resized; without preserve, the variables are cleared and all elements are set to Nothing. (Of course, even with the preserve keyword, if you make an array shorter than it was before, you lose any information stored in the elements that are dropped from the end.)

Variable Scope

By default, when a variable is declared or created in the main body of a script file, it has *global scope*; that is, it's also accessible to every procedure called in the script. Variables defined within functions or subroutines, however, have *private scope* by default. They're accessible only within the procedure in which they're declared. If a procedure containing a variable called var calls another procedure, that procedure can't access this variable. This protects variables in your procedures from being inadvertently altered by other procedures. When a procedure that defines the variable terminates, the variable is destroyed.

If you want to explicitly create variables with a global scope, you can do so by using the public statement. The same goes for private variables by using the private statement. Public variables are accessible to any procedure and are persistent until the script ends. For example, a procedure can use the following statement to declare a variable, Fsh, and an array, MyArray, that are available to all procedures in the script:

```
public Fsh, MyArray(10)
```

By default, variables can be used without being declared (or *dimensioned*) in advance. Seasoned programmers know that this can lead to hard-to-find bugs because it's difficult to detect typos; you could simply create a new misspelled variable where you had intended to change the value of a preexisting one. The `Option Explicit` statement fixes that by *requiring* you to declare all variables before using them, using a `dim`, `public`, or `private` statement. I recommend this in complex scripts. It takes a little extra work when you first write the program, but it helps eliminate a whole category of bugs.

To take advantage of this feature, put the statement `Option Explicit` as the first line of your script file. Then, follow this with `dim` statements listing each variable you use in the script. Yes, `Dim` is used to declare array variables, but it can also be used to define normal variables as well.

Here's an example of a script with a typo:

```
option explicit
dim myname
myname = "Brian"
wscript.echo "Hello", mynam
```

This script generates an error message when it runs into the undefined, misspelled variable `mynam`. Without `Option Explicit`, this script simply prints "Hello" and there is no other indication of the mistake.

Where to Go from Here

There's quite a bit more to VBScript than what I've shown you. There's probably a whole shelf of books devoted solely to VBScript at your local bookstore.

For a concise reference to all VBScript statements, functions, objects, and constants, download the VBScript Language Reference at technet.microsoft.com/scriptcenter. I gave instructions for browsing and downloading it at the beginning of the chapter.

Finally, I've found that some of the Microsoft public newsgroups can be a great source of information for everyone from beginners to old hands. The newsgroups at www.microsoft.public.scripting.vbscript and www.microsoft.public.scripting.wsh are particularly valuable. You can learn a lot by watching the discussions, and unlike most newsgroups I've tried, in these you have a reasonably good chance of getting a useful answer if you post a question. Although some of the conversations concern the use of VBScript in Web server and Web browser applications, most of the discussions are applicable to scripting as well.

3

Scripting and Objects

IN THIS CHAPTER

- This chapter introduces the concepts of objects, methods, and properties. It provides the background you need for the following seven chapters.

- Read this chapter to see how to use the objects provided with Windows Script Host with different scripting languages.

- To get the most out of this chapter, you should be familiar with at least one script programming language.

- The last section of the chapter shows how you can learn about the many undocumented objects provided with Windows.

Introduction to Objects

All the Windows Scripting languages that I discussed in Chapter 1, "Windows Script Host," provide the basic tools to control a script's execution and to manipulate strings, numbers, dates, and so on, but they don't necessarily provide a way of interacting with Windows, files, or application software. These functions are provided by *objects*—add-on components that extend a programming language's intrinsic capabilities. In this section, I discuss what objects are and introduce the terms you run into as you work with them. In the following sections, I discuss how objects are actually used in several programming languages.

In the most general sense, *objects* are little program packages that manipulate and communicate information. They're a software representation of something tangible, such as a file, a folder, a network connection, an email message, or an Excel document. Objects have properties and methods. *Properties* are data values that describe the attributes of the thing the object represents. *Methods* are actions—program subroutines—you can use to alter or manipulate whatever the object represents.

For example, a file on your hard disk has a size, creation date, and name. So, these are some of the properties you would expect a `File` object to have. You can rename, delete, read, and write a file, so a `File` object should provide methods to perform these tasks. An important aspect of objects is that they are self-contained and separate from the program that uses them. How the object stores and manipulates its data internally is its own business. The object's author chooses which data and procedures to make accessible to the outside world. In programming jargon, we say that an object *exposes* properties and methods; these items compose its *interface*. Figure 3.1 shows the interface of a hypothetical `File` object.

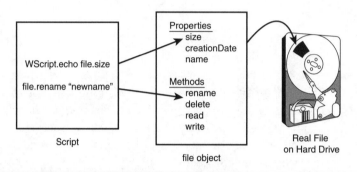

Figure 3.1   This hypothetical `File` object has an interface that can be used by other programs. How the `File` object actually stores its information and does its job are hidden.

Objects need a mechanism through which they can exchange property and method information with a program or script. Because each programming language has a unique way of storing and transferring data, objects and programs must use some agreed-upon, common way of exchanging data. For scripting and for most Windows applications, Microsoft uses what it calls the *Component Object Model* (COM). COM objects can be used by any compatible language, including VBScript, JScript, C, C++, C#, Visual Basic, Perl, and so on. COM objects can also be called *ActiveX Objects*, *Automation Objects*, or *OLE* objects, if they have certain additional features, but regardless of what they're called, the technology is based on COM.

In the next several chapters, you see objects that represent files, folders, network connections, user accounts, printers, Registry entries, Windows applications, email messages, and many more aspects of your computer and network. Windows comes with software to provide you with a wealth of objects. You can also download, buy, or create additional objects of your own devising.

Classes and Instances

Two other terms you're likely to run into while working with objects are *class* and *instance*. The distinction is the same as that between a blueprint for a house and the house itself.

The word *class* refers to the object's definition: its interface (the properties and methods it provides) and its implementation (the hidden programming inside that does the actual work). Hundreds of useful object classes are provided with Windows, and you can add or create more, as discussed in Appendix G, "Creating Your Own Scriptable Objects," which you can download at www.helpwin7.com/scripting.

When you use an object in a program, the class program creates one or more *instances* of the object. An instance is a parcel of computer memory set aside to hold the object's data. The class program then gives your program a *reference* to use when manipulating the object—some identifying value that the class program can use to determine which particular instance of the object your script or program is using. Figure 3.2 illustrates this point: Variables `file1` and `file2` are variables that reference two instances of a `File` object.

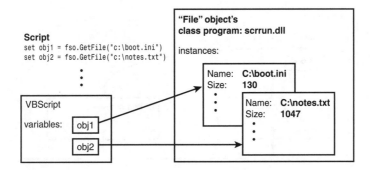

Figure 3.2 `File1` and `File2` refer to objects of the `File` class. This illustration shows two instances of the `File` object.

A reference is treated like any other variable in your program. Just as you can use functions such as `sqrt()` and `left()` to manipulate numeric and string values, you can use the object's methods and properties to manipulate an object reference.

Containers and Collections

As mentioned earlier, an *object* represents some real-world, tangible thing, such as a document or hard drive, and it has properties that represent the tangible thing's attributes. For example, an `apple` object might have attributes such as `color` and `tartness`. The actual data stored for the color might be a character string such as `"red"` or `"green"`. Tartness might be represented as number from `0` (sugary sweet) to `10` (brings tears to your eyes).

An object describing a file on a hard drive might have properties such as `name` (a character string) and `size` (a number). An object representing a hard drive might have properties describing the hard drive's size, volume name, and also the drive's contents.

Now, the contents of a hard drive could be represented as a list of filenames or an array of string values. However, it might be more useful if the hard drive could yield a list of file objects that you could then use to work with the files themselves. This is actually how many objects work. When appropriate, objects can return references to other objects. When an object needs to give you several other objects, it will give you a special object called a *collection*, which holds within it an arbitrary number of other objects. For example, a `Folder` object might represent a folder on your hard drive, and its `Files` property might yield a collection of `File` objects, which represent each of the files in the folder, as illustrated in Figure 3.3.

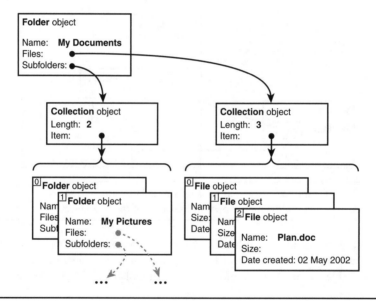

Figure 3.3   `File` and `Folder` objects can represent the contents of a hard drive. The contents of a folder can be represented by collections of `File` and `Folder` objects.

A collection object can actually hold *any* type of object inside it, and the collection object itself has properties and methods that let you count, extract, and work with these objects. This is a common thing to see in object programming: "container" objects that contain other objects of any arbitrary type.

Windows ActiveX objects use container objects that have two properties: `Item` and `Length`. The `Length` property indicates how many items are in the collection. The `Item` property retrieves one of the individual items. For some collections, you can extract individual objects from the Item collection using Item(0), Item(1), and so on. For many collections, though, the Item property requires a name or other arcane bit of identifying information. Therefore, each scripting language provides a more general way of letting you examine all the objects in a collection. I discuss this in more detail later in the chapter.

Collections are pervasive in Windows script programming, and some languages have special means of working with them. I give examples of using collections in each of the scripting languages discussed later in the chapter.

Object Naming

Because objects are separate program components, scripts and other programs that use them need a way to locate them and tell Windows to activate them. In this section, I describe how this is done.

Each programmer who creates an object class gives it a name that, with any luck, is fairly self-explanatory. For example, Scripting.FileSystemObject is designed to be used by Windows Script Host (WSH) programs to view and manage hard drives, files, and folders. Each of the programming languages you can use with WSH has a way of creating an object instance given just this name. For example, in VBScript, the statement

```
set fsobj = CreateObject("Scripting.FileSystemObject")
```

does the job, whereas in Open Object REXX, the comparable statement is

```
fsobj = .OLEObject~New("Scripting.FileSystemObject")
```

In either case, the statement causes the WSH interpreter to ask Windows to create an instance of the specified object. Windows looks up the object name in the Registry, finds the name of the program file that manages this object class (usually a file whose name ends in .dll or .ocx), and fires up the add-on program. The class program creates an instance of the object and gives your script a reference with which it can use and manipulate the object.

I show you how to do this in each WSH-compatible language later in this chapter. For almost all cases, this is all you need.

In the remainder of this chapter, I tell you how to use objects in VBScript and other languages. The next section on VBScript follows the tutorial style of Chapter 2, "VBScript Tutorial," whereas the descriptions for other languages assume more experience with programming.

Finally, at the end of the chapter, I tell you how to find useful objects not discussed in the later chapters of this book.

Using Objects with VBScript

To use objects in VBScript, you first need to create an instance of an object and store its reference in a VBScript variable. Then, the methods and properties of the object can be accessed using *variable.propertyname* or *variable.methodname*. This is easier to demonstrate than explain, so here's an example. This short script tells you whether your C: drive has a folder named \windows:

```
set fso = CreateObject("Scripting.FileSystemObject")
if fso.FolderExists("c:\windows") then
    WScript.echo "There is a folder named c:\windows"
end if
```

In the first line of the script, we create an instance of a `Scripting.FileSystemObject`. This is an object class provided with WSH that has handy properties and methods you can use when examining and manipulating disks and files.

Except for the word `set`, this looks just like a typical call to a function with the returned value being assigned to a variable. That's just what it is. `CreateObject` is a function that creates a new object instance. What's new is the word `set`, which VBScript requires you to use to indicate that an object reference is being stored rather than a regular value.

In general, the syntax to create an object instance in VBScript is

set *variablename* = **CreateObject("***objectname***")**

where *variablename* is the variable you want to use to hold the object reference and *objectname* is the type of object you want to create.

In the second line of the example, we use the `FolderExists` method to find out whether a specified folder exists. Remember that methods and properties are just like regular functions and subroutines; they just happen to "live" in a separate program that provides the object class. The presence of `fso.` before `FolderExists` tells VBScript that the `FolderExists` function is part of the object class to which `fso` refers, which in this example is `Scripting.FileSystemObject`.

Some properties and methods take arguments, as you saw with `FolderExists`. When they do, you have to use parentheses in the same way you would with any other VBScript function or subroutine call. If the method or property returns a function value, you must use parentheses:

```
variable = object.property("arguments", "in", "parens")
```

If a method doesn't return a value, you can omit the parentheses:

```
object.method "arguments", "without", "parens"
```

Does this look familiar? We used objects all through the VBScript tutorial in Chapter 2 in statements such as this:

```
WScript.echo "Today's date is", date
```

Now, you should recognize that WScript is an object reference and that echo is one of its methods. We never needed to use CreateObject to get WScript set up, though, because VBScript provides it automatically. The WScript object has several other handy methods and properties that I discuss later in this chapter.

As mentioned earlier, some properties and methods return another object as their values. For example, Scripting.FileSystemObject has a GetFile method that returns a File object. The File object can then be used to examine and manipulate the file. Here's a sample script that gives the size and creation date of the program file \windows\notepad.exe:

```
set fso = CreateObject("Scripting.FileSystemObject")
set file = fso.GetFile("c:\windows\notepad.exe")
WScript.echo "Notepad.exe was created on", file.DateCreated
WScript.echo "and is", file.Size, "bytes long"
```

The first line is the same as in the previous script, and it creates an instance of the helpful Scripting.FileSystemObject.

The second line asks the FileSystemObject to return a File object representing the file c:\windows\notepad.exe. Because I want to use this object several times, I saved it in the variable file, using the set keyword. (Although file is a reserved word in Visual Basic, it's not in VBScript, so it's available for use as a variable name.)

The next two lines use the File object's DateCreated and Size properties. Because these functions don't need arguments, there are no parentheses. The returned date/time and numeric values are printed by the WScript.echo method. On my computer, this prints the following:

```
Notepad.exe was created on 2/11/2008 6:56:09 PM
and is 151040 bytes long
```

Automation and Document Files

The GetObject function might be used to obtain an object that represents some already existing document file through a process Microsoft calls *Automation*. The GetObject function uses the name of the document file to find the appropriate object class server through the Windows standard file type/application association mechanism. You can see file type/associations on Windows XP in Windows Explorer by clicking Tools, Folder Options, File Types. On Windows 7 and Vista, you get there from Control Panel, Programs, Make a File Type Always Open in a Specific Program.

The following sample script uses the GetObject function to create a Word document object representing an existing file and print it:

```
set obj = GetObject("C:\docs\userlist.doc")   ' get object for existing document
obj.Printout                                   ' print the document
set obj = Nothing                              ' release the object
```

`GetObject` can also obtain a reference to an already existing object that was created by some other program, through a name called a *moniker*. Several preexisting objects can be used to manage networking, Windows, and Active Directory user accounts. We cover these in Chapter 7, "Windows Management Instrumentation," and Chapter 8, "Active Directory Scripting Interface."

The Difference Between Properties and Methods

I don't know about you, but for a long time I found the distinction between properties and methods to be confusing. Now, it's not crucially important to understand the difference, but if you're curious, I tell you how I finally came to an understanding of sorts.

If you look back in the preceding section, you see I mentioned the `FolderExists` method that is part of the object `FileSystemObject`. Why is `FolderExists` a method and not a property? It comes down to these main points:

- Properties relate directly to *aspects* of the object or, more precisely, of the thing the object represents.
- Properties act like variables: You just refer to them by their name.
- Every property returns a value of some sort. Retrieving a property's value doesn't change anything about the object or whatever it represents.
- Some properties let you assign new values to them. This changes the attribute of the object and the underlying thing it represents.
- Methods are the things the object's program can do for you.
- Methods act like functions and subroutines; they can have arguments passed to them.
- Methods don't have to return a value, but some do.
- Invoking a method can change something about the object or the real-world thing it represents.

Therefore, `FolderExists` is a method because it takes an argument (the name of the file it is to look up). Properties don't need arguments because they are intrinsic attributes of the object itself. As such, they don't need any additional information to return a value.

There is something else I should mention about properties: In many cases, you can both evaluate them (examine their values) and assign new values to them. They work just like variables in this regard. The difference is that when you assign a new value to a property, the object software makes a corresponding change in the actual thing the object represents. For example, assigning a new value to a `File` object's `Name` property changes the actual file's name, as shown here:

```
WScript.echo file.Name          ' evaluate the property
file.Name = "newname"           ' assign a new value to the property
```

Keep in mind, however, that some objects don't let you change a property's value. In this case, the object's documentation calls it a *read-only* property. And, a few specialized objects are designed so that changing the object's properties doesn't immediately change the underlying thing the object represents, until you use a special method that "commits" the change. Again, the object's documentation discusses this, and I point out a few objects of this sort in later chapters.

Nested Objects

One other thing I want to point out is that you don't necessarily need to save every object reference in a variable. In the previous example that displayed information about `Notepad.exe`, if I only wanted to see the creation date, I could have skipped the step of storing the `File` object in variable `file` and could have used these statements:

```
set fso = CreateObject("Scripting.FileSystemObject")
WScript.echo "Notepad.exe was created on",_
    fso.GetFile("c:\windows\notepad.exe").DateCreated
```

In this case, VBScript refers to `fso` to call the `GetFile` method, and the returned object is used to fetch the `DateCreated` property. It's not unusual to see several levels of objects this way; this is called a *nested object reference*.

When you're working with Microsoft Word objects, this is common. In scripts or Word macros, you might often see statements like these:

```
ActiveDocument.PageSetup.Orientation = wdOrientLandscape
ActiveDocument.PageSetup.TopMargin = InchesToPoints(0.5)
ActiveDocument.PageSetup.BottomMargin = InchesToPoints(0.5)
ActiveDocument.PageSetup.PageWidth = InchesToPoints(11)
```

In this example, the `ActiveDocument` object returns a `PageSetup` object, which has orientation and margin properties you can set. You could save yourself some extra keystrokes in creating this script by saving a reference to the `PageSetup` object, as follows:

```
set ps = ActiveDocument.PageSetup
ps.Orientation = wdOrientLandscape
ps.TopMargin = InchesToPoints(0.5)
ps.BottomMargin = InchesToPoints(0.5)

ps.PageWidth = InchesToPoints(11)
```

However, VBScript has a special program construct called the `With` statement that makes this even easier. The previous example could be rewritten this way:

```
with ActiveDocument.PageSetup
    .Orientation = wdOrientLandscape
    .TopMargin = InchesToPoints(0.5)
```

```
        .BottomMargin = InchesToPoints(0.5)
        .PageWidth = InchesToPoints(11)
    end with
```

The With statement lets you specify an object reference that is taken as the "default" object between With and End With. Inside the With statement, you can refer to the default object's methods and properties by preceding them with a period but no variable name. Not only can this save you a lot of typing, but it's easier to read, and it lessens the workload on VBScript, thus speeding up your script.

Note

If you need to, you can refer to other objects inside the With statement by using the fully spelled-out *object.method.etc* syntax.

Releasing Objects

When you create an object, Windows activates the object's class server program to manage the object for you. In the case of Scripting.FileSystemObject, you usually create one of these objects at the beginning of your script and use it throughout. When your script completes, Windows releases the object you've created. The class server program takes care of freeing up its memory and other housekeeping chores. You don't have to worry about it at all.

However, if you use a script to create multiple objects, you might find that it's appropriate to explicitly release them when you are through using them. For instance, a script that creates multiple Word documents should tell Word to close each document when you're finished with it; then, the script should release the document object, lest you end up with hundreds of documents open at once.

You can explicitly tell an object you're finished with it by setting the variable that holds the object reference to the value Nothing. Later in this book, there are examples of this in some of the sample scripts.

Working with Collections

If you ask Scripting.FileSystemObject for the files or subfolders contained in a folder or drive, it might need to return multiple File or Folder objects. To manage this, it actually returns a single *collection* object that contains all the File or Folder objects inside it. You can then examine the contents of the collection to look at the individual items.

A collection object has a Count property that tells how many items are inside and an Item method that returns a specific item from the collection. This would lead you to expect that you could write a script like this to print the names of the files of the root folder on your hard drive:

```
set fso = CreateObject("Scripting.FileSystemObject")
set files = fso.GetFolder("c:\").Files
for i = 1 to files.Count
    WScript.echo files.Item(i).Name
next
```

However, this script doesn't work. With a folder collection, Item doesn't allow you to retrieve items by number. It requires you to specify the *name* of the particular object you want, and if you don't yet know the names, this isn't very useful.

To scan through collection objects that can't be referenced by number, each scripting language provides a way to scan through collections without knowing what they contain. VBScript, for example, provides a special version of the For loop called For Each.

Pattern

To scan through a collection object named collection in VBScript, use the For Each loop as follows:

```
for each objectvar in collection
    :statements using objectvar
next
```

The For Each loop runs through the statements once for each object in *collection*, and the variable *objectvar* is made to refer to each of the individual objects in turn. Using For Each, and using a variable named file to hold the individual file objects, our folder-listing script now works:

```
set fso = CreateObject("Scripting.FileSystemObject")
set files = fso.GetFolder("c:\").Files
for each file in files
    WScript.echo file.Name
next
```

You could even use the following shorter version:

```
set fso = CreateObject("Scripting.FileSystemObject")
for each file in fso.GetFolder("c:\").Files
    WScript.echo file.Name
next
```

Now, if you don't plan on writing scripts in any other languages, skip ahead to the section titled "Using the WScript Object" on p. 111 of this chapter for more information about the built-in WScript object.

Using Objects with JScript

JScript, like VBScript, is a strongly object-oriented language—it's expected that programmers will use objects to extend its power. JScript supplies 11 built-in object types, and programmers can create generic and structured object types in scripts. I don't discuss the intrinsic object types here because this book focuses on external scripting and Windows management objects.

External COM/ActiveX objects are created using the `new` statement, as follows:

```
variablename = new ActiveXObject("objectname");
```

Here, *variablename* is the declared variable that is to receive the new object reference.

After you have an object variable in hand, its methods and properties are accessed using *variable.propertyname* or *variable.methodname*. For example, this is a short script that tells whether your C: drive has a folder named \windows:

```
var fso;
fso = new ActiveXObject("Scripting.FileSystemObject");
if (fso.FolderExists("c:\windows"))
    WScript.echo("There is a folder named c:\\windows");
```

Parentheses must be used on all method calls, even if the return value is not used—VBScript tolerates a statement such as

```
WScript.echo "There is a folder named c:\windows"
```

but JScript does not.

Case Sensitivity

In the WSH environment, JScript programs have access to a predefined object named `WScript`, which provides several useful methods and properties pertaining to the script's environment, execution, and debugging. Because JScript is a case-sensitive language, to use this object you must type `WScript` with a capital *W*, exactly as written here.

However, the method and property names of ActiveX and COM objects are *not* case sensitive. For example, JScript permits you to type `WScript.echo` or `WScript.Echo`.

Working with Collections

If you are used to using JScript with Internet Explorer in browser or server-side scripts, you might be familiar with objects that return collections of objects. Many Internet Explorer objects let you scan through the object collection using JScript's `for...in` statement.

However, most other objects' collections do not work with for...in and you must use an Enumerator object to work with them. This is true of most objects you encounter in the WSH environment. JScript's Enumerator object gives you a way of accessing a collection by stepping forward or backward through the collection's list of objects.

To use a collection provided by a scripting or other ActiveX object, you must first convert it to an enumerator:

```
enumObject = new Enumerator(collectionObject);
```

The Enumerator object has no properties (in particular, no Length property; if you need to know the number of items, you must get it from the original collection's Country property). It does have an internal concept of its "position" in the collection and has methods that let you move the current position forward or back to the beginning. Its four methods are listed in Reference List 3.1.

REFERENCE LIST 3.1   Methods of the JScript Enumerator Object

Item

Returns the current item from the collection. The return value is an object of whatever type the collection holds. If the collection is empty or the current position is undefined, it returns undefined.

AtEnd

Returns a Boolean value: True if the current item is the last in the collection, if the current position is undefined, or if the collection is empty. Otherwise, False is returned.

moveFirst

Makes the first item in the collection the current item. If the collection is empty, atEnd is immediately True.

moveNext

Makes the next item in the collection the current item. If the collection is empty or the current item is already the last in the collection, item is undefined.

Although a newly created enumerator should be positioned on the first item automatically, it's a better style to use moveFirst before examining atEnd or item.

Pattern

To scan through a collection object named obj, use an enumerator in this way:

```
e = new Enumerator(obj);
for (e.moveFirst(); ! e.atEnd(); e.moveNext()) {
    x = e.item();
    :statements using x
}
```

Here's an example. This script lists the names of all the files in the root folder on the C: drive:

```
var fso, e, file;

fso = new ActiveXObject("Scripting.FileSystemObject");

e = new Enumerator(fso.GetFolder("c:\\").files);
for (e.moveFirst(); ! e.atEnd(); e.moveNext()) {
    file = e.item();
    WScript.echo(file.name);
}
```

Now, if you plan on writing scripts only in JScript, you can skip ahead to the section titled "Using the WScript Object" for more information about the built-in WScript object.

Using Objects with ActivePerl

ActiveState's ActivePerl lets you run Perl scripts in the WSH environment. Perl's environment is already rich with file-management and network-communication tools, and if you're already a skilled Perl programmer, you might wonder what WSH can add. In other words, why use cscript or wscript to run Perl, when you could just run perl.exe directly?

The answer is that in the WSH environment, it's a simple matter to access COM, OLE (Automation), and ActiveX objects. The helpful $WScript object is predefined in the WSH environment. COM objects are the key to accessing network configuration, Active Directory, and Windows Management Instrumentation (WMI). Although you probably don't want to bother with the Windows script objects for file and directory management, the system-management tools make WSH worthwhile.

Running Perl Scripts in WSH

The ActivePerl installer creates two file associations for Perl files: .pl (Perl) is associated with Perl.exe, and .pls (PerlScriptFile) is associated with WSH.

If you use the familiar .pl filename extension for Perl programs that you want to run in the WSH environment, you have to use the command

```
cscript /engine:Perlscript myscript.pl
```

to fire them up. Because you might want to start scripts with the command line or from Explorer, your life is much easier if you use the extension .pls for programs meant to be used with WSH. This way, you can double-click the files in Explorer or use commands such as

```
start myscript.pls
myscript
cscript myscript.pls
```

to start script files; WSH knows what to do. You can also use PerlScript inside the structured .WSF files I discuss in Chapter 9, "Deploying Scripts for Computer and Network Management."

Here are some important things to remember when writing Perl scripts for use with WSH:

- You cannot use familiar Perl command-line switches such as -w. You need to directly set option values in the script.
- Any command-line arguments specified to cscript or wscript are not placed in the ARGV array. Instead, you must fetch command-line arguments from the $WScript->Arguments collection.

The Perl Object Interface

ActivePerl can interact with COM, ActiveX, and OLE (Automation) objects. The extended syntax for accessing methods is

```
$objectname->Method[(arguments[, …])];
```

Here's an example:

```
$myobject->SomeMethod
$myobject->Anothermethod("argument", 47);
```

The syntax for accessing Property values is

```
$objectname->{Propertyname}
```

Here's an example:

```
value = $myobject->{Length};
$myobject->[color] = "Red";
```

Because the syntax for accessing methods and properties is different, you must take care to check the COM object's documentation carefully to determine whether a value you want to use is a property or method.

▶ **Caution**

If you attempt to access an object property or method that does not exist or if you have misspelled the name, by default Perl does *not* generate an error. The result is simply undefined (undef). This makes it difficult for you to debug your script.

To avoid this pitfall, put

```
$^W = 1;
```

at the beginning of every script file. This causes Perl to print an error message if you attempt to reference an undefined method or property. I have found that the error message might not tell you clearly that the problem is an unrecognized property or method, but at least you get *some* warning.

To set a read/write property, you can simply assign a value to it, as in the following:

```
$file->{name} = "newname";
```

The standard `WScript` object, which I discuss in more detail later in the chapter, is predefined by the WSH environment and is available to a Perl script. For example, the current version of WSH can be printed with this script:

```
$WScript->Echo("The version is", $WScript->Version);
```

You could use conventional Perl I/O and write

```
print "The version is ", $WScript->Version;
```

instead. However, `print` writes to `stdout`, which is undefined when the script is run by WScript (the windowed version of WSH). A script using `print` works under Cscript, but not WScript. It's up to you, of course, but if you want your script to work equally well within either environment, use the `$WScript.Echo` method for output.

Note

Perl is a case-sensitive language, and object variable names such as `$WScript` must be typed exactly as shown here. However, an object's method and property names are *not* case sensitive.

To create an instance of an Automation, OLE, or ActiveX object, you can use either of two methods. The simplest is to use the `CreateObject` method provided with the built-in `$WScript` object, as in

```
$myobj = $WScript->CreateObject("Scripting.FileSystemObject");
```

You can also use the ActivePerl `Win32::OLE` extensions provided with ActivePerl:

```
use Win32::OLE;
$excel = Win32::OLE->new('Excel.Application')
    or die "OLE new failed";
```

For information on the OLE extensions, see the ActivePerl help file.

Working with Collections

Some of the COM objects you encounter in this book and elsewhere return *collection* objects, which are containers for a list of other objects. For example, the `Drive` property of `Scripting.FileSystemObject` returns a collection of `Drive` objects, and the `WScript.Arguments` property returns a collection of `Argument` objects. I discussed the methods and properties of the collection object earlier in the chapter.

Because the items of a collection object can't be obtained by an index value (at least, not directly), they must be "scanned" using an enumerator object. An enumerator gives you access to a collection object by maintaining the concept of a current location in the list, which you can then step through. To scan the list a second time, you must reset the current location to the beginning of the list and then step through the list again.

There are three ways to enumerate a collection. First, you can explicitly create an enumerator object, as in the following example:

```
$^W = 1;

$fso   = $WScript->CreateObject("Scripting.FileSystemObject");
$fls   = $fso->GetFolder("C:\\")->Files; # get collection of files in c:\
$n     = $fls->{Count};                  # just for kicks say how many there are
print $n, " files\n";

$enum = Win32::OLE::Enum->new($fls);     # create enumerator object
while (defined($file = $enum->Next)) {   # assign $file to each item in turn
    print $file->{Name}, "\n";           # print the file names
}
```

A second way uses the `in` function to hide the enumerator: The `in` operator returns `Win32::OLE::Enum->All(obj)`, which in turn returns a Perl array given a collection object. Instead of creating `$enum` and using a `while` loop in the previous example, I could have written the following:

```
foreach $file (in $fls) {
    print $file->{Name}, "\n";
}
```

Seeing this, you might guess that the third way is to use `in` to create an array of the subobjects, which you can then access explicitly:

```
@file = in($fls);
for ($i = 0; $i < $fls->{Count}; $i++) {
    print $file[i]->{Name}, "\n";
}
```

Of the three methods, the `foreach` method is the most straightforward, and it's the easiest on the eyes and fingers. Unless you really want to use an array, I recommend `foreach`.

Now, you might want to skip ahead to the section titled "Using the `WScript` Object" for more information about WSH built-in objects.

Using Objects with ActivePython

Many powerful CGI (Web-based) applications are written in Python, and ActiveState's ActivePython does a great job of integrating Python into the ASP scripting environment. This means it can also be used with WSH. Python, like Perl, has a rich set of built-in and add-on functions that give you complete access to the Windows API, so the scripting utility objects described in this book aren't going to be terribly interesting to the Python programmer. Still, you might want to use the scripting objects in the interest of increasing your scripts' language portability, and because COM/ActiveX objects are the only way to get programmatic access to Automation servers such as Microsoft Word.

Unlike Perl, Python was designed from the ground up as an object-oriented language. Objects, properties, and methods are its bread and butter, so to speak. If you're coming to Python from a background in other languages, there are a few points of which you should be aware:

- The WScript object discussed throughout this chapter is predefined. Python is case sensitive, so the object must be referred to as WScript, exactly.

- Although Python is generally case sensitive, the names of COM object methods and properties are not.

- Perhaps the easiest way to create ActiveX/COM objects is with the CreateObject method provided by WScript. Here's an example:

```
fso = WScript.CreateObject("Scripting.FileSystemObject")
files = fso.GetFolder("C:\\").Files
```

- You cannot directly assign a value to a COM object property. You must use

```
object.SetValue("propertyname", newvalue)
```

instead.

- Python automatically imports all predefined constants associated with an OLE object when you create an instance of the object. The constant values are created as properties of win32com.client.constants. For example, if you should create a Microsoft Word document, the value win32com.client.constants.wdWindowStateMinimize will be defined.

For more information about COM integration with Python, see the ActiveState documentation for the win32com package.

Working with Collections

Python automatically treats COM collection objects as enumerations. The easiest way to scan through the contents of an enumeration is with the for...in statement, as in this example:

```
fso = WScript.CreateObject("Scripting.FileSystemObject")
files = fso.GetFolder("c:\\").Files

for file in files:
    print file.name
```

Now, continue with the next section for more information about the built-in WScript object.

Using the **WScript** Object

WSH provides a built-in object named WScript for all scripts in all languages. We've used its Echo method in many of the examples in this book. WScript has several other methods and properties, as listed in Reference List 3.2, that you might find useful in writing scripts.

REFERENCE LIST 3.2   Properties and Methods of the WScript Object

Properties

Arguments

Returns a collection of WshArguments objects, representing the strings on the command line used to start WScript or Cscript. For example, if a script is started with the command

```
WScript myscript.vbs aaa bbb
```

or

```
myscript aaa bbb
```

then WScript.arguments.item(0) would yield "aaa" and WScript.arguments.item(1) would yield "bbb". WScript.arguments.length gives the number of arguments.

I discuss arguments in more detail in the next section.

BuildVersion

Returns a number identifying the current version of Windows Script Host. This number might vary between versions of Windows and as WSH is updated through Windows Update. I have seen WSH on Windows 7 return 0 for this property. I would not trust it to be usable.

FullName

Returns the full path and filename of the WSH program that is running your script (for example, c:\Windows\System32\cscript.exe).

Interactive

A Boolean value: True if the script is running in Interactive mode and False if in Batch mode. You might set this property using the //I or //B switch on the command line, or you might directly set the value in a script (for example, WScript.Interactive = False). In Batch mode, message and input boxes do not appear.

Name

Returns the name of the script host program (for example, `"Windows Script Host"`).

Path

Returns the name of the directory containing the script host program (for example, `"c:\Windows\System32"`).

ScriptFullName

Returns the full path and name of your script file (for example, `"c:\test\myscript.vbs"`).

ScriptName

Returns the name of your script file (for example, `"myscript.vbs"`).

StdErr, StdIn, and StdOut

These are file streams that can be used to read from the standard input or write to the standard output and error files. I discuss these in Chapter 4, "File and Registry Access." These properties are available with `cscript` only, not `wscript`.

Version

Returns the version of WSH (for example, `"Version 5.7"`).

Methods

CreateObject(*progid* [, *prefix*])

Similar to the built-in `CreateObject` function. With a *prefix* argument, it creates connected objects that can communicate events to the script. (Events are beyond the scope of this book.)

ConnectObject *object*, *prefix*

Connects an existing *object* to the script using event handler functions whose names begin with the string *prefix*.

DisconnectObject *object*

Disconnects the script from an object's events.

Echo *arg* [, *arg*]…

Displays any number of arguments of any type, formatted as strings and separated by spaces. Cscript writes them to the standard output, whereas WScript displays them in a pop-up message box.

GetObject(*filename* [, *progid*][, *prefix*])

Creates an object based on information stored in a file (for example, a document). If *progid* is not specified, it is determined from the file type. *prefix* might be specified to connect object events to the script.

`GetObject` can also obtain a reference to a preexisting object by specifying a special name called a *moniker*. This is illustrated extensively in Chapters 7 and 8.

Quit [*errorcode*]

Terminates the script. If a numeric value is specified, it is returned as the process's exit code—this can be useful when running scripts from batch files.

Sleep *msec*

Causes the script to pause for *msec* milliseconds. For example, WScript.sleep 1000 pauses for one second.

Of the properties and methods listed, the most useful are the Echo and Arguments properties. Let's see how you can use arguments to control what a script does when you run it.

Retrieving Command-Line Arguments

The use of command-line arguments is a common way of specifying information to a script at the moment it's run. The most common use for this is to write scripts that manipulate files, user accounts, or computers. The script can be written in a generic way, so that you can specify the particular files, people, or what-have-you at the time you run the script. For example, a script to process a file could be written like this:

```
filename = "specialdocument.doc"
'statements to operate on the file named filename
    ⋮
```

However, if you wanted to use this script to work with a different file, you'd have to edit the script. If you want a more general-purpose script, write the script to get the filenames from its command line, so you can simply type something like this:

```
C:\> myscript some.doc another.doc
```

Then, the script will operate on the files whose names you typed, rather than on a file whose name is built in to the script.

Usually, each programming language has its own way of providing command-line arguments to a program, but in the WSH environment, there is only one way they are obtained—through the WScript object's Arguments property.

The WScript.Arguments property returns a collection of objects, one for each item listed on the script's command line. You can write a script to use these arguments this way, more or less:

```
for each filename in WScript.arguments
    ' statements to operate on the file named filename
    ⋮
next
```

Of course, you have to use whatever method of manipulating objects and collections is appropriate to the script language you're using (this example is in VBScript). With script `myscript.vbs`, the command line

```
C:\> myscript some.doc another.doc
```

sets up the `WScript.Arguments` collection with two items: `some.doc` and `another.doc`. In VBScript, the `for each` statement lets your script process them in turn.

If you don't specify any command-line arguments, though, this script does nothing at all. It's best to have a script tell the user how to use it properly in this case. Here's a scheme for writing command-line scripts that you might find to be handy.

Pattern

When a script uses command-line arguments to specify what files (or users, computers, or whatever) to work with, it should explain how to use the script if no arguments are specified:

```
if WScript.arguments.length = 0 then
    ' no arguments on the command line? Display usage information, then quit
    WScript.echo "This script processes the named files"
    WScript.echo "by doing etc etc etc to them".
    WScript.echo "Usage: myscript file [file ...]"
    WScript.quit
end if
for each filename in WScript.arguments
    ' commands to process filename go here
    ⋮
next
```

Alternatively, you might want your script to operate on a default file if no files are named on the command line. Such a script should use a subroutine to do the actual processing of the files, so the subroutine can be called with either the default file or with specified files. In VBScript, it looks like this:

```
if WScript.arguments.length = 0 then
    ' no arguments on command line -- process file "default.file"
    process "default.file"
else
    ' process each of the files named on the command line
    for each filename in WScript.arguments
        process filename
    next
end if

sub process (filename)
    ' statements to process filename
    ⋮
end sub
```

In Chapter 9, I show you how to use more powerful types of command-line processing.

Locating and Using Unusual Objects

Several powerful, commonly used objects provided with Windows are documented by Microsoft in the Windows Scripting reference documents, and I discuss most of these in Chapters 4–9. If you're new to scripting, these should be enough to get you started, so you might want to skip ahead to Chapter 4.

In addition to these standard objects, many developers and companies provide add-in objects for free or for sale. There is, however, a wealth of objects already on your computer; hundreds of COM objects are supplied with Windows, and hundreds more are added if you install applications such as Word, Excel, and Visio. Many are designed just for the use of specific application programs and are of no use to script authors. Others are general-purpose objects for use by scripts and compiled programs. How can you tell which objects are installed on your computer and of those, which are useful for scripting? To be honest, identifying useful objects is tricky business, but if you enjoy detective work, read on.

To get an idea of what I mean by "hundreds of objects," take a look at the Windows Registry.

▶ **Caution**

Improper changes to the Windows Registry can make your computer nonfunctional. There is no undo command in the Registry Editor, so be very careful not to make *any* changes while examining the Registry.

To view the Registry on Windows 7 or Vista , click Start, type **regedit** into the search box, and press Enter. On XP, click Start, Run; type **regedit**; and press Enter. Expand the entry for HKEY_CLASSES_ROOT and scroll down past the .*xxx*-format entries to those that spell out names like "something dot something," as shown in Figure 3.4. Most of the entries from here down represent object classes; you can tell which ones do by the presence of a CLSID or CurrVer key under the object name.

In Figure 3.4, the FaxControl.FaxControl.1 entry has a CLSID entry, so it is an object. A CLSID (or *class ID*) is a long, essentially random number that object authors use to give their object a unique "fingerprint." A CurrVer entry, such as the one found under FaxControl.FaxControl, is used when there's a chance more than one version of the class program might be installed on your computer. The CurrVer value tells Windows where to look to find the class information for the most recent version of the object. Find that entry, and you find the object's CLSID.

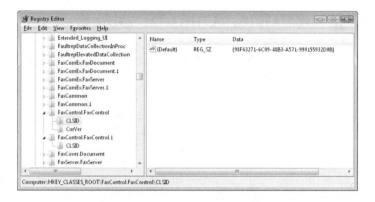

Figure 3.4   COM object classes are listed in the Registry under HKEY_CLASSES_ROOT, after the .xxx entries. Objects have an associated CLSID entry.

The first step in scouting out new and interesting objects is to peruse the Registry for names that sound interesting. For this example, I'll follow up on the FaxControl.FaxControl.1 object from Figure 3.4.

When you've found a CLSID value for a potentially interesting object, locate the matching value under My Computer\HKEY_CLASSES_ROOT\Clsid, where you find the information Windows uses to locate and run the program file that actually manages the object.

Figure 3.5 shows the class information for FaxControl.FaxControl.1. The InprocServer32 entry shows the actual program module (usually a DLL or OCX file) that manages the object. In this case, the program is \WINDOWS\system32\Setup\ fxsocm.dll. The name of this object and the location of its DLL make it sound like it might be used for setting up the Fax service. But how?

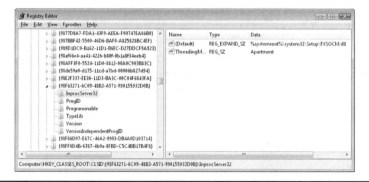

Figure 3.5   Class ID information for the FaxControl.FaxControl.1 object.

The first thing you have to check is whether the object is even suitable for use in script programs; some aren't. The first test, then, is to see whether you can create an object in your chosen scripting language. Use the *server.object* name you found under HKEY_CLASSES_ROOT. In VBScript, it looks like this:

```
set obj = CreateObject("FaxControl.FaxControl.1")
WScript.echo "CreateObject worked!"
```

If this script produces an error message, the object can't be used in scripts. If it runs without an error message, as it did when I tested FaxControl.FaxControl.1, the object has passed the first hurdle.

Your next step should be to search the Internet for references to the object name (for example, search for FaxControl.FaxControl.1 or FaxControl.FaxControl). I've found that Google is a great place to start. If you see references to pages on msdn.microsoft.com, these might point to complete documentation for the object in question. Be sure to search Google's "Groups" section, too. Many programmers haunt the comp.*xxx* groups, and if you're lucky, you might find an archived discussion about the object. (Unfortunately, if you do a Google search for FaxControl.FaxControl, you will most likely find only references to this very discussion from this book or from its first edition titled *Windows XP Under the Hood*, but no documentation.)

If you can't find documentation online, Microsoft or the object's creator might have supplied a help file describing the object. See whether the Clsid Registry values list a help file ending in .hlp or .chm. If it does, at a command prompt type

```
start pathname\helpfile.xxx
```

where *pathname\helpfile.xxx* is the full path to the help file listed in the Registry. This might show you how the object works. In the case of FaxControl.FaxControl.1, there is no help file.

> **Note**
>
> If the help file has the .hlp extension and you're using Windows 7, Vista or Windows Server 2008, you have to install the old Windows Help viewing program before you can open the .hlp file. Go to www.microsoft.com and search for "download winhlp32.exe".

If no help file is named, don't give up. Because COM objects are designed to be used by many programming languages, they can—if their developer wanted them to—provide a list of methods, properties, and their arguments to any program that asks. If your mystery object has this feature, you might be able to burrow into the object's program file to find its usage information.

The easiest way to do this is with an *object browser*, a program that's designed to do just this sort of burrowing. Microsoft provides one with many of its applications. If you have Microsoft Word, Excel, or PowerPoint, the Object Browser is included as part of the Macro Editor. Start the application and click Tools, Macro, Visual Basic Editor. Then, click View, Object Browser. If you have the full developer's version of Visual Basic installed, run it and click View, Object Browser.

To view information for a questionable class, you need to tell Word (or Visual Basic, and so on) to look into the class's program file. To do this, click Tools, References. Click Browse and locate the DLL or OCX file you found in the Registry. Click Open, and the library appears as a checked item in the Available References list, as shown in Figure 3.6.

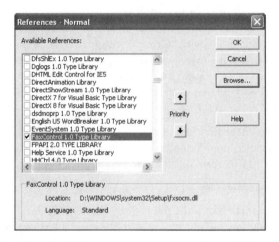

Figure 3.6   Selecting an object class type library to view in the Object Browser.

When the object type is listed and checked under Available References, click OK.

Then, select the class name from the library list in the upper-left corner of the Object Browser window, as shown in Figure 3.7. Choose object types in the left panel; the browser displays the object's methods, procedures, and predefined constants in the right panel under Members. You can select the objects in this list one by one, and in the bottom panel, the browser displays the method or procedure's arguments, if any, and any explanatory text it can dig up.

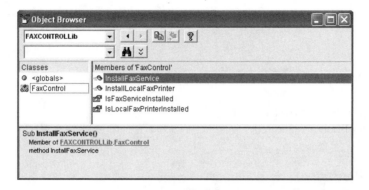

Figure 3.7   Viewing a class's type information in the Object Browser.

If you don't have any of the applications I've mentioned, another tool, called the OLE/COM Object Viewer, is provided with the Windows XP and Windows 2000 Resource Kits which you can download from www.microsoft.com. You can also download this tool directly from www.microsoft.com by searching for "OLE/COM Object Viewer."

The OLE/COM Object Viewer is much more difficult to use than the Object Browser. Here are some tips for using this viewer:

- Try to find the object of interest under Object Classes, All Objects. I've found that not all the objects I'm interested in are listed there. For example, `Scripting.Dictionary` is present, whereas `Scripting.FileSystemObject` is missing. If you can't find it there, look under Type Libraries.

- Double-click the library or object to view its class information. This information is designed for COM object programmers, not end users, so it's going to be tough to understand.

- `Typedef` items list some predefined constant values used by all the objects provided by the server.

- `Coclass` items define the objects the class server can create. If you view the contents of a coclass item, you find the class's predefined constants, properties, and methods.

Although either object browser can show you what sorts of values the methods and properties expect and return, it can't tell you what these values mean, so you have to experiment to find out if and how you can use them. In the case of `FaxControl.FaxControl.1`, the Object Browser showed two properties and two methods, as listed in Reference List 3.3.

REFERENCE LIST 3.3   Properties and Methods of the *FaxControl.FaxControl* Object

Properties:

IsFaxServiceInstalled
Returns a Boolean value.

IsLocalFaxPrinterInstalled
Returns Boolean value.

Methods:

InstallFaxService
Returns no value and takes no arguments.

InstallLocalFaxPrinter
Returns no value and takes no arguments.

This sounds pretty straightforward. There are no arguments to supply to these methods, so there's no detective work required there. Also, the names sound pretty self-explanatory. This object lets you know whether the Fax service and the Fax Printer are installed, and it can install them. But does it work?

Here's a sample script I wrote to check:

```
set obj = CreateObject("FaxControl.FaxControl.1")
WScript.echo "IsFaxServiceInstalled =", obj.IsFaxServiceInstalled
WScript.echo "IsLocalFaxPrinterInstalled =", obj.IsLocalFaxPrinterInstalled
```

The results when I ran it on a Windows XP computer that had a modem but did not have the fax service set up were

```
IsFaxServiceInstalled = 0
IsLocalFaxPrinterInstalled = 0
```

When I ran the script

```
set obj = CreateObject("FaxControl.FaxControl.1")
obj.InstallFaxService
```

Windows Setup asked for my Windows XP CD disk and installed the Fax service and printer. The first script's output became this:

```
IsFaxServiceInstalled = -1
IsLocalFaxPrinterInstalled = -1
```

Here, -1 means True (any nonzero value means True), so the object does the job you expect it to. Here's a script that can automatically be sure a user's Windows XP system has the Fax service as well as a fax and printer installed:

```
set obj = CreateObject("FaxControl.FaxControl.1")

if not obj.IsFaxServiceInstalled then
```

```
    WScript.echo "Installing Fax Service..."
    obj.InstallFaxServic
elseif not obj.IsLocalFaxPrinterInstalled then
    WScript.echo "Reinstalling Fax Printer..."
    obj.InstallLocalFaxPrinter
else
    WScript.echo "Fax printer is ready to go."
end if
```

This is a good example of the functionality you can find by digging into the many objects that come with Windows, and it shows the kinds of scripts you can write to manage Windows computers so other users don't have to poke around with the Control Panel themselves.

(On Windows Vista, this script works only on the Business, Enterprise and Ultimate editions. The Home editions don't come with built-in faxing support, but, all versions of Windows 7 include the Faxing service.)

4

File and Registry Access

IN THIS CHAPTER

- This chapter shows how to use "stock" objects provided with Windows Script Host to manipulate and read files, folders, the environment, and the Registry.

- You should be comfortable with the material in Chapter 3, "Scripting and Objects," before reading this chapter.

- Each object can do more than I have room to describe. I give examples of the most important functions, and you can use the reference information to see what other functions are available.

- The first time through each section, I suggest that you skim the lists of methods and properties, study the examples, and then go back through the reference tables.

Getting Real Work Done

The first three chapters of this book covered Windows Script Host (WSH), gave an overview of VBScript programming, and showed how to use Windows COM/ActiveX objects. Now, we get to start applying all that background information toward useful ends.

In this and the following chapters, I discuss several powerful objects provided with Windows you can use when writing scripts. These objects can manipulate files, run programs, reconfigure Windows, and help with network administration. As I introduce these objects, I give real-world examples of script programs you can use in their entirety or as the basis for writing scripts of your own.

In the rest of the chapters on scripting, I use VBScript almost exclusively. If you use a different language, remember that regardless of which programming language you use, the concepts remain the same, and the objects work in *exactly* the same way. You have to account for the peculiarities of your language's syntax and its way of handling collection objects, but the tips in Chapter 3 should make that job fairly straightforward.

Note

For beginning programmers, I start this chapter with a more tutorial approach to the `Scripting.FileSystemObject` object. Later in the chapter and in subsequent chapters, I adopt a more to-the-point style. Although I still use some short program fragments to illustrate points, I start presenting longer scripts to show how all the concepts fit together to make a useful program.

Manipulating Files and Folders

One of the principal reasons people write scripts is to work with files and folders. Although Windows Explorer makes it easy to use the mouse to copy and move files, when you have a large number of files and folders to work with, the graphical user interface can quickly become tedious. Here are some tasks that are a nightmare with Explorer but are a snap with scripting:

- Renaming several files
- Changing the attributes of all the files in a folder and in all levels of subfolders underneath it
- Printing all Microsoft Word files under 1MB in size from a USB drive with Word and all the image files with the Paint program
- Periodically scanning a folder for files with a certain name or file type and automatically printing or processing them in some way

Most scripting tasks involving files and folders use the object `FileSystemObject`, so we start there.

Scripting.FileSystemObject

The `Scripting.FileSystemObject` object is provided with WSH as a "helper" object. Its methods, properties, and subobjects give you most of the tools you need to work with files. Many VBScript scripts start with the statement

```
set fso = CreateObject("Scripting.FileSystemObject")
```

which creates an instance of `FileSystemObject` and stores it in the variable `fso`. It's only necessary to create one instance per script program—if you create it as a global variable, is available to all parts of your script and any of its subroutines or functions.

Note

In some of the script fragment examples that follow in this chapter, I use an object named `fso` but don't explicitly show the `CreateObject` call. You can assume that, in any example, `fso` is a `FileSystemObject` object created at the beginning of the script.

Reference List 4.1 lists the `FileSystemObject` methods and properties. We use many of them in the examples to follow throughout this chapter. Arguments to `Scripting.FileSystemObject` methods are strings, unless described otherwise.

> **Note**
>
> In these properties and methods, where a filename or folder name is called for, you can specify a full path starting with a drive letter, or you can enter a relative path. If the path you use doesn't start with a drive letter, the path is assumed to belong on the current drive. If the path doesn't start with a backslash, the path is assumed to be relative to the current working directory on the current or specified drive. For example, if the current directory is `c:\text` when you run your script, Windows interprets the path `\temp` as `c:\temp` and interprets the filename `subfolder\something.doc` as `c:\text\sub-folder\something.doc`.

REFERENCE LIST 4.1   Property and Methods of `Scripting.FileSystemObject`

Property:

Drives

Returns a collection of `Drive` objects, one for each physical or mapped network drive on the local machine.

Methods:

BuildPath(*path, name*)

Appends a file name to a pathname and returns the combined string. Takes care of adding any necessary : or \ characters. For example, `fso.BuildPath("C:\temp", "file.dat")` returns `"C:\temp\file.dat"`.

CopyFile *source, destination* [*,overwrite*]

Copies one or more files from one location to another. The `source` argument can contain wildcards in the filename, if desired. The `destination` argument can be a filename or folder name. If the Boolean argument `overwrite` is specified and is `False`, and if the destination folder already contains a file with the same name as the source file, the script terminates with an error; otherwise, existing files are over-written. The default value for `overwrite` is `True`. There is no return value, so you do not need to use parentheses when calling this method.

CopyFolder *source, destination* [, *overwrite*]

Copies a folder named by the `source` argument from one location to another. Any files and subfolders are copied as well. If the destination folder already exists, the contents of the source folder are added to it, and for the contents, the `overwrite` flag works the same as it does with `CopyFile`. You can copy multiple folders by specifying a wildcard in the `source` name. A wildcard can only be used in the last name in the path, however.

CreateFolder(*foldername*)

Creates a folder and returns a `Folder` object representing the new folder. The

method generates an error if the folder already exists, so you should use
`FolderExists` to check before calling `CreateFolder`. `CreateFolder` only creates the
lowest level folder in the specified path. The call

```
fso.CreateFolder("C:\a\b\c")
```

only works if `C:\a\b` already exists. Later in the chapter, I show you how to write a
subroutine that can create a subfolder even when the upper-level folders don't yet
exist.

CreateTextFile(*filename*[, *overwrite*[, *unicode*]]**)**
Creates a file with the specified name and returns a `TextStream` object that can be
used to read from or write to the file. Text streams are discussed later in the chapter.
The optional arguments are as follows:

- *overwrite*—If this argument is omitted or is `True` and the specified file already
  exists, the original file is deleted and a new one is created. If this argument is
  specified as `False`, an error occurs if the file already exists. The default value is
  `True`.

- *unicode*—If this argument is specified and `True`, the file is created using
  Unicode encoding. If this argument is omitted or `False`, the file is created using
  ASCII.

DeleteFile *filespec*[, *force*]
Deletes a specified file. The deleted file is *not* placed in the Recycle Bin—it's *gone*.
Read-only files are not deleted unless the Boolean parameter `force` is specified and
is `True`. You can delete multiple files by using a wildcard in the filename part of
filespec.

DeleteFolder *folderspec*[, *force*]
Deletes a specified folder and its entire contents. The deleted files and folders are
not saved in the Recycle Bin. Read-only folders and files are not deleted unless the
Boolean parameter `force` is specified and is `True`. If `force` is omitted or is `False`,
`DeleteFolder` stops with an error partway through the task if it encounters a read-
only file. You can delete multiple folders by specifying a wildcard in the source
name. A wildcard can be used only in the last name in the path, however.

DriveExists(*drive***)**
Returns `True` if the specified *drive* (for example, `"B:"`) exists; otherwise, it returns
`False`.

FileExists(*filename***)**
Returns `True` if the specified file exists; otherwise, it returns `False`.

FolderExists(*folder***)**
Returns `True` if the specified folder exists; otherwise, it returns `False`.

GetAbsolutePathName(*pathspec***)**
Returns a complete, fully qualified filename or pathname from any filename or
pathname. If the specified path is relative, the current directory is used to construct

the absolute path. For example, if the current directory is `c:\text` when you run your script, `fso.GetAbsolutePathName("some.doc")` returns `"c:\text\some.doc"`.

GetFileVersion(`filepath`**)**

Given the full path and filename of a Windows executable program or Dynamic Link Library (DLL) module, returns the version identification string stored in the file. Returns the empty string if there is no recognizable version information in the file or if the file does not exist. A typical return value might be something like "6.1.7600.0".

GetBaseName(`filepath`**)**

Returns the base name of the specified file, less any path or file extension. If `filepath` names a path and not a filename, it returns the last folder name in the path. Be warned, though: In this case, if the last folder has something that looks like a file extension in its name (`.xxx`), `GetBaseName` removes it. Use `GetFileName` if you want the final folder name in a path.

GetDrive(`drivespec`**)**

Returns a `Drive` object corresponding to the specified *drive*. Although it would make sense that `GetDrive` looks at the drive letter specified in `drivespec`, you cannot pass `GetDrive` a full pathname. If you try, the script generates an error. You can use `GetDriveName` to extract just the drive.

GetDriveName(`path`**)**

Returns the name of the drive used in the specified path.

GetExtensionName(`path`**)**

Returns the extension name for the last file or folder in a path—that is, any characters after the last period in the name. (This can be handy to get the extension of a file, but it isn't useful with folder names because the extension of a folder name is rarely given any meaning.)

GetFile(`filespec`**)**

Returns a `Scripting.File` object corresponding to the specified file. You can then use this object to change the file's name and attributes, as discussed later in this chapter.

GetFileName(`pathspec`**)**

Returns the name of the file or the last folder name in the specified path. `GetFileName` is like `GetBaseName` and `GetExtensionName`, but it returns the combined name and extension.

GetFolder(`folderspec`**)**

Returns a `Folder` object corresponding to the specified folder pathname (for example, `"C:\temp"`). You can then use this object to change the folder's name and attributes as well as to examine its contents, as discussed later in this chapter.

GetParentFolderName(`path`**)**

Returns everything up to the last item in `path`. This must be used with a path specification that does not contain a filename.

GetSpecialFolder(*folderspec*)

Returns the actual path of the specified special folder, as actually installed on the local computer. `Folderspec` is one of the following values:

Constant	Value	Description
WindowsFolder	0	Actual name of your Windows folder
SystemFolder	1	Actual name of the Windows\System32 folder
TemporaryFolder	2	Folder used for temporary and scratch files

Note

If you need your script to find personal folders such as your My Documents folder, see the WScript.Shell object discussed later in the chapter.

Caution

WindowsFolder, SystemFolder, and TemporaryFolder are *not* predefined constants. You should either define them in your script, as with the VBScript command

```
Const TemporaryFolder = 2
```

or use the values 0, 1 or 2 in your program. Be very careful about this. In VBScript, if you use one of these names without defining it, VBScript ends up using the default value 0, which always returns the path to the Windows folder.

GetStandardStream(*strm*)

Returns a TextStream object corresponding to the standard input, standard output, and standard error output streams for WSH. (Applicable only when a script is running under cscript.) The argument can be one of the following values:

Constant	Value	Description
StdIn	0	Returns the standard input stream
StdOut	1	Returns the standard output stream
StdErr	2	Returns the standard error stream

GetTempName()

Returns a randomly generated name that can be used as a scratch file. No folder name is provided. To make a temporary file in a designated temporary folder, use the name returned by

```
const TemporaryFolder = 2
fso.BuildPath(fso.GetSpecialFolder(TemporaryFolder), fso.GetTempName())
```

GetTempName doesn't create a file; it gives you a name that's unlikely to be used by an already existing file.

MoveFile *source, destination*

Moves one or more files from one location to another. *Source* can be a filename or a filename containing wildcards. *Destination* can be a folder name or a filename. If *destination* is a folder, be sure the name you specify ends with a backslash (\) so it's clear to Windows you're specifying a folder rather than a filename. If the destination is on the same volume (drive and partition), it is simply renamed; otherwise, it is copied, and the original is deleted. The destination folder must already exist.

If a destination file already exists or the source name contains wildcards and no files match, an error occurs. If an error occurs partway through moving files, any already moved files remain moved.

MoveFolder *source, destination*

Moves one or more folders from one location to another. Any subfolders are moved, too. If the last folder in the destination path does not already exist, it is created.

OpenTextFile(*filename*[, *iomode*[, *create*[, *format*]]])

Opens the specified file and returns a `TextStream` object that can be used to read from, write to, or append to the file. The optional arguments are as follows:

- *iomode*—Determines the way the file is to be used. Here's a list of the allowed values:

Constant	Value	Description
ForReading	1	Opens the file for reading. This is the default value.
ForWriting	2	Opens the file for writing. Any existing content in a preexisting file of the same name is erased.
ForAppending	8	Opens the file for writing and adds whatever is written to the end of any preexisting contents.

- *create*—Determines whether a new file is to be created if the specified file doesn't already exist. If this argument is specified and `True`, the file is created. If this argument is `False`, the file must already exist. The default value is `False`.

- *format*—Specifies the file encoding to use. Here's a list of the allowed values:

Constant	Description
TristateTrue	Opens or creates the file using Unicode.
TristateFalse	Uses ASCII.
TristateUseDefault	Uses the system default. This is the default value.

As you can see, the methods that `FileSystemObject` provides fall into two main categories: utility functions that help you manipulate filenames and test for file and folder existence, and methods that return objects corresponding to drives, files, and folders. We discuss the utility functions first, and then go over the drive, file, and folder objects.

Working with File and Pathnames

In scripts that manipulate files and folders, you often want to construct full pathnames to files by combining a filename with a pathname. You run into this when copying and renaming files, creating temporary files, and so on. Fully qualified pathnames look something like this:

```
c:\users\bknittel\documents\chapter.doc
```

Note

By the way, this shows the path to my Documents folder on my Windows Vista computer. On XP, the path would look something like c:\Documents and Settings\bknittel\My Documents. On your computer, the path is something else entirely. Later in the chapter, in the discussion of the WScript.Shell object, I show you how to get the correct path to your own folders in such a way that your script works on any version of Windows.

When you're creating a fully qualified name by joining a pathname (drive and/or folder) with a filename, it's not always as simple as sticking the two parts together with a backslash in between, as in this example:

```
filename = "chapter.doc"
path     = "c:\users\bknittel\documents"
fullpath = path & "\" & filename
```

The problem is that someone might specify the path as `"a:"`, intending to copy a file to the *current* folder of drive A:. However, this sample program produces the name `"a:\chapter.doc"`, which places the file in the *root* folder of drive A:. Furthermore, if someone enters a path such as `"c:\temp\"`, the program produces `"c:\temp\\chapter.doc"`, which is technically an improper filename. (Such a name works, but it's not good practice to count on it working in the future.)

The solution to this problem is to use the `BuildPath` method provided with `FileSystemObject`. Its job is to join paths with filenames, and it takes these details into account. The preceding sample program can be rewritten this way:

```
filename = "chapter.doc"
path     = "c:\users\bknittel\documents"
fullpath = fso.BuildPath(path, filename)
```

`FileSystemObject` comes with several additional methods to help you manipulate paths' filenames: `GetAbsolutePathName`, `GetBaseName`, `GetDrive`, `GetDriveName`, `GetExtensionName`, `GetFileName`, and `GetParentFolderName`. You can use these methods in scripts to tear apart filenames into their component pieces.

As an example, if you are writing a script to convert a folder full of GIF files to JPG files, you need a way to come up with the desired output filenames given the input names. The easiest way to do this is to use the `GetBaseName` method, which removes both a filename's path and its extension. Given the base name, we can stick on a new extension and folder name to get the desired output filename.

Here's a script fragment that processes all GIF files in a given input folder and from them creates JPG files in an output folder:

```
set fso = CreateObject("Scripting.FileSystemObject")
infolder  = "C:\pictures\received"
outfolder = "C:\pictures\converted"

for each file in fso.GetFolder(infolder).Files
    if ucase(fso.GetExtensionName(file.name)) = "GIF" then
        basename = fso.GetBaseName(file.name)
        giffile  = fso.BuildPath(infolder, basename & ".GIF")
        jpgfile  = fso.BuildPath(outfolder, basename & ".JPG")
        convertGIFtoJPG giffile, jpgfile

        ' if the conversion succeeded, delete the original file
        if fso.FileExists(jpgfile) then file.Delete
    end if
loop

sub convertGIFtoJPG (giffile, jpgfile)
    . . .
    (conversion routine to create JPG from GIF would go here.
     such a routine would probably use an image processing object of some sort)
    . . .
end sub
```

Here are several points to take note of:

- The `for each` loop runs through once for each of the files in `infolder`. `GetFolder` returns a `Folder` object; `.Files` returns a collection of all the files in that folder; and `for each` iterates through all the items in the collection. On each turn, `file` is a `Scripting.File` object representing one file.

- `fso.GetFileExtension(file.name)` returns just the extension part of the file's name, which it obtains from the file object's `name` property (we cover the file object shortly). `Ucase` turns it to uppercase before comparing it to "GIF"; otherwise, if the file's extension happens to be "gif" (in lowercase), is not matched.

- The statements inside the `if` statement process each of the GIF files in folder `infolder`. If `infolder` holds files other than GIF files, they aren't bothered by this script.

- The script uses `GetBasename` to extract just the part of the filename after the path and before ".gif", joins the extension ".jpg" to this, and uses `BuildPath` to join this with the output folder name. The result is that for each GIF file in `inpath`, the subroutine `convertGIFtoJPG` is called once with the input GIF filename and the desired output JPG filename.

Deleting and Renaming Files

The `DeleteFile` method is a straightforward counterpart to the command-line `del` command. For example, the statement

```
fso.Deletefile("c:\temp\somefile.tmp")
```

deletes file `c:\temp\somefile.tmp`. You should specify a full path to the file you want to delete unless you are sure you know what the script's current working directory is.

To rename a file, the best approach is to obtain its `Scripting.File` object and change the object's `Name` property. I discuss the `File` object later in this chapter, but as a sneak preview, you might use a statement like this:

```
fso.GetFile("c:\temp\newfile.tmp").Name = "newfile.doc"
```

You can also rename a file using the `MoveFile` method. However, `MoveFile` treats the *destination* name as a pathname, so the statement

```
fso.MoveFile("c:\temp\newfile.tmp", "newfile.doc")
```

not only renames the file `newfile.tmp`, but also moves it from the folder `c:\temp` to the script's current working directory. If this is not what you wanted, you would have to use the full pathname for the destination name:

```
fso.MoveFile("c:\temp\newfile.tmp", "c:\temp\newfile.doc")
```

Creating a Folder

If your task requires you to create or move files into a particular folder, it might be a nice idea to have the script ensure that the destination folder exists, especially if the script is meant to run on computers other than your own.

The `Scripting.FileSystemObject` object's `CreateFolder` method can do this for you. If you are planning on using a folder named `C:\myscript\output`, you might be tempted to put a statement like the following at the top of your script so the folder is always there if you need it:

```
fso.CreateFolder("C:\myscript\output")
```

However, there are two problems with this:

- If the folder already exists, WSH stops with an error message.

- `CreateFolder` can only create the lowest-level folder in a path. In the example, if `C:\myscript` doesn't already exist, `CreateFolder` can't create both `myscript` and `output` at once. Again, WSH stops with an error.

The way to solve a problem such as this is to *extend* the functionality of a built-in function. This can be done by writing a subroutine that your script can use to do a more thorough job. Here's a script containing such a subroutine to create folders—an extended version of `CreateFolder` called `CreateFullPath`. The first two lines of this script comprise a simple "main program"—they are the main body of the script. The rest of the script is the subroutine `CreateFullPath`. Here's the script:

```
                               ' Example file script0401.vbs
set fso = CreateObject("Scripting.FileSystemObject")
CreateFullPath "c:\myscript\output"

' ... rest of script would go here, doing something with folder \myscript\output


' ------------------------------------------------------------------
' Subroutine CreateFullPath creates the folder specified by 'path,'
' creating any intermediate folders as necessary. (Note: parameter 'path'
' is specified as 'byval' because we modify it inside the subroutine).
' ------------------------------------------------------------------
sub CreateFullPath (byval path)
    dim parent                       ' temporary variable

    path   = fso.GetAbsolutePathname(path) ' be sure path is fully qualified
    parent = fso.GetParentFolderName(path) ' get name of parent folder

    if not fso.FolderExists(parent) then   ' if parent(s) does not exist...
         CreateFullPath parent             ' ...create it
    end if

    if not fso.FolderExists(path) then     ' if subfolder does not exist...
        fso.CreateFolder(path)             ' ...create it.
    end if
end sub
```

You can use this subroutine in any script that needs to create a folder. This way, your script will never be tripped up because the desired folder already exists or because a parent folder doesn't exist.

How does it work? The `CreateFullPath` subroutine uses the `GetParentFolderName` method to get the name of the folder *above* the lowest one specified in `path`—its parent—and if it does not exist, creates it first. Only then, and only if necessary, does it create the final folder in `path`.

The trick in this subroutine is in the way it creates the parent folder: It calls *itself* to do the job. That way, `CreateFullPath` applies the same technique to ensure that the folder *above* the parent folder exists, and so on, up to the root folder.

Protecting Parameters

In the example used here, `path` isn't an ordinary variable; it's a parameter passed to `CreateFullPath` by the caller. What happens when you modify the value of a parameter to a function or subroutine?

There are two ways parameters can be passed: by *value* and by *reference*. When a parameter is passed by value, the subroutine gets a "copy" of the parameter value, so there is no problem if the subroutine modifies it. When a parameter is passed by reference, changes *can* make their way back to the calling procedure, if the value is a variable and not an expression.

In VBScript, you can explicitly declare parameters as `byval` or `byref`; the default in VBScript is `byref`, so if we don't add `byval` in `CreateFullPath`, modifications to `path` would be reflected back to the caller's variable. In this subroutine, it's best to specify `byval` so the change can't propagate back. In this example, it doesn't really matter, but if you used `CreateFullPath` in other scripts, it could.

Note that in JScript, this doesn't come up—all parameters are always passed by value.

This programming technique is called *recursion*, and it's quite powerful. It's used most effectively when you can divide a job into smaller pieces and use the same procedure to handle each piece. I show other examples of recursion later in this chapter. It's an especially common technique when working with folders because folders themselves are inherently recursive. Folders contain folders which contain folders.

If you want to write your own scripts or programs that use recursion, here are three tips:

- Initially, use debugging printout statements to have the script tell you what it's doing while it runs. For example, when I wrote `CreateFullPath`, I used `wscript.echo` to print `path` at the beginning of `CreateFullPath`; this lets me see if, when, and how it is called each time.

- Be sure that any variables you use to compute items inside the subroutine are local variables, which are created for each instance of the subroutine. Because several copies of `CreateFullPath` might be working at the same time, you have to be sure they don't attempt to use the same variables to store information. In `CreateFullPath`, this is done with the statement `dim parent`. If you use VBScript and want to modify the value of a subprogram's parameters, as I did with `path` in `CreateFullPath`, you probably want to use the keyword `byval` so any changes don't affect the subroutine's caller.

- The tricky part with recursion is getting it to stop! `CreateFullPath` keeps moving up directories as long as the parent folder doesn't exist. It could work its way up to the root folder but always stops there because the root folder always exists as long as the specified drive exists.

If recursion is a new concept for you, it's worth working through a few examples by hand, so you see how the subroutine works. Work out what happens if you call `CreateFullPath "C:\files\plans\april"` under the following circumstances:

- `C:\files\plans\april` exists before you start.
- `C:\files\plans` exists before you start, but not subfolder `april`.
- `C:\files` exists but not subfolder `plans`.
- `C:\files` does not exist.

In each case, you should see that `CreateFullPath` works correctly. Here's a geeky detail you need to know: A drive's top-level folder \ always exists, and technically speaking, its parent folder is itself, so `GetParentFolderName("\")` returns `"\"`. (You might recall that the `Shell.Folder` object behaves differently. When a `Folder` object represents a top-level folder, its `Parent` property returns the special value `Nothing`.)

Copying a Folder

Copying the contents of folders is also a recursive process because the folder being copied could contain subfolders that also need to be copied. The CopyFolder method does this automatically. You can easily copy a folder from one location to another, as shown here:

```
fso.CopyFolder "C:\book\04", "D:\bookbackup\04"
```

This copies the contents of `C:\book\04` to a folder on the D: drive, and all files and subfolders are copied, too. (I used a script like this while writing this book to keep backup copies of each chapter on an external disk and on a networked computer.)

Note that, by default, `CopyFolder` will overwrite preexisting files. If you want to ensure that existing files do not get overwritten, specify `False` as the third argument to `CopyFolder`.

The `Scripting.Drive` Object

The `Drive` object is returned by `FileSystemObject` and lets you find out how the drive is organized, how much free space it has, its online/ready status, and other useful information.

There are two ways to obtain a `Drive` object:

- You can get an object representing a specific drive using the `FileSystemObject` method `GetDrive`. Here's an example in VBScript:
    ```
    set drv = fso.GetDrive("C:")
    WScript.Echo "Drive C has", drv.FreeSpace, "bytes free"
    ```

- You can get a collection of all the drives in the computer using the `FileSystemObject` property `Drives`. You can then scan through the collection using the method appropriate to your scripting language. In VBScript, this might be as follows:

```
for each drv in fso.Drives
    if drv.IsReady then
        WScript.Echo "Drive", drv.DriveLetter, "has",_
            drv.FreeSpace, "bytes free"
    else
        WScript.Echo "Drive", drv.DriveLetter, "is not ready"
    end if
next
```

Then, if you want, you can use `if` statements inside the `for` loop to select certain drives or types of drives.

The `Drive` object has a passel of properties that can tell you about the drive's free/used space, its online status, and its drive type. Reference List 4.2 lists the `Drive` object's properties.

REFERENCE LIST 4.2   Properties of the `Drive` Object

AvailableSpace
Returns the number of bytes on the drive available to the script's user. Might be lower than `FreeSpace` if disk quotas are in effect. Works on both network and local drives. This property is read-only, which means you can use the property's value but you can't assign it a new value.

DriveLetter
Returns the drive letter of the `Drive` object as a string (for example, `"A"`). (Read-only.)

DriveType
Returns a value indicating the type of a specified drive. (Read-only.) Here are the possible values:

Value	Meaning
0	Unknown drive type
1	Removable disk (floppy, Zip, and so on)
2	Fixed disk
3	Network (mapped) drive
4	CD-ROM or DVD
5	RAM disk

FileSystem

Returns the type of file system in use for the specified drive. Possible return values include "FAT", "NTFS", and "CDFS". (Read-only.)

FreeSpace

Returns the number of free bytes on the disk. Might be greater than AvailableSpace if disk quotas are in use. (Read-only.)

IsReady

Returns the Boolean value True if the specified drive is online and ready; otherwise, it returns False. This property tells you whether a floppy or another removable disk drive has a disk inserted. (Read-only.)

Path

Returns the path for the drive (for example, "C:"). (Read-only.)

RootFolder

Returns a Folder object representing the root folder of the specified drive. (This property is read-only, although you can use the returned Folder object to do things to the root folder, as you see later.)

SerialNumber

Returns the unique decimal serial number that identifies all FAT and NTFS formatted fixed and removable disk volumes. (Read-only.)

ShareName

Returns the network share name for the specified drive, if the drive is a mapped network drive. Returns the empty string ("") if it's not a mapped drive. (Read-only.)

TotalSize

Returns the total space, in bytes, of the drive. (Read-only.)

VolumeName

Returns the volume name of the drive. This property is read/write, which means you can change a drive's volume name by assigning a new value to this property.

There are no methods for the Drive object. You can use the Drive object to collect and display information about drives, to check for sufficient free space, and to check whether drives actually exist and are ready before copying files to them.

Confirming That a Drive Exists

When you're copying or creating files, you should have a script ensure that the target drive letter exists and is ready to use—and to gracefully quit or offer a chance to amend the problem if it isn't.

Here's a script designed to copy files from one location to another. It first ensures that the destination drive exists and quits if the drive does not exist:

```
                                           ' Example file script0402.vbs
set fso = CreateObject("Scripting.FileSystemObject")

inpath  = "C:\book\04"
outpath = "G:\bookbackup\04"

set drv = fso.GetDrive(fso.GetDriveName(outpath))
if not drv.IsReady then
    msgbox "Removable Drive is not ready"
    WScript.quit 1
end if

CreateFullPath outpath
fso.CopyFolder inpath, outpath
msgbox "Backup of " & inpath & " complete."

' ------------------------------------------------------------------
sub CreateFullPath (path)
   dim parent                          ' temporary variable

   path   = fso.GetAbsolutePathname(path) ' be sure path is fully qualified
   parent = fso.GetParentFolderName(path) ' get name of parent folder

   if not fso.FolderExists(parent) then  ' if necessary create parent(s)
       CreateFullPath parent
   end if

   if not fso.FolderExists(path) then    ' if necessary create subfolder
       fso.CreateFolder(path)
   end if
end sub
```

The `if not drv.IsReady` statement is the important part of this example.
`fso.GetDrive` returns a `Drive` object corresponding to drive G:, and `IsReady` tests to
see whether the drive is turned on, has a disk, and is ready to go. If the drive is not
ready, the script displays a pop-up message and exits.

If the drive is ready, the script uses the `CreateFullPath` subroutine we discussed earlier
to ensure that the output folder exists and then copies the folder's contents.

Finding a Drive with the Most Free Space

This sample script shows how to locate which drive has the most free space of all drives on the computer. Note that it uses `IsReady` to ensure that the drive is online
before attempting to check the free space; otherwise, an offline disk drive makes the
script stop with an error message:

```
                                 ' Example file script0403.vbs
freedrv   = "?"           ' holds the best drive we've seen
freespace = 0             ' the amount of space free on freedrv
for each drv in fso.Drives
    if drv.IsReady then
```

```
        if drv.AvailableSpace > freespace then
            freespace = drv.AvailableSpace  ' this drive is better
            freedrv   = drv.DriveLetter     ' so remember its details
        end if
    end if
next
                                         ' report the results
Wscript.echo "Drive", freedrv, "has the most space:", freespace, "bytes."
```

At the end of the script, `freespace` is the amount of space on the drive with the most space, and `freedrv` is the name of the drive with the most room.

The `Scripting.Folder` Object

The `Folder` object returns information about the properties and contents of folders. Similar to the `Drive` object, you can obtain a `Folder` object to work with a specific, known folder, or you can get a collection of all the folders within a specific drive or folder.

To get information for a specific folder, use the `GetFolder` method. Here's an example:

```
set fso  = CreateObject("Scripting.FileSystemObject")
set fldr = fso.GetFolder("C:\temp")
```

To see all the folders contained inside another folder, use the `SubFolders` property, which returns a collection containing a list of all the subfolders:

```
fldrs = fldr.SubFolders
```

or

```
fldrs = fso.GetFolder("C:\temp").SubFolders
```

You can then use the `for each` statement to scan through all the folders in the collection.

▶

Note

The SubFolders collection does *not* include the subfolders named "." and ".." that the command prompt DIR command shows. These two "virtual" folders represent the current folder and its parent folder, respectively, but they're not really subfolders and they're not listed in the collection.

To get a `Folder` object for a special folder such as the Desktop or the Windows directory, don't try to guess or construct the path name yourself! The location of special folders can change from one version of Windows to another, and on a corporate network, it can be unpredictable. Instead, use the `FileSystemObject` object's `GetSpecialFolder` method or the `WScript.Shell.SpecialFolders` method to get the special folder's path name and pass that name to `GetFolder` to obtain the object. Here's an example that gets the `Folder` object for the `Temporary` file folder:

```
fldr = fso.GetFolder(fso.GetSpecialFolder(2))
```

Reference List 4.3 lists the `Folder` object's properties and methods.

REFERENCE LIST 4.3   Properties and Methods of the `Folder` Object

Properties:

Attributes

The file system attributes of the folder.

Folder attributes include read-only, system, hidden, compressed, and so on. Each possible attribute is represented by a numeric value, and the `Attributes` property is the sum of the values of the folder's actual attributes. (I demonstrate how this works in a sample program later in this section.) The `Attributes` property is basically read/write, although some attributes can't be changed by a script.

Table 4.1 lists the values of the `Attributes` property.

DateCreated

A date/time value indicating the date and time the folder is created. (Read-only.)

DateLastAccessed

The date and time the folder is last accessed. (Read-only.)

DateLastModified

The date and time the folder is last modified. (Read-only.)

Drive

The drive letter of the drive on which the folder resides. (Read-only.)

Files

A collection of `Scripting.File` objects representing all the files contained in the folder, including those with the hidden and system file attributes set. (Read-only.)

IsRootFolder

`True` if the folder is its drive's root folder; otherwise, `False`. (Read-only.)

Name

The name of the folder. Assigning a new value to the `Name` property renames the folder. (Read/write.)

ParentFolder

A `Folder` object representing the folder's parent (containing) folder. (Read-only.) For a root folder, this returns the special object reference `Nothing`, which causes an error if used. If your script might try to find the parent of a top-level folder, you need to check for this special value, with something like the following test:

```
...
set parent = fldr.ParentFolder
if parent is Nothing then
    wscript.echo "The folder was already a top level folder"
```

```
else
    wscript.echo "The parent folder is", parent.path
end if
```

Path

The fully qualified path of the folder.

ShortName

The name of the folder as seen by old DOS and Windows 3.1 programs that require the earlier 8.3 naming convention.

ShortPath

The full path of the folder as seen by old programs that require the earlier 8.3 naming convention. (Read-only.)

Size

The size, in bytes, of all files and subfolders contained in the folder. (Read-only.)

SubFolders

A collection of `Folder` objects representing all the folder's subfolders, including those with hidden and system file attributes set.

Type

Not too useful. For folders that have an extension in their name, `Type` is the descriptive name associated with files having that extension. For example, if a folder is named `folder.txt`, `Type` would be "Text File." (Read-only.)

Methods:

Copy *destination*[, *overwrite*]

Copies the folder from one location to another.

CreateTextFile(*filename*[, *overwrite*[, *unicode*]]**)**

Works as described under `CreateTextFile` in Reference List 4.1 on page 125, with one exception: If *filename* does not include a path or is specified with a relative path, the file is created in or relative to the folder represented by the `Folder` object.

Delete [*force*]

Deletes the folder. If the optional Boolean value *force* is passed and is true, the folder will be deleted even if is marked read-only..

Move *destination*

Moves the file or folder to a new location. It becomes a subfolder of *destination*.

File and Folder Attribute Values

File and folder attributes, such as system and read-only, are stored as a number. Each possible attribute has a numeric value associated with it, and the number stored in the `File` or `Folder` object is the sum of the values for whichever attributes apply. These values correspond to individual bits of a binary number. Table 4.1 lists the values.

Table 4.1   **Folder and File Attribute Values**

Attribute Name	Value	Attribute Protection	Description
Normal	0		If no attributes are set, the value is 0 and the file is called a "normal" file.
ReadOnly	1	R/W	The file is read-only.
Hidden	2	R/W	The file or folder is hidden.
System	4	R/W	The file is an operating system file.
Volume	8	R/O	This is a disk volume label.
Directory	16	R/O	This is a folder (directory).
Archive	32	R/W	The file has changed since the last backup.
Alias	64	R/O	This is a link or shortcut.
Compressed	128	R/O	The file or folder is compressed.

A file with just the ReadOnly bit set has an Attributes value of 1. A file with the Hidden and System attributes set has a value of 6 (2 + 4).

Testing File and Folder Attribute Values

Because the Attributes value can be the sum of several different individual attributes, you can't compare its value to a specific number. For example, the test

```
if file.Attributes = 1 then …
```

doesn't work if the file also has the Archive attribute set because the value is 33, not 1. The best way to work around this is to use *bitwise* testing of the attribute values. Each scriptable programming language has a way of performing bitwise testing. Here's an example in VBScript:

```
if file.Attributes and 1 then …
```

The value of the expression File.Attributes and 1 is 0 if the 1 bit is not set, and 1 if it is set; If considers 0 to be False and any nonzero value to be True. Therefore, the test is True if the Attributes value has the 1 bit set.

> **Tip**
>
> If you use file or folder attributes, your script will be easier to understand if you define named constants for the attribute values rather than use the numeric values. Put lines such as
>
> ```
> const ReadOnly = 1
> const Hidden = 2
> ```
>
> and so on at the top of your script, and then use these more meaningful names in attribute tests.

Using constants, we'd write this:

```
const ReadOnly = 1

if file.Attributes and ReadOnly then …
```

Testing Multiple Attributes

If you need to test multiple attributes, you must be careful. For example, the test

```
if file.Attributes and Hidden and Readonly then …
```

doesn't work. In fact, this test is *never* true. File attribute values are numeric quantities, and with numbers, the operators and and or don't work in the intuitive way you expect. With numbers, they perform *bitwise boolean* mathematics. Understanding bitwise math can take a bit of doing and is not something I get into here. However, you can use the following pattern and modify the examples given to fit your application.

> ### Pattern
>
> To select files that have *any one or more* of several file attributes, use the statement:
>
> ```
> if File.Attributes and (attribute or attribute or attribute…) then
> ```
>
> For example, to list all the files marked as either hidden or read-only or both hidden and read-only, you could use these statements:
>
> ```
> const Readonly = 1
> const Hidden   = 2
>
> for each file in fso.GetFolder("c:\windows\system32").Files
>     if file.attributes and (Hidden or Readonly) then
>         WScript.echo file.name
>     end if
> next
> ```
>
> However, to select files that have *all* of several file attributes, use the statement:
>
> ```
> if (File.Attributes and (attribute or attribute or attribute …)) =_
>     (attribute or attribute or attribute …) then
> ```
>
> For example, these statements list all the files marked as both hidden *and* read-only:
>
> ```
> for each file in fso.GetFolder("c:\windows\system32").Files
>     if (file.attributes and (Hidden or Readonly)) = (Hidden or Readonly) then
>         WScript.echo file.name
>     end if
> next
> ```

Changing File and Folder Attributes

You can change some of the attributes of a file or folder by assigning a new value to the Attributes property. However, only the attributes noted as R/W under "Attribute

Protection" in Table 4.1 can be changed from a script. You can't, for instance, set the `Directory` attribute; this corresponds to an attempt to turn a file into a folder.

To turn on and off individual attributes, you must use bitwise math. Bitwise math uses the `or` operator to add bit values together.

To turn on a bit, use the `or` operator:

```
file.Attributes = file.Attributes or (bit or bits to turn on)
```

Here's an example that gives a file the `ReadOnly` and `Hidden` attributes:

```
file.Attributes = file.Attributes or (ReadOnly or Hidden)
```

The advantage of this expression versus the following one is that the bitwise `or` expression works regardless of whether the attributes are set before you started:

```
file.Attributes = file.Attributes + ReadOnly + Hidden
```

The numeric + expression gives incorrect results if the `ReadOnly` or `Hidden` bits are already set—you end up adding in the `Attributes` value twice!

To turn off an attribute, use `and not`:

```
file.Attributes = file.Attributes and not (bit(s) to turn off)
```

This has the effect of leaving set all bits that are originally set, *except* the ones listed. For example, the statement

```
file.Attributes = file.Attributes and not (Hidden or ReadOnly)
```

removes the `Hidden` and `ReadOnly` attributes from a file.

Note

Files with the `Hidden`, `System` and `ReadOnly` bits set are called *super hidden*. They usually don't show up in Explorer windows unless you've enabled displaying both hidden and system files.

Additionally, the `Scripting.File` object lets you manipulate simple attributes such as Hidden, but it does not provide a way to manipulate user-level permissions for files and folders stored on an NTFS disk partition. For that, you can use the `cacls` command-line program, which is discussed in Chapter 14, "Windows PowerShell," or the Windows Management Instrumentation's (WMI) `Security` provider. WMI is discussed in Chapter 7, "Windows Management Instrumentation."

The `Scripting.File` Object

The `Scripting.File` object lets you see and alter information about individual files: names, attributes, sizes, and dates. As with the `Drive` and `Folder` objects, you can get the `Folder` object for a specific named file, or you can get a collection of all files in a given folder. If you want, you can run through all the members of a collection and select files based on name, extension, size, date, and so on.

Reference List 4.4 lists the properties and methods of the `File` object.

REFERENCE LIST 4.4   Properties and Methods of the `File` Object

Properties:

Attributes
Sets or returns the attributes of the file. Attribute values are listed in Table 4.1. This property is read/write or read-only, depending on the attribute.

DateCreated
Returns the date and time the specified file is created. (Read-only.)

DateLastAccessed
Returns the date and time the specified file is last accessed. (Read-only.)

DateLastModified
Returns the date and time the specified file is last modified. (Read-only.)

Drive
Returns the drive letter of the drive on which the specified file resides. (Read-only.)

Name
Sets or returns the name of a specified file. You can rename a file by assigning a new value to its `Name` property. (Read/write.)

ParentFolder
Returns the folder object for the folder in which this file lives. (Read-only.)

Path
Returns the fully qualified path to the file, including the filename. (Read-only.)

ShortName
Returns the short name used by programs that require the earlier 8.3 naming convention. (Read-only.)

ShortPath
Returns the short path used by programs that require the earlier 8.3 file naming convention. (Read-only.)

Size
Returns the size, in bytes, of the specified file. (Read-only.)

Type
Returns the descriptive name of the file type associated with the file's extension. For example, for files ending in `.txt`, "Text Document" is returned. (Read-only.)

Methods:

Copy `destination[, overwrite]`
Copies the file to a new location, which can be a folder name or filename. By default, if the destination file already exists, it is overwritten. If the Boolean

parameter *overwrite* is specified and is `False`, the script instead stops with an error message.

Delete *force*
Deletes the file. If the Boolean parameter *force* is specified and is `True`, a read-only file extension, so if you change deleted; otherwise, the script generates an error.

Move *destination*
Moves the file to a new location, specified as the path *destination*. If a file of the destination name already exists, the script generates an error.

OpenAsTextStream([*iomode*, [*format*]]**)**
Opens a specified file and returns a `TextStream` object that can be used to read from, write to, or append to the file. (We discuss this later in the chapter.)

Renaming a File

A script can rename a file by obtaining a `File` object for the file and changing its `Name` property, as in this example:

```
fso.GetFile("C:\folder\somefile.txt").Name = "somefile.bak"
```

Note you can only change the name, not the folder, during this operation. To actually move the file, you must use the `Move` or `Copy` method. The `Name` property includes the file's extension, so if you change the name of a file from `"test.doc"` to `"newname"`, the extension `.doc` will be lost.

Scanning for Files Based on Name, Type, Size, and So on

If you want to process, delete, rename, or copy files based on some properties of the file, you need to scan through a collection of all files in a folder. Here's a script that deletes all files with the extension .TMP or .BAK within a given folder:

```
                              ' Example file script0404.vbs
set fso = CreateObject("Scripting.FileSystemObject")
cleanpath = "C:\TEMP"

for each file in fso.GetFolder(cleanpath).Files
    upext = ucase(fso.GetExtensionName(file.Name))
    if upext = "TMP" or upext = "BAK" then
        wscript.echo "deleting", file.path
        file.Delete
    end if
next
```

In this example, we use `GetFolder` and its `Files` property to get the collection of all files in `C:\TEMP`. Inside the `for` loop, we use the `FileSystemObject` object's `GetExtensionName` method to get the file extension from each file's name and convert it to uppercase. Then, we match the extension against "TMP" and "BAK." If it matches, we delete the file.

Now, how would we clean up these files from \TEMP *and* from any folders within TEMP? We use the recursion technique we discussed earlier. What's needed is a subroutine to delete all junk files in a given folder and those in any of its subfolders. Here's what such a program might look like:

```
                                      ' Example file script0405.vbs
set fso = CreateObject("Scripting.FileSystemObject")
cleanpath = "C:\TEMP"

cleanup fso.GetFolder(cleanpath)

' - - - - - - - - - - - - - - - - - - - - - - - - - - - - - - - - - - - - - - - - - - -
sub cleanup (folder)
    dim file, subfolder            ' declare local variables

    for each file in folder.Files   ' clean up files
        upext = ucase(fso.GetExtensionName(file.Name))
        if upext = "TMP" or upext = "BAK" then
            wscript.echo "deleting", file.path
            file.Delete
        end if
    next
                                    ' clean up any subfolders
    for each subfolder in folder.SubFolders
        cleanup subfolder
    next
end sub
```

This script contains a subroutine to clean up temporary and backup files given a Folder object. The script starts out by calling cleanup with the Folder object for C:\TEMP.

Cleanup uses the same technique used in the previous example to remove all of this folder's BAK and TMP files.

The fun part comes next: Cleanup then scans through any subfolders within \TEMP. A folder's Folders property returns a collection of any folders within. Cleanup then calls *itself* with each of the subfolders, in turn.

As cleanup is invoked each time, it does what we want: It scans through files and deletes the BAK and TMP files, and it scans through and calls itself to remove these files from any deeper subfolders.

You can use this same technique to work on files based on size, attributes, modification or creation dates, and so on, based on your own needs. It's common enough that it should be noted as a pattern.

▶ **Pattern**
To process all files in a folder and all subfolders, use a recursive subroutine that works with a Folder object:

```
                                      ' Example file script0406.vbs
set fso = CreateObject("Scripting.FileSystemObject")
```

```
startfolder = "c:\xxx"                  ' identify starting folder name

dofolder fso.GetFolder(startfolder)
    ⋮


' ................................................................
sub dofolder (folder)
    dim file, subfolder                 ' declare local variables

    for each file in folder.Files    ' do something with the files
        wscript.echo "Processing file " & file.path
        ⋮
    next
                                       ' call again to process subfolders
    for each subfolder in folder.SubFolders
        dofolder subfolder
    next
end sub
```

You can use If…Then tests to limit the processing of files and/or folders to specific categories, if you want.

To select files more than a certain number of days old, you can subtract the file's modification date from today's date, as in this example:

```
if (Now()-file.DateLastModified) > 3 then
    wscript.echo file.Name, "is more than 3 days old"
    ⋮
end if
```

You can also select files based on file attributes. While writing this very chapter, in fact, I received an email from my editor, Rick Kughen, who asked if there is an easy way to remove the read-only attribute from all the MP3 files in his music folder and all subfolders. (Talk about perfect timing!) Here's a version of this pattern that solves his problem:

```
                                    ' Example file script0407.vbs
const ReadOnly = 1                  ' ReadOnly bit in file attributes
set fso = CreateObject("Scripting.FileSystemObject")

makerw fso.GetFolder("C:\music")    ' start in C:\music and work down


' ................................................................
sub makerw (folder)
    dim file, subfolder
                                    ' tell user where we are
    wscript.echo "Processing", folder.Path, "..."

    for each file in folder.Files    ' fix attribute on MP3 files only
        if (instr(ucase(file.Name), ".MP3") > 0) and _
            (file.Attributes and ReadOnly) then
```

```
            file.Attributes = file.Attributes and not ReadOnly
        end if
    next

    for each subfolder in folder.Subfolders
        makerw subfolder
    next
end sub
```

Given the number of file and folder properties available, you should construct `if` statements to meet just about any file selection needs you have.

Tip

When testing a file selection procedure, at first put only a `WScript.Echo` statement inside the `if` statement. When you know it's selecting the right files, only then go back and insert the statements that actually make changes, such as deleting or copying files.

I should add that after writing this script, I found that you can solve the problem by typing a single line at the command prompt. Scripting is very powerful, but as I show in Part II, "The Command Line Environment," the command line has its moments of glory, too. The solution, by the way, is to type `attrib -r *.mp3 /s` from the top-level folder `\music`. More about this in Chapter 13, "Command-Line Utilities."

Reading and Writing Files

It's often useful to read and write text files in a script. Here are some ways you can use this capability:

- Scripts often need to operate on a series of users, computers, files, or other targets. Rather than putting this information in the script itself, it might be better to keep the data separate from the script program in a text file, where it can be edited without molesting the script itself. The script can read this file to get the list of items to work with.

- Scripts can keep a log of their activities in a text file.

- Scripts can operate on externally generated data files such as comma-delimited export files from a spreadsheet program.

- Scripts can generate and place data into a text file for later printing, or they can import into a spreadsheet or database program.

- A script can act as a filter, like the `sort` and `more` commands, reading the standard input and writing to the standard output.

Text file input and output uses an object called `TextStream`. This object represents a file as a series of characters from which you can read or to which you can write new information.

The `TextStream` Object

Text files consist of characters using American Standard Code for Information Interchange (ASCII) or Unicode encoding. The encoding scheme maps letters and symbols to their numerical representation inside the file. ASCII is the default, and the usual format on the PC, so unless you use one of the Asian-language multibyte characters sets, ASCII is the symbol set of choice. If you need to use Unicode, you can tell Windows to use it when you open the file for reading or writing.

`TextStream` objects are created using the `FileSystemObject` object's `CreateTextFile`, the `OpenTextFile` method, or a `Scripting.File` object's `OpenAsTextStream` method. These methods were outlined earlier in the chapter in Reference Lists 4.1 and 4.4.

Pattern
Here are three typical ways to open a file:

- To open an existing file for reading, use `OpenTextFile`, as illustrated here:

      ```
      set stream = fso.OpenTextFile("some input file.txt")
      ```

  Alternatively, if you have a `File` object for the file, you can use the statement:

      ```
      set stream = file.OpenAsTextStream(forReading)
      ```

- To create a new text file, replacing any previous version of the file, use `CreateTextFile` with the `Overwrite` parameter set to `True`:

      ```
      set stream = fso.CreateTextFile("some input file.txt", True)
      ```

  If you have a file object, you can use the statement:

      ```
      set stream = file.OpenAsTextStream(forWriting)
      ```

- To create a new file or add to any previous contents if the file already exists, use `OpenTextFile` in `ForAppending` mode and with the `create` option set to `True`:

      ```
      set stream = fso.OpenTextFile("some input file.txt", ForAppending, True)
      ```

  With a `File` object, use this:

      ```
      set stream = file.OpenAsTextStream(forAppending)
      ```

The resulting object, `stream`, is a `TextStream` object you can use to read or write the file, as described in the remainder of this section.

Note
If you need to force the use of Unicode or ASCII, you can specify an additional argument to `CreateTextFile` or `OpenTextFile`, as described in Reference List 4.1. For example, to force the use of Unicode, the three statements in the preceding pattern is replaced with the following:

```
set stream = fso.OpenTextFile("some input file.txt", ForReading,_
    False, TriStateTrue)

set stream = fso.CreateTextFile("some input file.txt", True, True)

set stream = fso.OpenTextFile("some input file.txt", ForAppending,_
    True, TriStateTrue)
```

Between the codes for letters and numbers are special characters that indicate the end of each line of the file, tabs, and so on. On DOS- and Windows-based computers, each line is separated by the control characters carriage return (CR) and linefeed (LF; also called *newline*), which have the values 13 and 10, respectively. On Unix, Linux, and some other operating systems, the custom is to separate lines only by the linefeed (newline) character.

If you read and write files a character at a time, you encounter these special codes. For most applications, though, it's easiest to read and write text a whole line at a time; in this case, handy methods are provided as part of the TextStream object that let you ignore these line-delimiting control character details.

The TextStream object represents a text file's contents and keeps track of a "current location" in the file. As you read characters or lines from a file, the TextStream object remembers the next character waiting to be read. It also remembers how many lines you've read and how many characters you've read from the current line. As you write a file, it remembers the current line and column as well.

Reference List 4.5 lists the properties and methods of the TextStream object.

REFERENCE LIST 4.5   Properties and Methods of the TextStream Object

Properties:

AtEndOfLine
Boolean value. When reading from a stream, if this property is True, the next character to be read is a carriage return or linefeed control character.

AtEndOfStream
Boolean value. When reading from a stream, if this property is True, the entire file has been read and there is no more data left. (Read-only.)

Column
Returns the column number of the next character to be read or written. Goes back to 1 after a carriage return/linefeed has been read or written. (Read-only.)

Line
Returns the line number of the next line to be read or written. (Read-only.)

Methods:

Close

Closes the stream. After closing, the object can no longer be used. Use `Close` when you're finished reading or writing a stream to commit any changes to disk and to unlock the file so other applications can use it. If you do not explicitly close a `TextStream` object, the file is not be closed until the script ends.

Read(*nread*)

Reads up to `nread` characters from the stream and returns them as a string. If there aren't `nread` characters left in the file, one thinks that the method returns what's available. However, at least in WSH version 5.6, the script hangs if you try to read past the end of the file. Be careful, therefore, to get the file's length from the `File` object's `Size` property to be sure the file is as long as you expect.

ReadAll

Returns the entire contents of the file as a string object. This can be problematic with very large files (say, more than a few megabytes), but it does let you use string-manipulation functions to easily search and modify a file.

ReadLine

Reads a whole line of text from the file, up to and including a CR+LF or newline character, and returns the text as a string. The carriage return and/or linefeed is *not* included as part of the returned string.

Skip *nskip*

Skips over the next `nskip` characters in the stream without reading them.

SkipLine

Skips the next line in the stream without reading it. That is, it skips characters up to and including a CR+LF or LF.

Write *string*

Writes a string to the file. No CR+LF or newline is written unless these characters are in the string.

WriteBlankLines *nlines*

Writes `nlines` blank lines to the file; that is, it writes `nlines` CR+LF pairs.

WriteLine [*string*]

Writes the text of the string to the file, followed by a CR+LF. If `string` is omitted, it writes just a CR+LF.

Reading Text from Files

There are several ways to read all the lines of a file. Here is one basic pattern.

▶ **Pattern**

To read all the lines of a file, ignore blank lines, and process each line with a subroutine, you can use this pattern:

```
                                         ' Example file script0408.vbs
    ' set name of file to process; can also get this
    ' from a command line argument
filename = "c:\somefolder\somefile.txt"

set fso = CreateObject("Scripting.FileSystemObject")

    ' be sure the file exists and inform user if it doesn't
if not fso.FileExists(filename) then
    MsgBox "The file '" & filename & "' does not exist"
    wscript.quit 1
end if

    ' open the stream and read each line in turn
set stream = fso.OpenTextFile(filename)
do while not stream.AtEndOfStream
    str = stream.ReadLine
        ' if string is not blank, call the subroutine "process"
    if len(trim(str)) > 0 then process str
loop
stream.Close

' ...................................................................
' subroutine to process lines from the input file
sub process (str)
    Wscript.Echo "Input:", str

    ' (do something useful here)
end sub
```

In this pattern, the name of the file is fixed in the script. You can let the user specify it on the command line by retrieving it from the command-line argument collection:

```
if Wscript.Arguments.Length <> 1 then
    MsgBox "Usage: " & Wscript.ScriptName & " filename"
    Wscript.Quit 1
end if
filename = WScript.Arguments.Item(0)
```

The subroutine process can do anything you want. If this script is designed to create new user accounts, for example, you might want each line in the file to specify the information for one user. The subroutine process does the job of creating one user account.

Note

ReadLine works with either DOS-type (CR+LF-delimited) or Unix-type (LF-delimited) text files.

You can use your preferred scripting language's string-manipulation functions to work with the strings you read from an input file.

Writing Text to Files

You can easily write text files with a script. This is handy for creating log files of activity, for exporting data unearthed by the script to a spreadsheet or word processing program, or to create listings that can be printed.

As mentioned earlier in the chapter, to create a new file overwriting any previous file, use

```
set outstream = fso.CreateTextFile("\somefolder\filename.txt")
```

with whatever names you want to use for the `TextStream` object `outstream` and the filename. You can also add to a preexisting file using

```
set outstream = fso.OpenTextFile("\somepath\filename.txt", ForAppending, True)
```

which either appends to any previous content or creates the file if it doesn't already exist.

Tip

Appending is useful when you want your script to keep a log of what it does each time it runs. Keeping a log file is especially valuable when you run a script unattended using the Task Scheduler.

Tip

You can have your script send text output to a printer by using `CreateTextFile` with the name of a printer, if the printer is connected to a parallel port or is shared on the network. Use a name such as `"LPT1"` for a local printer connected to port LPT1 or `"\\sumatra\okidata"` to print to a network shared printer. (If your printer is connected via USB or a wireless connection, you have to share it and use its network share name because only parallel port printers have an LPT port name that `CreateTextFile` can write to.) If you're sending output to a laser printer, be sure to finish with a form feed character (ASCII character 12) before you close the stream so the last page prints. In VBScript, this might look like the following:

```
outstream.Write(vbFormFeed)
outstream.Close
```

After you have a `TextStream` object, writing files is made easy through the use of the `WriteLine` method; it writes a string and adds the appropriate carriage return/linefeed characters automatically.

For example, the following script lists the names of any MP3 or WMA files it finds in your [My] Music folder, or any subfolder, into a text file called `Music Listing.txt`:

```
                                      ' Example file script0409.vbs
set fso = CreateObject("Scripting.FileSystemObject")
set shl = CreateObject("WScript.Shell")
```

```
' get pathname of [My] Music, which isn't easy.
' The folder locations are different on XP vs Vista.
' On XP, it's in folder My Music, inside the My Documents folder.
' On Windows 7 and Vista it's folder Music, inside the User Profile folder.
' The shl.SpecialFolders method can give us the true location of [My] Documents,
' but there is no guaranteed way of finding Music. So:
' Use the USERPROFILE environment variable, and try the Win7/Vista location.
' If the Music folder doesn't exist, try the XP name and location.

musicfolder = shl.ExpandEnvironmentStrings("%USERPROFILE%\Music")
if not fso.folderexists(musicfolder) then
    musicfolder = fso.BuildPath(shl.SpecialFolders("MyDocuments"), "My Music")
end if

wscript.echo "Searching", musicfolder, "for MP3 and WMA files..."

                        ' create output file
set out = fso.CreateTextFile(fso.BuildPath(musicfolder, "Music Listing.txt"))

nfiles = 0              ' list the music files
listdir ""

out.Close               ' close the output file
                        ' tell user what we did
wscript.echo "Listed", nfiles, "files"


' ------------------------------------------------------------------
' listdir - list the music files in subfolder 'path' under My Documents.
' We print the path relative to [My] Music to make the listing more
' readable, but we must add this relative pathname to the music
' path (in variable musicfolder) to use GetFolder.

sub listdir (path)
    dim fldr, file, folder, extn, first

    first = True        ' we've seen no files in this folder yet
                        ' get the folder info by creating full path
    set fldr = fso.GetFolder(fso.BuildPath(musicfolder, path))

                        ' scan through files for MP3's or WMA's
    for each file in fldr.Files
       extn = ucase(fso.GetExtensionName(file.name))
       if extn = "MP3" or extn = "WMA" then
           if first then    ' print the folder name before first file
               out.WriteLine path
               out.WriteLine replicate("-", len(path))
               first = False
           end if
                            ' list the music file name
           out.WriteLine "   " & file.name
           nfiles = nfiles+1
       end if
```

```
          next

                                ' if we listed any files, print blank line
          if not First then out.WriteLine

                                ' now list contents of any subfolders
          for each folder in fldr.subfolders
              listdir fso.BuildPath(path, folder.Name)
          next
      end sub


      ' --------------------------------------------------------------
      ' replicate - return the string 'str' duplicated 'n' times

      function replicate (str, n)
          dim i
          replicate = ""          ' start with a blank string
          for i = 1 to n          ' append as many copies as requested
              replicate = replicate & str
          next
      end function
```

This script goes through some funny contortions to make the printout look good. Here are three things to look for in the script:

- The script prints the name of a folder it's scanning only if it actually finds a music file. This way, folders for artists, which generally contain only album folders, aren't listed. The variable first keeps track of whether any files have been listed on a given folder. If first is True, no files have been listed.

- The script prints the name of the folder, followed by a row of dashes the same length as the name of the folder. This gives the appearance of underlining. The function replicate copies the dash character (-) as many times as needed. After listing the folder, if any files have been listed (that is, variable first is False), a blank line is printed to visually separate each folder.

- The subroutine listdir uses the pathname in string form as its argument. In previous sample scripts that dive into folders, we use the Folder object itself, which is easier. In this script, however, we want to display just the part of the pathname *after* My Documents, so we keep track of just part of the string and use BuildPath to create the actual full path only when it's needed by GetFolder.

An ugly part of this script is how it locates the music folder. The WScript.Shell object is supposed to provide an operating-system–independent way of obtaining the path to special folders, but it doesn't know how to locate the Music folder. Worse, on XP, the My Music folder is a subfolder within My Documents, but on Vista, the folder is named Music and is not a subfolder of Documents but is in the user profile folder alongside Documents. Although

```
    fso.BuildPath(shl.SpecialFolders("MyDocuments"), "My Music")
```

works on XP, it does not work on Vista. Instead the script tries the Vista name and location first, and if the folder is not found, it tries the XP location.

The script produces a listing like this:

```
Baguette Quartet\Rendez-Vous
----------------------------------------
    Ça gaze.wma
    Si l'on ne s'était pas connu.wma
    Reine de musette.wma

Iris Dement\Infamous Angel
----------------------------------------
    Let the Mystery Be.wma
    These Hills.wma
    Hotter Than Mojave in My Heart.wma
```

Constructing More Complex Text Files

The previous example created a listing by writing whole lines at a time. You can create text files a bit at a time using the `TextStream` object's `Write` method. `Write` outputs any text it's given, but it doesn't add line breaks. You can generate text lines a bit at a time this way:

```
outstream.Write "The filename is: "
outstream.Write filename
outstream.WriteLine
```

This creates one line in the output file by writing two strings and adding a carriage return/linefeed afterward. You can also write a CR/LF with the `Write` command. In VBScript, these three variations all produce the exact same result in the output file:

```
outstream.Write "The filename is: "
outstream.Write filename
outstream.WriteLine

outstream.Write "The filename is: " & filename & vbCRLF

outstream.WriteLine "The filename is: " & filename
```

You can also insert tabs (ASCII 9) into text files; this is especially useful when you want to create a file to import into a spreadsheet, database, or word processing file. In VBScript, there's even a convenient predefined constant, `vbTab`, to make this easier. The following script is a variation of the MP3 listing program. Instead of making a nicely formatted text file meant to be viewed directly or printed, it creates a table with three columns (foldername, filename, and size):

```
                            ' Example file script0410.vbs
set fso = CreateObject("Scripting.FileSystemObject")
set shl = CreateObject("WScript.Shell")
```

```
' get pathname of [My] Music, which isn't easy.
' Use the USERPROFILE environment variable, and try the Win7/Vista location.
' If the Music folder doesn't exist, try the XP name and location.

musicfolder = shl.ExpandEnvironmentStrings("%USERPROFILE%\Music")
if not fso.folderexists(musicfolder) then
    musicfolder = fso.BuildPath(shl.SpecialFolders("MyDocuments"), "My Music")
end if

wscript.echo "Searching", musicfolder, "for MP3 and WMA files..."

nfiles  = 0               ' list the music files
listdir ""

out.Close                 ' close the output file
                          ' tell user what we did
wscript.echo "Listed", nfiles, "files"


' ------------------------------------------------------------------
' listdir - list the music files in subfolder 'path' under My Documents.
' We use the path relative to My Documents to make the listing more
' readable, but we must add this relative pathname to the music
' path (in variable musicfolder) to use GetFolder. This version creates a
' tab-delimited table rather than a formatted text listing.

sub listdir (path)
    dim fldr, file, folder, extn

                          ' get the folder info by creating full path
    set fldr = fso.GetFolder(fso.BuildPath(musicfolder, path))

                          ' scan through files for MP3's or WMA's
    for each file in fldr.Files
        extn = ucase(fso.GetExtensionName(file.name))
        if extn = "MP3" or extn = "WMA" then
                              ' format the path, name and size
            out.WriteLine path & vbTab & file.name & vbTab & file.Size
            nfiles = nfiles+1
        end if
    next
                          ' now list contents of any subfolders
    for each folder in fldr.subfolders
        listdir fso.BuildPath(path, folder.Name)
    next
end sub
```

This creates a file that looks like this:

```
Baguette Quartet\Rendez-Vous→Ça gaze.wma→1031008

Baguette Quartet\Rendez-Vous→Si l'on ne s'était pas connu.wma→883952

Baguette Quartet\Rendez-Vous→Reine de musette.wma→1286196

Iris Dement\Infamous Angel→Let the Mystery Be.wma→1349134

Iris Dement\Infamous Angel→These Hills.wma→1784372

Iris Dement\Infamous Angel→Hotter Than Mojave in My Heart.wma→1196018
```

This file can be imported into Excel in a snap.

Writing Unix-Compatible Text Files

`WriteLine` and `WriteBlankLines` write DOS-type files using CR+LF as the line delimiter. To write text files on a Windows system that will be usable on a Unix-based system, you have to write the line-ending codes yourself. Instead of using `WriteLine`, use `Write` and append a linefeed character yourself. In VBScript, at least, this is easy.

> **Note**
>
> VBScript has some predefined string constants that can be handy when writing text files. The value `vbCRLF` consists of a carriage return/linefeed pair, and `vbLF` is a linefeed only. `vbNewLine` is a "platform-independent" line delimiter you could use when writing a script that might run under either Unix or DOS/Windows; however, generally you probably want to exercise explicit control over the line delimiters by using `vbCRLF` or `vbLF` directly.
>
> To see the list of predefined strings, see Microsoft's VBScript Reference, under the heading "Constants."

In VBScript, instead of using `WriteLine`, you might write something like this:

```
stream.Write(str & vbLF)
```

This appends the linefeed character to the string before writing it. Instead of using `WriteBlankLines n`, you could write something like this:

```
for i = 1 to n
    stream.Write(vbLF)
next
```

Working with `Stdin` and `Stdout`

When you run a script from the command line using the `cscript` command, your script has access to the command-line environment's "standard input" and "standard output" files. These are, by default, input from your keyboard and output to the screen, but you can redirect them to files using the familiar command-line syntax

```
program arguments <infile >outfile
```

which instructs the program to read its input from file `infile` and write its output to file `outfile`.

→ To learn how to change the default host, **see** "Ways to Run a Script," **p. 29.**

→ To learn more about command lines and redirection, **see** Chapter 10, "The CMD Command-Line."

You can write scripts to take advantage of this, which can make your programs more "general purpose" in nature. For example, if we write a file-listing script that sends its output to the standard output, it does the following:

- Display the listing to the screen if the script was run with a plain command line.
- Display the listing a screenful at a time with | `more` added to the command line.
- Store the listing in a file with >`filename` added to the command line.
- Print the listing with >`prn` on the command line.★
- List only entries containing "jazz" by adding | `find /i "jazz"` to the command line

Likewise, a script that reads from the standard input takes its input from the following:

- The user's keyboard, if the script is run with a plain command line.
- A file with <`filename` added to the command line.
- The output of another program, if `program` | precedes the script command. (This is called a *pipe*.)

You can see that using standard input and output can give a script many runtime options, virtually for free.

All you have to do to take advantage of this is to use the predefined `TextStream` objects provided by WSH. Instead of using `fso.CreateTextFile` to create a stream for an output listing or `fso.OpenTextFile` to get a stream to read an input file, use the predefined objects listed in Table 4.2.

★*This works only if your printer is connected to parallel port LPT1 or if you've redirected LPT1 to a shared network printer using the* **net use** *command as described in Chapter 13.*

Table 4.2 **Predefined** *TextStream* **Objects**

Object	Use
WScript.Stdin	Standard input. Used to read input from the user's keyboard or, if redirected, from a file or program.
WScript.Stdout	Standard output. Used to write to the user's window or, if redirected, to a file or another program.
WScript.Stderr	Standard error output. Used primarily to print error messages you want the user to see, even if the standard output is redirected. Can be redirected with **2>filename**.

Tip

On Windows XP, WSH does not properly handle redirecting the standard input from a file or pipe if you run a script by simply typing its name. For example, if you type *scriptname* *<filename* and the script attempts to read from WScript.Stdin, the script terminates with an error. You must explicitly run the script with the cscript command (for example, cscript *scriptname.vbs* *<filename*, or *program* | cscript *scriptname.vbs*). On Windows 7 and Vista, redirection and pipes do work correctly, even if you run the script just by typing its name.

Here is a sample script that reads text lines from the standard input, replaces any tabs with commas, and writes the results to the standard output:

```
                                      ' Example file script0411.vbs
do while not WScript.Stdin.AtEndOfStream
    str = WScript.Stdin.ReadLine
    do
        i = instr(str, vbTab)
        if i <= 0 then exit do
        str = left(str, i-1) & "," & mid(str, i+1)
    loop
    WScript.Stdout.WriteLine str
loop
```

Programs that read from the standard input, massage the input in some way, and then write to the standard output are called *filters*. Filters can be handy tools because you can string them together like this:

```
someprogram | onefilter | anotherfilter > outfile
```

When writing scripts that process information, if you can write them with the filter concept in mind, you might find that you get more mileage out of your efforts.

Note

There is a bug in Windows XP that prevents you from using scripts as filters when you type just the script's name on the command line. For example, on XP

```
someprogram | script0411
```

does not work to take the tabs out of the output from `"someprogram"`. It displays an error message instead. You must type the `cscript` command explicitly, as in

```
someprogram | cscript script0411.vbs
```

This problem does not occur on Vista or Windows 7; you can use the simpler `someprogram |` `script0411` command line.

Prompting for User Input

You can use the standard input and output streams to interact directly with the user. WSH-based programs don't have much to work with in the way of user interaction and having to use the command prompt to enter information can seem like a trip back 20 years in computer history, but it still can be useful.

One simple way a program can receive user input is to *prompt* for it and then read from the standard output. Here's a rather silly sample script to show what I mean:

```
                             ' Example file script0412.vbs
wscript.stdout.WriteLine "Enter QUIT to stop the program"
wscript.stdout.WriteLine

do
    wscript.stdout.Write "What is your name? "
    if wscript.stdin.AtEndOfStream then exit do
    name = wscript.stdin.ReadLine
    if ucase(name) = "QUIT" then exit do

    wscript.stdout.WriteLine "Hello, " & name & "."
    wscript.stdout.WriteLine
loop
```

This script prompts for and reads names until the user types QUIT or indicates end of file by pressing Ctrl+Z. The script looks for both `QUIT` and `AtEndOfStream` so it works when the script is run with input redirected.

Note

If you use prompting, be careful to place the test for `AtEndOfStream` *after* the prompt has been typed. `AtEndOfStream` actually stops the script until Windows can determine whether you're going to type something or are going to press Ctrl+Z to end input. If you try to test `AtEndOfStream` before printing the prompt, the prompt does not appear.

Reading Binary Files

You can use the `TextStream` object to read binary files as well as text, if you're careful and you know the structure of the file you're reading. (This is a more advanced topic, so feel free to skip this section if you're new to programming and are still looking to build a foundation of knowledge.)

To read binary information using `TextStream`, you must use the `Read` method, not `readline`, to read in blocks of data. For example, to skip the first 10 bytes of a file and read the next 50, you could write the following:

```
stream.skip(10)
str = stream.read(50)
```

This reads 50 bytes into a string. To extract the binary information, you must then pick the string apart, character by character. In VBScript, you could display the bytes in the string just read with this:

```
for i = 1 to 50
    value = asc(substr(str, i, 1))
    wscript.echo "Byte", str(i,2) & ":", value
next
```

Here, `substr()` picks the string apart one character at a time, and `asc()` yields the byte value of the extracted character.

To interpret word values, you must pick the string apart two bytes at a time and then combine them, as in this example:

```
wordval = asc(substr(str,10,1)) + 256*asc(substr(str,11,1))
```

The preceding line extracts a 16-bit word value from bytes 10 and 11, assuming standard Intel-x86 byte ordering. (Although other computer architectures might use different ordering, most Microsoft-compatible file formats use the Intel ordering, so most files must be read this way.) In like fashion, you can construct a long or DWORD value by combining four bytes:

```
wordval = asc(substr(str,10,1)) + 256*asc(substr(str,11,1)) + _
    65536*asc(substr(str,12,1)) + 16777216*asc(substr(str,13,1))
```

To solve the problem in a general-purpose way and to make the script easier to read, it's handy to use a function to extract binary values from strings. Here is a function that retrieves an n-byte value starting at an offset position in string `str`:

```
function binaryval (byref str, offset, n)
    dim i
    binaryval = 0
    for i = offset+n-1 to offset step -1
        binaryval = binaryval*256 + asc(mid(str,i+1,1))
    next
end function
```

In this function, the offset value is zero based because that's the way most documentation describes the position of items inside file structures. The 10th character in a string corresponds to an offset of 9, so the statement

```
wordval = binaryval(str, 9, 4)
```

is another way to get the DWORD value illustrated earlier.

Example: Reading BMP Image Data

As an illustration of reading binary information, suppose we want to have a script fetch information about the properties of a Microsoft BMP image file. By searching the Internet for "BMP File Format Specification," I found that all BMP files start with the following information:

```
Offset

    0   WORD   bfType       the characters "BM"

    2   DWORD  bfSize       length of file

    6   WORD   bfReserved1  not used

    8   WORD   bfReserved2  not used

   10   DWORD  bfOffBits    offset in file to bitmap data

   14   DWORD  biSize       size of header information, usually 40

   18   LONG   biWidth      width of image in pixels

   22   LONG   biHeight     height of pixels

   26   WORD   biPlanes     number of image planes, always 1

   28   WORD   biBitCount   bits per pixel: 1, 4, 8, 16, 24, or 32
```

Therefore, if we read the first 30 bytes of a BMP file into a string named hdr, we can extract the width and height of the image in pixels using the binaryval function listed earlier. Here's an example:

```
width  = binaryval(hdr, 18, 4)

height = binaryval(hdr, 22, 4)
```

We can use this to write a script that displays the dimensions of any BMP files named on the command line:

```
                     ' Example file bmpsize.vbs
set fso = CreateObject("Scripting.FileSystemObject")
```

```
for each filename in Wscript.Arguments
    if not fso.FileExists(filename) then
        ' the file doesn't exist
        result = "does not exist"

    elseif fso.GetFile(filename).Size < 32 then
        ' the file is not long enough to be valid
        result = "is not a BMP file"

    else
        ' open the file and read the first 32 bytes
        set stream = fso.OpenTextFile(filename)
        hdr = stream.Read(32)
        stream.Close        ' close the stream

        if left(hdr,2) <> "BM" then
            ' the file didn't start with the required marker
            result = "is not a BMP file"
        else
            ' extract the size information
            width  = binaryval(hdr, 18, 4)
            height = binaryval(hdr, 22, 4)
            result = "Width: " & width & "  Height: " & height
        end if
    end if

    ' display whatever information we got for this file
    wscript.echo filename & ":", result
next


' ----------------------------------------------------------------
function binaryval (byref str, offset, n)
    dim i
    binaryval = 0
    for i = offset+n-1 to offset step -1
        binaryval = binaryval*256 + asc(mid(str,i+1,1))
    next
end function
```

When I ran the command

```
bmpsize test.txt xray.bmp "nasa sfbay.bmp"
```

the script dutifully printed the correct results:

```
test.txt: is not a BMP file

xray.bmp: Width: 980  Height: 980

nasa sfbay.bmp: Width: 1024  Height: 725
```

Example: Reading MP3 Tag Data

Another example of reading a binary file illustrates how to extract string information from a block of binary data. MP3 files contain an information block called a *tag* that describes the song's title, artist, album, and so on. Although various tag formats are being developed, the most common one puts this information in the last 128 bytes of the file and has the following format:

```
offset
    0   STRING(3)  Tag      must be the letters "TAG"
    3   STRING(30) Title    padded with spaces
   33   STRING(30) Artist
   63   STRING(30) Album
   93   STRING(4)  Year
   97   STRING(30) Comment
  127   BYTE       Genre    numeric code
```

To read this block, we can use the `TextFileObject` object's `Skip` method to skip all but the last 128 bytes of the file. Then, we can use `Read` to read the 128 bytes. We can use a script similar to the preceding example to read the MP3 file information. When extracting a string, however, we have to use the string position, which starts at 1, rather than the offset, which starts at 0. Here's a script to print the title information in any MP3 files named on the command line:

```
                    ' Example file script0413.vbs
set fso = CreateObject("Scripting.FileSystemObject")

genre = array("Blues","Classic Rock","Country","Dance","Disco",_
    "Funk","Grunge","Hip-Hop","Jazz","Metal","New Age","Oldies",_
        … (the full list is in the downloadble version of the script)
    "Punk Rock","Drum Solo","Acapella","Euro-House","Dance Hall")

for each filename in Wscript.Arguments
    if not fso.FileExists(filename) then
        ' the file doesn't exist
        result = "does not exist"

    else
        filelen = fso.GetFile(filename).Size
        if filelen < 128 then
            ' the file is not long enough to be valid
            WScript.echo filename, "is not an MP3 file"
        else
            ' open the file and get the tag information
            set stream = fso.OpenTextFile(filename)
            stream.Skip(filelen-128)
            hdr = stream.Read(128)
            stream.Close        ' close the stream

            if left(hdr,3) <> "TAG" then
                ' the block didn't start with the required marker
                WScript.echo filename, "has no title/artist info"
```

```
            else
                ' extract and print the size information
                WScript.echo filename & ":"
                WScript.echo "  Title: ", trim(mid(hdr,  4,30))
                WScript.echo "  Artist:", trim(mid(hdr,34,30))
                WScript.echo "  Album: ", trim(mid(hdr,64,30))
                WScript.echo "  Year:  ", trim(mid(hdr,94, 4))
                WScript.echo "  Genre: ", genre(binaryval(hdr,127,1)+1)
            end if
        end if
    end if
next

function binaryval (byref str, offset, n)
… (as seen before)
```

The sample output is as follows:

```
iris mojave.mp3:
  Title:  Hotter Than Mojave In My Heart
  Artist: Iris DeMent
  Album:  Infamous Angel
  Year:   1993
  Genre:  Folk
```

Of course, this works only if whomever created the MP3 file ensures that the tag information is added or downloaded correctly.

Reading and Writing XML

The Extensible Markup Language (XML) is an important tool for storing complex information in a way that's both easy to read for humans and easy to parse by computer. XML has become a popular form for storing information and for interchanging information between computers. Windows uses XML as a packaging format for scripts (which I discuss in in Chapter 9, "Deploying Scripts for Computer and Network Management," and in the Appendix G, "Creating Your Own Scriptable Objects," that you can download from www.helpwin7.com/scripting) and is becoming important as a tool for storing configuration information. Microsoft's latest .NET programming platform encourages programmers to start using text-based INI files again, rather than the Windows Registry, and many programmers are discovering that XML is the best format for human-readable information storage. Therefore, you might find it useful to read and write data in XML format in your scripts.

> **Note**
>
> This section is pretty geeky, so if you're just beginning to work with scripting, you might want to save this section for another day. And, when you do read it, as with all of this book's sections on objects, on the first pass through, you might find it most helpful to skip ahead to the examples that follow each reference section.

Also, take note that the XML object discussed here can also read and write XHTML, which is a version of the HTML web-page markup system that obeys XML's strict syntax rules. Most web browsers can read XHTML, so if you want to, you can use the XML object described here to work with XHTML data.

Some XML Basics

XML files contain both text and markup "tags," as in this example:

```
<?xml version='1.0' encoding='utf-8'?>
<!-- An XML representation of a slide show -->
<slideshow title="Sample Slide Show" date="1/1/2002" author="Yours Truly">
    <slide>
        <title>Wake up to WonderWidgets!</title>
    </slide>
    <slide>
        <title>Overview</title>
        <item>Why <em>WonderWidgets</em> are great</item>
        <item/>
        <item>Who <em>buys</em> WonderWidgets</item>
    </slide>
</slideshow>
```

In this example, `<slide>` and `<title>` are tags. Tags delimit and describe the meaning or purpose of the information in the file and are enclosed in angle brackets to distinguish them from the data they describe. Tags come in pairs called a *start tag* and an *end tag* (for example, `<slide>` and `</slide>`) because their purpose is to clearly define the beginning and ending of each block of information. The end tag version always uses the name of the start tag preceded by a slash (/).

Together, a start tag, an end tag, and everything in between is called an *element*. The "everything in between" is the element's *content*, and it can consist of text or combinations of text and other tags. In the slideshow example, the content of each `<title>` tag is plain text, whereas the content of each `<slide>` tag is a series of subsidiary tags. For the most part, any blank spaces and carriage returns between tags are ignored, so XML files can be formatted to be easy to read by humans.

Besides marking off information, tags can carry additional information called *attributes* that describe their content. For example, `<slideshow ...>` is a tag with attributes `title`, `date`, and `author`. If you're familiar with the HTML markup system used for web pages, this should look very familiar. Whereas HTML uses a fixed set of tags (such as `<TITLE>` and `<IMG>`), the tags in an XML file might be different—the list of allowed tags and their attributes are defined by a schema or document type definition (DTD) that varies from application to application—but the structure of XML is basically the same.

Unlike HMTL, though, XML requires strict attention to the use of end tags; they're never optional. To save space, there is a special format that can be used to indicate an element with no content. For any given tag `<xxx>`, the format `<xxx/>` is equivalent to (that is, a start tag immediately followed by its end tag with nothing in between). Notice that this was used in the slideshow example. The tag indicates a contentless item.

Clearly, XML files have a complex structure and can use several formats to represent the same information. Such a file would be excruciatingly difficult to read, parse, and use in a script if your only tools are the text file objects discussed in the preceding sections.

Fortunately, there's an object that does the work for you. The MSXML2.DOMDocument object (DOM stands for *Domain Object Model*) is not really a standard WSH object, but it's provided with all Windows XP, Vista, 7, and Windows Server computers, and you can get to it with WSH.

The MSXML2.DOMDocument object lets you write and read (parse) XML files as objects rather than as text files. You can read an XML file like the sample file provided earlier into an MSXML2.DOMDocument object. The object has methods and properties that let you examine and modify the XML data—for example, to scan through the slideshow data to find the item or title elements. The object also lets you create or modify XML data and then save the results to an XML text file. (Although it can save you a lot of time and programming effort, it's going to drive me crazy typing it over and over, so for the rest of this section, I just call it a DOMDocument object.)

There's a lot more to the DOMDocument object than I can present in this book—it would take several chapters to cover it thoroughly. I don't list all the object's properties and attributes here; I discuss only the some of the most useful ones in the examples that follow. I have also omitted all discussion of entity references (items such as HTML's &), which open whole new areas of complication. You can get more information on the DOMDocument system by visiting msdn.microsoft.com and searching for "Microsoft XML Parser." Here, I just give you enough information to let you read and write XML files of the sort you might encounter as a Windows system administrator working with installation scripts, setup files, and so on.

> **Note**
>
> Microsoft continually updates its XML software. The version included with Windows 2000 was version 2, and Windows XP, Vista, and 7 include version 3. You can download and install updated versions of the XML parser; just be sure to read the release notes that Microsoft provides because you might need to pass a different name to CreateObject to activate the new version.

As mentioned earlier, XML data is inherently hierarchical: Elements of XML data can contain other elements, and these, too, can contain other elements. Microsoft calls each XML document element a *node*, and any elements inside an element are called *child nodes*. When there is a list of consecutive items, these items are called *siblings*. The structure of the XML example given earlier is shown in Figure 4.1.

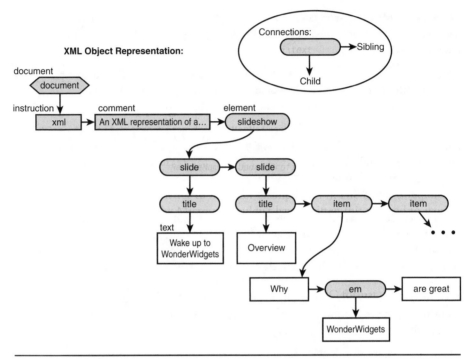

Figure 4.1 Node structure of the sample XML document.

The XML object system uses several objects, including `DOMDocument` (the root node of the XML data structure), `IXMLDOMNode` (a single node of the document tree; nodes can contain document text or subnodes), `IXMLDOMParseError` (information about errors discovered in the XML document structure), and `IXMLDOMNamedNodeMap` (a list of attributes and their values).

Reference List 4.6 lists the most important properties and methods of the `DOMDocument` object. `DOMDocument` describes the document as a whole and is the one you create with `CreateObject` to get things going.

REFERENCE LIST 4.6 Properties and Methods of the `DOMDocument` Object (Partial List)

Properties:

async
Determines whether the entire XML document is immediately loaded when the `Load` method is used (`async = False`) or if the XML system can return from `Load` and parse the document later (`async = True`). Note that you should set this property to `False` in scripting applications. (Read/write.)

childNodes

Returns a collection of IXMLDOMNode objects; these are the contents of the document. You can scan this collection for contents or use GetElements. (Read-only.)

documentElement

Returns the root (highest) element of the document; it might not be the same as firstChild if processing instructions, comments, or a document type exist at the beginning of the file.

parseError

Returns an IXMLDOMParseError object describing the last error encountered when the document is read in. This object has four interesting properties: errorCode is nonzero if there is an error, reason describes the problem, line gives the line number in the file on which the error is located, and srcText is the text of the line containing the error. You can use this information to see whether the XML system detected a problem, such as a missing end tag, and to report it to the script user. (Read-only.)

xml

Returns the representation of the entire document as XML text, in Unicode encoding. (Read-only.)

Methods:

createCDataSection(*data*)

The Create… methods create new IXMLDOMNode node objects. To add them to an XML document, you must populate the new nodes with information and then use the Insert… and Append… methods to add the new nodes to the existing document. We discuss this later in this section. createCDataSection creates a CDATA node, which contains arbitrary uninterpreted data. The data argument is a string.

createComment(*text*)

Creates a Comment node containing the text string.

createDocumentType(*name, publicid, systemid, internalsubset*)

Creates a Document Type node, which defines the DTD in use. If used, it must be added as the first child node of the document node.

createElement(*name*)

Creates a Document Element node with the given name. Elements correspond to tags in the XML file (for example, <slideshow>). Elements are generally populated with lists of other elements and text nodes.

createProcessingInstruction(*target, data*)

Creates a processing instruction (<? ?> tag). Most XML files start with a processing instruction with target "xml" and data something like "version='1.0' encoding='utf-8'".

createTextNode(*text***)**

Creates a Text node with the specified text. This is the actual document text.

getElementsByTagName(*name***)**

Returns a collection of all element nodes in the document that have the specified tag name. You can then scan the collection and examine the contents and subnodes of these elements. The collection lists matching elements in preorder: A parent node is listed first, followed by all its children, in order. More complex searches can be performed by the selectNodes method.

load(*XMLSourceFile***)**

Loads the named XML file. *XMLSourceFile* can be a filename or URL. Any previous contents in the object are discarded and replaced with the contents of the file. Returns False if the load failed; otherwise, it returns True.

loadXML(*XMLSourceText***)**

Like Load but loads XML source text directly. XMLSourceText is a complete XML document or well-formed fragment. Returns False if the load failed; otherwise, it returns True.

Save *destination*

Saves the current XML document in destination. For scripting purposes, this should be a filename, including the path.

selectNodes(*expression***)**

Returns a collection of all the nodes in the document that match a specified searching expression. The search expression syntax is called *XPath* (XSL Path Language). Note that SelectNodes is the meatiest part of the XML object. You can use it to zero in directly on the information you want to extract from an XML file. For example, "/book//name" returns all name elements that occur anywhere inside book elements. For more information, visit msdn.microsoft.com and search for "XSLT Reference."

selectSingleNode(*expression***)**

Like selectNodes but returns only the first node of any nodes identified by the search expression. This is handy when you only expect one, so you don't need to bother scanning the collection.

To read an XML file, create an instance of MSXML2.DOMDocument, use the Load method to read in the file or URL; then, use DOMDocument's other methods and properties to extract information from the file. We discuss those later in the section.

Here is a script fragment that loads the existing XML document:

```
set xdoc = CreateObject("MSXML2.DOMDocument")
xdoc.load("c:\mydata\test.xml")
```

After you have an XML document stored in a DOMDocument object, you can use the selectNode methods to identify certain components of the file from which you might want to extract information, or you can scan through the entire collection of objects. I show an example of this later in this section.

To create a new XML file, create an instance of `MSXML2.DOMDocument`, create data within the object using the `CreateNode` methods, and add these to the document structure using `IXMLNode`'s `Insert…` methods. Finally, use the `Save` method to store the document to a file.

Reference List 4.7 lists a few important properties and methods of the `IXMLDOMNode` object, instances of which describe the document's structure and content.

REFERENCE LIST 4.7   Properties and Methods of the MSXML2 `IXMLDOMNode` Object (Partial List)

Properties:

attributes

Returns an `IXMLDOmNamedNodeMap` list that enumerates the element's attributes. This isn't a collection that VBScript can peruse with `for each`. See the discussion of `Attributes` following this table. This property is read-only; use `setAttribute` to change or add an attribute.

childNodes

Returns a collection of the child nodes; these are the contents of the current element. You can scan this collection for contents, or you can use `FirstChild` and then `NextSibling` to visit the list of children. (Read-only.)

firstChild

Returns the first child object. (Read-only.)

lastChild

The last of an element's child nodes. (Read-only.)

nextSibling

The next node in a list of elements. This property is read-only. Unfortunately, due to a bug in the object, if you scan through the list by visiting `nextSibling` objects, the script will run off the end of the list. Be sure to stop when the current object is its parent's `lastChild`. In VBScript, this is detected by the expression `node is node.parentNode.lastChild`.

nodeName

For Element nodes, this is the tag name of the element (for example, `"Slideshow"`). For Document, Comment, and Text nodes, this is the fixed string `"#document"`, `"#comment"`, or `"#text"`. (Read-only.)

nodeType

As you might expect, this is the type of the node. Node type values are listed in Table 4.3. (Read-only.)

nodeTypeString

The node type as a descriptive string (for example, `"element"` or `"text"`).
(Read-only.)

nodeValue

The contents of a Text or Comment node. This is where you'll find the document
text. (Read/write.)

ownerDocument

Yields the `DOMDocument` object that's the "parent" document of this node.
(Read-only.)

previousSibling

The previous sibling in the list. If the current object is its parent's `firstChild`, there
is no previous sibling. (Read-only.)

xml

Returns an XML text fragment that describes this node and its content, including
any child nodes. (Read-only.)

Methods:

appendChild(*child*)

Appends a new child node `child` to the node's list of children. Returns the `child`
object.

hasChildNodes

Returns `True` if the node has any children. (Why this is considered a method and
not a property is beyond me.)

insertBefore(*newchild, child*)

Inserts a new node `newchild` before node `child` wherever it occurs in the
document.

removeChild(*child*)

Removes the specified child from the node's list of children. Returns a reference to
the removed child node (which should be the value of the parameter `child`.)

replaceChild(*newnode, oldnode*)

Requires two `IXMLDOMNode` arguments. Replaces `oldnode`, wherever it occurs in the
XML document, with `newnode`. You can use this to replace part of a document.
`ReplaceChild` doesn't care to which `IXMLDOMNode` you apply the method; any will
do (that is, `anynode.replaceChild(…)`). The method finds `oldnode` in the document
and replaces that node.

selectNodes

See `selectNodes` in Reference List 4.6.

selectSingleNode

See `selectSingleNode` in Reference List 4.6.

setAttribute(*name, value*)
Sets this node's attribute *name* to the string *value*.

Note
You can use DOMObject's xml or save method to save just a fragment of the XML data.

Table 4.3 lists the various types of node types you might encounter while scanning the structure of an XML document. (Other node types are described in Microsoft's XML DOM documentation, but you're not likely to encounter them while scanning a document.)

Table 4.3 **Important *nodeType* Values for** *IXMLDOMNode*

Value	Type
1	Element. Represents a <tag>.
3	Text. Contains document text in NodeValue.
4	CDATA. Contains arbitrary data.
5, 6	Entity reference and entity (not discussed here).
7	Processing instruction. Special markup that is not document text.
8	Comment. Descriptive text that again is not considered part of the document text.
10	Document type. Corresponds to a <!DOCTYPE > element, which specifies the document's DTD.

The attributes property of IXMLDOMNode returns an object representing all of the element's attributes. An element's attributes property describes the element's variable information. For example, a "font" element might have attributes to describe the typeface and the font size. In XML, this might look like <font face="Times" size="3">.

Here are a couple of problems with the attributes property:

- The attributes property is valid only on Element, Entity, and Notation nodes. On other node types, in VBScript at least, attributes should return null but instead returns what looks like but isn't a valid object.

- Unfortunately, attributes is not a collection object VBScript can scan with the for each statement. You can extract a specific attribute with getNameItem, or you can scan the list with a for loop, as shown following Reference List 4.8.

However, on the plus side, every Element, Entity, and Notation node has an attributes list, even if it is of zero length. The attributes list object has a property and two methods, which are listed in Reference List 4.8.

REFERENCE LIST 4.8   Property and Methods of the IXMLDOMNamedNodeMap Collection

Property:

length
The number of attributes in the collection. (Read-only.)

Methods:

getNamedItem(*name*)
Finds the attribute with the specified name and returns the attribute as yet another variant of an IXMLDOMNode object. (Its properties are covered next.)

item(*index*)
Retrieves attribute objects by index number, which ranges from 0 to the collection's length minus 1.

In working with XML files, you usually use getNamedItem to extract a specific attribute node by name. If you want to scan the entire list, though, you must use a loop, as shown here:

```
set alist = node.attributes
for i = 0 to alist.length-1
    set attr = list.item(i)
    wscript.echo attr.nodeName, "=", attr.nodeValue
next
```

Attributes are stored in IXMLDOCNode objects, with the interesting properties listed in Table 4.4.

Table 4.4   **Useful Properties of *IXMLDOCNode* When It Contains an Attribute**

Property	Description
NodeName	The attribute's name. Read-only.
nodeValue	The attribute's value. Read/write.
specified	A Boolean value. If True, the attribute's value is explicitly specified in the XML file. If False, the value is derived from the default value defined by the document's schema. Read-only.

As an example, the following script fragment displays the width attribute of all <img> tags in an XML document:

```
for each node in xmldoc.getElementsByTagName("img")
    wscript.echo node.attributes.getNamedItem("width").nodeValue
next
```

Reading an XML File

Now, with the reference material aside, let's see how these objects are used in practice.

The following script reads an XML file and lists its structure. The script first loads the document and then uses subroutine xmldump to list the first element; xmldump calls itself recursively to list any subelements, as deeply as necessary, until the bottom-level text nodes have been listed. Here's the code:

```
                          ' Example file script0414.vbs
const NODE_ELEMENT = 1

set xdoc = CreateObject("MSXML2.DOMDocument")

xdoc.load("test.xml")       ' load the file into the object

xmldump xdoc, 0             ' dump the entire document structure

' ------------------------------------------------------------------
' xmldump - list contents of XML object 'x'; lvl is current depth

sub xmldump (x, lvl)
    dim gap, child, i

    gap = space(lvl*3)  ' make an indenting string to show the depth
                        ' list the node type and name
    wscript.echo gap & "--------------------"
    wscript.echo gap & x.nodeTypeString, "'" & x.nodename & "'"

                        ' list any attributes
    if x.nodetype = NODE_ELEMENT then
        set alist = x.attributes
        for i = 0 to alist.length-1
            set attr = alist.item(i)
            wscript.echo gap & "Attribute", attr.nodeName, "=", attr.nodeValue
        next
    end if
                        ' if the node has any text content, list it
    if not isnull(x.nodeValue) then _
        wscript.echo gap & "nodeValue:",      "'" & x.nodeValue & "'"

                        ' now list any children, indented one level deeper
    if x.hasChildNodes then
        for each child in x.childNodes
            xmldump child, lvl+1
        next
    end if
end sub
```

The output of this script with the XML sample file introduced earlier starts out like this:

```
--------------------
document '#document'
    --------------------
    processinginstruction 'xml'
```

```
nodeValue: 'version="1.0" encoding="utf-8"'
--------------------
comment '#comment'
nodeValue: ' An XML representation of a slide show '
--------------------
element 'slideshow'
    --------------------
    element 'slide'
        --------------------
        element 'title'
            --------------------
            text '#text'
            nodeValue: 'Wake up to WonderWidgets!'
    --------------------
    element 'slide'
        --------------------
        element 'title'
            --------------------
            text '#text'
            nodeValue: 'Overview'
        --------------------
        element 'item'
            --------------------
            text '#text'
            nodeValue: 'Why '
            --------------------
            element 'em'
                --------------------
                text '#text'
                nodeValue: 'WonderWidgets'
            --------------------
            text '#text'
            nodeValue: ' are great'
```

Note

There are two ways to scan through the elements contained *within* an XML element. You can use for each to scan the list of child nodes, as in the previous example, or you can use a node's firstChild property to get the first subelement and then use nextSibling to walk through the list. The list is ended when you get to the special object reference "Nothing".

If you want to traverse a child list without using for each..., use this method:

```
* step through x's child list, sibling by sibling
set child = x.firstChild
do while not (child is Nothing)
   (process child)
   set child = child.nextSibling
loop
```

Creating an XML or HTML File

The XML object can produce HTML files as well as XML files. (Technically, it can produce "XHTML" rather than ordinary HTML because elements that have no content are written with a / at the end of the tag—for example, <HR/>. Most web browsers accept this syntax.) Creating XML or HTML with a script is much harder than reading it. The difficulty is that you have to create node objects individually and then stick them into the appropriate place in the document. It's tedious, as I show you.

For starters, let's create a simple HTML file that contains an unordered (bulleted point) list of three items. The script looks like this:

```
                          ' Example file script0415.vbs
set xdoc = CreateObject("MSXML2.DOMDocument")

                  ' create the outer HTML element
set html = xdoc.appendChild(xdoc.CreateElement("HTML"))

                  ' add the unordered list
set list = html.appendChild(xdoc.createElement("UL"))

                   ' add three list (LI) items
set item = list.appendChild(xdoc.createElement("LI"))
item.appendChild xdoc.createTextNode("This is item 1")

set item = list.appendChild(xdoc.createElement("LI"))
item.appendChild xdoc.createTextNode("This is item 2")

set item = list.appendChild(xdoc.createElement("LI"))
item.appendChild xdoc.createTextNode("This is item 3")

                   ' save the created structure as an HTML file
xdoc.save "test.html"
```

The resulting HTML output file looks like this:

```
<HTML>
<UL>
<LI>This is item 1</LI>
<LI>This is item 2</LI>
<LI>This is item 3</LI>
</UL>
</HTML>
```

(Although, it actually comes out as one long string, which is fine for a web browser but ugly in a book. I broke it into several lines.)

The script is so complex because each element in the file must be created and then placed into position. Adding text to an element, as the sample script did with the <LI> elements, adds another step.

If you want to use formatting tags such as <I> for italics, you must jump through some extra hoops. For example, to add an item to our HTML list with the content "This is *italicized* text," we need the following HTML:

```
<LI>This is <I>italicized</I> text</LI>
```

This is actually a string of three "sibling" items: a text item, an <I> element with text content, and a third text item. The script code to add this item is

```
set ital = xdoc.createElement("I")
ital.appendChild xdoc.createTextNode("italicized")

set item = list.appendChild(xdoc.createElement("LI"))
item.appendChild xdoc.createTextNode("This is ")
item.appendChild ital
item.appendChild xdoc.createTextNode(" text")
```

As you can see, creating HTML or XML in a script is not for the faint of heart, and probably isn't worth the trouble for simple output files. Still, it can be useful when the output file is complex or when its final structure can't be determined in advance but must be computed on-the-fly.

Here's an example. The following script file creates a "slideshow" XML file by reading lines from the standard input. If an input line starts with an asterisk (*), it's considered to be the title of a new slide. Any other lines are considered to be "item" points of the current slide. Here's the code:

```
                                 ' Example file script0416.vbs

set xdoc = CreateObject("MSXML2.DOMDocument")
                     ' add the standard XML version marker
xdoc.appendChild xdoc.CreateProcessingInstruction("xml", "version=""1.0""")
                     ' create the outer slideshow element
set slideshow = xdoc.CreateElement("slideshow")
xdoc.appendChild slideshow

curslide = null        ' there is no current slide yet
                       ' read lines from standard input
do while not WScript.Stdin.AtEndOfStream
    str = WScript.Stdin.ReadLine

    if left(str,1) = "*" then
                         ' this is a new slide. Create text node
        set text = xdoc.CreateTextNode(mid(str,2))
                         ' add text to a title element
        set title = xdoc.CreateElement("title")
        title.appendChild(text)
                         ' add title to a new slide element
        set curslide = xdoc.CreateElement("slide")
        curslide.appendChild(title)
                         ' append slide to the slideshow's list
        slideshow.appendChild(curslide)
```

```
        elseif isnull(curslide) then
                        ' can't add an item before first slide
            wscript.echo "File must start with a * slide item!"
            wscript.quit 1

        else
                        ' a new item: create text node
            set text = xdoc.CreateTextNode(str)
                        ' add text to a new item element
            set item = xdoc.CreateElement("item")
            item.appendChild(text)
                        ' add item to current slide's list
            curslide.appendChild(item)
        end if
loop
                        ' save as XML text
xdoc.save "myshow.xml"
```

With the input data

```
*first slide
an important point
another point
*second slide
final point
```

the script created the following XML file (and again, I added line breaks to make it more readable because the Save method writes the entire thing out as one long string):

```
<?xml version="1.0"?>
<slideshow>
<slide>
<title>first slide</title>
<item>an important point</item>
<item>another point</item>
</slide>
<slide>
<title>second slide</title>
<item>final point</item>
</slide>
</slideshow>
```

Although it's a difficult and tedious process, using the XML DOM object to create XML does have the advantage that the software is guaranteed to write a properly formatted XML file.

Manipulating Programs and Shortcuts

You sometimes might want a script to run an external program such as Notepad, the sort command, or some other type of utility program. You might do this when writing a script to automatically collect and process information. For example, if your script generates a lot of text, it might be nice to pop up the results in a Notepad window so the user can easily scroll through and read the results. You might also want to have a script create desktop and Start menu shortcuts, as part of an installation routine, during logon, or for network maintenance. All these tasks can be managed using the WScript.Shell object. The word *shell* is a generic term for the command interface computer users interact with to run programs. On Microsoft Windows, the shell is the desktop, a display managed by Windows Explorer.

The `WScript.Shell` Object

Like WScript.FileSystemObject, WScript.Shell is a utility object provided with WSH. WScript.Shell provides a way of interacting with the Windows program execution environment and Windows Explorer. This object's properties and methods let you interact with special folders, such as Desktop and My Documents; run programs; manage shortcuts; and examine environment variables such as PATH. WScript.Shell also lets you work with the Windows Registry, which is discussed in a later section. The properties and methods of the WScript.Shell object are listed in Reference List 4.9.

Reference List 4.9   Properties and Methods of the `WScript.Shell` Object

Properties:

`CurrentDirectory`
Returns the name of the "current directory" of the WSH program. The current directory is the one searched when you attempt to access files without specifying a drive and path. This property is read/write; you can change the script's current directory by storing a new string value to this property.

`Environment`[(location)]
The Environment property returns a collection of WshEnvironment objects, which represent a set of environment variables. Depending on the value of the location argument, Environment returns one of four distinct sets of objects. Location can be one of the following values:

Location	Description
"system"	The base set of predefined environment definitions that are provided to every user
"user"	User-specific environment variable definitions that can add to or replace the system-wide definitions
"process"	The current set of environment variables from this logon session, as provided to the script program when it started
"volatile"	A list of variables that are computed from dynamic data when you log on

This is tricky! If you specify "system" or "user," the collection of objects lets you view and modify the list of environment variables that will be set up the next time you log on, start a new application, or open a *new* Command Prompt window. Thus, you use the "system" and "user" lists when your intention is to reconfigure Windows. You might do this when you are writing a script to add a new folder to the PATH.

If you specify "process," the collection of objects represents the *current* list of environment variables inherited by WSH. You might use these values to find the name of the TEMP environment variable so you can store temporary files in the folder it names.

Note

There is no way to modify environment variables within a script so that the changes affect other running programs. This is unlike what happens with batch files—if you change an environment variable within a batch file, it affects subsequent programs run in the same Command Prompt window.

Also, please see the note at the end of this section about making changes to the "system" environment list on Vista and Windows 7.

Caution

If you omit the Location argument, Environment returns the "system" collection when the script is run on Windows 7, Vista, XP, NT, or 2000, and the "process" collection when running on Windows 9*x* and Me. You should *always* specify the location to ensure that you get the collection you need.

See the section "Working With the Environment" later in this chapter for more information. This property is read-only, although the elements of the collection it returns can be modified.

SpecialFolders[(*folder*)]

Returns a collection of SpecialFolder objects. These objects relate special user-specific Windows folders, such as the Desktop folder, to their actual locations on the hard disk. You can ask for the location of a specific folder by naming it as an argument to SpecialFolders. In this case, the return value is a string (*not* an object) naming the path to the folder. Here's a list of the special folder names:

"AllUsersDesktop"	"NetHood"
"AllUsersStartMenu"	"PrintHood"
"AllUsersPrograms"	"Programs"
"AllUsersStartup"	"Recent"
"Desktop"	"SendTo"
"Favorites"	"StartMenu"
"Fonts"	"Startup"
"MyDocuments"	"Templates"

This property is read-only. We talk more about SpecialFolders later in this chapter.

Methods:

AppActivate *title*

Activates an application window (brings it to the top and selects it for keyboard and mouse input). The window is chosen by matching its title text. Returns True if it finds and activates the window; otherwise, it returns False. If you know the process's process ID (PID) number, you can also pass that as a numeric argument to AppActivate. You can obtain an application's PID if you start it using Exec, or get it from the WMI objects discussed in Chapter 7.

CreateShortcut(*strPathname*)
Creates a new shortcut or opens an existing shortcut. Returns a WshShortcut or WshURLShortcut object. You must set this new object's properties to actually create a working shortcut. See the section "Creating and Modifying Shortcuts" for details.

Exec(*strCommand*)
Runs an application in a child command prompt shell. The application's standard input, standard output, and standard error streams might be read and written by the script. Returns a WshScriptExec object, which is discussed later in this chapter.

ExpandEnvironmentStrings(*strString*)
Replaces any occurrences of environment variable names marked by percent signs (for example, %path%) in the input string with the contents of the corresponding environment variables.

LogEvent *Type, Message*[, *Target*]
Adds an event entry to a log file. The Type value indicates the event severity level and must be one of the following values:

Value	Event Type
0	Success
1	Error
2	Warning
4	Information
8	Audit success
16	Audit failure

Message is a string, the text of the message to be recorded. If specified, Target specifies the network name of the computer whose Event Log is to receive the new entry. If desired, LogEvent can send an event to another computer across the network. If Machine is omitted, the event is stored in the local computer's log.

Popup(*strText*, [*nWait*], [*strTitle*], [*nType*])
Displays text in a pop-up message box. It's similar to the MsgBox function but has an optional timeout value that lets your script proceed if the user doesn't respond to the prompt (because the script was run as a scheduled task, for example). The arguments are

strText	The text to display.
nWait	The number of seconds to wait before closing the box; 0 means wait until the user clicks OK.

strTitle   The title to display at the top of the pop-up box.

nType   Indicates what sorts of buttons and icons to display.

The nType value can be any one the following values:

Constant	Value	Description
vbOKOnly	0	Displays the OK button only.
vbOKCancel	1	Displays the OK and Cancel buttons.
vbAbortRetryIgnore	2	Displays the Abort, Retry, and Ignore buttons.
vbYesNoCancel	3	Displays the Yes, No, and Cancel buttons.
vbYesNo	4	Displays the Yes and No buttons.
vbRetryCancel	5	Displays the Retry and Cancel buttons.

Any of the following additional constants can be added to nType to adjust the appearance of the popup message:

Constant	Value	Description
vbCritical	16	Displays the Critical Message icon.
vbQuestion	32	Displays the Warning Query icon.
vbExclamation	48	Displays the Warning Message icon.
vbInformation	64	Displays the Information Message icon.
vbDefaultButton1	0	The first button is the default.
vbDefaultButton2	256	The second button is the default.
vbDefaultButton3	512	The third button is the default.
vbDefaultButton4	768	The fourth button is the default.
VbSystemModal	4096	System modal. On Win32 systems, this constant provides an application modal message box that always remains on top of any other programs you may have running.

Popup returns one of the following values to indicate which button the user pressed to dismiss the message box:

Constant	Value	Button Title
vbOK	1	OK
vbCancel	2	Cancel
vbAbort	3	Abort
vbRetry	4	Retry
vbYes	6	Yes
vbNo	7	No

If the box closes itself due to a timeout, Popup returns -1.

Note

If WSH was run with the //B (batch) command-line argument, the PopUp method does nothing.

RegDelete *strName*

Deletes a key or one of its values from the Registry. strName is the path to the key or value. See "Working with the Registry," later in this chapter for details.

RegRead(*strName*)

Returns the value of a key or value from the Registry.

RegWrite *strName*, *value*[, *strType*]

Creates a new key, adds a value to an existing key, or changes the value of an existing value.

Run(*strCommand*, [*intWindowStyle*], [*bWaitOnReturn*])

Runs a program in a separate window. Here are the three arguments:

strCommand	The command to run. The string should list the name of the program and any arguments it requires.
intWindowStyle	The size of window to create. The values you can specify are 1, which opens the window normally; 3, which opens the window maximized; or 7, which opens the window minimized (as an icon).
bWaitOnReturn	A Boolean value. If this is specified and True, the script waits until the program terminates and returns its error status as the return value from Run. If this is omitted or False, the script continues running after the program is started, and the Run method returns 0.
SendKeys(*string*)	Sends one or more keystrokes to the active window (as if typed on the keyboard).

Running Programs

WScript.Shell can be used to run other programs at the behest of your script. You might do this as part of a complex procedure to gather and manipulate information or as a way of automating some repetitive task. Four of WScript.Shell's methods might come into play:

- **Run**—Starts a Windows program
- **SendKeys**—Sends keystrokes to the program as if you were typing them manually
- **AppActivate**—Selects the program with which SendKeys works
- **Exec**—Starts and interacts with a command-line program

Running Windows Programs

You can run Windows programs using the `WScript.Shell` object's `Run` method, which starts the program in its own window.

The first argument to `Run` is a string giving the name of the program (including the full path to the file, if the program is not in one of the standard folders found in the `PATH` environment variable) and any arguments required. For example, a script could write data to a text file and display it with the Notepad program, as in this example:

```
                                       ' Example file script0417.vbs
Const TemporaryFolder = 2

set shell = CreateObject("WScript.Shell")   ' create utility objects
set fso   = CreateObject("Scripting.FileSystemObject")
                                   ' get name of scratch file
tmpfile   = fso.BuildPath(fso.GetSpecialFolder(TemporaryFolder),_
    fso.GetTempName())

set file = fso.CreateTextFile(tmpfile)     ' create a text file
for i = 100 to 0 step -1
    file.WriteLine i & " bottles of beer on the wall!"
next
file.Close
set file = Nothing                         ' release the File object

' run notepad to display the file, and wait for it to terminate
shell.Run "notepad " & tmpfile, 1, True

' delete the scratch file
fso.DeleteFile(tmpfile)
```

In this example, the `Run` method starts Windows Notepad with the name of the created text file as its argument. The second argument, 1, tells Notepad to open a standard window, and the third argument, `True`, tells the script to wait until the user closes Notepad.

You can interact with programs you've run in a limited way, by sending keystrokes to them as if the user had typed them. I don't consider this terribly useful, so I only outline how it's done:

- You must know the title of the window you want to control. For programs that change their titles to the name of an open file, this can be tricky. Use `AppActivate("`*`title`*`")` to cause Windows to bring this desired program to the foreground. `AppActivate` returns `True` if successful; if it fails, there's not much you can do.

- You can send keystrokes to the application with the `SendKeys` method. `SendKeys` sends messages to the application that make it think the user has pressed keyboard keys. You can't simulate mouse movement, but you can send special keys such as END using `"{END}"` and Alt+F with `"%F"`; you can find the complete list of key symbols in the Microsoft Script Host documentation. Be sure to read this documentation as the +, ^, %, ~, { and } characters all have special meanings.

- It's best to have the script pause briefly between each keystroke it sends to an application to give the application time to process the request. `WScript.Sleep 100` pauses for 100 msec (one-tenth of a second), which should be adequate in most cases.

`SendKeys` lets you script interactions with Windows programs in the manner of a player piano. You can actually accomplish some sophisticated things using this method, which I call *key stuffing*, such as running a database report on a scheduled basis. However, writing this kind of script and debugging it can be nightmarish. It's usually better and easier to do "automated" processing using an application's Automation interface or command-line interface, if it has one.

Running Command-Line Programs

You can run command-line programs (actually, their proper name is "console applications") from a script using the `WScript.Shell` object's `Run` or `Exec` methods. If you only want to start the application and let it run in its own window, `Run` is adequate. However, `Exec` has two advantages over `Run`:

- You can start a program, let the script perform other tasks, and later determine if and how the program is terminated.
- When running a command-line program, `Exec` lets you send data directly to the program through its standard input file stream, and you can read data from the program's standard output and standard error output using `TextStream` objects.

Start a command-line program using the `Shell` object's `Exec` method, specifying a full command line, as shown here:

```
set shell = CreateObject("WScript.Shell")
set program = shell.Exec("ping www.someplace.com")
```

You can specify a full path to the program you're running, or—if it can be found in PATH—you can just specify its name, as in the preceding example.

Notice that `set` is used to get the return value of Exec. `Exec` returns a `WshScriptExec` object that gives you control over the program you just started. The properties and methods of `WshScriptExec` are listed in Reference List 4.10. After the reference list, I show you a sample script, and after that is a section on avoiding tricky problems that can arise when you run a command-line program from a script.

REFERENCE LIST 4.10   Properties and Method of the `WshScriptExec` Object

Properties:

ExitCode
Returns the application's exit status after it has terminated. If the process is still running, `ExitCode` and `Status` are 0.

ProcessID

Returns the PID for the application. You can use this number as an argument to the AppActivate method.

Status

Indicates whether the program is still running: 0 means it's running, and 1 means it has terminated.

StdErr

A TextStream object that might be read to get any output the program writes to the standard error output.

StdIn

A TextStream object that might be written to; anything written to StdIn is sent to the standard input of the program.

StdOut

A TextStream object that might be read to get any output the program writes to the standard output.

Note

When you call the AtEndOfStream method of the StdOut or StdErr objects, the script pauses until either the program writes something to the stream or the program terminates and you've read all the data. I talk more about this later in this section.

Method:

Terminate

Terminates the program if it's still running. Usually this is only used in an abnormal situation (for example, when a program that was expected to have completed within a few seconds is still running after a longer time).

After starting a command with Exec, you usually interact with it by writing to its standard input or reading from its standard output or standard error. Therefore, you can use an external program to perform any sort of task to assist the script.

In this example, a script uses the ping program to test a list of Internet hosts to ensure they're online. If any are offline, a message is printed. Here's the code:

```
                                  ' Example file script0418.vbs
set shell = CreateObject("WScript.Shell")
hosts     = array("www.netsol.com", "www.google.com","www.yahoo.com")

failed    = ""                    ' list of failed hosts
for each host in hosts
    if not pingtest(host) then
        failed = failed & " " & host ' if failed, add name to list
    end if
next
                                  ' if any failed, display the list
if len(failed) > 0 then MsgBox "Warning: can't reach" & failed
```

```
' --------------------------------------------------------------
' pingtest - try to ping the host named 'host'. If even one ping
' returns, consider the test a success.

function pingtest (host)
    pingtest = False                      ' assume failure

    wscript.echo "Pinging", host

    set ping = shell.Exec("ping " & host) ' run the command

    do while not ping.Stdout.AtEndOfStream
        str = ping.Stdout.ReadLine        ' read its results

        if instr(str, "could not find") > 0 then exit do

        if instr(str, "Reply from") > 0 then
            pingtest = True               ' a reply means success
            exit do                       ' we can stop right now
        end if
    loop
    ping.Terminate                        ' stop ping if it's still going
end function
```

In most cases you want your script to wait until the program has completed its job
before it proceeds. If your script reads all of the program's output in a loop controlled
by StdOut.EndOfStream, as in the previous example, you're covered because
EndOfStream does not return True until the program has exited and you've read all its
output.

However, if you don't read the program's output, you must have the script test repeatedly check to see whether the program is still running (Status = 0), and if so, wait a
moment, as in this example:

```
set shell = CreateObject("WScript.Shell")

set program = shell.Run("someprogram")

do while program.status = 0  ' while program is still running
    WScript.Sleep 100        ' pause 100 msec before trying again
loop
```

The Sleep method is used here to pause the script while waiting for the program to
terminate. If you didn't put the pause in, the do loop would circle at a furious pace
waiting for the program to end. With the script program making this kind of demand
on the processor, the external program has a harder time getting its job done.

If you want to give the program, say, five seconds to terminate on its own, and if it
doesn't force it to stop, you could use a for loop to limit the number of times the
loop is executed:

```
for nwait = 1 to 50
    if program.status <> 0 then exit for
```

```
    WScript.Sleep 100
next
program.Terminate
```

Here, we wait 100 msec up to 50 times, for a total of at most five seconds. If the program terminates earlier, `exit for` keeps us from waiting longer than necessary. After the loop, `Terminate` stops the program if it hasn't already stopped by itself.

Reading Text from a Console Application

If the external application generates text output, your script might fail to run properly unless you run the program and read its output in this specific order:

```
set program = Shell.Exec(command line)

do while not program.StdOut.AtEndOfStream
    txt = program.StdOut.ReadLine
    ' (do something with txt, if appropriate)
loop

' if you care about whatever might have been written to stderr, use this loopl,
' otherwise omit it:
do while not program.StdErr.AtEndOfStream
    txt = program.StdErr.ReadLine
    ' (do something with txt, if appropriate)
loop
```

Even if you don't do anything with the text this script reads from the application, if you don't write the script this way, your script or the application might get "stuck" with one waiting for the other indefinitely.

Here's the background: The console application you run might write text to the standard output stream, the standard error stream, or both. When it does so, Windows collects whatever text is written and holds onto it until your script reads it using the `StdOut` and `StdErr` TextStream objects. This is called *buffering*. But it works only up to a point—if more than 4,096 characters accumulate, Windows halts the application until your script reads the collected text. If your script never gets around to reading the text, the application is never permitted to resume and complete its task.

There's another complication. When you use a `TextStream` object to read from a file stored on the disk, Windows knows in advance how much information is stored in the file. Here, however, we're reading from a running program and Windows has no way of knowing what text, if any, might appear in the future. So, as long as the program is still running, the `AtEndOfStream` method has a tricky job. Here's how it works:

- If the application is still running and has written some text you haven't yet read, `AtEndOfStream` returns `False` so you can go ahead and read it.

- If the application has finished its job and exited and you've read all of whatever text it wrote, `AtEndOfStream` returns `True` so your loop can terminate and your script can go on. However,

- If the program is still running and there is no text waiting to be read, AtEndOfStream halts your script until the external program writes some text, or it terminates. Either way, at that point, AtEndOfStream is able give an answer and it does return either False or True.

The pitfalls you have to watch out for are these:

- If you know that the program can never generate more than 4,096 characters of text, you don't have to worry about its getting "frozen" waiting for you to read the text, so you can construct whatever type of loop you want and interact with the program any way you want. The loop I showed earlier that waits for Status to change from 0 to 1 works fine. Just remember that your script might pause if you reference the AtEndOfStream property.

- If the program might write a lot of text to StdOut right after starting the program, you must read whatever text it generates, using a loop like this:

```
do while not program.StdOut.AtEndOfStream
    txt = program.StdOut.ReadLine
    ' (do something with txt, if desired)
loop
```

  At the call to AtEndOfStream, the script might halt for an arbitrary amount of time, waiting for the program to either write or terminate, so you can't ask your script to do anything other than crank around this loop reading from StdOut.

- If the application writes text to StdErr, generally there isn't much of it (usually just a short error message). If you care to read that text, use a loop controlled by while not program.StdErr.AtEndOfStream *after* the StdOut loop. If you try to read the StdErr text first, and the application writes a lot of text to StdOut, Windows might halt it waiting for your script to catch up—and it never will. You have to read all of StdOut first and then StdErr. (Because AtEndOfStream can lock up the script, you can't write a loop that reads from both StdOut and StdErr in alternation.)

- If the application might generate a lot of text to both StdOut and StdErr, you must not run it directly. One stream or the other will buffer enough text to stop the application, and your script will then stop in a call to the other stream's AtEndOfStream method. Instead, write a batch file to run the application and redirect all its output to a file, to the standard output, or handle the output some other way. For example, this batch file runs a program named "someprogram" and sends both its standard output and standard error streams to the standard output:

```
@echo off
someprogram 2>&1
```

  Have your script run this batch file, like this:

```
set program = Shell.Exec("cmd.exe /c ""c:\full\path\to\batchfile.bat""")
```

  Read StdOut from this batch file process, and the program doesn't stall.

If your script gets stuck while running a console application and never finishes, it's almost certainly either stuck in a call to `AtEndOfStream` or in a loop waiting for the program object's `Status` property to become 1, and the application is likewise stuck waiting for your script.

If this happens, press Ctrl+C to cancel the script, put `WScript.Echo` statements before every reference of `AtEndofScript`, `ReadLine`, and so on or run it in the Script Debugger, so you can see where your script is getting stuck.

Creating and Modifying Shortcuts

`WScript.Shell` can also be used to create and modify shortcuts on the desktop and Start menu. You could use this feature to ensure that a necessary shortcut is always installed on every user's desktop or as part of an installation procedure for a new program. You can create both standard program shortcuts and so-called "URL shortcuts" that link to a website.

Shortcuts are actually small files that contain the data Windows Explorer uses to fire up the program represented by a shortcut. Normal shortcut files use the extension `.lnk`, whereas URL shortcuts use the extension `.url`. The data inside shortcut files isn't plain, readable text, so `WScript.Shell` provides an object to represent this data and make it easy to manage.

Here's how it works: You first use `WScript.Shell`'s method `CreateShortcut` or `ModifyShortcut` to "open" a new or existing shortcut for editing. This creates an instance of a `WshShortcut` object that represents the shortcut with which you're working. Then you can change this object's properties, and Windows updates the corresponding shortcut.

Note

Windows actually has two varieties of the `WshShortcut` object: `WshShortcut`, for standard short-cuts, and `WshURLShortcut`, for links to Web pages. You create regular shortcuts with a `.lnk` extension and URL shortcuts with a `.url` extension. When you modify a shortcut, the methods and procedures are identical for both types.

The properties and the one method of `WshShortcut` and `WshUrlShortcut` are listed in Reference List 4.11.

REFERENCE LIST 4.11   Properties and Method of the `WshShortcut` **and** `WshUrlShortcut` **Objects**

Properties:

Arguments

Specifies any arguments to be passed to the program. This is a string value. (Read/write.)

Description

The shortcut's description text, which appears as a tooltip if you hover the mouse over the shortcut icon. (Read/write.)

FullName

The fully qualified path to the shortcut object's target program, which is set by the TargetPath attribute. (Read-only.)

Hotkey

Identifies the key combination to activate the shortcut. (Read/write.)

IconLocation

The icon assigned to the shortcut. (Read/write.)

The format of the IconLocation property is "*filename, iconnumber*" where filename is the name of an executable EXE or DLL file containing one or more icons and iconnumber is the zero-based index into the file's list of icons. For most applications, the first icon is the one used for shortcuts, so "filename.exe,0" is the usual IconLocation setting.

RelativePath

Sets or returns the path to the target program relative to the location of the short-cut. I recommend you ignore this property. When you create a new shortcut, specify a full path, and assign it to the TargetPath property. (Read/write.)

TargetPath

The path to the shortcut's target program or a URL in the case of a link to a web page. (Read/write.)

WindowStyle

Assigns a window style to a shortcut or identifies the type of window style used by a shortcut. (Read/write.)

WindowStyle determines how the application is started. The possible values are 1, which opens the window normally; 3, which opens the window maximized; and 7, which opens the window minimized (as an icon).

WorkingDirectory

The working directory used by a shortcut. (Read/write.)

Method:

Save

Saves a new or edited shortcut object to disk. This method must be used after the shortcut object's properties are changed to commit the changes to the .lnk file.

Here is a script to create a desktop shortcut to a text file containing a to-do list that you edit with Notebook:

```
                                  ' Example file script0419.vbs
set shl = CreateObject("WScript.Shell")  ' make objects
set fso = CreateObject("Scripting.FileSystemObject")
desktop = shl.SpecialFolders("Desktop")  ' get folder locations
mydocs  = shl.SpecialFolders("MyDocuments")
```

```
                                       ' create shortcut object
set sc  = shl.CreateShortcut(fso.BuildPath(desktop, "\To Do.lnk"))

sc.TargetPath       = "notepad.exe"      ' set program to run
sc.WorkingDirectory = mydocs             ' set working folder
sc.Arguments        = fso.BuildPath(mydocs, "todo.txt") ' specify file
sc.WindowStyle      = 1                   ' open as normal window
sc.Hotkey           = "Ctrl+Alt+T"        ' set hotkey
sc.IconLocation     = "notepad.exe, 0"    ' use normal notepad icon
sc.Description       = "View and Edit To Do List"
sc.Save                                   ' create the shortcut
```

The script first creates the utility objects it needs and then looks up the locations of the Desktop and [My] Documents folders. (The value of `SpecialFolders("MyDocuments")` gives the correct location of your Documents folder no matter what version of Windows you're using). It creates the new shortcut, named to `do.lnk`, in the Desktop folder. The shortcut runs Notepad with a file named `todo.txt` in [My] Documents.

If the program or file specified by `TargetPath` can't be found in the environment variable `PATH`, you must specify the full path the program or document named in `TargetPath`. Windows finds `notepad.exe` by itself, but we could have specified its full path with

```
sc.TargetPath = shl.ExpandEnvironmentStrings("%WINDIR%\notepad.exe")
```

or, equivalently, with

```
sc.TargetPath = fso.BuildPath(_
    fso.GetSpecialFolder(WindowsFolder), "notepad.exe")
```

You can add items to the Start menu by adding shortcuts to the special folders used to populate the menu. You can't add icons to the large Start menu panel with a script, but you can add them to the [All] Programs list.

To create Start menu items, create shortcuts in a subfolder of one of these two main folders:

- To create a shortcut that is seen by all users on the computer, create the shortcut under `SpecialFolders("AllUsersStartMenu")`.

- To create a shortcut for the current user only, create the shortcut under `SpecialFolders("StartMenu")`.

For example, to create a "Special Tools" folder and shortcut for all computer users, you could write a script based on this outline:

```
set shl   = CreateObject("WScript.Shell")' make objects
set fso   = CreateObject("Scripting.FileSystemObject")

startmenu = shl.SpecialFolders("AllUsersStartMenu")
toolfolder = fso.BuildPath(startmenu, "Special Tools")

CreateFullPath(toolfolder)                ' create folder if necessary
```

```
set sc = shl.CreateShortcut(fso.BuildPath(toolfolder, "first tool.lnk"))
  … set shortcut properties
sc.Save

sub CreateFullPath (path)
   …
  (the CreateFullPath subroutine was shown earlier in the chapter)
```

This script constructs the name of the folder under the Start menu in the variable `tool-folder`. It uses the subroutine `CreateFullPath` to ensure that the folder exists and then creates one or more shortcuts in the new folder.

Working with the Environment

Environment variables such as the program `PATH` and the temporary file folder name `TEMP` can be examined by looking through the `Environment` property of `WScript.Shell`. `Environment("process")`, which returns a collection of `WshEnvironment` objects that define the current set of environment variables. You can examine this collection to extract environment variable definitions. Here are some reasons you might want to do this:

- To find the name of the folder to be used for scratch files, which is named by the `TEMP` environment variable.

- To look through the program search path (variable `PATH`) to see where a program is installed.

- To look up special settings communicated in the environment, such as the location of library files (variable `LIB`), the logged-on user's name (variable `USERNAME`), or the current processor type (`PROCESSOR_ARCHITECTURE`). Although the computer's user might tamper with these, they're convenient when security is not at stake.

You might also use the `Environment` property to modify the settings Windows uses to set up the environment each time you log on. This is somewhat complex and needs some explanation.

Every time you log on, Windows sets up a list of environment variables. It gets these from several sources. Windows keeps a list of default "system-wide" environment variable definitions that every user receives when he logs on. In addition, each user can have an additional set of personalized variables; these can add to or override the system default values. In addition, a set of dynamic or "volatile" values are computed when you log on, such as the name of your logon server and the current computer name.

When you log on, Windows first initializes your environment with the dynamic "volatile" variables, then adds in the "system" definitions, and then adds the "user" definitions to come up with your initial environment.

You can modify these initial definitions either through the Computer Properties dialog box or through scripting. `Environment("system")` and `Environment("user")` return collections of `WshEnvironment` objects that represent the initial settings. If you modify the values in these collections, Windows makes the changes apply for future logons. (Another set of values in `Environment("volatile")` lists the variables that are computed "dynamically" using current logon information, but there is no need ever to modify these.)

After logging on, you might change environment variable values within a Command Prompt window using the `set` command, as described in Chapter 10. Changes made with the `set` command affect only the copy of the Command Prompt window in which you issue the command, and they persist only as long as you stay logged on. Every time you start a program, the program inherits a copy of the current settings, which is called the *process environment*. The process set is the sum total of all definitions and changes. However, any changes made to the process environment by a program aren't seen by other programs, and they don't persist when the program terminates.

> **Note**
>
> This is the reason for the important distinction between the collections returned by the `Environment` property. The `"process"` collection gives you *current* environment values. Use this collection to extract the environment values WSH inherited when it was started. The `"system"` and `"user"` collections are used for management purposes to set the initial values for logon sessions and Command Prompt windows opened in the future.

The `Environment` collection's properties and methods are shown in Reference List 4.12.

REFERENCE LIST 4.12   Properties and Methods of the `Environment` Collection

Properties:

Item(*name*)
Returns the contents for the environment variable `name`. The value returned is the definition of the named variable. If the variable is undefined, the property returns the empty string (`""`).

This property is read/write: You can assign a new value to it to alter an environment variable's definition or to create a new environment variable definition. If you alter a value in `"process"` collection, the change is visible only to the instance of the script that makes the change. If you alter a variable in the `"system"` or `"user"` collection, the definition affects only Command Prompt windows or Windows applications you start after making the change.

Length
Returns the number of Windows environment variables in the collection. (Read-only.)

Methods:

Count

Returns the number of environment variables in the collection; appears to be the same as `Length`.

Remove *strName*

Removes an existing environment variable by name. If you remove a variable from the process collection, the change is visible only to the instance of the script that makes the change. If you delete a variable in the "system" or "user" collection, the change affects only Command Prompt windows or applications you start up after making the change.

Extracting Environment Information

The `Environment("process")` collection contains the entire current set of environment variables (those with names and those without). To retrieve individual environment variables (and their values) from this collection, use the environment variable name as the index. For example, the `TEMP` environment variable can be fetched with the following:

```
username = shl.Environment("process").Item("TEMP")
```

> **Caution**
>
> You must specify `"process"` as the `Environment` method's *location* argument if you want to view current environment settings. On Windows 7, Vista, XP, 2000, and NT, if you omit the argument, Windows returns the system default environment—not the complete current environment.

You can list all the current environment variables with this script:

```
                                ' Example file script0420.vbs
set shl = CreateObject("WScript.Shell")
for each env in shl.Environment("process")
    wscript.echo env
next
```

Printing the environment object itself (env in the sample script) prints `"name=value"`, in contrast to the `Item(name)` method, which extracts just the value.

If you only need to convert an environment variable to its value, the `Shell.ExpandEnvironmentStrings` method might be more useful. `ExpandEnvironmentStrings` scans a string for items that look like %*XXX*%, where *XXX* is the name of an environment variable. %*XXX*% is replaced with the definition of the environment variable. This method makes short work of filling out pathnames that are based on the Windows directory, as mentioned earlier in the discussion of shortcuts. This expression

```
shl.ExpandEnvironmentStrings("%WINDIR%\notepad.exe")
```

replaces `%WINDIR%` with `C:\WINDOWS`, or whatever the Windows directory is on the current computer, and returns the proper path, `C:\WINDOWS\notepad.exe`.

> **Tip**
>
> Using `ExpandEnvironmentStrings` is a handy way to get environment variable values. You can simply use the expression
>
> `shl.ExpandEnvironmentStrings("%varname%")`
>
> where you need the value of variable `varname`. This is especially useful with environment variables that are defined recursively; some variables contain *%XXX%* items in their definitions. `ExpandEnvironmentStrings` takes care of expanding all the items until no more instances of `%` are left.

Managing Environment Settings

As mentioned earlier, when you start a new Windows application or open a new Command Prompt window, your environment settings are obtained from a set of calculated values, plus a list of system-wide default settings, merged with user-specific settings. These initial values are stored in the Registry, and they can be edited by modifying items in the `Environment("system")` or `Environment("user")` collections. To modify the system-wide environment definitions, you must have Administrator privileges.

The following sample script shows how to add a new folder to the `PATH` list so all users will have access to a folder for scripts:

```
set shl = CreateObject("WScript.Shell")
                    ' obtain system-wide default environment collection
set env = shl.Environment("system")
                    ' append semicolon plus "c:\scripts" to the path
env.Item("PATH") = env.Item("PATH") & ";c:\scripts"
```

(If you run this script repeatedly, though, it adds the folder to the path more than once. I show you a better way to write this script this shortly.)

Changes made to these collections don't affect Command Prompt windows that are already open or applications that are already running.

As we've discussed, you can make the definitions of environment variables apply to all users or just to your own user account. The previous script adds the `c:\scripts` folder to the `PATH` variable for all user accounts, while

```
set shl = CreateObject("WScript.Shell")
set env = shl.Environment("user")
env.Item("PATH") = env.Item("PATH") & ";c:\scripts"
```

changes the `PATH` definition just for your own user account.

Special Handling of the PATH Variable

As I mentioned previously, when you open a new Command Prompt window or start a Windows application, Windows provides it with a list of environment variables. To make this list, Windows predefines some values (the "volatile" variables), adds in the "system" collection, and then adds the personalized "user" collection.

If a variable is defined in both the "system" and "user" collections, the user-specific value is the one that is used. However, the PATH variable is handled a different way. If a user-specific definition of PAT exists, it is *appended to* the system-wide definition, rather than replacing it. This lets you define your user-specific PATH variable listing just your own personal program and script folders, and you don't have to worry about putting the standard Windows system folders in it.

This main reason for doing it this way is to protect you. If it didn't work this way, and you accidentally left out the standard list of Windows folders, your PATH list would be incomplete and most programs don't work.

In any case, if you use a script to add a folder to either the "user" or "system" PATH definition, you should still *append* it to the original value, in case some other folders are already listed, like this:

```
if len(env.Item("PATH")) = 0 then   ' if PATH was empty, set to new folder
    env.Item("PATH") = newfolder
else                                ' add to what was there before
    env.Item("PATH") = env.Item("PATH") & ";" & newfolder
end if
```

Better yet, if you want to have script add a particular folder to the path (for example, as part of installing an application, as part of setting up new computers, or as part of a login script), you should check whether the required folder is already in the path before adding it. Here is a script you could use as a starting point for such a task:

```
' addtopath.vbs - adds the specified folder to the "all users" path
    dim shl, env

    set shl = CreateObject("WScript.Shell")
    set env = shl.Environment("system")

    add_folder_to_path "c:\scripts"       ' add c:\scripts to the PATH


' ------------------------------------------------------------------------
' add_folder_to_path - add a specified folder to the PATH if it's not already
    there

sub add_folder_to_path (newfolder)
    dim curpath, i, testfolder

    curpath = ucase(trim(env.Item("PATH")))   ' get a copy of the current PATH
    do while len(curpath) > 0                  ' check each folder in the list
        i = instr(curpath, ";")                ' ... find semicolon (separator)
        if i = 0 then                          ' ... if none found, curpath has
```

```
        testfolder = curpath                '    just one folder. Take it,
        curpath    = ""                      '    and there are no more left
    else                                     ' ... otherwise take up to but not
        testfolder = trim(left(curpath, i-1)) '  including the ; as a name
        curpath    = trim(mid(curpath, i+1))  '  and this is that's left
    end if                                    '  for next time through

    if ucase(newfolder) = testfolder then exit sub  ' folder was already in
PATH
  loop                                       ' ... keep picking apart curpath

  ' if we never found it, add newfolder to the PATH
  env.Item("PATH") = env.Item("PATH") & ";" & newfolder
end sub
```

> **Note**
>
> On Windows 7 and Vista, to modify the "system" environment list, you have to run the script with ele-
> vated privileges. On XP, you have to run it from a Computer Administrator account. You don't need ele-
> vated or administrator to modify the "user" environment settings.
>
> To run a script with elevated privileges, run it from an elevated Command Prompt window or right-click
> it in Windows Explorer and select Run As Administrator.

Working with the Registry

The Windows Registry is a repository of system and user information that is accessible
to any Windows program. The Registry provides a centralized, well-managed place to
store settings, preferences, and security information.

> **Note**
>
> You might remember horror stories from the days of Windows 95, 98, and Me about peoples' Registry
> databases becoming corrupted after a power failure or a blue-screen crash. A damaged Registry is a
> nightmare because if the Registry gets mangled, Windows can't function. Luckily, the Registry is now well
> protected against *inadvertent* crashes and corruption.
>
> However, this doesn't help you if your script deliberately deletes or alters important Registry information.
> Be very careful when modifying Registry information, especially in the `Control`, `System`, and
> `Classes` sections and under any section titled `Windows`. You should do a full system backup before
> you start any project that involves making serious changes to the Registry.

Despite this obligatory warning, I can say that the Registry doesn't have to be all
that scary, and scripts can take good advantage of the capability to read and write
Registry data.

The Registry is organized much like a file system. Just as a disk drive holds folders and folders can contain files and nested folders, the Registry holds information in *keys* and keys can contain *values* and nested keys. The syntax for specifying the location of information in the Registry is even similar to the file path. For example, `HKEY_CURRENT_USER\Software\Microsoft` is a typical key name.

Just as a computer can have several disk drives, the Registry has several separate branches of keys, whose names all start with `HKEY_`. When specifying the names of keys or values with the script objects we're about to discuss, you must specify the full path to any key or value in which you're interested and each path must start with one of the five standard branches. You must use the full names or one of the abbreviations listed in Table 4.5.

Table 4.5   **Registry Key Root Names and Abbreviations**

Root Name	Abbreviation
HKEY_CLASSES_ROOT	HKCR
HKEY_CURRENT_CONFIG	—
HKEY_CURRENT_USER	HKCU
HKEY_LOCAL_MACHINE	HKLM
HKEY_USERS	—

Values are named items within keys and are specified by adding the value name to the key's pathname. For example, under Windows Vista and XP, the Registry key `HKEY_CURRENT_USER\SessionInformation` has a value named `ProgramCount` that tracks the number of programs the user is running. The pathname for this value is `HKEY_CURRENT_USER\SessionInformation\ProgramCount`.

Examining Registry Keys and Values

The `WScript.Shell` object's `RegRead` method lets you read values from Registry entries. You can get values just by specifying their pathnames. (A key can also have a *default value*, which is specified by the name of the key itself with a trailing backslash but no value name.)

The `RegRead` method returns the value for a specified value, as in this example:

```
set shell = CreateObject("WScript.Shell")
wscript.echo shell.RegRead("HKCU\SessionInformation\ProgramCount")
```

`RegRead` can return one of several types of values, depending on the type of data stored in the Registry value. The Registry data types and the corresponding data types returned by `RegRead` are listed in Table 4.6. The most common two types are listed first.

Table 4.6   **Registry Value Types and** `RegRead` **Results**

Registry Type	RegRead Return Type	Purpose
`REG_DWORD`	Integer	Single number
`REG_SZ`	String	Text data
`REG_EXPAND_SZ`	String	Text with embedded environment variables
`REG_MULTI_SZ`	Array of strings	Multiple lines of text
`REG_BINARY`	Array of integers	Generic binary data

The requested item must exist in the Registry when you use `RegRead`; otherwise, the script generates an error.

Saving Information in the Registry

You might use a script to modify Registry settings as part of network management (for example, to enforce certain settings upon logon). Also, the Registry can be a handy place to store information used by scripts because it's *persistent*. That is, information placed in the Registry stays there between runs of your script and between logon sessions. You can take advantage of this to store counters of the number of times a script is run, default parameter values, and so on.

▶

Caution

Saving information in the Registry requires care—trust me, you really can mess up your computer. It's best to do a backup of the Registry and your important files before embarking on the adventure of debugging a Registry-modifying script.

Also, please see the note at the end of this section regarding making changes to the `HKEY_LOCAL_MACHINE` Registry section on Windows 7 and Vista.

The `RegWrite` method creates Registry values. You can use `RegWrite` to create a key by assigning it a default value. Here are the three arguments to `RegWrite`:

- **`strName`**—The path of the value or key to be created. To specify a key, the path should end with a backslash (\).
- **`Value`**—The data to assign to the value. Only string or integer values are accepted; arrays are not.
- **`strType`**—The name of a Registry data type to use, specified as a string. Allowed values are `"REG_SZ"`, `"REG_DWORD"`, `"REG_BINARY"`, and `"REG_EXPAND_SZ"`. If `strType` is omitted, the object automatically chooses between `REG_DWORD` or `REG_SZ`, depending on whether `Value` is a number or string.

Although modifying system settings is fairly dangerous, you can safely use the Registry to store configuration information you like to make available to scripts, such as default server names, important IP addresses, and usernames, or to run counts or error counts. The Registry is a good place to store information you want to have persist from one run of the script to another. You can also store setup information, such as the name of a user who should be informed of problems, and so on. This way, the settings can be changed without modifying the script itself and the same information can be used by several scripts.

You can fairly safely store information in the Registry if you adopt a standard location. Here's the method I use:

- For information that is unique to each user, store values under
  HKCU\Software*YourCompanyName**ScriptName* but substitute your actual company name and the actual name of your script. This way, your keys don't collide with those used by manufactured software or by your other scripts.

- For information that is common for all users of a given computer, use
  HKLM\Software*YourCompanyName**ScriptName*.

The following example shows how a script can store a number in the Registry that counts how many times the script has been run:

```
                                    ' Example file script0422.vbs
set shell = CreateObject("WScript.Shell")

nruns = shell.RegRead("HKCU\Software\Mycompany\RunCount\number of runs")
nruns = nruns+1
wscript.echo "Number of runs:", nruns

Shell.RegWrite "HKCU\Software\Mycompany\RunCount\number of runs",_
    nruns, "REG_DWORD"
```

However, the script starts by reading from the "number of runs" value, so this must exist before the script is run for the first time.

In general, you must either manually create the keys your application needs or create an "install" script that creates the keys the first time around. And just as you must create a top-level folder on the disk before creating a subfolder, you must create upper-level Registry keys before lower-level keys. An "install" script for the counting example might look like this:

```
                                    ' Example file script0423.vbs
set shell = CreateObject("WScript.Shell")

Shell.RegWrite "HKCU\Software\Mycompany\", ""
Shell.RegWrite "HKCU\Software\Mycompany\RunCount\", ""
Shell.RegWrite "HKCU\Software\Mycompany\RunCount\number of runs",_
    0, "REG_DWORD"
```

This ensures that the keys Mycompany and RunCount exist, and then it initializes the number of runs value to 0. The Software key always exists; it is created when Windows is installed.

Another example shows how a maintenance script might use the Registry to store the name of a server that is to be managed. This script gives you the option of specifying the server name on the command line. If the server is specified, the script stores the name in the Registry for future use. If the server is not specified, the script uses the name previously stored in the Registry. Here's the code for this example:

```
                                              ' Example File script0424.vbs
set shell = CreateObject("WScript.Shell")

if WScript.Arguments.Count = 0 then
    ' server was not named on command line. Get default value from Registry.
    'Don't stop on errors, in case the value is not defined.
    on error resume next
    servername = shell.RegRead("HKCU\Software\Mycompany\ServerClean\servername")
    if isempty(servername) or err.Number <> 0 then
        ' there was no default name found... display message and quit
        MsgBox("You must specify the server name on the command line "&_
               "the first time you run this script")
        WScript.Quit 1
    end if
    on error goto 0    ' restore normal stop-on-error behavior
else
    ' server was named on command line. Save in Registry. Be sure to
    ' create MyCompany and ServerClean keys if they don't already exist.
    servername = WScript.Arguments(0)
    Shell.RegWrite "HKCU\Software\Mycompany\", ""
    Shell.RegWrite "HKCU\Software\Mycompany\ServerClean\", ""
    Shell.RegWrite "HKCU\Software\Mycompany\ServerClean\servername",_
        servername, "REG_SZ"
end if

WScript.echo "Cleaning up server \\" & servername & "..."

' now manage the server: clean up temporary files, etc.
⋮
```

Note

On Windows 7 and Vista, to modify the HKEY_LOCAL_MACHINE part of the Registry, you must run your script with elevated privileges. To run a script with elevated privileges, run it from an elevated Command Prompt window or right-click it in Windows Explorer and select Run As Administrator.

If you do not run the script with elevated privileges, Vista's "registry redirection" mechanism kicks in and it appears that the script is working when it's really not. What happens is that any changes the script attempts to make to keys under HKEY_LOCAL_MACHINE are written to HKEY_CURRENT_USER\Software\Classes\VirtualStore\MACHINE instead. Any programs or scripts *you* run "see" these Registry changes as if they had really been saved under HKEY_LOCAL_MACHINE, but other users do not.

5

Network and Printer Objects

- This chapter shows how to use the `WScript.Network` object to control mapped network drives and network printer connections.

- You should be comfortable with the material in Chapter 3, "Scripting and Objects," before reading this chapter.

- You can use `WScript.Network` to control printing from DOS applications as well as Windows applications.

- The last section shows how you can send output from a script directly to a printer—this is especially useful with scripts you run unattended from the Task Scheduler.

Managing Network and Printer Connections

Windows Script Host (WSH) programs can query and manage your computer's network and printer connections. You might want to do this for several reasons, such as the following:

- You want to collect and report network information as part of a documentation-generating script.

- You want a logon script to ensure that every time your users log on, the correct network drives and printer connections are available, regardless of how badly the users might have mangled things during their previous sessions. (Although, if you're using Windows 7 or Vista and Windows Server 2008, Active Directory might take care of this for you. I discuss this later in the chapter.)

- Your network environment changes frequently, so you want to use a script to record and invoke the proper settings.

- You want to standardize and simplify the setup of newly installed computers in your organization.

- You use a workstation or server on a test bench and want to easily select one of several standard configurations.

WSH can help you accomplish all these tasks. Although the command line's net command can perform some of the same tasks, WSH scripts offer more detailed control and can work with the Registry, files, and other system components at the same time as the network.

Scriptable objects can also let you use printers and/or the fax service to automatically generate output from your scripts. After discussing network and printer management, I cover printing from scripts and faxing in Chapter 6, "Messaging and Faxing Objects."

Note

Remember, too, that you can use the objects described in these chapters in Microsoft Word macros and in other scripting applications, not just WSH.

The first object I introduce is the WSHNetwork object, which is created with the name "WScript.Network", as in the following statement:

```
set wshNetwork = CreateObject("WScript.Network")
```

This is a "utility" object. As with Scripting.FileSystemObject, you need only one instance of WScript.Network in your script to perform network tasks. Its properties and methods are shown in Reference List 5.1.

REFERENCE LIST 5.1   Properties and Methods of the WshNetwork Object

Properties:

ComputerName
Returns the computer name set on the Computer Name tab in the System Properties dialog box. This is the computer's name for Windows Networking. (Read-only.)

UserDomain
Returns the Windows networking domain name of the currently logged-on user's account. For nondomain or local account logons, this is the same as the computer name. (Read-only.)

UserName
Returns the logon name of the currently logged-on user. (Read-only.)

Methods:

AddPrinterConnection *LocalName, RemoteName*[, *UpdateProfile*
[, *UserName, Password*]]
Redirects one of the emulated LPT printer ports available to MS-DOS applications on the local computer to a remote networked printer.

Here are the arguments:

- **LocalName**—The name of the DOS printer port ("LPT1", "LPT2", or "LPT3") to redirect to the network printer. You cannot redirect an LPT port that is already being used by a physical local printer.

- **RemoteName**—The share name of the network printer in Universal Naming Convention (UNC) notation (`\\`*machine*`\`*sharename*).You can specify the printer's short share name or its "friendly" name (for example, `"\\sumatra\ okidata"` or `"\\sumatra\Okidata OL 810"`).

- **UpdateProfile**—Optional Boolean value. If it's `True`, the printer mapping is saved to the current user's profile so that is restored upon the next logon.

- **UserName**—Optional. The name of a user account valid on the remote computer to use for this network connection. It does not work if there is already a network drive or printer connection to the same remote computer using the default username or some other username. (Only one set of credentials at a time can be used to connect to a given remote computer.) This can be specified as `"`*username*`"` to use one of the remote machine's local accounts or as `"\\`*domain*`\`*username*`"` to use a domain account.

- **Password**—Optional. This is the logon password associated with the specified *UserName*.

An error is generated if the port is already redirected or is used by a locally attached printer.

AddWindowsPrinterConnection *PrinterPath* [, *DriveName* [, *Port*]]
Adds a connection to a remote network printer that is then available to Windows applications. This adds an icon to the user's `Printers` folder.

The `PrinterPath` argument specifies the share name of the network printer in UNC notation (for example, `"\\`*machine*`\`*sharename*`"`). You can specify the printer's short share name or its friendly name as displayed by the remote computer.

The `DriverName` and `Port` arguments are required only when the script is run from Windows 98 or Me computers, so I don't discuss them. Omit these arguments from your scripts.

No error is generated if a connection icon for the indicated printer already exists.

EnumNetworkDrives()
Returns a collection of objects that lists drive letters mapped to remote network drives. The objects are strings and come in pairs. The first item, `.Item(0)`, is the name of a mapped drive name—for example, `"F:"`. The second item, `.Item(1)`, is the UNC share name to which the drive is redirected. Likewise, `.Item(2)` is a drive name, `.Item(3)` is the corresponding share name, and so on. I show you how to work with this odd arrangement later in this section.

EnumPrinterConnections()
Returns a collection of objects that lists LPT ports that are redirected to remote network printers. As with `EnumNetworkDrives`, these objects are simple text strings and come in pairs. The first item in each pair is a local port name (for example,

"LPT1").The second item in each pair is the name of the remote printer.The names returned might not be short UNC share names but might instead be the remote machine's "friendly" printer name. For example, instead of \\sumatra\ okidata, the name might be listed as "\\sumatra\Okidata OL 810".

MapNetworkDrive *LocalName, RemoteName* [, *UpdateProfile*
    [, *UserName, Password*]]
Redirects a local drive letter to a remote shared folder. Here are the arguments:

- **LocalName**—The drive letter to redirect.This can also be an empty string to establish a connection to the remote share without mapping a letter; this can increase the speed with which the remote drive can be subsequently accessed.

- **RemoteName**—The UNC share name of the remote folder (for example, "*server**sharename*").

- **UpdateProfile**—Optional Boolean argument. If passed and True, the drive mapping is added to the current user's profile so the mapping is reestablished upon the next logon.

- **UserName**—Optional.This is the name of a user account valid on the remote computer to use for this network connection. It does not work if there is already a network drive or printer connection to the same remote computer that is using the default username or some other username. (Only one set of credentials at a time can be used to connect to a given remote computer.) This can be specified as "*username*" to use one of the remote machine's local accounts or as "*domain**username*" to use a domain account.

- **Password**—Optional.This is the password to use to authenticate the specified UserName.

The method fails if the drive letter is already mapped, if the letter corresponds to a local physical disk drive, or if the network path does not exist.

RemoveNetworkDrive *Name* [, *Force* [, *UpdateProfile*]]
Disconnects a mapped drive letter from a remote shared folder.

Here are the arguments:

- **Name**—The drive letter to unmap (for example, "F:"). Note that the colon is required. If the network path was attached without a network drive, specify the remote network path instead of the drive letter.

- **Force**—Optional Boolean argument. If specified and True, the drive mapping is disconnected even if the mapped drive is currently in use. Otherwise, if the drive is in use, the script generates an error. *In use* means that a local program is using a file or viewing a folder on the remote drive or that a Command Prompt window has the mapped drive as its current drive.

- **UpdateProfile**—Optional Boolean argument. If specified and True, the drive mapping is deleted from the current user's profile so the mapping is not automatically reestablished at the next logon. If the mapping is in your profile and `UpdateProfile` is not specified or is `False`, the drive is mapped again the next time you log on.

An error is generated if the connection does not exist.

RemovePrinterConnection *Name* [, *bForce* [, *bUpdateProfile*]]
Removes redirection from a local emulated LPT port to a remote network printer.

Here are the arguments:

- **Name**—The name of the redirected port (for example, "`LPT1`") or the UNC share name to which a port is redirected; the latter can unmap multiple LPT redirections to the same printer. To cancel DOS redirection, set *Name* to the name of the local redirected DOS port (for example, "`LPT2`").

- **Force**—Optional Boolean argument. If specified and `True`, the redirection is removed even if a program on the local computer is currently spooling output to the printer.

- **UpdateProfile**—See `RemoveNetworkDrive` for a description.

An error is generated if the specified connection or printer does not exist.

SetDefaultPrinter *PrinterName*
Sets a shared network printer to be the local computer's default printer. `PrinterName` is the UNC share name of the remote printer. This must be done after using `AddWindowsPrinterConnection` to make a connection to the same shared printer.

This method cannot select a local printer as the default printer, nor is there any way to determine the current default printer.

You should note that `WScript.Network` is limited in its capabilities. It can perform the following tasks:

- It can view, but not modify, the logged-on user's name, the computer name, and the current logon domain.

- It can list, add, and delete drive mappings, but it cannot share folders or printers on the network.

- It can list, add, and delete connections to shared network printers but cannot install local (directly connected) printers.

- It can set the default printer to be one of the network printers, but not a local printer.

To perform more advanced network management functions, you have to turn to Chapter 7, "Windows Management Instrumentation," and Chapter 8, "Active Directory Scripting Interface." Still, `WScript.Network` is useful for many basic networking tasks, as you'll see in the next several sections.

Retrieving Network User Information

The WScript.Network object's three properties retrieve information about the current user, computer, and domain from which the user logged on, as illustrated in the following sample script:

```
set sn = CreateObject("WScript.network")
WScript.echo sn.userName
WScript.echo sn.computerName
WScript.echo sn.userDomain
```

On my computer, for example, this prints as follows:

```
bknittel
JAVA
JAVA
```

As you might guess, my login username is bknittel, and the computer I was using at the time is named Java. The UserDomain property is also Java, even though that's not my workgroup's name. Why? UserDomain tells you who authorized this account. This is either a domain name or the name of the local computer because user accounts come from one of two places:

- **Local accounts**—These are set up only on the individual computer. When the current user logs on using a local account, the UserDomain reported is the computer's name.

- **Domain accounts**—These are set up by an administrator on a domain network. If permitted by the network's security setup, users of one domain might log on to computers that are part of another domain. Therefore, the UserDomain reported might not necessarily be the domain to which the computer belongs, and in any case, is not the same as the computer name.

On a computer that's a member of a workgroup rather than a domain network, including all Windows Home Edition computers (which cannot be domain members), all accounts are local accounts, so UserDomain always matches the computer name.

Displaying the user and domain information might not seem terribly useful. However, it can be handy to have access to this information in scripts that are used by more than one user or on more than one computer. Writing a script that can be run by all users on all computers can make your life as a network administrator easier, but you might still need to accommodate different setups based on the computer or username. Here are some ways this can be done:

- You can write a script to set up drive mappings, environment variables, or the program PATH to include folders that are based on the user's name. For example, your network can have a set of shared folders of the form \\SERVER\homefolders\username, one for each user, in which users can store files in a standard place that is backed up daily. Mapping a drive to this "home" folder can be automatic on a domain network, but you're on your own on a workgroup network. It can still be done, though: In a logon script program, you can use the `UserName` property to construct the desired shared folder name and use this to map a drive.

- You can write a script that performs certain actions only for specific users or computers. For example, after setting up standard programs and mappings, you might have a logon script start up certain programs only on those computers that are known to have extra hardware, or you might make special settings for specific users.

Here's an example that shows how a general-purpose logon script might perform special operations for each user:

```
                                        ' Example file script0501.vbs
set wshNetwork = CreateObject("WScript.Network")
set wshShell   = CreateObject("WScript.Shell")

user = ucase(wshNetwork.userName)

MapDrive "H", "\\bali\home\" & user    ' map home drive

select case user
    case "BKNITTEL"          ' map drive F and G
        MapDrive   "F:", "\\sumatra\photos"
        MapDrive   "G:", "\\ambon\software"
        wshShell.run "notepad c:\todo.txt" ' display to-do list
        UsePrinter "\\bali\okidata"

    case "NALEKS"                    ' just map the simulator folder
        MapDrive   "F:", "\\bali\ibm360"

    case "ACCOUNTING"
        MapDrive   "X:", "\\sumatra\quicken"

    case else ' for any other user, just set up network printer
        UsePrinter "\\bali\hp laserjet"
end select

function MapDrive (byval drive, path)
    ⋮
```

I show you the functions `MapDrive` and `UsePrinter` later in the chapter. Logon scripts are discussed further in Chapter 9, "Deploying Scripts for Computer and Network Management."

This script maps two drives, fires up Notepad, and ensures that a specific printer is available if `bknittel` logs on, maps a different drive for user `naleks`, and so on. As you can see, a script like this can let you embed all logon information in one script. If you place a shortcut to this script in the All Users startup folder, it will be run when any user logs on. This is folder `\ProgramData\Microsoft\Windows\Start Menu\Programs\Startup` on Windows 7 and Vista, and folder `\Documents and Settings\All Users\Start Menu\Programs\Startup` on Windows XP.

Tip

This type of user-specific setup is as valuable on a small workgroup network as on a large corporate domain. With a large number of users, you might find it most useful to perform setup operations based on group membership rather than by individual usernames. I show you how to test group membership in Chapter 8.

However useful it is to know these usernames and computer names, `WScript.Network` doesn't let you *change* them or learn anything about the users' privileges or account settings. For that, you need to use the Windows Management Instrumentation (WMI) tools described in Chapter 7.

Managing Drive Mappings

One of the most common network functions needed in scripts is the mapping of drive letters to shared network folders. Usually, drive mappings are made by a user utilizing Explorer or by using the command-line command `net use`. Mappings made in one logon session are usually recorded in the user's profile and are made available again the next time the user logs on. However, sometimes you might want to take more direct control of mappings, such as the following:

- In a logon script, you might want to set up standard drive mappings that your users always need. The script should override changes made by the user in a previous logon session so the correct mappings are guaranteed to be available. (That's a nice way of saying "even if the user messes things up.")
- In utility, backup, and maintenance scripts, you might want to create temporary drive mappings so files can be moved to another network location.
- In a script that is run automatically by the Task Scheduler, you might want to use mapped drive letters. However, by default, the Task Scheduler runs scripts in the context of a special system user account and not your own user account. Therefore, your own personal standard drive mappings are not available. The script will need to create any drive mappings it needs to use.

The `WScript.Network` object provides methods to enable you to control drive mappings in these situations.

Listing Drive Mappings with `EnumNetworkDrives`

The `EnumNetworkDrives` property returns a collection of objects that describes any existing drive letter mappings. However, this collection is not like those we've seen so far, where the collection contains full-fledged objects, each with its own properties and methods. This collection is one of a few that must be examined by looking at its `Item` properties in numerical order; the collection is simply a list of text strings that, when taken in pairs, describes the current mappings.

→ To learn more about collections and the `Item` property, **see** "Containers and Collections," **p. 95.** (Chapter 3).

The values of this collection can be extracted with the `Item` property. The first string (item 0) gives a mapped drive name (for example, `"F:"`). The second string (item 1) gives the share name to which the drive is mapped, in UNC path format. The collection continues on in this way with pairs of strings—the third string (item 2) gives another mapped drive name, and so on. For example, the script

```
set wshNetwork = CreateObject("WScript.Network")
set maps = wshNetwork.EnumNetworkDrives
```

might yield the collection similar to Listing 5.1.

Listing 5.1 Sample `EnumNetworkDrives` **Collection**

```
maps.item(0)                  "F:"               ┐
maps.item(1)                  "\\sumatra\chapters" ┘── first drive name and path
maps.item(2)                  "H:"               ┐
maps.item(3)                  "\\bali\home\bknittel" ┘── second drive name and path
                     .
                     .
                     .
maps.item(maps.Length-2)      "X:"               ┐
maps.item(maps.Length-1)      "\\bali\incoming faxes" ┘── last drive name and path
```

A straightforward way to examine this collection is to use your preferred scripting language's version of the `for` loop. In VBScript, the following script prints the drive mappings by stepping through the list of items by twos:

```
                                      ' Example File script0502.vbs
set wshNetwork = CreateObject("WScript.Network")
set maps = wshNetwork.EnumNetworkDrives
for i = 0 to maps.Length-2 step 2
    WScript.echo "Drive", maps.item(i), "is mapped to", maps.item(i+1)
next
```

On each turn through the loop, `maps.item(i)` is a drive name and `maps.item(i+1)` is a shared folder path. On my computer, this script produces the following output:

```
Drive F: is mapped to \\sumatra\chapters
Drive H: is mapped to \\bali\home\bknittel
Drive J: is mapped to \\bali\shared documents
Drive X: is mapped to \\bali\incoming faxes
```

Printing a list of mapped drives typically isn't a useful thing to do because typing net use at the Windows command prompt does the same thing. However, you might find it useful when debugging scripts that are run from the Task Scheduler. Using the file-writing tools covered in Chapter 4, "File and Registry Access," you can create a log file and record the drive mappings, like this:

```
set fso = CreateObject("Scripting.FileSystemObject")
set wshNetwork = CreateObject("WScript.Network")

' create log file and record date and time in it
set log = fso.CreateTextFile("c:\temp\myscript.log", True)
log.writeline "The script was run at " & now()

' map drive letters needed by the script
⋮

' list current drive mappings to be sure they're correct
set maps = wshNetwork.EnumNetworkDrives
for i = 0 to maps.Length-2 step 2
    log.writeline "Drive " & maps.item(i) & " is mapped to " & maps.item(i+1)
next

' do things with these mapped drives
⋮

' close the log file
log.close
set log = Nothing
```

After the script is supposed to run, you could check c:\temp\myscript.log to ensure that the date and time are as expected and that the correct drives have been mapped.

What the EnumNetworkDrives property is really useful for is to check to see whether specific drive mappings exist before attempting to create a new one or before deleting a mapping. A script will terminate in an error if you attempt to map a drive letter that belongs to a local drive, attempt to map a drive letter that is already mapped, or try to delete a drive mapping that does not exist.

Here are two subroutines that can help in scripts that need to manipulate drive mappings. The first tests whether a given drive letter is already a mapped network drive,

▶ **Pattern**

To determine whether a drive letter is a mapped network drive, use the following IsDriveMapped function in your scripts:

```
                                      ' Example File IsDriveMapped.vbs
function IsDriveMapped (byval drive)
' use only the letter, not :, and make sure it's uppercase
    drive = ucase(left(drive,1))

    ' assume it's not mapped
    IsDriveMapped = False
```

```
    ' if no such drive, return False right now
    if not fso.DriveExists(drive) then exit function

    ' get Drive object and check its type: 3 = mapped
    isDriveMapped = (fso.GetDrive(drive).driveType = 3)
end function
```

To use this function, you will need to create the `FileSystemObject (fso)` just once at the beginning of your script with the following statement:

```
set fso = CreateObject("Scripting.FileSystemObject")
```

Then, the function can be used in this way:

```
if IsDriveMapped("G") then
    actions to take if G is already mapped
end if
```

The second handy function returns the network path to which a given drive is mapped. It returns the empty string if the drive letter is not mapped.

Pattern

To determine the network path of a mapped network drive, use this `GetDriveMapping` function in your scripts:

```
                                          ' Example File GetDriveMapping.vbs
function GetDriveMapping (byval drive)
    dim i, maps

    ' use only the letter, not :, and make sure it's upper
    drive = ucase(left(drive,1))

    ' get list of mappings
    set maps = wshNetwork.EnumNetworkDrives

    ' assume it's not mapped
    GetDriveMapping = ""

    ' scan the list of mapped drives
    for i = 0 to maps.Length-2 step 2
        if ucase(left(maps.item(i),1)) = drive then
            ' the letter was listed, we have our answer
            GetDriveMapping = ucase(maps.item(i+1))
            exit for
        end if
    next
end function
```

To use this function, you need to create the `wshNetwork` object just once at the beginning of your script with the statement:

```
set wshNetwork = CreateObject("WScript.Network")
```

Then, the function can be used in this way:

```
if GetDriveMapping("G") = "\\BALI\TEXT"
    actions to take if drive G is mapped to \\bali\text
end if
```

Adding Drive Mappings

The WScript.Network object provides the MapNetworkDrive method to create drive letter mappings. It takes between two and five arguments:

MapNetworkDrive *LocalName*, *RemoteName*, [*UpdateProfile*], [*UserName*], [*Password*]

- *LocalName*—The drive letter to map (for example, "F:"). The colon is required, although I don't see why Microsoft couldn't have written this method to work with or without it. You can pass the empty string to create a connection to the remote computer without mapping a drive letter; an open connection makes subsequent accesses to the shared folder faster when you use UNC names in file open, copy, move, and delete operations.

- *RemoteName*—The shared network folder to use, in UNC format ("*server**sharename*" or "*server**sharename*\\subfolder"); *server* is the name or IP address of one of the computers on your network, and *sharename* is the name of the shared folder. If you specify subfolder names, the mapped drive connects to the specified folder and the user is not able to "see" folders above this. (Novell network users might recognize this as the "map root" feature.)

- *UpdateProfile*—An optional Boolean value that is either True or False. The default is False. If specified and True, the mapping is saved in the current user's profile, so the next time she logs on, the drive mapping is restored. This is the equivalent of checking the Reconnect at Logon box when mapping network drives with Explorer or specifying the /persistent:yes option when using the net use command-line program.

  For temporary mappings created and then deleted by a script, you can omit this value or specify False. For mappings that are to be reset at each logon, specify True.

- *UserName* and *Password*—Optional arguments that can let you connect to a remote computer using a username and password different from the one you used to log on. This has some pitfalls that I discuss in a moment.

Here is an example of the MapNetworkDrive method's use:

```
set wshNetwork = CreateObject("WScript.Network")
wshNetwork.MapNetworkDrive "F:", "\\bali\Shared Documents"
```

As you can see, the MapNetworkDrive method is pretty straightforward to use. There are, however, some shortcomings you should be aware of:

- If the drive letter is already mapped or belongs to an existing physical drive, the method causes the script to fail with an error.

- If you want to use an alternative username and password to connect to the shared folder, you must be sure that there are no other connections (mapped drives or Explorer views) to the same computer using your own or any different username. Windows permits only one connection to each remote computer, so all drives mapped to a given computer must use the same credentials.

- If you need to connect using an alternative username that requires a password, the script has to either prompt the script user for the password or store the password in the script. The latter can be a huge security risk: Anyone able to read your script can obtain a username and password valid on the remote computer. For this reason, I suggest that you try *not* to use alternative credentials. If you must, it's best to prompt the user for a password or, if that's impossible, ensure that the remote user account has as few privileges as possible. You could set up a special account that is set not to allow local logon and has access to only a limited number of necessary files.

Even if you supply a valid shared folder name and drive letter, the mapping can still fail if network problems exist or if the remote computer is down. You can let the script fail with an error, or you can catch the error and report it gracefully. I show you a way of doing this in the next pattern.

Deleting Drive Mappings

When a drive mapping is no longer needed, your script can delete it with the `RemoveNetworkDrive` method. Your script can delete a named drive mapping or a "nameless" connection made by calling `MapNetworkDrive` with an empty string as the drive name. It takes one to three parameters:

`RemoveNetworkDrive(Name, [Force], [UpdateProfile])`

- **Name**—The name of the drive to unmap (for example, `"F:"`) or the UNC path to disconnect if there is no associated drive letter (for example, `"\\bali\sharedfolder"`).

- **Force**—An optional Boolean parameter. If `True`, the mapping is undone even if some program is still using a folder or file on the shared drive. This can happen if an application has a document open on the shared folder, if you have an active Explorer view of the shared folder or any subfolder, or if you have a Command Prompt window open with the shared drive as the current drive. The default is `False`. When *Force* is omitted or `False`, rather than sever an active connection, the `RemoveNetworkDrive` method fails.

- **UpdateProfile**—Another optional Boolean parameter. If `True`, the mapping is be removed from the user's profile so that it is not reestablished the next time the user logs in. If *UpdateProfile* is omitted or specified as `False`, and the mapping is stored in the user's profile, it remains there.

`RemoveNetworkDrive` causes the script to fail if the drive or connection in question does not exist, so you should either verify that it does exist or trap the error. The following pattern shows how this can be done.

Pattern

To delete a network drive mapping in a script, use the following function in your script:

```
                                                      ' Example File UnMap.vbs
function UnMap(byval drive)
    UnMap = True                              ' assume success

    if len(drive) = 1 then drive = drive & ":" ' ensure there's a colon

    on error resume next                      ' try to unmap, but don't halt
    err.Clear                                 ' clear any previous ➥errors
    wshNetwork.RemoveNetworkDrive drive, False, True ' if an error occurs

    if err.Number <> 0 then                   ' there was an error
        UnMap = False                         ' report failure
    end if
    on error goto 0
end function
```

This function returns `True` if the unmapping is successful or `False` if it fails. You can call this as a function if you care about the return value. Here's an example:

```
if not UnMap("G:") then
    WScript.echo "Drive unmap failed, can't continue"
    WScript.quit 1
end if
```

In VBScript, you can call it as a subroutine if you don't care whether the operation succeeded:

```
Unmap "G:"
```

You must create the **wshNetwork** object once at the beginning of your script with the following statement:

```
set wshNetwork = CreateObject("WScript.Network")
```

Setting Up Mappings in a Script

Because there are numerous ways a drive mapping can fail, and because the correct drive mapping might already exist when your script runs, you should use a function to handle all the various possibilities. This way, the coding needs to happen just once and your script can take advantage of it as many times as necessary. Here is an example of such a subroutine you can use in your scripts.

Pattern

To map a network drive letter in a script, you can use the following function in your script:

```
                                          ' Example File MapDrive.vbs
function MapDrive(byval drive, byval path)
    MapDrive = True                        ' assume success

    if len(drive) = 1 then drive = drive & ":" ' ensure there's a colon

    if IsDriveMapped(drive) then               ' already mapped?
        if GetDriveMapping(drive) = ucase(path) then
            exit function                      ' ...as desired; quit now
        end if
        UnMap drive                            ' ...unmap before proceeding
    end if

    err.Clear
    on error resume next                   ' try to map, but don't halt
    wshNetwork.MapNetworkDrive drive, path ' if there is an error
    if err.Number <> 0 then                ' there was an error
        MapDrive = False                   ' report failure
    end if
    on error goto 0
end function
```

You can add the optional `UpdateProfile` parameter to the `MapNetworkDrive` method call if it's appropriate for your script. (The function `IsDriveMapped` was presented earlier in this chapter.)

The function returns `True` if the mapping is successful or `False` if it fails. You can call this as a function if you care about the return value. Here's an example:

```
if not MapDrive("G:", "\\myserver\someshare") then
    WScript.echo "Drive mapping failed, can't continue"
    WScript.quit 1
end if
```

In VBScript, you can call it as a subroutine if you don't care whether the operation succeeded:

```
MapDrive "G:", \\myserver\someshare
```

This function requires the IsDriveMapped, GetDriveMappings, and UnMap functions listed earlier in the chapter. You must create the `fso` and `wshNetwork` objects once at the beginning of your script with the following statements:

```
set fso       = CreateObject("Scripting.FileSystemObject")
set wshNetwork = CreateObject("WScript.Network")
```

Managing Network Printer Connections

The `WScript.Network` object has methods to manage network printer connections comparable to the methods for managing mapped drives, as shown in Reference List 5.1. Adding and deleting connections to networked printers adds and deletes icons from the current user's Printers folder, so you can use scripts to ensure that your computer's users have the most up-to-date and appropriate set of network printer choices. This is a good task for logon scripts.

In the next few sections, I cover the topics of listing, adding, and deleting printer connections. There is also a way to control the redirection of output from DOS programs to network printers—through the mapping of the DOS environment's virtual LPT devices.

Displaying Printer Information

The `EnumPrinterConnections` method returns a collection that describes the printers set up on the current computer—both locally connected and networked. Similar to `EnumNetworkDrives`, the collection returned by this method is not a standard list of objects but rather a set of pairs of strings, each of which describes one printer. The discussion of `EnumNetworkDrives` earlier in this chapter explains this type of collection, so I don't repeat that discussion here.

The pairs of strings returned by `EnumPrinterConnections` list the printers' ports and names. The first string in each pair lists the port to which the printer is connected, for both local and network printers. (This information isn't terribly useful for networked printers.) The second string in each pair lists the name of the printer. For local printers, this is the printer's full name. For networked printers, it's the share name of the printer.

The following sample script lists the current printer connections:

```
                                       ' Example File script0503.vbs
set wshNetwork = CreateObject("WScript.Network")

set maps = wshNetwork.EnumPrinterConnections
for i = 0 to maps.Length-2 step 2
    WScript.echo "Port:", maps.item(i), " Name:", maps.item(i+1)
next
```

On my computer, this produces the following odd listing:

```
Port: LPT1:   Name: HP LaserJet 4V
Port: LPT2    Name: \\sumatra\okidata
Port: LPT1:   Name: \\sumatra\Okidata OL810
Port: SHRFAX:   Name: Fax
Port: XPSPort:   Name: Microsoft XPS Document Writer
Port: Microsoft Document Imaging Writer Port:   Name: Microsoft Office Document
    Image Writer
```

The first printer listed is a local printer, directly connected to my computer. It's connected to port LPT1.

The second printer is the result of redirecting DOS device `LPT2:` to `\\sumatra\` `okidata` using the command-line `net use` command, as shown here:

```
net use lpt2: \\sumatra\okidata
```

Note that the port value returned by `EnumPrinterConnections` does not include a colon in this case—it just says "`LPT2`".

The third printer is a network printer for which I've set up a printer icon. It's also listed as using port `LPT1:`. This is the port to which the printer is connected on the remote computer, Sumatra, and has nothing to do with my own computer's LPT1 port.

The remaining printers represent standard Windows printing services. The fax printer device represents the Windows Fax service I use to send faxes through my modem. The port is listed as `SHRFAX:`, but this is not a standard Windows device and, as tantalizing as it sounds, it can't be used from DOS applications, nor can it be shared with other computers. The XPS and Office Document Writer entries are software services that create formatted files. They act like local printers.

You can use this information in the same way we used the `EnumNetworkDrives` information earlier in the chapter (that is, in procedures to create or delete network printer connections), although you must be careful how you interpret the values, as detailed in the following list:

- If `Name` starts with two backslashes (`\\`) *and* `Port` includes a colon (`:`), the entry describes a Windows Network printer connection and icon. `Name` is the network share name. Other than noting the presence of the colon, the `Port` value can be ignored.

- If `Name` starts with `\\` but `Port` does *not* include a colon, the entry describes redirection for DOS applications to a network printer. `Name` is the network share name, and `Port` names the local DOS device that is redirected.

- If `Name` does not start with `\\`, the entry describes a local printer. `Name` is the printer's device drive name, and `Port` is the device or service to which the printer is connected.

Yes, it's strange.

Connecting to Network Printers

The `AddWindowsPrinterConnection` method lets you install a new network printer connection (and icon). Like mapped network drives, this is done on a per-user basis. Unlike mapped network drives, though, printer connections are always permanent and persist from one logon session to another. This means you need to set them up only once and they stick. The method's parameters are as follows:

```
AddWindowsPrinterConnection PrinterPath [, DriveName [, Port]]
```

PrinterPath is the server name and printer share name for the network printer in UNC format (for example, `"\\sumatra\okidata"`). You can use either the official short share name (for example, `"okidata"`) or the longer friendly name that Windows displays on the Printers page (for example, `"Okidata OL810"`).

The remaining two arguments were used only by Windows 98 and Me and are ignored if specified under under Windows 7, Vista, 2000, and XP. You can simply omit them.

The `AddWindowsPrinterConnection` method does *not* fail with an error message if you attempt to duplicate an existing printer connection, so if your script wants to ensure that a specific printer icon exists, it's fine to simply attempt to add it. The printer is added if necessary; otherwise, nothing happens.

The following pattern shows a reliable way of adding network printer connections.

Pattern

To add a network printer connection in a script, you can use the following function:

```
                                        ' Example File UsePrinter.vbs
function UsePrinter (path)
    UsePrinter = True                 ' assume success

    err.Clear
    on error resume next              ' make connection, don't stop on error
    wshNetwork.AddWindowsPrinterConnection path
                                      ' if error occurred, return False
    if err.number <> 0 then UsePrinter = False
    on error goto 0
end function
```

The function returns `True` if the printer was added (or already exists) and `False` if it could not add the printer. In VBScript, you can call this function as a subroutine if you do not care about the return value—for example, you can use the following statement:

```
UsePrinter "\\sumatra\okidata"
```

For you to use this function, the `wshNetwork` object must be created at the beginning of your script with this statement:

```
set wshNetwork = CreateObject("WScript.Network")
```

You will probably only use `AddWindowsPrinterConnection` or the function `UsePrinter` as part of a logon script that verifies that all necessary network printer connections are installed. It can be handy to set up such logon scripts in advance. Then, if your network environment changes, you don't have to instruct tens to thousands of users to set up new printer icons.

▶

Tip

If you manage a domain network with Windows Server computers, you might know that Active Directory (AD) can make network computers visible to Windows client computers, so users can easily search for printers located near them. Until recently, there was no way to have AD automatically install the network printers on client systems. Network managers had to resort to installing them via logon scripts, as discussed in this section.

Windows Server 2008 introduced a new Deploy With Group Policy option that lets AD automatically deploy network printers, so you don't have to use logon scripts anymore, for this particular purpose, at least. However, it works with Windows Vista and Windows 7 client computers only. A workaround lets you deploy network printers from Windows Server 2008 Active Directory to Windows XP and Windows Server 2003 clients, which involves running the program PushPrinterConnections.exe on the client computers, in place of or in a logon script. To read about this trick, go to technet.microsoft.com and search for "deploy pushprinterconnections.exe."

Redirecting DOS Session Printers

If you (or your organization) use legacy DOS applications, you know that it can be difficult to manage printer output from these applications. Whereas Windows applications can choose from a list of installed printers that are connected locally or through the network, most DOS applications can't; they only know how to use parallel ports LPT1, LPT2, and LPT3. To enable DOS applications to print to network printers, Windows provides a way of *redirecting* the DOS printer devices to network printers. (On Windows 9*x* and Me, this was called *capturing*.) Whatever it's called, the effect is that DOS applications see a simulated printer port that appears to be connected to a printer; it happily accepts print output, which Windows then funnels through the network to a real printer. In the absence of printer redirection, if a DOS application attempts to direct output to an LPT port, Windows attempts to use the indicated port hardware.

The `WScript.Network` object's `AddPrinterConnection` method can be used to set up printer redirection so DOS applications can send output to a selected network printer. Unlike `AddWindowsPrinterConnection`, this method does *not* create a printer icon or make the printer accessible to Windows applications. It simply makes the network printer available to DOS applications. As shown in Reference List 5.1, the method's arguments are as follows:

```
AddPrinterConnection LocalName, RemoteName [, UpdateProfile] _
    [, UserName, Password]
```

Note that this method provides for making the connection using an alternative user account, whereas `AddWindowsPrinterConnection` does not. Specifying an alternative username adds complications; see the discussion in the section "Adding Drive Mappings," earlier in this chapter, for more information.

Also, this method *will* fail with an error if the connection already exists, so you should examine `EnumPrinterConnections` before attempting to make the connection or catch errors while making the attempt. I show you how to do this after we discuss how to delete Windows printers and cancel printer redirection.

Tip

MS-DOS programs don't know how to print to USB-connected printers, but you can work around this limitation using printer sharing and redirection—even if you don't have a network. Here's how: Share the printer, giving it a short and sensible share name like "laserjet." Then, redirect an unused LPT port name to the shared printer. The MS-DOS program is then able to print to this redirected LPT port.

You can set up the redirection with the Command Prompt command,

> `net use lpt3 \\computername\laserjet`

or you can call the `RedirectPrinter` function that I describe shortly from a script, with

> `RedirectPrinter "lpt3", "\\computername\laserjet", True`

using the actual name of your computer in place of *computername*, and the printer's actual share name in place of *laserjet*.

Deleting Printer Connections

You can delete network printer connections (and the associated Printers folder icon) and cancel DOS printer direction with the `RemovePrinterConnection` method. It takes from one to three arguments, which are described in detail in Reference List 5.1:

> `RemovePrinterConnection` *Name*, [*bForce*], [*bUpdateProfile*]

The optional *Force* parameter determines what happens if some application is currently using the printer. The default is `False`. When *Force* is omitted or `False`, rather than sever an active connection, the `RemovePrinterConnection` method fails.

The `RemovePrinterConnection` method generates an error if the designed printer connection does not exist, so you should check whether it does before attempting to delete a connection. The following function shows you how.

Pattern

To delete a Windows networked printer, use the following function:

```
                                         ' Example File DeletePrinter.vbs
function DeletePrinter (byval path)
    dim maps, i, ismapped                ' local variables

    path = ucase(path)                   ' be sure path is uppercase

    DeletePrinter = True                 ' assume success
```

```
        ismapped = False                          ' see if printer is exists
        set maps = wshNetwork.EnumPrinterConnections
        for i = 0 to maps.Length-2 step 2
            if ucase(maps.item(i+1)) = path then
                ismapped = True                   ' we are using this printer
                exit for
            end if
        next

        if not ismapped then exit function        ' printer not used, just return

        err.Clear
        on error resume next                       ' delete connection
        wshNetwork.RemovePrinterConnection path, True, True

        if err.number <> 0 then
            DeletePrinter = False                  ' we failed
        end if
        on error goto 0
    end function
```

If you change your network configuration, you can use `UsePrinter` and `DeletePrinter` in a logon script to remove obsolete printers and add new ones so your users see the correct printers automatically.

Now that you have seen how to cancel printer redirection, we can write a function to safely set up printer redirection.

Pattern

The following function takes three arguments: `device`, `path`, and `updateProfile`. `device` is the name of a DOS printer port to redirect, `path` is a network printer name in UNC format, and `updateProfile` determines whether the assignment is made permanent. It handles the situation where the redirection might already have been done and correctly changes the mapping to the specified path. It returns `True` if the redirection is complete or `False` if it could not be performed:

```
                                                ' Example File RedirectPrinter.vbs
    function RedirectPrinter (byval device, byval path, byval updateProfile)
        dim maps, i, ismapped                     ' local variables
        dim devcolon, devnocolon

        device = ucase(device)                    ' put port name in uppercase
        i = instr(device, ":")                    ' get versions of name with
        if i > 0 then                             ' and without the colon
            devcolon   = device
            devnocolon = left(device, i-1)
        else
            devcolon   = device & ":"
            devnocolon = device
        end if

        RedirectPrinter = True                    ' assume success
```

```
    ismapped = False                            ' see if port already mapped
    set maps = wshNetwork.EnumPrinterConnections
    for i = 0 to maps.Length-2 step 2
        if maps.item(i) = devnocolon and _
                left(maps.item(i+1),2) = "\\" then ' port is already redirected
            ismapped = True
            exit for
        elseif maps.item(i) = devnocolon then ' port hooks to a local printer
            RedirectPrinter = False             ' we cannot redirect it
            exit function
        end if
    next

    if ismapped then
        err.Clear
        on error resume next                    ' delete existing  connection
        wshNetwork.RemovePrinterConnection device, True, updateProfile

        if err.number <> 0 then
            RedirectPrinter = False             ' return False if error
            exit function
        end if
        on error goto 0
    end if

    err.Clear
    on error resume next                        ' try to make the connection
    wshNetwork.AddPrinterConnection device, path, updateProfile

    if err.number <> 0 then RedirectPrinter = False   ' return False if error
    on error goto 0
end function
```

For you to use this function, the **wshNetwork** object must be created at the beginning of your script with the following statement:

```
set wshNetwork = CreateObject("WScript.Network")
```

Setting the Default Printer

A final issue in managing network printers with WScript.Network is ensuring that users always have an appropriate default printer selected. Of course, users can change the default printer at any time with the Printers and Faxes control panel (or with any of several add-on utilities that enable users to change the default printer with a pop-up menu). Still, when you've added or deleted printers in a logon script, you should select an appropriate default printer using the **SetDefaultPrinter** method; simply pass it the network share name of the desired printer, as in this example:

```
wshNetwork.SetDefaultPrinter("\\sumatra\okidata")
```

The `SetDefaultPrinter` method can select only a network printer, not a local printer; if your script deletes all network printers, you or the user must manually select a preferred local default printer.

Printing from Scripts

Thus far we've discussed how to manage printers from scripts. Now let's take a short look at *using* printers in scripts. You might want to have your script generate printed output if it generates reports you want to view in printed form or it runs automatically under the Task Scheduler.

> **Tip**
>
> In a business environment, for scheduled scripts that perform critical tasks such as backups, I recommend printing a report every day. This way, if the scheduled task stops working, you'll know that something is wrong by the details in the report or by the report's absence. If you're concerned about the wasted paper, you can write a script to summarize the results of all the scheduled tasks and print a single sheet, or you can use the email tools discussed in the next chapter. In any case, automatic status reports can help you avoid losing track of those things that go crash in the night. I talk about this in more detail in Chapter 9.

You can send printed output to a network printer in one of these ways:

- You can use Word or other applications that expose themselves as an automation object. For example, you can create a `Word.Document` object, use methods such as `Selection.Type` to insert text, and then use the `.Print` method to print the document.
- If you have a plain-text file and you simply want to send it to the default printer, you can execute the following command line, using the `Shell.Run` method described in Chapter 4:

  ```
  notepad.exe /p "filename.txt"
  ```

  It's best to specify the full path to the text file in the command line.
- If your printer can accept plain ASCII text directly, there is a third option: You can use `AddPrinterConnection` to redirect an unused LPT device to a network printer. Use the `FileSystemObject`'s `CreateTextFile` method to write to the LPT device (for example, if your computer has no physical LPT2 printer port, you can redirect LPT2 and use the name `"LPT2:"` with `CreateTextFile`). Write report output to the `TextStream` object. Finish the output with a Form Feed control character, so the last page is printed and ejected. After the `TextStream` object is closed, the report prints.

Whereas the first method can create nicely formatted reports, the last method can be done on any Windows computer and doesn't need any additional installed applications, but it does require that your printer have enough "intelligence" to render text using its own internal processing power. (Some bottom-of-the-line laser and inkjet printers don't.) Here is an example that shows how you can print directly to a network printer from a script:

```
                                            ' Example File script0504.vbs
' create utility objects
set wshNetwork = CreateObject("Wscript.Network")
set fso = CreateObject("Scripting.FileSystemObject")

' use the RedirectPrinter function shown earlier in the chapter
' to set up LPT2 for remote printing
if not RedirectPrinter("LPT2", "\\sumatra\laserjet", False) then
     wscript.echo "* Unable to print report:", err.description
        wscript.quit
end if

' Open a TextStream object, with output to LPT2
set pfile = fso.CreateTextFile("LPT2:")

' write the report
pfile.WriteLine "---------- " & now() & " ----------"
pfile.WriteLine "This is the report"
pfile.WriteLine "This more of the report"
pfile.WriteLine "This is end of the report"

pfile.Write chr(12)    ' end with a Form Feed control character
pfile.Close            ' close the text stream so printing can begin
wshNetwork.RemovePrinterConnection "LPT2"    ' remove the printer redirection

' (function from earlier in the chapter:)
function RedirectPrinter (byval device, byval path, byval updateProfile)
    :
end function
```

6

Messaging and Faxing Objects

IN THIS CHAPTER

- Scripts can send email or faxes to report problems and automate workflow.

- Collaboration Data Objects (CDO) can send plain text and HTML-formatted text messages with any number of attachments. The faxing objects send documents via fax through your fax modem.

- The CDO and faxing objects are complex, but they're easier to use than you'd first guess. Use the examples provided here as your starting point.

Sending Email from Scripts with CDO

Although we usually think of email as a person-to-person medium, you can also send email directly from Windows Script programs. Here are some examples:

- For automated, scheduled scripted operations such as backups, reports, or disk cleanups, it's important to know whether the scheduled operation completed successfully. You might want to have scripts used with the Task Scheduler send an email message to a system administrator with a report of the operation's success or failure. If the daily message is missing or contains error reports, you know something is amiss.

- You can write scripts to automatically send information to network users, such as reports of excessive disk usage, distribution of incoming files or faxes, and so on.

- You can create a script that emails any files specified on its command line to a particular destination. If you create a shortcut to this script, Explorer lets you drag and drop files onto it. Any file(s) you drag onto the icon are automatically mailed to the chosen destination. This might be handy in some work environments—for example, to forward purchase orders or edited files to another person in the organization.

So, how do you send email messages from a script? The answer is that you use the Collaboration Data Objects (CDO) package.

Microsoft developed CDO as an add-on tool for Microsoft Office and Outlook, but it has evolved into a standalone tool that can be used by Windows Script Host (WSH) scripts, `.asp` web pages, and standard Windows applications. CDO provides a complex set of objects that can be used to send, receive, and display email and newsgroup messages; handle attachments; and even perform some of the tasks of an email server. Most of these topics are beyond the scope of this book. Here, I show how CDO can be used to send text or HTML-formatted email messages. It can send anything from plain text, to complete web pages, to complex formatted messages with multiple attachments.

> **Note**
>
> You can find more about CDO on the Microsoft Developers website at msdn.microsoft.com. Search for "CDO for Windows 2000" (using the quotes), or open the index listings for MSDN Library, Messaging and Collaboration, Collaboration Data Objects, or CDO for Windows 2000. I have to warn you, though; if you think *my* writing is obtuse, wait until you read Microsoft's.

Oddly enough, the CDO version distributed with Windows 7, Vista, XP, and 2000 is called CDO for Windows 2000. Although several other CDO flavors are mentioned in Microsoft's documentation, for the remainder of this chapter, CDO refers only to CDO for Windows 2000. It's installed on your computer in the `\windows\system32` folder as file `cdosys.dll`.

If the `cdosys.dll` file is missing from your system, your best option is to copy it from another Windows system. Put it in the `system32` folder, open a Command Prompt window (an elevated Command Prompt window on Windows 7 or Vista), and type `regsvr32 %windir%\system32\cdosys.dll`.

The CDO Object Model

CDO uses several object types to represent an email message. Here are the primary objects you use:

- **CDO.Message**—Represents a single email message. It contains several other objects within it: BodyPart, which is the content of the message; Attachments, which is a collection of objects representing any attached documents or images; and Fields, which describes the sender, subject, and other message attributes.

- **BodyPart**—An object that represents a message component. BodyPart can contain other BodyPart objects nested inside it, which represent subelements of the message.

- **CDO.Configuration**—A collection of `Field` objects that tell CDO how to deliver the message.

- **Field**—An object that defines one parameter, such as the subject line or the sender of the message.

The objects and their relationships are illustrated in Figure 6.1. If this doesn't make sense right away, hang in there. The text that follows should help clear things up.

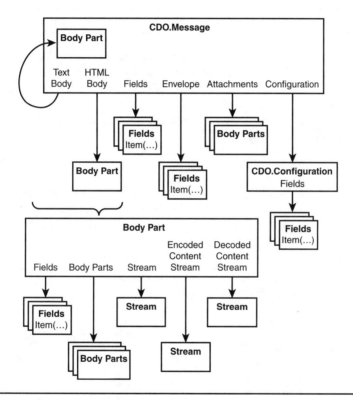

Figure 6.1   The `CDO.Message` object is composed of several other objects that together describe the contents of the message, the destination, and the delivery method.

In a simple message containing only a single text message, the message content is stored in the `CDO.Message` object's internal `BodyPart` object, as shown in Figure 6.2. The `TextBodyPart` property, which the `Message` object uses to provide quick access to the text version of the message, refers to this internal `BodyPart` object.

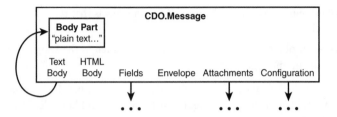

Figure 6.2 CDO objects for a simple text-only message.

CDO also lets you send a message in both HTML and plain text using the "multipart/alternative" MIME format. In this case, two sub-`BodyPart` objects are under the main message. One contains the text version of the message, and one contains the HTML version. The HTML version might contain further subparts—for example, images referenced by the formatted message. The objects and the resulting message structure are illustrated in Figure 6.3.

Note

MIME stands for Multipart Internet Mail Extensions. It's a standardized way of packaging text, images, documents, and other data into plain-text files that can be moved about through the Internet's email systems. For detailed information about MIME formats, see the documents RFC 2045, RFC 2046, and RFC 2047, which you can view at www.ietf.org/rfc.

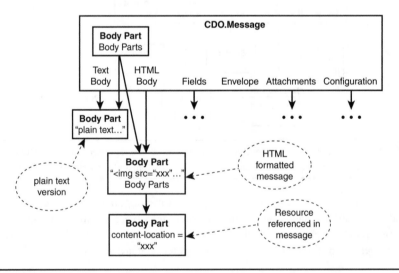

Figure 6.3 The CDO objects and MIME message structure for a multipart/alternative message with both HTML and plain-text versions.

This might seem confusing at first, but it makes more sense when you look at the steps necessary to send a message:

1. Create a `CDO.Message` object.
2. Create a `CDO.Configuration` object and link it to the `CDO.Message` object.
3. Set `Field` values in the `CDO.Configuration` object to describe how the message is to be delivered (for example, the name of your network's Simple Mail Transport Protocol [SMTP] mail server).
4. Assign the subject line, the recipients, the sender's address, and so on to properties of the `CDO.Message` object. This information is stored in the `Message` object's `Fields` collection.
5. Add text content or formatted HTML content to the message's `BodyPart` object.
6. Optionally, attach additional documents to the message by adding more `BodyPart` objects to the `Attachments` collection. This can be done with just one line of code per attachment.
7. Finally, use the `CDO.Message` object's `Send` method to deliver the message.

This procedure sounds complex, but it's easy to use and extend after you have a working script in hand. It was no piece of cake getting my first message script to work, but all the subsequent examples were easy to create. You can download these sample scripts from www.helpwin7.com/scripting and take it from there.

The next several sections provide reference listings or these objects. (You can see the full list of methods and properties on the MSDN website that I mentioned earlier.) I recommend that the first time through this material you skip ahead and look at the examples, which start with "Sending a Message with CDO" on page 256, just to see how this stuff looks in actual use, before looking through the reference material.

The `CDO.Message` Object

The `CDO.Message` object is the primary object used to work with email and newsgroup messages. The properties and methods used to send email are described in Reference List 6.1. The properties and methods used to process incoming messages or send messages to Usenet newsgroups are not covered in this chapter.

The properties that involve email addresses use standard email format. Multiple addresses can be entered, separated by commas. Each address can take any one of the following forms:

- `"Full name" <emailaddress@domain>`
- `"Full name" emailaddress@domain`
- `Full name <emailaddress@domain>`
- `emailaddress@domain`

If you put email addresses inside your scripts and use a format with quotation marks, remember that you might need to escape the quotation marks to enter them in your scripting language. For example, in VBScript, you would have to type

```
msg.from = """Brian Knittel"" <brian@somedomain.com>"
```

to use the first format.

REFERENCE LIST 6.1   Properties and Methods of the CDO.Message Object (Partial List)

Properties:

Attachments

Returns a BodyParts collection that holds the message's attachments. Attachments can be added with the AddAttachment method. Read-only.

AutoGenerateTextBody

A Boolean value. If this property is set to True, a TextBodyPart is automatically generated for this message from the HTMLBodyPart. You should only set the HTMLBodyPart in this case. The examples show how this is done.

BCC

A text string listing the Blind Carbon Copy (BCC) recipients for this message. The BCC addresses are not shown in copies of the message sent to others.

BCC and several other properties are actually stored in the Fields collection but are made available through properties to make viewing and setting them more convenient.

BodyPart

Returns a reference to the main message BodyPart object contained in the CDO.Message object. This is the primary message part, the root of the hierarchy of elements in the message. You work with this object to set the message content. Read-only.

CC

A text string listing Carbon Copy (CC) recipients for this message.

Configuration

Returns or sets the CDO.Configuration object associated with this message.

DSNOptions

An integer value that requests downstream mail servers to send you email messages (*delivery status notifications* [DSNs]), indicating success or failure in transferring or delivering your message. The permitted values for DSNOptions are listed in Table 6.1. Multiple options can be selected by adding the values 2, 4, and/or 8 together. For a convoluted explanation of DSNs, see www.faqs.org/rfcs/rfc1894.html. You need to worry about this property only if you want delivery notifications.

Fields

The collection of `Field` objects for this message. The fields describe the sender, recipient, and other message information. You can alter the collection by changing individual `Field` items and then using the collection's `Update` method. For convenience, some of the fields can be set using properties such as `From` and `Subject`. The object automatically puts values assigned to these properties into the `Fields` collection.

From

The email address of the message's author.

HTMLBody

The main body of the message in HTML format, as a text string. You can set the HTML content of the message in several ways; one is by assigning a string value to this property. You don't *have* to format an email message with HTML. In many cases, it's fine to create a plain-text message and store it in the `TextBody` property.

HTMLBodyPart

Returns a reference to the `BodyPart` object holding the main body of the message in HTML format. This refers to an object in the `BodyPart.BodyParts` collection if the message is being sent in multipart/alternative format or the main `BodyPart` itself if the message is being sent as HTML only. If no HTML content has been defined, attempting to read this property causes an error.

The `HTMLBody` property reflects the *content* of this object. If you want to send an HTML-formatted message, in most cases it's sufficient to assign a string value to the `HTMLBody` property. You usually don't need to work with the `HTMLBodyPart` object itself. Read-only.

MDNRequested

A Boolean value. If this property is `True`, the message is sent with a header that requests delivery notification. More detailed control of delivery notifications is available by setting the To Disposition-Notification-To and Disposition-Notification-Options fields. Values of these fields are inserted as header lines of the same name. These options are discussed in RFC 2298, available at www.ietf.org/rfc.

MIMEFormatted

A Boolean value. If you want to send a message that can be displayed either as plain text or as formatted HTML at the option of the recipient, set this property to `True` and either set both the `TextBodyPart` and the `HTMLBodyPart` properties to equivalent versions of the message or set the `HTMLBodyPart` to the HTML version and set property `AutoGenerateTextBody` to `True`. The message is sent with MIME type "multipart/alternative."

If you want to send the message as plain text only, or HTML only, leave this property set to `False` and set either the `TextBodyPart` or the `HTMLBodyPart` property, not both.

Organization

The organization (company) name of the message sender. This can be left blank.

ReplyTo

The preferred address for replies to this message. Usually the same as the From address. If this is left blank, most email clients use the Sender or From address for replies.

Sender

The email address of the message sender, if different from the author (From). This field corresponds to the rarely used "Sender:" line in an email message.

Subject

The subject line of the message. Although supplying a subject line is always a good idea, it is optional in email messages.

TextBody

The main body of the message in plain-text format, as a string. This is the content of the TextBodyPart object. Multiple lines are delimited with carriage return/line-feed characters. You can set the text body in several ways, as discussed later in the chapter.

TextBodyPart

A BodyPart object that represents the text version of the message. Similar to HTMLBodyPart, this refers to a subelement of the main BodyPart if the message is being sent in multipart/alternative format, or to the main BodyPart itself if the message is being sent as text only. The TextBody property reflects the content of this object.

As with the HTMLBodyPart object, you probably don't need to reference TextBodyPart directly. You can simply format your messages as a string value and assign it to the TextBody property. Read-only.

To

The principal recipient(s) of the message, as a text string. The message is also sent to CC and BCC addresses. If you want the message to go to more than one recipient, separate each email address with a comma and a space.

Methods:

AddAttachment(*path* [, *username*, *password*])

Creates an attachment to the message and returns a reference to the new BodyPart object. The object is added to the message's Attachments collection.

Path can refer to a filename, or it can be a URL pointing to a web page. If you want to attach a file, you *must* specify a drive letter and the full path to the file.

If you want to attach content picked up from a web page or FTP site, specify the full URL including the protocol (for example, "http://"). If the content is in a password-protected directory, you can specify the optional parameters *username* and *password* as the credentials to use when picking up the content.

Attachments are transmitted as MIME-encoded parts, and you should be sure that the attachment is assigned the correct MIME *content type*, which describes how to interpret the attachment data. Examples of content types include "text/plain", "text/html", "application/MS-Word", and "application/octet-stream". If you specify a filename that includes an extension such as ".doc" or ".gif", Windows attempts to determine the correct content type for you using information in the Registry. If you find that your attachments are not given the correct content type, you can use the object reference returned by `AddAttachment` to make adjustments to its `ContentMediaType` property. The properties and methods of the `BodyPart` object are discussed shortly.

▶

Note

Because `AddAttachment` expects a URL-formatted name, if you are sending a file stored on your computer, you must either use the prefix `file://` or start the filename with a drive letter and colon. You should also specify the full path to the file. Correct examples are `"file://c:/Users/bknittel/documents/report.doc"` and `"c:\Users\bknittel\documents\report.doc"`.

If you omit `file://` or fail to specify a drive letter, you get this confusing error message: `The specified protocol is unknown.`

If you are sending a web page, you must use the `http://` prefix. You can also use the `ftp://` and `https://` prefixes to obtain a file using FTP or Secure HTTP, respectively.

AddRelatedBodyPart(*path*, *reference*, *referencetype* [, *username*, *password*])
Used with HTML-formatted messages to embed subsidiary items (*resources*), such as graphics and frame contents, that are referenced by the main message body. Returns an object reference to the added `BodyPart`. Using this method automatically sets the `MIMEFormatted` property and sets up a multipart-MIME message. *Path*, *username*, and *password* work as with `AddAttachment` and specify the filename or URL of the content to add. *Reference* specifies the name to give the embedded component. This is the name that the main body document uses to reference the items. There is an example of this usage later in the chapter. *Referencetype* is a value that indicates how the main document references the attached resources. The allowed values for *referencetype* are listed in Table 6.2. `AddRelatedBodyPart` returns a reference to the added body part.

You do not need to use this method if you use `CreateMHTMLBody` to construct an HTML-formatted message; `CreateMHTMLBody` automatically adds any related elements to which the message refers.

The usual method is to use `cdoRefTypeLocation` for *referencetype* and to specify a simple name for the *reference* value. For example, if the main document had an embedded image that was tagged with `<IMG SRC="aname">`, the image could be attached with:

```
msg.AddRelatedBodyPart "c:\images\some.gif", "aname", cdoRefTypeLocation
```

As with `AddAttachment`, `AddRelatedBodyPart` requires a prefix that indicates how to pick up the file. *Path* must start with a drive and folder name, or a protocol label such as `file://` or `http://`.

CreateMHTMLBody(*path* [, *flags* [, *username, password*]])

This method converts the HTML document specified by the filename or URL indicated in *path* to a multipart HTML message and saves it as the message's `HTMLBodyPart`. The method should not be used with a message object that already contains HTML content.

As with `AddAttachment`, *path* must start with a drive and folder name, or `file://`, `http://`, and so on.

Subsidiary components of the web page, such as graphics and frame contents, are automatically attached, unless you indicate otherwise with the *flags* value. If *path* is a URL that refers to a password-protected web folder, the optional parameters *username* and *password* specify the credentials to use. The optional *flags* value indicates which, if any, subparts of the document should be omitted; the default value is `CdoSuppressNone`. The possible values for *flags* are listed in Table 6.3. Multiple flags can be specified by adding their numeric values.

Send

Sends the email message to the specified recipient(s) using the method that was set in the `CDO.Configuration` object. This method is used only to send email messages. After calling `Send`, you can release the message object from memory, as in this example:

```
msg.send
set msg = Nothing
```

Table 6.1 lists the constant values used by the `DSNOptions` property. You can add any of the values `cdoDSNFailure`, `cdoDSNSuccess`, and `cdoDSNDelay` together to indicate that you want notifications in multiple circumstances.

Table 6.1   *cdoDSNOptions* **Constants**

Name	Value	Description
cdoDSNDefault	0	Issue no status notifications.
cdoDSNNever	1	Issue no status notifications.
cdoDSNFailure	2	Issue a notification if the delivery fails.
cdoDSNSuccess	4	Issue a notification if the delivery succeeds.
cdoDSNDelay	8	Issue a notification if the delivery is delayed.
cdoDSNSuccessFailOrDelay	14	Issue a notification if the delivery succeeds, fails, or is delayed. (Note that 14 is the sum of 2, 4, and 8.)

▶ **Note**

If you enclose your script in a WSH format file, as discussed in Chapter 10, "The CMD Command-Line" you can use a <reference> tag to have WSH define these constants automatically.

Otherwise, if you write a .vbs or .js file, you'll either have to put definitions for the constants you need in your script program or use the numeric values directly. To make it easier to add constant definitions, you can download a file containing VBScript constant definitions for all the CDO constants listed in this chapter from www.helpwin7.com/scripting.

Table 6.2 lists the constant values used by the *referencetype* parameter of the AddRelatedBodyPart method.

Table 6.2   *cdoReferenceType* **Constants**

Name	Value	Description
cdoRefTypeId	0	The *reference* parameter contains a value for the "Content-ID" MIME header. The HTML message refers to this resource using this Content-ID header.
cdoRefTypeLocation	1	The *reference* parameter contains a value for the "Content-Location" MIME header. The HTML message refers to this resource using this message-relative Uniform Resource Locator (URL). This is the usual method.

Table 6.3 lists the constant values used by the `flags` parameter of the `CreateMHTMLBody` method. Multiple flags can be specified by adding their values together.

Table 6.3   *cdoMHTMLFlags* **Constants**

Name	Value	Description
CdoSuppressNone	0	Omit nothing; download all the items referred to in the HTML document (default).
CdoSuppressImages	1	Don't include images referenced in `<IMG>` elements.
CdoSuppressBGSounds	2	Don't include sound resources specified by `<BGSOUND>` elements.
CdoSuppressFrames	4	Don't include frame contents specified in `<FRAME>` elements.
CdoSuppressObjects	8	Don't include object resources specified by `<OBJECT>` elements.
CdoSuppressStyleSheets	16	Don't include style sheets referenced by `<LINK>` elements.
CdoSuppressAll	31	Omit all referenced objects.

Working with Fields

Several CDO messaging objects use a collection of named values called `Fields`. A `Fields` collection operates a bit like an array, except it is indexed by a text name rather than by a number.

Some `Field` values can be viewed or set through properties on the object that contains the `Fields` collection; those properties are provided as a convenience so you don't have to fool around with the `Fields` collection. If you need to examine or alter a `Field` value for which no helpful property is provided, you must manipulate the `Fields` collection directly.

Note

The `Fields` collection is borrowed from another Microsoft object toolkit called ActiveX Data Objects (ADO). There is quite a bit more to it than we'll need for its use with CDO, so I present only the most important details. You can find out more about the `Field` object and `Fields` collection at msdn.microsoft.com. Search for "ADO API Reference" (using the quotation marks).

For our purposes, each `Field` object contains these three important properties:

Property	Description
`Name`	The name of the field
`Value`	The associated value
`Type`	The value type

`Type` indicates the type of the value (integer, string, and so on), but, because most scripting languages convert all values to type `Variant`, this is not relevant. However, if a `Field` object's `Type` is `0`, the value is undefined and an error can occur if you attempt to display it.

A `Fields` collection contains one or more `Field` objects. The properties and the one method of the `Fields` collection are listed in Reference List 6.2.

REFERENCE LIST 6.2   Properties and Method of the `Fields` Collection

Properties:

`Count`
Returns the number of items in the collection.

`Item(`*index*`)`
Returns an individual item from the collection. *Index* can be a string (the `Name` of the desired `Field` item) or a number (the ordinal index of the desired item in the range `0` to `Count-1`).

Method:

`Update`
`Update` sends any changes made to the `Fields` collection back to the parent message object. If you fail to invoke `Update`, any changes you make to items in the `Fields` collection will have no effect and the mail message is not delivered correctly.

The following example sets a `Field` for a `CDO.Message` object named `msg`:

```
set fields = msg.Fields      ' get copy of Fields from object msg'
                             ' make alteration
fields.Item("http://schemas.microsoft.com/cdo/configuration/name") = value
fields.Update               ' store changed value
```

As an alternative, you could use the VBScript `with` statement:

```
with msg.Fields
    .Item("http://schemas.microsoft.com/cdo/configuration/name") = value
    .Update               ' store changed value
end with
```

In actual use, *name* would be replaced with one of the names listed in the tables that follow. The field names are quite long and consist of a long prefix plus a parameter name.

Several `Field` objects with the same prefix tend to be in each collection; only the *name* part varies from item to item. The fields in the upcoming tables are grouped by prefix to make the lists easier to read.

You can examine a `Fields` collection using your scripting language's normal method for examining collections. In VBScript, you can use a `For Each` loop or a `For` loop, as shown in the following example:

```
set msg = CreateObject("CDO.Message")

for each fld in msg.Fields        ' use a "for each" loop
    if fld.type = 0 then
        wscript.echo fld.name, "is undefined"
    else
        wscript.echo fld.name, "=", fld.value
    end if
next
                        ' -- OR --
set flds = msg.Fields          ' use a for loop and numeric indexing
for i = 0 to flds.Count-1
    if flds.item(i).type = 0 then
        wscript.echo flds.item(i).name, "is undefined"
    else
        wscript.echo flds.item(i).name, "=", flds.item(i).value
    end if
next
```

Fields for the `CDO.Message` Object

The `Field` values for the `CDO.Message` object contain the message's sender and recipient names, the message's subject, and other "overall" message settings. The list of possible values is shown in Table 6.4. Note that the fields in the `httpmail` category contain the most important message header information and can use the full local character set.

> **Note**
>
> Several of the fields can be viewed or set through the `CDO.Message` properties that were listed in Reference List 6.1. For brevity's sake, those fields are omitted from this listing.

Table 6.4   **Partial List of Values in the** *CDO.Message* **Object's** *Fields* **Collection**

Name	Description
PREFIX "URN:SCHEMAS:HTTPMAIL:"	
content-disposition	Corresponds to the "Content-Disposition" MIME header for a BodyPart.
content-media-type	Corresponds to the "Content-Type" in the MIME message header. It's usually something such as "image/gif", "text/html", and so on.
Date	The date on which the message is sent. This is automatically set by the Send or Post method.
Fromemail	The email address part of the From string.
Fromname	The name part of the From string.
Htmldescription	The HTML version of the message (the HTMLBodyPart content) as a text string.
Importance	The message's importance. It must be one of the cdoImportanceValue constants specified in Table 6.5.
Normalizedsubject	The Subject string with prefixes such as Re: or Fwd: removed.
Priority	The message's priority. Must be one of the cdoPriorityValue constants specified in Table 6.6.
Senderemail	The email address; part of the sender string.
Sendername	The name part of the sender string.
Textdescription	The plain-text content of the message body. This is the content of the TextBodyPart as a text string.
PREFIX "URN:SCHEMAS:MAILHEADER:"	
content-base	The base URI Uniform Resource Identifier (URI), which is often called a URL, to use for relative URIs in the other header fields, and for any HTML message parts that do not contain a <BASE> tag.

In addition, the mailheader category contains ASCII text RFC 1522–encoded versions of the fields in the httpmail category. It's not necessary to view or alter the fields that are duplicated; the CDO.Message object sets them automatically from the httpmail versions.

Tables 6.5 and 6.6 list constants that define the acceptable values for the Importance and Priority fields, respectively.

Table 6.5   *cdoImportanceValues* **Constants**

Name	Value	Description
cdoLow	0	Low importance
cdoNormal	1	Normal importance
cdoHigh	2	High importance

Table 6.6   *cdoPriorityValues* **Constants**

Name	Value	Description
cdoPriorityNonUrgent	-1	Not urgent
cdoPriorityNormal	0	Normal priority
cdoPriorityUrgent	1	Urgent

The CDO **BodyParts** Collection

Email messages can contain multiple parts: a text version, an HTML version, attached documents, attached web pages with resources such as images and frames, and so on. Also, messages that are forwarded can contain a hierarchy of messages. (Have you ever gotten one of those email jokes that has been forwarded from person to person to person?) These are known as multipart-MIME messages, and the text file that carries such messages contains markers that show where one piece ends and another begins.

The CDO.Message object represents these compound messages using an object structure called a BodyPart and a collection called BodyParts. A BodyPart object contains one piece of a multipart message (for example, a message or an image). The message subelements contained within a BodyPart are represented by a BodyParts collection.

Reference List 6.3 lists the properties and methods of the CDO BodyParts collection. If you're only interested in sending simple text messages, you don't need to bother with BodyParts and can skip ahead to the section "The CDO.Configuration Object."

The BodyParts collections can be examined using a for each loop or a for loop, as with the Fields collection described earlier in the chapter.

REFERENCE LIST 6.3   Properties and Methods of the BodyParts Collection

Properties:

Count
Returns the number of items in the collection. Read-only.

Item(*n***)**
Returns the specified BodyPart object from the collection, where *n* can range from 0 to .Count-1.

Methods:

Add([*n*]**)**
Adds a new, empty `BodyPart` to the collection and returns an object reference to the new object. If a numeric argument is given, the new object is inserted as the *n*th item in the list (for example, 1 to `.Count+1`). If *n* is `-1` or is omitted, the new `BodyPart` is added to the end of the collection. If *n* is 1, the new `BodyPart` is added to the beginning of the list. Note that *n* cannot be 0.

Delete *x*
Deletes the specified object from the collection, where *x* can be either an ordinal number from 1 to `.Count` or an object reference to the `BodyPart` to be deleted.

DeleteAll
Removes all `BodyPart` objects from the collection.

Just to emphasize the point, `Item()` uses index numbers from 0 to `.Count-1`, whereas `Add` and `Delete` use numbers from 1 to `.Count` to represent the existing objects. Although inconsistent, this is the way Microsoft designed it.

The CDO BodyPart Object

An individual component of the message is represented by a `BodyPart` object. Every `CDO.Message` contains a `BodyPart` object that represents the message to be sent, which in turn can contain nested `BodyPart` objects. The properties and methods of the `BodyPart` object are described in Reference List 6.4.

REFERENCE LIST 6.4   Properties and Methods of the CDO `BodyPart` Object (Partial List)

Properties:

BodyParts
Returns a reference to the `BodyParts` collection that represents all the subparts of this message element. The easiest way to add a new item to this collection is with the `AddBodyPart` method.

Charset
The standard descriptor for the character set used in the message (for example, `us-ascii` or `shift-jis`). Corresponds to the `charset` parameter of the Content-Type field in the message header.

ContentMediaType
Describes the MIME type of a subdocument (for example, `text/plain` or `image/gif`). This is used with the `Charset` value to construct the message's Content-Type header line.

ContentTransferEncoding

Describes the method to be used to encode the content of the message. The default type is 7bit. Text should usually be encoded as 7bit or quoted-printable. Image and binary data are usually encoded using base64. The permitted encoding types are listed in Table 6.8.

Fields

Returns the Fields collection attached to this BodyPart. Many of the object's properties are actually stored in Fields; the properties simply provide a more convenient way to get to them. See the section "Working with Fields" earlier in the chapter for more information. This property is read-only; you can alter it by changing individual Field items and then using the collection's Update method.

Filename

Corresponds to the filename specified by the MIME header's Content-Disposition line. Read-only.

Parent

Returns a reference to the object that contains this message element (that is, the BodyPart's parent BodyPart or the primary BodyPart in the Message object).

Methods:

AddBodyPart(*n*)

Adds a new, empty BodyPart to the list of message subelements contained within this BodyPart as well as returns an object reference to the new object. Using this method is the same as using the Add method of the object's BodyParts property; that is, the statements

```
set newpart = bp.AddBodyPart(n)
```

and

```
set newpart = bp.BodyParts.Add(n)
```

are equivalent. See the discussion for the Add property in the section "The CDO BodyParts Collection," earlier in the chapter.

GetEncodedContentStream()

Returns an ADO Stream object, which can be read to view the encoded contents of the message part. This method is not useful when sending or receiving messages, but again, I think it could come in handy if you needed a way to just encode a file in base-64 or another format.

SaveToFile *filename*

Writes the contents of the BodyPart object to a file. The filename can be specified in normal format using a full path (for example, "C:\message.doc") or URI format (for example, "file://c:\message.doc").

The values in a `BodyPart` object's `Fields` collection are listed in Table 6.7. Fields that are accessible as `BodyPart` properties are not listed. (In addition, the `Fields` collection of the primary `BodyPart` object contained within a `CDO.Message` object contains all the fields listed earlier in Table 6.4. These are `CDO.Message` fields, not `BodyPart` fields, so they are not listed in the Table 6.7 either.)

Table 6.7   **Values in the *BodyPart* Object's *Fields* Collection**

Name	Description
PREFIX "URN:SCHEMAS:HTTPMAIL:"	
`attachmentfilename`	Corresponds to the "filename:" parameter of the Content-Disposition mail header in an attachment `BodyPart` object. (Read-only.)
`content-disposition-type`	The type part of a content-disposition header. It can be one of the values `unspecified`, `other`, `attachment`, or `inline`.
PREFIX "URN:SCHEMAS:MAILHEADER:"	
`content-description`	A comment describing a part of a multipart message.
`content-disposition`	The Content-Disposition MIME header for this part of a multipart message.
`content-id`	A unique identifier for the resource.
`content-language`	The two-letter code describing the language used in the resource (for example, `en` or `de`).
`content-location`	The URI that corresponds to the resource (for example, where the embedded part came from).
`content-type`	The Content-Type MIME header for this `BodyPart` object, containing a content-media type and optionally a character set identifier.
PREFIX "HTTP://SCHEMAS.MICROSOFT.COM/"	
`sensitivity`	Defines the sensitivity level of the message and corresponds to the "Sensitivity:" mail header. It is set to one of the integer values listed in Table 6.9.

Tables 6.8 and 6.9 list constants used by the `ContentTransferEncoding` property and the `sensitivity` field, respectively.

Table 6.8 *cdoEncodingType* **Constants**

Name	Value	Description
cdo7bit	7bit	Simple 7-bit ASCII.
cdo8bit	8bit	8-bit coding with line-termination characters.
cdoBase64	base64	Three octets encoded into four sextets with offset.
cdoBinary	binary	Arbitrary binary stream.
cdoMacBinHex40	mac-binhex40	Macintosh binary-to-hex encoding. CDO can decode but not encode binhex.
cdoQuotedPrintable	quoted-printable	Mostly 7-bit, with 8-bit characters encoded as =*HH*.
cdoUuencode	uuencode	Unix Uuencode encoding.

Table 6.9 *cdoSensitivityValues* **Constants**

Name	Value	Description
cdoSensitivityNone	0	Not specified (default)
cdoPersonal	1	Personal
cdoPrivate	2	Private
cdoCompanyConfidential	3	Confidential

The ADO **Stream** Object

The contents of a CDO.Message or BodyPart object are exposed (made available) as a Stream object that can be saved to a file. Stream is another object borrowed from the ADO system, and there isn't enough room to cover it completely here. Stream objects aren't important for sending messages, but if you're working with CDO to manipulate received messages or encode or decode data files, some of Stream's methods and properties can be helpful. The ADO Stream object's methods and properties are listed on the Microsoft website mentioned at the beginning of this chapter.

The **CDO.Configuration** Object

The CDO.Configuration object contains Field values that tell the Message object how to deliver the email message. The two ways the message can be delivered are as follows:

- By sending the message to an SMTP or Network News Transfer Protocol (NNTP) mail or news server, either on your own network or at your Internet service provider (ISP). This is the most direct way of delivering the message.

- By dropping the message into a folder, your mail server periodically scans for outgoing messages. This technique can be used if you are using the Microsoft SMTP or NNTP server that is part of Internet Information Services (IIS) system If the "drop directory" for the SMTP server is on the computer running the script or is reachable through the network, you can use this method.

The `CDO.Configuration` object contains just one property: `Fields`. The `Fields` collection contains a list of values that describe the method to be used to deliver the message. The field values are set using the methods described earlier, in the section "Working with Fields." One method—`Load`—lets you pull in default server delivery information from other applications.

Reference List 6.5 describes the property and method. The values of the configuration object's `Fields` collection are listed in Table 6.10.

REFERENCE LIST 6.5   Property and Method of the `CDO.Configuration` Object

Property:

Fields
Returns a `Fields` collection object containing the `Field` values that determine how the message is to be sent. The `Field` values are listed in Table 6.10.

Method:

Load *loadFrom*
Sets `Fields` with default settings made for the Outlook Express and Internet Information Services SMTP and NNTP server connections. If your script will always runs on a computer that has IIS installed and is configured for outbound mail, or if you always run the script from a user account that has a default identity set up for Outlook Express, you can use this method to avoid having to "hard-wire" the outgoing delivery method and server information. The *loadFrom* value must be one of the `cdoConfigSource` constants listed in Table 6.11.

For most scripting applications, it's probably best to ignore the `Load` method, assume that all values need to be set, and set them in your script.

The `Fields` values for the `CDO.Configuration` `Fields` collection used for email are shown in Table 6.10.

Table 6.10   **Partial List of Values in the** `Fields` **Collection of** `CDO.Configuration`

Name	Description
PREFIX: "HTTP://SCHEMAS.MICROSOFT.COM/CDO/CONFIGURATION/"	
`Autopromotebodyparts`	Boolean value. If this value is `True`, any `BodyPart` objects containing only one embedded `BodyPart` are sent as a single part.
`Httpcookies`	List of cookies (separated by semicolons) to send to HTTP servers when fetching pages using `CreateMHTMLBody` or `AddAttachment`.
`Languagecode`	RFC 1766 Language Code (for example, `en` or `de`) to use when generating response text for reply or forwarded messages.
`sendemailaddress`	The sender's default email address. This is used as the From address with the SMTP server.
`sendpassword`	The password to use when connecting to the SMTP server, if `smtpauthenticate` is set to `cdoBasic`.
`sendusername`	The username to use when connecting to the SMTP server, if `smtpauthenticate` is set to `cdoBasic`.
`senduserreplymailaddress`	The sender's "reply-to" email address to use in email messages. If this is not specified, the message's "From" address is used.
`sendusing`	Method to use when sending email messages. It must be one of the `cdoSendUsing` constants defined in Table 6.13.
`smtpaccountname`	The SMTP account name as displayed by Outlook Express; it's not actually used for anything.
`smtpauthenticate`	Authentication method to use when sending messages to a mail server. The value must be one of the `cdoProtocolsAuthentication` constants listed in Table 6.12.
`smtpconnectiontimeout`	Number of seconds to wait before timing out an SMTP connection. The default is 30 seconds or, if loaded, the Outlook Express setting.
`smtpserver`	Name of server to use when posting email messages via SMTP. This can be a DNS name or an IP address in dotted decimal format and can be loaded from Outlook Express setup.
`smtpserverpickupdirectory`	Path to the pickup directory to use when posting email messages via a pickup directory.

Name	Description
smtpserverport	TCP port to use when posting mail messages with SMTP. The default is 25 or, if loaded, the setting used in Outlook.
smtpusessl	Boolean value that indicates whether to use Secure Sockets Layer (SSL) when posting via SMTP. If you set smtpusessl to True, you generally need to also set smtpserverport to 465 or the port number specified by your ISP.
urlgetlatestversion	Boolean value. If this value is True, AddAttachment and CreateMHTMLBody always fetches a specified page rather than use a cached local copy.
urlproxyserver	The proxy server to use when fetching HTTP resources. It must be specified as an IP address or a server name plus port (for example, "1.2.3.4:80" or "proxy.mycompany.com:80").
urlproxybypass	String value. If set to "<local>", local addresses do not use the proxy server.
Prefix: "urn:schemas:calendar:"	
timezoneid	Time zone identifier to use when adding timestamps to outgoing messages and when reading incoming messages. Defaults to the local computer's setting. It must be one of the cdoTimeZoneId constants listed in Table 6.14.

Table 6.11 lists the constants used in the LoadFrom method.

Table 6.11   *cdoConfigSource* **Constants**

Name	Value	Description
CdoSourceDefaults	-1	Loads default values from both Internet Information Services and Outlook Express
CdoSourceIIS	1	Obtains server settings from the SMTP configuration values for IIS on this computer
cdoSourceOutlookExpress	2	Obtains server settings from the default identity in the current user's Outlook Express configuration

Table 6.12 lists the constants used by the nntpauthenticate and smtpauthenticate fields.

Table 6.12   *cdoProtocolsAuthentication* **Constants**

Name	Value	Description
cdoAnonymous	0	Do not authenticate.
cdoBasic	1	Use basic (clear-text) authentication. The specified username and password are sent. Use this option for non-Windows mail services that require authentication before sending (GMail for example).
cdoNTLM	2	Use Windows NTLM authentication. The current process's credentials are used (that is, the credentials of the user running the script).

Table 6.13 lists the constants used by the sendusing field.

Table 6.13   *cdoSendUsing* **Constants**

Name	Value	Description
cdoSendUsingPickup	1	Send the message by dropping into the IIS SMTP service pickup directory.
cdoSendUsingPort	2	Send the message directly using SMTP. This is the most common method.

Table 6.14 lists the constants used by the timezoneid field.

Table 6.14   *cdoTimeZoneId* **Constants**

Name	Value	GMT Offset	Locations
cdoUTC	0	0:00	Universal Coordinated Time
cdoGMT	1	0:00	Greenwich Mean Time; Dublin, Edinburgh, and London
cdoLisbon	2	+1:00	Lisbon and Warsaw
cdoParis	3	+1:00	Paris and Madrid
cdoBerlin	4	+1:00	Berlin, Stockholm, Rome, Bern, Brussels, and Vienna
cdoEasternEurope	5	+2:00	Eastern Europe
cdoPrague	6	+1:00	Prague
cdoAthens	7	+2:00	Athens, Helsinki, and Istanbul
cdoBrasilia	8	-3:00	Brasilia
cdoAtlanticCanada	9	-4:00	Atlantic Time (Canada)
cdoEastern	10	-5:00	Eastern Time (United States and Canada)

Name	Value	GMT Offset	Locations
cdoCentral	11	–6:00	Central Time (United States and Canada)
cdoMountain	12	–7:00	Mountain Time (United States and Canada)
cdoPacific	13	–8:00	Pacific Time (United States and Canada), Tijuana
cdoAlaska	14	–9:00	Alaska
cdoHawaii	15	–10:00	Hawaii
cdoMidwayIsland	16	–11:00	Midway Island and Samoa
cdoWellington	17	+12:00	Wellington and Auckland
cdoBrisbane	18	+10:00	Brisbane, Melbourne, and Sydney
cdoAdelaide	19	+9:30	Adelaide
cdoTokyo	20	+9:00	Tokyo, Osaka, Sapporo, Seoul, and Yakutsk
cdoHongKong	21	+8:00	Hong Kong SAR, Perth, Singapore, and Taipei
cdoBangkok	22	+7:00	Bangkok, Jakarta, and Hanoi
cdoBombay	23	+5:30	Bombay, Calcutta, Madras, New Delhi, and Colombo
cdoAbuDhabi	24	+4:00	Abu Dhabi, Muscat, Tbilisi, Kazan, and Volgograd
cdoTehran	25	+3:30	Tehran
cdoBaghdad	26	+3:00	Baghdad, Kuwait, Nairobi, and Riyadh
cdoIsrael	27	+2:00	Israel
cdoNewfoundland	28	–3:30	Newfoundland
cdoAzores	29	–1:00	Azores and Cape Verde Island
cdoMidAtlantic	30	–2:00	Mid-Atlantic
cdoMonrovia	31	0:00	Monrovia and Casablanca
cdoBuenosAires	32	–3:00	Buenos Aires and Georgetown
cdoCaracas	33	–4:00	Caracas and La Paz
cdoIndiana	34	–5:00	Indiana (East)
cdoBogota	35	–5:00	Bogota and Lima
cdoSaskatchewan	36	–6:00	Saskatchewan
cdoMexicoCity	37	–6:00	Mexico City and Tegucigalpa
cdoArizona	38	–7:00	Arizona
cdoEniwetok	39	–12:00	Eniwetok and Kwajalein
cdoFiji	40	+12:00	Fiji Islands, Kamchatka, and Marshall Islands

continues

Table 6.14   **Continued**

Name	Value	GMT Offset	Locations
cdoMagadan	41	+11:00	Magadan, Solomon Islands, and New Caledonia
cdoHobart	42	+10:00	Hobart
cdoGuam	43	+10:00	Guam, Port Moresby, and Vladivostok
cdoDarwin	44	+9:30	Darwin
cdoBeijing	45	+8:00	Beijing, Chongqing, and Urumqi
cdoAlmaty	46	+6:00	Almaty and Dhaka
cdoIslamabad	47	+5:00	Islamabad, Karachi, Sverdlovsk, and Tashkent
cdoKabul	48	+4:30	Kabul
cdoCairo	49	+2:00	Cairo
cdoHarare	50	+2:00	Harare and Pretoria
cdoMoscow	51	+3:00	Moscow and St. Petersburg
cdoInvalidTimeZone	52		Invalid time zone identifier

Okay, enough with the reference information. Let's see how you can make use of all this information.

Sending a Message with CDO

The reference material in the previous section describes a complex set of objects for sending messages. All that complexity is there to make it possible to construct and manipulate multipart, multiformat messages. It turns out that in real-life applications, you'll likely use only a few of all those methods and properties.

The basic steps involved in sending a message are as follows:

1. Create one `CDO.Message` and one `CDO.Configuration` object and give the `Message` object a reference linking it to the `Configuration` object.

2. Add message content to the `CDO.Message` object.

3. Add delivery method information to the `CDO.Configuration` object.

4. Send the message.

The first step is to create objects, using standard object calls. For example, in VBScript, the following statements create and link `Message` and `Configuration` objects named `msg` and `config`, respectively:

```
set msg = CreateObject("CDO.Message")          ' create objects
set config = CreateObject("CDO.Configuration")
set msg.Configuration = config                 ' link msg to config
```

The third statement tells `msg` that its associated `Configuration` object is `config`. In the remaining examples, if these `CreateObject` calls aren't shown, you can assume that they're part of the script.

In the next few sections, I show you how to go through the remaining steps, with several variations.

Constructing the Message

In most cases, you just want to send a simple text or HTML-formatted message. The content of the message can come from a text string, a file, or, if you want to send a web page as a message, a URL.

The `CDO.Message` object contains one `BodyPart` object that can be used in one of two ways: If you are sending a simple text or HTML message, it holds the message content. If you are sending a multipart message, with alternative and/or subsidiary parts, this `BodyPart` object holds the component parts of the message in its `BodyParts` collection, as illustrated earlier in Figures 6.2 and 6.3.

Therefore, to construct a simple message, you assign content to the main `BodyPart` object. To construct a multipart message, you add components to the `BodyPart`.

Sending a Text String

If you are sending a simple text message, you only need to put the message text into the CDO message's `BodyPart` object. It's easiest to use the `TextBody` property to do this. If no other message content has been added to the object, the `TextBodyPart` property refers to the main `BodyPart` (as illustrated earlier in Figure 6.2) and the `TextBody` property to its content. If you assign a text string to `TextBody`, that becomes the content of the message.

A text message should consist of lines of text of at most 75 characters or so, separated by carriage return/linefeed pairs. This lets the message display properly in text-based email programs. For example, you could construct a message using these statements:

```
reminder = "This is a reminder message:" & vbCRLF & _
           "Go to your weekly meeting at 1:15" & vbCRLF & _
           "Bring a pencil."
```

You could construct a message that lists all the Microsoft Word .doc files in a certain directory with statements such as:

```
                              ' Example File Script0601.vbs
set fso = CreateObject("Scripting.FileSystemObject")
set dir = "C:\Documents and Settings\All Users\Documents\Orders"
```

```
txt = ""
for each file in fso.GetFolder(dir).Files     ' scan for .DOC files
    if instr(".DOC", ucase(file.Name)) > 0 then
        if txt = "" then                       ' first one, start the message
            txt = "There are new documents in the Orders folder:" & _
                    vbCRLF & vbCRLF
        end if
        txt = txt & file.Name & ", " & _
              file.DateCreated & vbCRLF         ' add name to the list
    end if
next

if txt = "" then WScript.Quit(0)      ' no files to announce, just quit
set msg.TextBody = txt                ' assign the message content
```

This creates a message such as the following:

```
There are new documents in the Orders folder:

fromPTP.doc, 3/11/2002 1:13:10 PM
fromZandar.doc, 3/11/2002 2:13:15 PM
```

Sending a Message from a Text File

You can tell CDO to use the contents of a text file as the message body by reading the text into a string variable and assigning it to the TextBody property we used in the previous section. Here's an example:

```
sendfile = "C:\temp\message.txt"          ' file to send
set fso = CreateObject("Scripting.FileSystemObject")

set infile = fso.OpenTextFile(sendfile)   ' read file into a string
txt = infile.ReadAll
infile.Close
set infile = Nothing

msg.TextBody = txt                        ' set message content
```

Sending the Output of a Program

You can email the output of a command-line program through the aid of the WScript.Shell object, which is covered in Chapter 4, "File and Registry Access." For example, the following statements grab the output of a ping command as a text email message:

```
set shell = CreateObject("WScript.Shell")
set ping  = shell.Run("ping www.someplace.com")
txt = "The ping test results are:" & vbCRLF & ping.Stdout.ReadAll
set ping = Nothing

msg.TextBody = txt                        ' set message content
```

Sending an HTML Message

HTML messages can be created by filling in the HTMLBodyPart object or assigning a string to the HTMLBody property. This can be the sole message component, or part of a multipart/alternate message that contains both text and HTML versions.

You can create HTML-based messages by inserting the appropriate HTML tags into a text string. The file listing message shown earlier could be sent in HTML using a <UL> unordered list, with these statements:

```
                                           ' Example File script0602.vbs
txt = ""
for each file in fso.GetFolder(dir).Files     ' scan for .DOC files
    if instr(".DOC", ucase(file.Name)) > 0 then
        if txt = "" then                      ' first one, start the message
            txt = "There are new documents in the Orders folder:" & _
                    "<P><UL>"
        end if
        txt = txt & "<LI>" & file.Name & ", " & _
                file.DateCreated              ' add name to the list
    end if
next

if txt = "" then WScript.Quit(0)     ' no files to announce, just quit
txt = txt + "</UL>"                   ' end the list
set msg.HTMLBody = txt               ' assign the message content
```

In this script, a new list item is added for each file using an HTML <LI> tag. The entire list is displayed as a <UL> (unordered, bulleted) list.

Sending a Web Page or HTML File

If you want to send an HTML message that is already contained in a file or is available as a web page, you can use the CDO.Message method CreateMHTMLBody to extract the file or web page as the message body.

CreateMHTMLBody takes a *flags* argument that indicates whether CDO is to obtain and embed into the message any images or other resources referred to by the main HTML document. Table 6.3 lists these constants. In general, you should use cdoSuppressNone (value 0) so that all referenced images, sounds, and other resources are included.

Tip

You can download a VBScript file with const definitions for all these values from www.helpwin7.com/ scripting. You can then copy these definitions into your scripts.

The following statements show how a file named servers.html can be sent as a formatted message:

```
const cdoSuppressNone = 0
msg.CreateMHTMLBody("file://C:\data\servers.html", cdoSuppressNone)
```

This statement takes the document `"c:\data\servers.html"` and uses it as the email message body. Any resources are fetched and included as well, as additional `BodyPart` objects.

`CreateMHTMLBody` can also obtain the message document from a web server, if you specify a standard URL rather than a filename. For example,

```
msg.CreateMHTMLBody("http://www.somewhere.com/somepage.html, _
    cdoSuppressNone)
```

visits www.somewhere.com, downloads the page and any included images or other resources, and uses this as the content of the message. You could use this technique in a script that runs on a schedule to automatically mail you, say, a network status page or a stock portfolio valuation.

If the web page requires a username and password, you can specify these after the *flags* argument. You should be careful about storing passwords in scripts, however, because anyone who obtains access to your script file will be able to see the password for the remote website.

> **Note**
>
> If the script is run more than once with the same URL, CDO might find that the page you are requesting is in the Temporary Internet Files cache of recently viewed pages, and it might send that copy. Although this speeds things up when you're sending a fixed page, if the page changes or is generated on-the-fly by a web server, CDO might send a stale copy. You can tell CDO never to look in the cache for pages by setting the `urlgetlatestversion` field in the `Configuration` object to `True`. The `Configuration` object is discussed later in the chapter.

Sending a Multiformat Message

If you want to send HTML-based messages, it's good to include an equivalent, plain-text version for people who don't like HTML or whose email programs can't read it.

You can manually construct both text and HTML versions and assign them using the statements used in the previous sections, or you can create just the HTML version and let CDO derive the text version automatically. This technique is the easiest way to produce a text version when you use `CreateMTHMLBody` to include a file or web page. Simply set the property `AutoGenerateTextBody` to `True`. Here's an example:

```
msg.CreateMHTMLBody("http://www.somewhere.com/somepage.html, _
    cdoSuppressNone)
msg.AutoGenerateTextBody = True
```

Adding Attachments

Email attachments are sent by adding `BodyPart` objects to the main message object's `Attachments` collection. Most of the work can be done using the message's `AddAttachment` method. This adds the new `BodyPart` object, loads the contents of a specified file into the `BodyPart`, and returns a reference to the new object. Here is an example:

```
set attach = msg.AddAttachment("C:\text\proposal.doc")
```

This is 99 percent of the job. The only other thing to worry about is that the attachment should be labeled with the correct content-type string (in property `ContentMediaType`), which describes the type of data inside the attachment. This information tells the message recipient's email program which application to use to open the attachment. A few common content types are listed here:

Content Type	Description
Text/plain	Plain ASCII text
Text/html	HTML formatted text
Image/jpg	A JPG image
Application/postscript	A PostScript document file
Application/octet-stream	Unspecified, binary data

Windows can often determine the proper content type from the attachment's file extension. If you want, though, you can set the content type explicitly and override what Windows guesses by using statements like these:

```
set attach = msg.AddAttachment("C:\text\proposal.doc")
attach.ContentMediaType = "application/msword"
```

If you don't need to worry about setting the content type, you don't need to store the object reference returned by `AddAttachment`, and you can simply use the method to attach files to your message with statements like these:

```
msg.AddAttachment "C:\text\proposal.doc"
msg.AddAttachment "C:\text\response.doc"
```

Finally, as with `CreateMHTMLBody`, you can give `AddAttachment` a URL instead of a filename, and it retrieves the specified document from a web server and adds it as an attachment. In this case, the content type is set to the value the web server provides. If the URL is password protected, you can pass a username and password as additional arguments to `AddAttachment`.

Including Images with an HTML Message

HTML-formatted messages can display images (for example, logos, photos, or a background pattern) stored on the web by specifying the images' URLs in <img> tags. Likewise, they can include references to sound and video resources, style sheets, and so on. However, in the interest of maintaining privacy, many email programs do not automatically download and display these external images and resources. To send a message that displays correctly, you have to include the resources as attachments to the message. Here's how you do it:

- For each image you want to use in the message, make up an identifying name. "image1", "image2", and so on are good enough.

- In the <img> tags in the HTML message body, use the notation src="*xxx*", where *xxx* is the identifying name you chose for the image.

- To attach an image file to the message, use the AddRelatedBodyPart method with three arguments: the full path to the image file, the identifying name you chose for the image, and the constant cdoRefTypeName (or the number 1).

- Set the attachment object's ContentMediaType property to "Application/ Octet-stream".

Here's how this looks:

```
                                        ' Example File mailimage.vbs
const cdoRefTypeName = 1

    imagefile1 = "C:\scripts\06\logo.gif"          ' specify full path
    name1      = "image1"

    html_msg   = "This is a message with an image:" & _
               "<P><img src='" & name1 & "'><P>Cool, huh?"

    set msg  = CreateObject("CDO.Message")              ' create objects
    set conf = CreateObject("CDO.Configuration")
    set msg.configuration = conf

    with msg                                    ' build the message
        .to   = "you@there.com"
        .from = "me@here.com"
        ...

    .HTMLbody = html_msg
        .AutoGenerateTextBody = True
                                    ' attach the image with an identifier
        set img = .AddRelatedBodyPart(imagefile1, name1, cdoRefTypeName)
        img.ContentMediaType="Application/Octet-stream"
        end with
    ...
```

The version of this script included in the set of downloadable files is complete and incorporates techniques that I discuss in the following sections.

Specifying the Recipients and Subject

The `CDO.Message` object has several properties that echo the familiar fields you fill in whenever you send an email message:

Property	Description
To	Primary recipient(s)
CC	Secondary recipient(s)
BCC	Private recipient(s) whose existence is invisible to the other recipients
From	The email address of the message author
ReplyTo	The address to which responses should be sent, if not the From address
Subject	A short description of the message

All but the Subject entry are email addresses that can be formatted as described earlier in the chapter in the section "The `CDO.Message` Object." If you enter multiple addresses, simply separate them with commas.

As an example, to send a message from `"sales@mycompany.com"` to `"orders@mycompany.com"`, with a carbon copy going back to `"sales@mycompany.com"`, you could use these statements:

```
msg.To      = "orders@mycompany.com"
msg.From    = "sales@mycompany.com"
msg.CC      = "sales@mycompany.com"
msg.Subject = "Orders received " & date()
```

Specifying the Delivery Server

The preceding sections described how to construct a message in the `CDO.Message` object. The next step is to set the `CDO.Configuration` object with the information needed to actually deliver the message.

CDO does not attempt to deliver the message directly to its recipients. Instead, it relies on a mail server to do the necessary work of finding the recipient's own mail servers and passing the message on. The forwarding server can be one run by your organization or ISP; whatever setup you use for sending email—with Outlook Express or some other email program—can be used to send mail from a script.

All the information in the `Configuration` object is stored in its `Fields` collection using the prefix `"http://schemas.microsoft.com/cdo/configuration/"`. It's strange and cumbersome, but we have to live with it. I've found that the easiest way to set the `Field` values is to store the prefix in a variable and to use the `with` statement, when using VBScript. These minimize the amount of typing and clutter. For example, you can set configuration properties using statements of this sort:

```
const cdoSendUsingPort = 2              ' standard CDO constants
const cdoAnonymous     = 0

set msg  = CreateObject("CDO.Message")  ' create objects
set conf = CreateObject("CDO.Configuration")
set msg.configuration = conf
                                        ' set delivery options
prefix = "http://schemas.microsoft.com/cdo/configuration/"
With conf.fields
    .item(prefix & "sendusing")             = cdoSendUsingPort
    .item(prefix & "smtpserver")            = "mail.mycompany.com"
    .item(prefix & "smtpauthenticate")      = cdoAnonymous
    .item(prefix & "urlgetlatestversion")   = True
    .update                             ' commit changes
End With
```

To route mail through an SMTP server in your organization or at your ISP, you must specify `cdoSendUsingPort` as the value for the `sendusing` field. This instructs CDO to send the message using standard Internet methods to a specified mail server. You must also tell CDO whether it needs to sign on to the mail server and how this is done. In most cases, no sign-on is necessary and you can use an "anonymous" connection. If your mail server requires a username and password to *send* email, you can use "basic" authentication and provide the name and password through `CDO.Configuration`.

In most cases, here are the field values you need to set:

Field	Value
sendusing	cdoSendUsingPort (2).
smtpserver	Name or IP address of your organization's or ISP's SMTP mail server.
smtpauthenticate	Refer to Table 6.12 for options.
sendusername	Username, if required.
sendpassword	Password, if required.

An example of this configuration was shown earlier in this section.

If your mail server uses a Secure Sockets connection, you might need to specify some of the other field values listed earlier in Table 6.10. Here's an example where email is sent through Google's gmail.com servers:

```
const cdoBasic = 1

.item(prefix & "sendusing")              = cdoSendUsingPort
.item(prefix & "smtpserver")             = "smtp.gmail.com"
.item(prefix & "smtpauthenticate")       = cdoBasic
.item(prefix & "sendusername")           = "MyUsername@gmail.com"
.item(prefix & "sendpassword")           = "MyPassword"
.item(prefix & "smtpusessl")             = True
.item(prefix & "smtpserverport")         = 465
.update
```

Sending the Message

The final step in sending an email message with CDO is to use the `Send` method to deliver the message. Because any number of things can go wrong during this process—the remote SMTP server might be down, there might be a network error, or the `Configuration` object might be missing some information—you should have your script catch and report the error rather than just failing. This is especially important with scheduled scripts that run unattended.

To send the message while detecting errors, you need to use your scripting language's exception-handling mechanism. In VBScript, this is done with the `on error` statement. Here's how to send the constructed message safely:

```
on error resume next       ' do not stop on errors
msg.Send                   ' deliver the message
send_errno = err.Number    ' remember error number
on error goto 0            ' restore normal error handling
if send_errno <> 0  then   ' if something went wrong...
    ' report the problem somehow
end if
```

After `.Send`, if the message is not delivered, `send_errno` is nonzero, so the `if` statement is true and you can take whatever action is appropriate.

Putting It All Together

Now, let's look at a few examples of sending a message, with all the steps put together.

This basic example sends a simple, no-frills text message every time the script is run:

```
' Example File script0603.vbs
const cdoSendUsingPort = 2                 ' standard CDO constants
const cdoAnonymous     = 0

set msg  = CreateObject("CDO.Message")     ' create objects
set conf = CreateObject("CDO.Configuration")
set msg.configuration = conf
```

```
With msg                                  ' build the message
    .to       = """Sue Smith"" <ssmith@somewhere.com>"
    .from     = """Mad Max"" <madmax@mycompany.com>"
    .subject  = "Message from a script"
    .textBody = "This is the message!"
End With

prefix = "http://schemas.microsoft.com/cdo/configuration/"
With conf.fields                          ' set delivery options
    .item(prefix & "sendusing")           = cdoSendUsingPort
    .item(prefix & "smtpserver")          = "smtp.mycompany.com"
    .item(prefix & "smtpauthenticate")    = cdoAnonymous
    .update                               ' commit changes
End With

on error resume next     ' do not stop on errors
msg.send                 ' deliver the message
send_errno = err.Number  ' remember error number
on error goto 0          ' restore normal error handling

if send_errno <> 0 then     ' if something went wrong...
    wscript.echo "Error sending message"
    wscript.quit 0
else
    wscript.echo "Message sent"
end if
```

This script generates and delivers the following message to the ssmith@somewhere.com email address:

```
Return-Path: <madmax@mycompany.com>
Received: from dualcore (dualcore.mycompany.com [6.5.4.3])
        by smtp.mycompany.com with ESMTPS id
e31xy8423775rvb.5.2009.01.22.18.11.28;
        Thu, 22 Jan 2009 18:11:29 -0800 (PST)
Sender: madmax@mycompany.com
thread-index: Acl8/+Y3D76b4rd+RrC7cDd4/qcINw==
Thread-Topic: Message from a script
From: "Mad Max" <madmax@mycompany.com>
To: "Sue Smith" <ssmith@somewhere.com>
Subject: Message from a script
Date: Thu, 22 Jan 2009 18:11:27 -0800
Message-ID: <5DDDD355AF9746E8AD31B20D95758855@dualcore>
MIME-Version: 1.0
Content-Type: text/plain
Content-Transfer-Encoding: 7bit
X-Mailer: Microsoft CDO for Windows 2000
Content-Class: urn:content-classes:message
Importance: normal
Priority: normal
X-MimeOLE: Produced By Microsoft MimeOLE V6.00.2900.5579
```

Now, in another example, we write a script that takes any files specified on its command-line arguments and mails them to a specific place. As mentioned earlier in the chapter, if you create a shortcut icon for this script, you can drag files onto it, and the script mails the file to the built-in recipient. You might use this if you have to frequently forward files to one specific person.

The `AddAttachment` method in the middle of the script does all the work:

```
                                        ' Example File mailfiles.vbs
    if WScript.arguments.count <= 0 then    ' no files were specified
        MsgBox "Usage: mailfiles filename..., or drag files onto shortcut"
        WScript.quit 0
    end if

    const cdoSendUsingPort = 2          ' standard CDO constants
    const cdoAnonymous     = 0

    sender     = "myname@mycompany.com"    ' sender of message
    recipient  = "somebody@mycompany.com"  ' recipient of this message
    relayserver = "mail.mycompany.com"     ' SMTP server

    set msg  = CreateObject("CDO.Message")   ' create objects
    set conf = CreateObject("CDO.Configuration")
    set msg.configuration = conf

    With msg                                ' build the message
        .to       = recipient
        .from     = sender
        .subject  = "Files for you"
        .textBody = "Attached to this message are files for you."

        nfiles = 0                          ' count of files attached
        for each arg in WScript.arguments   ' treat each argument as a
            .AddAttachment arg              ' file to be attached
            nfiles = nfiles+1
        next
    End With

    prefix = "http://schemas.microsoft.com/cdo/configuration/"
    With conf.fields                        ' set delivery options
        .item(prefix & "sendusing")         = cdoSendUsingPort
        .item(prefix & "smtpserver")        = relayserver
        .item(prefix & "smtpauthenticate")  = cdoAnonymous
        .update                             ' commit changes
    End With

    on error resume next    ' do not stop on errors
    msg.send                ' deliver the message
    send_errno = err.Number ' remember error number
    on error goto 0         ' restore normal error handling
```

```
if send_errno <> 0 then     ' if something went wrong...
    MsgBox "Error sending message"
else
    if nfiles = 1 then plural = "" else plural = "s"
    MsgBox "Sent " & nfiles & " file" & plural & " to " & recipient
end if
```

Tip

If you find this kind of script useful, be sure to check out Appendix G, "Creating Your Own Scriptable Objects" (which you can download from www.helpwin7.com/scripting), where I show you how to create your own simplified "send some email" object that encapsulates all this code.

As a final example, here is a script that can be run from the Task Scheduler to periodically scan a specified folder for files. Any file found in this folder is emailed to a fixed address, and the files are moved to an archive folder. This creates a drop-off folder that can be used in several ways:

- If you have your unattended scripts create log files in this folder, the logs can be mailed to an administrator for review.
- The folder can be shared on a network so users can drop off files for someone else to review or process.
- If the script scans your incoming fax folder, this automatically emails the faxes to a specified user.

The script takes care not to move the files out of the pickup folder unless the message is successfully sent. Also, the script stores the list of files it finds in an array and works with this array when sending and later moving the files. If the program uses one "for each file in folder" statement to add the attachments and a second to move the files, there is a chance that a file might be added between mailing and moving, and it never gets mailed. Here's the code for this script:

```
                                    ' Example File scanmail.vbs
                                    ' folder to scan for files
scanfolder    = _
    "c:\Documents and Settings\All Users\Documents\MailThese"


                                    ' folder to place mailed files
archivefolder = "c:\Documents and Settings\All Userss\Documents\Mailed\"

sender        = "sales@here.com"        ' sender of message
recipient     = "fulfillment@here.com"  ' recipient of this message
relayserver   = "mail.here.com"         ' SMTP server


' ----------------------------------------------------------------
' GET LIST OF FILES
' ----------------------------------------------------------------
```

```
WScript.echo "Scanning " & scanfolder & "..."

set fso = CreateObject("Scripting.FileSystemObject")
set folder = fso.GetFolder(scanfolder)

maxfiles = 50                       ' largest number of files expected
dim filelist()                      ' create resizable array to hold filenames
redim filelist(maxfiles)

nfiles = 0                          ' count of files stored

for each file in folder.Files       ' scan the folder
    if nfiles >= maxfiles then       ' if array is already full,
        maxfiles = nfiles+50         ' make it larger
        redim preserve filelist(maxfiles)
    end if

    WScript.echo "  Found", file.name ' list the files we find

    filelist(nfiles) = file.path     ' save filelist(0, 1, ...)
    nfiles = nfiles+1                ' add one to count of files
next

if nfiles = 0 then
    WScript.echo "No files to send"
    WScript.quit(0)                  ' nothing to do, just quit
end if

' ----------------------------------------------------------------
' COMPOSE THE MESSAGE
' ----------------------------------------------------------------

set msg  = CreateObject("CDO.Message")' create objects
set conf = CreateObject("CDO.Configuration")
set msg.configuration = conf

if nfiles = 1 then plural = "" else plural = "s"

With msg                              ' build the message
    .to       = recipient
    .from     = sender
    .subject  = "Files for you"

    .textBody = "Attached to this message are " & nfiles & plural &_
        " files for your attention."

    for i = 0 to nfiles-1            ' attach all of the files
        .AddAttachment filelist(i)
    next
End With
```

```
' ................................................................
' SET DELIVERY INFO
' ................................................................

const cdoSendUsingPort = 2                 ' standard CDO constants
const cdoAnonymous     = 0

prefix = "http://schemas.microsoft.com/cdo/configuration/"
With conf.fields                          ' set delivery options
    .item(prefix & "sendusing")           = cdoSendUsingPort
    .item(prefix & "smtpserver")          = smtpserver
    .item(prefix & "smtpauthenticate")    = cdoAnonymous
    .update                               ' commit changes
End With

WScript.echo "Sending message..."

on error resume next      ' do not stop on errors
msg.send                  ' deliver the message
send_errno = err.number
on error goto 0           ' restore normal error handling

if send_errno <> 0 then   ' if something went wrong...
    wscript.echo "error sending message"
    wscript.quit 1        ' just quit, as this is an unattended script
end if

wscript.echo nfiles & " file" & plural & " sent to " & recipient

' ................................................................
' ARCHIVE THE FILES
' ................................................................

WScript.echo "Moving files..."
for i = 0 to nfiles-1
    fso.MoveFile filelist(i), archivefolder
next

WScript.echo "Done"
```

Normally, a script like this is used with the Task Scheduler so it can run at appropriate intervals. If you use this technique, be sure to specify cscript as the command to use to run the script. The WScript.Echo statements, which are so useful for debugging, have no effect if the script is run under the Task Scheduler with cscript. However, they stop the program if run with wscript: Nobody ever sees the pop-up boxes or clicks their little OK buttons.

Faxing from Scripts

Microsoft provides faxing software with Windows XP Home Edition; XP Professional; 7; and Vista Business, Enterprise, and Ultimate editions (but not the Vista Home versions). This faxing service has a scriptable interface, so you can send faxes from scripts in much the same way that you can send email.

> **Note**
>
> Before it can send a document as a fax, Windows has to "render" the document as a black-and-white TIF image. This means that to fax a particular document type, you have to have a corresponding application installed and the application has to support printing from the Windows shell. To test this, right-click a document's icon on the desktop or in Windows Explorer, and select Print; it should come out of your default printer. If that doesn't happen, you can't fax this particular document type.

> **Note**
>
> The faxing objects provided with Windows XP can send only one document per fax call. The faxing objects provided with Windows 7 and Vista can send multiple documents as a single fax.

Several objects are used when working with the Fax service. The only three you have to use are `FAXCOMEx.FaxDocument`, `FAXCOMEx.FaxRecipient`, and `FAXCOMEx.FaxSender`. Reference Lists 6.6, 6.7, and 6.8 provide a list of the most important properties and methods of these objects.

REFERENCE LIST 6.6   Properties and Methods of the `FAXCOMEx.FaxDocument` Object (Partial List)

Properties:

Body

Full path and name of the file to send as a fax. The file must either already be a fax-encoded TIF image file or be a document of a type that Windows can automatically print using a standard or installed application associated with the file's extension (for example, Microsoft Word for a `.doc` file). The fax service uses the associated application to "print" the document to TIF image format.

Bodies

On Windows 7, Vista, and Windows Server 2008 (but not XP or earlier Server versions), you can transmit multiple documents in one fax by assigning an array of filenames to the `Bodies` property, rather than assigning a single file name to the `Body` property. Each element of the array must be a string containing the full path and name of a file.

CoverPageType

Specifies whether to send a cover page with the fax and where to locate the cover page template file. The possible values are listed in Table 6.15.

Table 6.15 **Values for** CoverPageType

Value	Description
fcptNONE (0)	No cover page is sent.
fcptLOCAL (1)	The cover page template is taken from the current user's custom cover page folder.
fcptServer (2)	The cover page template is taken from the computer's system-wide cover page template folder.

If CoverPageType is set to 1 or 2, property Coverpage must be set to the name of a cover page template file.

CoverPage

The name of the cover page template file (.cov file) to use for this fax.

If CoverPageType is set to fcptLOCAL (1), the name might specify a full path. If no path is specified, the script user's personal cover page folder is used (%userprofile%\[My]Documents\Fax\Personal Coverpages).

If CoverPageType is set to fcptServer (2), the CoverPage name must not include a path. The file is taken from the fax service computer's system-wide cover page folder, which is \Documents and Settings\All Users\Application Data\Microsoft\Windows NT\MSFax\Common Coverpages on XP, and \Program Data\Microsoft\WIndowsNT\MSFax\Common Coverpages\xx, where xx stands for your local language code—for example, en-US on Windows 7 and Vista.

You can create cover page templates with the Cover Page Editor tool provided with Windows. The editor lets you put text, graphics, and "fill-in fields" anywhere on the cover page. The fill-in fields are filled in with values you assign to the FaxDocument object's properties.

DocumentName

A descriptive name for this fax. The name is displayed in the Fax manager's queue and archive listing but is not transmitted to the recipient.

Note
Subject

Text to use to fill in the "Note" and "Subject" fields on the cover page. These values are optional.

Recipients

A collection of FaxRecipient objects, initially empty. You can add an arbitrary number of recipients using the collection's Add method. If you add more than one recipient, multiple faxes are queued up.

Sender

A `FAXCOMEX.FaxSender` object describing you, the fax sender. You need to create a `FaxSender` object separately and then assign it to this property.

Methods:

Submit(*servername***)**

Submits the fax document to the specified faxing computer for queuing and transmission. Use the empty string `""` to specify the local computer, or specify the name of a Windows Server computer running the shared fax service.

The return value is an array listing fax queue identification numbers, one for each recipient. Even if you specified only one recipient, the returned value is still an array with one element at index 0. If you want, you can use these ID numbers to locate and manage the fax using other fax service objects.

▶ **Note**

Windows occasionally fails to create and queue a fax but doesn't generate an error. The only way you'll know the submission failed is that the returned queue ID value is a string of all zero digits.

▶ **Note**

If you do want to use scripting to track and manage faxes, you should know that the fax queue ID is a 64-bit number. On Windows 7, Vista, and Windows Server 2008, `Submit` returns an array containing the ID values as 16-character hexadecimal strings, which you can pass to the other Fax Server objects to locate the fax. On XP and Windows Server 2003, however, the values in the array are *decimal* strings, which are useless as is. Worse, VBScript's built-in conversion functions can't convert such large numbers to hex for you. Later in this section I show you a routine that can do this for you.

ConnectedSubmit(*serverobj***)**

If your script created a `FAXCOMEX.FaxServer` object that is connected to your fax service, instead of `Submit` you can use `ConnectedSubmit`, passing it a reference to the `FaxServer` object.

REFERENCE LIST 6.7   Properties and Methods of the `FAXCOMEx.FaxSender` Object (Partial List)

Properties:

`City, Company, Country, Department, Email, FaxNumber, HomePhone, Name, OfficeLocation, OfficePhone, State, StreetAddress, Title, ZipCode`

Contact information and information about your location, which is used to fill in fields on the cover page. These are all string values and can be left blank or unset if you don't care to use them or if you are not using a cover page.

TSID

The transmitting subscriber identifier (TSID) string that is sent to the recipient's fax machine. This is limited to 20 ASCII characters and is typically your fax number. (The fax service ignores this value and sends its preconfigured TSID value if the server's `Configuration.UseDeviceTSID` value is `True`.)

Methods:

LoadDefaultSender

Fills in the property values (`City` and so on) with values set up when you configured the fax service on your computer or values saved earlier with the `SaveDefaultSender` method.

SaveDefaultSender

Saves the current property values as your user account's default values.

Reference List 6.8 lists the two properties of a `FaxRecipient` object. Generally, you do not create these objects directly. Instead, you typically use the `Add` method to add recipients to the `FaxDocument` object's `FaxRecipients` collection, as I show you in the sample script.

REFERENCE LIST 6.8   Properties and Methods of the `FAXCOMEx.FaxRecipient` **Object (Partial List)**

Properties:

FaxNumber

A string value specifying the recipient's fax number. This property determines who gets the fax. All dialing codes, area codes, and so on must be included. Dashes, spaces, and parentheses can be included but are ignored. A comma causes a 1-second delay and can be used to wait for a secondary dial tone. For example, "9,18005551212" dials the digit 9, pauses 1 second, and then dials 1-800-555-1212.

Name

The recipient's name. This value is used to fill in the corresponding field on the cover page.

Sending a Fax with a Script

To send a fax, perform the following steps:

- Create a `FAXComEx.FaxDocument` object. Set the `Body` or `Bodies` property with the full path to the document(s) you want to fax, and then set the cover page type and name.

- Call the `Faxdocument's Recipients.Add` method once for each desired recipient for the fax.

- If you are using a cover page, set any properties of the `FaxDocument`'s `Sender` object needed for the cover page.

- Finally, call the `FaxDocument`'s `Submit` method. Check the value(s) in the returned array to ensure that the fax is successfully queued.

The following sample script shows how this can be done:

```
                                        ' Example file script0604.vbs
set faxdoc = CreateObject("FAXCOMEx.FaxDocument")

with faxdoc
    .Body = "c:\scripts\06\memo.doc"        ' full path to document

    .Recipients.Add "1-510-500-5599", "John Doe" ' add recipient

    .DocumentName  = "Fax to John Doe"        ' set queue display name

    .CoverPage     = "generic.cov"        ' use shared "generic" cover
    .CoverPageType = 2                     ' (fcptSERVER)

    .Subject       = "Test Fax"           ' set cover sheet properties
    .Note          = "Remarks for the cover sheet"
    with .Sender
        .Name        = "My Name"
        .Company     = "My Company"
        .FaxNumber   = "1-510-555-1212"
        .OfficePhone = "1-510-555-2323"
        .TSID        = .FaxNumber
    end with
end with

faxdoc.Submit("")                         ' queue the fax
```

After the fax has been submitted, if you want, you can use other fax service objects to monitor the progress of your fax and see whether it was successfully delivered or failed due to a wrong or busy number. There isn't space to go into a lot of detail about that here, but I can give you some pointers.

First of all, as I mentioned previously, to track faxes you need to know the fax's queue ID value, which is returned by Submit. The return value from Submit is an array of one or more string values containing the ID number(s) of the fax(es) that was queued—one fax per recipient. The returned number is represented in hexadecimal on Vista and Windows 7. On XP, the value is returned in *decimal*, which is essentially useless: you have to convert it to hexadecimal before you can use it to look up the fax's status through other fax service objects. With that in mind, here's a bit of code that extracts the queue ID from a single-recipient fax:

```
...
id = faxdoc.Submit("")     ' submit the fax, and save the returned array
faxid = id(0)              ' get the ID string from the array
```

If you know that you are running the script on XP, add one more line of code to convert the ID string from decimal to hexadecimal, using this call:

```
faxid = ConvertDecToHex64(faxid)  ' convert decimal to hex
```

Note
Function `ConvertDecToHex64` is provided in `sendfax.vbs` in the set of sample scripts you can download from www.helpwin7.com/scripting.

If you won't know in advance whether the script will be run on XP, Vista, or Windows 7, use this code instead:

```
vistaOrBetter = False
for each os in GetObject( _
            "winmgmts:\\.\root\cimv2:Win32_OperatingSystem").Instances_
    if os.version >= "6" then vistaOrBetter = True
next
if not vistaOrBetter then faxid = ConvertDecToHex64(faxid) ' convert to hex
```

This uses Windows Management Instrumentation (WMI) to determine the operating system version. WMI is discussed in Chapter 7, "Windows Management Instrumentation."

After you have the fax's queue ID, you can look for it in the outgoing queue and the outgoing archive as follows:

```
set server = CreateObject("FAXCOMEx.FaxServer")  ' create server object
server.connect ""              ' connect to local computer's fax service

set ogQueue   = server.Folders.OutgoingQueue    ' get references to queue
set ogArchive = server.Folders.OutgoingArchive  ' and archive of sent faxes

Set ogFax = Nothing            ' try to find fax in the outgoing queue
on error resume next
Set ogFax = ogQueue.GetJob(faxid)
On Error GoTo 0
If Not ogFax Is Nothing Then
    ' found it in the queue; it's still pending, or it failed too many times
    wscript.echo "Fax is in the outgoing queue"
    wscript.echo "Status:", ogFax.status, _
                "Extended status:", ogFax.ExtendedStatusCode
else
    ' was not in the queue, so try to find it in the archive of sent faxes
    set sentFax = Nothing
    on error resume next
    set sentFax = ogArchive.GetMessage(faxid)
    on error goto 0
    if sentFax is Nothing then
        ' it's not in the archive either, must have been deleted
        wscript.echo "Could not find fax", faxid, "anywhere"
    else
        ' found it in the archive. Display delivery time and recipient CSID
        wscript.echo "Fax was delivered at", sentFax.TransmissionEnd, _
                "to", sentFax.CSID
    end if
end if
```

For faxes in the outgoing queue, the `status` and `ExtendedStatusCode` values tell whether the fax is still queued for sending or whether it is undeliverable. The full-length script `sendfax.vbs` included in the set of downloadable sample scripts shows how to decode these values.

Getting More Information About Faxing

For more information about the fax service objects, visit msdn.microsoft.com and search for "Fax Service Extended COM Reference." Be warned, though, that this documentation is confusing and has inaccuracies. Here are some tips to help navigate through it:

- Be careful not to get led by the search engine or links within the documenta-tion into any content under the heading "Fax Service Client API for Windows 2000." That documentation is not correct for Windows XP or later.

- Start with the section titled "Fax Service Objects" under Fax Service Extended COM Reference, and examine the `FaxServer` and `FaxDocument` objects.

- You will see object interfaces whose names end with a 2—for example, `IFaxDocument2`. The 2 refers to additional functionality, methods, and properties when you use the objects on Windows 7, Vista, and Windows Server 2008. Don't type the 2 when you're writing your script, however. Use the original object names as shown in the examples in this section.

- The documentation is aimed at programmers using Visual C++ or the full version of Visual Basic, not VBScript. In some cases, it makes references to arguments and return values that don't apply to scripting. To get the syntax right, use Google to search for sample scripts that use the objects, methods, or properties you're interested in, or use the Object Browser (discussed in Chapter 3, "Scripting and Objects") to look up the syntax for scripting. To use the Object Browser, you need to open a reference to the "Microsoft Fax Service Extended COM Type Library," file `fxscomex.dll`.

7

Windows Management Instrumentation

IN THIS CHAPTER

- This chapter shows how to use WMI to manage computers over a network.

- WMI can do something as simple as shutting down a computer or as complex as documenting its every setting.

- You cannot remotely manage Windows XP Home Edition with WMI scripts.

- This is hairy stuff. You should be familiar with the material in Chapter 3, "Scripting and Objects," and Chapter 4, "File and Registry Access," before reading this chapter.

- You might have run into the acronyms WBEM and CIM. This chapter discusses these as well.

Introduction to Windows Management Instrumentation

If you own even just one Windows computer, you know that maintenance can be a frustrating, time-consuming job. Multiply this by hundreds or thousands, and imagine what corporate IT managers face every day. Just keeping track of the computer inventory is a large-enough task; then there are the frequent network configuration changes, the addition and removal of network printers, updating applications and moving-target shared folders—not to mention crashes, hardware failures, and user-induced disasters. Keeping an organization's computers together is like trying to hold 50 Ping-Pong balls underwater with your bare hands. An IT job can be a one-way ticket to a padded cell and some very serious medication.

One way out of this mess is to eliminate, to the extent possible, the need to walk from computer to computer to make changes. On large networks, Active Directory can help by automating the installation of application software, enforcing consistent configuration, and restricting access to Windows components and settings. Windows Management Instrumentation (WMI) can help with the rest of the maintenance burden.

WMI provides a way to peer into the inner workings of Windows, to monitor settings, and make changes. Like the Performance Monitor, WMI has its fingers into just about every aspect of the Windows operating system, including device drivers, system services, and applications. WMI works over a network, so one computer running a WMI monitoring program (or script…hint, hint) can get into any computer on the organization's network.

WMI isn't just for management and maintenance. You can use it to create documentation describing your organization's computers, hardware configurations, connections, settings, operating systems, installed applications, applied hotfixes, and so on.

Needless to say, WMI is a huge topic—it could easily fill several books this size—so I can only provide a brief overview in this chapter. However, even though WMI is complex, and its details can be a bit confusing, in practice WMI is actually pretty straightforward to use. So that the background material that follows doesn't scare you off, here's a short sample script:

```
set ns = GetObject("winmgmts:\\.\root\CIMV2")
set disks = ns.InstancesOf("Win32_LogicalDisk")
for each dsk in disks
    wscript.echo dsk.name, "has", dsk.FreeSpace, "bytes free"
next
```

You can see at a glance that this script scans through a list of disk drives and displays the name and amount of free space on each drive. The "root\CIMV2" part is peculiar, but past that, it's not so bad.

On your first reading of this chapter, you might want to skip ahead to the section titled "WMI Examples," where you'll see WMI perform other practical tasks, and then come back and read the intervening sections that provide more detailed background. At the end of the chapter, I list some websites and books that can lead you to more information.

Note

In addition to WMI, Microsoft has another remote management system called Windows Remote Management (WinRM). I talk about WinRM later in the chapter.

WMI Functions

Because it's called on to manage many types of hardware and software, under many versions of Windows, one of the main goals for WMI is to standardize the way computer management information is organized. Every piece of hardware as well as every parameter and setting in every component of Windows has to be given a fixed name, so that WMI-aware programs can refer to them. WMI uses an organized system of names that look a lot like the path names of files and folders and of Registry keys.

This naming scheme is based on Common Information Model (CIM). CIM is an industry-wide standard concocted by the Distributed Management Task Force (DMTF), of which Microsoft is a member, along with Cisco, Hewlett-Packard, IBM, Intel, Oracle…in other words, everybody. (And, as you'd expect of the output of any such committee, it tries to be everything for everyone, and in doing so, it's hopelessly complex.)

Namespaces

In the CIM scheme, the various groups of setting and parameter names are organized into groups called *namespaces*, which are conceptually like folders. In each namespace is a set of objects that describe some aspect of the computer's hardware or software. The primary namespaces are listed in Table 7.1.

Table 7.1 **WMI Namespaces**

Namespace	Description
Root\aspnet	Objects representing ASP.NET (web service) applications and events.
Root\CIMV2	Objects representing Windows, hardware, and software. This namespace is the primary one you'll use for Windows management.
Root\Cli	Holds command aliases used by the command-line tool wmic; you can ignore this namespace.
Root\DEFAULT	Objects representing the Registry and System Restore.
Root\directory	Objects related to Active Directory.
Root\Interop	Contains CIM linkage information about configuration profiles such as power management plans.
Root\Microsoft\Homenet	Internet Connection Sharing and Personal Firewall configuration.
Root\nap	Configuration of the Network Access Protection system.
Root\Policy	Access to Group Policy configuration.
Root\RSOP	Access to Group Policy "Resultant Set of Policy" data for enterprise management applications.
Root\SECURITY	Objects related to WMI security.
Root\SecurityCenter	Information about installed antivirus, firewall, and other security products.
Root\SecurityCenter2	(Same stuff, different object model.)
Root\ServiceModel	Configuration for web services.
Root\subscription	Linkage information for handling of WMI events.
Root\WMI	Objects related to low-level networking and interface hardware performance statistics.

Other namespaces may appear as well, if you've installed WMI-integrated services and applications such as the Simple Network Monitoring Protocol (SNMP) service or Microsoft Office.

In each namespace are numerous objects that describe some aspect of Windows, software, or hardware. These objects can be viewed and modified to document or change Windows settings. Although there isn't room to describe all the objects in detail, Table 7.2 gives you an idea of what is available. The table lists just a few of the objects in the major namespace Root\CIMV2. Each of these objects represents some aspect of computer hardware or a Windows software component. In the following sections, I show you how to use a few of them.

Note

You'll see the acronym WBEM appear all over Microsoft's WMI literature. *Web-Based Enterprise Management* is another management standardization initiative, and the acronym WBEM is applied to WMI in an apparently random fashion. In fact, the objects you'll use to work with WMI are part of the WbemScripting object package.

Table 7.2   *Root\CIMV2* **Objects (Partial List)**

Win32_1394Controller	Win32_FloppyDrive
Win32_Account	Win32_IDEController
Win32_ApplicationCommandLine	Win32_IDEControllerDevice
Win32_ApplicationService	Win32_NetworkAdapter
Win32_Battery	Win32_NetworkAdapterConfiguration
Win32_BIOS	Win32_NetworkAdapterSetting
Win32_BootConfiguration	Win32_NTLogEvent
Win32_CDROMDrive	Win32_ODBCDriverAttribute
Win32_ComputerSystemProcessor	Win32_OperatingSystem
Win32_CreateFolderAction	Win32_OperatingSystemQFE
Win32_Desktop	Win32_PnPDevice
Win32_DesktopMonitor	Win32_Printer
Win32_DeviceBus	Win32_PrinterShare
Win32_DeviceSettings	Win32_Registry
Win32_Directory	Win32_Service
Win32_DiskDrive	Win32_Share
Win32_DiskPartition	Win32_ShortcutFile
Win32_DMAChannel	Win32_StartupCommand
Win32_DuplicateFileAction	Win32_SubDirectory
Win32_Environment	Win32_SystemAccount
Win32_Fan	Win32_Thread
Win32_FloppyController	Win32_UserAccount

Each of these object types has its own list of properties and/or methods that describe and control the hardware or software component the object represents. Table 7.2 lists just a small percentage of the available WMI management objects. There are actually hundreds of WMI objects and thousands of settings. Not all the objects' names start with WIN32_. Many objects defined by the CIM standards begin with CIM or other prefixes, but most of these objects have Windows-specific variants that do start with Win32. Those listed here are the ones you'll use most often.

> **Note**
>
> You can explore WMI and the WMI namespaces using the WMIC command-line program provided with Windows XP and later versions. For information about WMIC, open the Windows Help and search for WMIC. There's also a fantastic downloadable tool called Scriptomatic that I discuss later in the chapter.

Managing Windows Remotely

WMI not only lets you write scripts to manage Windows settings on your own computer, but also lets you write scripts to manage other computers, through the network, using Distributed COM (DCOM). DCOM technology lets a computer create and manipulate objects that "live" on another computer, via a network connection. It's no harder to write a script to manage other computers than to manage your own, although, as you are about to see, getting such a script to work can be dicey.

WMI was primarily designed for remote management of computers on a domain network by a domain administrator. So, not surprisingly, it works in this "corporate" scenario without any fuss at all. It *can* work on non-domain, workgroup networks (that is, on home and small office networks), but as you'll see in the following sections, there are conditions and restrictions with which you must contend. It's going to be an unfortunately complex discussion because Microsoft's network security rules are different on each version of Windows, and the rules depend on how the remote computer is configured. For this reason, I discuss each Windows version separately. I also point out issues with Windows Firewall.

> **Note**
>
> In the following sections, when I refer to the *remote* computer, I am referring to the computer that your WMI script is *managing*. When I refer to *your* computer, I am referring to the computer on which you are running the script.

On a Domain Network

If both the remote computer and your computer are members of the same Windows server domain, DCOM uses your domain account to create WMI objects on the remote computer, so your script needs to have the privileges granted to your domain account. Your account needs to be a member of the local Administrators group on the remote computer. This is the default case for any domain administrator (Domain Admin) account, so, remote WMI works for domain administrators without any issues.

If the remote computer runs Windows Vista or Windows 7 and has User Account Control (UAC) enabled, you *must* use a domain account that is a member of the computer's local Administrators group. This is the only situation where Windows gives full "elevated" privileges to objects created from other computers. By default, remote WMI requires elevated privileges.

Note

On the remote computers, Windows Firewall must be configured to permit WMI connections. On a domain network, this should be handled via Group Policy. A network administrator must set this up. Alternatively, you can open the firewall manually by following the instructions for each version of Windows discussed in the next sections.

If the remote computer is a domain member but your computer is not, or if your computer is a member of another, nontrusted domain, then in most cases. remote WMI does not work. In this case, the workgroup (non-domain) access rules apply, as discussed in the following section.

On a Workgroup Network

If either the remote computer or your computer is not a Windows domain member, the remote computer looks in its local user list for an account with the same name as the account you are using on your computer (or, for the account and password you specify in a call to the `ConnectServer` method).

If there is a matching account with the same password, WMI uses that account. If there is no account with the same name as your account, or if the passwords don't match, the remote connection fails.

By default, the matched account must be an Administrator account. If it is not a member of the Administrators group, the connection fails with a `Permission Denied` error.

If you successfully match an Administrator account, remote WMI might work, subject to the version-specific restrictions discussed in the next several sections.

Windows 95, 98, or Me

These obsolete versions of Windows have no user account-based security mechanism, so anyone who can use or connect to the computer can change any setting or file. (This is what makes these operating systems too vulnerable to be used in today's Internet- and network-connected world.) This would be a terrible security risk, but fortunately, WMI and/or DCOM are not enabled by default on these older versions. If you install and enable WMI and DCOM, anyone on your network could use a remote script to make any sort of change without restriction. I don't recommend that you do this.

Windows NT and Windows 2000 Professional

If the remote computer runs Windows NT or Windows 2000 and is a domain member, the rules described previously under "On a Domain Network" apply.

Otherwise, the rules discussed previously under "On a Workgroup Network" apply.

> **Note**
>
> WMI is installed and enabled by default only on Windows versions from XP on up. If you have computers running Windows 9x, 2000, or NT, you might have to enable WMI. You can do this manually, or if the computer is a domain member, you can do this through Group Policy. If you want to manage these older operating systems remotely, you have to be sure that the DCOM service is enabled on the computers as well.

Windows XP Home Edition

You cannot use WMI to manage XP Home Edition remotely. The Simple File Sharing feature is always enabled on XP Home Edition, so all network access to the computer occurs in the context of the Guest user account. The Guest account has insufficient privileges to create WMI objects via a network connection.

Windows XP Professional

If the remote computer runs Windows XP Professional and is a domain member, the rules described previously under "On a Domain Network" apply.

If the computer has Simple File Sharing enabled (which is the default setting), remote WMI does not work because all network access to the computer occurs in the context of the Guest account. If Simple File Sharing has been disabled, the account-matching rules discussed previously under "On a Workgroup Network" apply.

> **Note**
>
> On the remote computer, Windows Firewall must be configured to permit WMI connections. To do this on XP Pro, in a command prompt window, type the **command gpedit.msc**. Open Local Computer Policy, Computer Configuration, Administrative Templates, Network, Network Connections, Windows Firewall, Standard Profile. Double-click Windows Firewall allow Remote Administrative Exception, check Enabled, and enter the appropriate network address(es). For small networks, the entry `localsubnet` should work.

Windows Vista

If the remote computer runs Windows Vista and is a domain member, the rules described previously under "On a Domain Network" apply.

Otherwise, it's difficult to manage the computer remotely via WMI.

If Password Protected Sharing is turned off, remote WMI does not work because all remote access occurs through the Guest account.

If User Account Control is enabled, remote WMI does not work because it requires full, elevated Administrator privileges and remote connections get elevated privileges only in the domain scenario, as discussed previously. (You can get around this by reducing the privileges required by remote WMI. Follow the instructions under "Handling Remote Connections Under UAC" in the online article titled "User Account and WMI," which I discuss shortly. Be warned, though—it's a complex task, and you can't use remote WMI to change settings that require Administrator privileges.)

If User Account Control is turned off (which I *strongly* discourage) and Password Protected Sharing is enabled, remote WMI works, subject to the account-matching rules discussed previously under "On a Workgroup Network."

Note

On the remote computer, Windows Firewall must be configured to permit WMI connections. To do this on Windows Vista, open the Control Panel, click Allow A Program Through Windows Firewall, and check the box next to Windows Management Instrumentation (WMI).

Windows 7

If the remote computer runs Windows 7 and is a domain member, the rules described previously under "On a Domain Network" apply.

Otherwise, it's difficult to manage the computer remotely via WMI.

If User Account Control is enabled, remote WMI does not work because it requires full "elevated" Administrator privileges, as discussed in the previous section titled "Windows Vista."

If User Account Control is turned off (which I *strongly* discourage), remote WMI works, subject to the account-matching rules discussed previously under "On a Workgroup Network." There's an additional, weird condition: If your computer and the remote computer are both Windows 7 Homegroup members, even with User Account Control turned off, remote WMI doesn't work unless you use the ConnectToServer method and specify an Administrator account. Otherwise, the special HomeGroupUser$ account is used for the connection, and it does not have Administrator privileges.

▶ **Note**

On the remote computer, Windows Firewall must be configured to permit WMI connections. To do this on Windows 7, open the Control Panel and click System and Security, Allow A Program Through Windows Firewall. Locate the entry for Windows Management Instrumentation (WMI) and check the box in the Work/Home column.

The Bottom Line

I know this is terribly convoluted, but it's the result of Microsoft changing (improving?) the Windows network security scheme with every new version. On the bright side, you probably only want to use remote management on large networks, and because most large networks are domain networks, these version issues aren't a problem. For smaller organizations, you can always walk around and run management scripts directly on each computer, so the network—and the attendant security complications—aren't involved.

▶ **Note**

For more information about remote WMI, visit msdn.microsoft.com and search for the following articles:

- Connecting to WMI Remotely Starting with Windows Vista
- Connecting Between Different Operating Systems
- Connecting Through Windows Firewall
- Securing a Remote WMI Connection
- User Account Control and WMI

Making WMI Connections

WMI is one of the service processes that runs "behind the scenes" in Windows. It's always there, waiting for a client program—that is, a script or other management program—to connect to it. WMI provides COM objects that let a script interact with the underlying Windows settings and values. Figure 7.1 illustrates how this works. Your script uses WbemScripting objects that communicate with the WMI service on a selected computer. WMI returns information about the computer through the WbemScripting object's methods and properties and then saves changes back to the remote computer. The "remote computer" can be *any* computer on the network, even the same computer that is running the script, although there can be limitations due to network security, as discussed in the previous section.

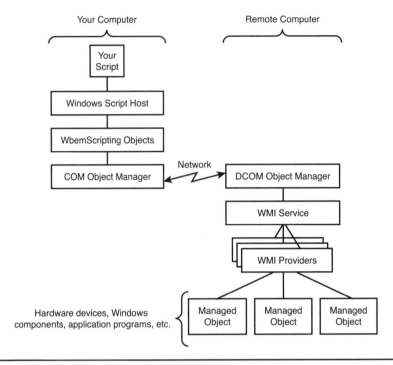

Figure 7.1   A WMI client program communicates with the WMI service on a specified computer, which dips into Windows settings through WMI provider services.

WMI Object Hierarchy

WMI uses several objects to represent the connection to another computer, its namespaces, the objects within the namespaces, and so on. The primary objects are listed in Table 7.3. On your first reading, just give this table a once-over and come back to it later after you've read the rest of the chapter and have seen these objects in use.

Table 7.3   The Primary `WbemScripting` **Objects**

Object	Purpose
`SwbemLocator`	Establishes a connection to a remote computer and returns one of the objects in this list.
`SwbemSecurity`	Configures the security settings that WMI is to use for a connection to another computer.
`SWbemServices`	Represents a connection to a namespace on a managed computer. This is an unusual object that is discussed later in the chapter.

Object	Purpose
SWbemObjectSet	A collection of SWbemObject objects, most commonly used to represent one of the major categories in a namespace (for example, one of the items shown earlier in Table 7.2). The collection represents the Windows components in the category.
SWbemObject	One instance of a managed item, such as a network connection, a file, a hard drive, or a user account. The methods and properties of SWbemObject are variable and depend on the type of item the object represents. This object is discussed later in the chapter.
	Because the methods and properties are variable, the remaining four object types can be used to provide a sort of self-documentation. As I'll show you, you can use them to see which properties and methods are provided as part of any WMI object you encounter.
SWbemMethodSet	A collection of SWbemMethod objects that lists the methods available for a given SWbemObject object.
SWbemMethod	Describes the purpose of and parameters used with a given method.
SWbemPropertySet	A collection of SWbemProperty objects that lists the properties available for a given SWbemObject object.
SWbemProperty	Describes the purpose and data type of a given property.

Note

For complete documentation on all the WMI objects, check out Microsoft's online WMI documentation, as discussed at the end of this chapter.

As mentioned earlier, WMI objects are nested like folders and files. For example, you might specify a file path as c:\documents\myproject\plan.doc. WMI objects can be specified using a similar path naming system. Table 7.4 lists paths starting from the CIMV2 namespace to a specific instance of a Win32_LogicalDisk object that manages the "C:" drive. Figure 7.2 illustrates the relationships between the various levels of objects in this example, and shows some of the methods and properties that can be used to obtain one from the other. GetObject can create an object at any level, given its path.

Note

If you are using a scripting language other than VBScript or JScript, the GetObject function might not be available. You can use the wscript.GetObject method instead.

In the previous example, only one property (`DeviceID`) is needed to select a specific object from an `ObjectSet`. Some objects require more than one property to be specified to get a single object.

Table 7.4 **Examples of WMI Path Specifications and Resulting Objects**

Path	Leads To
`\\Java\root\cimv2`	`SWbemServices`
`\\Java\root\cimv2:Win32_LogicalDisk`	`SWbemObject`
`\\Java\root\cimv2:Win32_LogicalDisk.Instances_`	`SWbemObjectSet`
`\\JAVA\root\cimv2:Win32_LogicalDisk.DeviceID="C:"`	SWbemObject

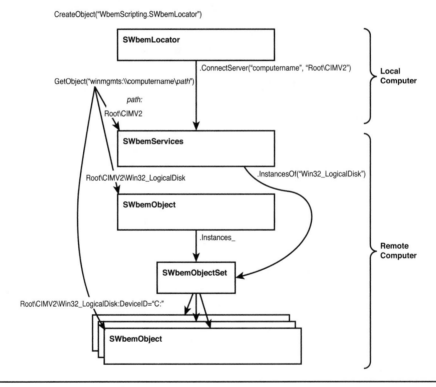

Figure 7.2 Relationship between various levels of the WMI object hierarchy.

When you create a WMI connection to a remote computer, you can specify how "deep" an object you want to extract. If you want to examine many objects, you might want to start with one of the top-level objects and then have your script scan through the objects within it. If you're only concerned with one specific item, you can specify the full path to the object and save yourself the trouble of digging for it.

> **Note**
>
> Because CIM is supposed to be operating system and platform independent, WMI treats / and \
> identically in pathnames. You can use either. Also, the object and parameter names are case insensitive.

You can establish a connection to a remote computer in two ways: You can use an
SWbemLocator object, or you can use object monikers to obtain objects from their
pathname. Both methods are discussed in the following sections.

Connecting with the WbemScripting.SWbemLocator Object

You can connect to WMI on the local computer or a remote computer by creating an
SWbemLocator object and using its ConnectServer method to establish a connection to
a desired computer. Let's suppose that we want to work with a computer named Java
and that we want to examine its CIMV2 namespace. The following statements show
how to make a connection using the Locator object:

```
set locator = CreateObject("WbemScripting.SWbemLocator")
set svcs = locator.ConnectServer("Java", "root\CIMV2")
```

This yields object svcs, which is an SWbemServices object that represents the
root\CIMV2 namespace on the computer Java. I'll show you how to use svcs to manage the remote computer later in the chapter.

The ConnectServer method can take several optional arguments. Its syntax is

ConnectServer(*servername*, *namespace* [, *username*, *password*], [*locale*],
    [*authority*], [*security*], [*namedvalueset*])

The parameters are described in Table 7.5.

Table 7.5 **Parameters for the** ConnectServer **Method**

Parameter	Description
Servername	The name of the computer to which to connect. If this parameter is blank or omitted, the connection is made to the local computer (the one on which the script is running).
Namespace	The namespace to which to connect (for example, "Root\CIMV2"). If this parameter is blank or omitted, the default namespace is used (usually CIMV2, but this can be changed by the WMI management tool described earlier).
Username	Optional. The username to use when connecting to the remote computer. You cannot specify an alternate username when connecting to the local computer. The default username is the name of the account you're using on the computer from which you run the script.

continues

Table 7.5 **Continued**

Parameter	Description
Password	Optional. The password to use when connecting to the remote computer.
Locale	Localization (language) code. For example, `"MS_409"` specifies American English. If this parameter is left blank, the Windows default locale is used.
Authority	The authentication method to use when connecting: `"kerberos"`, `"NTLM"`, or `"negotiated"`. If this parameter is omitted, `"negotiated"` is the default and is the best choice in almost all cases.
Security	This argument is not used, and it must be `0` (zero) or omitted.
Namedvalueset	This argument is not useful in scripts and should be omitted.

The username and password parameters might be required if you want to connect to a computer on which you have no account or on which you do not have Administrator privileges. Without Administrator privileges, you can sometimes connect to WMI and view properties, but cannot make changes. It's not a good idea to store passwords in scripts, however, so if you don't run your management script from a privileged account that has the necessary permissions by default, you should have the script prompt you for the necessary password.

➔ For more information about how Windows applies security rules to remote WMI connections, **see** "Managing Windows Remotely," **p. 283.**

The object returned by `ConnectServer` is an `SWbemServices` collection that you can examine or from which you can extract any desired `SWbemService` objects. I'll cover this in the section titled "`SWbemServices`."

Connecting with a Moniker

The second method of creating a connection uses a *moniker*—a pathname version of an object—and the `GetObject` function, which was discussed in Chapter 3. The moniker for a WMI object always starts with the string `"winmgmts:"`. The following statement shows how to make a connection using a moniker:

```
set svcs = GetObject("winmgmts:\\java\CIMV2")
```

This statement produces the same `SWbemServices` collection as the `ConnectServer` example in the previous section. With this method, however, you could specify a deeper pathname and get a specific management object, if that is all you needed. Table 7.4 shows how you might obtain lower-level WMI objects by specifying a longer path to `GetObject`.

Which method should you use? The moniker method is a bit easier to write, whereas the `Locator` method runs faster when your script needs to access many objects and/or computers. If you want to process a long list of computers, you might be better off using a script like this:

```
                          ' Example File script0701.vbs
set locator = CreateObject("WbemScripting.SWbemLocator")
manage "java"            ' manage each of the computers in turn
manage "bali"
manage "ambon"
manage "sumatra"
manage "kalimantan"
manage "buru"


' ---------------------------------------------------------
' subroutine 'manage' works with the specified computer

sub manage (computername)
    on error resume next ' make connection while trapping errors
    set svcs = locator.ConnectServer(computername, "root\CIMV2")
    errnum = err.number
    errmsg = err.description
    on error resume next
    if errnum <> 0 then  ' connection failed; say why and return
        wscript.echo computername, errmsg
        exit sub
    end if

    ' … (work with object svcs to manage the computer)

    set svcs = Nothing  ' delete the object and terminate the connection
end sub                 ' end of subroutine
```

▶ **Note**

If the computer name you specify after \ \ in the moniker string uses the dotted domain format (for example, `computer.mycompany.com`), Windows uses Domain Name System to resolve the name. If you specify a simple name, Windows tries to find the name with DNS first using the default domain name(s) associated with your computer and network connection(s). If the name is not found there, it tries the NetBIOS resolver. As a result, WMI does not work if your network's DNS system has the wrong IP addresses for your computers.

Although the moniker technique can be simpler to code, the `Locator` method lets you specify an Administrator account name and password. Therefore, you should use it if you want to connect to a remote computer and run your script from a non-Administrator account.

Connecting to the Local Computer

WMI lets you manage *any* networked computer, including the one on which you're running the script. You can connect to the "local" computer using either of the two connection methods described in the previous sections. Then, you can either specify the name of the computer directly, specify the name as ".", or *omit* the computer name entirely. For example, if the local computer is named JAVA, any of these statements returns the SWbemServices collection of JAVA's CIMV2 namespace:

```
set svcs = locator.ConnectServer("JAVA", "root\CIMV2")
set svcs = locator.ConnectServer(".", "root\CIMV2")
set svcs = locator.ConnectServer("", "root\CIMV2")

set svcs = GetObject("winmgmts:\\java\root\CIMV2")
set svcs = GetObject("winmgmts:\\.\root\CIMV2")
set svcs = GetObject("winmgmts:\root\CIMV2")
```

Because CIMV2 is the default namespace (unless you've changed the default), the following statements also produce the same result:

```
set svcs = locator.ConnectServer("JAVA", "")
set svcs = locator.ConnectServer(".", "")
set svcs = locator.ConnectServer("", "")
set svcs = GetObject("winmgmts:\\java")
set svcs = GetObject("winmgmts:\\.")
set svcs = GetObject("winmgmts:")
```

Note

You can change the default namespace if you want; right-click [My] Computer, select Manage, open Services and Applications, right-click WMI Control, select Properties, select the Advanced tab, and then click Change. Or, you can modify the Default Namespace value in the Registry key HKLM\SOFTWARE\Microsoft\WBEM\Scripting.

Connections to the local machine *always* use your user account, and you cannot specify an alternative account to ConnectServer. However, for local connections, you don't have to use an Administrator account if all you want do is to view Windows properties and settings.

Security and Authentication

If WMI can really do all it's cracked up to do, from altering network settings to shutting down a computer to creating or modifying user accounts, then you know it must be subject to strict security restrictions.

It is, and here's how these restrictions work: WMI security is based on the remote connection facilities that are part of DCOM. There are four aspects to DCOM security:

- **Authentication**—Identifies you to the remote computer.
- **Encryption**—Protects the information transmitted between computers from eavesdropping.
- **Impersonation**— Causes the remote DCOM service (and therefore WMI) to run in the context of *your* login account instead of the high-privilege SYSTEM account that most services use.
- **Permission** control—Lets you specify which system privileges a remote management task requires.

I regret to say that it's going to take several pages to go through this process, but it's necessary. WMI usually does not work properly without you making special consideration of these security details.

Authentication and Encryption

By default, the connection to a remote computer uses the identity of whatever account you use to run the script. This is *your* account when you run a script from the command line or the specified account if you use the Task Scheduler. The DCOM service on the remote computer checks your logon credential to see whether you are permitted to use that computer and what permissions you're allowed. On a domain network, the security identifier (SID) associated with your account is recognized by all computers on the network, and you'll have the permissions appropriate to your domain account. On a workgroup network or on a foreign domain, Windows might send your username and password in encrypted form to the remote computer. If an account with this name and password exists on the remote computer, you get access.

Tip

To use WMI on a workgroup (peer-to-peer) network, you'll have to make sure that each computer you want to manage has an account set up with the same username and password as the account you use to run the script. Furthermore, if Simple File Sharing is turned on (on XP) or Password Protected Sharing is turned off (on Windows 7 or Vista), WMI doesn't work because all network access uses the Guest account and Guest can't use WMI or DCOM.

Normally, your computer remains connected as long as your script maintains an object that refers to the remote computer, and one user-password check is enough. You can step up the security by having DCOM verify your logon credential every time it makes a request; this might help prevent someone with hostile intent and a direct connection to your network from hijacking the DCOM connection and making management operations on your behalf. The security can be turned up even further by making Windows encrypt each data packet sent between the two computers. Table 7.6 lists the various authentication and encryption options in ascending order of paranoia.

Table 7.6   **Authentication and Encryption Modes**

Name	Value	Constant Name/Description
Default	0	`wbemAuthenticationLevelDefault`—The default Windows setting. This varies between versions of WMI and of Windows, so it's best to specify one of the following levels explicitly.
None	1	`wbemAuthenticationLevelNone`—No authentication; the connection is made as Guest.
Connect	2	`wbemAuthenticationLevelConnect`—Authenticates just once, during the initial connection. This is the usual value to use.
Call	3	`wbemAuthenticationLevelCall`—Checks authentication at every WMI request.
Pkt	4	`wbemAuthenticationLevelPkt`—Authenticates every packet of data sent to WMI.
PktIntegrity	5	`wbemAuthenticationLevelPktIntegrity`—Like Pkt, but this mode additionally verifies that the data packets have not been tampered with.
PktPrivacy	6	`wbemAuthenticationLevelPktPrivacy`—This mode is like Pkt, but additionally every data packet is encrypted. This is the most secure value.

In most cases, Connect mode works and is the default. However, on some networks, the administrators might require a higher security level, so the default level might not work and attempts to use WMI results in error messages. In this case, you might need to specify a higher level when you make a WMI connection. You learn how to use alternate authentication modes in the next section.

Note

You can use the numerical values for these constants, or you can create named constants for these values and use them in your scripts. Alternately, you can write your scripts using the `.wsf` file format, which is discussed in Chapter 10, "The CMD Command-Line." In a `.wsf` file, you can use a `<reference>` tag to automatically import all of WMI's named constants.

Impersonation

Normally, WMI runs as a system service, part of the Windows operating system itself, and has unlimited access to all parts of Windows. Although WMI is designed to check your logon credentials and only perform tasks that your account is authorized to perform, WMI's designers understand the likelihood that WMI contains programming bugs and that these bugs could be exploited by an unscrupulous programmer.

Therefore, there's a chance that the authentication scheme might not be adequate to prevent network users from using WMI to gain access to all parts of the computer. WMI is set up to minimize this risk by running under *your* login account when you've connected to it remotely. This is called *impersonation*, and the result is that WMI can't do any more damage than you could if you are sitting right at the computer. When you connect with an Administrator-level account, WMI has that account's full access, but an "average Joe" isn't able to take over the computer.

Table 7.7 lists the various impersonation options that WMI can use.

Table 7.7 **Connection Impersonation Modes**

Name	Value	Constant Name/Description
Anonymous	1	`WbemImpersonationLevelAnonymous`—Prevents WMI from sending your user credentials to the remote computer. Note that most computers are configured to reject Anonymous connections.
Identify	2	`WbemImpersonationLevelIdentify`—Lets the remote WMI service verify the connecting user's identity but lets the service run at its "native" privilege level. This mode is not usually permitted.
Impersonate	3	`WbemImpersonationLevelImpersonate`—The remote computer's WMI service runs as if the authenticated user is logged on. This is the most likely setting to work and for most versions of Windows is the default mode.
Delegate	4	`WbemImpersonationLevelDelegate`—Lets the remote computer's WMI providers use the impersonated user's identity when connecting to yet another computer to gather information. This is supported only on a domain network with Kerberos authentication.

Normally, WMI requires that an *incoming* connection must use impersonation (options 3 or 4). However, versions of the WMI scripting objects prior to Windows XP Service Pack 2 might not specify impersonation mode by default when making connections *to* remote computers. If you know that all the computers on which your scripts will be run are Windows XP SP2 or better, the default impersonation setting should work. Otherwise, you should not count on the default setting being correct, and should specify that you want WMI to use impersonation. You learn how to specify impersonation options in the next section.

Note

You can check or set the default mode used by outgoing connections on a given computer by examining or changing the Registry value `Default Impersonation Level` in the key `HKLM\SOFTWARE\Microsoft\WBEM\Scripting` to one of the numeric values listed in Table 7.7. You can do a quick check by typing the following command:

```
reg query HKLM\SOFTWARE\Microsoft\WBEM\Scripting
```

Privileges

Thanks to the authentication and impersonation mechanisms, you can perform any action through WMI that the user account you're using is allowed to perform. However, some standard user privileges are not normally granted to WMI and have to be explicitly enabled when you make the WMI connection. If you need to perform operations governed by these privileges, you will have to inform WMI that you intend to use them by specifying privilege options when you make the WMI connection to the remote computer.

Note

You can't request a privilege that the user account WMI is using doesn't normally have. If you try to specify one, the connection to the remote computer fails. You can only indicate privileges the account already has, but that WMI doesn't enable by default. (Windows 7 users should be familiar with this concept because it's used in command elevation and with WMI.) As you might expect, privilege attributes are not required when managing computers running Windows 95, 98, or Me because these operating systems have no security mechanism.

Table 7.8 lists the specific privileges relevant to WMI and their numeric code values. The next section describes how to add them to a WMI connection.

Table 7.8   **Privileges Useful for WMI Connections**

Privilege Name	Value	Capability
MachineAccount	5	Create a machine account on a domain net work; that is, add a computer to the domain.
Tcb	6	Act as part of the operating system.
Security	7	Manage auditing and the security log.
TakeOwnership	8	Take ownership of files, for example.
LoadDriver	9	Load and unload device drivers.
Systemtime	11	Change the date/clock.
CreatePagefile	14	Create or modify pagefile settings.
CreatePermanent	15	Create a permanent object such as a device.

Privilege Name	Value	Capability
Backup	16	Back up the system.
Restore	17	Restore the system.
Shutdown	18	Shut down the computer while logged on locally.
SystemEnvironment	21	Modify firmware settings stored in Flash/EEROM.
ChangeNotify	22	Change directories to authorized subfolders, even if there is no access allowed to the parent. folders (also called *bypass traverse checking*).
RemoteShutdown	23	Shut down the computer from a remote connection.
Undock	24	Remove the computer from its docking station.
EnableDelegation	26	Let the computer or user account be trusted for delegation.
ManageVolume	27	Manage disk volumes (partitions).

Table 7.8 lists the privileges by their short names—for example, `ManageVolume`. There are actually four ways to refer to each privilege:

- **As a short name**—An example is `ManageVolume`. You can use short names when you specify privileges in a moniker, as I discuss shortly.

- **As a numeric value**—An example is `27` for the `ManageVolume` privilege. You use numeric values with the `.Add` method that I describe in the next section.

- **As a predefined constant**—If you are using the .wsf file format for your script and add the reference entry `<reference object="WbemScripting.SWbemLocator"/>`, you can use a predefined constant name in place of a numeric value with the `.Add` method. A privilege's constant name is its short name preceded by `WbemPrivilege`—for example, `WbemPrivilegeManageVolume`.

- **As a "C++ constant name"**—Add `Se` before the short name, and `Privilege` after. An example is `SeManageVolumePrivilege`. You can use the C++ constant name with the `AddAsString` method that I describe in the next section.

Specifying Security Options

If the default settings do not work for your network environment, you need to specify alternate authentication, impersonation, or privilege settings for each WMI connection. Unless you are sure that all computers on your network are running Windows XP Service Pack 2 or later, or, for earlier versions of Windows, have upgraded to WMI version 1.5 or higher, you'll at least need to specify Impersonate mode.

There are two ways to specify security options. One is used with the `SWbemServices` object that is returned by the `Locator` object, and the other method is used with the moniker system.

Specifying Security Options with the `SWbemServices` Object

If you connect to a remote computer with the `Locator` object, the result is an `SWbemServices` object. It has a property named `Security_` that returns an `SWbemSecurity` object that in turn has three properties: `AuthenticationLevel`, `ImpersonationLevel`, and `Privileges`, the last of which is a collection. After connecting to the remote computer, you can assign new values to these items. For example, the following script fragment establishes a connection to a computer named Java and requests the `SystemEnvironment` and `RemoteShutdown` privileges:

```
set locator = CreateObject("WbemScripting.SWbemLocator")
set svcs = locator.ConnectServer("Java", "root\CIMV2")

svcs.Security_.AuthenticationLevel = 2 ' Connect
svcs.Security_.ImpersonationLevel  = 3 ' Impersonate
svcs.Security_.Privileges.Add 21       ' WbemPrivilegeSystemEnvironment
svcs.Security_.Privileges.Add 23       ' WbemPrivilegeRemoteShutdown

' change the remote computer's System environment settings, then restart it
⋮
```

Note

You can also add privileges with the `AddAsString` method. `AddAsString` uses the C++ constant name of the privilege. Here's an example:

```
svcs.Security_.Privileges.AddAsString "seSystemEnvironmentPrivilege"
```

Specifying Security Options in Monikers

If you create WMI objects using moniker notation, you can specify alternate security and locale settings in the moniker string. The optional information goes just after `winmgmts:` inside curly brackets and is followed by an exclamation point, as in this example:

```
set svcs = _
    GetObject("winmgmts:{impersonationLevel=impersonate}!\\java\root\CIMV2")
```

One or more of the following items might be placed in the curly brackets:

- `AuthenticationLevel=`*name*, where *name* is one of the words listed in the Name column in Table 7.6, to specify an authentication and encryption scheme
- `ImpersonationLevel=`*name*, where *name* is one of the words listed in the Name column in Table 7.7, to specify an impersonation level

- **Authority=kerberos:***domain\server* or **Authority=ntlmdomain:***domain* to specify a specific Kerberos or Windows domain name in which to validate the user credentials

- **Privileges=(***name*[,*name*...]**)**, where the *name* items are one or more privilege names derived from the constants listed in Table 7.8 by stripping off the leading "wbemPrivilege" part, to specify additional privileges

- **Locale**=*name*, where *name* is one of the Microsoft MS_*xxx* locale identifiers, to specify an alternate language

If more than one item is used, separate the items with commas. Here is an example that does the same thing as the script fragment in the preceding section, but this time using moniker notation:

```
set svcs = GetObject("winmgmts:{authenticationLevel=Connect,ImpersonationLevel=3,"& _
    "privileges=(SystemEnvironment,RemoteShutdown)}!\\JAVA\root\CIMV2")
```

WMI Collections and Queries

As discussed in the previous section, you can connect to the WMI service on the local computer or a remote computer and obtain a WMI object at any of three levels in the namespace hierarchy:

- You can connect at the level of the entire namespace with a path such as "root\CIMV2". The resulting object is called an SWbemServices object, which has methods and properties that let you obtain lower-level objects representing the parts of Windows you want to manage. One of its methods lets you extract information from WMI using a special query language called the Windows Management Instrumentation Query Language (WQL).

- You can connect to a specific management object with a path such as "root\CIMV2:Win32_DiskDrive". The result is an SWbemObject object, but it represents a category, not a real manageable item. To obtain objects that represent items in the category, you can use its Instances_ property to obtain a collection called SWbemObjectSet.

- You can connect to a specific instance of a management object with a path such as root\CIMV2:Win32_DiskDrive="C". This isn't always easy because some of the qualifying parameters are very strange. I discuss this in a moment. These instances are represented by SWbemObject, whose properties and methods let you manage the part of Windows the object represents.

  In a few categories of objects, by design there can be just one instance of the object (called a *singleton*) and no qualifying parameter value that identifies the one instance within the category. For these, use =@ to indicate that you want the instance, rather than the category. For example, `root\Win32_CurrentTime` returns the object for the `Win32_CurrentTime` category and `root\Win32_CurrentTime=@` returns the one specific instance of the current time.

After you have obtained one of these three object types, you can manage the local or remote computer by modifying the WMI object. The next few sections describe how to do this.

SWbemServices

The `SWbemServices` object is returned by the `Locator` object's `ConnectServer` method, or by `GetObject` with a moniker that includes a namespace but no object name (for example, `"winmgmts:\\JAVA\Root\CIMV2"`). The most important of the methods and properties of the `SWbemServices` object are detailed in Reference List 7.1.

REFERENCE LIST 7.1   Property and Methods of the SWbemServices Object (Partial List)

Property:

`Security_`
Returns an `SWbemSecurity` object that you can use to configure the DCOM authentication, impersonation, and privilege settings for this connection to a remote computer. See "Specifying Security Options with the `SWbemServices` Object" earlier in the chapter for more information.

Methods:

`Delete(path)`
Deletes the `SWbemObject` instance specified by the *path* string. This is applicable only for certain nonphysical objects such as network drive mappings and files. The effect is to delete the Windows component or mapping represented by the object. *Path* must specify an object in the same namespace as the `SWbemServices` object. The syntax of object paths is discussed later in the chapter.

`ExecMethod(path, methodname, inparams)`
Executes one of the dynamic methods of the `SWbemObject` specified by *path*. The method named by the *methodname* parameter is called and given the parameters specified by the collection object *inparams*. `ExecMethod` is provided for languages that do not support output ("by reference") parameters, such as JScript. For more information about `ExecMethod`, check Microsoft's online WMI documentation, as discussed at the end of this chapter. `ExecMethod` is not needed with VBScript scripts.

`ExecQuery(query)`
Processes a query (search request) written in the WQL query language and returns an `SWbemObjectSet` collection of objects representing the results. For example, the query `"select * from Win32_LogicalDisk"` returns a set of objects representing all

the disk drives on the computer. With more complex queries, you can select objects based on criteria you provide. WQL is discussed in more detail in the next section.

InstancesOf(*class*)

Returns an `SWbemObjectSet` collection of objects representing all the instances of a given WMI category (class). For example, `InstancesOf("Win32_LogicalDisk")` returns the same set of objects as the preceding `ExecQuery` example.

The two main functions of `SWbemServices` in scripting applications are to provide access to `ExecQuery` and `InstancesOf`.

`InstancesOf` is the most straightforward of the two methods: You can get a collection of all objects of a given type and then scan through the collection to list or alter information. For example, you can list all the disk drives on the computer named JAVA and tell Windows to run `chkdisk` on the local hard disks during the next startup, with this script:

```
                                    ' Example File script0702.vbs
set svcs = GetObject("winmgmts:\\JAVA\root\CIMV2")
set drives = svcs.InstancesOf("Win32_LogicalDisk")
for each drv in drives
    wscript.echo drv.name
    if drv.DriveType = 3 then drv.ScheduleAutoChk
next
```

You don't always have to use the `SWbemServices` object and `InstancesOf` to get a list of objects. For example, you could get the `drives` collection directly by using this moniker:

```
set drives = GetObject("winmgmts:\\JAVA\root\CIMV2:Win32_LogicalDisk")
```

Which is best to use: the moniker format or the lengthier connection-and-query format? The moniker format is simplest to write if you want to do only one with thing with the connection to the remote computer. The connection format is faster if you want to perform several queries or changes.

WQL Queries

The other main reason to connect via the `SWbemServices` object is to gain access to its `ExecQuery` method. Through a query language that's similar to the Structured Query Language (SQL) used by databases, WQL lets you specify what set of objects you'd like to extract from WMI. There are three forms of WQL queries:

- **select**—These queries return a set of objects based on matching the object type and/or parameter values.
- **references of**—These queries return all objects that are directly related to a specified object. This can return, for instance, all Windows services that depend on a particular service.

- **associators of**—These queries return all objects that are indirectly related to a specific object. For example, `associators of {Win32_LogicalDisk.DeviceID="C:"}` might yield a connection containing objects representing the computer system itself, the C: drive's root directory, and the disk partition that contains logical drive C:.

There isn't enough room to describe `associators of` and `references of` in any more detail than this, but you can find more information in Microsoft's online WMI documentation. described at the end of this chapter.

`Select` queries can be used to extract WMI objects based on specific criteria, such as drive letters, disk types, network provider types, and so on. Although you can use a moniker or the `InstancesOf` method (discussed earlier) to get *all* objects of a given class, `select` gives you more fine-grained control.

Here's the basic format of a `select` statement for object queries:

> **select** *propertylist* **from** *class* [**where** *conditions*]

Propertylist can be a comma-delimited list of the object properties you're interested in or * to return all the object's properties. You can use * for most scripting applications. If you find that the `ExecQuery` method takes too long to run, you might enter a list of just the object properties you're interested in to reduce the amount of data that has to be transmitted back from the remote computer.

Class is one of the object classes in the namespace—for example, one of the items in Table 7.2. However, you are not limited to the `Win32_xxx` classes and instead might choose one of the superclasses from which these are derived. For example, superclass `Device` includes all the device classes, including `Modems`, `Keyboards`, and so on.

`Where` *conditions* is an optional clause with a Boolean expression. `Where` limits the result set to only those objects whose properties match the conditionals—that is, those objects for which the expression evaluates as `True`.

When you're using queries in your script, the query expression is entered as a text string, so remember you might have to pay special attention to any quotation marks *inside* the query to enter them in your chosen scripting language. In VBScript, for example, they have to be doubled up. Alternately, you can use single quote characters in the query. Here are some sample `select` statements:

```
set disks = svcs.ExecQuery(_
    "select * from Win32_LogicalDisk where Filesystem = ""NTFS""")

set codes = svcs.ExecQuery(_
    "select * from Win32_Codecs where Group = 'Video'")

set dirs = svcs.ExecQuery(_
    "select Name, LastModified from Win32_Directory")
```

You must also double up any backslashes (\) in your queries because WMI treats them as special characters. This means that in JScript and other scripting languages that also treat the backslash as a special character, you need to enter *four* backslashes when coding a query string.

You can use WQL queries not just to list items, but to locate items to be managed. For example, you can use WMI to terminate application programs by name. To kill all copies of Notepad, for instance, you could run the following script:

```
                                        ' Example File script0703.vbs
dim processes

set processes = GetObject("winmgmts:").ExecQuery(_
    "select * from Win32_Process where Name='notepad.exe'")
for each process in processes
    process.Terminate
next
```

SWbemObjectSet

SWbemObjectSet is a collection object that holds a number of SWbemObject items. SWbemObject can be treated like any standard scripting collection object. It has Count and Item properties that you can use to select individual objects, or you can use an enumerating procedure such as VBScript's for each statement to scan through the collection.

It can be difficult to know in advance how to select a specific item from the collection. The Item property doesn't take a numeric index, so you can't view the items with collection.item(0), collection.item(1), and so on. In some cases, the indexing value is reasonable. With disk drives, for example, it's the drive letter. However, for many other object types, the indexing value is a strange internal Windows identifying code.

For objects that occur only singly, such as the Win32_ComputerSystem object that represents the computer as a whole, it's a common practice to use a for each or other enumeration loop to scan through the collection object and save a copy of the first (only) object found.

This is a common pattern in fact, so let's write it up.

▶ **Pattern**

To obtain from a collection a single WMI object whose full pathname isn't known in advance, use a for each loop to pick the object out of the collection. For example, to get the first (and only) instance of the Win32_OperatingSystem object from the Win32_OperatingSystem collection, use these statements:

```
set loc  = CreateObject("WBemScripting.Locator")
set svcs = loc.ConnectServer("JAVA", "Root\CIMV2")
set oss  = svcs.ExecQuery("select * from Win32_OperatingSystem")
```

Then, use a loop to pick the object out of the collection:

```
for each item in oss  ' examine the collection
    set os = item     ' save the first item and stop
    exit for
next
```

Now, you can use the object in the remainder of the script. Here's an example:

```
os.ShutDown()
```

SWbemObject

Ultimately, all system information returned by WMI is represented by the `SWbemObject` object, either alone or in a collection.

`SWbemObject` has a base set of methods and properties common to all instances. These are called *static* methods and properties because they're fixed and present on every `SWbemObject`. Then, there are additional methods and properties that vary depending on what system component the object represents. These are called *dynamic* properties and methods because they appear only when appropriate. For example, an `SWbemObject` object that is representing a `Win32_CDROMDrive` object has additional properties, such as `Drive` and `VolumeName`. An `SWbemObject` object representing a `Win32_NetworkConnection` object has properties relevant to network connections, such as `UserName` and `RemotePath`.

This is the meat of WMI! Each of the objects listed in Table 7.2 has a number of dynamic properties and methods to let you examine and manipulate all the internal aspects of Windows.

If the important methods and properties are dynamic, how do you know what their names are, and how do you use them in your scripts? There are so many objects, each with its attendant properties and methods, that I can't begin to list them all here or even in the appendices. Your best bet is to read the online WMI documentation or use the Scriptomatic tool that I discuss later in the chapter.

Reference List 7.2 shows the most useful of the static (fixed) properties and methods of `SWbemObject`.

REFERENCE LIST 7.2   Static Properties and Methods of `SWbemObject` (Partial List)
Properties:

`Methods_`
Returns a collection of `SWbemMethodSet` objects that describes all the dynamic methods for this object. The `SWbemMethodSet` object is discussed in the next section.

Path_

Returns a full path description of this particular object in moniker format. You can use this path to obtain this object directly with `GetObject()`.

Properties_

Returns a collection of `SWbemPropertySet` objects that describe all the dynamic properties for this object. The `SWbemPropertySet` object is discussed in the next section. `Methods_` and `Properties_` are used not to manage Windows, but to let you write scripts that document what WMI objects can do. I discuss this in the next section.

Methods:

Delete_

Deletes the object and deletes the Windows information that it represents, such as a Registry entry or a file. This method is allowed only on objects that represent something that can be deleted.

Instances_

Returns an `SWbemObjectSet` collection of *all* instances of the object class to which this object belongs.

Put_

Saves any changes made to the object back to the computer that the object represents. WMI objects are *copies* of information about Windows. You can modify an object through its properties and methods, but the changes don't affect Windows until you use the `Put_` method.

▶ **Note**

The last method in Reference List 7.2 is very important. If you change the value of any property of a WMI object, you must use `Put_` to actually make the change take effect in whatever part of Windows the object represents.

Now, let's take a look at some concrete applications of WMI in managing computers across a network.

SWbemMethodSet and SWbemPropertySet

As mentioned in the previous section, every instance of `SWbemObject` sprouts whatever properties and methods are appropriate to the CIM model object it represents. It also has two static properties, named `Methods_` and `Properties_`, that provide descriptions of the dynamic additions. You can scan through these collections in the usual way to learn what the dynamic properties and methods are. As I mentioned previously, these let you document what the WMI object can do. If you use a WMI query to get a list of objects representing disk drives or operating systems, you can use these tools to see which methods and properties these objects have; then, you can write a script that uses them.

`SWbemMethodSet` is a collection of `SWbemMethod` objects, each of which describes one of the original object's dynamic methods. Here are the most relevant properties of `SWbemMethod`:

Property	Description
InParameters	An `SWbemObject` object whose `Properties_` collection describes the method's input parameters
Name	The name of the method
OutParameters	An `SWbemObject` object whose `Properties_` collection describes the method's output parameters

This is very tricky—`InParameters` and `OutParameters` each return another `SWbemObject` object whose `Properties_` property you have to examine to find the list of arguments. Kind of makes your head spin, doesn't it?

`SWbemPropertySet` is a collection of `SEbemProperty` objects, each of which describes one of the original object's dynamic properties. Here are the most relevant properties of `SWbemProperty`:

Property	Description
IsArray	Boolean value. If `True`, the associated property is an array value.
Name	The name of the property.
Value	The property's current value.

Here's an example of how you can use these tools. The following script lists the methods and properties of the `Win32_ComputerSystem` object:

```
                                 ' Example file listprops.vbs
set obj = GetObject("winmgmts:{impersonationlevel=Impersonate}!" & _
    "//./root/CIMV2:Win32_ComputerSystem")

wscript.echo obj.path_ & vbCRLF       ' List the object's full path

wscript.echo "Properties:"            ' List all property names

for each prop in obj.Properties_
    wscript.echo "   ", prop.name
next

wscript.echo                          ' List all methods
wscript.echo "Methods:"
```

```
for each meth in obj.Methods_
    arglist = ""                          ' construct list of parameters

    for each arg in meth.InParameters.Properties_
        if arglist <> "" then arglist = arglist & ", "
        arglist = arglist & arg.Name
    next

    for each arg in meth.OutParameters.Properties_
        if arg.Name <> "ReturnValue" then
            if arglist <> "" then arglist = arglist & ", "
            arglist = arglist & arg.Name
        end if
    next            ' ignore the ReturnValue item; it represents
                    ' the return value of the method itself

    wscript.echo "  ", meth.name & "(" & arglist & ")"
next
```

The output of this script looks like this:

```
\\JAVA\ROOT\CIMV2:Win32_ComputerSystem

Properties:
    AdminPasswordStatus
    AutomaticResetBootOption
    AutomaticResetCapability
    BootOptionOnLimit
    BootOptionOnWatchDog
    BootROMSupported
    ⋮
    WakeUpType
    Workgroup

Methods:
    SetPowerState(PowerState, Time)
    Rename(Name, Password, UserName)
    JoinDomainOrWorkgroup(AccountOU, FJoinOptions, Name, Password, UserName)
    UnjoinDomainOrWorkgroup(FUnjoinOptions, Password, UserName)
```

You can see from their names that the dynamic properties and methods of the Win32_ComputerSystem object could be useful tools for managing a workstation over the network.

However, you don't have to resort to using a script to find out which properties and methods are available to you. You can read the online WMI documentation, discussed at the end of this chapter, or you can use Microsoft's terrific Scriptomatic tool.

Scriptomatic

As you've seen, WMI is complex, the query language you have to use to get to specific parts of Windows is arcane, and the list of objects is vast. There's just too much to remember. Luckily, some wizards at Microsoft took pity on us and developed a software tool that helps us write WMI scripts using a simple point-and-click interface. The tool is called Scriptomatic, and you can download it from www.microsoft.com.

Using an Administrator-type account, follow these steps:

1. Open Internet Explorer, visit www.microsoft.com, and type **download scriptomatic** in the search box. This should let you locate the Scriptomatic 2.0 download page. Click Download, and then click Run to download and run the setup program.

2. In the WinZip Self Extractor dialog box, select a permanent location in which to store the two included files. Your profile folder is a reasonable place: On Windows 7 and Vista, the folder is \users*YourAccountName*, and on XP it's \Documents and Settings*YourAccountName*. Click Unzip, then OK, and then Close.

3. Right-click your desktop and select New, Shortcut.

4. Click Browse, locate the folder you selected in step 1, select the file ScriptomaticV2.hta, and click OK to close the Browse dialog box.

5. If you are using Windows XP, click Next and proceed to step 6.

   If you are using Windows 7 or Vista, put the cursor before the filename and type the letters B followed by a space. Then, click Next.

6. Change the shortcut name to **Scriptomatic**, and click Finish.

7. If you are using Windows XP, you're done.

   On Windows 7 or Vista, right-click the new shortcut and select Properties. On the Shortcut tab, click Advanced, and check Run As Administrator. Click OK, and then OK again.

Double-click the new shortcut to start Scriptomatic, which is shown in Figure 7.3. As you can see, you can select any of four scripting languages. The Run button runs the sample script and displays the results in any of five output formats. Command Prompt displays the results of the script's WScript.Echo statements in a console window. The other options save the results in a file; reformat them somewhat; and display them with Notepad, Internet Explorer, or Excel. I find the Plain Text version to be the easiest to work with.

Figure 7.3 Scriptomatic writes scripts that demonstrate
how to view all of a WMI object's properties.

A funny but disorganized `read_me.doc` file accompanies Scriptomatic. You'll need to
use Microsoft Word or the free Microsoft Word Viewer to open it. You might want to
read it, but you're probably better off just playing with the program. Select various
objects and click Run to see which properties it exposes. You can save any of the
sample scripts it produces to use as a starting point for your own scripts.

Tip

Scriptomatic writes scripts that just *display* object properties. If you modify the script so that it *changes*
object properties, remember that after changing properties, you have to use the object's `Put_` method to
save those changes; otherwise, the script has no effect.

Note

Scriptomatic demonstrates each object's properties, but it doesn't show you how to use any of the
object's methods. For that, you'll need to read the online WMI reference material, which is discussed in
the last section of this chapter.

WMI Examples

WMI is much easier to use than it is to describe, as you'll see. The remainder of the chapter shows several scripts that use WMI to monitor or manage one or more computers.

The sample scripts in this section are written to use a subroutine to process each computer. The subroutine is called for each computer that the script is to work with; you can extend the list of computers to suit your own network, or you can make the script operate on computers named on the command line by replacing the list of subroutine calls like this:

```
process "JAVA"
process "BALI"
process "SUMATRA"
```

with the following statements:

```
if WScript.Arguments.Count = 0 then
    WScript.echo "Usage: <scriptname> computername ..."
    WScript.quit
end if
for each arg in WScript.Arguments
    process arg
next
```

Use the actual name of your script in place of <scriptname> in the second line. This statement prints the script's command-line usage information if no computers are named on the command line. You then run the script with a command line like this:

```
script java bali sumatra
```

Collecting System Information

WMI scripts can extract information about your computer systems for documentation purposes. The following script collects network adapter information from each named computer:

```
                            ' Example File script0704.vbs
process "JAVA"
process "BALI"
process "SUMATRA"

sub process (name)
    wscript.echo name & ":"

    ' get collection of network adapters
    set adapters = GetObject("winmgmts:{impersonationlevel=impersonate}!" &_
        "//" & name & "/root/CIMV2:Win32_NetworkAdapterConfiguration")
```

```
              ' list information for each
        for each card in adapters.Instances_      ' display info for each adapter
            if not isnull(card.IPAddress) then
                wscript.echo "  ",     card.Caption

                for each addr in card.IPAddress    ' display each IP address
                    wscript.echo "    IP Addr ", addr
                next

                for each addr in card.DefaultIPGateway ' display each gateway
                    wscript.echo "    Gateway ", addr
                next

                wscript.echo       "    MAC Addr", card.MACAddress
                wscript.echo
            end if
        next
    end sub
```

Managing Printers

WMI can do a good job of setting up and configuring local and network printers.
Interestingly enough, Windows comes with several VBScript scripts that use
WMI to manage printers, so I don't take up space showing any here. Look for the
following files in the \windows\system32 folder on Windows XP, or in the
\windows\system32\Printing_Admin_Scripts\xxxx folder on Windows 7 and
Vista, where xxxx identifies your national language.

Filename	Description
prncnfg.vbs	Manages printer configuration
prndrvr.vbs	Manages printer drivers
prnjobs.vbs	Lists and manages print jobs
prnmngr.vbs	Installs and deletes local and network printers
prnport.vbs	Views and alters printer ports
prnqctl.vbs	Prints a test page

Although they're on the verbose side compared to the examples I've been giving, they
demonstrate many aspects of good "utility" scripts: the use of command-line options,
detailed error detection and reporting, and practical applications of WMI in managing
printers.

Monitoring Windows Service Packs and Hotfixes

The Win32_QuickFixEngineering object provides information about hotfixes installed
on the computer. Hotfixes are those "updates" provided by Windows Update. In a large
organization, the Windows automatic updating feature might create a nightmare of

incompatible and inconsistent updates. You can use WMI to monitor the updates installed on a given computer. Here's a list of the properties of `Win32_QuickFixEngineering`:

Caption	InstalledBy
CSName	InstalledOn
Description	Name
FixComments	ServicePackInEffect
HotFixID	Status
InstallDate	

The following script scans a list of computers and reports on the hotfixes installed on each. This script also shows how you might detect errors in connecting to the remote computer. This script prints an error message rather than stopping, if one of the remote computers doesn't cooperate:

```
                                    ' Example File script0705.vbs
set loc = CreateObject("WBemScripting.SWbemLocator")

process "BALI"
process "JAVA"
  ⋮

sub process (name)
    wscript.echo name & " ---------------------------------------"

    on error resume next      ' don't stop on errors

    set qfe = GetObject("winmgmts:{impersonationlevel=impersonate}!" &_
        "//" & name & "/root/CIMV2:Win32_QuickFixEngineering")

    errno = err.number        ' save info in case GetObject failed
    msg   = err.description
    on error goto 0           ' back to normal error handling
    if errno <> 0 then        ' oops, report the error
        wscript.echo "Connect to", name, "failed:", msg
        exit sub
    end if

    ' list information for each installed item
    for each hotfix in qfe.Instances_
        wscript.echo " ", hotfix.hotfixid, hotfix.description
    next
end sub
```

On my network, the listing looks like this:

```
BALI:
    Q147222
    Q293826 Windows 2000 Hotfix (Pre-SP3) [See Q293826 for more information]
    Q299553 Windows 2000 Hotfix (Pre-SP3) [See Q299553 for more information]
    Q300972 Windows 2000 Hotfix (Pre-SP3) [See Q300972 for more information]
JAVA:
    Q147222
    Q307869 Windows XP Hotfix (SP1) [See Q307869 for more information]
    Q308210 Windows XP Hotfix (SP1) [See Q308210 for more information]
    Q309521 Windows XP Hotfix (SP1) [See Q309521 for more information]
    .
    .
    .
```

`Win32_QuickFixEngineering` information is available on Windows 2000 and later versions but not on Windows 9x or NT.

Managing Services and Tasks

WMI provides the `Win32_Service` class to let you manage system services. Each instance of a `Win32_Service` object represents one installed service and indicates its current running status and its startup mode setting. The WMI documentation lists all the object's properties and methods. Some of the more interesting ones are provided in Reference List 7.3.

REFERENCE LIST 7.3   Partial List of the Properties and Methods of the `Win32_Service` Object

Properties:

DesktopInteract

Boolean value. `True` if the service can interact with the desktop Read-only. (By the way, on Windows 7 and Vista, the desktop used by services is not visible to users.)**DisplayName**

Short name for the service. (Read-only.)

Name

Longer descriptive name . (Read-only.)

PathName

Fully qualified path and name of the executable file that implements the service. (Read-only.)

Started

Boolean value. `True` if the service manager attempted to start the service. (Read-only.)

StartMode

Startup mode for this service. Can be any one of the strings `"Boot"`, `"System"`, `"Auto"`, `"Manual"`, or `"Disabled"`. (Read-only.)

StartName

The account name under which the service runs. If this value is `NULL`, the service runs under the LocalSystem account. (Read-only.)

State

Current run state of the service. Can be one of the following strings: `"Stopped"`, `"Start Pending"`, `"Stop Pending"`, `"Running"`, `"Continue Pending"`, `"Pause Pending"`, `"Paused"`, or `"Unknown"`. (Read-only.) It might be best to use the `InterrogateService` method before examining `State` or `Status`.

Status

The current status of the service. Can be one of the following strings: `"OK"`, `"Error"`, `"Degraded"`, `"Unknown"`, `"Starting"`, `"Stopping"`, `"Service"`, or `"Pred Fail"`. (Read-only.)

Methods:

StartService

Starts the service up.

StopService

Shuts the service down.

PauseService

Pauses the service.

ContinueService

Resumes the service after pausing.

InterrogateService

Requests the service to update its state and status properties.

ChangeStartMode(*newmode***)**

Sets the service's startup mode to a new value. *Newmode* must be one of the following string values: `"Boot"`, `"System"`, `"Automatic"`, `"Manual"`, or `"Disabled"`.

The `Win32_Service` object can let you write a script to monitor and manage services on remote computers; this can be especially helpful with servers running IIS, Exchange, or other critical services. Although Windows 7, Vista, and more recent versions of Windows Server include setup functions that enable Windows to automatically restart dead services, a script-based approach can let you combine service monitoring with reporting and recording.

The following shows how you can monitor crucial services on several computers with a script:

```
                                         ' Example File script0706.vbs
check "BALI",    "W3Svc"
check "JAVA",    "W3Svc"
check "BALI",    "DNS"
check "SUMATRA", "DNS"

sub check (server, servicename)
    set service = GetObject("winmgmts:{impersonationlevel=Impersonate}!" & _
        "//" & server & "/root/CIMV2:Win32_Service.Name='" & servicename & "'")

    state = service.state
    ' get a copy of the state, and make it stand out if abnormal
    if state <> "Running" then state = ucase(state) & " <<<"
    wscript.echo server, servicename, state
end sub
```

The output of the script looks like this:

```
BALI W3Svc Running
JAVA W3Svc STOPPED <<<
BALI DNS Running
SUMATRA DNS Running
```

For More Information

As I stated earlier, this chapter just gives the barest introduction to WMI. Personally, at first I found WMI to be fairly opaque, and it took quite a while to get the feel of it. I hope this introduction has given you enough of a start to tackle the Microsoft documentation and other resources. If you like what you've seen of WMI so far, you definitely want to dig deeper.

For more information about WMI, visit msdn.microsoft.com. Select the Library tab, and under MSDN library, select Win32 and COM Development, Administration and Management, Windows Management Instrumentation, WMI Reference. The sections you'll find most useful are WMI Classes, Scripting API for WMI, and WMI Command Line Tools.

I have found that the Microsoft newsgroup devoted to WMI (`microsoft.public. win32.programmer.wmi`) is a *terrific* source of information, sample scripts, and discussion. If you post a (sensible) question here, it'll probably be answered within a few hours. If your ISP doesn't offer this newsgroup, you can point your newsreader at news.microsoft.com. In Outlook Express, you can simply add an additional News account aimed at this server so you have access to this and your regular newsgroups.

You'll find many, many useful WMI scripts—or at least usable fragments of scripts—on the Web. Google "winmgmts" and you'll see what I mean.

Actually, you might find a few scripts already lurking on your own computer. If you still use Windows XP, look in `\windows\system32` for files ending with the extension `.vbs`. All but `pubprn.vbs` use WMI. These are lengthy and advanced programs, but they show you some practical applications of Windows Script Host and WMI.

Finally, you might check out the following books:

- *Windows Management Instrumentation (WMI)*, by Ashley Meggitt and Matthew M. Lavy (New Riders)
- *WMI Essentials for Automating Windows Management*, by Marcin Policht (Sams)

8

Active Directory Scripting Interface

IN THIS CHAPTER

- ADSI can manage workgroups, computers, NT domains, Active Directory domains, Novell networks, and IIS and Exchange.

- Although no single chapter can completely dissect ADSI, this chapter helps you get your foot in the door.

- You should be familiar with the material in Chapter 3, "Scripting and Objects," and Chapter 4, "File and Registry Access," before reading this chapter.

- If you want to write scripts to manage Active Directory, you need a strong background in LDAP syntax.

Managing the User Directory

One common task that network administrators face is the maintenance of user accounts. A new employee needs a computer account immediately to contribute, while the account of a terminated employee must be disabled instantly as a security measure. As employees' responsibilities change, so do their requirements for access to various secured network resources. In a large organization, with people being hired, fired, retired, released, relocated, and reassigned every day, keeping user accounts in sync is a huge job, and it isn't feasible to spend several minutes clicking through dialog boxes to make every change.

As you've guessed by now, the solution for this complex puzzle is scripting. Active Directory Scripting Interface (ADSI) objects give you scriptable access to almost all aspects of the Windows user account and security infrastructure. You can script additions, deletions, and changes to user accounts, passwords, logon preferences, and so on, as well as manage network resources such as shared folders and printers.

Note

ADSI's name makes it sound like it can be used only to manage the Active Directory security system on large corporate networks, but don't let that scare you off. ADSI doesn't *require* that your network use Active Directory. It can manage user accounts, network sharing and services on any network, and even on a single computer.

Uses of the Active Directory Scripting Interface

ADSI is especially well suited to work with Active Directory, the enterprise management system provided with Windows Server versions. However, ADSI works even without Active Directory and can give you access to the user directories of non–Active Directory–based domain and workgroup networks. ADSI can manage the following, at the very least:

- Active Directory on Windows Server systems.
- Windows NT–style domains.
- Novell NetWare Directory Services (NDS).
- Novell Bindery-mode servers (though, I suspect that these are rare beasts nowadays).
- Microsoft Exchange Server.
- Microsoft Internet Information Server (IIS).
- Any LDAP-based directory system. The Lightweight Directory Access Protocol (LDAP) is an industry standard for network access to user and network resource databases.
- Shared printers and folders on individual computers.
- Shared files in use.
- Local users and groups.
- Configuration of Windows Services.

You can see that with so many network databases covered, ADSI has the potential to "integrate" the management of a large heterogeneous network. The inclusion of Exchange, IIS, and other server types means that you can automate the maintenance of email and website accounts at the same time, making ADSI even more valuable for corporate and service provider administrators.

As you've probably also guessed, ADSI is based on a set of scriptable objects that represent the underlying user and network data. In the next few sections, I discuss some of the more important of these objects. I can't cover all of ADSI in this book, but as I did with Windows Management Instrumentation in Chapter 7, I can give you working code to get you started. At the end of the chapter, I list some resources you can use to get more information.

Limitations of ADSI with Windows Script Host

I'd like to comment on the practical usefulness of ADSI with Windows Script Host. *Very* large organizations probably want to purchase or develop an enterprise management system using a higher-level language than VBScript, out of performance and user interface considerations. With directories of tens to hundreds of thousands of objects, such companies will want to use advanced programming techniques to limit the amount of data that must be transferred over the network and packaged into objects. Such a system would probably be integrated with some sort of database system. All of this is beyond the scope of this book.

Another advanced topic that I can't cover here is the use of ADSI in Internet Information Server ASP scripts. With ASP, it's possible to develop an efficient Web-based interface to manage your organization's users. But again, this is beyond the scope of the book.

So, are ADSI, WSH, and this book still useful? Yes. Larger organizations can develop and test concepts for large applications and for ASP scripts with command-line scripts. Small to mid-size organizations often can't justify the purchase or development of a six-figure-price enterprise management system, so for most of us, WSH scripting is a good middle-of-the-road solution.

Finally, writing a script to perform a management task can not only make your job easier, but also serves as important documentation. For example, you might want to write a script to add a new user, with all the necessary bells and whistles of group membership, home directory sharing, and default profile configuration. When the script can do its job correctly, you've written complete and accurate documentation for the task. Scripting can make good business sense just for this reason alone.

Note

Most ADSI scripting only works when run from an account with Administrator privileges on the computer or domain to which ADSI is connecting. Throughout this chapter, keep in mind that you need to run ADSI scripts from an Administrator account.

For scripts that access a computer other than the one on which the script runs, you might also write your script using the `OpenDSObject` connection object that lets you specify an administrator account name and password.

Furthermore, User Account Control (UAC) can make remotely managing Windows Vista or Windows 7 computers that are not on a domain network difficult. To manage your own computer on Windows 7 and Vista, you need to run most ADSI scripts from an elevated command prompt.

For more information about the security issues caused by UAC, see "Managing Windows Remotely" on page 283.

ADSI Concepts

ADSI objects reflect the structure of the user directory information they represent. Microsoft's Active Directory and Novell's NDS were designed with an "object-oriented" approach in mind, so the objects have a natural, one-to-one correspondence with the structures of the directory.

For example, an Active Directory domain can "contain" many subgroups that represent corporate divisions or locations; these are further divided into subgroups or departments, possibly in many layers. Finally, there are the individual users, as shown in Figure 8.1.

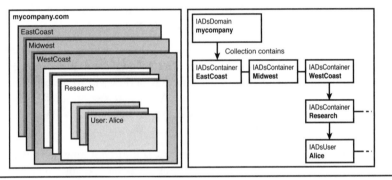

Figure 8.1   Active Directory or NDS can represent the structure of an organization, which is ultimately populated with users. ADSI objects exactly mimic the structure of the directory.

There is a corresponding ADSI object type to represent a domain, which contains a collection of subobjects representing the divisions, departments, and so on, until finally a collection contains only user and/or computer objects. You can manipulate the ADSI objects to add to, rename, delete, or reconfigure the directory items they represent using the same scripting techniques you've seen in the last several chapters.

As I mentioned earlier, although ADSI provides objects to represent Active Directory, it doesn't *require* that your network use Active Directory. ADSI can still manage computers, user accounts, and so on without it.

To start our introduction to ADSI, Table 8.1 lists the most significant of the ADSI objects—those that represent directory data and active network resources.

Table 8.1   **Description of ADSI Objects**

Object	Purpose
IADs	This is the base ADSI object. Its methods and properties are common to all ADSI objects.
IADsCollection	The base object for ADSI collections. You don't actually encounter this object in its plain form; you see other objects *derived* from it, which means they have all the properties and methods of IADsCollection, and then some.
IADsContainer	Another base class; represents directory containers and file system folders. Containers can hold other containers, computers, users, and so on (refer to Figure 8.1).
IADsComputer	Represents a single computer (either a server or a workstation) and has properties that describe the computer's name, location, capacity, operating system, and other information. It is also a container, and its child objects list the computer's users, groups, and services.
IADsDomain	Represents a domain or workgroup member computer. As a container, IADsDomain lists the domain or workstation's users, groups, and computer accounts.
IADsFileService	This is a variant of the IADsService object when it's describing a service that shares files. IADsFileService extends IADsService with additional descriptive properties. As a container, it lists active user connections, called *sessions*.
IADsFileShare	Represents a single shared folder.
IADsGroup	Represents a security group defined in the directory or on an individual computer. Oddly enough, IADsGroup is not a collection object itself, but its Members property is a collection of IADsUser and IADsGroup objects.
IASsNamespaces	A collection of all available directory providers.
IADsO	Describes the organization to which a container or user account belongs.
IADsOU	A container object that represents an organizational unit and its contents. This object has all the properties of IADsO as well.
IADsOpenDSObject	Provides a way of accessing a directory using an alternate user account and password.
IADsPrintJob	Represents a single pending print job waiting to print on a networked printer.
IADsPrintQueue	Represents a networked printer. As a collection, IADsPrintQueue lists pending and active print jobs.
IADsResource	Represents a shared file currently in use by a user.
IADsService	Describes a service task (for example IIS, file sharing, DNS, and so on) on a given computer.
IADsSession	Represents the connection between a user and a file server.
IADsUser	Represents a single computer user account.

You likely encounter other objects that are used to hold ancillary information, such as lists of what permissions are granted to which users. I describe some of these later in the chapter, and you can learn about the rest as you encounter them in practice. When you're beginning to tackle a particular directory or network-management task, start with Table 8.1 to see which object or objects represent the information you're interested in, and then delve into the Microsoft documentation for that object. This will lead you to any others you need to be aware of.

Multiple Inheritance

Multiple inheritance sounds like a great idea—I mean, who wouldn't love to have lots of rich, old relatives? But that's not what the phrase means here. Many ADSI objects are described in the Microsoft documentation as "implementing multiple interfaces." What this means in practical terms is that an object borrows methods and properties from other, simpler objects and then adds more of its own. It's the beautiful part of object-oriented programming systems, that objects can be based on each other. A new type of object can take care of a few additional details and let the original object do the heavy lifting. You run into this more with ADSI than with other object packages described in this book, and you need to be on the lookout for it because you might misinterpret the documentation otherwise.

A good example of this is in the write-up for the `IADsFileService` object. The documentation for `IADsFileService` lists only two properties: `Description` and `MaxUserCount`. However, there is a telling phrase in the object's description: "`IADsFileService` is a dual interface that inherits from `IADsService`." This means that `IADsFileService` sports of the methods and properties of `IADsService`, as well as its added `Description` and `MaxUserCount`. You have to look at the documentation for `IADsService` to get the rest of the details. There, you find 12 more properties: `HostComputer`, `DisplayName`, `Version`, and so on. All these apply to an `IADsFileService` object as well.

You find this happening with the various `IADsxxxOperations` objects as well. ADSI has objects that represent shared folders, printers, system services, and so on. When these resources are part of an operating system for which ADSI can perform management functions, the objects present an additional `Operations` interface that adds extra management properties and methods. You never see an `IADsServiceOperations` object by itself, but you will find its methods and properties available on an `IADsService` object.

It starts at the top. ADSI objects are based on an object called `IADs` that provides the foundation methods and properties shared by *all* the various objects. One of these common properties is `Class`, which identifies the particular flavor of object. You can use this value to determine the type of the objects you find in a collection and to create new objects, such as user accounts and security groups. You can also use it in the `Filter` property, which I describe under "Working with ADSI Collections," to select objects out of a collection based on their `Class`.

Table 8.2 lists the class names of the various ADSI objects you might encounter. Each of these objects is discussed in detail later in the chapter.

Table 8.2   **Class Property Values for ADSI Objects**

Class Name	Object Type	If a Collection, Contains...
`Computer`	`IADsComputer`	`Group`, `Service`, and `User`
`Container`	`IADsContainer`	`Container`, `OrganizationalUnit`, `Group`, and `User`
`Domain`	`IADsDomain`	`Computer`, `Group`, and `User`
`FileService`	`IADsFileService`	
`FileShare`	`IADsFileShare`	
`Group`	`IADsGroup`	(Not a collection!)
`OrganizationalUnit`	`IADsOU`	`Container`, `OrganizationalUnit`, `Group`, and `User`
`PrintJob`	`IADsPrintJob`	
`PrintQueue`	`IADsPrintQueue`	
`Resource`	`IADsResource`	
`Service`	`IADsService`	
`Session`	`IADsSession`	
`User`	`IADsUser`	

Creating ADSI Objects

For the most part, ADSI objects are created with the `GetObject()` function that is provided with VBScript. If you're using another programming language, you can use `WScript.GetObject()` in the same way. After you've used `GetObject()` to gain access to one ADSI object, you can use that object's properties and methods to extract other objects, collections, and information.

If you read Chapter 7 on Windows Management Instrumentation, you're now familiar with the *display moniker* system used to specify objects by name. `GetObject()` takes as its argument a display moniker, which is a string that names the type of object you want to create. For ADSI, this consists of the name of a network provider service to which you want to connect, a colon, and optionally, the path to an object within the provider's namespace.

Here's a list of the primary ADSI providers:

Provider	Description
WinNT:	Active Directory and other Windows user directories; File and Printer Sharing services. You *must* capitalize WinNT exactly as shown.
NDS:	Novell NetWare Directory Services.
NWCOMPAT:	Novell NetWare Bindery mode.
LDAP:	Other LDAP-based directories.
IIS:	Internet Information Server.
ADs:	The master list of all available providers.

For example, a VBScript program to manage a Windows Active Directory or Windows NT domain named "mycompany" can use this statement:

```
set obj = GetObject("WinNT://mycompany")
```

Whereas you could use

```
set obj = GetObject("NDS://mycompany")
```

to access a similarly named Novell NDS domain.

The path that follows the provider name—the part after the colon—depends on what kind of ADSI object you want. Here's where the fun starts. Table 8.3 lists the paths you use to directly obtain the most useful ADSI objects.

Table 8.3 **Paths Used to Obtain ADSI Objects and the Associated Object Type Created**

GetObject() Path*	Object
"ADs:"	IADsCollection
"IIS://*computer*/MSFTPSVC"	IISFTPService
"IIS://*computer*/MSFTPSVC/*n*"	IISFTPServer
"IIS://*computer*/MSFTPSVC/*n*/*folder*"	IISFTPVirtualDir
"IIS://*computer*/W3SVC"	IISWebService
"IIS://*computer*/W3SVC/*n*"	IISWebServer
"IIS://*computer*/W3SVC/*n*/*folder*"	IISWebVirtualDir
"LDAP://*ldapserver*/o=*orgname*[/ou=*unitname*]"	IADsContainer
"LDAP://RootDSE"	IADsContainer
"NDS://*treename*/O=*orgname*/OU=*ouname*"	IADsContainer
"NDS://*treename*/O=*orgname*/OU=*ouname*/CN=*groupname*"	IADsGroup
"NDS://*treename*/*orgname*/*ouname*"	IADsContainer
"NDS://*treename*/*orgname*/*ouname*/*username*"	IADsUser
"*provider*:"	IADsNamespaces
"*provider*://*computer*"	IADsComputer

GetObject() Path*	Object
"*provider*://*domain*"	IADsDomain
"*provider*://*domain*/*computer*[,*computer*]"	IADsComputer
"*provider*://*domain*/*computer*/LanManServer/*queue*"	IADsPrintQueue
"*provider*://*domain*/*computer*/LanManServer/*share*"	IADsFileShare
"*provider*://*domain*/*computer*/*service*"	IADsService
"*provider*://*domain*/*group*[,*group*]"	IADsGroup
"*provider*://*domain*/*user*[,*user*]"	IADsUser
"WinNT://*domain*/*computer*/LanManServer"	IADsFileService

Words in italics (such as provider, domain, *and* computer*) are meant to be replaced with an actual provider name, domain name, computer name, and so on. Square brackets, [ ], indicate an optional part, and ellipses, ..., indicate that the preceding part might be repeated.*

Caution

Although Windows usually accepts either the forward slash (/) or the backward slash (\) as the separator in pathnames, in ADSI paths, \ and / are *not* interchangeable. Always use the forward slash as a path separator.

Table 8.4 lists the more important ADSI objects and shows which providers support them. Only the providers with check marks can be used in GetObject calls to obtain the listed objects.

Table 8.4   ADSI Objects Available from the Primary Four Providers

Object	WinNT	NDS	NWCompat	LDAP
IADsComputer	✓		✓	
IADsContainer	✓	✓	✓	✓
IADsDomain	✓			
IADsFileService	✓		✓	
IADsFileShare	✓		✓	
IADsGroup	✓	✓	✓	✓
IADsMembers	✓	✓	✓	✓
IADsNamespaces	✓	✓	✓	✓
IADsO		✓		✓
IADsOU		✓		✓
IADsPrintJob	✓		✓	
IADsPrintQueue	✓	✓	✓	✓
IADsService	✓			
IADsSession	✓			
IADsUser	✓	✓	✓	✓

Caution

For complete and detailed documentation on ADSI providers and the interfaces they support, go to msdn.microsoft.com and search for "Provider Support of ADSI Interfaces" (using the quotes). There, you find a more complete version of what I've listed in Table 8.4.

Most importantly, after that table is a list of which specific properties and methods these objects actually support. Microsoft's online ADSI reference material for the various ADSI interfaces (objects) lists *many* more properties and methods than are actually available. If you just look at the reference material and don't check the list of "actually" available properties and methods, you go nuts trying to figure out why your scripts don't work.

Directory Security

Many ADSI objects cannot be used unless you are running the script under a user account that has Administrator privileges on the computer being managed.

If you find that the script does not run under an ordinary user account, your options depend on the provider you're using. `WinNT:` does not permit you to use an alternate username, so you have to run the script with an Administrator-level account.

For the `LDAP:` provider, which is used for Active Directory and LDAP management, you can use the `OpenDSObject` method to connect to ADSI using alternate user credentials. To use an alternate user account, create an `IADsNamespaces` object bound to LDAP with the statement

```
set ldap = GetObject("LDAP:")
```

and use the `OpenDSObject` method with this object. `OpenDSObject`'s syntax is as follows:

```
ldap.OpenDSObject(adspath, username, password, flags)
```

Like `GetObject()`, `OpenDSObject` takes an `ADsPath` name, the desired object's moniker. If you pass the value `NULL` for the username and password, the current process's security context is used. You can also specify a privileged account's username and password with one or more of the flag values listed in Table 8.5 to specify the level of security desired. Multiple flags can be specified by adding their values together. However, not all flags might be honored if the target LDAP server does not support them.

Table 8.5   `OpenDSObject` **Security Option Flags**

Constant	Value	Meaning
`ADS_SECURE_AUTHENTICATION`	1	Requests secure authentication to avoid sending the password as clear text. The WinNT provider uses NTLM. Active Directory uses Kerberos, if possible, or NTLM.

Constant	Value	Meaning
ADS_USE_ENCRYPTION	2	Forces ADSI to encrypt data transmitted over the network. Requires that the domain have a Certificate Server installed.
ADS_USE_SSL	2	Same as ADS_USE_ENCRYPTION.
ADS_READONLY_SERVER	4	Informs ADSI that no changes will be made; this might increase performance and enables ADSI to use backup domain controllers.
ADS_PROMPT_CREDENTIALS	8	Requests that the script user should be prompted for a password, if possible. Microsoft recommends against using this flag because it might not be supported in the future.
ADS_NO_AUTHENTICATION	16	Attempts to connect as an anonymous user. The WinNT provider does not accept anonymous connections.
ADS_FAST_BIND	32	Instructs ADSI not to add the dynamic object-specific methods and properties but rather to provide the base object methods and properties only. This can speed up requests in some advanced and unusual circumstances.
ADS_USE_SIGNING	64	Adds data-verification checks to inter-computer communications. The ADS_SECURE_AUTHENTICATION flag must also be used.
ADS_USE_SEALING	128	Adds Kerberos-based encryption to intercomputer communications. Requires ADS_SECURE_AUTHENTICATION.
ADS_USE_DELEGATION	256	Permits ADSI to delegate the user credentials when communicating across domains; that is, it permits the ADSI service on a remote computer to impersonate you in conversations with other domain controllers.
ADS_SERVER_BIND	512	Reduces network traffic and speeds performance when connecting to the LDAP provider with an ADsPath that includes a server name.

You can create other objects using the same alternate credentials by calling OpenDSObject repeatedly with the same username and Null for the password value.

Note

The NWCOMPAT: provider does not support OpenDSObject. If you need to connect to a NetWare server with alternative credentials, you must use the command-line net use program, as follows, before running your scripts:

net use *netwareserver* /U:*username*

Determining the Difference Between Containers and Leaves

You've probably heard the word *tree* used to describe hierarchical structures such as the folders on a hard disk or the series of containers in a directory. Figure 8.2 shows a directory structure laid out as a tree. The end objects, those that aren't containers, are appropriately enough called *leaves* because they sit at the end of the tree's branches. In a directory, user accounts and computer accounts are considered leaf objects because they're the final objects at the end of a series of containers.

Containers can hold both leaf objects and other containers at the same time. Figure 8.2 shows an example of this, where the main domain container holds a leaf—the Administrator user account—and also has subcontainers.

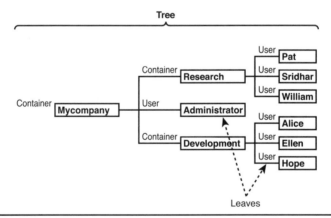

Figure 8.2   A directory structure is often called a *tree*, and the final objects—those that aren't folders or containers—can be called *leaves*. (It might help to turn the book counterclockwise 90°. Don't turn it clockwise or you end up with roots instead of leaves.)

When you scan the collection of objects inside a container, it's possible that the collection holds both container and leaf objects. When you scan through a container's contents with a script, you have to determine the type of each member object as you encounter it.

The Microsoft documentation tells you to use each object's `Schema` property, which returns the display moniker name of an `IADsClass` object that describes the object's data definition and structure—that is, its type. All ADSI object varieties have a `Schema` property because they are all derived from the basic `IADs` object and inherit `Schema` from `IADs`. Given an object's Schema name, you can use `GetObject` to obtain the `IADsClass` object, which has a Boolean property named `Container` that is `True` if the object is a container or `False` if it is a leaf. Got all that? The following code shows how Microsoft would have you do this:

```
set container = GetObject("WinNT://mydomain")
for each obj in container
    if GetObject(obj.Schema).Container then
        WScript.echo obj.name, "is a container"
    else
        WScript.echo obj.name, "is a leaf"
    end if
next
```

The thing is, *it doesn't work*. Some ADSI objects don't have all the expected properties. The script frequently crashes because the schema's `Container` property doesn't appear for every object type, or in some cases the Schema property itself is missing. This is the reality of ADSI.

To get around this, you're better off using the brute-force method of looking at each object's `Class` and `Name` properties and deciding for yourself whether the object is a container or a leaf. Table 8.2, shown previously, lists the most common object classes and indicates whether the object is a leaf or container. If the object has items listed in its "Contains" column, it's a container.

Because containers can contain leaves, or can be nested *ad infinitum*, it's the perfect situation to use recursion to list the contents of each level of container. For example, the following script lists the contents of the computer named Sumatra in the `GetObject` call:

```
                                        ' Example Script script0801.vbs
set comp = GetObject("WinNT://sumatra,Computer")' object to view

on error resume next          ' ignore inevitable errors
                              ' make services visible
comp.filter = array("Service","User","Group")

ListContainer comp, 0

sub ListContainer (obj, depth)
    dim member, cls           ' private local variables

                              ' list the object's class and name
    WScript.echo space(depth*3) & obj.class & ":", obj.name

    cls = lcase(obj.class)    ' check for container classes
```

```
    if cls = "container" or cls = "computer" or cls = "domain" then
        for each member in obj  ' list contents recursively
            ListContainer member, depth+1
        next

    elseif instr(cls, "group") then
                            ' list group members recursively
        for each member in obj.members
            ListContainer member, depth+1
        next
    end if
end sub
```

Even this script requires the on error resume next statement to bypass the inevitable errors in obtaining some groups' contents.

ADSI Objects for the WinNT: Provider

There are too many ADSI objects with too many methods and properties to list them all in this book. In this section, I give you an overview of the most important objects used to manage Windows networks and their most important properties. This reference should give you an overview of ADSI's capabilities and enough information to write useful scripts. You should, however, check the Microsoft ADSI documentation for the complete reference. Later in the chapter, I briefly cover the objects used for Active Directory management under the LDAP: provider as well as Internet Information Services management. There isn't enough room to cover the objects and techniques used to manage Novell NetWare, Novell NDS, Microsoft Exchange, and generic LDAP servers. At the end of the chapter, however, you find additional information sources listed.

Note

In your scripts, you must capitalize WinNT exactly as shown, with the "i" and "n" in lowercase, when you construct monikers that you pass to GetObject. You see this capitalization used throughout this chapter. If you type, for example, winnt, GetObject generates an Unspecified error. This is one of the only instances of case sensitivity in names to be found anywhere in Windows.

Important Notes Regarding the Microsoft Documentation

The ADSI objects are written in the Microsoft ADSI documentation that you can view at msdn.microsoft.com. Select the Library tab, then open—in turn—Win32 and COM Development, Administration and Management, Directory Identity and Access Services, Directory Services, Directory Access Technologies, Active Directory Service Interfaces, Active Directory Services Interfaces Reference, ADSI Interfaces. You need to use this documentation to get anywhere with ADSI, and you need to remember some quirky and important things when you're reading it:

- The references show all the properties and methods that *could* be provided by ADSI-compatible network services, but the reality is that not all the properties and methods listed actually exist. Plus, the list of which ones *do* work depends on which network directory provider you use (WinNT, LDAP, NDS, and so on).

  So, you *must* look at the information in the article titled "Provider Support of ADSI Interfaces," which is under "ADSI Service Providers" just after the "ADSI Interfaces" section I just mentioned. For example, under ADSI Interfaces, you'd expect that the `IADsComputerServices` interface should have a `ShutDown` method that you could use with any Computer object. No such luck. If you check the "Provider Support..." article, you see that no current ADSI provider actually supports this method.

- In these references, object methods are listed with names such as `Get_LastLogin` and `Get/put_Description`. You can ignore these and instead work with the corresponding properties with names such as `LastLogin` and `Description`. The `Get_` and `Put_` parts of the names are used only with compiled programming languages such as C++.

- If you get a script error message stating that a given property doesn't exist for the object you're using, try changing the reference in your code from *object.propertyname* to *object.Get("propertyname")* or *object.Put "propertyname", newvalue*. This sometimes solves the problem. If that doesn't help, see the first bullet point in this section; the property might not really exist.

- Remember that you *must* use the `.SetInfo` method to actually save any changes you make to ADSI object properties. `SetInfo` isn't be listed as a method for each object. It's inherited from the core `IADs` object, and you have to remember that it's there.

- Almost every ADSI object has an inherited property named `Schema` that refers to an object that describes the object type. Many objects have other properties, such as `Parent`, `AdsPath`, and `SeeAlso`, that appear to refer to other related ADSI objects. These are not actual object references that you can use to directly manipulate the related objects. They're monikers—string values—that you can print or can use as arguments to the `GetObject()` function, if you want to actually work to the other objects.

The following sections list the methods and properties of the most important objects.

IADs

The `IADs` object is the base object from which all other ADSI objects are derived. That is, all the other objects described in this chapter start with the methods and properties shown in Reference List 8.1 and add additional functions.

Note

To keep things brief, I do not repeat these properties in every one of the other objects, so you must remember that these are an integral part of *every* ADSI object.

REFERENCE LIST 8.1   Properties and Methods of the Base IADs Object Present on All ADSI Objects

Properties:

AdsPath

The moniker name of the object, of the form used by GetObject(); for example, "WinNT://*domain*/*computer*". If you've obtained an object from a collection, ADsPath gives the moniker you can use to create the object directly in the future.

Class

The class name of the object in question. This is one of the class names listed in Table 8.2: "User", "Domain", and so on.

GUID

The Globally Unique Identifier (GUID) for this object. It's a long string that identifies this object in the Active Directory (if the object is part of it).

Name

The name of the object. Most object names are what you expect for the object type: a user name for an IADsUser object, and so on.

Parent

The ADsPath name of the container object that holds this object, if applicable. You can use the Parent property value in a GetObject() call to create the object representing the container, if you need it.

Schema

This is a character string, the ADsPath of an IADsClass object that describes the properties expected on this object. For example, if obj is an IADs object, then

```
set sobj = GetObject(obj.Schema)
```

gives you sobj, which is an IADsClass object that can give you a list of the methods and properties of object obj. (Occasionally, you run into an IADs object that doesn't *have* a Schema property, so you can't get the corresponding IADsClass object.)

For more information about IADsClass, see the Microsoft documentation.

Methods:

Get(*propertyname*)

Returns the value of the property whose name is passed as a character string. In the WSH scripting environment, you can also manipulate properties using the usual object syntax. These two statements are equivalent:

```
wscript.echo object.someproperty
wscript.echo object.Get("someproperty")
```

When the property has a simple value, a normal variant value is returned. If the property has multiple values, an array is returned.

GetEx(*propertyname***)**

Like Get, but GetEx(*propertyname*) always returns an array containing the property value, even if there is just one value. You can use this method when examining properties that can have multiple values, so you don't need to check to see whether a single value or an array has been returned.

GetInfo

Forces ADSI to retrieve the property values for this object from the underlying Windows computer directory or service. This occurs automatically the first time you reference an object, but you can call GetInfo explicitly if you think the underlying information might have changed between the time you created an object and the time you want to view its properties.

GetInfoEx *namearray*, **0**

Forces ADSI to retrieve from the provider (for example, the computer or domain server being managed) the values of the parameters whose names are listed in the array *namearray*. The second argument must be zero. GetInfoEx is not normally needed in scripting applications.

Put *propertyname*, *newvalue*

Assigns the value *newvalue* to the property whose name is passed as the character string *propertyname*. In the WSH scripting environment, you will normally use the standard object property syntax, but for the record, the following two statements are equivalent:

```
object.someproperty = newvalue
object.Put "someproperty", newvalue
```

However, either way, modifying the value of an object's properties by either method does *not* automatically update the information stored in Active Directory or on the managed computer. The SetInfo method must be called to actually save the information.

PutEx *controlcode*, *propertyname*, *valuearray*

Updates the multiple-valued property *propertyname* using one or more values stored in the array *valuearray* according to the value of *controlcode*, which can be one of the following:

Constant	Value	Function
ADS_PROPERTY_CLEAR	1	Removes all values from the property
ADS_PROPERTY_UPDATE	2	Replaces the property's current values with the specified values

Constant	Value	Function
ADS_PROPERTY_APPEND	3	Adds the specified values to the current values
ADS_PROPERTY_DELETE	4	Deletes any of the listed values

SetInfo

Saves any changes made to the object's properties back to the underlying computer that the object represents.

Note

SetInfo must be used after any object is modified or created to actually change the associated user account, system service, Active Directory entry, or other managed object. This applies to *all* the ADSI objects discussed in this chapter.

IADsCollection and IADsContainer

IADsCollection and IADsContainer are also "base" object classes (interfaces) that are used as the foundation for ADSI objects such as IADsDomain.

IADsCollection is a collection object, so you can scan its contents using the normal means of enumerating a collection in your chosen scripting language. In VBScript, this can be done with the for each loop.

→ To learn more about enumerating collections, see "Containers and Collections," **p. 95**.

The combined properties and methods of IADsCollection and IADsContainer are listed in Reference List 8.2. Because IADsContainer expands on IADsCollection and adds additional properties and because they always appear together, I've mixed them together in this listing. In actual use, the objects that are derived from these interfaces have additional properties and methods, as discussed in the remaining sections of this chapter.

REFERENCE LIST 8.2 Properties and Methods of the IADsContainer and IADsCollection Interfaces

Properties:

Count

Returns the number of items in the collection. (Read-only.)

Filter

Can be used to limit the apparent number of objects in the collection to only those of a selected class or classes. To do this, create an array of class names (for example, "Group", "LocalGroup", "GlobalGroup", "User", and so on) and assign it to the Filter property. I discuss the Filter property in more detail in the next section.

Note

If you want to scan through one or more particular types of objects in a collection, you're better off setting the Filter property to limit the scope of the collection than trying to sort through all the object types
in your script's loop. Sometimes ADSI scripts hang when scanning through large containers without filtering.

Hints

This property lists object properties that should be cached for faster performance;
it's not relevant to VBScript programming.

Methods:

CopyHere(*sourcepath*, *newname*)

Adds a copy of an existing object to this container. *Sourcepath* is a string, the
ADsPath name of the object (for example, "//java/bknittel,User"). *Newname* is the
name the copy of the object is to have in this container. It can be Null, in which
case the copy has the same name as the original. This method returns a reference to
the new object. After creating the copy, you should set any required properties and
finish by using the SetInfo method on the new object. The new group, user, or
what-have-you is not actually created in the underlying directory until you use
SetInfo.

Create(*class*, *name*)

Creates a new object of the specified *class* in this container and gives it the specified *name*. *Class* is typically "OU", "Group", "User", or "FileShare". This method
returns a reference to the new object. After creating the object, you should set any
required properties and finish by using the SetInfo method on the new object. The
object is not actually created in the underlying directory until you use SetInfo.

For example, to create a new user, obtain the domain object for a domain account
or the computer object for a local account and use this:

```
set domain = GetObject("WinNT://domainname")   ' (or //computername)
set user = domain.Create("user", "username")
' set properties:
user.property = value
⋮
user.SetInfo  ' actually create the user account
```

A full-fledged script to create a user account would need to set various user properties, such as the home directory, the password, and the profile path. It would also
need to actually create the home directory and assign the new user full-control
privileges in it, which is beyond ADSI's ability. This last step can be done with the
cacls command-line program, however, and cacls can be run from the script. I
discuss cacls in Chapter 14, "Windows PowerShell."

Note

If you want to examine the new object or alter its properties, you should follow `SetInfo` with `GetInfo`. This reads back into the object all the actual properties of the newly created directory entry. `Create` does not fill in all the default values that a newly created physical directory entry receives. After `GetInfo`, you can view and alter the object's properties.

Delete *class, name*

Deletes an object in this container given its name and class. The action takes places immediately. There is no need to call `SetInfo`. Be sure to release any object references you might have stored to the deleted object. For example, this script deletes a user account:

```
                                          ' Example Script script0802.vbs
set domain = GetObject("WinNT://domainname")  ' (or //computername)
domain.Delete "user", "username"
```

GetObject(*class, name*)

When you have a collection of items, you can use `GetObject` to extract a particular object of interest, given its *class* and *name*. For example, I could extract the `IADsUser` object for a particular user, say `"Dave"`, from the domain with these statements:

```
set domain = GetObject("WinNT://mydomain")
set dave = domain.GetObject("user", "Dave")
```

Unless you need the larger collection object for other purposes, it's more efficient to get a single object directly with a more precise moniker. Here's an example:

```
set dave = GetObject("WinNT://mydomain/Dave,User")
```

The first method requires Windows to fetch the entire list of domain user and group names from the domain controller; the second only requests the one object.

MoveHere(*sourcepath, newname*)

Moves an object from another container into this container, given the object's `ADsPath` name. *Newname* is the name the moved object is to have in this container. It can be `Null`, in which case the object is not renamed. This method returns an object reference to the moved object. Here's an example of its use:

```
set user = container.MoveHere("WinNT://mydomain/someuser,User", Null)
```

Note

In the discussions of the other ADSI objects that follow, when any object is said to be derived from `IADsContainer`, remember that the object has all the properties and methods shown in Reference Lists 8.1 and 8.2, even if they're not listed again later.

Working with ADSI Collections

ADSI collections based on the `IADsContainer` object often contain a mixture of object types, reflecting the organization of real Windows objects; a domain can contain user accounts, computer accounts, and security groups. A computer contains all those plus system services. However, it can be difficult to sort through such a collection if you only want to examine objects of a particular type.

You can examine the `Class` property of each object to see whether it's an object of interest. For example, when printing a list of groups in a domain, you might write the following:

```
                                          ' Example Script script0803.vbs
set domain = GetObject("WinNT://mydomain")
for each object in domain
    if object.class = "Group" then
        WScript.echo object.name
    end if
next
```

This gets cumbersome if you're looking for more than one group at once. The `IADsContainer` object provides a special property named `Filter` to help out. If you assign an array value to a collection's `Filter` property, where the array contains one or more `Class` names, the collection will then appear to contain only objects of the named classes. The easiest way to create such an array in VBScript is with the `array()` function, which returns its arguments as an array. The previous script example can be rewritten as follows:

```
                                          ' Example Script script0804.vbs
set domain = GetObject("WinNT://mydomain")

domain.Filter = array("group")    ' view Groups only

for each object in domain         ' scan the collection
    Wscript.echo object.name
next
```

If you've set a container's `Filter` property, you can assign another array to view different objects, or you can assign it the value `Nothing` to remove filtering entirely. Also, you can create a filter that accepts more than one class type by simply creating a larger array:

```
domain.Filter = array("group", "user")
```

However, oddly enough, I have found that in VBScript, if you create the `Filter` array with a VBScript `dim` statement, the filter has no effect or the script generates an error when you attempt to assign the array to the `Filter` property. The preceding example works, but

```
dim flt(1)              ' create 2 item array (indexes are 0 and 1)
flt(0) = "group"
```

```
flt(1) = "user"
domain.filter = flt
```

does not. This appears to be a bug in either VBScript or ADSI.

IADsComputer and IADsComputerOperations

The `IADsComputer` object represents a computer account in a Windows Domain network. There is a computer account for each member computer in the domain. The `IADsComputer` object lets you view and manage information about each member computer. Its properties are listed in Reference List 8.3.

REFERENCE LIST 8.3   Properties of the `IADsComputer` Object

Division
The division, organization, or company name under which this computer's operating system is registered.

OperatingSystem
The operating system family that this computer is running. For Windows 7, Vista, XP, 2000, and NT, this is `"Windows NT"`.

OperatingSystemVersion
The version of the operating system on this computer. For Windows XP and 2000, this value is `"5.0"`. For Vista, it's `"6.0"`, and for Windows 7, it's `"6.1"`.

Owner
The name of the person who registered the operating system running on this computer.

Processor
The brand and model of CPU running in this computer (for example, my processor is reported as `"AMD64 Family 15 Model 35 Stepping 2"`).

ProcessorCount
Indicates whether Windows is configured for a single processor or multiple processors. This might be the string `"Uniprocessor Free"` or `"Multiprocessor Free"`. Here, `"Free"` doesn't refer to the price; it indicates that the installed version of Windows is a normal retail version. Software developers sometime use an alternative `"Checked"` version that has extensive internal debugging code built in.

You can obtain a computer object with a `GetObject()` call in one of these formats:

```
set computer = GetObject("WinNT://computername,Computer")
```

```
set computer = GetObject("WinNT://domainname/computername,Computer")
```

Be sure to specify `",Computer"` after the name to avoid ambiguity between computer, group, and domain names.

The Microsoft ADSI Interface documentation describes the `IADsComputer` object's properties as read/write, but in actuality you cannot change them through ADSI. To be more precise, you can modify the properties, but the `SetInfo` method is not available; thus, you can't actually make permanent changes to the properties.

The Microsoft documentation also lists additional, seemingly useful, properties, but you can't count on them being present on any particular instance of a `IADsComputer` object. `MemorySize`, for an example, is defined in the list of properties, but no current ADSI provider actually implements it. If you try to reference this property, your script generates an error.

You can handle this uncertainty in scripts by catching the error that occurs if you try to access a property that doesn't exist on a particular copy of the object you have:

```
name = "."                           ' name of computer to examine
set computer = GetObject("WinNT://" & name & ",Computer")
memsize = "Unknown"
on error resume next
    if len(computer.MemorySize) > 0 then memsize = computer.MemorySize
on error goto 0
wscript.echo "Computer", name, "memory size is", memsize
```

You can generalize this by writing a function to attempt to obtain objects' properties via the `Get` method, as follows:

```
                                        ' Example Script script0805.vbs
name = "mycomputer"                 ' name of computer to examine
set computer = GetObject("WinNT://" & name & ",Computer")
wscript.echo "Computer " & name & ":"
wscript.echo "Memory size:", getprop(computer, "MemSize", "Unknown")
wscript.echo "CPU type:", getprop(computer, "Processor", "Unknown")

function getprop (obj, propertyname, default_value)
    getprop = default_value          ' assume we'll fail, and set default value
    on error resume next             ' ignore errors
    getprop = obj.Get(propertyname)  ' try to set return value to property value
                                     ' if Get fails, original value is unchanged
end function
```

You can examine the object's actual set of properties by examining the `IADsClass` object that describes its structure:

```
                                        ' Example Script script0806.vbs
name = "java"    ' name of computer to examine
set computer = GetObject("WinNT://" & name & ",Computer")

set cls = GetObject(computer.Schema) ' get object that lists properties
' MandatoryProperties is an array of strings, the names of properites every
' IADsComputer object must have. OptionalProperties is an array of property
' names that an IADsComputer object for this particular computer may have.

For Each p In cls.MandatoryProperties
```

```
        wscript.echo p & ":", computer.get(p)    ' list property name and its value
    Next
    For Each p In cls.OptionalProperties
        wscript.echo p & ":", computer.get(p)
    Next
```

The `Computer` object also alleges to provide management properties and methods
through its `IADsComputerOperations` interface, which the ADSI documentation shows
as having a `Shutdown` method and a `Status` property. No current ADSI implementation
provides these, so you can't use ADSI to shut down (or restart) a Windows computer.
The `IADsComputerOperations` interface might be documented, but it is effectively not
present in actual use.

Finally, `IADsComputer` can potentially be treated as a collection. The objects in its collection include `IADsService` objects representing all installed services on the computer,
`IADsUser` and `IADsGroup` objects for the computer's local users and groups, and potentially other objects such as `"PrintJob"` and so on. These various object types are mixed
together in the collection, as you can see from the output of this sample script:

```
                                        ' Example script script0807.vbs
    ' name of computer to examine (change before running script):
    name = "computername"
    set computer = GetObject("WinNT://" & name & ",Computer")

    for each obj in computer              ' examine container's contents
        wscript.echo obj.class, obj.adspath ' print object's type and name
    next
```

I have found that this particular script might not always work correctly. On Windows
Server 2003, for instance, I have seen it list users, groups, and then nothing more; the
script gets stuck trying to move through the collection with the `"for each"` loop. You
should use the `.Filter` property to specify the type(s) of objects you want to examine
before using `"for each"`.

IADsDomain

The `IADsDomain` object represents a Windows or NetWare security domain, a group of
users and computers that share a common user account database. `IADsDomain` provides
methods and properties to view and manage the user accounts in a domain. Individual
computers—whether they are members of a domain or of a simple workgroup (peer-
to-peer) network—also have local user account databases, and `IADsDomain` can manage
these as well.

The properties and the one method of `IADsDomain` are discussed in Reference List 8.4.
`IADsDomain` is derived from the `IADsContainer` and `IADs` objects, so it has these
objects' properties and methods as well. A couple of these additional properties are
listed in Reference List 8.5, but you should remember that the other inherited properties and methods are present also.

REFERENCE LIST 8.4   Properties and Method of the IADsDomain Object

Properties:

AutoUnlockInterval

The time in seconds that an account remains disabled after a series of invalid password logon attempts.

Filter

Limits the view into the object's collection to only those object classes listed in the array assigned to the filter. See the discussion in the "Working with ADSI Collections" section for more information.

IsWorkgroup

A Boolean value that is True if this IADsDomain object represents a local computer's individual user directory, rather than a domain directory. This is true for all members of workgroup networks and for the individual computers of a domain network.

LockoutObservationInterval

The maximum time, in seconds, between invalid password login attempts for the attempts to be considered part of a cluster and to be counted. That is, the count of attempts resets to zero after LockoutObservationInterval seconds.

MinPasswordAge

The minimum time, in seconds, before a new password can be changed. This property can prevent users from rapidly changing their passwords back to a previously used value.

MinPasswordLength

The minimum password length allowed.

MaxBadPasswordsAllowed

The maximum number of bad password logon attempts allowed before the account is locked out.

MaxPasswordAge

The maximum time, in seconds, that a password can be left unchanged, after which a user is forced to change his password.

PasswordAttributes

A value indicating the required password complexity to be enforced by the system. It can be one of the following values:

Constant	Value	Description
PASSWORD_ATTR_NONE	0	No complexity requirement.
PASSWORD_ATTR_MIXED_CASE	1	Passwords must use upper- and lowercase characters.
PASSWORD_ATTR_COMPLEX	2	Passwords must use at least one punctuation or nonprinting character.

Note

For other scripting objects, I might have suggested that you encase your script in a .wsf file and use a <reference> tag to automatically import ADSI's predefined constants. However, for ADSI, sorry to say, this is not helpful. For ADSI scripts, you should define the constants yourself, as in this VBScript example:

```
const PASSWORD_ATTR_MIXED_CASE =    1
```

You can download a VBScript file with all the ADSI constants listed in this chapter from http://www.helpwin7.com/scripting.

PasswordHistoryLength

The number of previous passwords that the system remembers. This property is used to help prevent users forced to change their passwords from promptly switching back to their original passwords. A `PasswordHistoryLength` value of, say, 10, coupled with a large value for `MinPasswordAge` (say, 120 seconds) can make it too annoying for users to try to resist changing passwords. Instead, they choose a new password and attach it to their monitor with a sticky note.

Method:

SetInfo

As with all objects based on `IADs`, you must use the `SetInfo` method to commit any changes you make to the object's property values back to the Windows directory they represent. (`IADsDomain` sports all the other properties and methods of `IADs` and `IADsContainer` as well, which are listed in Reference Lists 8.1 and 8.2. I repeat this one here for emphasis.)

To obtain an `IADsDomain` object, use `GetObject()` as follows:

```
set domain = GetObject("WinNT://domainname")
```

`IADsDomain` is also a container object. The members of its collection can be a mixture of user accounts (`IADsUser`), security groups (`IADsGroup`), computer accounts (`IADsComputer`), and other objects.

You can scan through the entire collection using the normal method used by your scripting language, or you can use the `Filter` property to restrict the view to a limited set of object types. For example, this script lists only the users in a specified domain:

```
                                        ' Example Script script0808.vbs
set domain = GetObject("WinNT://domainname")
domain.Filter = array("User")    ' view only User-class objects
for each user in domain          ' scan collection and print each username
    wscript.echo user.name
next
```

IADsFileService and IADsFileServiceOperations

IADsFileService represents the File Sharing service on a given computer. You can use this object to examine and manage shared folders and even to disconnect or close shared files currently marked as "in use" (for example, after a workstation has crashed). It's based on the IADsService object, which represents any kind of system services. That is, this file service object has multiple interfaces, a feature discussed earlier in the chapter.

An IADsFileService object has all the properties and methods of IADsService and IADsServiceOperations, which are described later in the chapter, with additional functions specific to file sharing. On top of this, the IADsFileServiceOperations interface adds yet more properties and methods.

The net result is that this file service management object has all the properties listed under IADsFileService and IADsFileServiceOperations, which are discussed in Reference List 8.5.

REFERENCE LIST 8.5   Combined Properties of the IADsFileService and IADsFileServiceOperations Interfaces

Description
As I noted earlier in the chapter under "Important Notes Regarding the Microsoft Documentation" (page 332), some defined properties are not actually functional, and this is one of them. It always returns a blank string.

MaxUserCount
According to the Microsoft documentation, MaxUserCount returns or enables you to set the maximum number of users allowed to connect to shared files on the associated computer. However, this is another unimplemented property. MaxUserCount always returns a value of -1, and the script generates an error if you attempt to change the value.

Resources
Returns a collection of IADsResource objects listing each of the associated computer's shared resources (for example, files, named pipes, and so forth) that are actually in use. I describe the IADsResource object later in this section because it's not used elsewhere.

Tip
The Resources property can be a bit misleading. It describes shared resources that are *currently in use*. The IADsFileService object itself is a collection, and its contents are objects that represent *all* of the folders and printers the computer is sharing.

Sessions

Returns a collection of IADsSession objects that represent the connections between the associated computer and any clients (users) attached to the File Sharing service. See the section "IADsSession" later in the chapter for a description of this object.

You can obtain the IADsFileService object for a given computer by binding to the LanManService service with a statement like

```
set fs = GetObject("WinNT://computername/LanManServer")
```

or

```
set fs = GetObject("WinNT://domainname/computername/LanManServer")
```

As I just mentioned, in addition to the properties listed in Reference List 8.5, the IADsFileService object is itself a collection of IADsFileShare objects, which describe the resources that the computer has shared. I discuss IADsFileShare shortly.

The Resources property returns a collection of IADsResource objects, whose properties are noted in Reference List 8.6. This collection lists shared folders that are in use by network users.

REFERENCE LIST 8.6 Properties of the IADsResource Object

Name
Each IADsResource object has a name, as do all ADSI objects, but in this case it's a random string of digits assigned by the computer sharing the resource and isn't of any use.

User
Returns the account name of the user who has opened this resource.

UserPath
Returns the ADsPath of the user who has opened this resource. You can use GetObject() with this string to obtain the IADsUser object representing this user.

Path
Returns the path and filename of the resource on its host computer.

LockCount
Returns the number of file locks in place on this resource. (A *file lock* is an operating system mechanism used by multiuser databases and other programs to avoid having several people attempt to modify the same information at the same time.)

The following script lists all files shared by a specified computer that are currently in use:

```
                                        ' Example Script script0809.vbs
set cname = "sumatra"
set fs = GetObject("WinNT://" & cname & "/LanManServer")
```

```
wscript.echo "Shared files in use on", cname & ":"
on error resume next

for each resource in fs.Resources
    WScript.echo resource.path, "by", resource.user
next
```

The `on error resume next` statement is necessary because, when the `IADsFileService` object refers to a computer other than the one running the script, sometimes one of the objects returned in the `Resources` collection is invalid—it does not have a `Path` or `User` property and can't be listed. In all likelihood, the resource refers to the ADSI connection used to gather the remote resource information. But whatever these mystery objects are, they can't be detected in any way other than trying to view them and failing, so it's best just to have the script ignore the error that occurs.

This script doesn't display the user's computer name, though, and it's often useful to know where to go to get someone to stop using a file that you need to move, rename, or back up. This version of the script lists users by session, and then lists any files they have in use:

```
                                             ' Example Script script0810.vbs
cname = "sumatra"
set fs = GetObject("WinNT://" & cname & "/LanManServer")

wscript.echo "Shared files in use on", cname & ":"
on error resume next

for each session in fs.Sessions              ' list each session's user
    WScript.echo "*", session.user, "from", session.computer & ":"

    for each resource in fs.Resources        ' scan resources but only
        if resource.user = session.user then ' print items for this user
            WScript.echo "   ", resource.path
        end if
    next
next
```

IADsFileShare

The `IADsFileShare` object represents a single shared folder on a workstation or server. Its properties are described in Reference List 8.7.

REFERENCE LIST 8.7   Properties of the `IADsFileShare` Object

CurrentUserCount

Indicates the number of users currently connected to this shared folder. (Read-only.)

Description

A text description of the shared folder (perhaps its purpose).

HostComputer

The ADsPath name of the computer that is sharing this folder. You can use HostComputer with GetObject() if you need access to the corresponding IADsComputer object.

MaxUserCount

The maximum number of users that can connect to this resource at once. (Read-only.)

Name

The share name for this folder (This property is inherited from the base object IADs and is read-only.)

Path

The file system path of the shared file on the host computer.

You can obtain access to existing IADsFileShare objects through the collection of all shares on a specified computer:

```
                                         ' Example Script script0811.vbs
set lm = GetObject("WinNT://computername/LanManServer")
for each share in lm
    wscript.echo share.name, "=", share.path
next
```

Alternatively, if you know its name, you can use a moniker, as shown here:

```
set share = GetObject("WinNT://computername/LanManServer/sharename"
```

You can share a folder on a computer by creating a new IADsFileShare object, using the Create method:

```
                                         ' Example Script script0812.vbs
set lm = GetObject("WinNT://myserver/LanManServer")
set share = lm.Create("FileShare", "Sharename")
share.path = "C:\somefolder\some other folder"
share.description = "Some Descriptive Text"
share.SetInfo        ' save the altered object
```

Note

The Create method is discussed in Reference List 8.2.

Note

The current version of ADSI cannot set sharing restrictions (sharing permissions).

IADsGroup

The `IADsGroup` object represents a security group, which is a set of users who are all granted a given set of specific privileges and file access rights. The concept of a security group exits on Windows NT, 2000, XP, Vista, and 7, as well as on all versions of NetWare. The properties and methods of the `IADsGroup` object are described in Reference List 8.8. Interestingly enough, `IADsGroup` is *not* itself a collection object. To find the group's members, you have to use the `Members` method to retrieve a collection that represents the members.

REFERENCE LIST 8.8   Properties and Methods of the `IADsGroup` Object

Properties:

`Description`
A string describing the purpose of the group.

`Name`
The name of the group. (This property is inherited from the base `IADs` object.)

Methods:

`Add` *adsPath*
Adds a member to the group. `ADsPath` describes the user or group to add—for example, `"WinNT://domainname/username"`.

`IsMember(user)`
Tests whether the specified *user* is a member of the group and returns either `True` or `False`. *User* must be specified as an `ADsPath` representing the user account (for example, `"WinNT://domain/username"`).

`Members()`
Returns an `IADsMembers` collection listing all the users currently in the security group. The `IADsMembers` collection is described in the next section.

`Remove` *user*
Removes the specified user from the security group. *User* must be specified as an `ADsPath` representing the user account.

You can obtain an `IADsGroup` object for a specific group with `GetObject()`, as in this statement:

```
set group = GetObject("WinNT://domain/groupname,Group")
```

Alternatively, you can scan for all the groups in a given domain by examining the domain object's collection:

```
set domain = GetObject("WinNT://domain")

domain.filter = array("Group")
```

```
for each group in domain
    wscript.echo group.name, group.class
next
```

Note

In any of these examples, you can replace *domain* with a computer name to manage the local groups of a server or the security groups in the computers on a non domain network.

You can create a new local or global group using the IADsContainer method Create with the object representing a computer or domain. Here's an example:

```
                                         ' Example Script script0813.vbs
set server = GetObject("WinNT://mycomputer")

set newgrp = server.Create("Group", "IBM 1130 Enthusiasts")
newgrp.SetInfo    ' tell ADSI to save the new group

newgrp.Add("WinNT://mycomputer/bknittel,User")
newgrp.Add("WinNT://mycomputer/naleks,User")
```

IADsMembers

The IADsMembers object is a collection object that represents the individual user accounts belonging to a security group (an IADsGroup). It's the usual scripting collection object with a Count property indicating the number of items in the collection, plus an additional Filter property that can be set to a string value to limit the items seen in the collection.

The Filter property can be left to its default value, Nothing, or can be set to an array of strings naming object classes you want to see. The following scriptlet lists the users in a given security group and omits groups that are also members:

```
                                          ' Example Script script0814.vbs
set ptu = GetObject("WinNT://mydomain/PeachTree Users,Group")
set members = ptu.Members

members.filter = array("User")   ' list users in PeachTree Users
for each user in members
    wscript.echo "user:", user.name
next
```

The objects in the IADsMembers collection are potentially a mix of IADsUser and IADsGroup objects. You can determine the type of each object by examining its Class property. All objects based on IADs have this property, and it describes which particular flavor of ADSI object you have: "User", "Group", "PrintServer", and so on.

IADsNamespaces

The `IADsNamespaces` object is a collection of all ADSI providers available to the computer running an ADSI script. The collection lists the names of the providers as strings that can be used to form object monikers. The object is created with `GetObject("ADs:")`. On my test computer, the script

```
set namespaces = GetObject("ADs:")

wscript.echo "Namespaces ······"
for each ns in namespaces
    wscript.echo ns.name
next
```

printed the following:

```
Namespaces ······
WinNT:
NWCOMPAT:
NDS:
LDAP:
IIS:
```

The object is also purported to have one property named `DefaultContainer`, which can be set to an `ADsPath`. I say "purported to have" because every attempt I have made to reference it has failed with a "Object doesn't support this property" error.

Should this property be available on your systems, it can be set to the name of the default container for the current user's account. This is a good container to start with, for example, when displaying "neighboring" user accounts. `DefaultContainer` is said to be a read/write property; you can store a default container path there for the current user's future ADSI queries. You do not need to call `.SetInfo` after changing `DefaultContainer`.

IADsPrintJob and IADsPrintJobOperations

The `IADsPrintJob` object represents a single print job in a network printer's queue. You can use this object to view the name of the user who submitted the job and other job parameters. The object's properties are described in Reference List 8.9. If the print queue is on a Windows or NetWare server that can be managed by ADSI, the object contains the additional properties and methods defined by the `IADsPrintJobOperations` interface, which is described in Reference List 8.10.

REFERENCE LIST 8.9 Properties of the `IADsPrintJob` Object

Description

A string describing the print job. This is often the name of the document being printed, but it's sometimes blank. The cryptic description "Remote Downlevel Document" indicates output from a DOS application.

HostPrintQueue

The `ADsPath` name of the `IADsPrintQueue` object representing this job's print queue. Use this string with `GetObject()` if you need to obtain the corresponding object. (Read-only.)

Notify

The name of the user to be notified when this print job is completed or canceled.

NotifyPath

The `ADsPath` name of the `IADsUser` object representing the user account to be notified when the print job is completed or canceled. Use `NotifyPath` with `GetObject()` if you need the user object.

Priority

The priority of this print job, a number from 1 up.

Size

The size of the print job in bytes. (Read-only.)

StartTime

A date/time value indicating the earliest time of day that this job can be considered for printing. The date part is ignored.

TimeSubmitted

A date/time value indicating the time that the job is submitted. (Read-only.)

TotalPages

The total number of pages in the print job. (Read-only.)

UntilTime

A date/time value indicating the latest time of day that the job can be considered for printing. The date part is ignored. If `StartTime` and `UntilTime` are equal, the job can print at any time.

User

The name of the user who submitted this print job.

UserPath

The `ADsPath` name of the `IADsUser` object representing the user who submitted the print job. Use `UserPath` with `GetObject()` if you need the user object.

`IADsPrintJob` objects are obtained as a collection from the `IADsPrintQueue` object's `PrintJobs` property. Here's an example:

```
                                      ' Example Script script0815.vbs
set server = GetObject("WinNT://servername/sharename")
```

```
for each job in server.Printjobs
    wscript.echo job.User, job.TotalPages
next
```

For jobs on Windows and NetWare servers, IADsPrintJob sports the additional
IADsPrintJobOperations interface, which gives the object an additional set of properties and methods. These properties and methods are described in Reference List 8.10.

REFERENCE LIST 8.10   Properties and Methods of the IADsPrintJobOperations Interface

Properties:

Status

Returns one of the following values describing the current status of this print job:
Read-only.

Constant	Value (in Hexadecimal)
ADS_JOB_PAUSED	&H001
ADS_JOB_ERROR	&H002
ADS_JOB_DELETING	&H004
ADS_JOB_PRINTING	&H010
ADS_JOB_OFFLINE	&H020
ADS_JOB_PAPEROUT	&H040
ADS_JOB_PRINTED	&H080
ADS_JOB_DELETED	&H100

TimeElapsed

Returns the time elapsed, in seconds, since the print job started printing, or 0 if it
has not yet started printing. (Read-only.)

PagesPrinted

Returns the number of pages already printed. (Read-only.)

Position

Returns this job's position in the print queue. (Read-only.)

Methods:

Pause

Halts the processing of this print job. If the job has not yet started printing, other
jobs ahead of and behind this one can continue to print.

Resume

Permits this print job to continue printing or to be considered for printing.

Note

You must have Administrator privileges on the server hosting the queue to view or modify print jobs.

IADsPrintQueue and IADsPrintQueueOperations

The IADsPrintQueue object represents a network shared printer. This object lets you view the printer's location and description information as well as obtain lists of pending print jobs. The object's properties are described in Reference List 8.11. For print queues on Windows and NetWare servers, you can use the additional methods and properties provided by the IADsPrintQueueOperations interface to manage the print queue. These methods and properties appear as part of the same IADsPrintQueue object and are discussed in Reference List 8.12.

REFERENCE LIST 8.11 Properties of the IADsPrintQueue Object

BannerPage

Returns the pathname of the separator file inserted between print jobs or NULL if no separator page is configured.

Datatype

The default print data type preferred by this queue. This is a string with one of the following values: "RAW", "RAW [FF appended]", "RAW [FF auto]", "NT EMF 1.003", "NT EMF 1.006", "NT EMF 1.007", "NT EMF 1.008", or "TEXT".

DefaultJobPriority

The default priority value given to print jobs that do not specify a specific priority, an integer from 1 up.

Description

A brief descriptive name for the printer; this information displays in Active Directory and in Network Neighborhood. This information corresponds to the Description field in the Windows Printer Properties dialog box.

HostComputer

This property ostensibly names the computer that hosts the print queue. However, in my testing, a "Property does not exist" error occurred whenever I attempted to reference this property. The property is apparently not implemented in every ADSI provider.

Location

A brief description of the location of this printer. This corresponds to the Location field in the Windows Printer Properties dialog box.

Model

A text string naming the make and model of the printer. This is descriptive only. Changing this string does not change the associated printer driver.

Name

The name of the print queue. (This property is inherited from the base IADs object.)

PrintDevices

An array of strings that contain the names of the ports that serve this queue. If the queue uses printer pooling, more than one port might be listed.

PrinterPath

A string that gives the UNC pathname that refers to this printer (for example, "*servername**sharename*").

PrintProcessor

The name of the default print processor for this queue. For Windows printers, this is almost always "WinPrint".

Priority

The priority of jobs from this queue relative to any other queues that feed to the same printer ports. All jobs from the highest-priority queue are processed before any jobs from lower-priority queues are considered.

Starttime

A date/time value indicating the time of day that the queue begins processing jobs. The date part of the date/time is ignored.

UntilTime

A date/time value indicating the time of day that the queue stops processing jobs. The date part of the date/time is ignored. If StartTime and EndTime are the same value, the queue is always operational.

You can obtain IADsPrintQueue objects using GetObject, with statements like this one:

```
set queue = GetObject("WinNT://servername/sharename")
```

In this case, *servername* is the name of the computer hosting the print queue, and *sharename* is the name of the queue. You can also scan the list of all printers shared by a particular server with a filter:

```
                                        ' Example Script script0816.vbs
servername = "servername"
set server = GetObject("WinNT://" & servername)
wscript.echo "Print queues on", servername & ":"

server.Filter = Array("PrintQueue")
for each printer in server
    wscript.echo "***", printer.name
    for each job in printer.printjobs
        if job.totalpages = "1" then plural = "" else plural = "s"
        wscript.echo "   ", job.user & ":", job.totalpages, "page" & plural
    next
next
```

Here's some sample output from this script:

```
Print queues on sumatra:
***Okidata
    bknittel: 1 page
```

`IADsPrintQueueOperations` is an additional interface that provides management functions. If an `IADsPrinter` object refers to a Windows or NetWare print queue, the additional methods and properties described in Reference List 8.12 are available on the same object.

REFERENCE LIST 8.12   Properties and Methods of the `IAdsPrintQueueOperations` Interface

Properties:

PrintJobs
Returns a collection of `IADsPrintJob` objects representing all pending and active jobs in this queue. `IADsPrintJob` was described earlier in this section.

Status
Returns a value indicating the current status of this print queue. Read-only. `Status` is one of the values listed in Table 8.6 or possibly the sum of several values.

Methods:

Pause
Halts the processing of print jobs for this queue. If other queues are directed at the same printer(s), those queues might continue sending jobs to the printer(s).

Purge
Removes all pending print jobs from the queue.

Resume
Resumes the processing of print jobs.

You can use the `IADsPrintQueue` object to view and manage print queues but not create new ones.

Table 8.6 lists the status values returned by `IADsPrintQueueOperations`. The `Status` property can be one of these values or a sum of several values.

Table 8.6   **Status Values Returned by** `IAdsPrintQueueOperations`

Constant	Value (in Hexadecimal)
ADS_PRINTER_PAUSED	&H00000001
ADS_PRINTER_PENDING_DELETION	&H00000002
ADS_PRINTER_ERROR	&H00000003
ADS_PRINTER_PAPER_JAM	&H00000004

Constant	Value (in Hexadecimal)
ADS_PRINTER_PAPER_OUT	&H00000005
ADS_PRINTER_MANUAL_FEED	&H00000006
ADS_PRINTER_PAPER_PROBLEM	&H00000007
ADS_PRINTER_OFFLINE	&H00000008
ADS_PRINTER_IO_ACTIVE	&H00000100
ADS_PRINTER_BUSY	&H00000200
ADS_PRINTER_PRINTING	&H00000400
ADS_PRINTER_OUTPUT_BIN_FULL	&H00000800
ADS_PRINTER_NOT_AVAILABLE	&H00001000
ADS_PRINTER_WAITING	&H00002000
ADS_PRINTER_PROCESSING	&H00004000
ADS_PRINTER_INITIALIZING	&H00008000
ADS_PRINTER_WARMING_UP	&H00010000
ADS_PRINTER_TONER_LOW	&H00020000
ADS_PRINTER_NO_TONER	&H00040000
ADS_PRINTER_PAGE_PUNT	&H00080000
ADS_PRINTER_USER_INTERVENTION	&H00100000
ADS_PRINTER_OUT_OF_MEMORY	&H00200000
ADS_PRINTER_DOOR_OPEN	&H00400000
ADS_PRINTER_SERVER_UNKNOWN	&H00800000
ADS_PRINTER_POWER_SAVE	&H01000000

IADsService and IADsServiceOperations

The IADsService object represents and manages the settings for a system service installed on an individual computer. System services are the programs run "behind the scenes" by Windows to perform basic functions such as file sharing, UPS monitoring, event logging, and so on. The object's properties and one method are described in Reference List 8.13. All the IADsService properties are read/write, but you must use the SetInfo method to commit any changes you make.

IADsServiceOperations is an additional interface available on service objects that represent Windows computers. That is, for IADsService objects that represent Windows NT, XP, 2000, and .NET Server computers, and possibly NetWare servers as well, there are *additional* properties and methods that you can use to manage the service. The additional properties and methods are described in Reference List 8.14.

Note

You can also manage Windows services with the WMI objects described in Chapter 7. For service management, WMI is probably easier and faster.

REFERENCE LIST 8.13 Properties and Method of the IADsService Object

Properties:

Dependencies

An array of strings containing the names of services upon which this service depends (that is, services that must be started first). Each entry in the array consists of "Service:", followed by a service name, or "Group:", followed by a load order group name.

DisplayName

The "display" name of the service.

ErrorControl

Indicates how Windows should respond if the service fails to start. This property takes one of the values listed in Table 8.7.

HostComputer

The name of the computer running this service. It appears to be a read/write property, although I can't quite see what it would mean to change it—these properties apply only to the computer from which this object is obtained.

LoadOrderGroup

The name of the load order group to which this service belongs.

Name

The name of the service object. (This property is inherited from the base IADs object.)

Path

The path and filename of the executable program that provides this service.

ServiceAccountName

The name of the account that the service uses. This is usually "LocalSystem" or "NT AUTHORITY\LocalService".

ServiceAccountPath

This is purportedly the ADsPath string of the account associated with the service that could be used with GetObject() to examine the account's properties. However, in ADSI version 2.5, this property appears to be absent.

ServiceType

The type of service this program performs. It can one of the following values:

Constant	Value (in Hexadecimal)
ADS_SERVICE_KERNEL_DRIVER	&H01
ADS_SERVICE_FILE_SYSTEM_DRIVER	&H02
ADS_SERVICE_OWN_PROCESS	&H10
ADS_SERVICE_SHARE_PROCESS	&H20

StartType

Indicates when, during the Windows boot-up process, the service is started. This can be one of the following values:

Constant	Value (in Hexadecimal)
ADS_SERVICE_BOOT_START	&H00
ADS_SERVICE_SYSTEM_START	&H01
ADS_SERVICE_AUTO_START	&H02
ADS_SERVICE_DEMAND_START	&H03
ADS_SERVICE_DISABLED	&H04

StartupParameters

An optional string that is passed as the command-line argument to the service when it is started.

Version

The version information for this service.

Method:

SetInfo

Saves any changes you have made to the object's properties back to the Windows computer that the object represents.

Table 8.7 lists the values returned by the ErrorControl property.

Table 8.7   **Values for the** ErrorControl **Property**

Constant	Value	Error Action
ADS_SERVICE_ERROR_IGNORE	0	Windows logs the error and continues startup.
ADS_SERVICE_ERROR_NORMAL	1	Same as for ADS_SERVICE_ERROR_IGNORE. In addition, the user is notified with a dialog box.
ADS_SERVICE_ERROR_SEVERE	2	Windows logs the error and restarts the system in Last Known Good mode. If the error occurs in Last Known Good mode, startup continues.
ADS_SERVICE_ERROR_CRITICAL	3	Same as for ADS_SERVICE_ERROR_SEVERE, but if the error occurs in Last Known Good mode, startup is halted.

To obtain the list of services installed on an individual computer, you must first obtain an `IADsComputer` object for the individual computer and then scan through its collection contents looking for `IADsService` objects. The `Filter` property makes this easy:

```
                                          ' Example Script script0817.vbs
set computer = GetObject("WinNT://computername,Computer")
computer.Filter = Array("service") ' limit view to Services only

for each service in computer
   wscript.echo service.name, service.status
next
```

You must have Administrator privileges to view or modify service information.

For objects that represent services on Windows computers, one property and extra methods are available, as part of the `IADsServiceOperations` interfaces. These are shown in Reference List 8.14.

REFERENCE LIST 8.14   Property and Methods of the `IADsServiceOperations` **Interface**

Property:

Status

Returns the current status of the service. It can be one of the following values: Read-only.

Constant	Value (in Hexadecimal)
ADS_SERVICE_STOPPED	&H01
ADS_SERVICE_START_PENDING	&H02
ADS_SERVICE_STOP_PENDING	&H03
ADS_SERVICE_RUNNING	&H04
ADS_SERVICE_CONTINUE_PENDING	&H05
ADS_SERVICE_PAUSE_PENDING	&H06
ADS_SERVICE_PAUSED	&H07
ADS_SERVICE_ERROR	&H08

Methods:

Continue

Resumes the service after pausing.

Pause

Pauses the service.

SetPassword *newpassword*

Sets the password that is to be used with the service's associated user account.

Start

Starts the service. To restart a service, you need to stop it, wait for its status to equal ADS_SERVICE_STOPPED, and then start it again.

Stop

Stops the service.

You must have Administrator privileges to manage services.

IADsSession

The IADsSession object represents an active connection between a user on one computer and another computer that is sharing files, printers, or Remote Desktop (Terminal Services) connections. The session object describes only the connection between a user and another computer and doesn't contain detail information (for example, which files are in use). The object's properties, which are all read-only, are shown in Reference List 8.15.

REFERENCE LIST 8.15　Properties of the IADsSession Object

Computer

Returns the name of the user's client workstation.

ComputerPath

Returns the ADsPath moniker for the computer account for members of Active Directory networks only.

ConnectTime

Returns the number of seconds since the user connected to the shared resource. (The Microsoft documentation says minutes, but the value is in seconds.)

IdleTime

Returns the number of seconds since the user last accessed a shared resource. (The Microsoft documentation says minutes, but the value is in seconds.)

User

Returns the name of the user account for this session.

UserPath

Returns the ADsPath moniker for the user account; this can be used with GetObject() to obtain the corresponding IADsUser object.

You can obtain IADsSession objects as a collection from the IADsFileService object's Sessions property. The statements

```
                                            ' Example Script script0818.vbs
set fileserv = GetObject("WinNT://computername/Lanmanserver")
if not isempty(fileserv) then
    for each session in fileserv.sessions
```

```
            wscript.echo "User:", session.user, "Computer:", _
                session.computer, "idle:", session.idletime, "sec"
        next
    end if
```

list all the sessions being served by a specific computer. To find the session for a particular user, you have to scan through the collection and test the User property for a match to the desired name.

IADsUser

The IADsUser object represents a single computer user account in a domain or on an individual workstation. The IADsUser object has at least 47 properties and 3 methods that let you configure the account's username and contact information, set its password, login script, and profile, examine or alter group membership, and reset account lockout after the user has made too many attempts to log on with the wrong password. The Microsoft documentation lists all the properties, and you want to examine that documentation if you're going to use ADSI to manage accounts on an Active Directory network.

The most important properties are listed in Reference List 8.16, along with the three methods.

REFERENCE LIST 8.16 Properties and Methods of the IADsUser Object

Properties:

AccountDisabled
A Boolean value that is True if the account has been disabled. You can set this value to disable or enable the account. Remember to use .SetInfo after making any changes.

Description
The description text for this user account.

FullName
The user's full name.

Groups
This is an IADsMembers collection containing the security groups to which this user belongs. You can manipulate this collection to add or remove groups. See the listing for IADsMembers earlier in this section for more information.

HomeDirectory
The home directory path for this user.

IsAccountLocked
A Boolean value that is True if the account has been locked out due to too many attempts to log on with the wrong password.

LastLogin

Date and time of last logon to this account. (Read-only.)

LastLogoff

Date and time of the last logoff from this account. (Read-only.)

Profile

The user's profile path; on a local machine, this is usually a folder named
`\Documents and Settings\`*username*. On a domain network with roaming user
profiles, this is a path to a shared profile folder.

Methods:

ChangePassword *oldpassword, newpassword*

Changes the user's password from *oldpassword* to *newpassword*. You must use
`ChangePassword` rather than `SetPassword` and must know the account's old password if you do not have Administrator privileges.

SetInfo

Saves any changes you've made to the object's properties to the actual Windows
user directory. This method is inherited from object `IADs`.

SetPassword *newpassword*

Sets the user account's password to the new string value. The change takes place
immediately; you do not have to use `.SetInfo` to make the change permanent. You
must have Administrator privileges to use `SetPassword`.

You can obtain a specific user object with the statement

```
set user = GetObject("WinNT://domain/username,user")
```

where *domain* is the account's domain name for a global domain account or the name
of an individual workstation for a local or workgroup account, and *username* is the
name of the account. You can also create a new domain user account with the following statements:

```
set domain = GetObject("WinNT://domainname")
set user = domain.Create("user", "newusername")
```

You can create a new local workstation account with this:

```
set computer = GetObject("WinNT://computername,Computer")
set user = computer.Create("user", "newusername")
```

You should set all the relevant properties and finalize the account with

```
user.SetInfo
```

and then add the user to any necessary groups and directory containers. Because the
`IADsGroup` and `IADsContainer` objects' `Add` method takes a pathname argument, rather
than a direct object reference, you need to use statements like these:

```
set group = GetObject("WinNT://domainname,groupname,Group")
group.Add user.AdsPath
```

IIS and Exchange

Some of the most powerful applications for ADSI scripting are in the management of IIS and Microsoft Exchange. For managers of small to mid-size networks, maintaining the comings and goings of multiple websites and users can be a tedious job. ADSI scripting can give you a way of adding users or sites by typing one line at the command prompt; if you've ever spent 20 minutes poking at the IIS Manager, the Users and Groups Manager, and Windows Explorer to add one new server, you know what an improvement this can be.

However, it would take several chapters this size or larger just to delve into IIS management, and there simply isn't room to do that in this book. If you become familiar with the material in this chapter and gain experience writing scripts to manage user accounts and services, you find that extending your skills to manage IIS and Exchange should be a snap. The ADSI learning curve is steep, but it levels out fairly quickly. I show you where to get more information at the end of the chapter.

Managing Active Directory

Managing Active Directory shouldn't a huge conceptual leap ahead of anything we've discussed so far in this chapter. It's all about containers, about moving little people around in tidy little boxes—a simulacrum of life in the business world—and it's all represented by tidy little objects. What could be so difficult about it? Ah! If the mention of X.500 doesn't strike fear into your heart now, it will within a few minutes.

Because Active Directory is designed to work alongside other manufacturers' operating systems and network services, it is designed to conform to industry-wide standards for networkable directories. This is both a blessing and a curse. In the interest of interoperability, its syntax for specifying users, groups, containers, organizational units, and so forth is based on the X.500 standard, which was designed by a committee—a huge committee. That should give you a big clue right there!

Before we go into the objects and techniques involved in managing Active Directory, you need a quick introduction into X.500 and LDAP terminology.

X.500 and LDAP Terminology

Every item in an X.500 or LDAP-compatible directory has a unique name. Just as every file on your hard drive has a unique pathname, every ADSI object has its ADsPath. In LDAP, this is called a *distinguished name*, or DN. A directory object's DN is a full specification, naming this one person, group, computer, or whatever, out of the directory's entire universe of objects. If an Active Directory is organized as shown earlier in Figure 8.1, the user Alice has the following distinguished name:

```
o=mycompany.com/ou=WestCoast/ou=Research/cn=Alice
```

This looks a lot like a file's pathname, except that in a distinguished name, the name at each level of the hierarchy has to be marked with its structural significance: o = organization, ou = organizational unit, cn = common name, and so on. Because containers could conceivably hold different types of objects with the same name, these qualifiers make the path unambiguous.

The name shown previously is specified in what's called *Big-Endian form* because the name starts with the "big" end of the name—the organization. In Little-Endian form, Alice's DN is as follows:

```
cn=Alice, ou=Research, ou=WestCoast, o=mycompany.com
```

You can see that this starts with the little end, the lowest level of the directory organization, and works up toward the top. Active Directory accepts DNs in either format, but always returns them to you in Little-Endian form. Because a name could conceivably contain a comma, DNs use a backslash (\) to escape commas in the name. If a username is "Knittel, Alice", for example, the DN might look like this:

```
cn=Knittel\, Alice, ou=Research, ou=WestCoast, o=mycompany.com
```

The parts of a distinguished name are called *relative distinguished names*, or RDNs, because they specify an object relative to the container in which they're held. "Alice" is an RDN that uniquely specifies a user only within the West Coast Research division; there might be other Alices in other divisions.

The identifiers cn, ou and o are called *attribute names*. Here are the most commonly used attributes in Active Directory distinguished names:

Attribute	**Meaning**
dc	Naming context
o	Organization
ou	Organizational unit
l	Locality
cn	Common name (applies to containers, users groups, computers, and so on)

Note

Most of this discussion about the LDAP: provider applies to the Novell NetWare Directory Services NDS: provider as well because it is also based on LDAP. Some of the NDS: naming attributes differ, however.

Now, hopefully, with this background, it isn't too distressing to see how this works in practice. Given an Active Directory network user's distinguished name, you can obtain an IADsUser object using an LDAP moniker like this:

```
set user = GetObject(_
    "LDAP://CN=Alice,OU=Research,OU=WestCoast,O=mycompany.com")
```

This returns the same `IADsUser` object that you get if you specified this user with her "down-level" Windows NT domain name, as in

```
set user = GetObject("WinNT://mycompany/alice,User")
```

You can obtain the object representing an organization unit given its DN. Here's an example:

```
set user = GetObject("LDAP://OU=WestCoast,O=mycompany.com")
```

This returns an enhanced version of `IADsContainer` called `IADsOU`, which is discussed in the next section.

One last bit about constructing distinguished names: In most Active Directory networks, the top-level structure is specified not as `O=mycompany.com` but rather with "naming context" attributes specified in this way:

```
DC=mycompany,DC=com
```

That's the LDAP version of "mycompany.com" in Little-Endian form.

Rather than have to try to guess the name of the top level of your organization's network, ADSI provides a way of giving you the top-level distinguished name, called the *Default Naming Context*. The information is obtained from a property of a special object, called the *Root DS Entry*, with this script code:

```
set rootDSE = GetObject("LDAP://RootDSE")
context = rootDSE.Get("DefaultNamingContext")

wscript.echo "The top level name is", context
```

`RootDSE` is discussed in more detail in the next section.

Note

If you want to connect to a specific LDAP server, you can speed up the servicing of ADSI requests by connecting with the `OpenDSObject` method and specifying `ADS_SERVER_BIND` in the flag's argument. See the "Directory Security" section earlier in the chapter for more information.

You must use the `Get` method of the `IADs` object to obtain the most special Active Directory object properties because they are not part of the various `IADs` objects discussed earlier in the chapter. You can use this default context name to construct DNs in organization-independent scripts, as in this example:

```
set rootDSE = GetObject("LDAP://RootDSE")    ' get default naming context
context = rootDSE.Get("DefaultNamingContext")

set westcoast = GetObject("LDAP://OU=WestCoast" & context)
```

This fetches the `WestCoast` container from the top level of the organization, no matter how its top level is named.

Note

Because the Default Naming Context is returned in Little-Endian order, stick it onto the *end* of any DN you're constructing.

The collection of objects in this container can be scanned like any other ADSI enumeration. In fact, you can list the entire contents of Active Directory with a recursive program like this:

```
                                         ' Example Script script0819.vbs
set rootDSE = GetObject("LDAP://RootDSE")   ' get default naming context
context = rootDSE.Get("DefaultNamingContext")

set top = GetObject("LDAP://" & context)     ' get top level container
ListContainer top, 0                         ' start listing at the top

sub ListContainer (obj, depth)        ' subroutine to list a container
    dim member                        ' private local variable

    WScript.echo space(depth*3) & obj.name ' list the container's name

    on error resume next              ' ignore error if no collection
    for each member in obj            ' display anything inside
        ListContainer member, depth+1
    next
end sub
```

I have to tell you, though, that if you run this script in a Fortune 500 company, it might take a *long* time to run itself out.

Tip

To get acquainted with the structure of Active Directory, I suggest that you actually do run this script and redirect its output to a file so that you can examine it.

You can also browse through Active Directory with the Microsoft Management Console ADSI Edit plug-in. You can install it on desktop versions of Windows with `\support\tools\supptools.msi` on a Windows Server 2003 setup CD, or you can download the Windows Server 2003 Support tools from www.microsoft.com. After it's installed, open a command prompt window and type **start adsiedit.msc**. Select the default LDAP server. You can then browse through Active Directory in its raw form. You can read more about ADSI Edit by searching for that name on technet.microsoft.com.

For more information about Active Directory, LDAP, and X.500, you might want to visit technet.microsoft.com and search for "Active Directory Concepts." I have found www.kingsmountain.com/ldapRoadmap.shtml and www.tums.com to be helpful as well.

Active Directory Objects

A few special ADSI objects appear when you work with Active Directory and other LDAP directories. When you try to work with the added Active Directory properties found on these objects, the normal syntax you would expect to use, such as:

```
WScript.echo object.propertyname
object.propertyname = newvalue
```

might not work and might generate a script error. Instead, you might need to use the Get and Put methods, as shown here:

```
WScript.echo object.Get("propertyname")
object.Put "propertyname", newvalue
```

RootDSE

The RootDSE object describes the properties of the local LDAP server. There is no custom IADsRootDSE interface for this object, so you cannot access its properties using the standard object.*property* syntax. It's based on plain-old IADs, so you must use the Get() method to retrieve the special properties listed in Reference List 8.17.

REFERENCE LIST 8.17   Properties of the RootDSE Object (Partial List)

currentTime
Current date and time reported by the LDAP server.

defaultNamingContext
The default name context ("big end") of all DNs in the local domain.

dnsHostName
The current LDAP server's DNS hostname.

namingContexts
An array of string values listing the top-level sections of the directory. For Active Directory, these include the following:

- The Default Naming Context
- The DN of the Configuration section, which contains Active Directory's internal configuration information
- The DN of the Schema section, which contains lists of the structure, properties, and allowed values for all directory objects

rootDomainNamingContext
The name context ("big end") of all DNs in this directory.

serverName
The current LDAP server's DN.

supportedLDAPVersion
An array of LDAP version numbers supported by the current server.

You can obtain the `RootDSE` object with this moniker:

```
set rootDSE = GetObject("LDAP://RootDSE")
```

IADsO and IADsOU

`IADsO` and `IADsOU` are objects that represent an entire organization and a subunit of the organization, respectively. They are based on the `IADsContainer` object, so all of `IADsContainer`'s methods and properties appear as part of `IADsO` and `IADsOU`. In particular, they both act like collection objects and can contain computers, users, or other container objects. In addition, `IADsO` and `IADsOU` inherit the properties of `IADsLocality`, which describes such items as the local fax and telephone numbers.

For simplicity's sake, I've listed all the collected methods and properties available for these objects.

The properties and methods of `IADsO` and `IADsOU` are described in Reference List 8.18. The `IADsOU` object represents a subpart of an organization and has the same set of properties as `IADsO`, with the addition of `BusinessCategory`.

REFERENCE LIST 8.18   Properties and Methods of the `IADsO` **and** `IADsOU` **Objects**

Properties:

BusinessCategory
Describes the business function performed by this organizational unit. (`IADsOU` only.)

Count
The number of subobjects in the container (from `IADsContainer`). (Read-only.)

Description
A string describing the organization or unit (for example, the company name).

FaxNumber
A string describing the primary fax number.

Filter
See `IADsContainer`.

LocalityName
A string describing the physical location of the organization or unit.

Name
The name of the container. (This property is inherited from the base `IADs` object.)

Parent
The `ADsPath` name of the container that holds this object (also inherited from `IADs`).

PostalAddress

A string giving the primary mailing address.

SeeAlso

Any additional pertinent information.

TelephoneNumber

The organization or unit's primary telephone number.

Methods:

See `IADsContainer`.

You can obtain `IADsO` and `IADsOU` objects using their distinguished names or by scanning other containers, as described earlier in this section.

Developing ADSI Scripts

Throughout this chapter, I've provided scriptlets that you can modify and test to get acquainted with ADSI. These short scripts list the members of groups and individual properties. You can write more useful scripts by extending these beginnings with additional functions.

It's especially useful to write scripts that take arguments from the command line. You can use this technique to write scripts in a general-purpose fashion, and you specify the particulars on the command line when you run the script.

For example, on a small peer-to-peer workgroup network that doesn't use Simple File Sharing, it's useful for every user to have an account on each computer, with the same password on each. When a user changes his password on one computer, the password has to be changed on every computer—a real hassle. The following script can make this an easy job:

```
                                        ' Example script allpass.vbs
' change a password on all computers in the group

if WScript.Arguments.count <> 3 then  ' explain the command syntax
    WScript.echo "Usage: allpass username oldpassword newpassword"
    WScript.quit 0
end if
username = WScript.Arguments(0)        ' store the values
oldpass  = WScript.Arguments(1)
newpass  = WScript.Arguments(2)

Wscript.echo "Working..."              ' it may take a while, show we're alive

fix "bali"                             ' call fix once for each of the
fix "java"                             ' workgroup's computers.
fix "sumatra"
fix "ambon"
```

```
fix "kalimantan"

wscript.echo "Done."

sub fix (compname)                    ' subroutine to update one computer
    on error resume next              ' get user object
    set user = GetObject("WinNT://" & compname & "/" & username & ",User")
    if err then                       ' failed; tell them
        wscript.echo "Unable to change password on", compname
        exit sub
    end if
    user.changePassword oldpass, newpass
    if err then
        wscript.echo "Unable to change password on", compname
        exit sub
    end if
    user.setinfo    ' changePassword is immediate but best be sure
    wscript.echo compname & ": OK"
end sub
```

For example, when I type the command,

```
allpass bknittel myoldpassword anewpassword
```

this is what printed:

```
Working...
bali: OK
java: OK
sumatra: OK
ambon: OK
Unable to change password on kalimantan
Done.
```

This is reasonable because the computer named kalimantan was not turned on. That computer will have to be updated manually.

Caution

I suggest that when you start using ADSI to create and modify directory information, you develop your scripts on an isolated test computer and not your company's network. You need to be logged on with Administrator privileges, and if things go wrong, the damage could be catastrophic. When you're ready for a bigger test, if possible, use your script on a small "test" domain that you have set up strictly for testing purposes.

EzAD Scriptomatic

The scripting wizards at Microsoft created an ADSI version of the WMI Scriptomatic tool that I mentioned in the previous chapter. It's less detailed than the WMI Scriptomatic tool, but it can create the basic outline of scripts to create, read (examine), write (modify), and delete various objects in Active Directory. To set up this tool, log on to a Domain Admin account and follow these steps:

1. Open Internet Explorer, visit www.microsoft.com, and type **download ADSI scriptomatic** in the search box. Select the download page. Click Download, and then click Run to run the setup program.

2. In the WinZip Self Extractor dialog box, select a permanent location to store the two included files. Your profile folder is a reasonable place: On Windows 7 and Vista, this is usually \users*YourAccountName* and on XP it's \Documents and Settings*YourAccountName*. Click Unzip, then OK, and then Close.

3. Right-click your desktop and select New, Shortcut.

4. Click Browse, locate the folder you selected in step 2, select the file EZADScriptomatic.hta, and click OK to close the Browse dialog box.

5. If you are using Windows XP, click Next and proceed to step 6.

   If you are using Windows 7 or Vista, put the cursor before the filename, and type the letters **mshta** followed by a space. Then, click Next.

6. Change the shortcut name to **EzAD Scriptomatic**, and click Finish.

7. If you are using Windows XP, you're done.

   On Windows 7 or Vista, right-click the new shortcut and select Properties. On the Shortcut tab, click Advanced, and check Run As Administrator. Click OK, and then OK again.

Double-click the new shortcut to start EzAD Scriptomatic, which is shown in Figure 8.3. VBScript is the only supported language. EzAD Scriptomatic's basic script creates an object named by variable `strName`—for example, `"EzAdUser"` inside the directory's top-level container. To create an object in a subcontainer, you should set variable `strContainer` to the subcontainer's DN in Little-Endian format.

You can edit the generated script, click Run to run it, use copy-and-paste to move it somewhere else, or click Save to save it in a file. Then, you can use all or part of it to create your own, fully functional scripts.

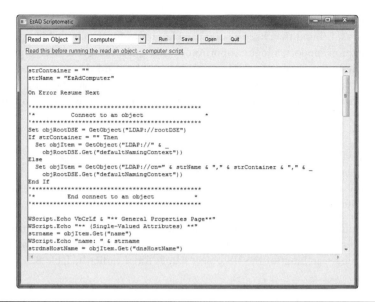

Figure 8.3 EzAD Scriptomatic writes simple scripts to create, examine, modify, or write Active Directory objects.

For More Information

This chapter has touched on the ADSI's capabilities. If you've found this interesting so far, I definitely encourage you to get more information. As with the previous chapter on Windows Management Instrumentation, the material in this chapter should be enough to show you how this stuff works and to give you enough background to make effective use of the Microsoft documentation that covers ADSI in its entirety.

On the Web, you can find Microsoft's online documentation at msdn.microsoft.com. Search for "Active Directory Services Interfaces." Be sure, however, to read my notes on interpreting this documentation from earlier in this chapter, in "Important Notes Regarding the Microsoft Documentation" on page 332.

There is also a moderately helpful set of tutorials and sample scripts at technet.microsoft.com. Search for "Scripting for Active Directory."

You can also find many websites that discuss ADSI scripting. A Google search for `getobject winnt` should give you enough to keep you busy for several days!

Microsoft's public newsgroup for ADSI programming support is `microsoft.public.adsi.general`. I found that, like the comparable groups for Windows Management Instrumentation support, a high proportion of user questions get answered promptly here, but the topics discussed on this newsgroup tend toward the esoteric. Most of the discussion centers on the `LDAP:` provider because most visitors are working with or trying to work with Active Directory. So, you might not find this newsgroup to be as rich a source of useful information as the WMI group, unless you want to (or have to) commit yourself to getting into the most arcane parts of ADSI.

For a printed reference, I recommend *Windows NT/200 ADSI Scripting for System Administration* by Thomas Eck, published by New Riders Publishing. It's well written and is full of useful sample scripts, presented cookbook style. Some of the examples are a bit too trivial, but it does do a good job of showing each ADSI object in action.

For more information about using ADSI for IIS management, visit msdn.microsoft.com and search for "IIS Admin Objects Reference." You can find tutorials and sample scripts on the Web by searching for the IIS object names listed earlier in Table 8.3.

9

Deploying Scripts for Computer and Network Management

IN THIS CHAPTER

- This chapter shows you how to write and distribute scripts for end users.

- You learn how to configure logon scripts on standalone, workgroup, and domain computers.

- You learn how to write scripts for unattended, scheduled processing.

- Windows has a tool that lets you create simple installation programs to distribute your own programs and scripts—if you know where to find it.

Using Scripts in the Real World

The previous chapters covered the basics of Windows Script Host (WSH) and the powerful data processing, management, and maintenance objects and functions it provides. If you've been experimenting with these tools along the way, you've probably already started using WSH to solve day-to-day problems.

It's one thing to write a quick-and-dirty script to address some immediate need—for instance, to fix a directory full of misnamed files. I find myself doing this all the time. For such one-time-use scripts, you don't have to worry about proper formatting, documentation, generality, reliability, portability, or any of the other hallmarks of good programming style.

However, in what's called a *production environment*—that is, in situations where your scripts might be used by other people, on other computers, or on a repeated basis—good programming style *is* a concern. In this chapter, I cover some of the tools that WSH provides to make it easier to write good, solid scripts that stand up to day-to-day use. Later, I give you some tips for deploying them in a real-world networked environment.

Designing Scripts for Other Users

It's one thing to write a script for your own use. You wrote it, and you know how it works, so you probably don't care to invest much effort in making it user friendly. However, when you're writing a script for others, you have to take into account that others haven't gone through the process of designing and writing the script, so they don't understand its nuances. They need some hand-holding. Even for your own scripts, chances are, six months after you write one, you'll have forgotten how it works yourself, and on inspection, the program will be about as comprehensible as a cuneiform tablet. So, for scripts that you intend to share or just keep around a while, it's worth investing some time to make them self-documenting and forgiving to the novice user.

Here are some of the attributes of a well-written, user-friendly script:

- The script should be written in as general a way as possible. For example, instead of writing a script to clean temporary files out of a particular named folder, you might write a script to clean any folder or folders named on the command line. If no folder is named on the command line, it might go ahead and clean a default folder, or you might have it display a description of how it's properly used. Making a script more general increases the likelihood that it can serve more than one purpose.

- As a programmer, you should use every tool at your disposal to help you write correct code. This means, for example, that if you're writing VBScript, you should use the `option explicit` statement, which requires you to declare *every* variable in a `dim` statement. This makes it possible for VBScript to detect any misspelled variable names. It doesn't catch other sorts of bugs, but this does take care of one whole category, for free. (Option Explicit is discussed in Chapter 2, "VBScript Tutorial," under the heading "Variable Scope," page 91.)

- The script should not make assumptions about its operating environment. For example, the Windows folder isn't always `C:\WINDOWS`. It could be `D:\WINDOWS`, `C:\WINNT`, or…who knows? Instead of writing a script that uses fixed paths to system folders, use environment variables and the `WScript.Shell` object to get the actual paths of various system and user folders. For details, see the entries for `GetSpecialFolder` in Reference List 4.1 (page 125) and `SpecialFolders` in Reference List 4.9 (page 182).

- The script should validate the existence of all files and folders named on the command line using the `FileExists` method discussed in Reference List 4.1 (page 125). If any specified files do not exist, have the script acknowledge that and quit before attempting to actually use the files. It's better to display a message such as "File input.dat does not exist" at the outset than to have the script get partway through its job, only to stop, and give the user a cryptic message such as the following:

```
C:\scripts\process.vbs(33, 1)
➥Microsoft VBScript runtime error: File not found
```

- The script should carefully check any command-line arguments for proper syntax. If errors are found, it should tell exactly what is wrong *and* display a concise, but helpful, description of what command-line arguments are allowed.

- The script should be written to assume sensible default values for optional command-line arguments. For example, if your script has an option to display lots of debugging information with `WScript.echo` statements, you might use the command-line argument `/verbose` to enable it, but have the verbose option default to "off" if it's not requested. We discuss these last two points in this chapter.

Writing a script with these properties takes time and makes the script larger and, ironically, increases the likelihood that there are bugs lurking in the script due to the added code. Therefore, when you're making a script for public consumption, you have to carefully test every possible variation and outcome. Still, in the long run, this is all worthwhile because it makes your programs much more reliable and user friendly.

One way to make it easier to write more user-friendly scripts is to package them as Windows Script Files (WSF) files.

Using WSF Files

In Appendix G, "Creating Your Own Scriptable Objects," which is included in the online version of this book and available for download at www.helpwinxp.com/scripting, I show you in detail how to create Automation objects by wrapping a script up in a Windows Script Component file. The Extensible Markup Language (XML) formatting that defines a WSC object can also be used to package regular scripts. In this case, the files are given the extension `.wsf`, so for the remainder of this chapter, I call them WSF files. There are several good reasons to put your scripts into WSF files instead of plain-old VBScript, JavaScript, Perlscript, or other plain script files:

- WSF files make it easy to process command-line arguments in a consistent way and to provide online help to script users.

- WSF files can give you automatic access to the symbolic constants associated with external objects so you don't need to manually define these constant values in your scripts.

- WSF scripts can refer to subroutines and functions stored in other WSF files. This lets you maintain just one copy of a WSF file that contains all the handy procedures you develop, and you can refer to this library from any number of WSF programs. If you need to change or fix one of the functions, you don't have to edit every file in which it's used.

If you're not familiar with XML file formatting, I suggest that you read "XML Basics" in the downloadable Appendix G. That section gives background on the format and structure of XML files.

The overall structure of a WSF file is shown next. Note that end tags are not shown, and not every one of the directives and elements listed must be used in every script. This just shows the ordering that is usually used in a WSF file.

```
<?XML?>              <!-- optional                              -->
<package>            <!-- required only if there is more than one job   -->
  <comment>                  <!-- can appear anywhere in the package   -->
  <job>
    <?job?>          <!-- optional                              -->
    <runtime>        <!-- definition of parameters & online help -->
      <named/>       <!-- optional definitions                  -->
      <unnamed/>
      <description>
      <example>
      <usage>
    </runtime>
    <object/>        <!-- zero or more -->
    <reference/>     <!-- zero or more -->
    <resource>       <!-- zero or more -->
    <script language="xxx">  <!-- one or more script elements    -->
  </job>...          <!-- can be followed by another job -->

</package>
```

Here are the main sections of a WSF file:

- **\<package\>**—Encloses all the scripts in the file.

- **\<job\>**—Encloses a single, independent script program. There might be more than one \<job\> in the file; you can specify which one or more WSH is to run when you type in the script's command line. Likewise, a \<job\> can contain more than one \<script\> element containing script program code, subroutines, and functions.

- **\<runtime\>**—Encloses the description of the job's command-line arguments. The information in \<runtime\> lets WSH print a nicely formatted command-line description and syntax help if the user types /? on the script's command line or if the user specifies command-line arguments incorrectly. This lets WSF scripts behave like all standard Windows command-line programs.

- **\<object/\>, \<reference/\>, and \<resource\>**—Set up references to objects and predefined data that the script program can use.

- **\<script\>**—These elements contain script program code for the job.

The next section describes all the valid WSF file tags in detail. After that, we go through their actual application.

WSF File Format Reference

Reference List 9.1 lists all the tags and attributes allowed in a WSF file. This reference lists only elements appropriate for enclosing script programs. Elements that are used only when creating WSC objects are not discussed here.

Note

XML ignores extra whitespace or line breaks between tags, attributes, or elements. However, text inside `<description>`, `<resource>`, `<helptext>`, and other display elements is displayed literally, so inside these tags you should only add whitespace and line breaks that you want to appear in the script's output.

REFERENCE LIST 9.1   WSF Tag Listing

`<?XML version="1.0" [standalone="yes"]?>`

The `<?XML?>` element requests that the WSH interpreter perform strict XML validation. With validation enabled, XML's stringent formatting and interpretation rules are applied. "Strict" mode is usually required when you will be editing the WSF file with an XML editor. For more information on strict XML validation, see the entry for `<?XML?>` in the downloadable Appendix G.

If present, the `<?XML?>` element must be the first line in the file and must not be preceded by blank lines. The `version` number should be specified as `1.0`. The optional `standalone` attribute indicates that the XML file does not reference an external Document Type Declaration (DTD) and can be omitted or specified as `"yes"`.

`<?job error="value" debug="value" ?>`

Enables the reporting of error messages from and the debugging of the job's script. By default, errors are *not* reported and debugging of scripts is *not* enabled. The `<?job?>` element lets you alter this default behavior by specifying `True` or `False` to enable or disable error message reporting, as well as debugging with the Windows Script Debugger or an equivalent script debugger.

Place this directive as the first item inside of a `<job>` element.

```
<! [CDATA[
    protected text
    ⋮
]]>
```

The CDATA section encapsulates script code inside a `<script>` element and indicates that it is not to be treated as XML markup; otherwise, the presence of characters such as <, >, and & in the script generates errors. The CDATA section must be used only in conjunction with the `<?XML?>` directive; without `<?XML?>` at the beginning of the file, the presence of a CDATA entry generates a syntax error.

```
<!-- any text
   ⋮
-->
```

Anything inside `<!-- ... -->` is treated as comment text, including any XML markup. This can be used to comment out blocks of code during testing or to enter comments or descriptive information. The `<comment>` element can also be used to enclose comments, but `<comment>` cannot contain any XML tags or other markup.

```
<comment>
    any text
    ⋮
</comment>
```

Indicates comment text that is to be ignored by the parser. You can embed multiple lines of text in a comment, but not XML tags.

```
<description>any text
</description>
```

Describes the purpose of the script. Any text inside the `<description>` element is displayed when the `WScript.Arguments.ShowUsage` method is executed or when the script is run with the `/?` command-line argument. The text can span multiple input lines if necessary. This element is an optional part of the `<runtime>` element.

Whitespace (line breaks, spaces, and tabs) between the start and end tags are significant. Output looks best if you begin the descriptive text immediately after the start tag, put any subsequent lines at the left margin, and put the end tag on a line by itself.

```
<example>Example: example usage text
</example>
```

Is used to give an example of proper usage of the script's command line. This is printed when the `WScript.Arguments.ShowUsage` method is executed or when the script is run with the `/?` command-line argument. Start the text with "`Example: .`" Whitespace is significant; see the comments under `<description>`. This element is an optional part of the `<runtime>` element.

```
<job [id="jobid"]>
    job content: <?job?>, <runtime>, <script>, etc.
    ⋮
</job>
```

Encloses a self-contained script program. More than one `<job>` can be placed in a single WSF file. If this is done, you should name each job with a distinct name for the `id` attribute. These job names are used on the command line to select which job or jobs to run. If there are multiple jobs in the file and you don't specify which to run, WSH runs each of them in turn, in the order in which they appear in the file.

```
<named name="argname" helpstring="description" type="argtype" required="boolean"/>
```

Defines an option (switch) argument that is permitted on the command line that runs the script. Named command arguments begin with a slash. Here's an example:

```
scriptname /someoption /otheroption=3
```

Here's a list of the attributes of `<named/>`:

- **name**—Name of the command-line option.
- **helpstring**—A brief description of the option's meaning or purpose.
- **type**—The type of data expected. This must be one of the following values: `"string"`, `"boolean"`, or `"simple"`. The default value is `"simple"`.
- **required**—`"True"` if the argument is always required or `"False"` if the argument is optional. The default value is `"False"`.

The `type` attribute specifies how you want the user to enter the command-line option. If you want the argument to have the form `/someoption=textvalue`, specify `type="string"`. If just the presence of the argument is all that matters (for example, `/verbose`), specify `type="simple"`. If you want the option to be an on/off switch of the form `/someoption+` or `/someoption-`, specify `type="boolean"`. However, this latter format is pretty strange. No Windows command-line program has ever used this form of argument, and I see no good reason to start using it now.

The information in `<named>` is used only when WSH is asked to display the script's usage information by calling the `WScript.Arguments.ShowUsage` method or by running the script with `/?` on the command line. Unfortunately, WSH does *not* use this information to automatically validate command-line arguments.

```
<object id="name" {classid="clsid:GUID" | progid="progid"}
    [events="boolval"]/>
```
Creates an instance of a specified object, in a global variable of the indicated *name*. You must specify either the object's progid name (for example, `"Scripting.FileSystemObject"`) or its classid. Be sure to close the object tag with `/>`.

The `events` attribute specifies whether the script is prepared to handle events fired by the object. Events are beyond the scope of this book.

```
<package>
    one or more <job> elements
    ⋮
</package>
```
Encloses one or more separate script programs in a WSF file. The `<package>` element is optional when the file contains only one job.

```
<reference {object="progid" | guid="GUID"}
    [version="version"]/>
```
Instructs WSH to load the type library for a specified object type. In effect, this loads all the predefined constants associated with the object. The object can be specified by its progid name (for example, to load the Windows Management Instrumentation (WMI) constants, use `object="WbemScripting.SWbemLocator"`) or by its GUID number. By default, WSH loads the most recent version of the object class, but if necessary, you can specify an older version with the `version` attribute. Be sure to close the tag with `/>`.

```
<resource id="resourceid"><![CDATA[text or number]]>
</resource>
or
<resource id="resourceid">text or number</resource>
```

Creates a named value that can be retrieved in the script using the `GetResource()` function. Note that `<resource>` tags provide a way to concentrate all language-specific text in one place in the file so that alternate language versions can be created at a later date. A `<resource>` tag assigns a name *resourceid* to some text or numeric data. The *resourceid* string is passed to `GetResource()` to retrieve the data into the script. The content should be encased in `<![CDATA[ ... ]]>` if the WSC file uses strict XML compliance. For more information about `<resource>`, see "Defining Resources" in the downloadable Appendix G.

```
<runtime>
    argument definitions: <named>, <unnamed>, <usage>,
    <description>, <example> tags
    ⋮
</runtime>
```

The `<runtime>` element contains tags that define the command-line syntax for a script job. The tags are described elsewhere in this reference list.

```
<script language="name">
<![CDATA[
    script code
    ⋮

]]>
</script>
or
<script language="name" src="location"/>
```

The first form of the `<script>` element encloses the actual script program code and/or subroutines and functions. You might find that you can get away with omitting the language attribute, but you should not trust that the default is correct on every computer. Always add `language="VBscript"` or whatever language you're using.

The second form of the script element indicates that WSH is to incorporate the script program stored at the location indicated by the `src` attribute. The location can be a filename (including the path), a UNC-formatted share name, or a URL, which must begin with `http://`. In this form, the script tag ends with `/>`, and there is no content or end tag. The file referenced by this "import" version of the script tag should be a plain script program file with no XML formatting.

If you use multiple `<script>` elements of either form, if more than one contains a program "body," the scripts are executed in sequence. For subroutine and function procedures to be shared across `<script>` elements, procedures must be defined in the same script element or in an *earlier* script element than the one in which it is used. In particular, if you want to use `<script src=…/>` to import a library of subroutines and functions, the importing tag must occur before the `<script>` in which you use the procedures.

If you used the `<?XML?>` strict-compliance directive at the top of your script, you should enclose the script code itself inside `<![CDATA[` and `]]>` to prevent any `<` or `>` characters in your script from being interpreted as tags. If you did not use the `<?XML?>` directive, do not use `<![CDATA[` and `]]>`. In either case, do not use the CDATA markup in any of the import files referenced by `<script src=…/>` elements.

`<unnamed name="`*argname*`" helpstring="`*description*`" many="`*boolean*`" required="`*value*`"/>`
In the `<runtime>` element, the unnamed element indicates a command-line argument that is unnamed (that is, does not start with the `/` character). These are typically filenames or items whose meaning is conveyed by their placement (order) on the command line.

Here's a list of the attributes of `<unnamed/>`:

- `name`—The name of the command-line option. At first it seems peculiar to give a name to an "unnamed" argument. There is a reason: This name is used if WSH has to print out the script's command-line syntax. This is the name it uses as a placeholder in the sample syntax line. Pick a name that represents the purpose of the argument: "filename," "username," or something along these lines.

- `helpstring`—A brief description of the option's meaning or purpose.

- `many`—A boolean value; `"True"` if the user can enter a variable number of these arguments or `"False"` if the user must enter a fixed number.

- `required`—The (minimum) number of occurrences of this item that are *required* to be entered. Valid values are `"0"`, `"1"`, `"2"`, and so on, `"false"`, which is the same as `"0"`, or `"true"`, which is the same as `"1"`.

As with `<named>`, the information in `<unnamed>` is used only when WSH is asked to display the script's usage information.

Note

These attributes determine how the ShowUsage method displays the command line syntax. For unnamed arguments, WSH does *not* verify whether a command line meets the syntax requirements specified by "many" and "required." Your script has to determine for itself whether the command line has the correct number of unnamed arguments. If you determine that the syntax is incorrect, call WScript.Arguments.ShowUsage and then call WScript.Quit.

`<usage>`*descriptive text*
`</usage>`
This element can be used in the `<runtime>` element. If present and if the script executes the WScript.Arguments.ShowUsage method or the user types `/?` on the command line, the text inside `<usage>` is printed instead of the automatically generated text that WSH normally produces from the `<named>`, `<unnamed>`, `<description>`, and `<example>` tags. If you use `<usage>`, there is no reason to specify the other tags.

Whitespace in <usage> is significant. For best formatting, start the text immediately after <usage>, begin any extra text lines at the left margin, and place the </usage> tag on a line by itself.

Now, let's go over ways to use the features of a WSF file.

Providing Online Help with WSF Files

As mentioned in Reference List 9.1, the WSF file format uses the <runtime> element to describe the command-line arguments that your script expects. This lets WSH automatically print help information for the user. This happens in two circumstances:

- If the user puts /? on the command line when he runs the script, WSH displays the script's usage information and quits. This is standard behavior for most Windows command-line programs, and it's nice that the WSF format makes your script behave the same way.

- If you execute the method WScript.Arguments.ShowUsage, WSH displays the usage information and continue.

The first circumstance happens all by itself. The second is under your control. I suggest that anytime you detect that the user has entered command-line arguments incorrectly, use WScript.echo to type a message explaining exactly what is wrong and then issue these statements:

```
WScript.Arguments.ShowUsage
WScript.Quit 1
```

This displays the correct usage information and stops the script with the exit status 1. A nonzero exit status indicates that something went wrong, and this can be detected if, for example, the script is run from a batch file or the Task Scheduler.

What does ShowUsage print? If you specified a <usage> element, it prints the contents of <usage>. Otherwise, it extracts the information from the other tags in <runtime> and prints it in the format

```
text from <description>
Usage: scriptname /named_arguments unnamed_arguments

Options:

name: description
text from <example>
```

with the named and unnamed arguments formatted with the usual syntax notation: square brackets around optional arguments, ellipses after repeatable arguments, and so on.

Here's an example. For a script that we want to take the optional arguments /volname (which takes a text argument) and /eject (which is a switch whose mere presence does something) as well as one or more filenames, the <runtime> markup might look like this:

```
<runtime>
    <named   name="volname"  required="false" type="string"
             helpstring="Name of volume for CD. Default is mm-dd-yy." />
    <named   name="eject"    required="false" type="simple"
             helpstring="Eject the disc after recording." />
    <unnamed name="name"     required="true"  many="true"
             helpstring="File or folder to burn to the CD." />
    <description>
This script burns the file(s) or folder(s) specified on the
command line to a CD or DVD.
    </description>
    <example>
Example: cdburn /volname:backup c:\files
    </example>
</runtime>
```

When a WSF file containing this information is run with the argument /?, this is the result:

```
This script burns the file(s) or folder(s) specified on the
command line to a CD or DVD.

Usage: cdburn.WSF [/volname:value] [/eject] name1 [name2...]

Options:

volname : Name of volume for CD. Default is mm-dd-yy.
eject   : Eject the disc after recording.
name    : File or folder to burn to the CD.

Example: cdburn /volname:backup c:\files
```

Note that the /volname and /eject options are automatically displayed in square brackets because they both are marked required="False". The unnamed argument is listed as name1 because one is required, and the option for entering more is shown because of many="True".

Although you could probably format this stuff yourself and enter it in a <usage> tag faster than you can enter all the other <runtime> tags, this method has the advantage that WSH always formats the information in a consistent way.

▶

Tip

Whatever method you use to display usage information, don't skip the task of writing this sort of help information into your scripts. I *promise* you it will help you at some future date, even if nobody else ever uses your script.

Processing Command-Line Arguments

The script's command-line arguments are made available through the built-in collection object WScript.Arguments. I discussed this collection in Chapter 3, "Scripting and Objects." It is a useful tool because it automatically sorts out the named and unnamed command-line arguments.

WScript.Arguments has two properties that return collections that are a subset of the contents of WScript.Arguments itself:

- WScript.Arguments.Named is a collection of the named (/*xxx*) command-line arguments passed to the script.
- WScript.Arguments.Unnamed is a collection of all the other command-line arguments (that is, filenames and the like).

I describe and discuss how to use both collection objects in turn.

Processing Named Arguments (Switches)

Reference List 9.2 lists the methods and properties of the Named collection.

REFERENCE LIST 9.2   Properties and Methods of the Named Collection

Properties:

Item(*name*)
Returns the *value* part of the command-line argument /*name*:*value*, as a string. If no argument with the given name is specified on the command line, it returns the value Empty. If the argument value has been enclosed in quotes, as in the following command line:

```
somescript /title:"This is the title I want to use"
```

then WScript.Named.Item("title") returns the string value This is the title I want to use without the quotation marks.

For simple arguments such as /*name*, the return value is always Empty; you should use the Exists method to determine whether the argument is specified.

For those weird boolean switches specified as /*name*+ or /*name*-, the return value is True (-1) if the argument ended with + or False (0) if the argument ended with -. (Personally, I don't ever use this syntax.)

Length
Returns the number of items in the collection. For named items, this isn't very interesting because you usually examine the contents of the collection with Item() or Exists().

Methods:

Count
Also returns the number of items in the collection.

Exists(*name*)

Returns `True` if the named argument is specified on the command line and returns `False` otherwise. Use this method to detect the presence of "simple" arguments such as `/verbose`.

As a simple example, for a script whose command line is in this format:

```
myscript /outfile:output.txt /verbose
```

you might use the `Named` collection this way:

```
verbose_mode = WScript.Arguments.Named.Exists("verbose")
output_file = WScript.Arguments.Named.Item("outfile")
if isempty(output_file) then output_file = "default.out"
if verbose_mode then wscript.echo "* output file = ", output_file
```

> **Note**
>
> If you scan through the `Named` collection, the values you see are the names of the arguments. To get their values, you have to use the `Item()` property. For example, this code lists all the arguments' names and values:
>
> ```
> for each arg in WScript.Arguments.Named
>     WScript.echo arg, "=", WScript.Arguments.Named.Item(arg)
> next
> ```

The problem with the simple approach is that if a user types, say `/verbse` instead of `/verbose`, the script would not notice. Although Windows Script Host ensures that arguments listed as required in the `<runtime>` section are present, it *ignores* named arguments that are not defined in the `<runtime>` section. So, `"verbse"` sits there in the `Named` collection, and the user never finds out she made a mistake. For a script that needs to stand up to daily use by other people, this isn't acceptable.

A good way to ensure that only valid arguments have been typed on the command line is to use the following pattern:

> **Pattern**
>
> To extract named command-line arguments (switches), perform the following steps:
>
> 1. In the `<runtime>` section, define each of the desired arguments. For "on/off" switches, forget about the "boolean" type and use "simple" instead. These default to off (`False`) if absent and on (`True`) if present.
>
> 2. If you need a feature to be on by default, use `"noxxx"` as the corresponding argument name so its presence means "turn feature xxx off."
>
> 3. In the script, declare variables for each of the arguments.
>
> 4. Initialize the variables to sensible default values.

5. Scan through the `WScript.Arguments.Named` collection and use your language's equivalent of the `"select case"` statement to handle each of the valid arguments. It's customary to treat argument names in a case-insensitive way. Have the "default" case print an error message and quit. It's also helpful to print information that lists all the valid arguments in this case.

6. For arguments that are supposed to provide a value, such as `/volname:xxx`, check to see that the value is actually provided (is not blank) and is valid. For example, if the user types just `/volname`, the value of `WScript.Arguments.Named.Item("volname")` is the empty string `""`, so you should check for that.

Here is an example. This script accepts a switch named `/verbose`, a negative switch named `/nolisting`, and a value switch named `/copies`:

```
option explicit
dim arg, verbose, listing, copies, val   ' declare variables

verbose = False                          ' set default values
listing = True
copies = 1

for each arg in WScript.Arguments.Named
    select case lcase(arg)
        case "verbose":         ' /verbose turns the verbose feature on
            verbose = True
        case "nolisting":       ' /nolisting turns the listing feature off
            listing = False
        case "copies":          ' /copies:n must supply a number
            val = WScript.Arguments.Named.Item(arg)
            if len(val) > 0 then
                copies = cint(val)
            else
                WScript.echo "/copies requires a number"
                WScript.Arguments.ShowUsage
                WScript.Quit 1
            end if
        case else:                  ' complain about any misspelled argument
            WScript.echo "Argument", "/" & arg, "is not valid"
            WScript.Arguments.ShowUsage
            WScript.Quit 1
    end select
next
⋮
```

Whether you validate argument names in this manner or not, be sure to check that all arguments with values have been assigned appropriate values.

Note

You can use these techniques in normal `.vbs` or `.js` script files, too; the `WScript.Named` and `WScript.Unnamed` collections are available even when you're not using a WSF file. You just don't get the automatic enforcement of "required" arguments, nor can you use the `ShowUsage` method. You have to write your own code to check for required arguments and print the usage information.

Processing Unnamed Arguments

The `WScript.Arguments.Unnamed` collection provides a list of all command-line arguments that don't start with /. Unnamed arguments; typically specify a list of files, users, or other items to process.

The properties and methods of the `Unnamed` collection are shown in Reference List 9.3.

REFERENCE LIST 9.3   Properties and Method of the Unnamed Collection

Properties:

Item(*n*)
Returns one of the arguments in the collection, where *n* is a number from 0 to Length-1.

Length
Returns the number of arguments in the collection.

Method:

Count
Also returns the number of arguments in the collection.

In most cases, you can write your script to process each of the items in turn, as indicated in the following pattern. If you want to ensure that a certain number of items is specified, you can check the value of `Length` or `Count`.

Then, you can use the usual collection iterator to handle each of the items. When all the arguments represent the same sort of items, such as filenames or usernames, it's often best to write a subroutine to process each item in turn. The following pattern illustrates this.

Pattern

When processing an arbitrary number of arguments that are identical in meaning, such as a list of filenames to be processed, it's best to use a subroutine to process each file. This makes it easier to see how the program works when you're reading the script. The following code illustrates a good way to do this:

```
if WScript.Arguments.Unnamed.Length < 1 then
    WScript.echo "You must specify at least one filename"
    WScript.Arguments.ShowUsage
    WScript.Quit 1
end if

' process each file in turn
for each arg in WScript.Arguments.Unnamed
    process arg
next

' process one file
sub process (filename)
    ⋮
end sub
```

Notice that the script explicitly checks to ensure that at least one unnamed argument is specified on the command line. You should do this even if you use the `<runtime>` tag in the WSF file to specify that an unnamed argument is required because WSH doesn't actually enforce this for you. The following XML:

```
<runtime>
    <unnamed name="filename" required="1" many="true"
            helpstring="file or files to process"/>
</runtime>
```

only controls the `ShowUsage` syntax display.

Enclosing More Than One Script

In a WSF file, there can be one or more `<job>` elements, each of which contains a complete script program. If there is more than one `<job>` in a WSF file, you can specify which job to run on the command line that you use to run the script. For example,

```
cscript somefile.wsf //job:cleanup
```

tells WSH to find the job section that is marked with the attribute `id="cleanup"` and runs the script inside. You can name more than one job. The command line

```
cscript somefile.wsf //job:report //job:cleanup
```

runs the script job named "report" and then "cleanup."

If you have multiple jobs in a file and don't put any `//job` parameters on the command line, WSH runs *all* the jobs in the order in which they appear in the file. Because of this, the multiple `<job>` format is probably not appropriate for many scripting applications. If your scripting application should do just one of several things, you might be better off writing just one script job that uses a regular command-line argument to determine which action to take.

Putting It All Together

The following sample script lets a user type a list of files or folders on the command line, which the script burns onto a recordable CD or DVD. The script ties together all the concepts in this section:

- It has built-in online help.
- It uses sensible default values.
- It validates its arguments before doing anything.
- It uses the `<reference>` tag to import predefined constants.

The script uses the built-in Image Mastering application programming interface (API) that comes with Windows 7 and Vista, which provides CD and DVD burning capability to programs and scripts.

You can also use this scripting technique on Windows XP and Windows Server 2003, if you first install the IMAPI update described at support.microsoft.com/kb/ KB932716. On XP, by default, only Administrators can burn CDs or DVDs using these tools. To let regular users burn CDs or DVDs, follow these steps:

1. Log on as an Administrator and open a Command Prompt window.

2. Type **start gpedit.msc** and press Enter. Open Local Computer Policy, Computer Configuration, Windows Settings, Security Settings, Local Policies, Security Options.

3. Double-click Devices: Allowed to format and eject removable media and select Administrators and Power Users or Administrators and Interactive Users.

4. If you are concerned that a network user might modify *writable* CD or DVD media that you mount, you could enable the policy Devices: Restrict CD-ROM Access to Locally Logged-On User Only. This precludes sharing your CD/DVD drives with the network, though. If your computer is a domain network member, a network administrator has to make these changes via Group Policy.

Note

For more information about burning CD and DVD media using the built-in tools, visit msdn.microsoft.com and select Library. In the left pane, select Win32 and COM Development, System Services, Device Services, Image Mastering API.

Here is the script:

```
<?XML?>                                        <!-- Example File cdburn.wsf -->
<job>
  <runtime>
    <named   name="volname"  required="false" type="string"
             helpstring="Name of volume for CD. Default is mm-dd-yy." />

    <named   name="eject"    required="false" type="simple"
             helpstring="Eject the disc after recording." />

    <unnamed name="name"     required="true"  many="true"
             helpstring="File or folder to burn to the CD." />

    <description>
This script burns the file(s) or folder(s) specified on the
command line to a CD or DVD.
    </description>

    <example>
Example: cdburn /volname:backup c:\files
    </example>
  </runtime>
```

```vbscript
<reference object="IMAPI2.MsftDiscMaster2" />      <!-- import constants -->
<reference object="IMAPI2FS.MsftFileSystemImage" /> <!-- (from two libs)   -->

<script language="vbscript">
<![CDATA[
  option explicit

  dim FSO, arg, fname, volname, i, eject, devname, canRecord, objMaster
  dim objRecorder, objDataDisc, objFileSystem, objRoot, objImage

  if WScript.Arguments.Unnamed.Count = 0 then ' be sure file(s) were named
      WScript.Arguments.ShowUsage
      WScript.Quit 1
  end if
                                              ' verify that files exist
  set FSO = CreateObject("Scripting.FileSystemObject")
  for each fname in WScript.Arguments.Unnamed
      if not (FSO.FileExists(fname) or FSO.FolderExists(fname)) then
          wscript.echo "File does not exist:", fname
          wscript.Quit 1
      end if
  next

  volname = ""                              ' set option defaults
  eject   = False

  for each arg in WScript.Arguments.Named    ' scan through options
      select case lcase(arg)
          case "volname":
              volname = WScript.Arguments.Named.Item("volname")
              ' (note that if the user just typed /volname,
              ' volname will still be a blank string)

          case "eject":
              eject = True

          case else:                         ' bail out on bad option
              wscript.echo "Option", "/" & arg, "is not valid"
              WScript.Arguments.ShowUsage
              Wscript.Quit 1
      end select
  next

  if len(volname) = 0 then                  ' if not present, or blank
      volname = cstr(date())                ' use today's date, but...
      do
          i = instr(volname, "/")           ' turn / characters into -
          if i = 0 then exit do
          volname = left(volname, i-1) & "-" & mid(volname, i+1)
      loop
  end if
```

```
' create Image Mastering API master object
Set objMaster = WScript.CreateObject("IMAPI2.MsftDiscMaster2")

if not objMaster.IsSupportedEnvironment then
    wscript.echo "Your computer has no recordable optical drives, " & _
                 "or you do not have permission to record"
    wscript.quit
end if
                                        ' create recorder objects
set objRecorder = CreateObject("IMAPI2.MsftDiscRecorder2")
set objDataDisc = CreateObject("IMAPI2.MsftDiscFormat2Data")

' look for first device that has blank media and recording capability
canRecord = False
for i = 0 to objMaster.Count-1               ' step through each drive
    devName = objMaster.Item(i)
    objRecorder.InitializeDiscRecorder(devName)

    ' Define the new disc format and set the recorder
    objDataDisc.recorder   = objRecorder
    objDataDisc.ClientName = "Script"

    If objDataDisc.IsRecorderSupported(objRecorder) and _
       objDataDisc.IsCurrentMediaSupported(objRecorder) and _
      (objDataDisc.CurrentMediaStatus & _
          IMAPI_FORMAT2_DATA_MEDIA_STATE_BLANK) then
        canRecord = True
        exit for
    end if
next

if not canRecord then
    wscript.echo "Could not locate CD/DVD drive with blank media"
    wscript.quit
end if

wscript.echo "Gathering files (this can take a while)..."
                                        ' prepare to ISO file system
Set objFileSystem = CreateObject("IMAPI2FS.MsftFileSystemImage")
objFileSystem.ChooseImageDefaults(objRecorder)
objFileSystem.FileSystemsToCreate = FsiFileSystemISO9660
objFileSystem.VolumeName = volname

Set objRoot = objFileSystem.Root              ' get root folder
for each fname in WScript.Arguments.Unnamed
    if FSO.FolderExists(fname) then
        objRoot.AddTree fname, True           ' copy subdirectory to the disc
    else
        objRoot.AddFile fname                 ' copy named file to the disc
    end if
next
                                        ' burn the disc
```

```
        wscript.echo "Burning disc..."
        Set objImage = objFileSystem.CreateResultImage()
        objDataDisc.Write(objImage.ImageStream)

        wscript.echo "Done."
        if (eject) then objRecorder.EjectMedia
    ]]>
    </script>
</job>
```

You might look at this and say, "There are about ten lines of actually useful code in there," and you'd be right. However, this script is nearly bulletproof, and the support it gives novice (or forgetful) users makes the extra effort worthwhile.

Deploying Scripts on a Network

The tools presented so far in this book give you the ability to manage a Windows computer. However, we've mostly discussed scripts from the standpoint of managing an individual computer. When you're managing a whole network of computers, you want to use scripts in several ways:

- On a single computer, to remotely manage many others. In this case, a script needs to manipulate a computer other than the one on which it's running.

- On multiple computers, with scripts stored in a common location. In this case, the goal is to have a repository of script programs and script components available for use wherever they're needed with only a single copy extant to reduce maintenance time and cost.

- On multiple computers, with scripts available on each computer. When a computer might not always be connected to a centralized network, but you still want to have scripts available for use by administrators or end users, you need a mechanism to distribute scripts and keep them up-to-date. Of course, this entails more work than keeping all scripts in one place.

- On multiple computers, during user logon. Windows provides for "logon scripts" that can reconfigure a user's computer every time he logs on. This lets you ensure a consistent work environment and provide automatic updating of required software tools.

WSH provides you with the tools to use scripts in all these scenarios. We discuss how in the next few sections.

Note

Remember that besides managing the deployment of scripts, you need to ensure that any required objects are also properly installed on every managed computer. If your script uses nonstandard objects you might need to copy the object's program files to the remote computers and run `regsvr32` on the remote computers to register the objects. You might be able to do this using the remote scripting tools discussed later in this chapter.

Creating Simple Installation Programs with IExpress

Windows 7, Vista, and XP come with a nifty program called IExpress that you can use to create simple setup-type installation programs. It was originally intended to help network administrators maintain Microsoft Outlook, but you can also use it to distribute scripts and programs to other users. (You can read a bit about it at .support.microsoft.com/kb/237803.)

IExpress provides a great way to disseminate the scripts, WSC components, and batch files that you might create using the tools described in this book, as well as regular Windows and command-line applications you've developed using other software development tools. The IExpress wizard creates an executable program (unfortunately, not a Windows Installer .MSI file) that walks an end user through the installation process and extracts files onto the hard disk. The installer can create Registry entries and can even run an installation program or a script to register WSC objects, modify the path, or perform other initial housekeeping actions.

The installation package created by IExpress copies your application's files into a temporary folder on an end user's system. You need to supply a script that asks the user for a permanent location for the files and copies them from the temporary folder to the chosen location. You can write your own script to do this, or you can use a batch file or an .INF file. I don't have room to describe .INF files here, but batch files and scripts are actually easier to deal with, so it's no loss.

A setup script or batch file could be quite complicated. However, to give you an example of how this might work, here is a simple batch file that copies all included .VBS files to a folder:

```
@echo off
set drv=%SYSTEMDRIVE%
if not exist %drv%\scripts mkdir %drv%\scripts
copy *.vbs %drv%\scripts
```

I discuss a more involved setup script written in VBScript later in this section.

To use IExpress, prepare the files you want to distribute as well as any of the following items:

- A license agreement explaining your terms for releasing the software, copyright notices, and so on. This is optional.

- An installation program, batch file, or script that copies the files to their permanent locations. The installation program can be an .exe or .inf file, a .vbs or .js script, or a .cmd or .bat batch file.

- A post-installation program that is to be run after the installation is finished. This program might perform housekeeping duties such as registering WSC or ActiveX components, creating folders, adjusting the PATH, or initializing Registry entries. It, too, can be an .exe or .inf file, a script, or a batch file. This item is optional.

When your materials are ready, type **iexpress** at the command prompt and step through the Wizard's screens as follows:

1. **Welcome dialog box**—Select Create New Self Extraction Directive File to create a new installer or Open Existing Self Extraction Directive File to edit a package you've created previously.

2. **Package Purpose**—Select the kind of installation file iexpress should make. It can create a program that extracts files and runs an installation command, a program that only extracts files, or a .cab file with no self-extraction functionality. In most cases, you want to automatically install the files in a target directory, so you should select the first option, Extract Files and Run an Installation Command.

3. **Package Title**—Enter a name to describe your software.

4. **Confirmation Prompt**—Choose whether you want the installer to confirm that the end user really wants to run the installer. You can type in the question that the user should be asked—something like, "Do you really want to install this program?" If the installation deletes or alters files, you should explain this in the confirmation question.

5. **License Agreement**—If you want, you can specify a text file that contains a license agreement the user should be shown and is asked to agree with as a condition of continuing the installation.

6. **Packaged Files**—Select all the files that comprise the programs or scripts you're distributing. You must also include the installation batch file, script, .inf file, or setup program that you specify in the next step. During installation, all these files are copied to a single temporary folder. Your setup program has to copy the files to the desired permanent location.

7. **Install Program to Launch**—Under Install Program, specify the program or script that copies the files from the temporary folder to their permanent location.

    Depending on the type of program or script you have created to copy and configure the files, use one of the following techniques:

    - **script**—Type **wscript**, followed by a space and then the name of the script file. For example, **wscript do_setup.vbs**. (I recommend wscript because, if you use cscript and the script encounters an error, the user does not see the error message.)

    - **batch file**—Type **cmd /c,** followed by a space and then the name of the batch file. For example, **cmd /c do_setup.bat.** *Do not* simply select the batch file from the drop-down list; if you do, the installer doesn't work on 64-bit versions of Windows. (You notice that batch files with .cmd extension don't show up in the drop-down list. No matter; just type the command as I indicated.)★

- **INF file**—Use the drop-down list to select the name of the INF file.

- **executable program**—Enter the name of the `.exe` file, followed by any necessary command-line arguments.

In any case, the program file must either be one of the files you selected in step 6 or be a standard Windows program. If you specify the name of a file that has spaces in its name, enclose the file name in quotation marks (").

Under Post Install Command, you could enter another command to be run after the Install Program has completed. In general, though, you don't need to use a Post Install command.

8. **Show Window**—Choose the type of window that the installer should display: Default, Hidden, Minimized, or Maximized. To create a silent, hidden installation procedure, select Hidden. (In this case, you should have entered no prompt in step 4 and no license agreement in step 5.) Otherwise, for a normal installer experience, select Default.

9. **Finished Message**—Enter a short text string that is to be displayed when the installation is complete. This might tell how to run the program or whom to call if problems are encountered.

10. **Package Name and Options**—Enter a path and name for the installer program that `iexpress` is to create. Don't bother adding the extension `.exe`; the wizard does that.

    Be sure to check Store Files Using Long File Name Inside Package.

11. **Configure Restart**—Specify whether the user's system should be restarted after the installation. The default is Always Restart, but in most cases this is unnecessary, so you should select No Restart.

12. **Save Self Extraction Directive**—Use this page to save the entries you've made in this wizard as a `.sed` file. This lets you rerun the wizard later to re-create the installation package or to change some of your choices without having to retype everything.

---

*I'm assuming that you're more likely to need to perform installations on 64-bit Windows than Windows 9x/Me. You can't support both categories of Windows if you use a batch file as the installation command. If you use the drop-down list to select a batch file, the installer that IExpress creates tries to run the batch file with the old command.com shell, which doesn't exist on 64-bit Windows. On the other hand, Windows 9x/Me don't have the cmd.exe shell. If you do have to support Windows 9x/Me, select the batch file name in the drop-down list and understand that the installer will not work on 64-bit versions of Windows. Better yet, write a script instead of a batch file. You can write a script that works on all these systems.

13. **Create Package**—Click Next, and then click Finish to complete the installer creation process.

You should find a new .exe file in the folder you specified in step 10. If you run this program, you are walked through the installation of your application.

Tip

After you've run the wizard once, you can re-create the installation program by typing the command

        iexpress /n *filename.sed*

where *filename.sed* is the name of the .sed file you created in step 12. You can use this command to quickly update the installation package after changing the files you're distributing.

The program file iexpress creates from these files can be distributed to end users over your network or through a web page, added to logon scripts, or delivered by any other means.

Tip

The version of IExpress provided with 64-bit versions of Windows creates installers that are 64-bit programs. These installers don't run on 32-bit versions of Windows. You can run a 32-bit installer on a 64-bit version of Windows without problems, but—as you might know—if it tries to write files in \windows\system32, Windows creates these files in \windows\sysWOW64. Similar redirection applies to changes made to parts of the Registry.

If you develop your installer on a 64-bit version of Windows, I suggest that you obtain a copy of iexpress.exe from a computer running Windows XP, name it iexpress32.exe, and copy it to a folder in your path. Then, you can run iexpress32 to create 32-bit versions of your installer packages, and if you want to provide your users with both options, run iexpress to create 64-bit installers.

Also, if your installer needs to create or modify files in \windows\system32 or in the HKEY_LOCAL_MACHINE area of the Registry, you probably do want to create separate 32-bit and 64-bit versions of both your installers and the installation scripts. That way, you can have better control over where the files and Registry keys are actually placed.

Creating IExpress Install Scripts or Batch Files

When the setup program IExpress creates has run on the target computer, it puts all the files you specified to the wizard in a temporary folder and runs the command you specified. As I mentioned, this can be a batch file, script, or .inf file. After the command has finished, the IExpress installer deletes all the files and removes the temporary folder.

So, at the very least, you have to provide a way to select a directory in which to install the files you're distributing and copy them to the target location. (Well, actually, you could skip asking the user where to install the files and use a wired-in target location, but you *do* have to copy the files somewhere.)

When you write a batch file or script to do this, you cannot make any assumptions about the location of the current directory. All you should assume is that the files you are distributing are all in the current directory; your batch file or script just has to copy or move them to the desired location. It can also set up any necessary Registry entries, register components, and so on, using any of the techniques discussed in this book. If you're installing a set of useful scripts, for example, you probably want to have your setup script add the script folder to the system PATH, if it's not already there. The following VBScript script named `copy_all.vbs` does the trick:

```vbscript
                                       ' Example file copy_all.vbs
option explicit
dim FSO, shl, target, file, pathlist, pathdir, I, env

on error resume next  ' don't stop on errors; user won't see message

set FSO = CreateObject("Scripting.FileSystemObject")
set shl = CreateObject("WScript.Shell")

' install to x:\scripts, where x: is the system (Windows) drive
set env = shl.Environment("process")
target = env.item("SYSTEMDRIVE") & "\scripts"
if not fso.FolderExists(target) then fso.CreateFolder(target)

' copy all distributed files except this script
for each file in FSO.GetFolder(".").Files
    if lcase(file.Name) <> "copy_all.vbs" then
        wscript.echo "Copying", file.Name, "to", target
        file.Copy fso.BuildPath(target, file.Name)
        if err.number <> 0 then
            msgbox "Unable to copy " & file.Name & " to " & target & _
                "; installation failed."
            wscript.quit
        end if
    end if
next

' see if target folder is in the PATH
pathlist = env.Item("PATH")    ' examine the PATH
do while len(pathlist) > 0
    i = instr(pathlist, ";")    ' find the dividing semicolon
    if i = 0 then
        pathdir = pathlist        ' no semicolon, this was the last entry
        pathlist = ""
```

```
    else
        pathdir = left(pathlist, i-1) ' text to the left of the semi
        pathlist = mid(pathlist, i+1) ' rest of text after the semi
    end if

    ' if the c:\scripts is already in the path, we're done
    if lcase(pathdir) = lcase(target) then wscript.quit
loop

' if we get here, the target folder is not already in the path; add it.
wscript.echo "Adding", target, "to the PATH"
set env = shl.Environment("system")
env.item("PATH") = env.item("PATH")& ";" & target
if err.number <> 0 then
    msgbox "I was unable to add " & target & " to the PATH"
end if
```

When you build your installation package, specify the following as the command to
execute on installation:

```
wscript copy_all.vbs
```

Note

If you use a batch file or script to run with `cscript` as the installation command and it encounters an
error when it runs, the user will *not* see an error message. The program's window closes before she can
see it. I suggest that you run an installation script with `wscript`. Also, you should use an error-handling
technique like that used in `copy_all.vbs` so your script detects any errors and notifies the user.

You can test and debug your script on a target computer by instructing the IExpress
wizard to display a Finished message (refer to step 9 in the previous section). When you
run the installer and it stops at this message, don't close the Finished dialog box. Open a
command prompt window and change to the installer's temporary folder (which is
named something like `IXP000.TMP` within your TEMP folder). Then, you can manually
run and debug the installation script and see any error messages. When you have tested
and fixed the installation script, be *sure* to copy it to some other folder, and then close
the Finished dialog box. The installer then deletes the temporary files and folder.

Dealing with User Account Control

On Windows 7 and Vista, User Account Control prevents normal applications and
scripts from writing files in or under the \windows and \program file folders, from
modifying the Registry under HKEY_LOCAL_MACHINE, and from making changes to the
system-wide environment variables unless the application is run with elevated
Administrator permissions.

Windows 7 and Vista recognizes an `.exe` file created by IExpress as an installer and automatically displays a User Account Control prompt if the file is named `setup.exe`. The installation script then runs with elevated privileges.

However, if you create an installer with a name other than `setup.exe`, your setup script is run without elevated privileges on Windows 7 and Vista target computers. Regardless of the name, if a user runs your installer on Windows XP and is not an administrator, he can't make changes in the protected locations.

Regardless of the target operating system, a well-designed setup script should ensure that it has the permissions it needs before it starts working. If your script finds that it doesn't have sufficient privileges to do its job, it can display a message instructing the user to use Run As or to log on as an Administrator and then try the installation again.

On a Windows 7 or Vista target that there is no simple way for the script to determine whether it has elevated Administrator privileges. One way to tell is to attempt to create a file in the windows\system32 folder, but the results of attempting this are hard to interpret.

There isn't room to discuss these details here, but I show you how to do this with a sample script you can download from www.helpwin7.com/scripting. The script is called `setup_admin.vbs`, and it determines whether it has elevated permissions. If it doesn't, it asks the user to use the Run As Administrator option. It also incorporates the Uninstall feature described in the next section.

> **Tip**
>
> To make everyone's life easier, if your installer needs to create files in protected Windows folders or change keys in the `HKEY_LOCAL_MACHINE` part of the Registry, name the installer program `setup.exe`.

> **Tip**
>
> You might want to digitally sign the installer `.exe` file that you generate to give greater assurance to users that the installer is actually produced by you and is safe to run. Use the signtool program that I talk about later in this chapter in the section "Signing Scripts." If you use a script as the installation command, you might want to sign that script before you run IExpress to create the `.exe` file. Then, use the `signtool utility` to sign the `.exe` file. You can automate both signing and building with a batch file named makeinstaller.bat that looks something like this:
>
> ```
> rem * sign the installation command script
> signtool sign /a /t http://timestamp.comodoca.com/authenticode copy_all.vbs
> rem *  build setup.exe
> iexpress /n myinstaller.sed
> rem * sign the installer program
> signtool sign /a /t http://timestamp.comodoca.com/authenticode setup.exe
> ```
>
> This way, you just have to type **makeinstaller** when you want to build a new version of `setup.exe`.

Providing an Uninstall Option

If you want to provide a way for users to uninstall whatever it is you delivered via your IExpress setup program, you must do two things:

- Write an uninstall script, batch file, or program that deletes the installed files and any shortcuts or Start menu items you created during installation. Then, add this uninstall script or file to the set of files included with your application and, during installation, copy it to whichever permanent folder you use to store your application's file(s).

- Make a Registry entry so the Add/Remove Programs Control Panel applet lists your program. If the user selects it, the Add/Remove Programs applet runs the uninstall script.

  To do this, in your initial installation script, use the Registry methods in object `WScript.Shell` or the `reg` command-line program to create a key named `HKEY_LOCAL_MACHINE\Software\Microsoft\Windows\CurrentVersion\Uninstall\`*YourApplicationName* with three `REG_SZ` string values:

Value Name	Value Contents
`DisplayName`	Name of application as you want it displayed in Add/Remove Programs.
`Publisher`	Name of your organization (or your own name).
`UninstallString`	Command line to use to run the uninstall script, batch file, or program. If you use a script to do this, you should specify `cscript.exe` followed by the full path to the uninstall script in its permanent location.

The `setup_admin.vbs` script I mentioned at the end of the previous section demonstrates how to do this.

Note

If you provide a way for users to run the uninstall script directly—for example, via a Start menu shortcut—have your uninstall script delete this Registry key so the application doesn't still appear under Add/Remove Programs. If you don't provide an alternative means to uninstall, don't worry about this; the Control Panel applet deletes the key automatically.

Writing Scripts to Manage Other Computers

This section covers a topic that is less about deploying *scripts* than about deploying *yourself*. If you have many computers to manage, you'll find that having to physically visit each one to apply updates or change settings, or even to run a handy management script you've written yourself, is a huge burden. So, not surprisingly, Microsoft and others have created ways to let you remotely manage computers.

There are several ways to accomplish this. The versions of Windows intended for business environments, include the Remote Desktop feature. Windows Server versions provide the comparable Terminal Services for Administration. Third-party applications, such as LogMeIn, GoToMyPC, PCAnywhere, and versions of the open-source application VNC (most of which are free,) provide the same functionality. With any of these technologies, you can "visit" another computer over the network and manage it without leaving your desk.

Yet, as valuable as these remote-control tools are, they can't automatically chug through a list of hundreds of computers and tweak a few settings on each in turn, as a script can. In Chapter 7, "Windows Management Instrumentation," and Chapter 8, "Active Directory Scripting Interface," we covered objects that can manage computers by name through your network.

One difficulty in using a script-based technique to deploy some sort of change through all of an organization's workstations is (a) obtaining and managing the list of all computers and (b) dealing with computers that are unavailable at the time you run the script. There are at least two ways to get the list of all workstations:

- If your organization uses a domain network with Active Directory, you can use the directory to scan for all computer accounts, using the techniques discussed in Chapter 8. You have to obtain the necessary containers and examine their collections and subcollections for computer accounts.

- If you don't have Active Directory available, or if your organization still (gasp!) uses Windows 9*x*/Me, you have to maintain a list of workstations by name and/or IP address by hand. You might be able to use network scanning to find all the names, but this is probably not as reliable as maintaining an inventory manually. You have to exercise lots of control of the network and over procedures to be sure that new computers don't get added without updating the list.

Regardless of the means you use to get the list of computers, when you need to deploy a change through the entire organization, I suggest that you create a text file listing all the computer names as a copy that is used *only* for this specific project. Then, write a script that scans this list, performs the required changes using WMI or ASDI, and removes the computer name from the list if the operation is successful. This way, you can rerun the script periodically until all the computers have been updated. Here is a sample script that does this sort of list editing:

```
                                  ' Example File deploy.vbs
option explicit
dim complist, maxcomputers, compname(), fso, s, nleft, str, i

complist = "update_printers.dat"  ' file containing names of computers to fix
maxcomputers = 100                ' initial size of array(grows automatically)
redim compname(maxcomputers)      ' list of computers still to be updated
nleft = 0                         ' number of computers in list

' *** read list of computers
set fso = CreateObject("Scripting.FileSystemObject")
set s = fso.OpenTextFile(complist)
do while not s.AtEndOfStream           ' read file line-by-line
    str = trim(s.ReadLine)
    if len(str) > 0 then               ' for each name
        if nleft >= maxcomputers then  ' grow the array if necessary
            maxcomputers = nleft+100
            redim preserve compname(maxcomputers)
        end if
        compname(nleft) = str          ' save name
        nleft = nleft+1
    end if
loop
s.close
set s = Nothing

' *** process each of the remaining computers: compname(0..nleft-1)
i = 0
do while i < nleft
    WScript.echo "Updating", compname(i) & "..."
    if process(compname(i)) then       ' if successfully updated
        nleft = nleft-1                ' remove the name from the array and
        compname(i) = compname(nleft)  ' fill the hole with the last name
        savelist                       ' write the list back without the
                                       ' just-fixed computer
    else
        WScript.echo "... FAILED"
        i = i+1                         ' skip this computer, get it next time
    end if
loop

' *** report on status
WScript.echo
select case nleft
    case 0   WScript.echo "ALL COMPUTERS HAVE BEEN UPDATED"
    case 1   WScript.echo "There is 1 computer left to update"
    case else WScript.echo "There are", nleft, "computers left to update"
end select

' savelist - write out the list of computers still to be fixed
sub savelist
    dim s, i
```

```
        set s = fso.CreateTextFile(complist, True)
        for i = 0 to nleft-1
            s.WriteLine compname(i)
        next
        s.Close
    end sub


    ' process - update whatever needs updating
    function process (computername)
        process = False           ' assume failure
        on error resume next      ' don't halt script on error

        '... update the named computer. Be very careful to check for
        '... errors. Set return value to True only if sure of success

        if (the update was successful) then
            process = True
        end if
    end function
```

In the script, the function `update` performs the actual work on a specific computer, and it must return `True` only if the update succeeds. After all computers have been updated, the project-specific computer list file will be empty.

Remote Scripting

Although WMI and ADSI are great for reaching into the insides of Windows on remote computers, another way to manage remote workstations is to copy scripts to the other computers and run the scripts there. If you can do this from one centralized computer, this can be called *remote scripting*.

Windows has a Remote Scripting feature built in, using the WSH Controller object that you might have read about at msdn.microsoft.com. Although it was at one time marginally useful on domain networks of Windows XP workstations, I've found it to be effectively useless in today's network environments for the following reasons:

- For Windows 7 and Vista target computers, it works only on Windows domain networks and only for domain administrators.
- To enable the feature, several settings have to be disseminated via Group Policy from the domain controller. In addition, a command has to be issued at each managed computer, individually, before you can use the technique to manage them remotely.
- It requires customized Windows Firewall exceptions.

Because you have to visit each computer before you can use the tool remotely, Remote Scripting is not an effective remote management tool. You might find it easier to use Remote Desktop, other remote control programs, special remote program execution tools like the Telnet service included with Windows, or the "psexec" tool from www.syinternals.com. I also talk about Windows PowerShell's remote management capabilities in Chapter 16, "Using PowerShell."

Replicating Scripts to Multiple Computers

For scripts that you need to use on several computers on your network, you can put the script files in a shared network folder, where they are available from any computer.

When you have to maintain computers that are *not* on your primary network—for example, workstations for home workers, field personnel, or computers on remote networks that might not be permanently connected—you need some means of distributing the script files in advance of needing them. It is most helpful if the distribution is automatic, and the files are up-to-date.

Between sites of a large corporate network, part of the job *can* be automated using the File Replication Service that is provided with Windows Server. The File Replication Service makes sure all server computers in a large internetwork have up-to-date copies of a set of shared, common files. Specifically, files and subdirectories under `\%windir%\sysvol\sysvol\`*domainname* on *any* domain server are copied to all other domain servers. There is no "master" copy in this case; if a file is created or edited on any server, it's copied to all the others. You can share a script's folder in one of the replicated directories and have the same set of scripts available on every local network in your organization. Scripts are also stored under the policy subdirectories.

Getting scripts copied to individual workstations, with or without a domain-based network, is another matter. For this, you have to be innovative. Here are some suggestions:

- On a domain network, you can have every user's logon script call a batch file or script subroutine that copies scripts from the replication folder on the domain server to a folder on each workstation. This way, whenever someone logs on, the workstations' cache of scripts is updated. The updating procedure should be "smart" and only copy new or changed files. Script files can do this by applying the `FileSystemObject` methods of Chapter 3; I give you a sample script to do this. A batch file calls a file-updating program such as `robocopy` to do this sort of job. `Robocopy` is provided with Windows 7 and Vista, and if you need it for XP, it's available in various versions of the Support Tools and Resource Kits.

- If you are not on a domain network, you can put an icon in a shared network folder to run a similar replication batch file or script. You just have to ask your users to click the update icon periodically. On small networks, this works quite well. It also works on domain networks when users work remotely, for example, over a virtual private network (VPN). I like to put a shortcut to a server-shared folder on each remote user's desktop. After they connect through dial-up networking or the VPN, they can open this shortcut to see a folder full of relevant network-related tasks.

The following script shows how you might replicate a folder full of script files from a server (or other central location) onto the local computer. This script can be run from a logon script or manually:

```
                                                    ' script REPL.VBS
' replicate a directory of files from the domain server onto a workstation

set fso     = CreateObject("Scripting.FileSystemObject")
set wshShell = CreateObject("WScript.Shell")
set environ = wshShell.Environment("Process")

' assume master copies are kept in a shared replicated folder on the domain
' logon server.  You can replace this with a fixed path name if your
' network does not have a domain controller or if you do not use replication.
' Here, we use the environment variable LOGONSERVER, since any DC could have
' logged the user on. This should work anywhere in the enterprise.
srcpath = environ("LOGONSERVER") & "\scripts\path"

' specify location to keep copies on all workstations
destpath = environ("WINDIR") & "\scripts"

wscript.echo srcpath
wscript.echo destpath

if fso.FolderExists(srcpath) then
    checkfolder fso.GetFolder(srcpath), destpath
end if

' checkfolder - replicate the contents of a master folder to a destination
' path. Folder is a Folder object, destpath is the name of the target
' directory.

sub checkfolder (folder, destpath)
    dim file, subfolder

    if not fso.FolderExists(destpath) then fso.CreateFolder(destpath)

    for each file in folder.Files   ' replicate each file
        checkfile file, destpath & "\" & file.Name
    next
                                    ' call again to process subfolders
    for each subfolder in folder.SubFolders
        checkfolder subfolder, destpath & "\" & subfolder.Name
    next
end sub

' checkfile - check one file and copy to destination if necessary.
' srcfile is a File object representing the master copy, destname is full
' pathname of the target copy.
```

```
sub checkfile (srcfile, destname)
    dim copyit, destfile

    if fso.FileExists(destname) then        ' file exists already?
        set destfile = fso.GetFile(destname) ' see if it needs to be replaced
        copyit = (srcfile.DateLastModified > destfile.DateLastModified) or _
                 (srcfile.size <> destfile.size)
    else
        copyit = True                        ' file does not yet exist
    end if

    if copyit then                           ' copy the file
        on error resume next                 ' don't stop if an error occurs
        fso.CopyFile srcfile.Path, destname, True
        if err.number then                   ' report error
           MsgBox "Unable to update " & srcfile.Name & ": " & err.description
        end if
        on error goto 0
    end if
end sub
```

Scripting Security Issues

As you've seen in the last few hundred pages, scripts are powerful tools and can get their fingers into every nook and cranny of Windows. It's bad enough that anyone can write and run a script on their own computer, but in this chapter, you've seen that they can be invisibly sent to and run on other computers. It's enough to keep a network security manager up nights with bad dreams and indigestion.

The good news is that most of the serious management functions require Administrator privileges. All scripts, including remote scripts, execute in the security context of the users who run them. Therefore, the damage they can do is limited to whatever damage the user can do sitting at the computer directly. This isn't much help if a user gets duped into running a malicious script contained in a Web page, sent in an email attachment, or just found lying around. On Windows 7 and Vista, User Account Control adds another layer of security, effectively limiting remote network scripting to administrators on a domain network.

One way to protect your organization's computers from unwanted WSH experimentation is to instruct WSH to run only *signed* scripts. Signing is the process of marking a script with a cryptographic signature that guarantees that the script was written by a known, trusted user. Windows Script Host versions 5.6 and later let you specify a Registry value that prevents unsigned scripts from running. The Registry value `HKEY_CURRENT_USER\Software\Microsoft\Windows Script Host\Settings\TrustPolicy` can be set to any of three `DWORD` values to determine how WSH treats unsigned scripts:

Value	Restriction Level
0	Run any script, signed or not.
1	Prompt the user if a script is unsigned.
2	Never run unsigned scripts.

Note

Word on the Windows support newsgroups is that the signed-scripts-only restriction can cause problems with the capability of Windows to run remote scripts. If you use remote scripts and then restrict scripting to permit signed scripts only, check to be sure that your remote scripts still work.

You can set this Registry value on all your organization's computers to whatever level you deem necessary. On a domain network, you can enforce this restriction through Group Policy. You can also make the setting manually by editing the Registry or by distributing a .reg Registry file.

Another area of concern is that end users might learn a bit too much by snooping around in the scripts on their computers and on the network. Scripts can contain a lot of fairly high-level information—the names of servers and possibly hidden shares, the location of important files, and even the techniques used by scripts to manipulate Windows. In a security-conscious environment, you should think twice about making this information easy to come by. I don't go so far as to suggest that you ban this book, but you can take the step of encrypting scripts so they're not easily readable.

In this section, I show you how to sign your own scripts so that they are trusted on your network and how to encrypt scripts for increased privacy.

Script Signing

Code signing is the process of attaching to a program file a cryptographically generated message that could only have been generated by a known, trusted person or organization. As it applies to scripts, signing marks a script as authentically produced by the trusted source and guarantees that the script has not been modified by others between signing and delivery. Signing can increase security if you take three steps:

- You or your organization must acquire a *certificate*, a special file that is issued by a Certification Authority (CA) that can vouch for your identity. A certificate file contains information and encryption keys and makes it possible to encode a file so anyone who receives the file can be sure that *you* sent it, insofar as they trust the certification authority. CAs include companies such as VeriSign, Comodo, Thawte, and others.

Certificates of this sort typically cost $200–$400 per year. (I show you how to get one for less shortly). Windows Server can generate certificates on their own for free for use within an organization, but without the "stamp of approval" of a CA, there is no way for these certificates to be verified outside the organization's domain network.

- Each script that you want your users to run must be digitally "signed" with this certificate. I show you how to do this in a moment.

- Each of your organization's computers should be set through Group Policy, Local Security Policy, or Registry settings not to run unsigned scripts or to at least warn users if they attempt to run an unsigned script.

Here are more detailed instructions.

Obtain Signing Tools

To install and use your code-signing certificate, you need two command-line tools developed by Microsoft: pvk2pvc.exe and signtool.exe. If you have a version of the Windows Software Development Kit (or Platform SDK, as it is formerly known) or any of Microsoft's Windows development products installed, search for either of these files under your \Program Files folder. If you find them, add the containing folder to your PATH, so you can run them from the command line.

If you don't already have the tools, download and install the most recent version of the Windows SDK from msdn.microsoft.com. At the time this was written, the most recent version was titled *Microsoft Windows SDK for Windows 7* and *.NET Framework 4*. Download and run its web-based installer and install the Win32 program development tools. You find signtool.exe and pvk2pvc.exe under \Program Files\Microsoft SDKs\ Windows\vxxx\bin. Add this folder to your PATH.

Obtaining a Code-signing Certificate

To sign scripts, you need to choose a CA. You can use a public, fee-based CA, or you can use your organization's own CA, if your scripts are for internal use only and you have Windows Server available.

Tip
I was able to purchase a one-year Comodo code-signing certificate for just $75 (a really good price) by signing up at author.tucows.com. If the discount offer is still available, you should be able to get to it by clicking Code Signing Certificates under Resources at the left side of the page.

Then, you must request and install a code-signing certificate. For a public CA, you do this on a website or by email, following the procedure specified by the CA. In most cases, the procedure goes something like this:

1. You apply for a code-signing (Authenticode) certificate via the CA's website. During this process, the website has you save a unique private key in a file on your computer with the extension `.pvk`. For example, you might select filename "signing.pvk." *Do not forget where you put this file!*

2. The CA later requests information from you or your company to verify that you are who you say you are. This might include copies of your business license, driver's license, utility bills, and so on.

3. You are notified when you can retrieve the public key part of your certificate.

Comodo's website installs the key directly into the Windows certificate store, but it's incomplete because the private key is not included. You must perform the following steps to reinstall the key:

1. Start the Certificate Manager with the command `"start certmgr.msc"`.

2. Under Certificates - Current User, open Personal, Certificates. Highlight the newly added certificate, right-click it, and select All Tasks, Export.

3. If the first page of the Export wizard asks whether you want to include the private key, there's no need to proceed. You're already all set. Otherwise, continue.

4. Select DER Encoded Binary X.509 (.CER) and click Next. Browse to the same folder that contains the private key (`.pvk`) file that you saved when you applied for your certificate and enter a filename like **signing.cer**. Click Next, and then Finish.

5. Open a command prompt window and change to the folder that now contains `signing.pvk` and `singing.cer`.

6. Type the following command:

   ```
   pvk2pfx -pvk signing.pvk -spc signing.cer -pfx signing.pfx
   ```

   If you specified a password to protect the `.pvk` file, add `-pi password` to the end of that command line.

   This combines the private and public keys.

7. Back in the Certificate Manager, delete the existing code-signing certificate; then, click Action, All Tasks, Import to import `signing.pfx`, which you just created.

This is what I had to do, but the exact instructions can vary depending on the CA you use. If you use your organization's own CA, follow the instructions specified by your network administrator.

When you have the certificate installed, you should see it in the Certificates MMC snap-in; an example is shown in Figure 9.1.

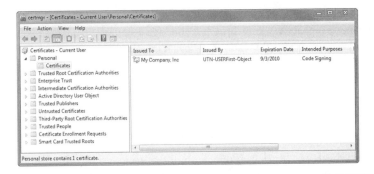

Figure 9.1   The Certificates Management Console
lists the certificates installed for your account.

Signing Scripts

WSH comes with an object that can sign script files using only a few statements. You might read about the "Scripting.Signer" object at msdn.microsoft.com. In the sample scripts you can download from helpwin7.com/scripting, I include a script named signscript.vbs that you can use to sign script files, which shows how this object can be used.

However, I suggest that instead of using that method to sign your scripts, you download and use the signtool.exe program from www.microsoft.com, as discussed earlier. The reason is that the digital signature on scripts signed using the Scripting.Signer object expires when the certificate expires (typically one to three years from the time it's purchased), and Windows will no longer considers the scripts safe to run. The signtool utility can add a digital timestamp, so the digital signature is considered valid indefinitely—so long as the script is not modified in any way.

In addition, when you obtain your code-signing certificate, check the CA's website to find the URL of its timestamp server. For example, for Comodo, the timestamp URL is http://timestamp.comodoca.com/authenticode.

To sign a script file from the command line, use the following syntax:

```
signool sign /a [/t "Certificate Name"] [/t timestampURL] scriptfile
```

For example,

```
signtool sign /a /t http://timestamp.comodoca.com/authenticode myscript.vbs
```

> **Tip**
>
> This is just the sort of command you want to put into a batch file to save you from typing and also to record the name and URL information for easy reference. You will learn how to write batch files in the subsequent chapters. My own version, named sign.bat, is included in the downloadable sample scripts.

For more information about signtool's command-line options, type **signtool sign** **/?**.

Whichever tool you use, after a script has been signed, you will see that a block of comments over a hundred lines long has been placed at the end of the script. The resulting file might look like this:

```
MsgBox "This is a signed script"
'' SIG '' Begin signature block
'' SIG '' MIIIMAYJKoZIhvcNAQcCoIIIITCCCB0CAQExDjAMBggq
'' SIG '' hkiG9w0CBQUAMGYGCisGAQQBgjcCAQSgWDBWMDIGCisG
   ⋮
'' SIG '' Hn7AhAQwZGWgpTbAYPWh0AT5Wz6rQdSpnuAj6w9zviVP
'' SIG '' qvCa6VFH9/0iE9VqBc+zuwIGYn11
'' SIG '' End signature block
```

If a script has been signed, when you view its Properties page in Windows Explorer, an additional tab labeled Digital Signatures appears, as shown in Figure 9.2. Clicking Details and then View Certificate lets you check the identity of the signer and of the CA.

Note

If you make any changes to a signed script, the signature is rendered invalid. You should either delete the signature comment lines or re-sign the file.

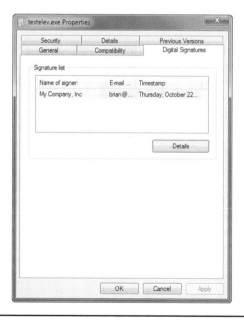

Figure 9.2   Signed script files gain a Digital Signatures tab in their Properties page that lets you check the identity of the signer.

Tightening Security to Require Signed Scripts

To secure a standalone or workgroup Windows workstation so that it requires WSH to check the authenticity of scripts, you must apply a security policy. On a domain network, this can be applied through Group Policy. On a standalone workstation, it can be applied through Local Policy, which is administered by the Group Policy MMC snap-in.

The settings are made through the policy entries under Computer Configuration, Windows Settings, Security Settings, Software Restriction Policies, Additional Rules. The administrator can add a "path rule" to block access to specific file types. For example, entering a "disallowed" rule for `*.vbs` without a pathname prevents the user from running any VBS file, from any location. Similar rules can be entered to block `.vbe`, `.js`, `.jse`, and `.wsf` files. The rules could also be written to block execution of scripts only in the temporary folders used by Internet Explorer and Outlook Express for downloaded files. In addition, the administrator should add "certificate rules" that specify trusted certificates—in particular, the certificate used to sign your scripts. Scripts signed by the listed certificates are allowed to run, while unsigned scripts are blocked by the other policy rules.

If a user under this policy regime attempts to run a script that is unsigned or has been altered since the signing, this message is displayed:

```
CScript Error: Execution of the Windows Script Host failed. (Windows cannot open
this program because it has been prevented by a software restriction policy. For
more information, open Event Viewer or contact your system administrator.)
```

Another security tool at your disposal is the DWORD Registry value `TrustPolicy` under key `HKEY_CURRENT_USER\SOFTWARE\Microsoft\Windows Script Host\Settings`. It can be created and set to any of the following values:

0   Scripts do not need to be signed (Default).

1   User is prompted if script is not signed.

2   Unsigned scripts do not run.

This value is only effective on a Windows Domain network with the value deployed via an administrative policy template or via Group Policy because, otherwise, a user (or a malicious program) could change the value and circumvent the restriction.

Caution

You should carefully test any restriction settings you make to be sure they work in your environment. Be sure that scripts that should run do run and that scripts that shouldn't don't.

The Script Encoder

The Script Encoder is a command-line utility that you can search for, download, and install from msdn.microsoft.com. Its job is to scramble the contents of .vbs or .js script files into a binary mishmash not easily read by humans, but which WSH can decipher as easily as the original script. This can give your scripts some measure of protection from snooping and theft. I say not *easily* read by humans because, unlike the strong encryption that the Windows Encrypted File System uses, the Script Encoder is fairly simpleminded. It's possible for a determined person to reverse the process and read the encrypted file. Consider script encoding a *mild* deterrent from *casual* snooping.

▶ **Caution**

In particular, don't hard-wire passwords in a script and then assume that encrypting the script keeps the passwords safe.

To use the Script Encoder, first make a backup copy of all the scripts you plan to encode and distribute, preferably on a different computer than the one you use to encode. This is to avoid the chance that you encode your only copy and lose the human-readable copy.

Encoded scripts use a different file extension than plain-text scripts. Table 9.1 lists the normal and encoded extensions.

Table 9.1   **File Extensions for Regular and Encoded Scripts**

Type	Regular File Extension	Encoded File Extension
VBScript	.vbs	.vbe
JScript	.js	.jse

The simplest syntax for encoding a script file is

```
screnc originalname newname
```

Here's an example:

```
screnc myscript.vbs myscript.vbe
```

This produces the encrypted version myscript.vbe, which you can then distribute to other users.

Although the Script Encoder permits the use of wildcards and has some other options, these are not applicable for encoding VBS and JS script files.

▶ **Note**

If you want to distributed signed encoded scripts, sign them before you encode them.

Setting Up Logon Scripts

One important use of scripts is to set up user accounts in a consistent way at every logon. This is important in business environments, where network resources might be moved from time to time or when users might inadvertently alter mapped network drives or other network settings. A script that runs whenever the user logs on can ensure that the user always has access to correct network resources. Logon scripts can also perform checks for software updates, clean up temporary folders, and otherwise perform maintenance tasks on a routine basis, automatically.

Windows lets you assign scripts on a per-user basis. A login script can be a WSH file or an old-style `.bat` or `.cmd` batch file; you can use whatever format you wish. A batch file can even launch WSH, if you need to use both environments.

In addition, Windows supports Group Policy–based script assignments that let you run a script upon user logon/logoff and computer startup/shutdown.

Note

Windows 7 and Vista can run scripts at logon, logoff, startup, shutdown, and other significant events, even without domain network membership, using the Task Scheduler. I discuss this toward the end of the chapter.

In this section, I show you how to assign logon scripts to users and groups.

User Profile Logon Scripts

The oldest and most common way to assign logon scripts is through the user profile mechanism. Windows lets you assign a script to a user account. This can be done both for domain accounts and for local computer accounts. Here's how to do this:

- On a Windows Server machine, run User Manager for Domains or Active Directory Users and Groups, whichever is appropriate.
- On a Windows workstation, for example, for a standalone or workgroup computer or for local accounts on a domain member, right-click My Computer, select Manage, and then select Local Users and Groups. (This isn't available on Windows Home versions.)

For local accounts and for standalone or workgroup computers, Windows looks for logon scripts on the local computer in a peculiar, fixed location: under the Windows directory in `\windows\system32\repl\import\scripts`. This folder is used because, historically, it was a folder that was automatically copied to all domain servers in an organization, as mentioned earlier in the chapter. If this folder doesn't already exist, you have to create it.

For domain user accounts, Windows retrieves scripts from the NETLOGON shared folder on the domain controller (server). On a Windows domain server, they are stored in `\windows\sysvol\sysvol\`*`domainname`*`\scripts`, which is shared as NETLOGON.

To assign a logon script, view the properties for a user and select the Profile tab, as illustrated in Figure 9.3. Enter the name of the logon script file, which can be of any registered script or batch file type. The filename you enter here is relative to `\windows\system32\repl\import\scripts`. You can enter either a plain filename (for example, `logon.vbs`) or a *`subfolder\filename`*, but you cannot enter an absolute path (that is, one starting with \), nor can you use `..` to attempt to climb to a higher folder. In most cases, logon scripts are stored in the top-level scripts folder, so you can simply enter the name without any path information.

Figure 9.3   Enter the location of the logon script in the Profile tab of a user's Properties page.

Caution

Because logon scripts can do anything the user can do, you *must* be sure no one can maliciously edit a logon script that belongs to another user.

Be careful to set proper access-control permissions on logon script files and on the scripts folder itself. Script files *must* be stored on an NTFS-formatted partition. They should be readable by everyone but writeable and modifiable only by an administrator.

The script is executed each time the user logs on, just after Windows restores any persistent network settings (that is, after network drives mapped with the Reconnect at Logon box is checked). The script can then rearrange network settings, Windows printers, software and Registry settings, and desktop icons or do whatever else is needed.

Scripts for Logon, Logoff, and Other Events on Windows 7 and Vista

Windows 7 and Vista let you specify commands to be run when significant system events occur, such as logon, logoff, startup, shutdown, resume from hibernate, and so on. You can assign scripts to these trigger events using the Scheduled Tasks tool. I cover this tool in the last section of this chapter.

Group Policy Logon, Logoff, Startup, and Shutdown Scripts

On a domain network, you can specify login scripts though Group Policy. Policy-based scripts are separate from the user profile script discussed in the previous section. Policy-assigned scripts run in addition to any script defined in the user profile. This feature is available even on standalone and workgroup computers, through each computer's Local Policy settings. With Active Directory, however, it's much more powerful because you can assign computer startup and shutdown scripts, as well as user logon and logoff scripts for Group Policy objects attached to users, groups, computers, organizational units, and so on.

To assign logon, logoff, startup, or shutdown scripts, first create and test the scripts. Then, assign the scripts in the Group Policy management tool using these steps:

1. To manage your own computer, click Start, Run; type **gpedit.msc**; and press Enter. Then, skip ahead to step 3.

2. To manage policy on a domain network, log on as a domain administrator. If you don't use Active Directory, run `gpedit.msc` as noted previously and continue with step 3. If you do use Active Directory, open Active Directory Users and Groups. Select an Active Directory object, view its properties, select the Group Policy tab, and add or edit a Group Policy object.

3. You should now have a Group Policy editor window open, as shown in Figure 9.4. To add a startup or shutdown script, view Computer Configuration, Scripts (Startup/Shutdown). To add a logon or logoff script, view Windows Settings, Scripts (Logon/Logoff). Then, double-click the Startup, Shutdown, Logon or Logoff entry, as desired.

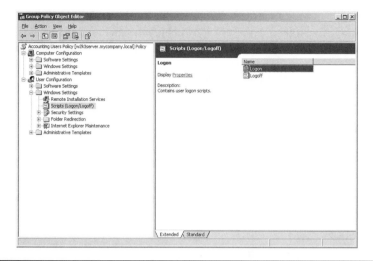

Figure 9.4   The Group Policy Editor lets you assign startup, shutdown, logon, and logoff scripts.

4. Click Show Files. This displays the folder that is used to hold scripts for this particular policy entry. It is one of the following folders:

Policy	Folder
Local	`\WINDOWS\system32\GroupPolicy\User\Scripts\Logon`
	`\WINDOWS\system32\GroupPolicy\User\Scripts\Logoff`
	`\WINDOWS\system32\GroupPolicy\Machine\Scripts\Startup`
	`\WINDOWS\system32\GroupPolicy\Machine\Scripts\Shutdown`
Group	`\\server\sysvol\`*domainname*`\Policies\{…}\User\Scripts\Logon`
	`\\server\sysvol\`*domainname*`\Policies\{…}\User\Scripts\Logoff`
	`\\server\sysvol\`*domainname*`\Policies\{…}\Machine\Scripts\Startup`
	`\\server\sysvol\`*domainname*`\Policies\{…}\Machine\Scripts\Shutdown`

(For standalone and workgroup computers, Local Policy is the only option available.)

5. Open another Windows Explorer window and locate the folder containing your new, tested script. Drag it to the policy folder, being sure to hold down the Ctrl key while you release the icon so you create a copy. You can close the Explorer windows now, if you want.

6. Back in the policy Properties dialog box, click Add, and then click Browse. Select the script you copied in the previous step, click Open, and then OK to confirm. The script now appears in the list of designated scripts, as shown in Figure 9.5.

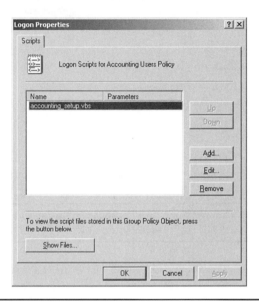

Figure 9.5 The Properties dialog box lists assigned scripts and any designated parameters.

7. You can add multiple scripts and use the Up and Down buttons to order them. These scripts are executed in turn, with one starting after the previous has exited. Click the Remove button to delete a script assignment. Click OK to save the script settings.

Here are some observations I've made about policy-based scripts:

- Policy-based logon scripts run after Windows establishes any memorized network connections; they are *started* before the user profile login script, but the logon process does not wait until any the policy-based script completes. Thus, the user profile logon script can't be sure when it starts up that the policy-based script has finished or even that it has begun to do its work. Meanwhile, after any startup scripts have been initiated, Windows proceeds to run startup programs listed in the Registry and in the All Users and personal Startup folders.

- Logoff scripts are run before Windows shuts down network connections, and the logoff process waits until the logoff script has exited before proceeding.

- The Local Machine Policy user logon script is *not* run for the Administrator account, but the logoff script is run for every account.

- Logon and logoff scripts are not run if the user signs off temporarily using Fast User switching. Even though the desktop is not visible, the user remains logged on. (On Windows 7 and Vista, though, you can run scripts at these events, using the Task Scheduler.)

Note

Using logoff and shutdown scripts is a neat idea, but there's no guarantee that either will run every time they should—sometimes Windows crashes, sometimes the power goes out, sometimes users log off with the reset button. Although you can use these scripts for cleanup and maintenance work, they're not reliable for billing, time tracking, or other applications where missing runs could make a significant difference.

Scheduling Scripts to Run Automatically

Besides writing Windows books, I work as a consultant and develop software for several companies. For large-scale database projects, I've found it useful to set up scheduled programs—scripts—that run on a nightly basis to create reports, archive old data, perform backups, and so on. This isn't a new idea: Nightly "batch" processing has been around almost as long as the computer itself.

Automatic scripting is a great way to be sure that important operations take place even if you forget to start them, and they can be performed during off hours so there is minimal disruption to your work. Often, the only convenient time to perform procedures, such as backups and database cleanups, is at night when most users are gone, because these tasks usually require all applications to be shut down and all data files to be closed.

Windows has a Task Scheduler tool that makes it easy to schedule scripts for automatic startup. In this section, I talk a bit about some extra considerations to make when writing scheduled scripts, and then I show how to use the Task Scheduler to set them up.

Writing Unattended Scripts

You usually write scheduled scripts for either or both of these reasons: to process information when nobody is around or to ensure that necessary processing isn't forgotten. In either case, this processing is usually important, and it's crucial that you know whether some problem is preventing it from occurring. Although automated processing is a great idea, it's easy and dangerous to succumb to an "out-of-sight, out-of-mind" obliviousness; there is no more horrifying experience in the computing realm than to find after a disk crash that the last year's worth of automatic backups never took place.

At the risk of laboring a point, I want to discuss some ways you can make scheduled scripts accountable for their proper operation. The key concepts here are logging and notification.

The problem with scheduled programs is that they don't interact with the user's desktop, so if they stop working, it could be some time before anyone notices.

As a sort of failsafe mechanism, I've found it useful to have every automatic process produce some sort of annoying reminder of its presence so that a missed run will be noticed. This can take the form of a log file, a printed report, or an email message.

As a matter of policy, every automated script should keep a log file record of its operation, indicating the date and time when key steps in the script have completed their task and certainly recording any errors or anomalous conditions that the script encounters, such as empty input files.

The following sample script has a procedure named `loggit` that can be used to record text messages in a log file. The procedure opens and closes the log file every time it records a message so that the information is sure to be written out. If the script crashes, you know that the problem occurred after the point in the script where the last message was written. Here's the script:

```
                               ' Example File sched.vbs
dim logfilename, fso
logfilename = "C:\scripts\logs\sched.log"
set fso = CreateObject("Scripting.FileSystemObject")

const ForAppending = 8

loggit "* Sched started"

' ... gather input

if input_file_was_empty then          ' (these are fictitious statements)
    loggit "Error: input file was empty"
    wscript.quit 0
end if

for each item in list_of_things_to_do
    loggit "starting to process item " & item
next

loggit "* Sched finished successfully"

' -----------------------------------------------
' loggit - write a message to the script log file

sub loggit (msg)
    set stream = fso.OpenTextFile(logfilename, ForAppending, True)
    stream.writeline date & " " & time & ": " & msg
```

```
      stream.close
      WScript.echo msg ' show on console window too in case someone is watching
   end sub
```

Logged messages should always use a consistent format. For example, error messages might always start with the string "Error." This helps you to automatically identify problems with a summarizing script, as we discuss shortly.

Controlling the Amount of Information Logged

When you're first debugging a script, you often add many logging and debugging `wscript.echo` statements. I suggest that you keep all these statements even after the script is working and change them all to logging procedure calls. To keep the log file from becoming bloated, control the amount of detail recorded with a "log-level" variable defined at the beginning of the script. For example, you could define three information levels: 0 = normal, 1 = moderate, 2 = maximum. Then, you can use `if` statements to control each log entry, as shown here:

```
   dim loglevel
   loglevel = 0   ' enable minimal logging
   ⋮
   if loglevel >= 0 then loggit "* this is always logged"
   ⋮
   if loglevel >= 1 then loggit "* this is logged at level 1+"
   ⋮
   if loglevel >= 2 then loggit "* this is only logged at level 2+"
```

If trouble occurs, all the debugging statements is still there. You can set the `loglevel` variable to its maximum value and run the script again to get more detailed information.

Sending Messages to the Event Log

You can also record logging information to the Windows Event Log. This should probably be reserved for errors because the Event Log tends to lose its usefulness if it's filled with "chatter" (that is, success and informational messages).

I covered event logging briefly in Chapter 4, "File and Registry Access," but here are the basics again: The `WScript.Shell` object has a `LogEvent` method that lets you store a message in the Event Log. The method call is

```
   LogEvent(intType, strMessage [,strTarget])
```

where *strTarget* is an optional argument giving the name of the computer whose Event Log the message should be sent to, *strMessage* is the text of the message to record, and *intType* is a number indicating the severity of the incident. Here are the values for *intType*:

Value	Meaning
0	Success
1	Error
2	Warning
4	Informational
8	Audit success
16	Audit failure

For script logging, only the first four values are appropriate. An Event Log entry can be recorded with the following statements:

```
                                           ' Example File script0903.vbs
set fso   = CreateObject("Scripting.FileSystemObject")
set shell = CreateObject("WScript.Shell")
⋮
' script program goes here

filename = "c:\scripts\data\input.dat"

if not fso.FileExists(filename) then
    shell.LogEvent 1, "SCHED.VBS - unable to find input file " & filename
    wscript.quit 1
end if
⋮
```

The information that is recorded in the Event Log is shown in Figure 9.6.

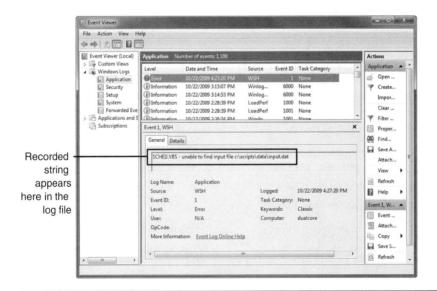

Recorded string appears here in the log file

Figure 9.6   The `WshShell.LogEvent` method writes an arbitrary string to the Application Log in the Windows Event Log.

If you prefer to collect all event information on a particular computer, perhaps one whose Event Log is monitored more carefully than the one on which the scheduled script runs, you can add the computer name as a third argument to `LogEvent`.

Printing and Messaging

Although it's not the "green" thing to do, you can write logging information to a printer where the physical presence of a report page calls attention to any problems the script might have reported.

Another, more environmentally correct way to make sure that information about a scheduled job gets the proper attention is to send log file results and error messages via email. I covered the CDO Messaging objects in Chapter 6, "Messaging and Faxing Objects," so I don't go through all that again here. I suggest that after running a scheduled script, you send the script's output or log file to an administrator or other responsible party.

You could mail the log file at the end of the script. However, if the script doesn't run to completion, the mail isn't sent, and the recipient has to notice the absence of the daily (or weekly or monthly) announcement to realize that something went wrong. When using printing or email to report on batch file results, it's better to schedule a separate script job to print or mail the results from the previous script(s). This way, the news goes out whether or not the processing scripts finish.

If you do this, the last thing the printing or emailing script might do is to archive the log file, and then create a new one saying something like "Scheduled script did not run." If tomorrow's scheduled task never gets started, the next time the printing or emailing script runs, it will print or send you the "Scheduled script did not run" message.

Summarizing Results

When several scheduled tasks are to be performed each night or if scripts are to be run on several different servers, it's useful to run one final scheduled task to summarize the night's processing after all the others have finished. It needs to only extract a simple success/failure note for each process. This way, if the nightly summary is missing or contains error messages, the administrative staff knows to look for a problem.

Sending such a report by email is a nifty way to go because it saves paper and is unlikely to get lost in the shuffle near a busy printer. Such a script might look like this:

```
                              ' Example File summary.vbs
option explicit
dim fso, summaryfile, recipient, summary, sum, msg
set fso = CreateObject("Scripting.FileSystemObject")
```

```
const ForAppending = 8

summaryfile = "c:\scripts\logs\summary.log"
recipient   = "Administrator@quarterbyte.com"

summary     = ""    ' summary text is accumulated in this string

' summarize all of the nightly scheduled scripts
summarize "c:\scripts\logs\sched.log"
summarize "c:\scripts\logs\cleanup.log"
summarize "c:\scripts\logs\backup.log"

' add a final line
summary = summary & string(64, "-") & vbCRLF

' create a new summary file
set sum = fso.CreateTextFile(summaryfile, True)
sum.Write summary
sum.Close

' then mail the summary using the object developed in Appendix F
set msg = CreateObject("ScriptMail.Message")
msg.To = recipient
msg.ScriptName = "summarize"
msg.Text = summary
msg.Send

' ------------------------------------------------
' summarize - record the last line and any errors from 'filename'

sub summarize (filename)
    dim stream, outstream, line, lastline

    ' first time through, note the date and time
    if summary = "" then
        summary = "Batch summary, " & date & " " & time & vbCRLF & vbCRLF
    end if

    ' note the file we're examining
    summary = summary & filename & ":" & vbCRLF

    ' if file doesn't exist, that's all we can say
    if not fso.FileExists(filename) then
        summary = summary & "    FILE NOT FOUND!" & vbCRLF & vbCRLF
        exit sub
    end if

    set stream = fso.OpenTextFile(filename)

    ' we don't want to summarize the same log info every night, so
    ' tack the log file contents onto the end of the same filename + ".old", and
    ' delete the original log when we're done.

    set outstream = fso.OpenTextFile(filename & ".old", ForAppending, True)
```

```
' run through the log file, picking up errors and saving the last line
lastline = "(empty file)"
do while not stream.AtEndOfStream
    line = stream.ReadLine             ' get line from log file
    outstream.WriteLine line           ' append to .OLD copy

    if instr(ucase(line), "ERROR") > 0 then
        summary = summary & "     " & line & vbCRLF
    elseif len(line) > 0 then
        lastline = line
    end if
loop
stream.close
outstream.close

' note the last line; it should be the "completed successfully" line
summary = summary & "     " & lastline & vbCRLF & vbCRLF

' we've copied the log to .OLD, so delete the original log file now
fso.DeleteFile(filename)
end sub
```

This script sends the last line from each listed log file on the assumption that the last line is something like "Sript completed successfully." If this line appears in the email, we know the script didn't crash before finishing. The message also includes any log entries with the word "error." Also, this script saves the logged data and deletes each log file, so it can detect whether the associated script has run. A missing log file indicates a big problem.

The email message generated by this script might look like this:

```
Batch summary, 4/15/2002 5:45:04 AM

c:\scripts\logs\sched.log:
    4/15/2002 2:12:02 AM: * Sched finished successfully

c:\scripts\logs\cleanup.log:
    4/15/2002 3:45:02 AM: ERROR: can't find folder \temp\database
    4/15/2002 3:47:35 AM: * Cleanup finished successfully

c:\scripts\logs\backup.log:
    FILE NOT FOUND!
-----------------------------------------------------------------
```

This summarizing script should be scheduled to run long after any other scheduled scripts should have been completed, but before the administrator arrives at work, if possible. It's nice to see a comforting "everything worked" message first thing every morning.

Such a system of daily or weekly reporting can go a long way to ensure that automated batch processing is functioning correctly, even if invisibly.

Scheduling Scripts with the Task Scheduler

Now, let's see how to schedule scripts for automatic processing. I describe the process of using the Task Scheduler. (The old Windows NT `at` command-line mechanism is also available—if you remember back that far—but it's not as flexible as the Task Scheduler, so we don't consider it here.)

To start the Task Scheduler, click Start, All Programs, Accessories, System Tools, Scheduled Tasks. Then, on Windows 7 and Vista, select Task Scheduler Library in the left pane. The Scheduled Tasks window displays any previously scheduled programs, the time each is next scheduled to run, the time each last ran, and the last run's status. (This indicates whether the program quit with a normal "0" exit status or returned a nonzero error status.) You might need to scroll the task list horizontally to see all of the recorded status information.

Scheduling a Script

To schedule a script for automatic execution on Windows 7 or Vista, follow these steps:

1. In the Actions column at the right, select Create Basic Task. Enter a name for the task (such as "Nightly Batch Processing") and click Next.

2. Select an interval at which the script should be run. Choose Daily, Weekly, or Monthly. If you want to run the script daily but only on certain days of the week, select Weekly. If you want a more complicated timed schedule, you can adjust it later. (Alternatively, you can elect to run a script when a specific Event Log entry is recorded, but I don't discuss that further here.) Click Next to proceed.

3. Select a start time for the script, as illustrated in Figure 9.7. You can also pick a starting date and choose the repeat frequency.

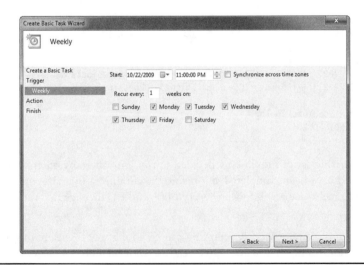

Figure 9.7   The Scheduled Task Wizard lets you choose the start time and days to run the script.

4. Select Start a Program, and click Next.

5. Click Browse, and then locate and select the script you want to run; then, click Open.

6. Position the cursor before the filename in the Program/Script box and type **cscript //B** , followed by a space. Be sure to use forward slashes (//) instead of backslashes (\\) and be sure there is a space after **B**. The entry should look like this:

    ```
    cscript //B c:\scripts\nightrun.vbs
    ```

    but with the path and filename for *your* script. Add any command-line arguments you want to pass to the script. Also, if you want the script's default folder to be something other than the folder in which the script resides, enter the desired default folder path. Then, click Next.

7. The Task Scheduler asks if you intended to run `cscript` with additional arguments. Click Yes.

8. Check Open Properties Dialog For This Task When I Click Finish; then, click Finish.

9. On the General tab, under Security Options, select Run Whether The User Is Logged On Or Not.

    If the script requires elevated Administrator permissions, check Run With Highest Privileges. Then, if your user account is not an Administrator Account or if you want to change the user account for other reasons, click Change User Or Group and select a different username.

10. If the script does not need to access shared files or folders on your network, check Do Not Store Password. This way, if you change the password on your account, the scheduled script still runs.

    If your script does need to access network resources, however, do not check Do Not Store Password. In this case, if you later change the password on your account, you have to remember to come back here and change the password associated with this scheduled task; otherwise, it does not run.

    You can modify the task's schedule on the Triggers tab. There, you can specify various other types of events that can cause Windows to run the script. The Conditions and Setting tabs have other settings you might want to investigate.

    Change any other settings you want, and then click OK to save.

11. If you did not check Do Not Save Password or if you selected an account other than your own, Windows should prompt you for a password. Enter the password, and click OK.

To schedule a script on Windows XP, you have to follow these slightly different steps:

1. Double-click Add Scheduled Task. Then, click Next to start the Scheduled Task Wizard.

2. Click Browse and locate the script file. Select the file and click Open.

3. Select an interval at which the script should be run. Choose Daily, Weekly, or Monthly. If you want a more complicated schedule, you can adjust it later. After selecting an interval, click Next.

4. Select a start time for the script, as illustrated in Figure 9.7. You can also pick a starting date and choose the repeat frequency—either Every Day, Weekdays, or Every *n* Days. Click Next.

5. Enter the username and password under which the script should run. Think carefully about this; use an account with sufficient privileges to read and write any necessary files and to perform whatever system operations are necessary, but no more. Don't use the Administrator account unless you really need its power. When you've entered an account and password, click Next.

6. Click Finish.

7. The script appears in the list of scheduled tasks. Double-click the entry to display its property pages. Select the Task page and edit the Run command line. It initially contains the full pathname to your script. Before this filename, insert **cscript //B** , as discussed previously. Be sure to use forward slashes (//) instead of backslashes (\\), and be sure there is a space after **B**.

8. Click OK to complete the scheduling process.

Tip

When entering scripts into the Task Scheduler, always use the full command line cscript //B *drive:\path\scriptfile arguments*…. Cscript forces the use of the command line rather than the Windowed version of WSH, and //B prevents cscript from displaying a message box or other dialog box that otherwise halts the script. If the script is run by the scheduler without //B, nobody may be there to click the OK button.

Note

If your computer is not turned on when a task is scheduled to run, it runs the next time your computer is started.

Testing a Scheduled Script

To test the scheduled item, you don't have to wait until its next scheduled run time. Just select the item in the task list; then, in the Actions column to the right, select

Run. Wait a while, and then press F5 to refresh the status list. Look in the Last Run Time and Last Run Result columns to see whether the script ran successfully. (If your script creates a log file or other diagnostic output, check that.)

If the status entry changes to "Could not start," you have probably entered the incorrect password or the incorrect path to the script file. If there are spaces in the pathname, the path must be enclosed in quotes.

If necessary, you can go back into the Properties dialog box to make changes:

- On the Task tab, you can change the script filename and the user account and password under which the script runs. You can also uncheck the Enabled box to temporarily stop future runs without deleting the scheduled entry.

- On the Settings tab, you can select how much time the script is given to run, after which it is terminated. The default setting is 72 hours, but most scripts should need much less time than this.

- On the Schedule tab, you can alter the run times and days or select Show Multiple Schedules, which lets you enter complex schedules with multiple periodic intervals.

However, after making any changes, you have to reenter the password used to run this script.

Caution

Be sure that script files you've set up to run under the scheduler can only be edited by the user whose account is used to run the script. This can be a *terrible* security hole. If a script runs with the Administrator privilege, but the file is editable by other users, then someone could modify the script to do whatever she wanted.

Be sure that scheduled scripts are stored only on an NTFS-formatted disk drive. Also, view the files' security permissions periodically to be sure that only appropriate users are listed as having write or modify rights to the file.

10

The CMD Command-Line

- This chapter introduces the command-line environment.
- Command-line programs can be powerful and useful. Honest.
- The CMD shell has many improvements over `COMMAND.COM`.
- The built-in commands provided by CMD perform many file and management functions.

The Command Prompt

I spent the first nine chapters of this book extolling the virtues of Windows Script Host (WSH) programming and proclaiming it to be the right tool for all Windows automation tasks. Now it's time to confess that "all" might not be the right word, and in the remainder of the book, I show you why.

Although most of the fanfare over programming advances in the last decade have been over windowed applications with pull-down menus, dialog boxes, and all that jazz, the old-fashioned command line has been quietly becoming more sophisticated and capable as well. If you click Start, All Programs, Accessories, Command Prompt, a window appears that looks a lot like what you would have seen back in the days of the original Microsoft MS-DOS. You can type the old commands such as `dir` and `cls`, and Windows dutifully prints a directory listing and clears the screen.

However, as much as this looks like the MS-DOS prompt, under the hood, it's a completely different animal. New commands, some spiffy new user interface tricks, and access to some of the most powerful maintenance and configuration tools in Windows make the command-prompt environment an effective place to work with programs and files.

For example, a large number of utilities are available for network and Internet file copying, troubleshooting, configuration, and management. Many Windows maintenance tasks can be performed from the command line, and many file- and graphics-conversions tools have command-line access. The batch file scripting language lets you write command-line tools of your own. I cover these topics in the next few chapters. This chapter covers the command-prompt environment itself.

CMD Versus COMMAND

One tip-off that the command prompt is not the same as it was back in the prehistoric MS-DOS days is that it's managed by a program called CMD.EXE. CMD was introduced in Windows NT and is the command shell on all modern versions of Windows. You might remember that the original MS-DOS command program was called COMMAND.COM; most people became aware of its name thanks to DOS's propensity to print "Cannot load COMMAND.COM" and then come to a screeching halt. Thankfully, that doesn't happen anymore.

Programs such as CMD and COMMAND are called *shells* because they encase an operating system. Their purpose is to mediate between the user and the programs he wants to run. Shells were the only user interfaces available in early mini- and microcomputer operating systems such as Unix, Multics, RSX-11M, and CP/M. In fact, the phrase *graphical user interface* came about as a way to distinguish the new generation of graphical interfaces from the old command-line shells.

The earliest shells could do little more than prompt for the name of a program and then locate and run the program. People got tired of typing the same commands over and over, so operating system developers provided ways to let the shell read a list of commands from a file and then run each in turn. Eventually, shells grew into little programming languages of their own, and the *shell script* or *batch file* was born. This concept blossomed on the Unix operating system back in the 1970s and ultimately made its way to MS-DOS, although in a much degraded form. The MS-DOS command prompt and its batch language were limited, peculiar, and inflexible.

Although CMD.EXE and its batch file language are still somewhat burdened with the legacy of COMMAND.COM, some significant new features make the command line a friendlier place to work. Personally, I use it on a daily basis, and I think that you'll find it to be just as useful as I do.

In this chapter, I focus on aspects of CMD that apply to direct use in the Command Prompt window. Everything in this chapter applies to batch files as well, which I discuss in more detail in the next chapter.

> **Tip**
>
> Microsoft's TechNet website has a good article about the command-prompt environment. It was originally published in *Windows NT Shell Scripting*. Although it's missing a few of the enhancements added between NT 4 and current versions of Windows, it's still a detailed and lucid paper. To find it, search www.microsoft.com for "The Windows NT Command Shell," using the quotes.

Running CMD

When you open a Command Prompt window, Windows starts the CMD.EXE program. CMD prompts for commands and executes them, until you close the window or type the exit command. There are several ways to open a Command Prompt window:

- Click Start, All Programs, Accessories, Command Prompt.

- On Windows 7, open a Command Prompt window as just described, right-click its icon in the task bar, and select Pin This Program to Taskbar. The icon is now always available.

- Click Start, and type **cmd** in the Search box. When the cmd.exe result appears, press Enter or click it.

- On Windows XP, or if you have customized the Start menu to show the Run command, click Start, click Run, type **cmd**, and press Enter.

You can change the properties of any of these shorcuts to preset the initial working directory. By default, it's your account's user profile folder.

> **Tip**
>
> You can also start a Command Prompt window from any Windows Explorer view, with a folder preselected as the current directory. This is a handy trick to know. In Windows 7 and Vista, hold down Shift, right-click a folder name in any Windows Explorer view, and select Open Command Window Here. On Windows XP, search www.microsoft.com for "Open Command Open Here Power Toy" and install it. This gives you Open Command Prompt Here as a right-click option on any folder without holding down the Shift key.

You can also open additional Command Prompt windows from the command line or from batch files, if there's a need. To open a new window from the command prompt, type **start cmd**. You can alter CMD's behavior by specifying additional command-line arguments, as I discuss shortly.

> **Tip**
>
> A good time to open an additional Command Prompt window is when you need to perform privileged administrative tasks. I describe this in the next section.

Opening a Command Prompt Window with Administrator Privileges

It's best to do your day-to-day work with a user account that doesn't have full Administrator privileges; this way, a runaway or malicious program can't get at Windows itself. It can be a pain, though, to have to use Switch Users every time you need to perform some management task. On Windows 7 and Vista, User Account Control (UAC) makes this somewhat easier, but in the Command Prompt world, things work a little differently.

On Windows 7 and Vista, command-line programs can't pop up a UAC dialog box. There is no command-line tool that can elevate a program you run from a command line—at least none that is provided with Windows. (More on this shortly.) So, to perform administrative functions with command-line programs, the Command Prompt window from which you run them must itself already be running with elevated privileges.

There are several ways to open an "elevated" Command Prompt window on Windows 7 and Vista:

- On Windows 7, pin the Command Prompt to the taskbar. Right-click its icon, right-click Command Prompt, and select Run As Administrator.

- On Windows Vista, create a shortcut to the Command Prompt in the Quick Launch bar. Right-click it and select Run As Administrator.

- Click Start, All Programs, Accessories. Right-click Command Prompt and select Run As Administrator.

- Create a desktop shortcut to cmd.exe. Right-click it and select Run As Administrator.

- Click Start and type **cmd** in the Search window. Then, right-click the `cmd.exe` result and select Run As Administrator.

- For most of the methods listed here, instead of right-clicking the icon or search result and selecting Run Aas Administrator, you can just hold down Ctrl+Shift and click the item.

Alternatively, you can create a desktop shortcut to cmd.exe (or a batch file, or script, and so on) and set its properties so that it always runs elevated. Just right-click the icon, select Properties, click Advanced, and check Run As Administrator. If you do this, I suggest that you rename the icon so its name indicates that it's a privileged version. For example, I named the icon Elevated Command Prompt.

When you start a Command Prompt any of these ways, you get a UAC prompt; the title of the Command Prompt window always starts with `Administrator:` to remind you that any program run from this window has full administrator privileges. (The word `Administrator` appears no matter what account name you're using, and it appears even if UAC is turned off.)

> **Note**
>
> There is no standard tool that lets you run a program with elevated permissions from a standard Command Prompt window or batch file. There are, however, a few third-party tools. You might consider installing one of the following:
>
> - From technet.microsoft.com, search for Script Elevation PowerToys for Windows Vista.
>
> - Do a Google search for the following four words: john robbins elevate wintellect. The result you want is the one at www.wintellect.com.
>
> - Try surun from www.sourceforge.net/projects/surun/.

On Windows XP, there is no UAC. You can still do most of your day-to-day work from a "Limited" or "Power User" account, and when you need to run a privileged command, you can quickly open a Command Prompt window that has Administrator privileges by typing

`runas /user:Administrator cmd`

on the command line or in the Start menu's Run dialog box. (If you're a Unix user, you can view this as the equivalent of the `su` command. I put this command into a batch file named `su.bat` on all my computers.) You can, of course, substitute any Computer Administrator account name.

The new window runs under the Administrator's logon name, and any programs you run from this command prompt also has administrator privileges. From it, you can, for example, type

`start compmgmt.msc`

to open the Computer Management window. However, you can't open an "Administrator" version of Windows Explorer or other windows that are based on Explorer, such as Network Connections, unless you first—just once—log on as Administrator. Open Explorer; click Tools, Folder Options, View; and check Launch Folder Windows in a Separate Process.

CMD Options

CMD has several command-line options. Although you don't often need to use these options, you might want to be familiar with them. To start the command shell with alternative settings, you can type **start cmd** with additional parameters or run `cmd` from within a shortcut, batch file, and so on.

The syntax of the CMD command itself is as follows:

`cmd [/a | /u] [/q] [/d] [/t:`*`fg`*`] [/e:on|off] [/f:on|off] [/v:on|off] [[/s] [/c | /k]`
`➥ [`*`command`*`]`

You can give CMD a specific command line to execute, or you can start it without a command. In the latter case, it repeatedly prompts for commands.

The options are described here. The features noted with an asterisk are discussed in the following sections:

Options	Description
/a	Causes standard output to use ANSI encoding.
/u	Causes standard output to use Unicode encoding.
/q	Turns the batch file echo default to off.
/d	Disables execution of AutoRun commands defined in the Registry. Use this if a rogue program (or you) sets up a bad AutoRun entry.
/t:*bf*	Sets the background (window) and foreground (text) colors for the window. For example, /t:80 specifies black text on a gray background. The color values are listed in Table 10.1.
/e	Enables or disables the command extensions.
/f	Enables or disables the file and directory name completion feature.
/v	Enables delayed environment variable expansion of !varname! items, as discussed in Chapter 11, "Batch Files for Fun and Profit"
/s	Modifies the treatment of quotation marks on the command line, as discussed in Chapter 11.
/c	Executes the command(s) in *command* and then quits.
/k	Executes the command(s) in *command* and then reads further commands from the standard input until end of file or until the exit command is received.

If used, the /c or /k option must appear immediately before the *command* string. Anything after /c or /k is treated as part of the command to be run, rather than an argument to CMD.

Several nonstandard command-line arguments are also recognized to maintain compatibility with batch files written for Windows NT 4.0:

Arguments	Description
/x	Same as /e:on. Enables command extensions.
/y	Same as /e:off. Disables command extensions.
/r	Same as /c. Executes *command* and quits.

The color codes used with /t are listed in Table 10.1.

Table 10.1 **Color Codes Used with** /t

Value	Color
0	Black
1	Blue
2	Green
3	Aqua
4	Red
5	Purple
6	Yellow
7	White
8	Gray
9	Light blue
A	Light green
B	Light aqua
C	Light red
D	Light purple
E	Light yellow
F	Bright white

Disabling Command Extensions

To run an old batch file that does not function with the extended version of CMD's built-in commands, you can explicitly disable extensions with /e:off on the CMD command line. For example, to run an incompatible batch file, use the following:

```
cmd /e:off oldbatch.bat
```

If this needs to be the rule rather than the exception, you have my sympathies, and you can disable extensions by default through the Registry key HKLM\Software\Microsoft\Command Processor\EnableExtensions. If this DWORD value is present and set to 0, command extensions are disabled. You can use /e:on on the command line to enable extensions for a particular instance of CMD.

Command-Line Processing

The Command Prompt window prompts for commands one line at a time. In this section, I describe how CMD interprets commands. Even if you are familiar with these concepts from MS-DOS, and even if you already know what > and < do, you should read through this section because there are several handy new features you might not yet know about.

CMD's most basic job is to read command lines that have this form:

```
programname arguments
```

Given this command, CMD tries to find an executable program file named
programname. If it does find such a file, it instructs Windows to start the program.
Any additional text typed on the command line—the command's *arguments*—
are passed to that program to interpret. Of course, in practice, things aren't quite
this simple:

- CMD recognizes some built-in commands such as set and cls. For these, CMD
  doesn't search for a file but rather handles the command itself.

- If the command isn't built in, CMD looks for a file named *programname* first in
  the current working directory, and then in a list of directories called the *search
  path*, which you can adjust. The default search path includes several of the subfolders under \WINDOWS. (Later in the chapter, I show you how to modify the
  path to include your own folders.)

- If you explicitly add a filename extension such as .EXE when you type the command, CMD looks through the search path only for this type of file. If you don't
  specify the file type, CMD looks for certain known file types. The list of file
  types is called the PATHEXT list, and you can modify the listed file types and their
  precedence if necessary.

- When CMD has located a file matching the name of the command you typed,
  CMD looks at the file's extension to determine what to do with it. If the file
  has the extension .EXE or .COM, it's an executable program and is run directly.
  Files with the extensions .BAT and .CMD are taken to be batch files, and CMD
  interprets them itself.

  For any other file type, CMD uses the file association information from the
  Windows Registry to determine what to do. If the file type is associated with an
  application program, CMD starts the associated application to open the file. For
  example, WSH is used to run files with the extensions .VBS, .WSF, and .JS, as we
  discussed in the first part of this book.

- Many characters—including < > ( ) ; , | ^ & % and !—have special meaning to
  CMD and alter the interpretation of the command. We cover this topic shortly.

After CMD has identified the program to run, it starts that program. If you've run a
Windows program, it pops up on the screen and leaves the Command Prompt win-
dow free to do other things. If you've run a command-line program, it occupies the
Command Prompt window until it completes or until you terminate it.

Stopping Runaway Programs

Occasionally you type a command that starts spewing page after page of text to the
screen or one that displays some sort of ominous warning about making a change to
Windows that can't be undone, and you want to stop it—pronto.

Most command-line programs quit if you press Ctrl+C. If that doesn't work, Ctrl+Break often works. As a last resort, you can simply close the Command Prompt window by clicking its close box in the upper-right corner. This kills the program in at most a few seconds.

You might also find the `tasklist` and `taskkill` command-line programs useful. I discuss them in detail in Chapter 13, "Command-Line Utilities."

Console Program Input and Output

Unlike Windows programs that display a window panel with menus and buttons, most programs designed to be run from a command prompt simply type out information line-by-line into the Command Prompt window. These programs are called *console programs* because they interact through plain-text input and output like old-fashioned programs that ran on a computer's main terminal; back then, the main terminal was often called a *console*.

The `tasklist` command is a good example of a console program. If you type **tasklist** in the Command Prompt window and press Enter, this program displays a list of all programs and services that are currently running on your computer, as shown in Figure 10.1.

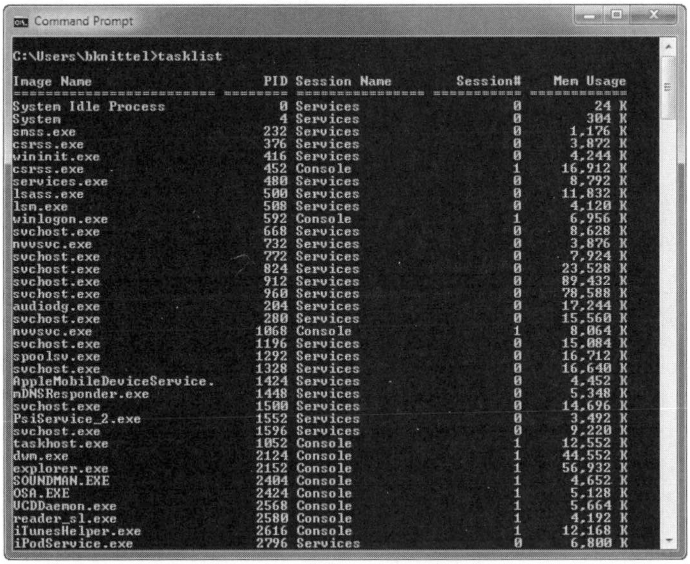

Figure 10.1   The Command Prompt window lets you type
commands—the names of programs to run—and view their output.

Each Command Prompt window has the concept of a *current directory*, its default folder, which is its starting place when looking for files. Although Windows Explorer displays its current directory in its status and address bars, it's most common for the Command Prompt window to show the current directory name in its *prompt*, the indicator it prints to tell you it's ready to accept another command. In Figure 10.1, the prompt is

```
C:\Users\bknittel>
```

Note

Because the prompt varies depending on the directory you are currently using, in this book I don't show the prompt when I give examples of commands to type.

Whereas you use dialog boxes and menus to tell Windows programs how to modify their behavior, you have to type this information into console programs. The `tasklist` command is another good example of this. The printout from the `tasklist` command in Figure 10.1 shows all the system's programs and services. If I want to see the tasks and programs running on the computer named bali, which is connected to my network, I can type the following command:

```
tasklist /s bali /u Administrator
```

In this command, `/s` tells `tasklist` that I want to query the networked computer named bali, and `/u` indicates that I want to use the Administrator logon to get this information. `/s` and `/u` are called *switches* or *options*. Most console programs display the list of options they accept if you enter `/?` on their command lines.

Those are the basics. Now, let's look at some of CMD's more involved features.

Using the Console Window

Normally, command prompt programs run in a normal window that has a title bar, resize points, a close button, and scrollbars.

Unlike a true DOS screen, in a console window, you can peer back in time to previously typed output using the scrollbars. This is particularly handy for programs that print more output than can fit on the screen at once. You can also halt a program's output momentarily by pressing Ctrl+S. When you've caught up with your reading, press Ctrl+S to let the program resume typing.

For better visibility, or to make a program look more like it's running with DOS, you can press Alt+Enter to run the program in *full-screen* mode. If you run a DOS graphics program, this happens automatically. In this mode, the program takes over the whole screen and all other Windows features disappear. You can press Alt+Enter again to bring back the Windows desktop.

You can set the screen mode and the number of lines that the window can scroll using the window's Properties dialog box, as shown in Figure 10.2. You can also set the window's colors and font. Usually, you don't need to adjust the font. It's best to simply resize the window in the normal way; Windows sizes the characters accordingly.

Figure 10.2   A Command Prompt window's Properties dialog box lets you select the screen mode, scroll length, editing properties, and screen colors.

I/O Redirection and Pipes

Normally, any output from a console program appears in the Command Prompt window, but you can *redirect* it into a file using the > character. For example, the command

```
tasklist >tasks.txt
```

generates the same listing as the previous example but stores it in a file named `tasks.txt`. Command-line programs send their output to what is called the *standard output stream*. By default, anything the program sends to the standard output is printed in the Command Prompt window. Figure 10.3 shows how this looks. The first `tasklist` command in the figure sends its output to the Command Prompt window. The second `tasklist` command has its output redirected into a file.

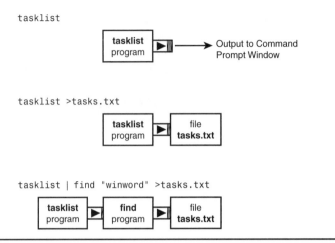

Figure 10.3 Output redirection sends the output of console programs to files or other programs.

Some programs read input through a *standard input* stream. By default, this is connected to your keyboard, and whatever you type is read by the program. For example, the `sort` command reads lines of text from the standard input, sorts them alphabetically, and writes the results to the standard output. If you type the following lines at the command prompt,

```
sort
c
b
a
Ctrl+Z
```

`sort` spits out the lines in order: a, b, c. (Note that Ctrl+Z on a line by itself indicates the end of input.) You can redirect the standard input with the < character. For example, the command

```
sort <somefile.txt
```

tells `sort` to read input from the file `somefile.txt`. You can use both input and output redirection at the same time. The command

```
sort <somefile.txt >sortedfile.txt
```

rearranges the contents of `somefile.txt` and creates a new file named `sortedfile.txt`.

You can also specify that the output isn't to replace an existing file but rather should simply be stuck onto the end (that is, *appended*) with the characters >>, as in this example:

```
dir /b c:\ >listing.txt
dir /b d:\ >>listing.txt
```

The first command creates the file `listing.txt`, and the second appends its output onto the end of `listing.txt`. (If the file `listing.txt` doesn't already exist, don't worry: >> creates it.)

Finally, you can hook the output of one program directly to the input of another by using the vertical bar symbol (|), usually found above the backslash (\) on a keyboard. For example, the `find` command reads lines from the input and passes only lines containing a designated string. The command

```
tasklist | find "winword"
```

has `tasklist` send its list of all programs through `find` which types out only the line or lines containing "winword." Finally,

```
tasklist | find "winword" >tasks.txt
```

connects `tasklist` to `find`, and `find` to a file, as illustrated in the third part of Figure 10.4.

Input and output redirection let you connect programs and files as if you are making plumbing connections. The | symbol is often called a *pipe* for this reason, and programs such as `find` are often called *filters*.

> **Note**
>
> One handy filter to know about is `more`, a program that passes whatever it's given as input to its output. What makes `more` useful is that it pauses after printing a screen full of text. `more` lets you view long listings that would otherwise scroll off the screen too quickly to read. For example, the command
>
> ```
> tasklist | more
> ```
>
> helps you see the entire list of programs. When you see the prompt - - More - - at the bottom of the screen, press the spacebar to view the next screen full.

The *standard error* is another output stream available to console programs. By default, if a program writes information to the standard error stream, the text appears in the Command Prompt window. Programs usually use this to display important error messages that they want you to see, even if the standard output is redirected to a file or pipe. You can redirect standard error too, though, if you want to capture the error messages in a file.

If you've worked with DOS, Linux, or Unix, this is probably already familiar to you. However, there are several input redirection variations you might not be familiar with. Table 10.2 lists all the redirection instructions that CMD recognizes.

Table 10.2   **Input and Output Redirection**

Redirection Option	Action
`<file`	Reads standard input from *file*.
`>file`	Writes standard output to *file*.
`>>file`	Appends standard output to *file*.
`1>file`	Writes standard output to *file*.*
`1>>file`	Appends standard output to *file*.
`2>file`	Writes standard error to *file*.
`2>>file`	Appends standard error to *file*.
`2>&1`	Directs standard error through the same stream as standard output. Both can then be redirected to a file or piped to another program.
`| nextcommand`	Sends output to the input of *nextcommand*.

* The number 1 refers to the standard output stream and the number 2 to the standard error stream.

Two special forms of output redirection are output to the NUL device and output to a printer. Windows recognizes the special filename nul in any folder on any drive and treats it as a "black hole" file. If you issue a command and redirect its output to nul, the output is discarded. This type of direction is useful in batch files when you want a command to do something, but don't want or need the user to see any error messages it might print. For example,

```
net use f: /del >nul 2>nul
```

runs the net use command and makes sure that no output appears to the user.

Special filenames LPT1, LPT2, and so on, represent your default printer and your local printer connected to ports LPT1, LPT2, and so on. You can direct the output of a command to the printer using redirection to these names. You can also direct output to network-connected printers by mapping these devices to network printers using the net use command, which I discuss in Chapter 13. Special name PRN is the same as LPT1.

In practical day-to-day use, standard output redirection lets you capture the output of a console program into a file, where you can edit or incorporate it into your documents. Standard error redirection is handy when you need to gather hardcopy evidence from a program that is printing error messages. Input redirection is used most often in a batch file setting, where you want to have a command run automatically from input prepared ahead of time.

Here are some examples:

```
cmd /? | more
```

This has the CMD command-line shell print its built-in help information, and it passes the text through `more` so it can be read a page at a time.

```
cmd /? > cmd.info
notepad cmd.info
```

This has CMD print its help information again, but this time, the text is stored in a file, and you view the file with Notepad. (Window-based programs can be useful on occasion.)

```
tasklist | sort /+60 | more
```

This has `tasklist` list all running programs, and it pipes the listing through `sort`, which sorts the lines starting with column 60. This produces a listing ordered by the amount of memory used by each running program. The sorted output is piped through `more` so it can be viewed a page at a time.

```
date /f >ping.txt
ping www.mycompany.com 2>&1 >>ping.txt
```

This checks whether the site www.mycompany.com can be reached through the Internet. The results, including any errors, are stored in a file named `ping.txt`. You could then view this file or analyze it with a program.

Copy and Paste in Command Prompt Windows

Although console programs don't have the display windows and menus of ordinary Windows programs, you can still use the mouse to copy and paste text to and from Command Prompt windows.

To copy text to the Clipboard, you have to extract a rectangular block of text—you can't select text line-by-line as you're used to. Position the mouse at the upper-left corner of the block of text you want, drag it down to the bottom-right corner, and then press Enter. While you're selecting text, the word *Select* appears in the window's title. Figure 10.4 shows how a Command Prompt window looks when selecting text.

You can also select text using the window's System menu. Click the upper-left corner of the window or press Alt+space, and then select Edit, Mark. Use the arrow keys to move the cursor to the upper-left corner of the desired area, and then hold the Shift key down while moving the cursor to the lower-right corner. Press Enter to copy the selected text.

```
Select Command Prompt                                        ─  □  X

C:\Users\bknittel\Documents>dir
 Volume in drive C is Win7
 Volume Serial Number is 505D-AA73

 Directory of C:\Users\bknittel\Documents

08/03/2010  04:15 PM    <DIR>          .
08/03/2010  04:15 PM    <DIR>          ..
06/02/2010  03:08 PM    <DIR>          CCWin
08/02/2010  02:17 PM    <DIR>          Corel User Files
08/02/2010  08:59 PM    <DIR>          Fax
06/02/2010  03:12 PM    <DIR>          HTML
08/03/2010  10:52 AM    <DIR>          Legal Documents
08/26/2009  10:03 AM    <DIR>          My Virtual Machines
07/13/2010  03:08 PM    <DIR>          New folder
06/26/2010  11:13 AM               228 PDF_Log.txt
12/07/2009  04:39 PM    <DIR>          Remote Assistance Logs
08/26/2010  10:12 AM    <DIR>          Scanned Documents
10/22/2009  01:34 PM    <DIR>          troubleshooting packs
11/21/2009  07:29 PM    <DIR>          Visual FoxPro Projects
06/02/2010  03:50 PM    <DIR>          Visual Studio 2005
08/27/2010  10:04 AM    <DIR>          Visual Studio 2008
08/27/2010  12:41 PM    <DIR>          WindowsPowerShell
06/02/2010  03:21 PM    <DIR>          Working Files
               1 File(s)            228 bytes
              17 Dir(s)   1,859,297,280 bytes free

C:\Users\bknittel\Documents>_
```

Figure 10.4   To copy text to the Clipboard, select a block
of text with the mouse or keyboard, and press Enter.

You can paste text into a Command Prompt window using the same menu, except to
paste, select Edit, Paste. To paste to a Command Prompt window, however, the program running in the window has to be expecting input.

Tip

The keyboard shortcut for Paste is worth memorizing: Alt+space, E, P.

By the way, "cut" isn't available—after something is typed in a Command Prompt
window, it's typed and can't be removed.

If you need to run a mouse-aware MS-DOS program in a Command Prompt window, you want to disable the Select feature so that mouse movements are sent to the
program rather than being interpreted by the console program window. To disable the
use of the mouse for copying text, select the window's Properties dialog box and
uncheck Quick Edit, as shown earlier in Figure 10.2.

Command Editing and the History List

Command lines entries can be long, convoluted lists of program names and arguments,
like this:

```
ibmfix -b -ic:\ibm\input\imports\filea.txt c:\ibm\output\impa.dat
```

Nobody expects you to type something like this without making errors. CMD lets
you edit a command before you press Enter so you can correct mistakes without having to retype the whole line. The additional editing functions provided by the optional

program DOSKEY in DOS and Windows 9*x* are standard in CMD. Here are some ways that CMD lets you edit a command under construction:

- The left- and right-arrow keys let you move the cursor back and forth within the line. Ctrl+left arrow and Ctrl+right arrow move the cursor back and forth by whole words. Home and End move the cursor to the beginning and end of the line, respectively.

- By default, any characters you type are inserted at the cursor point and the remaining text slides to the right. You can press the Ins key to toggle between insert and overwrite mode. (COMMAND.COM defaults to overwrite mode.)

- Command lines can extend in length beyond one line on the screen. If you type more characters than can fit on the width of the screen, CMD scrolls the line up. You can scroll to an earlier or later line with the left and right arrows. (COMMAND.COM doesn't let you scroll back to earlier lines.)

- If you press the F3 key, the command line is filled in with characters from the previously entered command, from the current cursor position to the end of the line.

- When you're finished editing, you can press Enter with the cursor at any place in the line.

Working with command-line programs can quickly get tedious if you have to type the same command over and over. Imagine typing in commands like this by hand, only to find that you should have typed -a instead of -b and need to do it all over again:

```
ibmfix -b -ic:\ibm\input\imports\filea.txt c:\ibm\output\impa.dat
ibmfix -b -ic:\ibm\input\imports\fileb.txt c:\ibm\output\impb.dat
ibmfix -b -ic:\ibm\input\imports\filec.txt c:\ibm\output\impc.dat
ibmfix -b -ic:\ibm\input\imports\filed.txt c:\ibm\output\impd.dat
```

Luckily, the CMD window keeps track of every line you type in, and it's easy to recall a previous command for editing or reuse. Here's how this works:

- You can press the up-arrow and down-arrow keys to scroll through the list of previously entered commands. If you find one you want to reuse, you can simply press Enter to run it again. Alternatively, you can edit the command using the keys described earlier.

- PgUp recalls the oldest command in CMD's list; PgDn recalls the most recent.

- If you press F7, CMD displays a list of recently entered commands. You can select one of these lines and press Enter to reuse it, or you can press Esc to dismiss the list of commands.

CMD has more editing features than I've listed here; these are just the most useful. To see the whole list, click Start, Help, and search for DOSKEY.

Tip

One feature you might want to read is the capability to define *macros*, which are whole command lines that you can call by typing a short abbreviation or keyword. Unix users know these as *aliases* and will be happy to know that they're available in Windows.

Name Completion

When you are typing command lines to CMD, you often need to type file and folder names. Name completion makes this easier—you can type just the first few letters of a file or folder name, strike a control key, and CMD finishes typing the name for you. This is a nifty but not widely known feature that, like most of the other fun new features in CMD, Microsoft has borrowed from the Unix operating system.

Here's how name completion works: If you press the filename-completion character (usually the Tab key), CMD examines the characters to the left of the cursor and uses this as the basis for a path and/or filename. The way to think of this is that when you type the completion character, CMD looks for any files whose names start with whatever you've typed so far. If there is a space or nothing at all to the left of the cursor, CMD looks for * (all files).

If CMD finds no matching file or folder name, it beeps and does nothing. If it does find a matching name, CMD finishes typing the name for you. It looks like this:

```
c:\batch> edit b          ← I type edit and the letter b, then press Tab

c:\batch> edit bills.bat ← CMD finds a matching file and completes the name
```

If this is the correct name, you can continue typing on the command line. This is a great timesaver! If the name that CMD types is not the one you are looking for, you can press the completion key again to see the next matching name. Pressing the key repeatedly cycles through all matching names. What's more, you can hold down the Shift key while typing the completion character to cycle backwards.

Tip

If you have to type a long pathname such as `\Users\bknittel\Documents`, you can use name completion for each part of the name. For this example, you could type the following:

`dir \u` (Tab) `\b` (Tab) `\d` (Tab) (Tab)

Try this on your own computer (and use your own username instead of `bknittel`). It's pretty slick—CMD adds the required quotation marks and moves them into the correct positions automatically.

Directory name completion works in an identical fashion, except that it matches *only* folder names. Name completion is enabled by default, but not directory name completion. If you're content enough to use the Tab key to cycle through both filenames and folder names, just leave everything as it is. If you want to use a separate key to indicate that you want CMD to look only for directory names, I show you how in the next section.

Enabling Directory Name Completion

As mentioned in the previous section, filename completion is enabled by default—the Tab key searches for a filename *or* folder name matching the characters to the left of the cursor. A similar feature called *directory name completion* lets you use a different key to match only directory names.

I will show you how to enable directory name completion shortly, but prepare yourself for some strangeness. First, there's the matter of the odd default control key settings:

- By default, name completion is enabled and uses the Tab key, whereas directory name completion is disabled.

- If you run CMD with `/f:on` on the command line, name completion is enabled but now uses Ctrl+F. Directory name completion is enabled and uses Ctrl+D.

- If you run CMD with `/f:off` on the command line, both name and directory name completion are disabled.

If you want directory name completion to be enabled all the time on Windows XP, the easiest approach is use the TweakUI tool, which you can download from www.microsoft.com. The setting is on the Command Prompt tab.

You can also edit the Registry to change the default settings on XP, Vista, or Windows 7. The values `CompletionChar` and `PathCompletionChar` set the key codes used for name completion and directory name completion, respectively. CMD looks for the values in the key

`HKEY_CURRENT_USER\Software\Microsoft\Command Processor`

which holds the settings for the current user. If they are not present there, CMD looks in

`HKEY_LOCAL_MACHINE\Software\Microsoft\Command Processor`

which sets the default for all users.

`CompletionChar` and `PathCompletionChar` are `DWORD` values that hold a number representing the associated control key. It's easiest to enter these values in decimal, where 1 = Ctrl+A, 2 = Ctrl+B, ... 26 = Ctrl+Z. Some handy values to know are listed here:

Value	Key
4	Ctrl+D
6	Ctrl+F
9	Ctrl+I (Tab)
32	Disables completion

To use Ctrl+F for name completion and Ctrl+D for directory name completion, follow these steps:

1. Run the Registry editor with the command `regedit`.
2. Open `HKEY_CURRENT_USER` and find `Software\Microsoft\Command Processor`.
3. Double-click the already-present `CompletionChar` entry, click `Decimal`, and enter the number **6**. Click OK.
4. Select Edit, New, DWORD Value. Type the name **`PathCompletionChar`**.
5. Double-click the new entry, click `Decimal`, enter the value **4**, and click OK.
6. Close the Registry editor and any Command Prompt windows.

From now on, when you start a Command Prompt window, Ctrl+F and Ctrl+D will work.

So you don't get surprised by CMD's behavior at some later date, when Registry settings have been made, CMD follows these rules for enabling name or directory name completion:

- If the Registry value is between 1 and 26, completion is enabled unless you specify `/f:off` when you run CMD.
- If the Registry value is 32, completion is disabled regardless of the `/f` option setting.
- If the `CompletionChar` value is defined as 9 (Tab) and the `PathCompletionChar` value is not defined, CMD displays the default behavior described earlier.

Now, back to our discussion of how the command prompt environment works.

Multiple Commands on One Line

CMD lets you type multiple separate commands on one command line, separated by an ampersand (&), as in this example:

```
dir & ping ftp.microsoft.com & ftp ftp.microsoft.com
```

CMD runs the three commands in turn, as if they had been entered on separate command lines:

```
dir
ping ftp.microsoft.com
ftp ftp.microsoft.com
```

This sounds trivial, but it can be handy. First, when you're typing the same several commands over and over, you can simply press the up-arrow key and use the history feature to recall all the commands at once.

Also, in batch files, which we cover in more detail in Chapter 11, this feature can be used to put several commands on one if statement, as in this example:

```
if not exist list.dat dir c:\in >list.dat & dir c:\out >>list.dat
```

If the file list.dat does not exist, then CMD runs the two dir commands in turn. This can simplify the batch program.

There are two other ways to specify multiple commands on the same line. If you separate commands with two ampersands instead of one, for example,

```
ping ftp.microsoft.com && ftp ftp.microsoft.com
```

the second and subsequent commands are only run if the preceding command is successful (that is, if it exited with an error status value of 0). This lets you create lists of commands that don't plow on after encountering an error.

Another variation lets you use || to indicate that the second command is to be run *only* if the first command fails—that is, if the first command exits with a nonzero error status, as in this example:

```
firstcommand || echo The first command failed
```

Grouping Commands with Parentheses

With CMD's command extensions, you can group several command lines inside parentheses, and CMD treats them as one command. This is useful with the if and for commands. For example, compound statements like the following are possible:

```
if exist c:\data\myfile.dat (
    echo Myfile.dat exists!
    copy myfile.dat d:\backups
    sort myfile.dat >myfile.out
    print myfile.out
)
```

Also, grouped commands can be used to collect the output of several programs into one file or pipe with redirection, as in this example:

```
(dir c:\data & dir c:\temp) >listings.txt
```

The commands must be separated by new lines or by the **&**, **&&**, or **||** separators I discussed earlier.

You can use grouped commands in batch files or at the command prompt. If you enter grouped commands at the command prompt and haven't yet entered the closing parenthesis when you press Enter, CMD prompts you to continue entering the command line(s) by printing the following:

```
More?
```

This isn't really a question, so don't type "yes." Just continue typing command lines and end with a closing parenthesis and whatever goes after it. Alternatively, you can press Enter by itself to stop the prompting.

Arguments, Commas, and Quotes

When a command-line program requires you to specify information such as the name of a file to process or an option to use, you usually type this information after the command name with the items separated by spaces. For example, the `delete` command erases the file or files named on its command line:

```
delete somefile.txt anotherfile.txt
```

You can also separate command-line arguments with the semicolon (;) or comma (,), but this is not recommended; CMD accepts this to be compatible only with good old `COMMAND.COM`.

Unfortunately, because Windows filenames can contain spaces in the middle of the name, the command

```
delete c:\Users\bknittel\Documents\My Music\mpeg files\files.txt
```

attempts to delete three files: `C:\Users\bknittel\Documents\My`, `Music\mpeg`, and `files\files.txt`. To solve this problem, CMD interprets quotation marks (") to mean that the text enclosed is to be treated as part of one single argument. For example, the command

```
delete "c:\Users\bknittel\Documents\My Music\mpeg files\files.txt"
```

deletes the one indicated file. The quotation marks are not seen as part of the filename; they just keep it all together.

Escaping Special Characters

As you've already seen, the following characters have special meaning to CMD:

```
< > ( ) & | , ; "
```

If you need to use any of these characters as part of a command-line argument to be given to a program (for example, to have the `find` command search for the character >), you need to *escape* the character by placing a caret (^) symbol before it. This indicates that the character is to be treated like any other character and removes its special meaning. To pass a ^ character as an argument, type ^^.

For example, the `echo` command types its arguments in the Command Prompt window. The command

```
echo <hello>
```

causes a problem because CMD thinks you want to redirect input from a file named `hello` and that you want to redirect output to…well, there is no filename after >, so CMD would print an error message. However, the command

```
echo ^<hello^>
```

prints <hello>.

Configuring the CMD Program

The previous section described how CMD reads and interprets commands. In this section, I tell you a bit about how CMD might be adjusted to better meet your own needs.

AutoRun

Normally, when it first starts, CMD examines the Registry for values under the keys

```
HKLM\Software\Microsoft\Command Processor\AutoRun
```

and

```
HKCU\Software\Microsoft\Command Processor\AutoRun
```

(HKLM and HKCU are short for HKEY_LOCAL_MACHINE and HKEY_CURRENT_USER, respectively.) Any values with type REG_SZ (string) or REG_EXPAND_SZ (string with environment variables to be expanded) are taken as commands to be run when an instance of CMD first starts up.

AutoRun settings can be used to perform some of the functions that used to be provided by the AUTOEXEC.BAT file in DOS. In particular, you might want to run DOSKEY to set macros via an AutoRun command.

If necessary, you can disable AutoRun commands by starting CMD with /D on its command line, as I discuss later in the chapter.

Environment Variable Substitution

As it examines command lines that you've typed or that it has read from a batch file, CMD replaces strings of the form *%name%* with the value of the named environment variable. For example, the command

```
echo %path%
```

turns into

```
echo c:\windows\system32;C:\WINDOWS;C:\WINDOWS\System32\Wbem
```

which then types this text. The command displays the value of the `path` variable. Environment variable substitution can be used anyplace on any command line, as long as the resulting text is a valid command. If you want to use an environment variable as part of a pathname, it's best to enclose the entire name with quotes because the environment variable might contain spaces. For example, to delete `testfile.txt` from the temporary folder, you should type

del "%temp%\testfile.txt"

> **Note**
>
> Environment variable names are not case sensitive. To CMD, %path%, %Path%, and %PATH% are all the same.

The Search Path

CMD has a mechanism that lets you store text information in named variables called *environment variables*. Environment variables are used to control the behavior of CMD and can also be used to store information in batch file programs. Environment variables can be defined in batch files, on the command line, or by WSH programs, and many are predefined by Windows.

One of the more important environment variables is `PATH`, which holds a list of directories that CMD searches to find programs. `PATH` is a list of folder names separated by semicolons. Its default value looks something like this:

```
C:\Windows\system32;C:\Windows;C:\Windows\System32\Wbem;
    ↪ C:\Windows\System32\WindowsPowerShell\v1.0\
```

This path list tells CMD that when you type a command, it should look for the command's program file in these directories, in precisely this order:

- The current directory, which CMD always searches first
- `c:\windows\system32`
- `c:\windows`

- `c:\windows\system32\wbem`
- `c:\windows\system32\WindowsPowerShell\v1.0`

If CMD finds the program file in one of these folders, it's run and no further folders are searched. This means that if there are command files or batch files with the same names in more than one search path folder, the one that is run when you type its name is the one whose directory appears earliest in the path.

Tip

If the same program or batch file is in more than one folder in your search path, and the first one that CMD finds is not the one you want, there is a workaround. You can type a full pathname before the command to eliminate any ambiguity about which copy of the program you want to use. For example,

> `c:\windows\system32\ping`

tells CMD exactly where to find the PING program.

Windows sets the PATH variable when it starts CMD, and you should be careful when changing it; if you remove the important Windows directories, CMD isn't be able to find many of the programs you want to use.

You can change the path to include your own directories using the `path` command. If you plan on writing your own batch files, WSH programs, or other application programs, it's a good idea to place them in a special folder of their own and then add that folder to the path. I show you how to do this in the next section.

Changing the Path

You can change the search path in two ways: First, you can set a new value for the `path` environment variable using the `set` command, as in this example:

> `set path=c:\batchfiles`

Second, you can use the "shortcut" command, as shown here:

> `path c:\batchfiles`

Both have the same effect: They set the environment variable `path` to `c:\batchfiles`, so CMD only looks for programs in this folder. This is probably not a good idea, though, because it removes the Windows folders from the path and makes all the standard command-line programs unavailable.

Note

The `path` and `set` commands only change environment variables for the current, running instance of the CMD program. If you open a new Command Prompt window, you are back to the original, default values.

If you want to make a permanent change to `path` or any other environment variable so that the change appears in all future CMD prompt windows, you need to make the change on the System Properties dialog box, as I discuss later in the chapter under "Setting Default Environment Variables." Alternatively, you can use a script, as we discussed in Chapter 4, "File and Registry Access," or on Windows 7 and Vista, you can use the `setx` command.

Most of the time, what you need to do is add a new folder to the existing path list, usually at the beginning, so that any batch files you write or new programs you install can be run just by typing their name. This is a particularly good time to use environment variable substitution and is such a common thing to do that it's a pattern.

Pattern

To add a directory to the beginning of the search path, use the following statement:

```
set path=directorypath;%path%
```

Here, *directorypath* should be the fully qualified folder name. Here's an example:

```
set path=c:\batchfiles;%path%
```

When CMD encounters this command—that is, if you type it at the command line or in a batch file—CMD first replaces the text `%path%` with the current value of PATH, so the command turns into this:

```
set path=c:\batchfiles;c:\windows\system32;C:\WINDOWS;C:\WINDOWS\System32\Wbem; ...
```

Now, the new path starts with `c:\batchfiles` but still includes the standard Windows folders. If you place a batch file named `test.bat` in `c:\batchfiles`, and then type **test** on the command line, your batch file runs.

You could also add a new folder to the *end* of the search path with a statement like this:

```
set path=%path%;c:\batchfiles
```

The ordering only matters if there are versions of the same command in more than one folder in the path; the version in the first folder to be searched is the one that Windows runs.

Tip

If you mess up the path with one of these commands and CMD stops working, just close the Command Prompt window and open another. This restores the path to the default setting.

Putting your own folders ahead of the Windows folders in the list can be a blessing or a curse. If you create a program or batch file with the same name as a standard Windows program, yours runs instead of the standard program. If this is what you want, great, but if not…the result can be confusing.

Predefined and Virtual Environment Variables

Environment variables can be set in any of six places. If a given variable name is set in more than one place, the last definition is used. The sources are processed in the following order:

1. Predefined, built-in system variables (for example, APPDATA).

2. System-wide variables defined in the System Properties dialog box.

3. User-specific variables defined in the System Properties dialog box (as I mentioned in the previous section). However, a user-specific PATH definition does *not* replace the system-wide definition. Instead, it's added to the end of whatever is in the system PATH definition. Windows does this so that you can easily add more directories to the PATH for your own account without any risk of messing up the required system-wide PATH directories.

4. Variables defined in logon scripts (batch or WSH-type).

   These first four sources are processed when a user logs on, and they form the user's default environment; the remaining sources are processed each time a new CMD process is started, and any changes are lost when CMD is closed.

5. Variables defined in AUTOEXEC.NT, if a DOS program is run.

6. Variables defined on the command line, in batch files, or in WSH scripts through WshShell.Environment("Process").

The following variables are defined by default for all users (systemwide):

Variable Name	Usual Value on Windows 7
ALLUSERSPROFILE	C:\ProgramData
APPDATA	C:\Users*username*\AppData\Roaming
CommonProgramFiles	C:\Program Files\Common Files
COMPUTERNAME	*computername*
ComSpec	C:\WINDOWS\system32\cmd.exe
HOMEDRIVE	C:
HOMEPATH	\Users*username*
LOCALAPPDATA *	c:\Users*username*\AppData\Local
LOGONSERVER	(Varies)
NUMBER_OF_PROCESSORS	(Varies)
OS	Windows_NT
Path	C:\WINDOWS\system32;?C:\WINDOWS; C:\WINDOWS\System32\Wbem; C:\Windows\System32\WindowsPowerShell\v1.0\, but this varies depending on the location of Windows

PATHEXT	.COM;.EXE;.BAT;.CMD;.VBS;.VBE;.JS;.JSE;.WSF; .WSH;.MSC
PROCESSOR_ARCHITECTURE	(Varies)
PROCESSOR_IDENTIFIER	(Varies)
PROCESSOR_LEVEL	(Varies)
PROCESSOR_REVISION	(Varies)
ProgramFiles	C:\Program Files
ProgramData *	C:\ProgramData
PROMPT	PG
PSModulePath *	C:\Windows\system32\windowsPowerShell\v1.0\ ➡Modules\
PUBLIC *	c:\Users\Public
SESSIONNAME	(Varies)
SystemDrive	C:
SystemRoot	C:\WINDOWS
TEMP	C:\Users*username*\AppData\Local\Temp
TMP	C:\Users*username*\AppData\Local\Temp
USERDOMAIN	*computername* or *domainname*
USERNAME	*username*
USERPROFILE	C:\Documents and Settings*username*
windir	C:\WINDOWS

Entries marked with an asterisk (★) are not defined by default on Windows XP.

In addition, when command extensions are enabled, several "virtual" environment variables are available. The following environment variable names are computed dynamically if used on a command line or in a batch file:

Name	Value
CD	The current directory drive and path
DATE	The current date, formatted as by the **DATE** command
TIME	The current time, formatted as by **TIME** command
RANDOM	A random number between 0 and 32,767
ERRORLEVEL	The exit status of the previous program
CMDEXTVERSION	The version number of command extensions
CMDCMDLINE	The command line used to start CMD itself

However, if you define a variable with one of these names, your defined value always supercedes the dynamic value.

The maximum size for an individual environment variable (name, equals sign, and value) is 8,192 bytes. The total size of all environment variables must be smaller than 65,536KB.

Setting Default Environment Variables

To define environment variables permanently so that they are defined whenever you log on, click Start, right-click My Computer, and select Properties. Next, view the Advanced tab and click Environment Variables. Windows displays the dialog box shown in Figure 10.5.

Figure 10.5   The Environment Variables dialog box lets you edit default environment variables for your account or for all users.

The top part of the dialog box lets you define the default variables for your account. You can click New to add a new variable, or you can click Edit or Delete to modify an existing entry.

The lower part of the dialog box edits the default variables provided to *all* user accounts. These settings can only be edited by an Administrator account, and the settings can be overridden by user-specific entries.

> **Note**
> You can also modify the default environment variables with WSH scripts by modifying the `Environment("system")` and `Environment("user")` collections, as discussed in Chapter 4, in the section "Working with the Environment."

Built-in Commands

CMD recognizes and interprets several commands directly. Many of these commands are helpful when writing batch files, as we discuss in the next chapter. In this section, Reference List 10.1 lists the built-in commands. I discuss some in more detail after the listing and cover others in more detail in Chapter 11.

Many commands have features called *command extensions*. Command extensions are enabled by default in Windows 7, Vista, and XP, but they can be disabled if necessary.

REFERENCE LIST 10.1   CMD's Built-in Commands

:label
Defines the target for a goto or call statement. Useful only in batch files.

@command
Executes *command* without echoing it to the console, if echoing is enabled. This is mostly used at the beginning of batch files to disable all command echoing: @echo off.

a:
b:
c:
etc
A command consisting solely of a letter and a colon changes the default or "current" drive to the indicated disk drive. Use the cd or pushd command to change the default or "current" directory.

assoc [*.extension*[=[*filetype*]]]
The assoc command displays or sets associations between file extensions such as .DOC and file types such as "Word.Document.12." (This is the information behind the associations that Explorer displays and edits in its Tools, Folder Options, File Types dialog box.) The assoc command can take several forms:

Command	Result
assoc	Lists all associations.
assoc *.xxx*	Lists the association for extension *.xxx*.
assoc *.xxx=*	Deletes the association for *.xxx*.
assoc *.xxx=type*	Sets the association for *.xxx* to *type*. *Type* must be a file type listed in the Registry under HKEY_CLASSES_ROOT.

The assoc command isn't too useful, but it can help you to quickly find the application associated with a given file extension. Use assoc to list the file type for the extension, and then use the ftype command to find the linked application.

break

This command does nothing. Under MS-DOS, it is used to enable and disable
Ctrl+C checking.

call *batchfile* [*arguments…*]
call :*label* [*arguments…*]

Performs a "subroutine" call. Executes a secondary batch file or transfers control to
a specified label within the current batch file. Control returns to the statement after
the call when the subroutine reaches the end of file or an **exit** /B statement.

cd [/**d**] [[*drive:*]*directory*]

Changes the current working directory to the specified path, which might be a relative or absolute path. If a drive letter is specified, the default directory for that
drive is changed, but the working drive (the Command Prompt window's default
drive) is not changed unless you add the /d option. With no arguments, **cd** prints
the current directory.

As a convenience, you do not need to use quotes, even if the directory name contains spaces. For example,

```
cd \Program Files
```

works correctly. You can also use name completion to help fill in long pathnames if
you are typing **cd** commands on the command line. For example, **cd** \Pr followed
by the Tab key should complete the path "\Program Files" with Windows
automatically adding the quotes.

chdir

Chdir is identical to the **cd** command and takes the same arguments.

cls

Clears the screen (the Command Prompt window).

color [*bf*]

Allows you to change the background and text colors of the current Command
Prompt window. The argument to **color** is a two-letter code. The first letter is the
code for the screen background color, taken from the values listed in Table 10.1.
The second letter is the code for the text color. For example, the command **color**
1e requests yellow text on a dark blue background. With no arguments, **color**
restores the screen's colors to their initial settings.

You can also set a Command Prompt window's colors using its Properties
dialog box.

copy [/**d**] [/**v**] [/**n**] [/**l**] [/**y**|/**-y**] [/**z**] [/**a**|/**b**]
  source [/**a**|/**b**] [+*source* [/**a**|/**b**]]… [*destination* [/**a**|/**b**]]

The **copy** command copies files from one location to another and can also make a
copy of a file in the same directory but with a different name. The simplest version

of the command just lists the name of the original (source) file and the name to give the copy:

```
copy mydata.dat e:\files\april2002data.dat

copy mydata.dat mydata.backup
```

The destination name can be a full filename, or if the copy is to have the same name as the original, just a folder pathname.

Wildcards can be used in the source filename to copy multiple files. If this is the case, the destination name must be a folder name.

If you list multiple source files on the command line separated by + signs, they are combined (concatenated) into one destination file. If you want to copy multiple files separately and can't write their names using a wildcard format, you need to issue multiple copy commands.

Other options might be specified on the command line, as listed here:

Option	Result
/a	Copies the file in ASCII (text) mode. A Ctrl+Z character in the file is taken to mean "end of file" and no more data is read.
/b	Copies the file in binary (data) mode.
	(I have never needed the /a and /b options, but should you find them necessary, you can specify one or the other at the beginning of the copy command to apply to all files, or you can add them after individual file names.)
/d	The destination file will be unencrypted, even if the original file is encrypted.
/l	If the named file is a symbolic link, the link is copied, not the file to which the link refers.
/n	Gives the destination copy a short "8.3" filename.
/v	Windows should read the copied file back and compare it to the original to be sure that the copy is correct. This option is especially useful when copying to floppy, Zip, or other removable disks.
/y	Lets copy overwrite any existing files without asking for confirmation.
/-y	Makes copy always ask for confirmation before overwriting an existing file.
/z	Lets copying resume after a temporary network disconnection and displays a percentage-complete indicator while copying. Used for copying across a network.

The /y argument makes copy silently overwrite any existing files of the same name as the destination file. If / -y is specified, copy always prompts before overwriting.

The default behavior is to prompt if copy is entered from the command line, and not to prompt if copy is used in a batch file. You can change these defaults by assigning the value /y or / -y to the COPYCMD environment variable. In any case, if you specify /y or / -y on the command line, this overrides the default setting.

Any other copy options might be included in the COPYCMD environment variable to set the command's default behavior. The COPYCMD environment variable also affects the move command.

date [/t | *newdate*]

With no arguments, date displays the current date and requests that you type in a new date. You can press Enter to keep the current date. You can also set the date by specifying the new date on the command line. The date must be formatted according to the localized date format. For example, in the United States, the format is mm-dd-yyyy or mm/dd/yyyy also see the time command). With /t on the command line, date displays the date without prompting for a replacement. (This is useful if you want to just print the date in the text output of a batch file, for example.)

del [/p] [/f] [/s] [/q] [/a[[:]*attributes*]] *filename* …

Deletes files named on the command line. One or more filenames might be named, and wildcards might be used. The filenames can include a path. If no path is specified, they are deleted from the current directory.

Caution

Files deleted by del are removed immediately and permanently. They do not go to the Recycle Bin.

If a directory name is listed by itself, all the files in the directory are deleted, although the directory itself is not removed (for that, use the rd command). For example, the following two commands have the same effect:

```
del c:\temp\*.*
del c:\temp
```

Here are the command-line options:

Option	Effect
/p	Prompts to confirm deleting each file.
/f	Forces deletion of read-only files.
/s	Recurses subdirectories of the current or named directories, deleting any files with the specified name(s).
/q	Quiet mode. Does not ask for confirmation if you enter *.* as the filename.

Option	Effect
/a	Selects files to delete based on specified file attributes. After /a and an optional colon, enter one or more of the following attribute codes:

r—Read-only files

s—System files

h—Hidden files

a—Files with the archive bit set

i—Files marked *not to be indexed*

l—Reparse points and symbolic links

-—Before an attribute code, means *not*

You can specify more than one attribute. For example, /a:hr indicates that only files that are both hidden *and* read-only are to be deleted.

Here are some examples of `del` commands:

- `del myfile.doc`

  Deletes `myfile.doc` from the current directory

- `del /q c:\temp\*.*`

  Deletes all files in `C:\temp` without prompting

- `del /s c:\temp\*.tmp`

  Deletes `.TMP` files from `C:\temp` and all subfolders

- `del /a:h *.*`

  Deletes all files from the current directory, even hidden files

dir *pathname* … [**/p**] [**/q**] [**/r**] [**/w**|**/d**|**/b**|**/n**|**/x**] [**/s**] [**/l**] [**/c**] [**/4**]
[**/a**[[**:**]*attributes*]] [**/o** [[**:**]*sortfields*]] [**/t**[[**:**]*timefield*]]
The `dir` command lists the names of files and/or subfolders found in specified folders. With no arguments, the `dir` command lists all the files and folders in the current directory. The basic directory listing includes a title, a list of files with their sizes and last-modified dates, and a total count of files and bytes used. I discuss the `dir` command in more detail after this reference listing.

echo on|off
echo *text*
echo.
The first version enables or disables echoing of batch file commands to the console during execution. The second version writes the specified *text* to the standard output, which either appears in the console window or is written to another file or program, if the standard output is redirected. The third version prints a completely blank line—that is, just a carriage return and line feed. Echo, by itself, prints its on/off status.

endlocal

(See setlocal.)

erase

Erase is identical to the del command and takes the same arguments.

exit [/**b**] [*exitcode*]

Terminates the current Command Prompt console window or batch file. In a batch file, exit /b terminates the batch file (or the batch file subroutine) without terminating CMD as well. The optional numeric *exitcode* argument specifies an exit code. With /b, this command sets the ERRORLEVEL environment variable to the specified value; otherwise, it sets CMD's exit code.

for [*modifiers*] %*variable* **in** (*set*) **do** *command* [*arguments*]

   or, in batch files,

for [*modifiers*] %%*variable* **in** (*set*) **do** *command* [*arguments*]

Executes *command* repeatedly, with variable taking on one of the values from a specified set of values at each iteration. The variable name is a single letter and is case-sensitive. In the usual usage, set is a list of strings or filenames (possibly specified with wildcards).

If the for command is used in a batch file, the percent signs must be doubled up to prevent them from being interpreted as argument or environment variable substitutions.

If an environment variable is used on the command line and its value changes as the for command proceeds, the results might not be what you expect. See the section titled "Delayed Expansion" in Chapter 11 (page 511) for more information.

The for command is discussed in more detail after the reference list.

ftype [*.extension*[=[*filetype*]]]

The ftype command is a partner to the assoc command and displays or sets the associations between file types such as "Word.Document.8" and the commands used to open the files for editing. The ftype command can take several forms:

Command	Result
ftype	Lists all associations
ftype *FileType*	Lists the association for the named *FileType*
ftype *FileType*=	Deletes an association
ftype *FileType=command*	Sets the open command for the named *FileType* to *command*

In the command string, symbols of the form %1 and %* indicate how any other arguments from the original command line are to be passed to the open command. To get more information on the argument format for ftype commands, open a

Command Prompt window and type **ftype /?**.

The `ftype` command isn't all that useful, but it can help you to find the application associated with a given file extension. Use the `assoc` command to list the file type for the extension, and then use `ftype` to find the linked application. For example, I wanted to find out what program was used to run Perl programs on my computer. Here are the two commands I typed, shown in boldface, and the results printed by CMD:

```
C:\book\10>assoc .pl
.pl=Perl
C:\book\10>ftype Perl
Perl="D:\Perl\bin\perl.exe" "%1" %*
```

goto *label*
goto :EOF
Directs CMD to jump to the line in the batch file starting with :label and to continue reading statements from that point. Goto :EOF jumps to the end of the file and, in effect, terminates the batch file. Exit /B does the same thing. This is used to terminate batch processing and to exit from a batch file subroutine started with the `call` statement.

if *condition command1* [**else** *command2*]
or

if *condition* (
   commands…
) [**else** (
   commands…
)]
The `if` command is used mostly in batch files to perform commands based on conditions encountered as the batch program runs. If, call, and goto are what make the batch file language a real programming language.

If commands can execute one or more commands if the *condition* test is true. An optional `else` clause lets you specify a command to run if *condition* is not true.

md *foldername*
The `md` command creates a new directory (folder). The folder name can be a fully qualified path such as c:\musicfiles, or it can be specified relative to the current directory.

When command extensions are enabled, which is the default, `md` creates any intermediate directories in the path, if they do not already exist. This is another big improvement in CMD over COMMAND.COM. For example,

```
md "c:\musicfiles\folk\baguette quartette"
```

works even if c:\musicfiles does not already exist.

Note

If the directory you are creating contains spaces in the name, you must enclose the *foldername* argument in quotation marks. If you omit the quotation marks, CMD ignores anything on the command line after the first space.

mkdir *foldername*

Mkdir is identical to the md command and takes the same arguments.

move [/y|/-y] [*drive:*] [*path*]*filename*[,…] *destination*

or

move [/y|/-y] [*drive:*] [*path*]*foldername newname*

The move command moves files from one folder or drive to another, and it can also rename directories.

When moving files, move has the same effect as dragging the files to a new location with Windows Explorer. If the files are moving to a new directory on the same drive, they are not physically copied; Windows needs only to alter the directory entries. If the files are being moved from one drive to another, move copies the files to the new location and then deletes them from the original drive. The *filename* argument or arguments can include wildcards to move groups of files. The *destination* argument should be the path to the new folder, or if you are only copying one file, a path including a new filename.

The /y argument makes move silently overwrite any existing files of the same name in the destination folder. If /-y is specified, move prompts before overwriting. The default behavior is to prompt if move is entered from the command line and not to prompt if move is used in a batch file, unless the default is changed by the COPYCMD environment variable or overridden by /y or /-y on the command line. See the copy command earlier in this section for information about COPYCMD.

The second form of the command simply renames a directory to maintain compatibility with older versions of Windows. Because CMD still implements the old meaning of move, you must use wildcards if you want to move all files in a folder. Here are two examples:

- The command move c:\temp*.* datafiles moves all files in c:\temp into datafiles, which is interpreted as a subfolder of the current directory.
- The command move c:\temp datafiles renames c:\temp to c:\datafiles.

Note

On Windows 7, Vista, and XP, the rename command can rename directories, so I recommend you use rename instead of move for this purpose.

path *pathlist*

Sets the search path to *pathlist*, a list of folder pathnames separated by semicolons. The path command with no arguments prints the current path. You can also set the path by assigning the *pathlist* value to the environment variable PATH in a set statement. If there are spaces in any of the names, the name should be enclosed in quotes, as in this example:

```
path "c:\program files\microsoft office";c:\windows\system32;c:\windows
```

The PATH value is used by DOS and Windows programs, so if you use DOS programs, you should use only the short 8.3 version of each name in the path. For example, the setting

```
path c:\progra~1\micros~1;c:\windows\system32;c:\windows
```

specifies the same list of folders but is compatible with both DOS and Windows programs.

pause

The pause command is used in batch files to let the user read some output before continuing. It prints the famous message "Press any key to continue" in the Command Prompt window and waits for the user to press…well, any key except Ctrl+C or Ctrl+Break, which terminate the batch file.

In new batch files, you might want to use the set /p command to print a more friendly message. I discuss this in Chapter 11.

popd

(See pushd.)

prompt [*text*]

Sets the prompt displayed in the Command Prompt window before each command line to *text*. If the prompt command is used without any arguments, the prompt is set back to the default setting, pg.

I don't have the space to describe all the prompt options in detail here, but you can get a listing by typing prompt /?. If you regularly work with many computers, the prompt setting

```
prompt %computername%\%username% $p$g
```

can help you remember with which machine you're working at any given moment.

pushd *path*
popd

Changes the current directory to the specified *path*. The previous current drive and directory are remembered, and popd restores the previous path. Pushd saves as many directory changes as you care to make, and each popd returns to the directory in effect before the corresponding pushd. Unlike with cd, if the path specified to pushd contains a drive letter, the current drive is changed as well.

When command extensions are enabled, you can specify a network path (for example, `\\server\sharename\path`) in a `pushd` command, and it automatically maps a drive letter to the network path, starting with the letter Z and working backwards. `Popd` automatically deletes the temporary drive mappings.

rd [`/s`] [`/q`] *path*

The `rd` command removes the directory named *path*.

You can delete a folder, including all of its files and subfolders, by specifying the `/s` option. This is very dangerous because the files are deleted immediately and are not moved into the Recycle Bin. Be careful when using `/s`. As a precaution, CMD prompts you to confirm whether you really do want to delete the entire subdirectory tree. You can add `/q` on the command line to eliminate this prompt.

Without `/s`, the specified directory must be empty; otherwise, the command print an error message and not delete the directory.

> **Tip**
>
> If you attempt to delete an apparently empty directory with `rd` but Windows complains that the directory is not empty, look for hidden files or folders by typing `dir /ah` *path*.

rem *text*

Allows you to enter a remark (comment) in a batch file. The text is ignored. Special characters such as `|`, `>`, `<`, and `&` are also ignored after `rem`, so you can use these characters in the remark.

ren [*path*]*oldname newname*

Same as `rename`.

rename [*path*]*oldname newname*

Renames a file or folder from *oldname* to *newname*. If the file or folder is not in the current directory, you can specify its path. Note that *newname* must not include a path.

rmdir

`Rmdir` is the same as `rd` and takes the same arguments.

set [*name*[=[*value*]]]
set `/a` *expression*
set `/p` *name=promptstring*

Sets and displays environment variables. The basic set command has several useful variations:

Command	Result
set	Displays the list of all environment variables.
set *name*	Displays any variable(s) starting with the letters *name*.

Command	**Result**
set *name*=	Deletes the variable *name*.
set name=value	Sets the variable *name* to the specified *value*. *Value* is taken literally—do not put spaces after the = sign and do not use quotation marks unless you want those characters recorded in the variable.

You can use environment variable substitution in a **set** command. For example, to add c:\batchfiles to the beginning of the existing PATH value, you could use this command:

set path=c:\batchfiles;%path%

You can insert special characters, such as >, <, &, and |, into environment variables, but you must use ^ before them to prevent them from being interpreted as redirection commands or command separators. For example,

set envvar=some^|text

defines an environment variable named envvar with the value some|text.

With command extensions enabled, the **set** command lets you perform numerical calculations and prompt for input. For information on calculating with **set**, see "Performing Numerical Calculations in Batch Files," later in this chapter. For information on prompting, see "Prompting for Input" in Chapter 11 (page 514).

setlocal [ENABLEEXTENSIONS|DISABLEEXTENSIONS]
    ➥[ENABLEDELAYEDEXPANSION|DISABLEDELAYEDEXPANSION]
commands
⋮
endlocal
Setlocal saves and restores the batch file environment state. Setlocal saves a record of all environment variables, the current drive letter, the current working directory of all drives, and the state of command extensions and delayed environment expansion. Endlocal restores these settings to their previous values. The optional arguments to setlocal let you enable or disable the command extensions and/or delayed expansion. (Delayed expansion is discussed in Chapter 11.)

The settings revert to the previous state after endlocal or at the end of the batch file. This means that you cannot use setlocal in a batch file that is to change environment variables that remain changed when the batch file ends and the command prompt returns.

shift [/*n*]
This command shifts the batch file arguments to the left. The optional argument /*n* lets you start shifting at argument number *n*, leaving the lower-numbered arguments alone. The shift command is discussed in more detail in Chapter 11.

The `shift` command is used when you want to process a variable number of arguments given to a batch file; your batch file can process argument %1, shift, and repeat the process until the argument is blank.

```
start "title" [/Dpath] [/I] [/MIN | /MAX]
    [/SEPARATE | /SHARED] | [/AFFINITY value] |
    [/LOW  | /BELOWNORMAL | /NORMAL | /ABOVENORMAL |
    /HIGH | /REALTIME]
    [/WAIT] [/B] command [arguments]
```

Starts a *command* in a new window. The specified command can be a Windows program, a console program, or even the name of a document file, in which case CMD starts the associated application. If `start` is used in a batch file, the batch file continues without waiting for the program to exit.

Tip

This is an incredibly useful command. You can type a command such as `start somefile.doc` to run Microsoft Word and open the named file. How great is that?!

Optional command-line parameters control how the program is run:

Parameter	Description
`"title"`	Sets the window title to the specified string. By default, the name of the program file is used.
`/Dpath`	Starts the program in the specified directory.
`/I`	Starts the program with the default initial environment variable settings, rather than with a copy of the current settings.
`/MIN`	Starts the window minimized.
`/MAX`	Starts the window maximized.
`/SEPARATE`	If the program is a 16-bit Windows program, this parameter starts it in a separate memory space with its own copy of the Win16 environment.
`/SHARED`	If the program is a 16-bit Windows program, this parameter starts it in the shared memory space where it can interact with other 16-bit Windows programs. (/SEPARATE and /SHARED are not applicable on 64-bit Windows systems because they cannot run 16-bit Windows programs.)
`/AFFINITY value`	On a multicore or multiprocessor system, it limits the process to run on processors corresponding to the bits set in the hexadecimal value. For example, value 1 restricts the process to the first processor, whereas value 3 limits it to the first two processors.

/LOW /BELOWNORMAL /NORMAL /ABOVENORMAL /HIGH /REALTIME	Runs the program in the indicated priority class. Be cautious of using /REALTIME, which lets the program run to the exclusion of nearly anything else. If the program is ill-behaved, you might have a difficult time running the Task Manager to stop it.
/WAIT	Makes the start command wait until the program exits before continuing. This is useful in batch files to let you run a program with an altered priority.
/B	For command line (console) programs, this parameter runs the program in the current window. Ctrl+C handling is disabled by default, but Ctrl+Break should still work if you need to interrupt the program.

time [/t | *newtime*]

With no arguments, time displays the current time of day and requests that you type in a new time. You can press Enter to keep the current setting. With /t on the command line, time displays the time without prompting for a replacement. This is meant to be used in batch files. For example, to record the date and time that a batch file was run, you might use the following commands:

```
echo batch file run on >batchlog.txt
date /t >>batchlog.txt
time /t >>batchlog.txt
echo. >>batchlog.txt
other commands >>batchlog.exe
```

However, it might be neater to print both the date and the time on the same line with the statement echo %date% %time% >>batchlog.txt.

You can also set the time by specifying the new clock setting on the command line. The time must be formatted according to the localized time format. You enter times with or without seconds, in 24-hour format or in AM/PM format, as in these examples:

```
time 18:58
time 6:58:20 PM
```

title [*string*]

Sets the title of the current Command Prompt window to the specified string. By default, the title is Command Prompt, and when a program is running, it's Command Prompt - *command line*.

type [*path*]*filename*

Writes the specified file to the standard output. Normally this means that the file is displayed in the Command Prompt window. (For long files, the more command is a better choice because it displays the file a page at a time.) You can also use `type` to append one file onto another. For example, the following commands run a `ping` command, display the result, and also add the result to a log file that accumulates new information every time the commands are run:

```
@echo off
cls
echo Testing connection to mycompany.com...
ping www.mycompany.com 2>&1 >ping.out
echo The results are:
type ping.out

echo.            >>ping.log
echo Test run at >>ping.log
date /t          >>ping.log
time /t          >>ping.log
type ping.out    >>ping.log
del ping.out
```

ver
displays the version of Windows on your computer.

verify [**on** | **off**]
Verify on instructs Windows to read back all data written to the hard disk by application programs immediately after writing, to ensure that the data can be read correctly. This is especially useful when writing to floppy or other removable disks. Verify off disables read-after-write checking. Verify with no arguments displays the current setting; the default is off. You can specify the /V option with the `copy` command to enable verification just for the copy operation.

vol [*drive:*]
Displays the label and volume serial number for a disk drive. By default, `vol` displays the information for the current drive. You can specify an alternative drive on the command line.

Extended Commands

CMD's built-in commands are a superset of the ones recognized by the old COMMAND.COM shell, and many have been extended with new features. The command extensions are enabled by default in Windows 7, Vista, and XP, although they can be disabled if necessary. Table 10.4 lists the extended commands and their added features.

If the extensions cause problems for you—for example, if you have to use old batch files that do not work with the new command versions and you cannot update them—you can start CMD with the extensions disabled. I discuss this in the section "Running CMD."

Table 10.4   **Commands Modified by Command Extensions**

Command	Features Added by Command Extensions
assoc	Only available with extensions enabled.
call	call :label Argument substitution modifiers (for example, %~f1).
cd / chdir	Option /D changes current drive. The current directory uses the directory's actual upper/lowercase.
color	Only available with extensions enabled.
date	Option /T prints the date without prompting for a new date.
del / erase	Option /S displays names of files being deleted.
endlocal	Restores EXTENSIONS and DELAYEXPANSION settings.
for	(Many options are available; see the description of for.)
ftype	Only available with extensions enabled.
goto	goto :EOF
if…else	/I, IF CMDEXTVERSION, IF DEFINED Comparisons such as LEQ.
md / mkdir	Creates intermediate directories if necessary.
prompt	$+ and $M options.
pushd / popd	Accepts a network path and maps a drive letter.
set	/A and /P options. The set command with a partial name displays matching names.
setlocal	ENABLE... and DISABLE... arguments.
shift	/n option.
start	Starts nonexecutable files via file extensions. Uses PATHEXT expansion. Doesn't wait for Win32 commands to exit before prompting again. Uses the COMSPEC path when the command is CMD. Runs Explorer if the command is a folder name.
time	Option /T prints the time without prompting for a new time.

In the next few sections, I provide some additional detail on some of the more important commands.

Listing Files with the **Dir** Command

The dir command is one of the most helpful command-line programs. Although it's often more efficient to use Explorer to view folder contents, dir has a few tricks up its sleeve that make it worth knowing about.

Without any command-line arguments, dir prints a listing of files and directories (folders) in the current directory. Here's a sample listing:

```
Volume in drive C has no label.
Volume Serial Number is 7AC1-7AC5

Directory of C:\Users\bknittel\Documents

05/27/2010  06:27 PM    <DIR>          .
05/27/2010  06:27 PM    <DIR>          ..
04/30/2009  06:23 PM    <DIR>          Fax
05/21/2009  04:15 PM    <DIR>          Remote Assistance Logs
05/26/2009  06:28 PM    <DIR>          Book Files
04/30/2009  06:23 PM    <DIR>          Scanned Documents
05/27/2009  05:02 PM            28,672 book outline.xls
               1 File(s)         28,672 bytes
               6 Dir(s)   1,132,052,480 bytes free
```

(If you've only ever used Macintosh- or Windows-based computers, you might find it hard to believe that not too many years ago, this was the *only* way to view and locate files.)

So what are . and ..? These two odd entries represent the current directory and its parent directory. They serve no real purpose today; they're the software equivalent to your appendix, a remnant of MS-DOS's distant Unix ancestry, and you can ignore them.

The rest of the listing shows the names of the directory's files and subdirectories as well as their sizes and last-modified dates. The listing ends with a summary of file counts and sizes.

In Reference List 10.1, I showed all the command-line options you can use with dir. In this section, I go over a few of the ones that are particularly useful.

Paginating Long Listings

If dir prints more names than you can see on the screen at one time, you can scroll back through the listing using the Command Prompt window's scrollbar. You can also ask dir to print only 24 lines at a time—the amount that fits in the default window size—by adding /p to any dir command. When you've caught up with the listing, press Enter to print the next screenful. For example, dir %windir% /p lists the contents of the Windows folder a page at a time.

Searching for Particular Files

You can specify individual filenames or folder names, using wildcards if desired, to limit the listing to specific files and locations. The command dir *.exe lists only files ending in .exe, and dir m*.* lists only files starting with the letter *m*.

You can add /s to any dir command to make the listing include all subdirectories of the folder in which dir starts its search. For example, dir c:*.mp3 /s /p locates all

MP3 files anywhere on drive C: because it starts in the root directory `C:\` and examines all subdirectories. Of course, you can use the Windows Search window to perform this sort of task, but when you already have the Command Prompt window open, it can sometimes be quicker to type a command like this than to poke around with Windows. Of course, whether you use `dir` or the Search window, you only see files in folders for which you have read permission.

Making Columnar Listings

The options `/w` and `/d` print listings of filenames that are arranged in several columns; the exact number of columns is difficult to predict because `dir` makes the columns wider or narrower depending on the length of the longest filename it finds. The difference between the two options is that `/w` lists the names by rows, whereas `/d` sorts them into columns. The `/w` listing looks like this:

```
 Volume in drive C has no label.
 Volume Serial Number is DC77-E725

 Directory of C:\simh\ibm1130\sw\dmsr2v12

[.]            [..]            ABOOTPT.asm     ABOOTPT.bin     ABOOTPT.lst
ASYSLDR1.asm   ASYSLDR1.bin    ASYSLDR1.lst    CSYSLDR2.asm    CSYSLDR2.bin
CSYSLDR2.lst   DBOOTCD.asm     DBOOTCD.bin     DBOOTCD.lst     DCILOADR.asm
DCILOADR.bin   DCILOADR.lst    dmsr2v12.zip    DSYSLDR1.asm    dsysldr1.bin
dsysldr1.lst   FSYSLDR2.asm    FSYSLDR2.bin    FSYSLDR2.lst    JADUPCO.asm
...
```

The `/w` and `/d` options are particularly useful to get printable listings of your files.

Printing Directory Listings

Don't you find it annoying that Windows Explorer has no "print" command? Ha! Here's an area where the command-line environment is much more capable. You can easily print a directory listing from the command line.

You can redirect the output of any `dir` command to a network printer or to your local printer if you've shared it, using commands such as the following:

```
cd \Users\\bknittel\Documents\My Music
dir >\\localhost\printername
```

where *printername* is the share name of your printer. This technique doesn't tell the printer to finish the last page of the listing, however, and you probably have to manually eject the last page.

Tip

You can gain a bit more control over the process by redirecting the listing to a file and then printing it with Notepad or a word processor. However, if you redirect the directory listing into a file in the same directory you're listing, the listing file will appear in the output. You can avoid this by directing the listing file into another directory, as with these commands:

```
cd \Users\bknittel\Documents\My Music
dir /s >..\list
notepad ..\list
del ..\list
```

Note that .. represents the directory one level above the directory being listed. After printing the listing with Notepad, you can delete the scratch file.

Getting Lists of Filenames

The default directory listing format lists dates, sizes, times, header information, and a summary. The /b option asks dir to print a list of names only. The output of such a listing can be redirected to a file, where it can be used as input to programs, batch files, or WSH scripts that want, as input, a list of filenames.

When you use /s and /b, the dir command lists the full path for all files it displays. For example, from my Windows directory, dir /b /s *.wav prints a long list of files starting with these:

```
C:\WINDOWS\Help\Tours\WindowsMediaPlayer\Audio\Wav\wmpaud1.wav
C:\WINDOWS\Help\Tours\WindowsMediaPlayer\Audio\Wav\wmpaud2.wav
⋮
C:\WINDOWS\Help\Tours\WindowsMediaPlayer\Audio\Wav\wmpaud9.wav
C:\WINDOWS\Media\chimes.wav
C:\WINDOWS\Media\chord.wav
C:\WINDOWS\Media\ding.wav
C:\WINDOWS\Media\notify.wav
⋮
```

Sorting Listings

By default, dir sorts files by name. You can list files in some other order by using the /o option, followed by one or more letters indicating which parts of the file information to use for sorting. Reference List 10.1, earlier in this chapter, shows the whole list of sort options. Some of the most useful combinations are listed here:

Option	Sorts
/o-s	By size. Largest first
/odn	By date. Oldest first, then by name
/o-dn	By date. Newest first, then by name
/oen	By type (extension), then by name

Listing Hidden Files

Normally, hidden files are omitted from dir listings. (What would be the point otherwise?) However, you can ask dir to list hidden files by adding /ah to the command line. The /a flag instructs dir to list files with specified attributes, and the h indicates that you want to see hidden files.

You can use the /a option to select files based on the other attributes listed in Reference List 10.1. For example, /as lists only system files, /a-s lists only files that are *not* marked as system files, and so on.

Locating Alternate File Streams

The Windows NTFS file system has a feature that lets it store more than one file inside a file. The feature is called Alternate File Streams, and it lets Windows store information separate from, and parallel to, the main content of any file. Windows uses this feature to store encryption information with every file protected by the Encrypted File System and to hold the marker that labels a downloaded file as having come from a potentially unsafe source. Rogue software can also store viruses inside alternate file streams; if you open such a file with Notepad, for example, you see only innocuous text because Notepad only looks at a file's "primary" stream.

You can get a listing of any alternate streams associated with a file or files by giving dir the /R switch. For example, the dir /r listing for a program file I downloaded from the Internet looks like this:

```
Directory of C:\Users\bknittel

05/27/2010  06:43 PM            526,848 demo5.exe
                                     26 demo5.exe:Zone.Identifier:$DATA
               1 File(s)        526,848 bytes
               0 Dir(s)   1,134,792,704 bytes free
```

Notice that two names are listed, but it counts for just one file. The additional stream is named "Zone.Identifier," and it was added to the demo5.exe by Windows when I downloaded it. Most programs (Notepad, for instance) don't let you see the contents of alternate streams unless you type the full name without the final :$DATA. For example, notepad "demo5.exe:Zone.Identifier" works.

To scout for all files with alternate streams, a command like this might help:

```
dir /s /r | findstr /c:"$DATA"
```

You find lots of such files in your Internet Explorer temporary files folder.

Setting Variables with the Set Command

From the days of MS-DOS version 1, Microsoft's batch file language had two striking deficiencies: the inability to perform string and numerical calculations and the inability to prompt for input. With the command extensions enabled, alternate versions of the set command help remedy these problems to a great extent.

Performing Numerical Calculations in Batch Files

The command set /A *expression* evaluates a string as a mathematical expression. Any assignment statements in the expression cause CMD to format the result as a string and assign it to a named environment variable. *Expression* uses standard mathematical syntax. The operators allowed in the expression are listed in order of decreasing precedence:

Operators	Description
( )	Expression grouping.
! ~ -	Unary operators: boolean NOT, bitwise invert, and arithmetic negative.
* / %	Multiply, divide, remainder.
+ -	Add, subtract.
<< >>	Bitwise shift left, shift right.
&	Bitwise AND.
| ^	Bitwise OR and exclusive OR.
= *= /= %= += -= &= ^= |= <<= >>=	Assignment, and the combined operator/assignment operators borrowed from the C programming language. A += 3 is the same as A = A + 3.
,	Separates multiple expressions.

Any alphanumeric words are taken to indicate environment variables. In an expression, if a named environment variable is undefined or does not contain a number, it is treated as the value 0. Variables are treated as decimal numbers, except that numbers starting with 0x are interpreted as hexadecimal (base 16) and numbers starting with 0 are treated as octal (base 8). Here are some examples:

```
set A=3
set /A B=A*2, C=2*(B+5)
```

These statements set environment variables A to 3, B to 6, and C to 22.

If you use set /A in a batch file, it is silent, but if you type it on the command line, it displays the last value it calculates. For example, the command

```
set /A 3+3
```

types the result 6 without storing the result to any environment variable. It turns the command prompt into a nice, quick calculator.

String calculations—for example, to remove the extension from a filename—are not quite as cleanly implemented, but I'll show you what's available later in the section on environment variable substitution.

Conditional Processing with the `if` Command

The `if` command lets you run specific commands only if certain conditions are true. If is one of the central requirements of a true programming language, and the extended `if` command provided by CMD makes the batch file language much more useful than it was in the days of COMMAND.COM. You use the `if` command in batch files far more often than directly at the command prompt.

The basic formats of the `if` command are

> **if** condition *command*

and

> **if** condition (*command1*) **else** *command2*

The first version tests some condition and, if it's true, executes *command*. If the condition is not true, the command is ignored.

The second version provides a second command that is run if the condition is false. In this version, one command or the other is run, depending on the condition.

You can group multiple commands in an `if` statement using parentheses. For example, the statements

```
if not exist input.dat (
    echo Attention: creating new input.dat file
    dir /b c:\inputs >input.dat
)
```

check to see whether file `input.dat` exists and, if it doesn't, run the `echo` and `dir` commands. Grouped commands make CMD batch files much easier to read and write than the DOS format, where you would have had to write this instead:

```
if exist input.dat goto haveinput
    echo Attention: creating new input.dat file
    dir /b c:\inputs >input.dat
:haveinput
```

You can use the `else` clause with grouped commands as well, in the following format:

> **if** *condition* (
>   *commands*
>
>   ...
>
>) **else** (
>   *commands*
>
>   ...
>
>)

The indenting is optional; it just makes the commands easier to read.

There are several *condition* tests, as listed here:

- **[not]** *strng1* **==** *strng2*

  Compares *strng1* to *strng2* and is true if the strings are exactly equal, including case. The sense can be reversed by preceding the test with the word not.

- **[not] errorlevel** *number*

  Examines the exit status value of the last program that is run. The condition is true if the exit status is greater than or equal to *number*. Not reverses the sense; the test is true if the exit status is less than *number*.

- **[not] exist** *[path]name*

  The test is true if the named file or directory exists. The sense can be reversed with not. To test for a directory, add a backslash (\) to the end of the directory name. For example, if exist c:\temp\ will detect the existence of directory c:\temp, but will not be fooled by a file named c:\temp.

- **[/i]** *strng1 compareop strng2*

  Compares two strings and returns the result of the comparison. If both the strings consist only of digits, the comparison is made numerically; otherwise, it's made alphabetically. If /i is used, the test is case-insensitive. *Compareop* is one of the following:

  EQU—Equal to
  NEQ—Not equal to
  LSS—Less than
  LEQ—Less than or equal to
  GTR—Greater than
  GEQ—Greater than or equal to

- **cmdextversion** *number*

  The test is true if the version number of the CMD extensions is greater than or equal to *number*. The command extension version number for Windows 7, Vista, and XP is 2. The test is always false if the command extensions are disabled.

- **defined** *variable*

  The test is true if the named environment variable is defined and is not empty.

The extended if statement is one of CMD's biggest improvements. Combined with environment variables, you have a decent programming language.

Scanning for Files with the **for** Command

You often need to perform some command repeatedly with each of several files. CMD provides a command named for that helps save typing; it repeats a command for each item in a specified list.

At its simplest, for runs a command for every item placed in its *set* (a list of items in parentheses). For example,

```
for %x in (a b c) do echo %x
```

prints out three lines:

```
a
b
c
```

The set consists of the strings a, b, and c. For creates a temporary variable named x and issues the command echo %x three times, with x taking on the values a, b, and c in turn. In the command, any occurrence of %x is replaced by the value of x, so this for command is the equivalent of issuing these three commands:

```
echo a
echo b
echo c
```

(By the way, the choice of which letter to use for the variable is completely arbitrary. I picked x, but you can use any of the lowercase letters a to z or the uppercase letters A to Z. Oddly enough, case matters here.)

If any of the items in the set contain the wildcard characters * or ?, CMD replaces the items with the list of all matching filenames. Therefore, the command

```
for %x in (*.doc) do echo %x
```

runs the echo command once for each .doc file.

Note

One tricky thing about for is that the percent sign (%) is considered a special character in batch files. When you use a for command in a batch file, you have to double up all the % signs used with the for variable. The previous for statement would have to be written this way in a batch file:

```
for %%x in (*.doc) do echo %%x
```

If you write lots of batch files, you get used to this, but then you have to remember to use only one % sign if you type a for command directly at the command prompt.

I show you how to exploit the for command in batch files in the next chapter.

The for command in CMD is much more powerful than its COMMAND.COM equivalent. Several modifiers can be placed between the word for and the set to make for perform several useful tricks.

Using the `for` Command's Variable

As the `for` command runs through each of the files or words named in the *set* list, the variable you specify on the command line takes each of the set's values in turn. If the variable is specified as, say, `%x`, wherever `%x` appears after the keyword `do`, it is be replaced by the variable's value. CMD has added some additional ways to extract information from the variable, most of which treat the variable as a filename and let you extract just specific filename components. This makes it possible to construct for loops that could, for example, run through all the `.DOC` files in a folder and copy them to files named `.BACKUP`.

CMD edits the value of the variable based on extra characters you place after the `%` symbol and substitutes the edited version into the command line. The variable edits that CMD offers are listed in Table 10.5. (The same edits are available for the command line and subroutine arguments in batch files.)

Table 10.5   **Variable-Editing Functions**

Expression	Result
`%n`	Argument or variable *n* without editing.
`%~n`	Removes surrounding quotes (`" "`).
`%~fn`	Fully qualified pathname.
`%~dn`	Drive letter only.
`%~pn`	Path only.
`%~nn`	Filename only.
`%~xn`	File extension only.
`%~sn`	Short DOS 8.3 file and path.
`%~an`	File attributes.
`%~tn`	Modification date/time of file.
`%~zn`	Length of file in bytes.
`%~$PATH:n`	Fully qualified name of first matching file when `PATH` is searched. If no file is found, the result is a zero-length string. The filename must include the proper extension; `PATHEXT` is not used.

The filename modifiers can be used in combination (for example, `%~dpn` returns the combined drive and path).

Tip

When using variable edits, it's best to use uppercase letters for your variable so that CMD can distinguish between the editing characters, which must always be in lowercase, and your variable. (You might notice that $PATH: is not in lowercase—the dollar sign and colon make it clear to CMD that this is an editing function and not the variable P.)

As an example, the following `for` loop copies only files under 1MB in size to a network folder:

```
for %X in (*.*) do if %~zX LSS 1000000 copy %X \\bali\myfiles
```

Processing Directories

The `for` command has several variations that change the way it interprets the contents of the listed set of names.

The variation **for /d %variable in (set) do command** works much like the standard for command, except that wildcards in *set* match only directory names. You can use this variation to perform a command or run a batch file in any or all of the subfolders of particular folders. For example, on Windows 7,

```
for /d %d in ("%homepath%\Documents\My Music\*.*") do echo %d
```

lists the names of all the subfolders under the user's My Music folder.

Processing Files in Directories and Subdirectories

The variation **for /r path %variable in (set) do command** runs the complete `for` command in the directory named by *path* and then in each of its subdirectories and their subdirectories, and so on. The wildcard matching operation on *set* is performed in each of these directories. For example, the command

```
for /r c:\data %x in (*.txt) do notepad %x
```

visits the folder `c:\data` and each of its subfolders, and in each one, it runs a copy of Notepad to display and edit every `.txt` file it finds. (This can open a lot of copies of Notepad.)

Numerical **for** Loop

The variation **for /l %variable in (start#,step#,stop#) do command** makes the variable take on numeric values from *start#* to *stop#*, incrementing by step# at each turn. For example, the statement

```
for /l %v in (1,1,10) do echo %1
```

prints numbers from 1 to 10. The step value can be positive or negative. The set (1,1,5) generates the sequence (1 2 3 4 5), whereas the set (5,-1,1) generates the sequence (5 4 3 2 1).

Parsing Text

In its most unusual variation, the `for` command reads strings, the contents of a file, or the output of a command, and from this text extracts a series of values to use as the set.

This is the most complex use of the `for` command. In the simplest version, the command extracts just the first word from each line of text it reads. The definition of "word" is text delimited by one or more spaces or tabs. The command can be written to use any of three sources of data:

```
for /f %variable in (filenames) do command

for /f "usebackq" %variable in (`command1`) do command2

for /f %variable in ("literal text") do command
```

The first version examines all the files named in the filename set, which might use wildcards. The files are read as text files, and the first token (word) from each line is used as the source of values for the variable.

The second version runs *command1* as a CMD command line and then gathers its output. The first token on each output line is used as the source of values for the variable.

The third version looks at the literal text surrounded by quotes. This form would only make sense if used with environment variables within the quotes. The first token is used as the value for the variable.

If you use a set of one or more filenames and must use quotes to protect spaces in the filenames (to indicate you are specifying files and not literal text), use the `usebackq` modifier as in this version:

```
for /f "usebackq" %variable in ("filename"...) do command
```

Now, reading the first word from each line is not very interesting. Luckily, the parsing system also lets you choose which tokens to extract, specify token delimiters, specify a line-terminating character, and pick up more than one token from each input line. You can specify any of the following items in quotes after `/f`:

Modifier	Description
`eol=c`	Indicates that all text after the character *c* is to be ignored.
`skip=n`	Skips the first *n* lines of the file before extracting tokens.
`delims=xyz…`	Uses the specified character(s) as the token delimiters, rather than a space and tab. For example, `delims=,` specifies the comma as the delimiter.

Modifier	Description
tokens=*x*,*y*,*m*-*n*	Selects which tokens on the input lines to return as variables. If more than one is listed, the for command assigns the values to additional variables in increasing alphabetical order after the one specified with %. Numbers separated by a dash indicate a range. For example, tokens=1,4-7 would select input tokens 1, 4, 6, and 7 and would define four variables.
usebackq	Indicates that quotation marks in *set* indicate filenames, not literal text, and that single quotes indicate literal text.

The following for command runs the arp command to get a list of the computer's network adapter information. The arp command lists each of the computer's IP addresses and physical MAC addresses. The for command skips three headers lines and extracts two tokens from each remaining output line. The first is stored in the named variable %a, and the second in the next letter up, %b:

```
for /f "skip=3 tokens=1,2 usebackq" %a in (`arp -a`) do (
    echo IP address %a, MAC address %b
)
```

Note

One thing that for /f cannot do is parse the common comma-separated value (CSV) text format because these files use quotation marks to surround text items and can have commas inside the items. The for statement is not smart enough to parse comma- and quote-delimited text.

Also, the command I just showed works when typed directly at the command prompt, but you must double-up the percent signs when you put these commands inside a batch file. I discuss this in the next chapter.

Getting More Information

There's quite a bit of information about the command-line environment tucked away in Windows, but it's scattered far and wide. To read about the CMD program itself and the built-in commands, click Start, Help and Support and then search for the following strings:

- cmd
- command shell overview
- command-line reference
- command-line reference A-Z

On Windows 7 and Vista, nothing is likely to come up, but click the Search IT Pro Content on the Microsoft Technet website link and you are led to the content.

Microsoft has mostly eliminated Command Prompt information from the Help files distributed with Windows 7 and Vista. Steer toward the pages that describe the Server versions of Windows.

You can also get information from the command-line `help` program. Type commands of the form

```
help cmd
help dir
help for
```

and so on, using any of the command or program names listed in this chapter. The `help` command automatically sends its output through `more` so you can view it a page at a time. Almost all command-line programs display help information if you run them with `/?` as a command-line argument, so if help doesn't work, try running the program like this:

```
cmd /? | more
more /? | more
ping /? | more
```

11

Batch Files for Fun and Profit

IN THIS CHAPTER

- Batch files let you automate repetitive tasks and create nifty command shortcuts.

- The batch file language in current versions of Windows is greatly improved over the DOS/Win9x version.

- Like scripts, batch files can serve as documentation of critical business procedures.

- You should be familiar with the material in Chapter 10, "The CMD Command-Line" before starting this chapter.

Why Batch Files?

Although Windows Script Host (WSH) is a powerful scripting and programming environment, the old-fashioned batch file can still be a useful, powerful tool in the Windows environment. Why? Whereas WSH programs use objects as tools to perform Windows management and data-processing tasks, batch files use *entire programs* as their tools. WSH scripts give you great control of the details of a task, whereas batch files let you work at a grosser, macro level. So, just as it's an advantage to have both small and large wrenches in your toolbox, it's an advantage to know how to write both scripts and batch files. Furthermore, like Windows Script programs, batch files serve as a form of documentation because they capture critical business management information— procedures and configuration data—in written form.

In my work as both a software developer and writer, I've found that the batch files I write fall into three categories:

- Tiny files to manipulate the command-line environment. For example, I have several little batch files that change the working directory to the correct folder for specific projects and perhaps add a directory to the search path. This way, I can open a Command Prompt window, type one word, and be ready to work with a particular project's files.

- Medium-sized files that perform a specific series of commands that I find myself typing over and over. For example, I frequently have to send updated versions of a particular set of files to a client. I use a batch file to update a ZIP file and email the results so the whole job is taken care of with one command.

- Monster batch files that perform a long sequence of tasks and handle a variety of command-line options. In my work, these tend to involve custom-developed command-line programs for data-processing applications or Microsoft-provided utilities used to manage Windows—both the standard tools and those provided with the Windows Resource Kits. For example, I have a batch file that documents all the Internet domains managed by my Windows Server's DNS service. This batch file could reconstruct the entire set of domains if it is necessary to move to a new server. This kind of job is a snap for a batch file but would be a nightmare to reenter through the graphical user interface.

In Chapter 10, I discussed all the commands built in to the CMD shell. In this chapter, I discuss the commands that are particularly useful in batch files and give you some examples of the three categories of batch files I find useful.

Creating and Using Batch Files

Batch files are plain-text files. You can most easily create and edit them with Notepad. I suggest that you create a special folder just for your own batch files and add this folder to your search path (as discussed in Chapter 10), so you can run them from any folder in any Command Prompt window.

You can place them in any folder you want. You can place them on your own hard drive, or you might want to place your batch files on a shared network folder so they can be used from any computer. I place my personal batch files in a folder named `c:\bat`. To create this folder, open a Command Prompt window and type these commands at the prompt:

```
c:
mkdir \bat
cd \bat
```

To add this folder to the search path, follow these steps:

1. To get started:

   - On Windows 7, click Start, right-click Computer, and select Properties. Select the Advanced tab and click Environment Variables.

   - On Windows Vista, click Start, Control Panel, User Accounts and Family Safety, User Accounts. Then, under Tasks, click Change My Environment Variables.

   - On Windows XP, click Start, right-click My Computer, and select Properties. Select the Advanced tab and click Environment Variables.

- Alternatively, on any of these versions of Windows, this is what I find easiest: Type **start sysdm.cpl** in a Command Prompt window, select the Advanced tab, and click Environment Variables.

2. Look in the list of variables defined in the upper section under User Variables for *your-user-name*.

3. If there is already an entry named PATH, select it and click Edit. At the beginning of the Variable Value field, insert C:\bat and add a semicolon to separate this name from the names that are already there. The result should look something like what's shown in Figure 11.1.

Figure 11.1   When adding a directory to the beginning of the path, be sure to place a semicolon after the new directory name.

If there is *not* already an entry named PATH, click New and enter PATH as the variable name. Enter C:\bat as the variable value.

4. Click OK three times to close the three dialog boxes. Close the Command Prompt window and open another one. Type path and press Enter. You should see c:\bat at the beginning of the path.

Note

If you want to make your batch files available to *every* user on your computer, you need to edit the lower System Variables section. Follow the preceding procedure, except, on Windows Vista, in step 1, use the instructions I gave for Windows 7. On Windows XP, you have to be logged on as a Computer Administrator.

Alternatively, just type **start sysdm.cpl** in a privileged Command Prompt window. I discussed privileged command prompts in Chapter 10.

After c:\bat has been added to your path, any batch files you create in this folder can be run by typing their names at the command prompt.

Batch files should be given the extension .cmd or .bat. Either is fine. The .bat extension is more traditional, whereas .cmd makes it clear that the batch file is written for the new command interpreter because DOS and Windows 9*x* do not recognize such files as batch files.

To create a sample batch file, open a Command Prompt window or use the one opened earlier in this section. Type the command:

```
notepad test.bat
```

and then click Yes when Notepad asks, "Do you want to create a new file?" In the empty Notepad window, type the following lines:

```
@echo off
cls
echo The command line argument is %1
pause
```

Save the file and at the command line type this:

```
test xxx
```

The Command Prompt window should clear, and you should see the following:

```
The command line argument is xxx
Press any key to continue . . .
```

Press Enter, and the command prompt should return. You can use this procedure to create any number of batch files. One batch file you might want to create right now should be named `bat.bat` with this one line inside:

```
pushd c:\bat
```

This falls into the "tiny handy" batch file category mentioned earlier. With this in place, if you type `bat` at any command prompt, your current directory is changed to `c:\bat` so you can edit or create batch files. Type **popd** to go back to whichever directory you were using before.

Of course, you could type `pushd c:\bat` directly. It can seem silly to create a batch file just to save nine keystrokes, but when you're actively developing batch files, you quickly find that this does make life easier.

I have about a dozen batch files like this that I use on a daily basis to move into directories for specific projects. For projects that use special command-line programs, the batch file has a second line that adds the program directory to the beginning of the search path, using a command such as this:

```
path c:\some\new\folder;%path%
```

If you find yourself frequently working with command-line programs, you will want to make "tiny, handy" batch files for your projects as well.

Batch File Programming

In the following sections, I discuss programming techniques that take advantage of the extended commands provided by the CMD shell. The commands that are most useful in batch files are listed in Table 11.1.

Table 11.1   **Batch File Commands**

Command	Use
`call`	Calls batch file subroutine
`echo`	Displays text to the user
`setlocal/endlocal`	Saves/restores environment variables
`exit`	Terminates batch file
`for`	Iterates over files or folders
`goto`	Used for flow control
`if`	Executes commands conditionally
`pause`	Lets the user read a message
`pushd/popd`	Saves/restores the current directory
`rem`	Used for comments and documentation
`set`	Sets environment variables, performs calculations, and prompts for user input
`shift`	Scans through command-line arguments
`start`	Launches a program in a different window

The syntax and options for these commands were described in Chapter 10. If you've written batch files for DOS, Windows 9x, and Windows NT, you find that most of these commands have been significantly enhanced, so even if you are familiar with these commands, you should read their descriptions in Chapter 10.

Displaying Information in Batch Files

By default, batch files display or echo every line inside them to the Command Prompt window as they run. For complex batch files, this can be distracting, as page after page of commands and messages scroll by. It's hard to read, and you might miss important error messages buried in the middle of the mess. Therefore, it's traditional to disable batch file echoing with the statement

```
@echo off
```

at the beginning of the file. `Echo off` turns off the echoing feature, and the `@` at the beginning of the command prevents the `echo` command itself from being echoed before it can work its magic.

> **Tip**
>
> When you're debugging a batch file, it can be helpful to leave echoing turned on so that you can see which commands are being run. To turn echoing on temporarily, add `rem` so that the batch file's first line reads
>
> ```
> rem @echo off
> ```
>
> Rem turns this line into a comment. You can remove it later when the batch file is working correctly.

However, it's nice to have batch files tell you what's going on inside so that you know that something is actually happening. The echo command is great for this—it echoes whatever text follows the word echo, so you can put helpful comments throughout the batch file like this:

```
@echo off
echo Starting to sort files...
⋮
echo Sending results to the printer...
⋮
echo Done.
```

Tip

Sometimes it's beneficial to see exactly how a program is going to be run by a batch file, especially when the program's command line is constructed on-the-fly with environment variables and arguments. To do this, put @echo on just before the program's command line and @echo off just after it. This way, CMD displays the actual command line as it runs the program.

You can also have echo commands display the environment variables and command-line arguments with which the program is working. For example,

```
echo Your user name is %username%
```

prints Your user name is followed by the contents of the username environment variable. I show examples of this kind of informational message throughout the chapter.

Argument Substitution

Many times you find that the repetitive tasks you encounter use the same programs but operate on different files each time. In this case, you can use command-line arguments to give information to the batch file when you run it. When you start a batch file from the command line with a command such as

```
batchname xxx yyy zzz
```

any items after the name of the batch file are made available to the batch program as arguments. The symbols %1, %2, %3, and so on are replaced with the corresponding arguments. In this example, anywhere that %1 appears in the batch file, CMD replaces it with xxx. Then, %2 is replaced with yyy, and so on.

Argument substitution lets you write batch files like this:

```
@echo off
notepad %1.vbs
cscript %1.vbs
```

This batch file lets you edit and then run a Windows Script Host program. If you name the batch file `ws.bat`, you can edit and test a script program named, say, `test.vbs` just by typing this:

```
ws test
```

In this case, CMD treats the batch file as if it contained the following:

```
@echo off
notepad test.vbs
cscript test.vbs
```

This kind of batch file can save you many keystrokes during the process of developing and debugging a script.

Besides the standard command-line arguments `%1`, `%2`, and so on, you should know about two special argument replacements: `%0` and `%*`. `%0` is replaced with the name of the batch file, as it is typed on the command line. `%*` is replaced with *all* the command-line arguments as they are typed with quotation marks and everything left intact.

If I have a batch file named `test.bat` with the contents

```
@echo off
echo The command name is %0
echo The arguments are: %*
```

then the command `test a b c` prints the following:

```
The command name is test
The arguments are: a b c
```

`%0` is useful when a batch file has detected some problem with the command-line arguments the user has typed and you want it to display a "usage" message. Here's an example:

```
if "%1" == "" (
    rem - no arguments were specified. Print the usage information
    echo Usage: %0 [-v] [-a] filename ...
    exit /b
)
```

If the batch file is named `test.bat`, then typing `test` would print out the following message:

```
Usage: test [-v] [-a] filename ...
```

The advantage of using `%0` is that it is always correct, even if you rename the batch file at a later date and forget to change the "usage" remarks inside.

Argument Editing

CMD lets you modify arguments as they're replaced on the command line. Most of the modifications assume that the argument is a filename and let you extract or fill in various parts of the name. When command extensions are enabled, CMD can insert edited versions of the arguments by placing a tilde (~) and some additional characters after the % sign. The editing functions let you manipulate filenames passed as arguments. Table 11.2 lists the edit options, using argument number 1 as an example.

Table 11.2   **Argument Editing Expressions**

Expression	Result
%~1	Removes surrounding quotation marks (").
%~f1	Fully qualified pathname.
%~d1	Drive letter only.
%~p1	Path only.
%~n1	Filename only.
%~x1	File extension only.
%~s1	Short DOS 8.3 file and path.
%~a1	File attributes.
%~t1	Modification date/time of file.
%~z1	Length of file in bytes.
%~$PATH:1	Fully qualified name of the first matching file when searching PATH. If no file is found, the result is a zero-length string. The filename must include the proper extension; PATHEXT is not used.

For example, if I ran a batch file with the argument "under the hood.doc", the results would be as follows:

Expression	Result
%~1	under the hood.doc
%~f1	C:\book\ch11\under the hood.doc
%~d1	C:
%~p1	\book\ch11
%~n1	under the hood
%~x1	.doc
%~s1	C:\book\ch11\UNDERT~1.DOC
%~a1	--a------
%~t1	04/20/2002 12:42 PM
%~z1	45323
%~$PATH:1	

Here's how these features might be used: Suppose I have a series of files that I need to sort. The input files could come from any folder, but I want to store the sorted files in C:\sorted and give them the extension .TAB regardless of what the original extension is. I can write a batch file named sortput.bat to do this:

```
@echo off
sort <%1 >c:\sorted\%~n1.tab
```

The sort command reads the file as I've specified it on the command line, but the output file uses only the base part of the input file's name. If I run the command

```
sortput "c:\work files\input.txt"
```

the substituted command is

```
sort <"c:\work files\input.txt" >c:\sorted\input.tab
```

Conditional Processing with **If**

One of the most important capabilities of any programming language is the capability to choose from among various instructions based on conditions the program finds as it runs. For this purpose, the batch file language has the if command.

The Basic **If** Command

In its most basic form, if compares two strings and executes a command if the strings are equivalent:

```
if string1 == string2 command
```

This is used in combination with command-line variable or environment variable substitution, as in this example:

```
if "%1" == "ERASE" delete somefile.dat
```

If and only if the batch file's first argument is the word ERASE, this command deletes the file somefile.dat.

The quotation marks in this command aren't absolutely required. If they are omitted and the command is written as

```
if %1 == ERASE delete somefile.dat
```

the command still works as long as some command-line argument is given when the batch file is run. However, if the batch file is started with no arguments, then %1 is replaced with nothing and the command turns into this:

```
if == ERASE delete somefile.dat
```

This is an invalid command. CMD expects to see something before the == part of the command and barks if it doesn't. Therefore, it's a common practice to surround the items to be tested with some character—any character. Even $ works, as shown here:

```
if $%0$ == $ERASE$ delete somefile.dat
```

If the items being tested are identical, they are still identical when surrounded by the extra characters. If they are different or blank, you still have a valid command.

The if command also lets you reverse the sense of the test with the not option:

```
if not "%1" == "ERASE" then goto no_erase
```

Checking for Files and Folders

The exist option lets you determine whether a particular file exists in the current directory:

```
if exist input.dat goto process_it
    echo The file input.dat does not exist
    pause
    exit /b
:process_it
```

Of course, you can specify a full path for the filename if that's appropriate, and you can use environment variables and % arguments to construct the name. If the filename has spaces in it, you need to surround it with quotation marks.

The not modifier can be used with exist as well, as in if not exist *filename*....

Tip

The exist test works if the specified name exists as either a file or a folder. If you want to ensure that the test works only if the name exists as a folder, perform the test this way:

```
if exist c:\foldername\ command
```

to see whether the folder *c:\foldername* exists. The backslash at the end will prevent Windows from matching a file name, but it ignores the backslash when testing a folder name.

Checking the Success of a Program

When a command-line or even a Windows program exits, it leaves behind a number called its *exit status* or *error status* value. This is a number that the program uses to indicate whether it thinks it did its job successfully. An exit status of zero means no problems; larger numbers indicate trouble. There is no predetermined meaning for any specific values. The documentation for some programs might list specific error values and give their interpretations, which means that your batch files can use these values to take appropriate action. How? Through the `errorlevel` variation of the `if` command.

After running a command in a batch file, an `if` statement of the form

```
if errorlevel number command
```

executes the command if the previous program's exit status value is the listed number or *higher*. For example, the `net use` command returns `0` if it is able to map a drive letter to a shared folder, and it returns a nonzero number if it can't. A batch file can take advantage of this as follows:

```
@echo off

net use f: \\bali\corpfiles
if errorlevel 1 goto failed
    echo Copying network data...
    if not exist c:\corpfiles\nul mkdir c:\corpfiles
    copy f:\*.xls c:\corpfiles
    exit /b
:failed
    echo Unable to access network share \\bali\corpfiles
    pause
```

Note

The `net use` command is discussed in Chapter 13, "Command-Line Utilities." Its purpose is to map a drive letter to a network shared folder.

You can also use `not` with this version of the `if` command. In this case, the command is executed if the error status is *less* than the listed number. The error testing in the previous example can be rewritten this way:

```
if not errorlevel 1 goto success
    echo Unable to access network share \\bali\corpfiles
    pause
    exit /b
:success
    echo Copying network data...
    if not exist c:\corpfiles\nul mkdir c:\corpfiles
    copy f:\*.xls c:\corpfiles
```

In this version, the flow of the batch file is a bit easier to follow. However, even this can be improved upon, as you see next.

Performing Several Commands After **If**

Often, you want to execute several commands if some condition is true. In the old days, before the extended CMD shell came along, you had to use a `goto` command to transfer control to another part of the batch file, as in the `if exist` example given in the previous section. With the extended version of `if`, this is no longer necessary.

The extended `if` command lets you put more than one statement after an `if` command, by grouping them with parentheses. For example, you can place multiple commands on one line, as shown here:

```
if not errorlevel 1 (echo The network share was not available & exit /b)
```

Or you can put them on multiple lines:

```
if not errorlevel 1 (
    echo The network share was not available
    pause
    exit /b
)
```

I recommend the second version because it's easier to read. Look how much clearer the network file copying example becomes when parentheses are used instead of `goto`:

```
@echo off

net use f: \\bali\corpfiles
if errorlevel 1 (
    echo Unable to access network share \\bali\corpfiles
    pause
    exit /b
)
echo Copying network data...
if not exist c:\corpfiles\nul mkdir c:\corpfiles
copy f:\*.xls c:\corpfiles
```

You can also execute one set of commands if the `if` test is true and another if the test is false by using the `else` option, as in this example:

```
if exist input.dat echo input.dat exists else echo input.dat does not exist
```

You can use `else` with parentheses, but you must take care to place the `else` command on the same line as `if`, or on the same line as the closing parenthesis after `if`. You should write a multiple-line `if...else` command using the same format as this example:

```
if exist input.dat (
    echo Sorting input.txt...
    sort <input.txt >source.data
) else (
    echo Input.txt does not exist. Creating an empty data file...
    echo. >source.data
)
```

Extended Testing

The extended `if` command lets you perform a larger variety of tests when comparing strings, and it can also compare arguments and variables as numbers. The extended comparisons are listed in Table 11.3.

Table 11.3 **Comparison Operators Allowed by the `if` Command**

Variation	Comparison
if *string1* **EQU** *string2*	Exactly equal
if *string1* **NEQ** *string2*	Not equal
if *string1* **LSS** *string2*	Less than
if *string1* **LEQ** *string2*	Less than or equal to
if *string1* **GTR** *string2*	Greater than
if string1 **GEQ** string2	Greater than or equal to
if **/i** (comparison)	Case-insensitive
if **defined** *name*	True if there is an environment variable *name*
if **cmdextversion** *number*	True if the CMD extensions are version *number* or higher

As an added bonus, if the strings being compared contain only digits, then CMD compares them numerically. For example, you could test for a specific exit status from a program with a statement like this:

```
some program
if %errorlevel% equ 3 (
    echo The program returned an exit status of 3 which
    echo means that the network printer is offline.
)
```

Processing Multiple Arguments

When you have many files to process, you can get tired of typing the same batch file commands over and over, like this:

```
somebatch file1.dat
somebatch file2.dat
somebatch file3.dat
...
```

You can write batch files to handle any number of arguments on the command line. The tool to use is the `shift` command, which deletes a given command-line argument and slides the remaining ones down. Here's what I mean: Suppose I started a batch file with the command line

```
batchname xxx yyy zzz
```

Inside the batch file, the following argument replacements would be in effect before and after a `shift` command:

Before Shift	**After Shift**
%0 = *batchname*	%0 = xxx
%1 = xxx	%1 = yyy
%2 = yyy	%2 = zzz
%3 = zzz	%3 = (blank)
%4 = (blank)	%4 = (blank)·

The batch file just has to repeatedly process the item named by %1 and shift until %1 is blank. This is a common process, so I list it as a pattern.

Pattern

To process a variable number of command-line arguments, use the `shift` command to delete arguments until they're all gone, as in this example:

```
@rem                                    Example File batch1201.bat
@echo off
if "%1" == "" (
    rem if %1 is blank there were no arguments. Show how to use this batch
    echo Usage: %0 filename ...
    exit /b
)

:again
rem if %1 is blank, we are finished
if not "%1" == "" (
    echo Processing file %1...

    rem ... do something with file %1

    rem - shift the arguments and examine %1 again
    shift
    goto again
)
```

You can also use the `for` command, which appears in a pattern later in this chapter.

If you want to have the program process a default file if none is specified on the command line, you can use this variation of the pattern:

```
@rem                                    Example File batch1202.bat
@echo off

if "%1" == "" (
    rem - no file was specified - process the default file "test.for"
    call :process test.for
) else (
    rem - process each of the named files
:again
```

```
    rem if %1 is blank, we are finished
    if not "%1" == "" (
        call :process %1
        rem - shift the arguments and examine %1 again
        shift
        goto again
    )
)
exit /b

:process
echo Processing file %1...
⋮
```

In this version, if no arguments are specified on the command line, the script processes a default file—in this case, `test.for`. Otherwise, it processes all files named on the command line. This version of the pattern uses batch file subroutines, which are discussed later in the chapter in the section "Using Batch File Subroutines."

The extended version of the `shift` command, `shift /n`, lets you start shifting at argument number *n*, leaving the lower-numbered arguments alone. The following illustrates what `shift /2` does in a batch file run with the command "`batchname xxx yyy zzz`":

Before Shift	**After Shift**
`%0` = *batchname*	`%0` = *batchname*
`%1` = xxx	`%1` = xxx
`%2` = yyy	`%2` = zzz
`%3` = zzz	`%3` = (blank)
`%4` = (blank)	`%4` = (blank)

In actual use, you might want to use this feature if you need to have the batch file's name (`%0`) available throughout the batch file. In this case, you can use `shift /1` to shift all the remaining arguments but keep `%0` intact. You might also want to write batch files that take a command line of the form

```
batchname outputfile inputfile inputfile …
```

with an output filename followed by one or more input files. In this case, you could keep the output filename `%1` intact but loop through the input files with `shift /2`, using commands like this:

```
@rem                                    Example File sortmerge.bat
@echo off

rem be sure they gave at least two arguments
if "%2" == "" (
    echo Usage: %0 outfile infile ...
    exit /b
```

```
)

rem collect all input files into SORT.TMP

if exist sort.tmp del sort.tmp

:again
if not "%2" == "" (
    echo ...Collecting data from %2
    type %2 >>sort.tmp
    shift /2
    goto again
)

rem sort SORT.TMP into first file named on command line

echo ...Sorting to create %1
sort sort.tmp /O %1
del sort.tmp
```

Working with Environment Variables

Although environment variables were initially designed to hold system-configuration information such as the search path, they are also the "working" variables for batch files. You can use them to store filenames, option settings, user input from prompts, or any other information you need to store in a batch program. Environment variables were covered in Chapter 10. In the discussion of environment variable substitution, the set command was introduced as the way to set and modify environment variables.

However, you should know that, by default, changes to environment variables made in a batch file persist when the batch file finishes because the variables "belong" to the copy of CMD that manages the Command Prompt window and any batch files run in it. This is great when you want to use a batch file to modify the search path so you can run programs from some nonstandard directory. However, it's a real problem if your batch file assumes that any variables it uses are undefined (empty) before the batch file starts. Here's a disaster waiting to happen:

```
@echo off
set /p answer=Do you want to erase the input files at the end (Y/N)?
if /i "%answer:~,1%" EQU "Y" set cleanup=YES
… more commands here
… then, at the end,
if "%cleanup%" == "YES" (
    rem they wanted the input files to be erased
    del c:\input\*.dat
)
```

If you respond to the prompt with Y, the environment variable cleanup is set to YES, and the files are erased. However, the next time you run the batch file, cleanup is *still* set to YES, and the files are erased no matter how you answer the question. Of course, the problem can be solved by adding the statement

```
set cleanup=
```

at the beginning of the batch file. In fact, good programming practice requires you to do so in any case (you should always initialize variables before using them), but the point is still important: Environment variables are "sticky."

In the old DOS days, a batch file program would usually add set statements to the end of batch files to delete any environment variables used by the program. However, CMD provides an easier method of cleaning up.

If you plan on using environment variables as working variables for a batch file, you can use the setlocal command to make any changes to the variables "local" to the batch file. At the end of the batch file, or if you use an endlocal command, the environment is restored to its original state at the time of the setlocal command. It is prudent to put setlocal at the beginning of any batch file that does not require its environment changes to persist outside the batch file itself.

Environment Variable Editing

As with the old COMMAND.COM, in any command, strings of the form %var% are replaced with the value of the environment variable named var. One of CMD's extensions is to let you modify the environment variable content as it is being extracted. Whereas the edits for command-line arguments are focused around filename manipulation, the edits for environment variables are designed to let you extract substrings.

The following types of expressions can be used

Expression	Result
%name:~n%	Skips the first n letters and returns the rest
%name:~n,m%	Skips n letters and returns the next m
%name:~,m%	First (leftmost) m letters
%name:~,-m%	Last (rightmost) m letters

Using the environment variable var=ABCDEFG, here are some examples:

Command	Prints
echo %var%	ABCDEFG
echo %var:~2%	CDEFG
echo %var:~2,3%	CDE
echo %var:~,3%	ABC
echo %var:~,-3%	EFG

Expressions of the form %name:*str1*=*str2*% replace every occurrence of the string *str1* with *str2*. *str2* can be blank to delete all occurrences of *str1*. You can start *str1* with an asterisk (*), which makes CMD replace all characters up to and including *str1*.

Using the environment variable var=ABC;DEF;GHI, here are some examples:

Command	Prints
echo %var:;= %	ABC DEF GHI
echo %var:;=%	ABCDEFGHI
echo %var:*DEF=123%	123;GHI

The first example listed is particularly useful if you want to use the PATH list in a for loop; for wants to see file or folder names separated by spaces, whereas PATH separates them with semicolons. I discuss this in more detail later on.

→ For more details on working with environment variables, **see** "Setting Variables with the Set Command," **p. 480**.

Processing Multiple Items with the **for** Command

You often need to write batch files that process "all" of a certain type of file. Command-line programs can deal with filename wildcards: For example, you can type delete *.dat to delete all files whose name ends with .dat. In batch files, you can accomplish this sort of thing with the for loop.

Note

If you have a Unix background, the need for special statements to deal with wildcards can seem confusing at first. On Unix and Linux systems, the command shell expands all command-line arguments with wildcards into a list of names before it starts the command, so to the command it appears that the user typed all the names. This is called *globbing*. On DOS and Windows, the shell doesn't do this. When command-line arguments contain wildcard characters, it's up to the command or batch file to expand the name into a list of filenames.

The basic version of the for command scans through a set or list of names and runs a command once for each. The format for batch files is

```
for %%x in (set of names) do command
```

where *set of names* is a list of words separated by spaces. The for command executes *command* once for each item it finds in the set. At each iteration, variable x contains the current name, and any occurrences of %%x in the command are replaced by the current value of x. You can choose any alphabetic letter for the variable name. Also, upper- and lowercase matters, meaning *a* and *A* are different to the for command.

Note

When you type a **for** command directly at the command prompt, you only use single percent signs. In a batch file, you must double them up. Otherwise, they confuse CMD because they look sort of like command-line arguments or environment variable replacements. This dates back to the MS-DOS days, and we're still stuck with it.

For example, the command

```
for %%x in (a b c d) do echo %%x
```

prints four lines: a, b, c, and d. What makes **for** especially useful is that if any item in the set contains the wildcard characters ? or *, **for** assumes that the item is a filename and replaces the item with any matching filenames. The command

```
for %%x in (*.tmp *.out *.dbg) do delete %%x
```

deletes any occurrences of files ending with .tmp, .out, or .dbg in the current directory. If no such files exist, the command turns into

```
for %%x in () do delete %%x
```

which is fine—it does nothing. To get the same "silent" result when specifying the wildcards directly in the **delete** command, you have to enter

```
if exist *.tmp delete *tmp
if exist *.out delete *.out
if exist *.dbg delete *.dbg
```

because **delete** complains if it can't find any files to erase.

As another example, the command

```
for %%F in ("%ALLUSERSPROFILE%\Documents\[wrap]
    ➥My Faxes\Received Faxes\*.tif") do echo %%~nF: received %%~tF
```

prints a list of all faxes received from the Windows Fax service and the time they were received.

Note

If you use variable substitution edits, choose as your **for** variable a letter that you don't need to use as one of the editing letters. **for** stops looking at the editing expression when it hits the **for** variable letter. For instance, in the example, if I had needed to use the ~f editing function, I would have had to choose another variable letter for the **for** loop.

Several other forms of the **for** command are covered in Chapter 10, and you should make sure you're familiar with them. The extended **for** command lets you scan for directories, recurse into subdirectories, and do several other useful things that you can't do any other way.

Using Multiple Commands in a `for` Loop

CMD lets you use multiple command lines after a `for` loop. This makes the Windows `for` command much more powerful than the old DOS version. In cases where you would have had to call a batch file subroutine in the past, you can now use parentheses to perform complex operations.

For example, this batch file examines a directory full of Windows bitmap (BMP) files and ensures that a corresponding GIF file exists in another directory; if the GIF file doesn't exist, it uses an image-conversion utility to create one:

```
@echo off
setlocal
echo Searching for new .BMP files...

for %%F in (c:\incoming\*.bmp) do (
    rem output file is input file name with extension .GIF
    set outfile=c:\outgoing\%%~nF.gif
    if not exist %outfile% (
        echo ...Creating %outfile%
        imgcnv -gif %%F %outfile%
    )
)
```

Therefore, every time you run this batch file, it makes sure there is a converted GIF file in the `\outgoing` folder for every BMP file in the `\incoming` folder. This sample script uses several of the techniques we've discussed in this chapter:

- A `setlocal` statement keeps environment variable changes in the batch file from persisting after the batch is finished.
- The `for` loop and `if` command use parentheses to group several statements.
- The environment variable `outfile` is used as a "working" variable.
- The batch file uses `echo` statements to let you know what it's doing as it works.

A batch file like this can make short work of maintaining large sets of files. You might accidentally overlook a new file if you are trying to manage something like this manually, but the batch file doesn't.

As a final example, the following handy batch file tells you what file is actually used when you type a command by name. I call this program `which.bat`, and when I want to know what program is run by, say, the `ping` command, I type the following:

```
which ping
```

The batch file searches the current folder and then every folder in the PATH list. In each folder, it looks for a specific file, if you typed a specific extension with the command name, or it tries all the extensions in the PATHEXT list, which contains EXE, COM, BAT, and the other usual suspects:

```
@rem                                      Example file which.bat
@echo off

if "%1" == "" (
    echo Usage: which command
    echo Locates the file run when you type 'command'.
    exit /b
)

for %%d in (. %path%) do (
    if "%~x1" == "" (
        rem the user didn't type an extension so use the PATHEXT list
        for %%e in (%pathext%) do (
            if exist %%d\%1%%e (
                echo %%d\%1%%e
                exit /b
            )
        )
    ) else (
        rem the user typed a specific extension, so look only for that
        if exist %%d\%1 (
            echo %%d\%1
            exit /b
        )
    )
)
echo No file for %1 was found
```

As you can see, the `for` command lets you write powerful, useful programs that can save you time and prevent errors, and the syntax is cryptic enough to please even a Perl programmer.

Delayed Expansion

Environment variables and command-line arguments marked with % are replaced with their corresponding values when CMD reads each command line. However, when you're writing `for` loops and compound `if` statements, this can cause some unexpected results.

For example, you might want to run a secondary batch file repeatedly with several files, with the first file handled differently, like this:

```
call anotherbatch firstfile.txt FIRST
call anotherbatch secondfile.txt MORE
call anotherbatch xfiles.txt MORE
```

You might want to do this so that the first call creates a new output file, while each subsequent call adds onto the existing file.

You might be tempted to automate this process with the `for` command, using commands like this:

```
set isfirst=FIRST
for %%f in (*.txt) do (
    call anotherbatch %%f %isfirst%
    set isfirst=MORE
)
```

The idea here is that the second argument to `anotherbatch` is `FIRST` for the first file and `MORE` for all subsequent files. However, this does not work. CMD replaces `%isfirst%` with its definition `MORE` when it first encounters the `for` statement. When CMD has finished processing `%` signs, the command looks like this:

```
set isfirst=FIRST
for %%f in (*.txt) do (
    call anotherbatch %%f FIRST
    set isfirst=MORE
)
```

Because `FIRST` is substituted before the `for` loop starts running, `anotherbatch` does not see the value of `isfirst` change, and the result is

```
call anotherbatch firstfile.txt FIRST
call anotherbatch secondfile.txt FIRST
call anotherbatch xfiles.txt FIRST
```

which is not at all what you wanted.

There is a way to fix this: Delayed expansion lets you specify environment variables with exclamation points rather than percent signs, as an indication that they are to be expanded only when CMD actually intends to execute the command. Because `!` has not traditionally been a special character, this feature is disabled by default. To enable delayed expansion, specify `/V:ON` on the CMD command line or use `SETLOCAL` to enable this feature inside the batch file. The statements

```
setlocal enabledelayedexpansion
set isfirst=FIRST
for %%f in (*.txt) do (
    call anotherbatch %%f !isfirst!
    set isfirst=MORE
)
```

works correctly.

Another way delayed expansion is useful is for collecting information into an environment variable inside a `for` list. As an example of how this might work, the following batch file adds `c:\mystuff` and every folder under it to an environment variable named `dirs`:

```
setlocal ENABLEDELAYEDEXPANSION
set dirs=
for /R c:\mystuff %%d in (.) do set dirs=!dirs!;%%d
```

The for statement recursively visits every folder, starting in c:\mystuff, and %%d takes on the name of each folder in turn. The set statement adds each directory name to the end of the dirs variable.

Using Batch File Subroutines

The CMD shell lets you write batch file subroutines using the call command. Although the new capability to group statements with parentheses makes batch file subroutines somewhat less necessary than they were in the past, the subroutine is still an important tool in batch file programming.

For example, in a task that involves processing a whole list of files, you might write a batch file subroutine to perform all the steps necessary to process one file. Then, you can call this subroutine once for each file you need to process.

In the old days of COMMAND.COM, batch file subroutines had to be placed in separate BAT files. You can still do this, but with CMD, you can also place subroutines in the same file as the main batch file program. The structure looks like this:

```
@rem                              Example File batch1203.bat
@echo off

rem MAIN BATCH FILE PROGRAM -----------------------

rem call subroutine "onefile" for each file to be processed:
cd \input
for %%f in (*.dat) do call :onefile %%f    <---subroutine called here

rem main program must end with exit /b or goto :EOF
exit /b

rem SUBROUTINE "ONEFILE" -------------------------
:onefile
echo Processing file %1...
echo … commands go here …
exit /b
```

The call command followed by a colon and a label name tells CMD to continue processing at the label. Any items placed on the call command after the label are arguments passed to the subroutine, which can access them with %1, %2, and so on. The original command-line arguments to the batch file are hidden while the call is in effect.

Processing returns to the command after the call when the subroutine encounters any of these conditions:

- The end of the file is reached.
- The subroutine deliberately jumps to the end of the file with the command `goto :EOF`.
- The subroutine executes the command `exit /b`.

Normally, any of these conditions indicates the end of the batch file, and CMD returns to the command prompt. After `call`, however, these conditions end the subroutine, and the batch file continues.

> **Caution**
>
> You must be sure to make the main part of the batch file stop before it runs into the first subroutine. In other scripting languages such as VBScript, the end of the "main program" is unmistakable; in the batch file language, however, it is not. You must use `goto :EOF` or `exit /B` before the first subroutine's label; otherwise, CMD plows through and runs the subroutine's commands again.

Prompting for Input

If your batch file has to print a message you definitely don't want the users to miss, use the `pause` statement to make the batch file sit and wait until they've read the message and acknowledged it. Here's an example:

```
echo The blatfizz command failed. This means that the world as
echo we know it is about to end, or, that the input file needs to
echo be corrected.
pause
exit /b
```

If you want to ask a user whether to proceed after a mishap, or if you want the batch file to prompt for input filenames or other data, you can use the new extended `set /p` command. `set /p` reads a user's response into an environment variable, where it can be tested or used as a command argument. Here's an example:

```
:again
    echo The input file INPUT.DAT does not exist
    set /p answer=Do you want to create it now (Y/N)?
    if /i "%answer:~,1%" EQU "Y" goto editit
    if /i "%answer:~,1%" EQU "N" exit /b
    echo Please type Y for Yes or N for No
    goto again
```

These commands ask the user to type a response, examine the leftmost letter with `%answer:,1%`, and take the appropriate action only if the user types a valid response. In fact, this is a good pattern to remember.

▶ **Pattern**

To prompt a user for a yes/no answer, use a series of commands following this pattern:

```
:again
    echo If the question is long or requires an explanation,
    echo use echo commands to display text before the question.
    set /p answer=Ask the question here (Y/N)?
    if /i "%answer:~,1%" EQU "Y" command to execute for Yes
    if /i "%answer:~,1%" EQU "N" command to execute for No
    echo Please type Y for Yes or N for No
    goto again
```

Put a single space after the question mark on the `set /p` command. If you use this pattern more than once in the same batch file, be sure to use a different label for each one. I used `again` in this version, but you can use any word as the label.

You can modify this pattern to create a menu. You can write a prompt like this:

```
echo Options: [A]dd, [D]elete, [P]rint, [Q]uit, [H]elp
set /p answer=Enter selection:
```

In this example, instead of comparing the response to the letters Y and N, you would compare it to A, D, P, Q, and H.

Useful Batch File Techniques

As mentioned in Chapter 9, "Deploying Scripts for Computer and Network Management," I like to make scripts and batch files user friendly—not only so that they can be used more easily by other people, but also because I know that three weeks after I write one, I have forgotten how to use it, what it does, and how it works. I also frequently find myself standing in front of the refrigerator wondering what I was after when I opened it, so this isn't surprising. But, even if this doesn't happen to you, the principle is still a good one: If you write your batch file well, you are doing yourself a future favor.

With this in mind, in this section, I cover a few techniques and tricks that I use to make batch files more helpful, useful, and reliable.

Processing Command-Line Options

You might want your batch files to act like the Windows built-in commands and have them recognize options that begin with / or -. It's helpful to have a batch file recognize /? as a request to display information about the program itself.

The `shift` command is useful here. At the beginning of the batch file, you can examine the first argument (%1) and see whether it starts with /. If it does, it's an option. You can set an environment variable, delete the argument with `shift`, and then repeat the process until all options have been removed.

The following three command options can be useful to implement:

Option	Meaning
/?	Help. Prints help info and quits.
/v	Verbose. Turns on debugging printouts.
/q	Quiet. Disables normal printouts.

Here's how I process these options at the beginning of a batch file:

```
@rem                                    Example File batch1204.bat
@echo off
setlocal
rem - initialize options to their default values
set verbose=NO
set quiet=NO
:again
    set arg=%1
    if "%arg:,1%" == "/" (
        if "/i" %arg% EQU "/v" (
            set verbose=YES
        ) else if "/i" %arg% EQU "/q" (
            set quiet=YES
        ) else (
            :usage
            echo Usage: %0 [/v ^¦ /q] filename...
            echo.
            echo This batch file copies each of the files to the
            echo network folder. Other helpful information goes here.
            exit /b
        )
        shift /1
        goto again
    )
```

Here are some notes about the programming in this example:

- To examine the leftmost character of each argument, the program copies it to the environment variable arg and then examines the first character with %arg:,1%. Because the argument could be empty, the first if statement has to use quotation marks around the strings being compared.

- Because the remaining if commands are only reached if arg starts with /, it definitely is not empty, so there is no need to use quotation marks around the other tests. However, it's a good habit to use them anyway.

- The final else prints the usage information if the user types /? or any invalid option.

- The shift command uses /1 so that %0 is left alone and always contains the name of the batch file.

Later in the batch file, you can use the values of the environment variables verbose and quiet to determine whether to print messages. Extra debugging information can be printed like this:

```
if "%verbose%" == "YES" echo Got to the part where we'll clean out the folder
```

Similarly, normal messages such as Processing file %1 and pause commands that stop the batch file can be disabled if the /Q option is given:

```
if not "%quiet%" == "YES" echo Processing file %1...
```

I use the strange if not test in this case as a failsafe measure. If the variable quiet is not defined, I'd rather have the output appear. (This is an important part of making reliable programs. To the extent possible, have programs anticipate things that should never happen and try to make the best of the situation should they occur.)

Tip

The "quiet" option is a good one to provide if you want to run the batch file with the Command Scheduler. If the quiet option is enabled, the batch file should never use pause.

After the batch file has read and eliminated any command-line options, %1 indicates the first filename or whatever the command-line argument means in your application. If you expect at least one argument, you can print out the usage information and quit if it's missing:

```
if "%1" == "" goto usage
```

This sends the batch program back to the label :usage, which you find back in the part of the batch file that processes the command-line options.

Then, if your batch file processes an arbitrary number of input items, you can process each of them in turn using a batch file subroutine:

```
for each %%x in (%*) do call :process %%x
exit /b
```

In this example, %* is replaced with all the remaining command-line arguments. Any wildcards in the names are expanded into matching filenames, and the for command calls the batch file subroutine process with each item in turn.

The batch file subroutine process receives the item as argument number 1, so it usually starts like this:

```
:process
if not "%quiet%" == "YES" echo Processing %1...
```

Managing Network Mappings

If your batch file uses network folders, you might want to map one or more drive letters to shared folders. The problem is that the drive letter you want to use might already be in use. You have to use a creative strategy to deal with this. I have three suggestions.

Use UNC Pathnames

In many cases, you can avoid mapping a drive letter entirely. Most Windows command-line programs accept Universal Naming Convention (UNC) network pathnames, so you can use the *server**sharename*\... format directly. For example, I used a batch file while I was writing this book to save backup copies of the content on another computer:

```
@echo off
echo Backing up chapter files
xcopy c:\book\*.* \\bali\brian\bookbackup /S/Z/Y/M
```

This copied the files to the server \\bali, to subfolder bookbackup of the shared folder brian.

Use pushd to Assign a Random Drive Letter

The pushd command assigns a random drive letter if you specify a network path. If you can write your batch file commands to use the current directory so you don't need to know the drive letter, so much the better. My backup batch file could have been written this way:

```
pushd \\bali\brian\bookbackup
xcopy c:\book\*.* . /S/Z/Y/M
popd
```

You can also determine the drive letter that pushd creates using the %cd% environment variable. This "virtual" variable always returns the current drive letter and path. After the pushd command, it might have the value Y:\.

Be sure to end the batch file with popd to release the temporary drive letter.

Remember, too, that if your batch file *does* need to know the drive letter that is mapped to the network location, you can retreive it. After the pushd command, the %cd% environment variable will return the full current path. You can use a command like

```
set drv=%cd:~,2%
```

to pick up the mapped drive letter. This command might be set to something like Y:.

Delete Previous Mappings Before Starting

If you want or need to use fixed, mapped network drive letters, you should take a heavy-handed approach to mapping. Delete any preexisting mapping of your desired drive letter first, and then map it to the desired network folder.

Because the network drive might or might not be mapped when the batch file starts, I like to use `net use` to delete any existing mapping. If you redirect its output to the nul file, any error messages simply disappear. This prevents the batch file from displaying an error message if the drive letter is not mapped when it starts. Here's an example:

```
rem - map drive G to the network folder

net use g: /del >nul 2>nul         & rem - delete previous mapping if any

net use g: \\server\sharename      & rem - make new mapping
if errorlevel 1 (
    echo The network folder is not available
    if not "%quiet%" == "YES" pause
    exit /b
)
```

Checking for Correct Arguments

If your batch file accepts filenames as input, it's possible that the batch file's user types a name incorrectly. It's best to detect this as quickly as possible, rather than letting whatever programs the batch file runs encounter invalid filenames. Before taking any other action with the files, you can perform a quick check of the names the user entered with a loop like this:

```
for %%f in (%*) do (
    if not exist %%f echo Error: file %%f does not exist & exit /b
)
```

Of course, this assumes that all the command-line arguments are filenames—you have to write a checking procedure that's appropriate to your own needs. The idea is that whenever possible, you should validate all input before starting to work with it.

Keeping Log Files

If you write batch files to use with the Command Scheduler, you aren't able able to see any error messages your batch program prints if it runs into trouble. As mentioned in Chapter 9, it's important to have unattended programs keep a record of their activity so that you can confirm whether they're working correctly; if they're not, you can find out what is going wrong.

When I write a batch file for unattended use, I usually have it create a log file as its first step and store the current time and date in the file. Then, I sprinkle `echo` commands throughout the program to add a running commentary to the log file. The structure looks like this:

```
@echo off
set logfile=MYBATCH.LOG
echo Batch command: %0 %* >%logfile%
echo Started at %date% %time% >>%logfile%
echo ---------------------- >>%logfile%
```

I use an environment variable for the name of the log file so that if it's necessary to change its name, I only need to edit the `set` command at the beginning of the file. Adding the time and date lets you quickly determine whether the scheduled batch process is actually being run.

Then, throughout the batch file you can use `echo` commands similar to the ones used at startup to add to the log file. Record the names of files processed, add a note at the beginning of each major group of commands and definitely record any problems encountered. It's best to display messages to the standard output as well as to the log file:

```
@rem                                    Example File batch1205.bat
set logfile = mappit.log

echo Mapping network drive...
echo Mapping network drive... >>%logfile%

net use m: \\server\sharename
if errorlevel 1 (
    echo Unable to use shared folder \\server\sharename
    echo Unable to use shared folder \\server\sharename >>%logfile%
    echo Quitting prematurely! >>%logfile%
    exit /b
)
```

This way, you can see the output yourself if you run the batch file manually.

Finally, it's a good idea to record a final entry just before the batch file exits so that you know it didn't get stuck just before the last command. The final commands in the batch file's main program section might look like this:

```
echo --------------------- >>%logfile%
echo Ended at %date% %time% >>%logfile%
```

You might want to have the program jump down to these final statements even after encountering a fatal error. Instead of using `exit /b` after encountering the network error, I could have written `goto done` and put this at the end of the batch file:

```
:done
echo --------------------- >>%logfile%
echo Ended at %date% %time% >>%logfile%
```

This way, the log file should *always* end like this:

```
---------------------
Ended at Thu 05/02/2002 23:54:12.90
```

If it doesn't, I know that something quite unexpected must have happened.

Tip

If you use many scheduled batch files, you might want to use the techniques described in Chapter 9 to create a "management summary" showing the results of each of them.

12

The MS-DOS Environment Under Windows

MS-DOS Programs on Windows

Old programs never die; they just get harder to maintain. That's an old programmer's proverb—well, no, it's not really. But you quickly find that it's true if you have to use or support MS-DOS programs on modern versions of Windows. Some programs that are based on this original 16-bit, character-based PC operating system are still in use today (mostly in businesses), and whereas Windows 95 and 98 had MS-DOS running underneath, MS-DOS is nowhere to be found on a computer running Windows 7, Vista, XP, 2000, or NT.

Instead, the 32-bit versions of these Windows NT–based operating systems *emulate* DOS for the old programs. That is, Windows provides a software environment that simulates the same disk, keyboard, printer, and screen functions that MS-DOS provided. It's called the Windows NT Virtual DOS Machine (NTVDM).

Note

The 64-bit versions of Windows 7, Vista, and XP do *not* provide support for directly running MS-DOS applications, for legitimate technical reasons. If you have a 64-bit version of Windows, you can still run MS-DOS applications inside a virtual machine, by running Windows XP or MS-DOS inside Microsoft Virtual PC, VMWare, or another virtual machine program, or, on Windows 7, the Windows XP Mode feature that is available as a free download. You can use the configuration techniques described in this chapter to configure the virtualized copy of 32-bit Windows.

The Virtual DOS Machine

MS-DOS programs interacted directly with the computer's hardware; they could directly manipulate the display adapter to change the screen resolution, they could directly address the computer's serial and parallel ports to control modems and printers, and they interacted with the operating system through special processor instructions called *software interrupts*. None of these are allowed of a Windows program today. All hardware is strictly controlled by the operating system kernel and its device drivers so that errant user programs can't bring down the operating system. (Of course, errant device drivers can and do.)

When you attempt to run any program, Windows examines the program file to determine which operating system environment it requires. Program files ending with .COM are always MS-DOS programs. Files ending with .EXE could be Win32, Windows 3.1, or MS-DOS programs. In this case, Windows examines the first few bytes of the program file, which indicate the difference.

When it finds that it has been asked to run an MS-DOS program, Windows starts a program called ntvdm.exe, which in turn reads and interprets the DOS program. NTVDM acts as the mediator between the DOS program and Windows and performs the following functions:

- It allocates memory organized in the fashion of the old PC architecture: 640KB of memory is available for the simulated DOS environment and the application program, and the expanded and extended memory interfaces that let MS-DOS reach beyond the 1MB point are simulated as well.

- NTVDM handles any software interruptions that the program issues, and it translates the MS-DOS system requests into Windows equivalents.

- NTVDM sets aside memory that appears to the MS-DOS program to be the display adapter's memory. NTVDM monitors this memory and, when changes occur, draws corresponding changes in the Command Prompt window.

- If the program issues instructions to put the display adapter into a graphics mode, NTVDM changes the Command Prompt window to full-screen mode. Windows then switches the display adapter to the requested graphics mode and relays any "safe" hardware instructions from the MS-DOS program to the display adapter. All the modifications are monitored, however, and control can be taken back at any time.

- Printing and serial port access is monitored in a similar way. NTVDM intercepts any processor instructions that attempt to manipulate the printer or serial ports, determines the program's intent, and uses Windows functions to produce the same effect.

- NTVDM provides mouse support through the DOS standard mouse device driver. This driver is built in to NTVDM and does not have to be loaded separately.

This sounds like a lot of work, and it is. NTVDM is nearly 400KB in length, larger than the entire memory available in early PCs. Happily, only 32KB of this appears in the 640KB memory space seen by the MS-DOS program. The simulated device drivers are tiny because most of the real work is done elsewhere in the NTVDM program.

Note

One side effect of the emulation scheme is that when you run an MS-DOS program, the program appears in the Task Manager's Processes list as `ntvdm.exe`. If you run DOS WordPerfect, for example, you don't see `wp.exe` listed. I talk more about this at the end of the chapter.

By the way, if asked by an application program, NTVDM advertises itself as running MS-DOS version 5.0. I have no idea why Microsoft chose DOS 5 over DOS 6.

In most cases, DOS programs work well. NTVDM is not perfect, however. For example, NTVDM's emulation of some hardware is not quite perfect. Also, NTVDM doesn't mimic old MS-DOS-type networking functions quite precisely enough to fool all programs. I've run into these sorts of problems:

- DOS programs that use network printers, such as the old DOS FoxPro database program, don't always eject a page after printing or sometimes eject too many pages.

- Modem software like Norton-Lambert's Close-Up remote-control software doesn't work perfectly. Data is lost between the software and the modem, resulting in slow communications and even modem hang-ups.

- Games that attempt to use NTVDM's Sound Blaster emulation might generate hideous screeching sounds or might crash entirely.

Unfortunately, when problems like these do occur, there is little or nothing you can do about it.

Besides NTVDM.EXE and COMMAND.COM, in the name of compatibility (but probably just for sentimental reasons), Windows comes with some old DOS 5.0 utility programs. These are the original MS-DOS 16-bit programs. They work just as they always did—no improvements have been made. These old-timers include the following:

append	fastopen★	mem
debug	graftablnlsfunc	setver
edit	graphics	share★
edlin	loadfix	
exe2bin	loadhigh	

The programs marked with an asterisk (★) do nothing because Windows performs these functions automatically. They are provided for compatibility. Presumably, they're there to pacify any old applications, batch files, or installation programs that require these now-unnecessary commands. One additional compatibility program deserves special mention: forcedos.

forcedos

When you attempt to run any program, Windows examines the program's executable file to determine what sort of program it is: 32-bit Windows, 16-bit Windows, OS/2, DOS, and so on. Usually, Windows does a good job of determining the environment required by a program, but it sometimes fails. If you find that it fails to correctly identify a program as a DOS program, you can force Windows to run the program in the MS-DOS environment by adding forcedos to the beginning of the command line. Here is the syntax:

```
forcedos [/d folder] program arguments…]
```

MS-DOS and COMMAND.COM

As mentioned in Chapter 10, "The CMD Command-Line," and Chapter 11, "Batch Files for Fun and Profit," Windows uses a new command prompt shell program named CMD.EXE. As it turns out, to maintain maximum compatibility with old MS-DOS programs and old batch files, the original COMMAND.COM is actually still available. The clunky old version of its batch file language we all knew and "loved" is still there.

Here's how it works: If you run an MS-DOS program in a Command Prompt window, CMD assumes that you're going to work in the 16-bit world for a while. When the DOS program finishes, the window switches to the COMMAND.COM shell. You notice several differences:

- The current directory name is changed to its old-style 8.3 equivalent. For example, if your current directory had been `C:\program files`, when the DOS program exits, the directory is displayed as `C:\PROGRA~1`.

- Environment variable names change to all uppercase letters, except the variable `windir`, which is not present.

- The extended versions of the built-in commands are unavailable. Table 11.4 lists the affected commands.

- If you've run `COMMAND.COM` explicitly, you cannot close the window by clicking its close button—`COMMAND.COM` doesn't get the message to quit. You have to type **exit** to close the window.

These changes make it more likely that old programs and batch files will be able to run. However, if you want, you can keep `CMD.EXE` as your command shell even when using MS-DOS programs, by configuring the MS-DOS environment. I discuss this in the following sections.

Configuring the MS-DOS Environment

To maintain compatibility with as many old DOS programs as possible, NTVDM can be configured in several ways to mimic an older environment. You can configure NTVDM's memory and window options through a properties dialog box, and you can configure the virtual DOS environment itself through configuration files that mimic the old `CONFIG.SYS` and `AUTOEXEC.BAT` files. Here is how the default configuration works:

- By default, NTVDM gives the MS-DOS program as much regular and DOS Protected Mode Interface (DMPI) memory as it asks for. No Extended (XMS) or Expanded (EMS) memory is available unless you change the settings.

- NTVDM reads configuration options from `\windows\system32\config.nt` and executes the batch file `\windows\system32\autoexec.nt` before running the program. These files are installed along with Windows and contain important default settings that permit the use of high memory, networking, and emulated Sound Blaster sound hardware.

These settings should work for most MS-DOS programs. However, if you need specially tuned DOS environments for special applications, you might want to configure Windows shortcuts for these applications or at least create shortcuts that open custom-configured Command Prompt windows.

To create a customized MS-DOS environment, right-click the name of the MS-DOS program you want to run and select Properties. If you change any of the default properties and save the settings, Windows creates a file with the same name as the program file, but with extension `.PIF`. This PIF file holds the customized settings. It is listed in Explorer as a "Shortcut to MS-DOS Program." Use this shortcut to run the program. If you need to run a batch file before running the program, follow this same procedure, but create a shortcut to the batch file instead of the program. I cover this in the next section.

Note

You must use the shortcut to start the MS-DOS program to take advantage of any configuration changes you've made. If you run the EXE file directly, Windows does not know to look at the PIF (shortcut) file.

Window and Memory Options

The Properties dialog box for a MS-DOS application shortcut (PIF file) lets you set the virtual MS-DOS environment's memory display and mouse properties. To customize these properties, right-click the MS-DOS application file itself, or if you've already created customized properties, you can right-click the MS-DOS Application Shortcut icon and then select Properties.

Here are the most common settings to change:

- The working folder on the Program page
- The Extended Memory and Initial Environment options on the Memory page
- The Always Suspend option on the Misc page

In the next sections, I describe all the property pages in more detail so you can see what configuration options are available. The General, Security, Summary, and Backup pages (if they appear on your system) are the same as for any other Windows file, so I don't describe them here.

Program Settings

The Program tab displays a typical Shortcut property page and has the following settings (see Figure 12.1):

Figure 12.1   The MS-DOS Shortcut Program tab. The Advanced
button lets you specify a custom `config.nt` or `autoexec.nt` file.

- **Cmd Line**—The path to the MS-DOS program file or batch file and any additional command-line arguments you need. If you enter **?** on the command line, Windows prompts you for command-line arguments when you run the shortcut. Whatever you type is used in place of **?**.

- **Working**—The drive and folder to use as the initial working directory for the program. If you leave this field blank, the initial directory is the one containing the MS-DOS program. If several people use the shortcut, you might want to start the path with the string `%userprofile%` to represent the path to the current user's profile folder and specify the rest of the path relative to that.

- **Batch File**—Ostensibly, the name of a batch file to run before starting the program. As far as I can tell, however, this feature does work.

- **Shortcut Key**—Optional. Specifies a hotkey that is supposed to start the program. However, this feature does not appear to work either.

- **Run**—Selects the initial window size: Normal, Maximized, or Minimized (icon). Full Screen is different; see the screen settings.
- **Close on Exit**—If this option is checked, the window closes when the program exits. If this option is unchecked, the window remains open but inactive and the title includes the word Inactive. You should leave this checked in most cases.

Tip

If a DOS program fails to run, uncheck this box and try to run the program again. You then have time to read any error messages that appear.

The Program tab also lets you specify alternative configuration and startup batch files to use instead of CONFIG.NT and AUTOEXEC.NT. To change the configuration files associated with a shortcut, click the Advanced button and enter the paths and names of the desired files. The default values are %SystemRoot%\SYSTEM32\CONFIG.NT and %SystemRoot%\SYSTEM32\AUTOEXEC.NT. I describe the settings in these files shortly.

Tip

If your MS-DOS program has timing or speed problems, it might expect to change the settings of the PC's timer chips. If you click the Advanced button on the Program tab and check Compatible Timer Hardware Emulation, the problem might go away.

Font Settings

The Font tab lets you select the font used when the program is running in a window. The default setting, Auto, lets Windows resize the font as you resize the window, but you can specify a fixed size. If you do, the window is not resizable.

Tip

If you want to switch to a fixed font size, you can do it while the program is running. Right-click the upper-left corner of the program's window, select Properties, and view the Font tab. Make any desired changes and then select Save Properties for Future Windows with the Same Title when Windows offers you this option.

Memory Settings

The Memory tab, shown in Figure 12.2, lets you specify the type and amount of memory to make available to the MS-DOS program. The plethora of memory types came about as different ways of coping with the original PC's limited memory hardware options. Some programs can use any type of memory, but others specifically require access to XMS or EMS memory. Here's a list of the settings:

Figure 12.2   The Memory tab lets you make various
memory formats available to the DOS program.

- **Conventional Memory, Total**—The amount of memory between 0 and
  640KB. The Auto setting provides up to 640KB. You will probably never need to
  alter this setting.

- **Initial Environment**—The number of bytes to set aside for environment
  variables. Auto directs NTVDM to use the amount specified in the SHELL setting
  in CONFIG.NT. If you use complex batch files, you might want to increase this
  setting to 2,000 bytes or more.

- **Protected**—If checked, this option prevents the program from altering memory
  in the range occupied by the simulated MS-DOS system components. Check
  this box only if you experience unexplained crashes.

- **EMS Memory**—If your program requires EMS (paged) memory, set this to
  Auto or a fixed number.

- **XMS Memory**—If your program can use XMS expanded memory, set this to
  Auto or a fixed number.

- **Uses HMA**—This option normally has no effect because the High Memory
  Area is used by the simulated MS-DOS program.

- **DPMI Memory**—By default, this option is set to Auto. You can disable or
  permit a fixed amount of DPMI memory, if necessary.

Screen Settings

The screen settings let you determine whether the program has "direct" access to the whole screen at startup. These settings include the following:

- **Usage**—Lets you select between full-screen and window as the initial display mode. In full-screen mode, the MS-DOS program takes over the primary display and can display graphics.

- **Restore Settings at Startup**—If this option is checked, the most recently used window size and font is reused the next time you start the program. If you want to provide a consistent environment for multiple users, uncheck this box, make the appropriate initial settings, and then make the PIF file nonwritable by other users using file security settings.

- **Fast ROM Emulation**—When this option is checked, the Virtual DOS Machine emulates the graphics functions normally provided by the display adapter's built-in (read-only memory) BIOS program.

- **Dynamic Memory Allocation**—When this option is checked, Windows releases memory assigned to the virtual graphics display when the program switches from graphics to text display. If you get a blank screen when the program switches back, try unchecking this box.

When the MS-DOS program is running and attempts to change the display from text-based to graphical, Windows automatically switches to full-screen mode. You can manually switch back and forth between full-screen and window mode by pressing Alt+Enter. If the program is using a text display, you can continue using it in window mode. If it is displaying graphics, however, the program is suspended (frozen) and minimized unless it's in full-screen mode. Windows, unfortunately, can't display a little windowed version of the DOS graphical display.

Miscellaneous Settings

The Miscellaneous Settings tab determines how the program behaves when it's running in a window. Most of the settings are self-explanatory. The tab is shown in Figure 12.3. Here are the less obvious settings:

- **Always Suspend**—If this option is checked, the MS-DOS program is frozen when it's not the active window. Because MS-DOS programs didn't anticipate multitasking, they tend to burn lots of CPU time even when idle. Suspending the program when you're not using it makes your system more responsive. However, if you are running a communications or database program that needs to run while you do other things, uncheck this box.

Figure 12.3   The Miscellaneous Settings tab lets you
control the program's use of the mouse and keyboard.

- **Idle Sensitivity**—This is also related to the idle CPU issue. Windows tries to
  guess when the DOS program is just spinning its gears doing nothing and gives
  it a lower priority when it thinks this is the case. A high Idle Sensitivity setting
  means that Windows leans toward thinking the program is idle, resulting in snap-
  pier performance for other applications. A lower Idle Sensitivity setting makes
  Windows give the DOS application more time. The DOS application is better
  able to perform background (noninteractive) processing, while making your
  Windows applications more sluggish. Raise this setting if your DOS program
  makes everything else too slow or lower it if your DOS program can't get its job
  done. In the latter case, also uncheck Always Suspend.
- **Exclusive Mode**—Dedicates the mouse to the DOS program.
- **Fast Pasting**—Determines how quickly Windows stuffs simulated keystrokes
  into the MS-DOS programs when you paste in text from the Windows clipboard using Alt+space, Edit, Paste. If characters are lost when pasting, uncheck
  this option.

- **Windows Short Keys**—These check boxes let you determine which special keystrokes should be passed to Windows rather than to the MS-DOS programs. If your MS-DOS program needs key combinations such as Alt+Tab and Alt+Enter, you must uncheck the relevant boxes on this page. The DOS program will then get these keystrokes in full-screen mode or when its window is active, so be prepared to lose the corresponding Windows shortcut.

  It's especially tricky if you uncheck Alt+Enter and the program switches to full-screen mode. You will have to type Ctrl+Alt+Del to bring up the Task Manager if you want to switch back to the Windows desktop before the program exits.

Compatibility Settings

Windows' compatibility settings let you limit the capabilities of the virtual display adapter seen by the MS-DOS program. The relevant settings are Run in 256 Colors and Run in 640×480 Screen Resolution. If your MS-DOS program has problems displaying graphic screen, try checking these boxes.

CONFIG.NT

Just as MS-DOS used `CONFIG.SYS` to make initial memory allocations and to load device drivers, NTVDM uses `CONFIG.NT` to configure the virtual DOS environment.

The default `CONFIG.NT` file as installed by Windows is located in `\windows\system32` and contains several pages of comment text, which you might want to read. Here are the default settings in this file:

```
dos=high,umbdevice=%systemroot%\system32\himem.sys
files=40
```

You can edit `CONFIG.NT` to modify the defaults for all MS-DOS applications, or you can create alternative files using a different name for use with specific applications. In the latter case, use the Advanced button on the Program Settings properties page for the program's shortcut to enter the alternative filename. I use the name `CONFIG.NT` in the discussion that follows to refer to any config file.

> **Note**
> If you use MS-DOS database applications, you probably want to increase the `FILES=` setting in `CONFIG.NT` to `100` or more. You might also want to add the ANSI cursor control module with the line
>
>   device = %systemroot%\system32\ansi.sys
>
> Otherwise, you rarely need to change these settings.

The full set of options for `CONFIG.NT` is provided in Reference Listing 12.1.

REFERENCE LIST 12.1   `Config.NT` **Settings**

COUNTRY=*xxx*[,[*yyy*][, [*path*]]*filename*]

Tells MS-DOS to use an alternative character set and date/time format. *xxx* is a country/region code, *yyy* is an optional code page designator, and *filename* designates an optional driver containing country code information. If you use the virtual MS-DOS environment outside the United States, view the Help and Support Center and search for "country."

DEVICE=[*path*\]*filename* [*parameters*]

Loads a device driver. Hardware device drivers almost certainly do *not* work in Windows, but certain software services implemented as drivers do. Examples include `himem.sys`, which is required to let MS-DOS programs access memory above 640KB, and `ansi.sys`, which interprets character sequences that some DOS programs use to control the cursor. These drivers are located in folder `%systemroot%\system32`.

DEVICEHIGH=[*path*\]*filename* [*parameters*]
or
DEVICEHIGH [**SIZE**=*xx*] [*path*\]*filename* [*parameters*]

Similar to *device* but attempts to load the device driver into upper memory blocks, leaving more conventional memory for MS-DOS applications. If there is insufficient room in upper memory or if the device `himem.sys` has not been loaded, the driver is loaded into conventional memory. The alternative `size=`*xx* format lets you specify the number of bytes of high memory that must be free; *xx* must be specified in hexadecimal.

DOS=[**HIGH**|**LOW**][, **UMB**|**NOUMB**]

`DOS=HIGH` specifies that MS-DOS should move parts of itself into the high memory area (the first 64KB past 1MB). The default is `LOW`, where DOS resides entirely in conventional memory. The optional keyword `UMB` indicates that DOS should make upper memory area blocks (the memory beyond 1MB+64KB) available for DOS, devices, and programs.

DOSONLY

If this keyword is present in `CONFIG.NT`, `COMMAND.COM` is only permitted to run MS-DOS programs. Normally, if you type the name of a Windows program at its command prompt or in a batch file, it runs the Windows program in a separate environment. This might disrupt some DOS terminate-and-stay-resident (TSR) programs, so the `DOSONLY` option lets you prevent this from happening.

ECHOCONFIG

If the command `ECHOCONFIG` appears, `CONFIG.NT` commands are echoed to the Command Prompt window while NTVDM is initializing. The default is for the commands not to be displayed.

FCBS=_n_

File Control Blocks (FCBs) are an archaic structure used by DOS version 1.0 programs to manage files. Few, if any, surviving MS-DOS programs require FCBs, but if you have one, you can use the FCBS statement to instruct NTVDM to allocate space for _n_ of them. (At this late date, if you do need them, you already know it, as you have had to deal with this on every prior version of DOS and Windows.)

FILES=_n_

Sets the maximum number of concurrently open files available to MS-DOS applications. The default value is 20. You might want to increase this number to 100 or more if you use database applications such as MS-DOS FoxPro.

INSTALL=[path\]_filename_ [_parameters_]

Loads a TSR into memory prior to running AUTOEXEC.NT.

One program that you might need to install in AUTOEXEC.NT is setver.exe. Setver intercepts programs' requests to find out what version of DOS is running, and it lies to them. Its purpose is to let you run programs that would otherwise be unhappy to find that they're running on DOS version 5.0, which is what NTVDM would tell them. If your MS-DOS application complains about the DOS version number, open the Help and Support Center and search for "setver."

NTCMDPROMPT

By default, when an MS-DOS program is run from the command line or a batch file and exits, CMD runs COMMAND.COM to handle all further commands. This makes it possible to run old MS-DOS batch files. If you specify NTCMDPROMPT in CONFIG.NT, CMD does not run COMMAND.COM but remains in control between MS-DOS programs. This lets you write modern batch files to use with MS-DOS programs.

SHELL=[path\]_filename_ [_parameters_]

Specifies an alternative shell program to use if you do not want to use COMMAND.COM as the MS-DOS shell. You can also use this command to specify COMMAND.COM with startup options. For example, the entry

```
shell=%systemroot%\system32\command.com /E:2048/P
```

requests 2048 bytes for environment variables. The /P option is required to prevent COMMAND.COM from exiting after processing one command.

STACKS=_n_,_s_

When a hardware interrupt occurs, NTVDM needs "memory stack" space to temporarily store information for the interrupt handler. The stacks option lets you instruct NTVDM to allocate separate stack space for interrupt handlers. The numbers _n_ and _s_ instruct NTVDM to allocate _n_ blocks of _s_ bytes each. _n_ can be 0 or 8 through 64. _s_ can be 0 or 32 through 512. The default values are 9 and 128, respectively. If necessary, you can save memory for program use by specifying `stacks=0,0`; this might or might not cause a program crash. You can specify `stacks=8,512` to allocate plenty of stack space if you suspect that interrupt handlers are causing DOS crashes.

SWITCHES=/K

Makes MS-DOS programs treat the keyboard as a "conventional" 96-key keyboard even if it uses the extended 102+ key layout. If you use this switch and also load `ansi.sys`, specify `/k` after `ansi.sys`.

The following items are permitted in `CONFIG.NT` for compatibility with historical `CONFIG.SYS` settings but have no effect in Windows:

- `buffers`
- `driveparm`
- `lastdrive` (`lastdrive` is always `Z`)

AUTOEXEC.NT

`AUTOEXEC.NT` serves the same purpose `AUTOEXEC.BAT` did on MS-DOS systems: It is a batch file that lets you run programs that set up the command environment before you begin working. The default version of `AUTOEXEC.NT` installed with Windows is located in `\windows\system32` and contains the following commands:

```
lh %SystemRoot%\system32\mscdexnt.exe
lh %SystemRoot%\system32\redir
lh %SystemRoot%\system32\dosx
SET BLASTER=A220 I5 D1 P330 T3
```

MSCDEXNT provides support for CD-ROM drives, REDIR is the network interface, DOSX provides upper-memory support (it serves the same purpose `EMM386.EXE` did on MS-DOS), and the `SET` command provides DOS programs with information about the simulated Sound Blaster sound hardware. No matter what kind of sound system your computer has, MS-DOS programs "see" a Sound Blaster–compatible card (although the emulation is less than perfect).

In addition, if you've installed the Client for Novell Networks, `AUTOEXEC.NT` also runs `nw16.exe` and `vwipxspx.exe`, which gives DOS applications access to the Novell application programming interface (API).

You can load other programs and set environment variables in `AUTOEXEC.NT`, but remember that they are loaded every time you run an MS-DOS program. If you need particular TSR programs only for some MS-DOS applications, set up a customized AUTOEXEC file just for those applications.

Tip

If you used DOSKEY under MS-DOS, you might have been pleased to see that DOSKEY is provided with Windows. However, this version works with cmd.exe only and does *not* work inside the emulated DOS environment, so it's not useful to add it to AUTOEXEC.NT.

MS-DOS Environment Variables

In MS-DOS, memory is a limited resource, and MS-DOS is particularly stingy with environment variable space. If you need to define more than a dozen or so environment variables in any MS-DOS–style batch files, you probably need to extend the amount of space allocated to environment variables either on the Properties dialog box of an associated shortcut or in a shell= command in a CONFIG.NT file. These techniques were described earlier in the chapter.

When you first start an MS-DOS program or COMMAND.COM, NTVDM inherits the default Windows environment, but with the following changes:

- All variable names are changed to uppercase. MS-DOS programs do not expect to find lowercase letters in environment variable names.
- The COMSPEC variable is added, which contains the path and filename of the command shell (usually COMMAND.COM).
- The TEMP and TMP variables are reset to the system default, rather than the user-specific setting.
- Path names in all environment variables are changed to use DOS-compatible 8.3-character names.

MS-DOS and Networking

In the days of MS-DOS, networking was an expensive and fairly uncommon option. Networking software for DOS was bulky, balky, and an afterthought to boot. Microsoft's networking product required you to load hardware-specific device drivers, followed by programs that managed network protocols, followed finally by a software layer that provided file services to DOS.

One lucky result of this was that MS-DOS application programs never dealt with network hardware directly; they let DOS and its underlying network layers take care of the details. The NTVDM environment supplies the same services through the redir.exe program that is loaded in AUTOEXEC.NT, so MS-DOS programs can use today's fast, inexpensive networks.

Note

If you create custom AUTOEXEC files and want your DOS applications to use networking, you must load `redire.exe` in your custom files just as it's loaded in `AUTOEXEC.NT`.

DOS programs, however, usually are not designed to handle Universal Naming Convention (UNC) network format filenames—that is, filenames such as `\\myserver\officefiles\march\plans.doc`. If you want to access network files from MS-DOS applications, you have to map a drive letter to connect to the network folder and then have the MS-DOS program use that drive letter for file access.

You can map drive letters with Windows Explorer using the Tools, Map Network Drive menu, or you can map drive letters from the command prompt using the `net use` command. I talk about `net use` in Chapter 13, "Command-Line Utilities."

Note

DOS applications do not expect to see computer names or folder and printer share names longer than eight letters. You have to be careful to use short names when you configure your network if you want any network-aware MS-DOS applications to see the shared resources.

Printing from MS-DOS

MS-DOS applications ran in an environment where there was no competition for computer hardware. Only one program ran at a time, so it was acceptable for a program to send data directly to printer hardware. On Windows, because many programs can run at once, the operating system must mediate between programs and resources.

NTVDM takes care of this discrepancy by providing "virtual" LPT printer ports to MS-DOS applications. When an MS-DOS application issues instructions that would send data to a printer, NTVDM intercepts the instructions and instead sends the data to the Windows spooler so that output from the MS-DOS program and other concurrent Windows applications aren't mixed together. If you look at the printer queue while a DOS application is printing, you see these print jobs labeled as `Remote Downlevel Document`.

Because DOS programs were completely responsible for managing the attached printers, Windows spools output from MS-DOS in "raw" mode, meaning the output is sent to the printer verbatim. This can include text, control sequences, and graphics commands. If the MS-DOS printer uses control sequences for the wrong printer model, you get some strange printouts. But, it was this way back in the old days as well.

For local printers that are connected to hardware port LPT1, LPT2, or LPT3, you might instruct your MS-DOS programs to use the port directly.

Print Redirection

If you need to use network printers or printers connected to USB ports, it's another matter. MS-DOS programs have no idea what USB is and, with few exceptions (WordPerfect being one of them), DOS programs didn't provide for explicit connections to remote printers either.

However, you can work around this by mapping LPT ports to shared printers using the `net use` command. Just as you can map drive letters to shared folders, you can map printer ports to shared printers. I discuss the `net use` command in more detail in Chapter 13, but here are some specific tips for using this command to set up printing for MS-DOS applications:

- There is no law that says that you can only use printers shared by *other* computers. If you want to use a USB-based printer on your own computer, you can share it and use a `net use` command to map it to a virtual LPT port. Your MS-DOS applications will then able to send information to the printer.

- You must map shared printers to LPT ports that are *not* actually in use on your computer. For example, if you have a printer connected to LPT1, you cannot map a network printer to LPT1.

- You are not necessarily limited to LPT1, LPT2, and LPT3. You can map shared printers to devices LPT1 up to LPT9. Some MS-DOS programs accepts these larger numbers; some don't. You have to experiment.

The basic `net use` command to map a printer looks like this:

```
net use lpt3: \\server\printname
```

Here's the command to undo a mapping:

```
net use lpt3: /d
```

For more details, see Chapter 13.

Print Screen

On Windows, the Print Screen function does not work as it did in the real MS-DOS. When an MS-DOS program is running in window mode, the Prt Scr key works just as it normally does in Windows; it copies a bitmap picture of the screen or current window to the Clipboard. In full-screen mode, the Prt Scr key doesn't send the screen to the printer. Instead, it copies the screen's *text* to the Clipboard. To print it, you need to paste the text or bitmap into a document and print it as a separate step.

Configuring Serial Communications with MS-DOS

The NTVDM environment tries to make the computer's COM ports available to MS-DOS programs through a bag of virtual hardware tricks. NTVDM captures attempts by the DOS program to issue instructions to the serial port's hardware, and from the pattern of commands, determines what the program is trying to do. It then performs these actions through the Windows programming interface.

DOS-based serial communication software uses direct hardware control and interrupt drivers that receives information directly from the hardware when information arrives from the modem or other remote serial device. NTVDM simulates these hardware interrupts *fairly* successfully. Some DOS-based serial communications programs work under Windows, although some don't.

This can be a point of difficulty for businesses upgrading communications, remote access, and remote support systems from DOS and older versions of Windows. If your software doesn't work under Windows, there is unfortunately nothing you can do to improve the situation. If your old application does not function correctly, you have to dual-boot your computer between Windows and DOS, revert to Windows Me or 98, or develop new software.

Using Special-Purpose Devices for MS-DOS

NTVDM provides limited hardware support for MS-DOS applications. As mentioned, it intercepts and simulates interaction with LPT parallel ports, COM serial ports, the keyboard, and the video display. It provides DOS-mediated network and file access, and it provides a mouse driver and fools MS-DOS programs into thinking that there is Sound Blaster–compatible hardware, if your system has any sort of sound support. But that's the end of the virtual hardware support.

If you depend on access to special-purpose hardware, either through direct control or through device drives, you are probably out of luck. If your program attempts to access any other hardware devices, NTVDM either stops the program dead in its tracks or, at best, prevents the hardware access from occurring.

If you depend on custom hardware and can't afford to develop a proper Windows-based device driver for it, there *is* one thing you can try. I can't vouch for it, and I must warn you that it could severely compromise the integrity of your Windows system. My attorneys insist that I tell you this is completely *at your own risk*, but here it is: There is a way to open a "window" in the Windows barrier between user programs and the system hardware. It lets you issue INP and OUT instructions to a range of physical I/O ports. You can find software to do this at www.beyondlogic.org/porttalk/porttalk.htm. With the device's physical ports made available, you can communicate with the device. However, interrupts and DMA do not work, and this technique only works on a 32-bit Windows system. Again, this is a last-resort option. It is better to invest in developing a proper Windows device driver.

Managing MS-DOS Programs

You can use MS-DOS applications as you always did. However, whereas the old programs think they're back in 1985, you're not, and there are a few points to remember:

- MS-DOS programs can't deal with long file or folder names. You have to use the so-called "8.3" filenames that Windows provides just for this purpose. You might have seen these mangled names before. They look like this:
  `C:\PROGRA~1\MICROS~1`.

  For files that you use *only* with DOS applications, you should use only short file and folder names that don't need to be mangled. For example, you can create folders such as `C:\offdocs`, instead of `C:\office documents` and filenames such as `feblist.doc` instead of `february resource lists.doc`.

- If you need to find the mangled name of an existing file or folder, use the `dir` command-line command with the `/x` option. This displays the short version along with the full name.

- The mouse should work if the program is mouse-aware. If your mouse simply highlights blocks of text on the screen instead of controlling the application, right-click the window's title bar, select Properties, view the Options tab, and uncheck Quick Edit.

- For programs that are not designed for use with the mouse, you can use the Quick Edit feature to copy text from the screen, and you can paste text to the DOS application with the shortcut Alt+space, E, P.

When Things Go Awry

As mentioned earlier, when you run MS-DOS programs under Windows, as far as Windows is concerned, the actual application in use is called `ntvdm.exe`. Even though the application is running in a simulated MS-DOS world, NTVDM intercepts the usual Windows key combinations that control window behavior: Alt+space opens the system menu, and so on. In addition, Ctrl+C or Ctrl+Break usually terminate a DOS application, although some programs have special exit key sequences.

As mentioned earlier, you can disable the Windows keyboard functions if these keystrokes are needed by the DOS application. This will make you rely more on the mouse to manage the application window, but it's a small price to pay.

If you need to terminate an MS-DOS application that's run amok, you are pleasantly surprised that the Reset button probably does not have to be used. In most cases, you can click the Close button on the application's window. After a few seconds, Windows ask whether you want to terminate the application. If you click Yes, it's summarily dispatched and the problem is solved. (Of course, if you haven't saved your data, you lose it, and there's a chance that the application has corrupted one or more of its data files, but this is also the case under MS-DOS.)

You can also use the Windows Task Manager to remove unruly DOS applications. This might be necessary if you are running a DOS application in full-screen mode and cannot return to the Windows desktop with Alt+Enter. In this case, you should do what you would have done under MS-DOS: Press Ctrl+Alt+Del. Instead of rebooting the computer, however, this switches you out of full-screen mode and displays the Windows Task Manager.

If you're happy enough to let the DOS program keep running, you can just press Esc to dismiss the Task Manager.

If you need to kill the DOS application, you have two choices: If the task is clearly identifiable on the Applications tab, you can select the task name and click End Task. After a few seconds, you can terminate the program.

However, the window title might not reflect the name of the current DOS application. It's more likely to say "Command Prompt - command" or just "Command Prompt." If you have several MS-DOS applications open, you might have a hard time finding the right one to terminate. I suggest closing the applications that are still responding to narrow the choices. You can also use the Processes tab, look for `ntvdm.exe`, and terminate this task.

13

Command-Line Utilities

IN THIS CHAPTER

- More than 250 command-line programs are provided with Windows 7, up from about 150 provided with Windows XP.

- You can get some jobs done more quickly with a command-line utility than with a Graphical User Interface (GUI) program.

- This chapter covers the most important command-line programs—the ones you really need to know how to use.

- Windows has a tool that lets you create simple installation programs to distribute your own programs and scripts—if you know where to find it.

Windows Command-Line Programs

Hundreds of executable programs are installed along with Windows; some of these are familiar, standard Windows programs such as Notebook, Windows Media Player, Solitaire, and Internet Explorer. Many are system service programs that we never interact with directly. However, it might surprise you as much as it did me to find that over one-third of them are command-line programs. The operating system is called *Windows*, after all, not *Prompts*, so what's with all these command-line programs?

It turns out that the command-line programs fall into three general categories:

- **Maintenance and administrative programs**—These have graphical equivalents. The command-line versions enable you to perform maintenance operations with batch files and scripts. Also, it's sometimes easier to type a command line with filenames and wildcards than it is to poke at individual files with Explorer.

- **Batch file and command-line tools**—These programs include cmd, more, and findstr and are useful when creating and using batch files, when working with text files, and when navigating through the command-line environment.

- **TCP/IP networking tools and utilities**—These are mostly inherited from the Unix operating system, where today's Internet grew up. These utilities are used to manage Windows networking and to interoperate with Unix systems.

All the command-line programs are listed in Appendix C, "Command Line Program Reference," which starts on page 735. You might want to take a look at that listing to get a feel for the type of programs available.

So, how do you use these programs? As I've mentioned before, many command-line programs are self-documenting; you can type the command name followed by **/?** or type **help *commandname*** at the command prompt to see the program's description, syntax, and sample uses. Many are also written in the Windows Help and Support Center. Therefore, it doesn't make a lot of sense for me to reproduce all that information in this book.

Instead, I'm going to focus on describing what I consider the essential command-line programs—the ones that give you the biggest boost in productivity and power as you use and manage Windows XP.

The Essential Command Line

Besides the built-in commands that are part of the CMD shell (discussed in Chapter 10, "The CMD Command-Line"), about 20 other command-line programs come in handy on a day-to-day basis. They fall into five categories:

- **Graphical User Interface (GUI) shortcuts**—Standard Windows programs that you can activate just by typing their names: `calc`, `control`, `mmc`, `notepad`, and `regedit`. The `start` command is also useful.

- **General-purpose shell programs**—Utilities to simplify life on the command line: `findstr`, `more`, `tree`, and `xcopy`.

- **File-management tools**—Programs that manage file permissions and access controls: `attrib` and `cacls`. (`cacls`, by the way, is the only tool available that lets you manage file permissions on NT File System (NTFS)-formatted disks under Windows XP Home Edition without booting it up in Safe Mode.)

- **Management power tools**—Programs that control Windows as well as its services and applications: `driverquery`, `runas`, `sc`, `tasklist`, and `taskkill`.

- **Networking utilities**—Tools for using and managing Windows Networking in general and TCP/IP networks in particular: `ipconfig`, `net`, `netstat`, `nslookup`, `ping`, and `tracert`.

I describe these programs in this chapter.

GUI Shortcuts

The first set of essential command-line programs aren't actually command-line programs at all—they're standard Windows GUI programs. However, I've added them here to illustrate an important point: If you enter the name of a GUI program file on the command line, Windows runs the program in the normal way. So, when you're working at the command prompt, if you know a GUI program by name, you can spare yourself a lot of poking around on the Start menu or Control Panel. Seven commands that you may find beneficial to know are listed here:

- **calc**—Runs the Windows Calculator accessory.
- **control**—Opens the Control Panel. I discuss this command in more detail in moment.
- **mmc**—Opens the Microsoft Management Console (MMC). From the MMC menu, you can click File, Add/Remove Snap-In to add any MMC tool that you like to use.

  On Windows 7 and Vista, you can type the name of a MMC plug-in as a command and it opens. For example, type **compmgmt** to open the Computer Management console. On XP, you have to type **start** *plugin*.**msc**—for example, **start compmgmt.msc**.

- **notepad**—Runs Windows Notepad. To edit a particular file, type the file's name after **notepad**.
- **regedit**—Runs the Registry Editor, which is not normally found on the Start menu.
- **start**—Followed by the name of a file, this command launches the associated application and opens the file. For example, **start somefile.xls** launches Microsoft Excel and opens **somefile.xls**. For many registered programs, **start** *programname* runs the program even if the program file isn't in the search path. For example, **start excel** and **start winword** open Excel and Word, respectively.

  If the filename you are opening contains a space, insert **""** before the name and put the name in quotation marks. For example, **start "" "some file.doc"**.

You might find that you often want to run other GUI programs while working at the command prompt. If you hate taking your hands off the keyboard to use the mouse, just find the program's name and you can run it directly.

Tip

To find the name of a Windows program file, right-click the program's menu entry or shortcut. Select Properties, and then look at the Target field on the Shortcut properties page.

The Control Panel is actually a "shell" program, much like MMC. The actual work is done by plug-in programs or *applets* called CPL files. If you know the name of a plug-in, you can enter its name on the command line after the `control` command and jump directly to the desired Control Panel applet. If you want to access the Control Panel from the command line, it's enough to type **control** and use the GUI from there. However, if you want to run a particular control applet from a batch file, script, or shortcut, this is a great way to make the user's job easier.

The standard Control Panel applets are listed in Table 13.1. Some CPL files contain more than one applet. In these cases, you can specify which to run by adding more words after the name of the CPL file.

Table 13.1   **Control Panel Applets**

Command **Arguments**	**Control Panel Applet Displayed**
access.cpl	Accessibility Options (XP Only)
appwiz.cpl	Add/Remove Programs
collab.cpl	People Near Me (Win7/Vista only)
desk.cpl	Display Properties
firewall.cpl	Windows Firewall
fonts	Fonts Folder
hdwwiz.cpl	Add Hardware Wizard
inetcpl.cpl	Internet Properties (used by Internet Explorer and Outlook Express)
Intl.cpl	Regional and Language Options
Joy.cpl	Game Controllers
main.cpl	Mouse Properties
main.cpl keyboard	Keyboard Properties
main.cpl pc card	PCMCIA Card Properties (XP Only)
mmsys.cpl	Sounds and Audio Devices
ncpa.cpl	Network Connections
nusrmgr.cpl	User Accounts
odbccp32.cpl	ODBC Data Source Administrator
powercfg.cpl	Power Options
sysdm.cpl	System Properties
tabletpc.cpl	Pen and Touch
telephon.cpl	Phone and Modem Options
timedate.cpl	Date and Time Properties
wscui.cpl	Action Center (Windows 7 and Vista only)

For example, you can open the Network Connections Control Panel directly by typing

```
control ncpa.cpl
```

on the command line, in a shortcut, in the Start menu's Run dialog, or in a batch file.

> **Note**
>
> To make setting changes that are restricted to Computer Administrators, you need to issue the command from an elevated (privileged) command prompt window. For more information, see "Opening a Command Prompt Window with Administrator Privileges," on page 436.
>
> In addition, on Windows XP, the `control` command does not work for the Network Connections control panel `ncpa.cpl` and other applets based on Windows Explorer unless you first instruct Windows to use a separate instance of explorer.exe for each Explorer window. To do this, open Windows Explorer; click Tools, Folder Options, View; and check Launch Folder Windows in Separate Processes.
>
> If your user account is not a Computer Administrator account and you have to use `runas` to open an Administrator command prompt window, you need to make that Separate Processes setting change while actually logged on to the Computer Administrator account you are using.

> **Tip**
>
> You don't have to open a Command Prompt window to run a command-line program. Just type [window key]+R and the Run dialog box pops up. Then, type in your command line and press Enter. If the command requires elevated privileges, though, you have to open an elevated command prompt first, as discussed under "Opening a Command Prompt Window with Administrator Privileges" on page 436.

General-Purpose Shell Programs

At the command prompt, you find yourself using the built-in commands, such as `pushd`, `cd`, and `dir`, quite frequently. There are four other programs you should know about: `findstr`, `more`, `tree`, and `xcopy`. These are useful in many situations—to examine the contents of text, script, and batch files; to examine directories; and to copy files.

findstr

`findstr` is an enhanced version of the old text-searching program `find`. In its basic form, `findstr` scans one or more files, or the standard input, for text strings and prints those lines that contain the desired string. This is handy when you know what you're looking for but can't remember what file contains it or to extract and condense specific information from files. It's especially helpful in batch files that gather information from programs that generate more text than you need; `findstr` can help you automatically cull the information.

In its most basic usage, `findstr` prints any lines that contain the string or strings specified on its command line. For example, suppose I have a file named `afile` with this text inside:

```
Now is the time for
all good men to
come to the aid of their party.
The rain in Spain falls
mainly in the plain.
```

The command `findstr "to all" afile` prints the following text:

```
all good men to
come to the aid of their party.
```

It found both `to` and `all` on the first line and `to` on the second. The words on the command line can be specified in any order, and they don't have to be complete words: `findstr "a"` extracts any input lines that contain the letter *a*.

To find a string that contains spaces, you must use the `/c` option and put the string in quotes, like this: `findstr /c:"in Spain"`. You may also want to add the `/i` option to make the search case-insensitive.

You can search multiple files by specifying them at the end of the command line. Here's an example:

```
findstr "to all" afile *.txt d:\input\*.txt
```

`findstr` is a filter, which means that if you don't name any files on its command line, it reads from the standard input and always writes its results to the standard output. You can use `findstr` to find any files with the uppercase letters *FOR* in their name by using a command such as this:

```
dir | findstr "FOR"
```

Also, you can direct the output of the `findstr` command to a file or another program by using the > or | symbol.

Tip

In batch files, `findstr` can be especially useful with the extended `for /f` command, which can parse the output of a command, as discussed in Chapter 10. For example, you can write a command such as this:

```
for /f "usebackq" %%n in (`someprogram | findstr "text"`) do (
    somecommand %%n
)
```

This command runs a program named `someprogram` and filters the output through `findstr`. The first token on each output line is passed to `somecommand`.

`findstr` has many options, which you can view by typing `findstr /?` on the command line. I don't list them all here, but I discuss several of the most useful ones.

Case-Insensitive Searching

You can specify /I before the search pattern to have findstr ignore uppercase/lowercase when matching strings. You will find that you need /I more often than not. For example,

```
dir | findstr /i "for"
```

prints the name of any file containing *for*, *FOR*, or *foR*, or any other combination of upper- or lowercase.

Literal String Matching

As mentioned earlier, if you specify several words on the findstr command line, it searches for any of the words. You can instruct findstr to search for an exact string, including spaces, with the /C option. Using the sample input afile listed earlier, the command

```
find str /i /C:"the rain" afile
```

prints just the line, "The rain in Spain falls."

Positional Searching

The options /B and /E instruct findstr to look for the desired search text only at the very beginning or end of each text line, respectively.

Searching Multiple Files

To search more than one file, you can specify more than one filename on findstr's command line. In this case, when findstr finds a matching text line, it precedes each output line with the name of the file in which it found the text. When it's displaying this directly to the Command Prompt window, it highlights the filename in a brighter color. The output might look like this:

```
C:\book\14>findstr "text" *.txt
a.txt:this is more text
b.txt:this is a text file
c.txt:when entering text
```

You can instruct findstr to search the specified files and any subdirectories of the paths you specify by adding the /S option. Here's an example:

```
findstr /s "text" c:\book\*.txt
```

You can also tell findstr to look in a file for a list of files to search by using /G:*filename*. For example, the command findstr /I /F:filelist "computer" opens the file named filelist. It's assumed that each line of this file is the name of a file to be searched. findstr looks into each of these files for the word *computer*. Also, /F:/

instructs `filelist` to read the list of files from the standard input. For example, the command

```
dir /od /b *.log | findstr /F:/ "Administrator"
```

uses `dir` to create a list of `.log` filenames in date order. `Findstr` then searches these files for the word *Administrator*.

Getting Extra Information

Several `findstr` options add or remove information from the output line. These options are listed here:

Option	Output
/V	Prints lines that do *not* match
/N	Prints line numbers before each line
/M	Prints only names of files that contain a match
/O	Prints the character offset to each matching line
/P	Skips files with nonprinting (binary) characters

Matching Text with Wildcards

The most powerful feature of `findstr` is its capability to match text using wildcards, or more precisely *regular expressions*, which lets you specify how to match strings with variable information.

Regular expressions are composed of characters to be matched, plus special items that describe how the matching string can vary. The special regular expression items are listed in Table 13.2.

Table 13.2 **Special Items for Regular Expressions**

Item	Matches
. (period)	Any one character.
*	Zero or more occurrences of the previous item.
^	The beginning of the line.
$	The end of the line.
[*xyz*]	Any of the characters listed inside the brackets. The list can contain individual letters and/or ranges of letters. For example, [A-Za-z] matches the letters *A* through *Z* and *a* through *z*.
[^*xyz*]	Anything *but* the characters in set *xyz*.
\<	The beginning of a word.
\>	The end of a word.
x	Literal character *x*, usually used with *, ., and so on.

If you haven't encountered these before, regular expressions take some getting used to. To start with, forget about the asterisk (*) as you remember it from its use with DOS wildcards, as in del *.txt. In regular expressions, * indicates that the search character or expression that comes *before* it is both optional and repeatable. For example, ab*c matches ac, abc, abbc, abbbc, and so on, but not abxyzc because this search pattern looks for a, followed by zero or more b's, followed by c.

In regular expressions, the period (.) is the wildcard character. A single period matches exactly one character, any character. For example, a.c matches axc, a-c, and a c— even a space counts as a character. Join . with *, and you now have the DOS-type wildcard: a.*c matches ac, axc, a123c, and so on. In other words, it matches anything starting with *a* and ending with *c*.

> **Note**
>
> findstr interprets the following special characters as regular expression operators by default:
>
>   . * ^ $ [ ] \
>
> If you want to search for a string with these characters but don't want to use regular expressions, you can either precede the special characters with a backslash (\ *, \ ^, \ \, and so on) or use the /L option to tell findstr to be "literal."

As an example of how powerful regular expressions can be, suppose we want to extract from a file (or a program's output) all lines that begin with a date. We could use this search:

```
findstr "^[0-9][0-9]/[0-9][0-9]/[0-9][0-9]*" filename
```

The first character, ^, anchors the search to the beginning of each input line; dates that don't start in column 1 aren't matched. Then, the pattern matches lines starting with dates such as 12/03/02 as well as 12/03/2002.

As another example, suppose you are stuck on the morning's crossword puzzle and want to find all five-letter words starting with the letter *A* and ending with the letter *E*. You could use this:

```
findstr /i "\<a[a-z][a-z][a-z]e\>" dictionary.txt
```

If you are sure that the file contains no spaces, you could also write the following:

```
findstr /i "a...e" dictionary.txt
```

With spaces in the input file, however, this pattern might match something such as "the area I entered," which is not what you are after.

Note

Regular expressions are powerful pattern-matching tools. If you haven't run into them before, search www.google.com for "regular expressions" to read more about them. Beware, though: They come in many flavors. `findstr`'s version is fairly limited and is missing ?, +, ( ), and other operators to which Unix users are accustomed.

`more`

I briefly mentioned `more` in Chapter 10, but it has some extra options and functions that I want to describe in more detail. Here's its full set of command line options:

`more` [/E [/C] [/P] [/S] [/Tn] [+n]] [filename...]

With no extra arguments, `more` displays the standard input or the named files a page at a time. If you use the /E option, `more` gains some extra capabilities that can be handy. After /E, you can add any of the following options:

Option	Description
/C	Clears the screen before displaying text.
/P	Expands formfeed characters into blank lines.
/S	Squeeze. Displays multiple blank lines as a single blank line.
/Tn	Sets tab stops at every *n* spaces. The default is 8.
+n	Starts displaying the file at line number *n*, skipping lines 1 through *n*–1.

If you find that you use any of these all the time, you can put them into an environment variable named MORE to make them the default settings. For example,

```
set MORE=/E /C /P /S
```

in your logon script, or similar settings made in the System Properties' Environment Variables dialog box, make the /E, /C, /P, and /S options active by default.

As cool as `more` is, it can't scroll backward through the file. For this reason, I sometimes find that the Notepad accessory makes a better text viewer. To turn Notepad into a command-line filter, I wrote the following batch file, named `view.bat`, which is in a folder that's in my standard search path:

```
@rem                                              Example File view.bat
@echo off
if "%1" == "" (
    rem --- save standard input to temp file and display it
    more >C:\temp\view.tmp
```

```
        notepad C:\temp\view.tmp
        del C:\temp\view.tmp
) else (
        rem --- open file(s) with notepad
        for %%f in (%*) do start notepad %%f
)
```

→ To learn more about the search path, see "Creating and Using Batch Files," **p. 492.**

If this batch file is given the name of one or more files on its command line, it displays the files with Notepad. Otherwise, it acts as a filter—it uses more to save the standard input to a temporary file, and then displays the temporary file with Notepad. Therefore, you can enter a command like this:

```
dir c:\windows\system32 | view
```

It's a nice marriage of the GUI and command-line worlds.

(It might seem odd to use more this way. When its output is directed to a file rather than the console window, it doesn't perform its paging duties but rather just copies the standard input through to the output. It's the only standard Windows utility that can do this, so it's the only way to create a batch file filter.)

tree

tree is a nifty, simple command-line tool that answers the question, What subdirectories are inside this folder? You often wonder this as you poke around in the command-line environment.

If I type tree at the command prompt, the output looks like this:

```
C:.
├───batch files
├───figures
│   ├───line
│   └───screen
├───review
└───scripts
```

Using text-based graphics, this shows that the current directory has four subdirectories: batch files, figures, review, and scripts. Also, figures has two subdirectories of its own (line and screen).

You can specify a starting drive and path on the command line, if you want to view another directory, and you can add the /F option, which makes tree list filenames and folders.

Tip

In directories with many subdirectories, the output of `tree` can be confusing and might scroll off the screen. If this happens, I have another useful batch file for you. It's called `e.bat`, and it has only two lines:

```
@rem                                                      Example file
e.bat
@echo off
if "%1" == "" (explorer /e,.) else explorer /e,"%1"
```

This batch file fires up Windows Explorer with the current directory selected in the Folder view. If you get lost at the command prompt, just type **e** and press Enter to get the GUI view. Problem solved in two keystrokes! (As you might have guessed by now, I'm somewhat impatient.)

xcopy

If you need to copy a large group of files, xcopy is the tool of choice. Granted, you can click files and folders with Windows Explorer and drag them around on the screen, and that's fine when you only want to do it once, but sometimes the command-line method is much more sensible. Here are some examples:

- If you want to copy the same set of files repeatedly, or on a scheduled basis, creating a batch file that uses xcopy lets you set the process up once and use it as many times as necessary.

- If you want to maintain a backup copy of files and folders in the most efficient way possible, xcopy can automatically copy only changed files to minimize the amount of time required and the amount of data moved.

xcopy is similar to its simpler cousin copy. In the most basic usage, you type xcopy *from to*, where *from* is the name of the file or folder you want to copy and *to* is the location in which you want to make the copy. However, xcopy has a staggering number of command-line options—27 in all—that can make it do several more interesting things. I describe them all here, but several "save the forest" groups are already staging protests outside my office as it is (notwithstanding the fact that I'm a member). So, I just describe some useful xcopy applications. You can see the full list by typing xcopy /? | more at the command prompt, or you can open the Help and Support Center and search for xcopy.

Copying Subdirectories

If you add the /S option, xcopy copies all subfolders as well, recursively, except for empty subfolders. The /E option copies even empty folders, thus retaining the exact directory structure of the original. If you use either of these options, you should also use the /I option to indicate the destination name is a folder, not a filename. For example,

```
xcopy c:\book e:\book /E /I
```

copies the directory C:\book and all files and folders within it to drive E:.

Making Backups

You can use xcopy to make backup copies of files and folders into another folder, onto another disk drive or a CD-RW drive, or to a network shared folder. When making backup copies, add the /K option so that xcopy preserves file attributes such as System and Read-Only in the copies. In addition, when copying to a network folder, add /Z so that xcopy can continue copying after brief network interruptions. Here's an example:

```
xcopy c:\book \\bali\bookfiles /K /E /I /Z
```

You can easily make a backup of your own personal Documents folder. It's easiest to use the userprofile environment variable to specify the path, as in this example:

```
xcopy "%userprofile%\Documents" e:\backup /K /E /I
```

This doesn't copy hidden files, however, and doesn't back up your personal settings and Registry entry files. You can't do this with xcopy while you're logged in because the hidden Registry file NTUSER.DAT cannot be opened for copying while the account is logged on. If you have Administrator privileges, though, you can copy another user's entire profile by specifying the /H option to copy even hidden files with a command like this:

```
xcopy "C:\Users\username" e:\backup /H /K /E /I
```

Here, *username* is the name of one of the computer's user accounts. (You can't use the userprofile environment variable in this case because it points to the Administrator account's folder, not the desired user's.)

To back up *all* the profiles on the computer, you could use the command

```
xcopy "C:\Users" e:\backup /H /K /E /I
```

or on Windows XP

```
xcopy "C:\documents and settings" e:\backup /H /K /E /I
```

although you would need Administrator privileges to do this because it requires xcopy to read other users' files.

Copying Only Updated Files

If you do use xcopy to create backups of a set of files and folders, you want to run the xcopy command periodically to keep the backup up-to-date. In this case, you don't want to have to copy files that haven't been changed. Use the /D option to instruct xcopy only to copy files that are newer than any copy in the backup set. This saves time and reduces network traffic. You also need to add the /R option so that xcopy can write over old copies of read-only files. /Y lets xcopy overwrite old files without prompting for confirmation. Now, you can see xcopy in its full alphabet-soup glory. The command

```
xcopy "%userprofile%\Documents" e:\backup /H /K /R /E /D /I /Y
```

or on Windows XP

```
xcopy "%userprofile%\My Documents" e:\backup /H /K /R /E /D /I /Y
```

copies your My Documents folder and all subfolders, but it only copies files that are newer than any already copied to e:\backup. Also, all file attributes are preserved.

The /D option serves double duty—you can also use it to specify a date, and xcopy only copies files changed or created on or after the specified date. See the online help for more information on this usage.

Unattended Backups

xcopy can't copy files that are in use by application programs, nor can it copy the personal Registry information of a user who is logged on. For backup purposes, it's helpful to put xcopy commands into a batch file and use the Task Scheduler to run the batch when users are not likely to be logged on. If you do this, you should add the /C option to tell xcopy to continue even if it encounters errors. If someone is up late and has a document file open, for example, /C lets xcopy continue to copy other files and folders.

For instance, you could write a batch file to copy all users' Documents folders onto a network folder using this command:

```
pushd %userprofile%\..
for /D %%d in (*.*) do (
    xcopy "%%d\Documents" "\\server\backups\%%d" /H/K/R/E/C/D/I/Z/Y
)
```

which works on Windows 7 and Vista. The pushd command changes to the directory above the current user's profile folder, which holds the profiles for everyone. The for loop then scans into everyone's profile folder. The equivalent version for Windows XP is

```
pushd %userprofile%\..
for /D %%d in (*.*) do (
    xcopy "%%d\My Documents" "\\server\backups\%%d" /H/K/R/E/C/D/I/Z/Y
)
```

You have to be sure to set up a network shared folder for this purpose before running the batch file and to use the correct server and share name in the xcopy command.

Note

Some other good general-purpose programs you might want to look into on your own are `sort` and `find`. `find` is a simplified version of `findstr`; `sort` lets you sort text files alphabetically.

File-Management Tools

Windows gives users the choice of formatting their hard disks with either of two file system structures: File Allocation Table (FAT) and NTFS. Both systems provide ways to make files invisible (hidden) and unalterable (read-only). In addition, NTFS provides a user and group security scheme that lets the user determine exactly who can view, create, modify, and delete files on a file-by-file and folder-by-folder basis. Although you can control these file attributes from the Windows Explorer GUI, Microsoft has also provided command-line tools to manage file attributes.

Note

On Windows 7 and Vista, the drive that holds Windows itself must be formatted with NTFS, but other drives can be formatted with either system. Windows XP can be installed on a FAT disk, although this is a huge security risk.

These utilities can be used in batch files to set up and maintain user folders. For example, you can make a batch file that creates a folder on a file server for each newly added user and then adds the appropriate NTFS permissions to secure the folder.

In addition, Windows XP Home Edition does its best to entirely conceal the existence of NTFS file permissions. The Explorer GUI has no means of viewing or modifying permissions, yet they still exist and still affect users' access rights to the file system. The `cacls` command lets you view and modify NTFS permissions on Windows XP Home Edition, either to create restricted folders outside the users' normal profile folders or to repair problems.

Note

XP Home Edition users can gain access to the NTFS Security Properties tab in the Windows GUI by booting up in Safe Mode and logging on as Administrator.

attrib

Microsoft's FAT and NTFS file systems support a set of primitive file "attributes" that can be used to indicate that a file is to receive special treatment. For example, the read-only attribute prevents Windows or DOS from writing data to the file or deleting it. These attributes don't offer as much protection as the user-level security system used on NTFS formatted disks, but they do help prevent accidents.

The `attrib` command displays and changes the basic file attributes, which are listed here:

Code	Attribute	Description
R	Read-Only	The file can be read but not written.
A	Archive	The file has been modified since the last backup. The Archive attribute is rarely used.
S	System	The file is an operating system file.
H	Hidden	The file is not visible to `dir` and most other commands.

These attributes can be viewed and changed in Windows Explorer, but it can be helpful to monitor them from the command line as well. The syntax of the `attrib` command is

attrib [+|-*x* ...] *filename* [/**S** [/**D**]]

where *x* is one of the attribute code letters R, A, S, or H. *filename* can contain wild-cards. Specifying +*x* sets the attribute, and -*x* clears the attribute. If you do not specify any + or - options, `attrib` lists the current attribute settings of the named file.

The /S option makes `attrib` apply itself to files in all subfolders of the specified or current folder, and /D makes `attrib` apply attributes to folders and files.

Finding Hidden Files

The command `attrib` with no arguments lists all files in the current directory, including hidden files. This makes it easy to find hidden files. Here's a sample listing:

```
A         C:\Users\bknittel\book.txt
A  SH     C:\Users\bknittel\NTUSER.DAT
A  SH     C:\Users\bknittel\ntuser.dat.LOG
A  SH     C:\Users\bknittel\ntuser.ini
A         C:\Users\bknittel\test.bat
```

All these files have their Archive attribute set. Three are hidden, and NTUSER.INI is marked as System and Hidden. SH files are also called *super hidden* because no program touches them unless you remove the S and H attributes.

The command `dir` /ah also lists hidden files but doesn't show you which files are hidden and which are not.

Setting and Clearing Attributes

Attrib lets you set and clear attributes. To remove the Read-Only attribute from all files in the current folder, type this:

```
attrib -r *.*
```

Alternatively, to make all files read-only, type

```
attrib +r *.*
```

To edit a "super hidden read-only" file such as the Windows XP boot configuration file C:\BOOT.INI, you could use the System Properties dialog box, or you could remove the S, R and H attributes manually, as in this example:

```
attrib -s -h -r boot.ini
notepad boot.ini
attrib +s +h +r boot.ini
```

After editing a file such as boot.ini, it's good practice to restore the file attributes to their original settings, as shown in the example.

The recursive option /S lets you modify attributes in subdirectories. For example, if you've copied a set of MP3 files from a CD-ROM drive onto your hard disk, you find that all the files are marked Read-Only. The following commands show how to fix this:

```
cd \music
attrib -r *.mp3 /s
```

For fun, compare this to sample script script0407.vbs in Chapter 4, "File and Registry Access."

cacls

On disks formatted with the NTFS file system, in addition to the Read-Only, Hidden, System, and Archive attributes, files and folders can have user-level security attributes as well. User-level security allows users and administrators to control who has access to files and folders and to determine exactly what these users can do. Separate attributes determine whether one can create, delete, read, write, execute, or manage each file and folder.

On all editions of Windows 7 and Vista, in most cases, you can manage these properties most effectively with the Properties dialog box in Windows Explorer. However, in some situations the command line is an important alternative:

- On Windows XP, when Simple File Sharing is enabled, Windows hides the GUI for file permissions and instead manages all file permission settings automatically.
- On Windows XP Home Edition, Simple File Sharing cannot be disabled. Short of restarting Windows in Safe Mode, there is no easy way to gain GUI access to file and folder permissions, even though they are active on NTFS-formatted disks.
- Network and system managers might want to modify file permissions with batch files so the task can be automated and documented.

A Problem with User Folders

If a file is created in a user's private directory, it has all access rights enabled for the owner but no permissions enabled for any other user. This is how Windows makes the files "private." When you drag files from one folder to another using Windows Explorer, Explorer on Windows 7 and Vista (usually) updates the file's security settings to match the destination folder's settings. Thus, if you drag a file from a private folder to a public folder, it becomes readable by everyone, which is usually your intent.

On Windows XP with Simple File Sharing turned off, this does *not* happen, and the file is visible but not accessible to other users on the computer and network. On all versions of Windows, if you move files with the command-line move command, the files' permission settings are *not* changed. You can, of course, modify file permissions using the Windows GUI on all versions of Windows (except XP Home Edition). The easiest fix is to modify the properties of the folder that contains the file, select the Security tab, click the Advanced button, and check Replace All Child Permissions With Inheritable Permissions From This Object. This gives all files in the folder the same permissions as the folder itself.

Sometimes, though, it can be easier to do this from a command prompt window. Enter **cacls**, which can alter file permissions from the command line. If you're a system manager or a Windows XP power user, you need to remember this command in case you ever end up with files stranded by inappropriate file permissions.

XP Home Edition users can also boot up in Safe Mode and log on as Administrator to gain access to the file Security properties page in the Explorer GUI.

cacls modifies the Access Control List (ACL) that's attached to each file on an NTFS disk. ACLs list users and user groups, along with the associated permissions to read, write, execute, and change files. Files and folders can also inherit permissions from the folder that contains them.

The syntax for the cacls command is

```
cacls filename [/T] [/E] [/C] [/G user:perm ...]
    [/R user ...] [/P user:perm ...] [/D user ...]
```

where *filename* is the name of the file or folder whose permission you want to modify. You can specify wildcards in the name.

With no other options, cacls lists the file or folder's current permission settings. The listing includes the names of users and groups with permissions to the file or folder, followed by code letters that indicate what rights the user or group has. The permission codes can be one of the following:

Code	Meaning
R	Read an existing file or folder's contents
W	Write (create a new file)
C	Read, write, and change an existing file
F	All of the above, plus modify permissions

In some cases, when unusual combinations of permissions are applied to a file (for example, Read and Write but not Change), `cacls` might print a more detailed list of specific permissions. `cacls` can list but not modify these custom permission combinations.

When listing the permissions for a folder, `cacls` might also print the additional codes (`OI`), (`CI`), and (`IO`), which have the following meanings:

Code	Meaning
CI	Container Inherit. The entry applies to subfolders of this folder.
OI	Object Inherit. The entry applies to files in this folder.
IO	Inherit Only. The access entry applies to subfolders and files but not to the folder itself.

For a typical private file, the `cacls` listing might look like this:

```
C:\plans\strita.xls JAVA\bknittel:F
                    NT AUTHORITY\SYSTEM:F
                    BUILTIN\Administrators:F
```

This indicates that three entities have Full permissions to this file. The entities are as follows:

- **JAVA\bknittel**—A standard local user account. Local user account names begin with the name of the computer.
- **NT AUTHORITY\SYSTEM**—The Windows operating system itself. SYSTEM is usually granted rights to all files.
- **BUILTIN\Administrators**—The local "Administrators" group. The Administrator account and any other Computer Administrator users are members of this group.

These are the normal settings for a private file. For public files, an additional entry, either `Everyone:R` or `Everyone:RWC`, gives all other users the ability to read or to read and change the file.

With command-line arguments, `cacls` modifies file permissions. The arguments are described in Table 13.3.

Table 13.3 **Options for the `cacls` Command**

Option	Description
/T	Recursively processes all subfolders, seeking the specified name or names. With filename `*.*`, this option processes all files in all sub folders.

continues

Table 13.3 **Continued**

Option	Description
/E	Edits the file or folder's ACL. Permissions on the command line are added to any existing permissions. Without /E, the file's ACL is deleted and then replaced with the permissions specified on the command line.
/C	When the filename is specified with wildcards, /C makes `cacls` continue with other files if it encounters an error. An error can occur if you do not have permission to modify the settings of a file or if the file is in use.
/G user:perm	Grants (adds) the listed permissions for the specified user or user group. perm can be any or all of the letters R (Read), W (Write), C (Change), and F (Full Control). You can list more than one user:perm item to add permissions for multiple users or groups.
/R user	Removes all permissions for the specified user or group. This option is only applicable when used with /E.
/P user:perm	Replaces the permissions for the specified user or group with the listed codes. In addition to the four codes listed under /G, you can specify /P user:N, which means *no permissions*. This is the same as specifying /R.
/D user	Denies access by the specified user. Be careful with /D because it "trumps" any permissions to access the file.

Checking Permissions

If users have difficulty accessing a file, the easiest way to identify the problem is to view the file's properties in Windows Explorer. Select the Security tab and view the settings for each entry. If the Security tab doesn't appear on Windows XP Professional, you can temporarily disable Simple File Sharing to make it appear. Click Tools, Folder Options, View and uncheck Simple File Sharing at the bottom of the Advanced Settings list.

If you don't want to do this or if you have Windows XP Home Edition, log on as a Computer Administrator, open a Command Prompt window, change to the directory containing the file in question, and then type `cacls filename`. The listing should show you whether the user has access to the file.

Granting Permissions to Everyone

If a file has been moved to a public, shared folder but isn't accessible by other users, you can fix the problem with `cacls`. Log on as a Computer Administrator or as the owner of the file, open a Command Prompt window, change to the folder containing the file, and type the command

```
cacls filename /E /G everyone:RWC
```

where *filename* is the name of the file you want to make available. You can use wild-cards (for example, `*.*`) to fix multiple files with one command. You can also name specific users. For example,

```
cacls filename /E /G norm:RWC bob:RWC
```

grants permissions to the user accounts Norm and Bob, without making the file available to Everyone. (However, if Simple File Sharing is enabled, Norm and Bob can't be able to access the file over the network. You have to grant access to Everyone for network users to use a file when Simple File Sharing is in effect.)

Making a File or Folder Private

To make a file private, it's best to remove specific users and groups using the `/R` command. For example, to remove access by Everyone, use the following command:

```
cacls filename /E /R everyone
```

To modify a folder and all the folder's contents, you can modify the folder's properties, and then use the recursive option to modify all files and subfolders, as in this example:

```
cd \foldername
cacls . /E /R everyone
calcs *.* /T /E /R everyone
```

> **Caution**
>
> Be *very* careful when using `cacls` with folders. If you remove essential permissions from a system folder such as `\Windows`, the operating system might stop working. Use the GUI to make changes in file permissions whenever you can.

Making Files Inherit Permissions from Their Folders

When you encounter the "unreadable file in a public folder" problem discussed in the sidebar, the fix is to make all files in the folder inherit their permissions from the containing folder. `cacls` can't fix this. You can easily use the GUI, as mentioned, or the sidebar. Alternatively, you can use the alternative file-permissions utility `icacls`, which is provided with Windows 7 and Vista. On XP, you have to obtain it from one of the Windows Resource Kits discussed at the end of the chapter. Never do this on a sensitive folder such as `\windows` or any of it subfolders:

```
cd \users\public\documents
icacls *.* /reset
```

Management Power Tools

Quite a few command-line utilities are available that make short work of some tedious Windows management tasks. If you've ever tried to find the names of all the system services or device drivers running on a given Windows computer, you know what I mean. This section shows you some handy tools to help you manage Windows XP computers from the command line.

driverquery

driverquery lists the names of all device drivers installed on a computer. You can list the drivers for the local computer or another computer on your network. The default listing format looks like this:

```
Module Name  Display Name            Driver Type   Link Date
============ ====================== ============= ======================
1394ohci     1394 OHCI Compliant Ho Kernel        4/21/2009 8:50:20 PM
ACPI         Microsoft ACPI Driver  Kernel        4/21/2009 8:08:37 PM
AcpiPmi      ACPI Power Meter Drive Kernel        4/21/2009 8:13:46 PM
adp94xx      adp94xx                Kernel        12/5/2008 3:59:55 PM
adpahci      adpahci                Kernel        5/1/2007 10:29:26 AM
adpu320      adpu320                Kernel        2/27/2007 4:03:08 PM
AFD          Ancillary Function Dri Kernel        4/21/2009 8:09:58 PM
⋮
```

You can run driverquery with no arguments to display the list for the local computer, or you can add /S *computername* to list the drivers on another computer. If you are denied access to the remote computer, you can add the additional options /u *username* /p to use an alternative account, such as Administrator. driverquery prompts you for the account's password.

Note

If you have a network drive mapped to the remote computer using your own user account, you cannot specify an alternative account name to driverquery because Windows only permits you to attach to a given remote computer with one account at a time.

By default, driverquery prints a table formatted as shown in the earlier example. If you want to import the information into a spreadsheet, you can add the option /FO CSV to format the results with quotation marks and commas between the columns.

driverquery has a few other options that you can try. The most interesting are /V, which adds additional columns such as the device driver's filename and its running/not running status, and /SI, which adds information about the driver's installation file and manufacturer. Despite what the online help says, /SI displays information about unsigned drivers as well as signed drivers.

To see the whole list of options, type driverquery /?.

runas

The runas command is more useful on Windows XP than on Windows 7 and Vista because on XP there is no User Account Control and use the user account named Administrator is typically used to perform administrative functions. When you need to perform a management operation, though, it can be inconvenient to log off and back on as Administrator.

The runas command lets you run some applications as another (usually privileged) user while remaining simultaneously logged on with your own user account. runas is great when you want to run a setup program or examine files you don't normally have access to.

Here's the syntax of runas:

```
runas [(/noprofile|/profile)] [/env] [/netonly] [/smartcard]
    /user:username command
```

If *command* contains spaces or command-line arguments, you must surround it with quotation marks. The primary usage is to open a command prompt window as a Computer Administrator, using this syntax:

```
runas /user:accountname cmd
```

replacing *accountname* with a Computer Administrator account name such as Administrator. I don't go into runas in any more depth here. On Windows 7 and Vista, it's not terribly useful; instead, you open an elevated command prompt window. If your account is not a Computer Administrator account, you select an alternative account name from the User Account Control prompt.

> ⊛ I discussed elevated (privileged) command prompts on page 436 in the section "Opening a Command Prompt Window with Administrator Privileges".

On XP, you might also use runas to run other programs such as setup programs and copies of Windows Explorer. However, you cannot run Windows Explorer or any of its derivative programs—Control Panel, My Computer, My Documents, Network Connections, and some other control panel applets—unless you first change a setting. To do this, log on to the account that you will be using with runas, and open Windows Explorer. Click Tool, Folder Options. Select the View tab. In the Advanced Settings list, check Launch Folder Windows in a Separate Process. Click OK and log out. Now, Explorer windows will work from runas. This useful tip is described in more detail at blogs.msdn.com/aaron_margosis/archive/2004/07/07/175488.aspx

tasklist

tasklist displays a list of all running processes on the system. This information is helpful when you want to see whether a program is running inappropriately or if you suspect that some essential program or system service is no longer running. It can also display information about the Dynamic Link Library (DLL) program files in use by each process.

`tasklist` has several options that you can see by typing `tasklist /?`. Here, I just discuss the most interesting options. With no option, `tasklist`'s default output looks something like this:

```
Image Name                   PID Session Name     Session#    Mem Usage
========================= ====== ================ ======== ============
System Idle Process            0 Console                 0         20 K
System                         4 Console                 0        216 K
smss.exe                     484 Console                 0        348 K
csrss.exe                    540 Console                 0      2,756 K
winlogon.exe                 568 Console                 0      2,896 K
⋮
setiathome.exe              1516 Console                 0     16,324 K
cmd.exe                     2604 Console                 0        900 K
tasklist.exe                2112 Console                 0      2,824 K
```

The columns are explained in Table 13.5.

Table 13.5 **Column Headings in the `tasklist` Printout**

Heading	Description
Image Name	The name of the program file.
PID	Process identifier. A number that uniquely identifies each running program.
Session Name	This field is blank for programs started as Windows services and displays `Console` for programs started by users physically at the computer. The session name is different for users attached via Remote Desktop or Windows Terminal Services.
Session#	Windows supports the concept of sessions, which allow for simultaneous logons from different users. On desktop versions of Windows, only one user can actively work at a time but multiple users can be logged on. Fast User Switching lets you switch between sessions. On Windows 7 and Vista, session 0 is used solely for system services. The first person to log on gets session #1, the second simultaneous logon gets session #2, and so on. On Windows XP, the first user to log on at the physical desktop (as opposed to Remote Desktop) connects to session #0, which is already running system services.
Mem Usage	The amount of memory in use by the program. This might total more than the amount of physical memory because some programs can be paged out.

The listing shows both system service processes and user programs. The /V option adds additional columns: the program status (running/not responding), the program's username, total CPU time, and window title, if any.

You can export `tasklist`'s output to a spreadsheet by adding the /FO CSV option. For example, the command

```
tasklist /fo csv >tasks.txt
```

saves the current task list into a text file that you can then import into an Excel spreadsheet as a comma-delimited file.

System service tasks can actually provide several distinct services. The /SVC option lists the services provided by each task, as in this example:

```
Image Name               PID Services
==================== ====== =======================================
services.exe             612 Eventlog, PlugPlay
lsass.exe                628 PolicyAgent, ProtectedStorage, SamSs
svchost.exe              796 RpcSs
svchost.exe              940 Dnscache
svchost.exe              968 LmHosts, RemoteRegistry, SSDPSRV, WebClient
spoolsv.exe             1036 Spooler
⋮
```

Software developers might be interested in seeing which DLL files are loaded by each task. The /M option prints this information, as in this example:

```
Image Name               PID Modules
======================== ====== =======================================
cmd.exe                 2876 ntdll.dll, kernel32.dll, msvcrt.dll,
                             USER32.dll, GDI32.dll, ADVAPI32.dll,
                             RPCRT4.dll, Apphelp.dll
```

You can also view the task list information for another computer by adding the /S *computername* option. As with `driverquery`, you might need to use a privileged account name by adding /U *username* /P.

`tasklist` is most helpful when a program has crashed but left "pieces" of itself running. Microsoft Word is notorious for this; sometimes Word crashes and disappears from the normal Task Manager Applications display, but `tasklist` shows that a process named `winword.exe` is still running. You can't start Word again until this rogue process has been terminated with `taskkill`.

Note

`tasklist` and `taskkill`, which I describe next, are not provided with Windows XP Home Edition. However, they are provided with all editions of Windows 7, Vista, and XP Professional. XP Home users could copy `tasklist.exe` and `taskkill.exe` from a computer running XP Pro.

taskkill

taskkill lets you terminate programs running on your computer or another networked computer based on the program's username, session number, process ID (PID) number, or program name. taskkill is especially useful because it can sometimes terminate tasks that refuse to disappear when you try to kill them with the Task Manager dialog box.

taskkill has many options, more than you will ever need. In fact, it should have been named overkill. (Sorry, I had to.) You can see the whole list by typing taskkill /?. Here, I discuss a few of the most useful options.

Killing a Process by PID Number

If you can find the PID number of an errant program either in the output of tasklist or in the Task Manager dialog box, then you can type

> **taskkill /pid *pidnumber* /f /t**

entering the actual process ID number in place of *pidnumber*.

The /F option tells Windows to terminate the task "forcefully," and /T terminates any child tasks or subprograms started by the program in question. In most cases, this solves the problem. If this doesn't work, you might try running the taskkill program as Administrator:

> runas /user:Administrator taskkill /pid *pidnumber* /f /t

taskkill can also terminate processes on a remote computer using the /S *computername* option, following the same format described earlier for tasklist.

Killing the Processes of Another User

If you have to kill tasks belonging to another user (for example, one who has logged off using Fast User Switching), you must use an Administrator account. It's probably best to log on as Administrator and use the Task Manager dialog box to fix this, but you can use taskkill as well. The command is

> taskkill /FI "USERNAME eq *username*"

where *username* is the account's name; it can be a plain name for a local account, or it can be username@domain or domain\username for a domain account. You can run this from a nonprivileged account by opening an elevated (privileged) command prompt window, as discussed earlier.

Use this form of the command first to let any programs that are willing to exit gracefully do so. Then, repeat the command with /F /T at the end to dispatch any stragglers.

Killing Processes by Program Name

You can terminate a task based on its program name using this form of the `taskkill` command:

```
taskkill /IM programfile
```

Here, *programfile* is the name of the program's EXE file (for example, `winword.exe`). You can use wildcards with this name; for example, `note*` kills `notepad.exe` as well as *note*-anything-else. Be *very* careful when using wildcards because you don't want to terminate any essential Windows services by accident.

sc

`sc` is called the Service Controller program, and for good reason. `sc` can manage just about every aspect of installing, maintaining, and modifying system services and device drivers on local and networked Windows computers. It's another command with a huge number of options, which you can list by typing `sc /?`. It has so many options that after printing the /? help information, it prompts you to see whether you want to view additional information about its `query` and `queryex` subcommands.

The basic format of an `sc` command is as follows:

sc [*servername*] *command* [*servicename* [*option* ...]]

If the *servername* argument is omitted, `sc` operates on the local computer. There is no provision for entering an alternative username or password, so you need to run this command from an elevated (privileged) command prompt window to do more than just list the installed services.

In the next sections, I list some of the more useful `sc` commands. If you maintain Windows computers, you should carefully examine the complete list of commands yourself, though, because you might have different ideas about what makes a command interesting.

Listing Installed Services

The command `sc queryex` prints a long list of installed services along with their current run states. A typical service listing looks like this:

```
SERVICE_NAME: Dhcp
DISPLAY_NAME: DHCP Client
        TYPE               : 20  WIN32_SHARE_PROCESS
        STATE              : 4  RUNNING
                                (STOPPABLE,NOT_PAUSABLE,ACCEPTS_SHUTDOWN)
        WIN32_EXIT_CODE    : 0  (0x0)
        SERVICE_EXIT_CODE  : 0  (0x0)
        CHECKPOINT         : 0x0
        WAIT_HINT          : 0x0
```

```
PID                : 844
FLAGS              :
```

The most useful parts of this listing are detailed in Table 13.6.

Table 13.6   **Useful Fields in** *sc queryex* **Printout**

Field	Description
SERVICE_NAME	The "short" name for the service. This name can be used with the net command to start and stop the service.
DISPLAY_NAME	The "long" name for the service. This name is displayed in the Services panel in Windows Management.
STATE	The service's current activity state.
PID	The service's process identifier.

You can add type= driver or type= service (with a space after the equals sign) to the sc queryex command to limit the listing to just drivers or just services.

Starting and Stopping Services

System managers occasionally need to start and stop services for several reasons: to reset a malfunctioning service, to force a service to reinitialize itself with new startup data, or to temporarily stop a service while other services are being maintained. You can manage services using the GUI Windows Management tool, but when you have to perform this sort of task frequently, it's more convenient to use a batch file. For instance, I use a batch file to stop and restart my company's mail server after I make changes to its configuration file. Typing the batch file's name (downup, in case you're curious) is much easier than navigating through Computer Management.

To use sc to start and stop services on a local or remote computer, you must know the service's "short" name. The easiest way to find a service's short name is to use sc queryex to get the listing of all service names. Then, you can use the commands

```
sc stop servicename
sc \\computername stop servicename
```

to stop a service on the local computer or on a remote computer specified by *computername*, respectively. Likewise, you can use the commands

```
sc start servicename
sc \\computername start servicename
```

to start services.

Note

sc has many other commands that let you install and configure services as well as interrogate their operational status and dependency lists. The installation commands can be especially useful if you need to deploy services in an enterprise environment.

Networking Utilities

Networking is one the strongest features of Windows, and this shows in the breadth of command-line utilities provided for network management and debugging. Besides the tools provided to manage Windows networking for file and printer sharing, Windows comes with a whole set of standard TCP/IP programs that any Unix user will find instantly familiar. The Berkeley Unix "r" programs and the Unix printer programs lpq and lpr are here, as are standard TCP/IP tools such as ping, ftp, and nslookup. I don't have room to describe all the networking tools provided with Windows, but I've chosen six that I've found to be extremely useful. You can find the others listed in Appendix D, "Index of Patterns and Sample Scripts."

ipconfig

ipconfig is a handy utility that shows you the status of your computer's TCP/IP networking configuration. It's especially useful when you use dial-up networking, Virtual Private Networking (VPN), or Local Area Network (LAN) adapters with automatic IP address assignment, because ipconfig can tell you what IP address information has been assigned to these dynamically configured connections. ipconfig can also release and re-request automatically assigned IP addresses for your LAN adapters.

Listing IP Address Information

In its simplest form, the command ipconfig displays the current IP address, subnet mask, and gateway address for any active LAN adapters and dial-up networking connections, including dial-up Internet connections. The output looks like this:

```
Windows IP Configuration

Ethernet adapter Local Area Connection:

        Connection-specific DNS Suffix  . : mycompany.com
        Link-local IPv6 Address . . . . . : fe80::3cb4:bfdb:442f:6315%11
        IPv4 Address. . . . . . . . . . . : 192.168.0.3
        Subnet Mask . . . . . . . . . . . : 255.255.255.0
        Default Gateway . . . . . . . . . : 192.168.0.1
```

With the /all option, ipconfig displays additional information about each connection. The output looks like this:

```
Windows IP Configuration

        Host Name . . . . . . . . . . . . : java
        Primary Dns Suffix  . . . . . . . :
        Node Type . . . . . . . . . . . . : Unknown
        IP Routing Enabled. . . . . . . . : No
        WINS Proxy Enabled. . . . . . . . : No
        DNS Suffix Search List. . . . . . : mycompany.com


Ethernet adapter Local Area Connection:

        Connection-specific DNS Suffix  . : mycompany.com
        Description . . . . . . . . . . . : SMC EZ Card 10/100 PCI
        Physical Address. . . . . . . . . : 00-E2-4F-11-39-47
        Dhcp Enabled. . . . . . . . . . . : No
        Link-local IPv6 Address . . . . . : fe80::3cb4:bfdb:442f:6315%11
        IPv4 Address. . . . . . . . . . . : 192.168.0.3
        Subnet Mask . . . . . . . . . . . : 255.255.255.0
        Default Gateway . . . . . . . . . : 192.168.0.1
        DNS Servers . . . . . . . . . . . : 192.168.0.2
```

This is helpful information to have when you're diagnosing network and Internet problems. What's more, if you're using a dial-up connection or a dynamically (DHCP)-configured LAN connection, this is the only way to get this information. The most important items are listed in Table 13.7.

Table 13.7   **Information Displayed by** ipconfig /all

Heading	Description
Host Name	This computer's name for TCP/IP purposes; does not necessarily match the Windows Networking computer name.
Primary DNS Suffix	The primary Domain Name Service (DNS) domain name for the computer. This is set in the System Properties dialog box by clicking Change, More.
Node Type	The NetBIOS node type. This is usually Hybrid on systems that use NetBIOS networking.
Connection-specific DNS Suffix	The DNS domain name for a specific connection.
Description	The name of the network adapter or dial-up networking adapter for this connection.
Dhcp Enabled	Yes, if the connection is set for automatic configuration.
IP Address	The IP address assigned to this connection.
Subnet Mask	The subnet mask for this connection.

Heading	Description
Default Gateway	The default gateway (router) for this connection.
DNS Servers	The IP addresses of the server(s) used to perform DNS (domain name) lookups.

`ipconfig` information can be especially helpful in debugging certain networking problems:

- If the IP address is listed as Autoconfiguration IP Address, then Windows is unable to locate a DHCP server for this LAN adapter. Unless you have built a small network without a DHCP server, a connection-sharing router, or Windows Internet Connection Sharing, this usually indicates a failure of the network wiring or of the DHCP server.
- If the IP address is listed as 0.0.0.0, the indicated adapter is disconnected.
- If the IP address is inappropriate for the network to which you are connected, you have probably relocated your computer from one network to another and need to reset and renew your IP address. I show how in a moment.

Resetting Automatically Assigned Addresses

If your network uses DHCP to automatically assign IP addresses to computers, you might occasionally run into problems where an address is not assigned to your computer or is not reassigned when you unplug from one network and connect to another. You can quickly fix this problem with ipconfig by typing the commands from an elevated (privileged) command prompt window:

```
ipconfig /release
ipconfig /renew
```

Tip
These commands can often restore a disabled cable modem or DSL Internet connection.

Examining and Clearing the DNS Cache

When Windows has to find the IP address for a given hostname, it remembers the results for a short time to save time when making subsequent connections to the same site. If Windows fails to find an address for a given name, this is also remembered for a short time—again, to save time and trouble for future lookups. The information is stored in what's called the DNS Resolver Cache.

You can display the contents of this cache with the command `ipconfig /displaydns`. You can erase all the cached information with `ipconfig /flushdns`. This can be helpful if, for example, your organization changes IP addresses or if a site is temporarily offline but has been restored. Clearing the DNS cache removes all obsolete information.

Note

You must type these commands in an elevated (privileged) command prompt window.

Other variations of the `ipconfig` command let you reset the DHCP information for individual adapters and let you assign a DHCP "class" name. Type **ipconfig /?** for more information.

net

The `net` command provides several tools for configuring network mappings and shares, and it can even add user accounts. It's a strange command that dates back to the earliest days of networking with PCs. The `net` command has 22 subcommands. You can view the list of commands online by typing **net help**, and you can get additional help for any individual command by typing **net help** *command*, where *command* is one of the names listed in the following sections. If you type net /? or net command /?, you still get online help, although the text is less detailed.

I don't describe all 22 of the `net` commands in the following sections. The three most useful, important commands are `net help`, `net use`, and `net view`. These are useful on a day-to-day basis. Several others can be utilized to manage Windows and user accounts.

net continue

The command `net continue` resumes a system service that is suspended by `net pause`. The `net` command, like `sc`, can be used to control system services. The syntax is `net continue "servicename"`, where *servicename* is the "display" name for the service. If the name contains spaces, you must surround it in quotation marks.

`net continue`, `net pause`, `net start`, and `net stop` work only with the local computer. The `sc` command, discussed earlier in the chapter, can work with the local computer or with any networked computer, so for service management, I recommend that you use `sc` instead of the `net` commands.

net file

The command `net file` displays the names of all the local computer's shared files that are currently opened by remote network users. The output looks like this:

```
ID        Path                        User name          # Locks
-----------------------------------------------------------------
17        c:\book\test1.bat           ADMINISTRATOR      0
```

The listing shows the local names of the files and the user account that is using each file, but not the computer from which the remote user has connected. If necessary, you can close a file opened by a remote user by typing `net file` *id* `/close`, where *id* is one of the ID numbers displayed in the `net file` listing. You only want to do this if you are sure that the remote user has gone away or that his computer has crashed.

net help

The command `net help` displays online help for any of the `net` commands. Type **net help** for a complete listing of the documented commands.

net helpmsg

The command `net helpmsg` *number* displays the error message text for a numerical Windows error code. These numerical codes are displayed by some programs.

net localgroup

The command `net localgroup` creates local security groups on the local computer. `net localgroup` works on any version of Windows based on Windows NT but not Windows 9*x*.

The syntax for creating and deleting local groups is as follows:

```
net localgroup groupname [/comment:"text"] /add [/domain]
net localgroup groupname [/comment:"text"] /delete [/domain]
```

The optional /comment option adds a text description of the group. The /domain option adds the group as a Domain Local group on the current domain controller, rather than on the local workstation.

You can add users to and delete users from the group with the following commands:

```
net localgroup groupname username… /add
net localgroup groupname username… /delete
```

net pause

The command `net pause` temporarily suspends a system service. The syntax of the command is

```
net pause "servicename"
```

See the `net continue` command discussion for more information about the service control. You can get a list of currently running services by typing `net start`.

net print

The command `net print` lets you view and manage the print queues of the local computer.

Here's the syntax to view a remote printer queue:

net print *computername**sharename*

This lists any pending print jobs. For example, on my network, the command `net print \\sumatra\okidata` printed this listing:

```
Name                       Job #     Size        Status
------------------------------------------------------------
okidata Queue              1 jobs
    bknittel                 109     12380         Waiting
```

The listing shows that one print job is pending, which `bknittel` submitted. The job identification number is 109.

You can suspend, release, or delete a print job with the following command:

net print *computername jobnumber* {**/hold** | **/release** | **/delete**}

For example, `net print \\sumatra 109 /delete` deletes the job pending in my printer's queue.

`net print` is not as useful as the Printers & Faxes Control Panel display, but it might be useful if you are connecting to a Windows computer using text-based `telnet`. If you want to automate print job management, though, it's probably best to write a script that uses Windows Management Instrumentation, as described in Chapter 7.

net send

The command `net send` was formerly used to send messages to other network users. The messaging service proved to be a security risk, so it's now disabled by default, and the `net send` command is consequently no longer useful.

net session

The command `net session` displays all the connections from other computers to your computer's shared files and printers. A session represents the connection itself, and there is only one per remote computer, regardless how many files the other computer is using. (There might be an additional session listed for a given remote computer if that computer is using your computer's shared Internet connection.) The output of the `net session` looks like this:

```
Computer          User name        Client Type       Opens Idle time
------------------------------------------------------------------------
\\BALI            ADMINISTRATOR    Windows 2000 2195    1 00:00:00
\\SUMATRA                          Windows 2000 2195    3 00:00:17
```

The listing shows the names of the remote computers connected to yours, the remote user's name (if known), the remote computer's operating system, the number of files or folders that the remote user has open, and the amount of time since the last activity.

You can find out more about the activities of an individual connection with the command

> **net session** *computername*

which lists the shared folders and printers that the remote user is currently using.

In case of an emergency, you can forcibly disconnect a remote user with the following command:

> **net session** *computername* /**delete**

net share

The command net share displays and manages shared folders offered by your computer. The basic command net share displays a list of all folders currently shared by your computer. On my computer, for instance, the listing looks like this:

```
Share name   Resource                  Remark
-------------------------------------------------------------------
IPC$                                   Remote IPC
C$           C:\                       Default share
ADMIN$       C:\WINDOWS                Remote Admin
CDROM        E:\
Users        C:\Userse
```

The IPC$, C$, and ADMIN$ shares are set up by Windows for administrative use. Windows 7 and Vista, by default, share the Users folder, which contains all user profile folders. (Windows keeps remote users from seeing even the existence of folders and files that they don't have permission to read, so this is not a security risk. Remote access to each user's shared folders and files is controlled by changing standard file and folder security settings.) Windows XP automatically shares the All Users "My Documents" folder as "SharedDocs." Other folders that you explicitly share appear as well.

You can also use net share to add and delete shared folders from the command line. There are three versions of the command. Here's the first version:

> **net share** *sharename=drive:path* [/**users:***number* | /**unlimited**]
>   [/**remark:***text*] [/**cache:**{**Manual** | **Documents** | **Programs** | **None**}]

This shares the folder specified by *drive:path* as shared folder *sharename*. You can optionally limit the number of connections to the share with the /users option. You can record descriptive text with the /remark option, and you can specify how the files in this folder are to be treated if the remote user requests them to be made available while offline.

> **net share** *sharename* [/**users:***number* | /**unlimited**]
>   [/**remark:***text*] [/**cache:**(**Manual** | **Documents** | **Programs** | **None**)]

This version of the command changes the user restrictions, remark text, and offline usage hints for an existing share.

> **net share** (*sharename* | *devicename* | *drive:path*} **/delete**

This final version of the command cancels sharing of a folder or printer. You can specify the share name or drive and path to cancel folder sharing, or you can specify the name of a printer queue to cancel printer sharing.

net share is a convenient way to share and "unshare" folders, and it can be faster to use than the Windows Explorer GUI.

net start

The command net start lists active services. The names listed by this command are the long "display" names that you can also view with the sc queryex command, described earlier in the chapter. net start, however, lists only running services.

You can start an inactive service with the command net start "*servicename*". However, net start can only start services on the local computer. The sc command is more useful because it can also start services on remote computers.

In most cases, you must issue net start and net stop, which I discuss shortly, from a privileged Command Prompt window. However, on Windows XP, a Power User account can usually start and stop most services.

net statistics

The command net statistics workstation displays information about your computer's use of remote network resources. It lists the number of bytes sent and received, the total read and write operations, and error statistics.

The command net statistics server displays information about other computers' use of files and printers shared by your computer, including bytes sent and received, password errors, and the number of files opened.

net stop

The command net stop "*servicename*" stops a system service on your computer. You must specify the long "display" name of the service, as listed by sc queryex or net start.

Tip

If you suspect that someone is inappropriately accessing shared files on your computer, you can instantly stop file sharing by typing **net stop server** from an elevated command prompt. On XP, if you are not a computer administrator, you must type **runas /user:Administrator "net stop server"**.

net use

The command `net use` is the most important and useful of the `net` commands because it lets you map network drives and network printers from the command line. It's useful not only while working directly at the command prompt, but especially in batch files, where it can automatically configure the necessary network environment before the batch file starts copying or printing files.

Here are the most useful variations of the command:

net use

This version of the command displays a list of all network drive and printer mappings currently in effect. This is a *very* useful command because it instantly shows you what network drives are available and where they point.

net use *drive:* *computer**sharename*

This version of the command maps drive letter *drive* to a network shared folder named *computer**sharename*. This is the plain-vanilla version of the command. The next variation shows all the available options.

net use *drive:* *computer**sharename*[*subfolder…*]
 [[*password*] {**/user:***username* | **/smartcard**} [**/savecred**]]
 [**/persistent:**{**yes**|**no**}]

If you specify one or more subfolder names after the share name, the mapped drive considers that subfolder to be the root directory of the drive, and it cannot "see" upper-level directories. Novell NetWare users are familiar with this as the "map root" function.

The **/persistent** option lets you specify whether the mapping is automatically reinstated when you log off and back on. The default setting is **yes**, although you can change the default.

By default, the connection to the remote computer is made using your username and password. If you want to use an alternative account, you can add the **/user** option or the **/smartcard** option. If you specify a username, you can enter it in any of the standard formats: *username*, *domain**username*, or *username@domain*.

> ### Note
> You can connect to a given remote computer with only one user account at a time. You can't map one drive letter using your own account and a different drive letter with an alternative account.

You can specify the alternative account's password on the command line just before the **/user** option. It's a security risk to store passwords in batch files, however. Fortunately, two better alternatives are available. If you omit the password or specify * in its place, net use prompts you for the password. You can also instruct net use to prompt once and then remember the password by adding the /savecred option.

net use lpt*N***: ***computer\sharename* [*user and persistence options*]

This version of the command maps a remote network printer to an LPT port for use by DOS programs. You can map ports LPT1 through LPT9, if desired; however, you cannot map an LPT port name that is used by a physical port interface on your computer. This version of the command supports the same alternative user and /persistent options as the drive-mapping command described previously.

net use *device*: /**del**[**ete**]

This version of the command deletes a drive or printer mapping. *device* is the drive letter or LPT port to delete.

net use *drive*: /**home**

This version of the command maps a drive letter to your account's designated "home" directory. This command works only when you are logged on to a domain user account and when the system administrator has specified a home directory for your account. This command can be helpful in batch files and logon scripts.

As mentioned earlier, net use by itself displays all network mappings. The listing looks like this:

```
Status      Local    Remote                Network
-------------------------------------------------------------
OK          K:       \\sumatra\cdrive      Microsoft Windows Network
OK          LPT1     \\sumatra\okidata     Microsoft Windows Network
```

This shows that drive K: is mapped to shared folder \\sumatra\cdrive, and that DOS printer LPT1 is mapped to \\sumatra\okidata.

The Status column shows that the connections to \\sumatra are currently active. You might see the status change to Disconnected when you first log on or after 20 minutes or so of inactivity, but this usually is not an indication of a problem. Windows reestablishes the connection automatically when you attempt to use the drive or printer.

I have found net use to be of most use in making batch files that I use for automatic backups and to use networked applications. Here's one automatic backup batch file I use:

```
@rem                                     Example File batch1301.bat
@echo off
net use z: /del >nul 2>nul
net use z: \\bali\backups
if errorlevel 1 (
    echo The network drive is not available
    exit /b 1
)
xcopy "%userprofile%\Documents" "z:\%username%" /H/K/R/E/D/I/Z/C
```

```
if errorlevel 1 (
    echo The backup copy encountered errors
    exit /b 1
)
net use z: /del
```

The first net use command in this program deletes any existing mapping for drive Z: Because there might not be a current mapping and I don't want to see the error message if there isn't, the standard output and standard error streams are redirected to the "null" file—the output just disappears.

The second net use command maps drive Z: to a backup folder on my file server. Then, xcopy copies my Documents folder to my own personal subdirectory on the file server. The environment variables %userprofile% and %username% let any user on my network use the same batch file. The script ends by removing the drive mapping as part of a general good-housekeeping practice.

Note

On Windows XP, I use the folder name My Documents rather than just Documents.

There are three additional variations of net use that I've found to be of little or no practical use. Here's the first variation:

```
net use \\computer\sharename[\subfolder…]
    [[{password | *}} {/user:username | /smartcard} [/savecred]]
    [/persistent:{yes|no}]
```

This version of the command establishes a connection to a shared folder without mapping a drive letter. This allows quicker access if you later connect to the shared folder using its UNC name (\\computer\sharename) in Windows Explorer or other applications.

```
net use \\computer\sharename /delete
```

This version of the command disconnects a shared folder that is attached without a drive letter.

```
net use /persistent:{yes | no}
```

This version of the command sets the default persistence setting to yes or no. This default applies when you issue future net use commands without specifying the /persistent option.

Most of the time, you use the basic versions of net use.

net user

The command net user without options lists all local user accounts on the computer. net user username lists information for the specified user account, including the last logon date, the user's full name, time and station restrictions, profile and home directories, logon script setting, and group memberships.

You can also use `net user` to create and manage accounts. There are several variations. Here's the first:

net user *username* [*password*] **/add** *options* [**/domain**]

This version of the command creates a user account with the specified username. If you omit the password, the account is created with no password. You can set the account's password on the command line, or you can specify `*`, which makes `net user` prompt you to enter the new account's password. The **/domain** option adds the account as a domain account rather than as a local account.

I don't discuss `net user` further, except to note that if you need to set up the multiple user accounts on several machines, `net user` might be helpful. For example, you can write a batch file to create user accounts for a college class using a program similar to this:

```
@rem                             Example File mkaccount.bat
@echo off

rem --------------------------------------------------
rem Create a student account
rem Be sure the command line contains a classname, username and password
rem --------------------------------------------------

if "%3" == "" (
    echo Usage: mkaccount classname username password
    exit /b
)

rem --------------------------------------------------
rem Attempt to create the account. Throughout this
rem batch file %1 is the class name (e.g. CS101),
rem %2 is the new logon name (e.g. asmith), and
rem %3 is the initial password (e.g. xyz123)
rem --------------------------------------------------

net user "%2" "%3" /add /passwordreq:yes /domain

if errorlevel 1 (
    echo Unable to create account %2
    pause
    exit /b
)

rem --------------------------------------------------
rem Add the new user to the class group and the
rem students group
rem --------------------------------------------------
```

```
net group "%1" "%2" /add
net group students "%2" /add

rem -------------------------------------------
rem Create the user's profile folder and grant
rem Full access rights to the new student account. The
rem teacher already has full rights to
rem \classes\classname so she or he will inherit rights
rem to the student's directory.
rem For the roaming profile to work, the "students" group
rem must have read permissions on the class folder but
rem but this permission must not apply to subfolders.
rem -------------------------------------------

mkdir "d:\home\classes\%1\%2"
cacls "d:\home\classes\%1\%2" /E /G "%2:F"

rem -------------------------------------------
rem Assign the profile folder using the network path
rem \\server\classes to the folder d:\home\classes
rem -------------------------------------------

net user "%2" /profilepath:"\\server\classes\%1\%2" /domain
```

This batch file uses net user to create a student account, adds the account to the domain groups for the class and for all students, creates the account's profile folder, grants the new account full rights to its profile, and then assigns the profile folder to the account. This batch file can be called from a batch file containing the class roster. Here's an example:

```
@echo off
call mkaccount CS101 abaker DK@$g931xC
call mkaccount CS101 bsmith OXD2ba-12#
call mkaccount CS101 cfong  PXc43L$*Qf
⋮
```

net view

The command net view displays the networked computers that your computer has seen (that is, it can display the "Network Neighborhood"), and it can also list the shared folders and printers available on a remote computer. For this reason, net view is quite useful in debugging Windows networking problems.

The plain command net view displays the list of known active computers in the current workgroup or domain. The list looks like this:

```
Server Name        Remark
-------------------------------------------------------------
\\BALI             Our Humble File Server
\\JAVA             Brian's Workstation
```

You can add the option /domain to display a list of all known domains and work-groups on the current network, or you can add /domain:*domainname* to display a list of computers in the specified domain or workgroup.

The command net view *computername* displays a list of folders and printers shared by the specified computer. The list looks like this:

```
Shared resources at \\bali

Share name  Type   Used as  Comment
-----------------------------------------------------------
cdrive      Disk
faxes       Disk   F:
Laserjet    Print           Two bins
temp        Disk   X:
```

This is a good way to get a quick list of network resources that you can then use with net use. Items with drive letters listed under the Used As column are already mapped.

You can view the offline file-caching settings for a set of shared folders by adding the option /cache after *computername* (for example, net view \\bali /cache). In this case, the Comments column is replaced with the file-caching settings for each shared folder. This applies to shares provided by Windows XP Professional, Windows 2000 Pro and Server, and Windows .NET server only.

Finally, if your network includes Novell NetWare file servers, two additional forms of net use let you view a list of available NetWare servers and a server's shared resources:

```
net view /network:nw
net view /network:nw \\servername
```

netstat

netstat lists the status of your computer's TCP/IP protocol subsystem. Its main use is to list the names of remote computers to which your computer is attached; the listed connections indicate either that your computer is using a resource offered by another computer or that another computer is connected to yours. netstat can list TCP and UDP ports that your computer has open for listening. These indicate services that your computer is offering to the network or the Internet. netstat can also print statistics about TCP/IP networking traffic and errors.

You can view the full syntax by typing netstat /?. In the following section, I describe the most useful options.

Listing Active Connections

The netstat command with no options lists all current TCP connections between your computer and others. By default, netstat attempts to convert the remote computers' IP addresses into names. This can take a long time, so you can print a faster all-numeric listing by adding the -n option. The connection table looks like this:

```
Proto  Local Address      Foreign Address                      State
TCP    java:4273          sumatra.mycompany.com:microsoft-ds   ESTABLISHED
TCP    java:4319          bali.mycompany.com:netbios-ssn       ESTABLISHED
TCP    java:netbios-ssn   sumatra.mycompany.com:2430           ESTABLISHED
TCP    java:4564          msgr-cs122.msgr.hotmail.com:1863     ESTABLISHED
```

Each line represents one connection. The Local and Foreign Address columns indicate the names of the computers involved in the connections and the port number or name for the connection. The port indicates the type of network service: http or 80 indicates a Web server connection, 137 through 139 or netbios-x indicate Windows File Sharing, and so on.

It's sometimes possible to tell from the port numbers which computer—yours or the remote computer—is offering the service and which is the client or consumer of the service. In *most* cases, the server side of a TCP connection uses a port number below 1024, whereas the client side uses a port number above 1024. This is not always the case because some services use large port numbers on the server side. For example, TCP port 3389 is used by Microsoft's Remote Terminal Services and Remote Desktop, port 5190 is used by the AOL Instant Messenger service, and port 1863 is used by Microsoft Messenger. In these cases, the end of the connection that is using the "standard" port number is the server side.

The preceding sample listing shows that the local computer, Java, is using shared files on both Sumatra and Bali because it has a connection to these computers' NetBIOS session (netbios-ssn) ports. Bali, in turn, is using shared files on Java because it has made a connection to Java's NetBIOS port. Finally, Java has a connection to Microsoft's Messenger service.

Tip

The list of "well known" ports is in the file \windows\system32\drivers\etc\services. You can add to this file if you want netstat to be capable of printing the names of additional network services. For starters, you could add the following entries to the end of your computer's services file:

```
msmsgs      1863/tcp    #Microsoft Messenger
tsc         3389/tcp    #Microsoft Remote Desktop Services
aim         5190/tcp    #AOL Instant Messenger
pcaw-ssn    5631/tcp    #PC Anywhere session
pcaw-scan   5632/udp    #PC Anywhere server discovery
```

On Windows 7 and Vista, you can edit the services file only from an elevated command prompt. On XP, you must be logged on as a Computer Administrator or use an Administrator command prompt.

The State column indicates the status of the connection and is usually one of the following values:

State	Meaning
LISTEN	Your computer is awaiting incoming connections on this port.
SYN_SEND	Your computer is attempting to open this connection. The other computer has not yet replied.
ESTABLISHED	There is an active connection.
FIN_WAIT_1 or 2	The connection is being shut down
CLOSE_WAIT	The connection has been closed. This entry will remain for a while.

Listing Open Ports (Servers)

You can see the full list of ports to which your computer answers with the command netstat -a. This adds to the listing all ports that have no current connection but for which your computer is listening. Each one of these potentially indicates a service that your computer is offering to other networked computers or to the Internet at large if you have no firewall in place. The list of ports printed by a Windows XP computer is alarmingly long, and most of the port numbers are not standard numbers associated with well-known services.

If you add the -o option, netstat additionally prints the PID number of the program that has opened each port. You can combine this information with the output of tasklist to determine which program is associated with each connected or waiting port. Alternatively, use the -b option, and netstat prints the name of the listening program's executable file.

Listing Statistics

The -e, -s, and -p options display Ethernet and per-protocol summary statistics. See the online help for descriptions of these options.

Constant Monitoring

You can add a number (*n*) to the end of the netstat command line to make it repeat its printout every *n* seconds. This makes it possible to watch connections come and go during debugging or to watch statistics change over time.

nslookup

nslookup is a tool that interactively queries DNS servers. nslookup lets you find IP addresses given hostnames, and vice versa, and can also help you identify Internet miscreants—spammers and hackers.

Note

nslookup is a complex program and could easily take up an entire chapter itself. The Help and Support Center has fairly detailed information about each of its commands but does not provide much in the way of a tutorial. For a thorough introduction to DNS and nslookup, the acknowledged "bible" is *DNS and Bind*, by Paul Albitz and Cricket Liu, published by O'Reilly.

In this chapter, there isn't room to document all of nslookup's commands, but I describe a few practical applications to show you what it can do.

Finding an IP Address Given a Hostname

To look up the IP address for a given DNS hostname, type **nslookup** *hostname*. If the host is in your default domain, you can omit the domain name from the command. Otherwise, it's best to spell out the full domain name and add a period at the end. For example,

```
nslookup www.microsoft.com.
```

prints the following text:

```
Server:  sumatra.mycompany.com
Address:  192.168.0.2

Non-authoritative answer:
Name:    www.microsoft.akadns.net
Addresses:  207.46.230.218, 207.46.197.100, 207.46.197.113, 207.46.230.219
Aliases:  www.microsoft.com
```

The "Server" lines tell which DNS server provided the answer; in this case, the one on my network. The "Non-authoritative answer" heading indicates that my DNS server already had the requested information on hand from an earlier lookup, so it did not need to contact Microsoft's primary, or *authoritative*, DNS server directly. Finally, nslookup prints out a choice of several IP addresses for this website. Take your pick.

Finding the Hostname for an IP Address

The Internet's DNS system provides a reverse-lookup mechanism that lets you find the name associated with an IP address. You can type nslookup **207.46.230.218** and nslookup prints the following:

```
Server:  sumatra.mycompany.com
Address:  192.168.0.2

Name:    microsoft.com
Address:  207.46.230.218
```

This indicates that the standard or *canonical* name for this IP address is microsoft.com. Other hostnames might also return this IP address (you saw earlier that www.microsoft.com is one), but this is the main name. It's not uncommon for companies to set up several names, such as `mycompany.com`, `ftp.mycompany.com`, `www.mycompany.com`, and `mail.mycompany.com`, all pointing to the same IP address.

One good use of this reverse-lookup capability is to help identify the source of spam e-mails. If you can identify the name of the computer from which the spam originated, you might be able to report the miscreant to the responsible Internet Service Provider and get the account shut down. Although spammers always use a fake computer name and return address in their mailings, the IP addresses in the "Received by:" lines don't lie and indicate the mail's origin.

However, many ISPs and companies do not maintain reverse name lookup information, so the `nslookup` command cannot tell you the domain name of some IP addresses. `nslookup` can still help, if you look up Start of Authority information.

Examining Start of Authority Information

When you cannot determine the hostname and domain of a specific IP address, you *might* be able to determine the name of the company that owns the IP address through additional `nslookup` queries. For this, we can't use the simple command-line interface but rather must start `nslookup` without options. In this mode, it prompts for commands in its own query language.

Here's how this authority search works: IP addresses have the familiar format *aaa.bbb.ccc.ddd* (four groups of numbers between 1 and 255—for example, `63.194.114.254`). If `nslookup` can't find the name of address *aaa.bbb.ccc.ddd*, it can at least determine what company is responsible for the block of all addresses starting with *aaa.bbb.ccc*. To check, type the following commands:

```
nslookup
set type=any
ccc.bbb.aaa.in-addr.arpa.
```

That is, enter the three sets of numbers in reverse order, from last to first, followed by `in-addr.arpa`. To investigate the block containing address 63.194.114.254, we type `114.194.63.in-addr.arpa`. With any luck, `nslookup` prints something like this:

```
114.194.63.in-addr.arpa nameserver = ns1.pbi.net
114.194.63.in-addr.arpa nameserver = ns2.pbi.net
114.194.63.in-addr.arpa
        primary name server = ns1.pbi.net
        responsible mail addr = postmaster.pbi.net
        serial  = 200203060
        refresh = 3600 (1 hour)
        retry   = 900 (15 mins)
        expire  = 604800 (7 days)
        default TTL = 3600 (1 hour)

ns1.pbi.net     internet address = 206.13.28.11
ns2.pbi.net     internet address = 206.13.29.11
```

This shows the name of the DNS server that is responsible for this block of IP addresses, and the attached domain name should tell you the name of the company that owns the IP addresses, or the ISP that manages them.

If you're pursing a spammer or hacker, this information should point you in the right direction for reporting the problem or obtaining further information. You might try contacting the "responsible mail address" contact listed by `nslookup`. Turn the first period into an at sign (@) to get the mail address; `postmaster@pbi.net` in this example. For big companies, however, this e-mail address is probably not monitored. You might have better luck with `abuse@`*`domainname`*.

If `nslookup` can't find information about the IP addresses, you can try typing the following:

```
bbb.aaa.in-addr.arpa.
```

However, even if this does result in information, the responsible party is probably a top-level national ISP, and it's unlikely that they are interested in assisting you with whatever project you're working on.

To get out of `nslookup`'s prompt mode, type `exit`.

Testing a DNS Server

You can use `nslookup`'s prompt mode to test a specific DNS server. You might want to do this after setting up a server in your organization. To do this, type the following commands:

```
nslookup
server hostname or ipaddress
```

Here, *`hostname`* or *`ipaddress`* is the name or address of the server you want to test. Then, as `nslookup` continues to prompt you for input, enter hostnames or IP addresses. `nslookup` sends the requests to the specified server for resolution. Type **`exit`** when you're done.

ping

This venerable tool sends small data packets to a designated target computer or network router, which is supposed to send them right back. `ping` tallies up the percentage of data packets that make a successful roundtrip. `ping` therefore lets you know whether the target computer and all Internet connections between you and that computer are working. For example, when I typed `ping www.berkeley.edu`, I received the following printout:

```
Pinging arachne.berkeley.edu [169.229.131.109] with 32 bytes of data:

Reply from 169.229.131.109: bytes=32 time=22ms TTL=242
```

```
Reply from 169.229.131.109: bytes=32 time=21ms TTL=242
Reply from 169.229.131.109: bytes=32 time=22ms TTL=242
Reply from 169.229.131.109: bytes=32 time=20ms TTL=242

Ping statistics for 169.229.131.109:
    Packets: Sent = 4, Received = 4, Lost = 0 (0% loss),
Approximate round trip times in milli-seconds:
    Minimum = 20ms, Maximum = 22ms, Average = 21ms
```

(There's that canonical name business again; ping looked up the IP address for the name I typed, and then looked up that address's canonical name. That's why the listing says arachne.berkeley.edu instead of www.berkeley.edu.) You can see that all four of the test probes that ping sent are returned. Each roundtrip took about 20 milliseconds.

If you're testing a network wiring problem, you might find ping's -t option useful. ping -t tests the network connection constantly, instead of just four times, so you can poke around with your network's wiring and hubs. Look for the telltale flashing lights that show ping's data packets traveling by.

Tip

When you're trying to diagnose a flaky Internet connection, start by pinging your computer's gateway IP address and its DHCP server IP address first. The ipconfig program can give you these numbers. This test tells you whether your computer is capable of communicating with its nearest neighbor. If the ping test fails, then you have a problem with your network or modem connection itself, and the Internet is not to blame.

ping lets you specify the size of the data packets it sends. I have found that a flaky DSL Internet connection can sometimes transmit short packets without any problems but can't send large packets at all. Because ping sends small 32-byte packets by default, this can make it appear that the DSL connection is working. It's confusing when you can ping Internet sites but not connect to them with Internet Explorer. Adding the option -s 800 tells ping to send 800-byte packets. If you consistently find that small packets get through your Internet connection whereas large ones don't, you might have a problem with the wiring between your DSL modem and the telephone company's central office.

Note

Many Internet hosts do not return ping packets. Don't even bother trying to ping www.microsoft.com or www.intel.com. They don't respond. If you're trying to determine whether your Internet connection is working, try pinging one of your ISP's mail or DNS servers; they're more likely to respond.

tracert

The Internet consists of hundreds of thousands of computers and network routers connected to one another through various types of data connections: fiber optic,, Ethernet, telephone line, microwave, and others. To get from your computer to an Internet host, your data has to "hop" across anywhere from 4 to 20 such connections as it zigzags its way around the globe. (If you've ever flown Southwest Airlines cross-country, you know what this is like.) If there's a failure anywhere along the way, your data doesn't reach its destination. The problem is, when you can't reach an Internet host, you don't know if the desired computer is down or if there's an Internet outage somewhere in between.

tracert can tell the difference. Here's how it works: The command tracert *hostname* sends a small data packet to the specified computer, just like ping. However, the packet carries a marker that says it's allowed to make only one hop towards its goal. After it makes one hop, it's considered undeliverable and is sent back by the first router. This is a good thing—if this packet makes it back to you, you know that the connection from your computer to at least one Internet router is working. tracert then sends another packet with only enough "postage" to make *two* router hops. If this one makes it back, you know that the connection from the first router to the second is working. tracert repeats this repeatedly until the packet either reaches the desired destination, as illustrated in Figure 13.1, or stops coming back. In the former case, you know that the entire network path is working. In the latter, you have found out how far your data goes before it stops, and this tells you where the outage is.

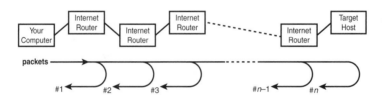

Figure 13.1   *tracert* maps out the path from your computer to a remote Internet host.

Here's an example: Suppose my mail program says it can't connect to my mail server, mail.pacbell.net. If I type tracert mail.pacbell.net and see the message

```
Tracing route to mail.pacbell.net [64.164.98.8]
over a maximum of 30 hops:

  1    3 ms    2 ms    2 ms  11.22.33.1
64.220.177.1 reports: network unreachable
```

then I know that the data made one successful hop to 11.22.33.1, which is my DSL router. However, that router said it could not pass the data any further. This means that the problem is close to me; my network connection is down, and I should call my ISP for assistance.

On the other hand, if the report looked like the following, then the entire network path is working:

```
Tracing route to mail.pacbell.net [64.164.98.8]
over a maximum of 30 hops:

  1     3 ms     2 ms     2 ms  64.220.177.1
  2    25 ms    15 ms    16 ms  65.104.11.1
  3    17 ms    15 ms    20 ms  205.158.11.61
  4    16 ms    19 ms    20 ms  64.0.0.129
  5    22 ms    19 ms    17 ms  64.220.0.62
  6    18 ms    19 ms    24 ms  64.220.0.21
  7    23 ms    21 ms    19 ms  bb1-p3-2.pxpaca.sbcglobal.net [151.164.8
  8    18 ms    23 ms    19 ms  bb2-p9-0.sntc01.pbi.net [64.161.1.21]
  9    27 ms    19 ms    27 ms  64.161.1.26
 10    18 ms    19 ms    19 ms  bb1-p15-0.pltn13.pbi.net [64.161.124.253
 11    22 ms    18 ms    19 ms  srvr1-vlan40.pltn13.pbi.net [64.164.97.2
 12    19 ms    22 ms    23 ms  mta7.pltn13.pbi.net [64.164.98.8]
Trace complete.
```

If the mail server is not responding, it's not due to a connection problem. The mail server itself is probably not working.

If tracert's test showed that data made three or more hops but failed to reach the destination, then we would conclude that the problem is with routers that belong to the Internet's "backbone," and there is not much we mere mortals can do about that.

Tip

tracert is a great tool for diagnosing problems, and it's even more valuable when you know what its output should look like when your Internet connection is working properly. You should point tracert at a few distant locations and record the result, direct the output into a file, and save or print it. This way, you have something to compare it to if things break down.

Note

Some other handy networking programs you might want to look into on your own are arp, ftp, nbtstat, netsh, pathping, and route. netsh lets you configure network adapters, routing tables, and filters, and it has a complex command-line environment of its own. Most of its commands, however, work only on Windows 2000/.NET Server.

Getting More Utilities

You can get hundreds more useful command-line utilities by downloading the Windows Resource Kits from Microsoft's website. Visit www.microsoft.com and search for the words download windows resource kit. The Windows Server resource kits are particularly rich in command-line utilities, and you don't need a Windows Server installation to use them. When you download and install a Resource Kit, it includes help files that document all the provided tools.

14

Windows PowerShell

- This chapter introduces Windows PowerShell, a truly unique scripting and management tool.

- This chapter describes how PowerShell works as a command-line environment. The following chapters discuss the PowerShell programming language and PowerShell commands.

- You'll see that PowerShell commands work with objects instead of text.

- You'll learn about an important security setting you'll have to change before you can run PowerShell scripts.

Introduction to Windows PowerShell

In 2006, Windows Script Host (WSH) and the Command Prompt shell got a new sibling when Microsoft released a completely new environment called Windows PowerShell. PowerShell has some similarities to the older tools: Like the Command Prompt shell, it lets you type commands interactively as well as put them into script/batch files, and you can easily use pipes and redirection to string files and programs together. Like WSH, it provides a powerful object-oriented programming language for complex scripting.

But PowerShell is a *very* different, strange animal, and it has powerful features that go way beyond what WSH and the Command Prompt offer. I show you what I mean in the following sections.

An Object-Oriented Command Shell

Here's one way that that PowerShell is different and strange. Recall that if you type dir into a regular Command Prompt window, the dir command spits out a bunch of text onto the screen, giving the names, sizes, and timestamps of the files in a directory. You can direct that text into a file using the > redirection operator, or you can "pipe" the text to another program using the | operator. For example, the command

```
dir /s /b | sort
```

lists the files in the current directory and its subdirectories as a stream of text, and the text is sent to the sort program that sorts them alphabetically. If you read Chapter 10, "The CMD Command-Line," or if you've used a command-line environment in nearly any computer operating system in the last, say, 30 years, this should be familiar.

Windows PowerShell command lines appear to work in the same way, but its commands deal with *objects* rather than just text. These are the same sort of objects I talked about in Chapters 3–9: objects that represent files, folders, Windows device drivers, network services, documents any of the hundreds of objects defined in the .NET Framework library). What flows from one command to the next, via that pipe symbol (|), is a stream of objects. The various PowerShell commands let you generate, manipulate, invoke methods on, change properties of, and extract information from these objects.

As an example, here's what happens when you type dir in a PowerShell window. The PowerShell dir command is actually an alias (shorthand) for the Get-ChildItem cmdlet. You can type either name and get the same result.

Wait, cmd-what? *Cmdlet*, pronounced "command-let," as in "cute tiny little command." PowerShell's built-in commands are called cmdlets. Maybe they were out of vowels up in Redmond that year? No, the reason for the odd name is that they're not completely built in to PowerShell, like cmd.exe's commands, nor are they really completely independent of it, like exe files. They're implemented in a new way, so they needed a new word. In any case...

With no other arguments, Get-ChildItem emits File and Folder objects for all the files and subfolders in the current directory. If I type the command dir with no arguments, Get-ChildItem spits out a list of File and Folder objects, and because there is no pipe or output redirection, the results spill into the Windows PowerShell command window.

When objects land in the PowerShell window, PowerShell prints one line for each object, in a nice columnar format, listing the most important properties of each object. For File and Folder objects, this includes the Name, Length, LastWriteTime, and Mode properties. The resulting list looks like this:

```
    Directory: C:\users\bknittel
Mode              LastWriteTime      Length Name
----              -------------      ------ ----
d-r--         6/2/2010   1:27 PM            Contacts
```

```
d-r--        6/15/2010   11:35 PM                 Desktop
d-r--        6/14/2010    8:47 AM                 Documents
d-r--        6/2/2010     1:27 PM                 Downloads
  ⋮
d-r--        6/2/2010     1:27 PM                 Videos
d-r--        6/23/2010   11:01 AM                 Virtual Machines
-a---        8/21/2009    6:07 PM           1889  listprops.vbs
-a---        8/20/2009   12:34 PM           1020  nets.vbs
-a---        8/20/2009   11:54 AM           3668  tempfile.txt
-a---        9/14/2009    7:13 PM           1605  test.vbs
-a---        6/23/2010    2:19 PM           3650  x
```

The headings at the top of the columns are just the names of the properties that are being displayed. The listing would be similar for any other type of object a cmdlet generated.

The thing to ponder here is that the dir command in the regular Command Prompt environment generates text in a fixed format. The dir cmdlet in Windows PowerShell generates a list of File and Folder objects, which PowerShell formats into a text listing after the fact.

You can redirect the output of a PowerShell cmdlet to a file, using the familiar > character, and the same thing occurs: the stream of objects gets formatted into a nice, text listing.

The innovation in PowerShell is what happens when you use the pipe redirection symbol (|). PowerShell lets you direct a stream of objects from one cmdlet to another, and they can change the properties of and call methods on these objects, doing real work as they get passed along. It's only when the objects finally hit the screen that text appears. One cmdlet might generate a list of objects representing files, computers, services, and network objects; the next in the pipeline might filter and pass on just the ones that are of interest; and the next might call methods to perform actions on the objects. This is a truly unique feature of Windows PowerShell.

So, to do what used to require a loop in WSH:

```
fso = CreateObject("Scripting.FileSystemObject")
for each file in fso.GetFolder("c:\temp").Files
    file.Delete
next
```

you can do with a single command line in Windows PowerShell:

```
dir c:\temp | remove-item
```

dir generates a list of File and Folder objects representing the contents of directory c:\temp and passes it to the remove-item command, which deletes the "real world" thing behind any object it's passed.

You could also type the following:

```
(dir c:\temp).delete()
```

which generates the same stream of File and Folder objects and calls the `delete` method on each object. The result is the same: The files are deleted.

(And, as you might expect, you could also just type `remove-item c:\temp\*.*`. That would be the most straightforward command, but it doesn't show how PowerShell differs from the regular command prompt.)

Here's another example of how a pipeline command can work:

```
dir | where-object {$_.LastWriteTime -lt (get-date).addmonths(-6)} | remove-item
```

`dir` generates an object for each file in the current directory, `where-object` passes along only those that are more than six months old and `remove-item` deletes the old files. So, we've constructed a disk cleanup command of out of general-purpose cmdlets. (Don't type this command, by the way—it's just an example!)

This is very peculiar and powerful, and it takes some getting used to.

Based on the .NET Framework

The .NET Framework is Microsoft's answer to Sun Microsystem's Java programming language. In both cases, programs are generated not using the instruction set of your computer's Intel or AMD hardware processor (CPU), but of a different, fictitious computer processor. The underlying .NET Framework (or in Java's case, the Java Virtual Machine) examines the instructions and carries out their directives. In other words, .NET programs are for the most part *interpreted* by a lower-level program, with some sophisticated engineering to make them run nearly as fast as a program that's directly driving your CPU. What this interpretive layer does is make it nearly impossible for an incorrectly written or rogue program to take down Windows or interfere with other applications. It also gave the .NET Framework authors the freedom to design a fictitious CPU with an instruction set that is well-suited for modern programming languages not derived from the antiquated Intel instruction set. In theory, at least, .NET programs should be more reliable than "native" programs. In addition, .NET programs are written in languages that take care of the low-level details of managing computer memory and objects, so the programmer doesn't have to struggle with them, and this—again, in theory—leads to even better reliability.

The "Framework" part of the name comes from the fact that there is a huge library of programming functions and objects that any .NET Framework program can use. The .NET Application Programming Interface (API) is *far* more sophisticated than the original Windows API that older-style Windows applications were built on. It includes hundreds of objects that let you work with graphical user interfaces (GUIs), database access, network communications, web interaction, cryptography, number-crunching, and more.

Here's what's in it for you: (You knew I was going somewhere with all this, didn't you?) All the power of the .NET Framework is available in Windows PowerShell command lines and scripts. Besides managing Windows and doing the sort of routine data processing tasks that you can do with WSH or batch files, PowerShell scripts can interact with web services, manipulate databases, display dialog boxes, and more. If you've worked with both Visual Basic for Applications (VBA) scripting in, say Microsoft Word, and with VBScript in WSH, you know that VBScript can't access core Windows API functions the way that VBA can. Windows PowerShell doesn't have this limitation. The entire .NET Framework API is available to scripts.

The only real barrier is the learning curve. In three chapters, I, of course, can't give you general .NET and PowerShell expertise, but I'll get you started and show you how to learn more for yourself.

An Extensible Environment

PowerShell can run three sorts of programs: built-in commands, external programs, and scripts. This is analogous to the regular Command Prompt environment, where you could use the built-in commands that are handled by the cmd.exe program itself, run external programs, or create batch files that let you orchestrate either type of command to perform the steps of a more complex task. In PowerShell, the built-in commands are cmdlets. Unlike the Command Prompt shell, however, these built-in commands are not wired into the PowerShell program but are added to it through a snap-in mechanism as one or more .DLL files stored on your hard disk. So, custom cmdlets can be added to the environment. The idea is that Microsoft and third parties can add install management cmdlets for their applications and servers, so that they can be managed by PowerShell scripts. Microsoft SQL Server, Microsoft Exchange, and VMWare servers have custom cmdlet snap-ins, for example. If you're a skilled .NET programmer, you can create your own custom cmdlets using the Windows PowerShell 2.0 Software Development Kit (SDK) and Microsoft Visual Studio Express Edition, both of which you can download free from Microsoft.

In addition, PowerShell responds to command keywords that are part of its built-in script programming language which is a unique language, all its own. It's not VBScript, it's not VB.NET, it's not C#. It's PowerShell. I discuss the PowerShell language in detail in Chapter 15, "PowerShell Programming."

You can also create and use .NET and COM objects not just in scripts, as you do with WSH, but right at the PowerShell command prompt.

This means that every cmdlet, Windows program, command-line program, .NET object, and COM object (including WMI and ASDI) is available right at your fingertips.

> **Note**
>
> As an aside, it's interesting to know that just as VBA provided an object-oriented, full-scale programming language that could be integrated into applications such as Microsoft Word, programmers can "host" PowerShell inside their .NET applications. PowerShell is intended not just for helping you automate your routine tasks, but to serve as the scripting/macro language for Windows applications and services.

Obtaining Windows PowerShell

Two versions of PowerShell are available: versions 1.0 and 2.0. I only discuss version 2.0 in this book for three reasons:

- It's somewhat more advanced and better behaved.
- It's the version that's installed by default on Windows 7.
- It includes a nifty graphical script editing and debugging tool called the PowerShell Integrated Scripting Environment (ISE).

As I mentioned, Windows PowerShell 2.0 is installed by default with Windows 7 and Windows Server 2008 R2. You can download it for Windows XP, Vista, Windows Server 2003, Windows Server 2003 R2, and Windows Server 2008, as I discuss later in this chapter.

Note

On Windows 7 or on older version of Windows, after installing the PowerShell update that I describe shortly, you might notice that your PATH environment variable includes the entry \windows\ system32\WindowsPowerShell\1.0. The 1.0 doesn't mean that you have an old version of PowerShell. You have version 2. It just uses the same path for its components that the earlier version did.

The following section describes the procedure for installing Windows PowerShell 2.0 on each version of Windows for which PowerShell is available.

Windows 7

Windows PowerShell 2.0 is installed by default on Windows 7. You don't need to do anything special to set it up.

Windows Vista and Windows XP

To install PowerShell 2.0 on older versions of Windows, follow these steps:

1. Be sure that you have .NET Framework 3.5 installed. If you need to install it, download and install the highest available service pack version. At the time this was written, .NET Framework 3.5 SP1 was available.

Note

PowerShell 2.0 requires Microsoft's .NET Framework 2.0 or better, while the GUI PowerShell editor/debugging tool that I describe later in this chapter requires .NET Framework 3.5. At the time this was written, .NET Framework 4.0 had been released, but the PowerShell installer doesn't see it as meeting the Framework prerequisite. Therefore, in these installation procedures, I give instructions for installing .NET Framework 3.5.

2. Download and install an update called the Windows Management Framework Core. At the time this was written, you can find it at support.microsoft.com/kb/ 968930. If that URL fails, search microsoft.com for "KB968930" or for "Windows Management Framework download."

   Find the link to download the appropriate update for your version of Windows. The update is available for the following desktop Windows editions:

   - Windows Vista, x86 (32-bit) and x64 (64-bit) versions
   - Windows XP SP3 and Windows Embedded, x86 (32-bit) versions only

   The update installs Windows PowerShell 2.0 and Windows Remote Management (WinRM) packages. It also enables and starts the Windows Firewall and Internet Connection Sharing Service on XP.

3. Run Windows Update to download and install any available security update, hotfixes, and/or .NET Framework service packs.

After you have Windows PowerShell installed on your computer, take it for a test drive, as I describe shortly in "The PowerShell Environment."

Windows Server 2008 R2

Windows PowerShell 2.0 is installed by default on Windows Server 2008 R2.

Windows Server 2008 R2 Server Core

To install PowerShell 2.0 on a Server Core R2 installation, run `sconfig` and then select Configure Remote Management, Enable Windows PowerShell. Or, type the following commands:

```
dism /Online /Enable-Feature /FeatureName: NetFx2-ServerCore
dism /Online /Enable-Feature /FeatureName: MicrosoftWindowsPowerShell
```

Windows Server 2008 (pre-R2), 2003 R2, and 2003

Follow the instructions given previously for Windows Vista and XP, but in step 2, select the update package appropriate for your version of Windows Server. The update is available for the following Server editions:

- Windows Server 2003, x86 and x64 versions (includes Windows Server 2003 R2)
- Windows Server 2008, x86 and x64 versions

At the time this was written, Microsoft did not plan to provide PowerShell 2.0 for Itanium versions of Windows Server other than 2008 R2. If that hasn't changed by the time you read this, your only option might be to download and install Windows PowerShell 1.0 for Windows Server 2003 Itanium, by searching for Microsoft KB926140.

Windows Server 2008 (Pre-R2) Server Core

You can't install PowerShell 2.0 on a Windows Server 2008 Server Core installation. You can install PowerShell 1.0, but it involves jumping through several hoops. The biggest difficulty is in getting the .NET Framework installed. For the procedure, do a Google search for "Dmitry's PowerBlog PowerShell on Server Core."

The PowerShell Environment

You should be able to click Start, All Programs, Accessories and see Windows PowerShell as a choice (although you might have to scroll down; by default, it's below System Tools). On 32-bit Windows versions, there are normally two choices:

- **Windows PowerShell**—This is the interactive command-line environment. I discuss this first.
- **Windows PowerShell ISE**—This is a GUI editing/debugging tool that you can use to help develop PowerShell scripts. I discuss this later in the chapter.

On 64-bit versions of Windows, these two menu selections run the 64-bit version of Windows PowerShell. In addition, there are selections for Windows PowerShell (x86) and Windows PowerShell ISE (x86), which run the 32-bit versions of PowerShell. These are provided in case you have to use a cmdlet snap-in that is available only in a 32-bit version, but they are otherwise probably not of much interest.

Alternatively, you can open a regular Command Prompt window and type `powershell` or type `powershell` in the Windows Search box or Run dialog box.

> **Note**
> If you run PowerShell inside a regular Command Prompt window, you won't get the default white-on-blue color scheme that you get when you open PowerShell from the menu, but it's the same program. You can return to the regular cmd.exe command prompt by typing `exit`.

> **Note**
> Windows PowerShell is subject to the same security issues as the regular Command Prompt. To modify system files or perform other administrative actions on Windows 7 and Vista, you must run PowerShell with elevated privileges. On Windows XP, to perform privileged tasks, you must be logged on as a Computer Administrator or run PowerShell under an Administrator account using `runas`.
>
> I discuss this in more detail toward the end of this chapter in the section "PowerShell Security."

Whichever method you use to start PowerShell, the next prompt you see should have the letters PS at the left, as shown in Figure 14.1. Type **dir** and press Enter, just to prove to yourself that this is *not* the old Command Prompt. The format of the directory listing is very different.

Figure 14.1 The PS to the left of the prompt tells
you you're using Windows PowerShell.

I discuss the command-line environment more in the next section.

The PowerShell Command Prompt

Windows PowerShell prompts for commands just as the old Command Prompt environment does. It prompts, you type a command, you press Enter, it displays some sort of results, and you repeat the process over and over.

One thing that's really improved with PowerShell, though, is that the command language is really a full-fledged programming language and creating, working with, and displaying variables is easy. For example, you might recall that you could use the `set` *name=xxx* command in batch files to store data in named variables and use the `%name%` syntax to retrieve the data.

In Windows PowerShell, you define variables by putting a dollar sign ($) in front of the variable's name to both define and retrieve its value. For example, you can type the commands

```
$a = 40 + 7
$a
```

and Windows PowerShell obediently displays the computed value of a, which is 47.

Every PowerShell command is just an expression with a value, so it's perfectly legal to type 40+7 as a command line. PowerShell prints the result. These are trivial examples, but it can be quite powerful when you're working with objects—just type the name of an object and its property to display the value of the property, for example:

```
$f.path
```

to print the Path property of an object you've put into variable $f.

I describe PowerShell's programming syntax in more detail in the next chapter. For now, remember that whatever you can put into a script, you can also type directly at the PowerShell command prompt.

Command-Line Editing

PowerShell lets you use the backspace, arrow, and other editing keys on your keyboard to modify command lines as you're typing them and to recall, modify, and reuse previously typed commands. This will be very familiar if you've worked with the Command Prompt because the editing keys are identical. (There's a reason for this: PowerShell is a standard console application just like cmd.exe.)

The arrow key functions are the most important to remember:

- The left and right arrow keys (← and →) let you move within a command line that you're typing, so you can go back and change a mistake at the beginning of the line without erasing and retyping the whole thing.

- Ctrl+← and Ctrl+→ move back and forth a whole word at a time. This can save a lot of keystrokes.

- The Home and End keys move instantly to the beginning or end of the line.

- Normally, if you move backward in the edited line and start typing, what you type is inserted ahead of what's already there. This is usually very handy. If you need to replace a lot of text, though, instead of erasing what's there and then typing in the new, press the Ins key once and your typing *replaces* what's already there—just type over it. The cursor changes to a solid block to remind you that this is what will happen when you type. You can press Ins again to return to Insert mode. PowerShell automatically switches back to Insert mode when you press Enter, so you can edit the next command normally.

- The up and down arrow keys (↑ and ↓) let you step back to commands you typed previously. You can use ↑ to locate a previous command and press Enter to reissue it, or you can locate it and then edit it before pressing Enter.

There are some other function keys that you might want to know about. These shortcuts actually work in *any* Powershell or Command Prompt window, and with any console application:

Key	Does the following...
F2	F2 followed by a single character copies text from the previously entered command line into the current command line, up to but not including the first occurrence of the character you type. For example, if the previous command was

`get-childitem c:\temp | get-member`

then pressing F2 | copies `get-childitem c:\temp` into the current input line.

F3	Types in whatever was in the previous command line from the cursor position to the end of the line. For example, if you mistype a single character in a command line:

`fet-childitem c:\temp`

and don't realize it until you've pressed Enter, just type g and then press F3 to recall the rest of the line. You'll end up with

`get-children c:\temp`.

F4	F4 followed by a single character deletes text from the cursor up to but not including the first occurrence of that character.
F7	Pops up a list of recently typed commands. You can scroll through it using the arrow keys and press Enter to reissue the command.
F9	Lets you type in the number of a previous command. The numbers are the ones shown in the F7 pop-up. (This one would have been useful if the numbers ran backward, so that 3 meant the third command back, but they don't, so it's not.)

To be honest, you can work through an entire IT career without ever using these F-key shortcuts and not suffer for it, but if you can manage to remember them, they could come in handy some day. I keep meaning to remember F7, but I never do.

Copying and Pasting

Copying and pasting in the PowerShell environment works exactly as it does in any Command Prompt or console program window, again, because PowerShell *is* a normal console program, just like cmd.exe.

You can't cut text out of the window; you can only copy text from a rectangular region to the clipboard. To copy from the PowerShell screen with the mouse, click the upper-left corner of the PowerShell window and select Edit, Mark. Point to the upper-left corner of the text you want to copy, press the mouse button, and drag to the lower-right corner of the text you want. Then, right-click the screen, or press Enter, to copy the text.

Note

If all the text you want isn't visible, remember that you can scroll the window up and down during the process.

There are also keyboard shortcuts for these steps. Press Alt+Space E K to begin. You can then use the arrow keys to move the cursor to the upper-left corner of the desired text; then, hold down Shift and while holding it, use the arrow keys to move to the lower corner. Press Enter to complete the operation.

Personally, I find it easiest to type Alt+Space E K to start, switch to the mouse to mark the rectangle, and then go back to the keyboard to press Enter.

To paste text from the clipboard into the PowerShell window, click the upper-left corner of the window and select Edit, Paste. You might find it quicker to use to the keyboard shortcut: Alt+Space E P.

Pausing Output and Stopping a Runaway Program

As in the regular Command Prompt environment, you can type Ctrl+C to cancel a running PowerShell program or script.

In addition, Ctrl+S stops a printout that's scrolling by so fast you can't read it, and another Ctrl+S starts things up again. You can also use the scrollbar to look back through the contents of the PowerShell window.

Still, if a command is going to generate a lot of output, just as in the Command Prompt environment, it's best to either pipe the output through the `more` command, which pauses after every screenful, or direct the output into a file, and then view the file with Notepad or a word processor.

Command-Line Syntax

PowerShell's command-line syntax is at once familiar and a bit strange. I discuss this in the following sections.

Command Types

As I mentioned previously, PowerShell has built-in language statements, and it can run internal cmdlets, external commands, and scripts that contain multiple PowerShell commands.

With the exception of the PowerShell language keywords like `if` and `foreach`, which can have complex structures, commands are evaluated one line at a time, just as in the Command Prompt world.

The first word on the line is the name of the command you want to run. Any remaining text on the line is passed to the command as its arguments. Normally, spaces delimit the command name and the arguments, but you can use the single or double quotation mark (") character to embed a space in an argument, as in the following command:

```
command /abc "argument with spaces"
```

In an unusual twist, to type a program name that has spaces in its name or path, you must use single or double quotes around the name and must precede the command with an ampersand, as in this example:

```
&"command with spaces" /abc argument
```

PowerShell finds the program that corresponds to the command name by searching the following places in this order:

1. PowerShell first looks through its *alias* list, which is a list of shorthand names for commands. PowerShell is installed with nearly 150 built-in aliases predefined. For example, `cd` is set up as the alias for the `Set-Location` cmdlet. As you work with PowerShell, you'll find that you'll soon want to define your own custom aliases for the commands you use most often.

   If an alias name is matched, PowerShell replaces the command name in your command line with the alias definition and the search process over.

2. PowerShell then scans the names of functions that have been defined by the current script, if you're running a PowerShell script, or that have been defined at the command line. If a function with the specified name is found, the function is called and passed the command-line arguments. As I explain in the next chapter, you can define your functions in the PowerShell language in scripts or at the command prompt. They work and act just like cmdlets.

3. If the command name is not found in the alias list, PowerShell searches the list of cmdlets that come preinstalled with Windows PowerShell or have been added by a snap-in that came with an added application or service. If it's found, the cmdlet is run.

4. If the name doesn't match a cmdlet, PowerShell uses the standard search path mechanism to look for an external program, much as cmd.exe does. It looks first in the current directory and then through the directories listed in the PATH environment variable for a file with the stated command name and whose extension is a recognized program extension. In each folder searched, PowerShell does the following:

   a. It first looks for the extension `.ps1`, which is used for PowerShell scripts in PowerShell versions 1.0 *and* 2.0. If a script file is found, PowerShell runs the script (subject to the security restrictions that I discuss shortly).

   b. If a `.ps1` file is not found, it scans through the extensions listed in the PATHEXT environment variable, just as cmd.exe would. This mechanism lets it find and run standard Windows executable files (`.exe` files), both

GUI and console applications. PATHEXT also includes `.cmd` and `.bat`, so that PowerShell can run normal Command Prompt batch files—it fires up a copy of cmd.exe to do so. Likewise, for `.vbs`, `.js`, `.vbe`, and `.jse` files, it fires up WSH to run these scripts, and for `.MSC` files, it runs the snap-in through the Microsoft Management Console.

Thus, you can run PowerShell cmdlets and scripts, console applications, Windows programs, batch files, or any other sort of program from the PowerShell environment. `notepad` still starts Notepad.

There are exceptions to the normal search processing, though:

- If your command includes an explicit path as part of the command name, PowerShell runs the specified file. For example, the command `c:\bin\sort.exe` would run that specific copy of `sort.exe` and would not try to search for `sort` as an alias or in the PATH locations.

- To improve security, PowerShell will not run a `.ps1` PowerShell script that it found in the current directory before it searched the PATH list. It will tell you about it, but it won't run it. It will run only PowerShell scripts that it finds in the PATH or those to which you've explicitly typed a path.

  You can run a file in the current directory by preceding its name with `.\`, as in `.\myscript.ps1`. This is an explicit path, so it satisfies PowerShell's security requirement.

  Even then, PowerShell might not run scripts at all, depending on additional security settings that I discuss in the next section.

- It's conceivable that more than one PowerShell snap-in might define a cmdlet with the same name. PowerShell searches through snap-ins from the most recently installed back toward the first installed, and the first snap-in found that defines the cmdlet name is the one that's used. Also, you can import (load) new snap-in cmdlet modules while PowerShell is running, and the same ordering applies: Snap-ins are examined from the most recently imported toward the oldest.

  Or, you might have defined an alias that has the same name as an existing cmdlet. If you type the aliased name, you'll get the command that the alias specifies, not the original cmdlet.

  To run a specific cmdlet from a specific snap-in without hitting this ordering or aliasing problem, you can precede the cmdlet name with the name of the snap-in module, followed by a backslash. For example, Microsoft.PowerShell.Utility\ Get-Date runs the Get-Date cmdlet in the Microsoft.PowerShell.Utility module even if you've defined an alias for Get-Date or another module has defined a cmdlet with the same name.

- For more information on command searching, type **help about_command_ precedence** at the PowerShell command prompt.

I know this can seem tedious in an introduction, but you need to know the details of the search system to get your own scripts to run and to diagnose problems if someday the program that runs isn't the one you expected.

The main thing you should take from this is that if you want to develop and use your own PowerShell scripts, you will want to create a specific folder to hold them and put that folder name into the Windows PATH environment variable. If you've already set up such a folder for batch files or WSH scripts, you can use the same folder for PowerShell scripts.

➜ To see how to set up a script folder and put it in the PATH, **see** "Adding Scripts to the Path", p. 37.

Then, follow the instructions in the section on scripting security later in this chapter to let your scripts run.

Redirection and Pipes

You can redirect the output of commands you run from the PowerShell prompt and in PowerShell scripts into files using the same syntax that I described in Chapter 10. The usual operators—|, >, <, >>, and so on—work as they do in the Command Prompt environment.

In PowerShell, though, remember that most cmdlets emit objects, not text. The output of these cmdlets turns into text listings only when they land in the PowerShell window, are redirected to files, or piped to standard Windows console commands. You can control the formatting of these text listings using cmdlets that I describe in chapter 16 "Formatting Cmdlet Output."

Cmdlets and Objects and Scripts, Oh My!

The PowerShell world introduces new, somewhat confusing concepts and terminology, and I suspect that your first reaction will be similar to mine: I looked at a few PowerShell scripts; scratched my head; and thought, "I wonder if there are any donuts left in the kitchen?" At first, it all seemed pretty opaque and possibly not worth investigating. Fortunately, this feeling didn't last long. (Neither did the donuts.)

The biggest obstacles are the strange names of the cmdlets and the unusual command-line syntax. Cmdlets have names like Remove-ItemProperty, Get-Content, Wait-Job, New-Alias, and so on. This can help make sense of it:

- Cmdlet names are case insensitive. You can type `wait-job` just as well as `Wait-Job`. The capitalization is used to make the words more distinct when you read the documentation.

- Microsoft's programmers chose to use a noun–verb convention for naming the cmdlets to make the names more clearly say what the cmdlets actually do. The dash is just part of the name. `Rename-Item` isn't some sort of combination of a `Rename` command and an `Item` command. The name is all one word: `Rename-Item`, and you can guess from this name that it probably renames whatever items it's given.

  Yes, the names tend to be long and cumbersome to type. A Unix programmer would have chosen a name like `ri` for that `Rename-Item` command. But, `ri` doesn't really tell what it does. As it turns out, PowerShell *does* have a built-in alias for `Rename-Item`, and the alias is…`ri`.

  As you learn PowerShell's commands, you might start by using the long names to help remember what the commands do and then scan through the alias list and start learning their shorter abbreviations.

- The names of cmdlet command-line options are similarly long. For example, the `get-process` cmdlet can take the following optional arguments:

  ```
  -Name "string"
  -ComputerName "string"
  -FileVersionInfo
  -Module
  -Id integer
  -InputObject object
  ```

  Again with the long names! Who can type `-InputObject` quickly without making three typos along the way? Well, it turns out that you don't have to type the entire option name, just enough to distinguish the desired option from any others that start with the same letters. So, you can type `-input` or even `-in` instead of `-InputObject`. You just can't shorten it to just `-i` because that's not enough to distinguish between `-Id` and `-Inputobject`.

- Some command can be shortened even more. For example, a typical `new-alias` command looks like this:

  ```
  new-alias -name shortname -val realcommandname -descr "Brief description"
  ```

  But, you even can omit the parameter switches, in this really short version of the command:

  ```
  new-alias shortname realcommandname
  ```

  The two arguments in this case are called *positional parameters* because PowerShell has to figure out what they are based on their position in the command line. You can see which parameters can be specified this way by looking at a cmdlet's syntax description. If you type `new-alias -?`, you can see that the syntax is

  ```
  New-Alias [-Name] <string> [-Value] <string> [-Description <string>]
  [-Force] [-Option {None | ReadOnly | Constant | Private | AllScope}]
  [-PassThru] [-Scope <string>] [-Confirm] [-WhatIf] [<CommonParameters>]
  ```

Notice that the `-Name` option indicator itself is listed in [ ] brackets, so it's optional, but the `<string>` value after it isn't. This argument must always be there, so it can be interpreted by its position. The `-Value` string is listed the same way, but none of the other arguments are.

The other main obstacle to learning to use PowerShell is the strange syntax with commands like the example I gave earlier

```
dir | where-object {$_.LastWriteTime -lt (get-date).addmonths(-6)} | remove-item
```

The `dir` and `remove-item` parts are self-explanatory, but the middle part is, well, non-obvious. This where you hit the PowerShell learning curve, and the only thing to do is expose yourself to a lot of it. It will start to make sense pretty quickly. My advice is to read as many PowerShell scripts as you can. Read them like literature, get a feel for the language, and work out what they do. The next chapter explains a lot of the syntax. I'll just point out a couple of things about that example command here.

The `where-object` cmdlet is a filter. It reads a stream of objects from the previous command in the pipeline, evaluates a true/false value for each one, and passes along only the objects for which the value is true. In the example, the true/false value is provided by the part within curly brackets:

```
{$_.LastWriteTime -lt (get-date).addmonths(-6)}
```

Caution

This command is great for cleaning out a temp folder, but don't run it in your user profile folder or anywhere else! The files don't go to the recycle bin and can't be recovered if you delete the wrong ones!

It's important to know that this expression isn't handled directly by `where-object`. If it was, then conceivably every cmdlet might have a different way of constructing these expressions, which make would things inconsistent and difficult to master.

Instead, this expression format is part of the PowerShell language itself. Technically, `where-object` expects the body (code) of a function on its command line. The curly brackets signify that you're typing the body of a function that you're defining on-the-fly without giving it a name, and that function is given to `where-object` to use to evaluate each of the file objects it scans. (This little function is technically called a *lambda*, but that's not too important here.)

Let's pick it apart. There are three parts:

`$_.LastWriteTime`	`$_` is a placeholder for the object that `where-object` is examining. `$_.LastWriteTime` picks up the `LastWriteTime` property from that object. For a file or folder object, it's the date and time that the file was last modified.

`-lt`	This does a comparison of two values, and it's true if the first value is less than the first. In other words, the expression `{a -lt b}`, is true if value *a* is less than value *b*. In this instance, the test is true if the file's LastWriteTime is less than (earlier than) the time that comes after `-lt`.
`(get-date).addmonths(-6)`	This is the oddest part, but watch how it works: The `get-date` cmdlet is run. With no arguments, it spits out a .NET `System.DateTime` object representing the current date and time. In this simplest form, it's like `Now()` in VBScript. The parentheses around it indicate that we are going to treat the result of the cmdlet as a value. `addmonths` is one of the standard methods of the `System.DateTime` object. In this case, we end up with the current date with six months subtracted from it—in other words, the date six months back.

The end result is that this expression is true if the file was last written more than six months ago. The curly brackets turn this expression into a function so that `where-object` can evaluate it for each of the objects it examines.

The output of this `where-object` command is just those file objects that were last modified more than six months ago. The rest of the command line feeds that stream of objects to `remove-item`, which deletes the files they represent. The end result is that this command purges a directory of old, abandoned files.

Now, I didn't just write that command off the top of my head. I had to learn the basics of cmdlets first, so I knew to write:

```
dir | where-object {some expression} | remove-item
```

Then, I had to learn about the properties of the file and folder objects to know to use `LastWriteItem` and the `System.DateTime` object to find the `addmonths` property. To help with that job, interestingly enough, there are cmdlets that describe the properties of any object they encounter. I describe that next.

Getting Help

The most important PowerShell command to learn first is the one that helps you learn about the others! It's called `get-help`, but it has a predefined alias named `help`, so you can use either of these command names interchangeably. PowerShell has a lot of built-in help—477 different topics, in fact, at the time I wrote this.

Here are some tips:

- Type the word `help` by itself to get a quick introduction to the online help system.

- After `help` or `get-help`, you can type a word, cmdlet name, or partial cmdlet name. You can also type a phrase enclosed in quotation marks.

    If more than one topic, cmdlet name, or description matches what you typed, `get-help` prints a list of all matching help entries. You can then type `help` followed by the specific entry name that interests you to get the details.

    If exactly one name or description contains the word or phrase you typed, `get-help` prints the help information for that topic.

- Some cmdlets have additional help information available. For example, you can see some examples of using the `new-alias` cmdlet by typing `help new-alias -examples`. Common options for additional information are `-examples`, `-detailed`, and `-full`. The main help page for a topic tells you whether these expanded pages are available.

- The help text appears in the console window and by default is piped through `more` so it stops after every screenful. Press Enter to go on to the next page.

- Alternatively, you might find it easier to direct help output into a file by adding, for example, `>x` to the end of the help command line; then, type `notepad x` to read the text.

- There are help entries covering every one of the installed cmdlets and additional articles on different topics. These articles start with `about_`. For example, `help about_execution_policies` prints information about the scripting security restriction system. (You can also type `help about_exec` and get the same result because only one entry contains the string "about_exec" in its title or description.)

    To see a list of all of these "about" entries, type `help about`.

This online help system is great for locating cmdlets based on words in the description of the job they do and for learning about their command-line syntax after you've found a cmdlet that interests you.

> **Tip**
>
> In the online syntax descriptions, the following conventions are used:
>
> [ ] square brackets indicate optional command arguments.
>
> { } curly braces usually indicate a series of options from which you can choose, with a vertical bar | between the options.
>
> < > angle brackets surround a value that you have to supply yourself. For example, [`-Description <string>`] indicates an optional argument. You can omit it, or you could type something like `-description "some text"`. As I mentioned in the previous section, you could probably abbreviate this to `-descr "some text"`.

Prompting to Complete Commands

If you type a PowerShell command that requires specific arguments, but omit some or all of the required arguments, PowerShell prompts for them by name. Here's an example: If you type `set-alias` without any arguments, PowerShell prompts for the required `-name` and `-value` arguments. Here's how it looks:

```
PS C:\Users\bknittel> set-alias

cmdlet Set-Alias at command pipeline position 1
Supply values for the following parameters:
Name: ax
Value: get-alias
```

(I typed the responses in italics.) This mechanism can help you as you learn to use the cmdlets, but remember that PowerShell won't prompt for *optional* arguments, just the required ones.

Personally, I don't find this mechanism that useful and never trigger it deliberately. You should know it exists though because if you omit a required argument from a command, PowerShell might prompt you in this way and you might find it confusing at first.

Aliases

As I mentioned previously in "Command-Line Syntax," when you type a command, PowerShell looks through list of aliases, functions, cmdlets, and external programs to find the program you want to run.

Because people who do a lot of work at the command prompt are so used to typing commands like `cd` and `dir`, PowerShell comes with predefined aliases for many of these familiar commands. Because the names of many of the cmdlets are tediously long, there are predefined aliases for many of the cmdlets that are only two or three characters long. (This should make Unix users happy!) The idea is that you'll find that there are just a few commands you tend to use over and over. After you know which these are, you can look up their short aliases and use those to save time typing.

One serious limitation of aliases, though, is that they can map only one command name to another. An alias definition can't include command-line arguments. I would really like to define an alias named `h` that issued the command `cd $home`, which changes back to your user profile "home" directory, but this isn't supported. It's really unfortunate.

How to Get a Listing of Aliases

You can see a list of all the built-in aliases by typing `alias` (which, as you'll see, is an alias itself, for the real command name `get-alias`). I find it easiest to view this list in a text file by typing two commands:

```
alias >x
notepad x
```

You'll notice the alias named %, for ForEach-Object, and the alias named ?, for Where-Object. The latter, used in that "delete old files" command example I gave earlier in the chapter, would look like this:

```
dir | ? {$_.LastWriteTime -lt (get-date).addmonths(-6)} | remove-item
```

Personally, I don't think it this reads well, but if I got used to typing it, it might save some time. It's up to you whether you want to use shortcuts like this, so nobody's forcing anything on you. The idea is to use the shortcuts that make sense to you and ignore the others.

How to Define a New Alias

You can define a new alias by typing a command like this:

```
new-alias -name shortname -value realcommandname -description "Brief description"
```

but substituting the name of the alias you want to create for *shortname* and the command that the alias should run for *realcommandname*. If the alias already exists, you have to add -force to the command to replace the old one. I show you how you can shorten this command later in this chapter.

You should know that alias definitions don't survive when you close your PowerShell window. The next time you run PowerShell, your custom alias will be gone. If you come up with favorite aliases you want to keep, see the section on Profiles at the end of this chapter.

Navigating Directories and Other Locations

In the command-line world, you use typed commands to navigate up and down through folders and disk drives. Windows PowerShell uses the same cd command as the Command Prompt to change directories, so familiar commands like

```
cd \Users
cd ..
cd subfolder
```

still work. You can use the Tab key to automatically fill in partially typed file and folder names, just as in the Command Prompt environment.

You can also take advantage of directory names stored in PowerShell variables. Your user profile folder path is stored in variable $home, so you can use the command cd $home to return to your profile directory from any location.

Now, here's something really interesting: You're used to using cd to move around the file system. In PowerShell, you can also navigate through the Registry!

Here's how it works: Just as Windows recognizes different drive letters, like this:

```
c:\users\bknittel
d:\saved_pictures\February2010\Yosemite
e:\setup.exe
```

PowerShell recognizes additional drives, which it calls *providers*, that treat the Registry and the lists of environment variables, aliases, PowerShell variables, defined functions, digital certificates, and Web Services for Management just like disk drives. You can specify paths to these elements, list them with `dir`, and in some cases even use `cd` to navigate through them.

The default provider drives on Windows 7 are listed in Table 14.1.

Table 14.1   **Provider Drives on Windows 7**

Drive Name	Contains
A:, B:, C:, and so on	Disk drives (FileSystem provider)
Alias:	List of PowerShell aliases
Cert:	Digital certificates
Env:	Environment variables
Function:	Defined functions
HKCU:	Registry section HKEY_CURRENT_USER
HKLM:	Registry section HKEY_LOCAL_MACHINE
Variable:	PowerShell variables
WSMan:	Windows Services Management connections to the local and remote computers

Name completion works with these drives, too. For example, if you type `dir hklm:soft` and press the Tab key, PowerShell changes `soft` to `SOFTWARE`, which is the first Registry key that matches the partial name you typed. You can continue the path by typing \ and another part of a key name.

Try typing these commands at the PowerShell prompt (and notice that you don't have to capitalize them; the names are case insensitive):

`dir hklm:\software`	This lists the keys under HKEY_LOCAL_MACHINE\SOFTWARE.
`cd hklm:\software`	Makes the Registry your "current location."
`dir`	Lists the keys in this current location.
`cd $home`	Returns to the file system in your profile folder.
`dir cert:\currentuser`	Lists certificates associated with your use account.

`dir variable:`	Lists all variables currently defined in Windows PowerShell.
`dir env:`	This lists all defined environment variables.

Many PowerShell cmdlets can work with objects specified by their paths whether the paths point to a file, a Registry key, a certificate, or whatever. For example, the `del` command (which is an alias for `delete-item`) can delete a Registry key just as easily as a file, with a command like `del hkcu:\software\badkey`.

PowerShell Security

Because Windows PowerShell can be used to change Windows settings and has the potential, if run by a privileged user, of undermining Windows' security system, Microsoft has taken care to be sure that it's difficult to run PowerShell scripts without your taking intentional steps to enable them. There are additional barriers to running scripts that come from the Internet, via email, Instant Messaging programs, and so on. This was done to avert the possibility that hackers might figure out ways to exploit potential flaws in, say Internet Explorer, to install and run PowerShell scripts on your system without your permission.

PowerShell Scripts and User Account Control

Windows PowerShell was designed first and foremost for managing Windows, so you will end up wanting it to do things that require Administrator privileges. On Windows 7 and Vista, PowerShell, requires *elevated* privileges—just running it from a Computer Administrator account isn't enough. Either open an elevated command prompt and then type `powershell` or use any of the methods you'd use to run cmd.exe with elevated privileges, but run powershell.exe instead.

On Windows XP, to perform administrative functions, you'll have to be logged in as a Computer Administrator when you start PowerShell. Alternatively, you can use the `runas` command to start powershell.exe in the context of an Administrator's user account. You could use the `su` batch file that I described in Chapter 10 and then type `powershell` to start the shell, or you could write a new batch file that runs `powershell.exe` instead of `cmd.exe`—it's up to you. The same discussion that I just mentioned, starting on page 437, discusses `runas` on Windows XP.

→ For instructions on opening an elevated command prompt, see "Opening a Command Prompt Window with Administrator Privileges" on page 436.

Whatever version of Windows you're using, you'll probably want to try this right away, as you want to use a privileged PowerShell command to let you run PowerShell script files. I describe this command next.

Script Execution Policy

As initially installed, PowerShell is set up so that it can be used interactively at the command prompt but will not run scripts. This does make sense. The majority of Windows users will never touch PowerShell, and nobody knows what future bug might be discovered that would let hackers silently send them malicious PowerShell scripts via Internet Explorer, Adobe Acrobat, YouTube, or who knows what. Better to be safe than sorry.

But, you're a power user, and you want to use PowerShell scripts. No problem, you just have to change the default script execution policy from Restricted to, as I recommend, RemoteSigned. Table 14.2 lists the possible policy settings.

Table 14.2   **PowerShell Script Execution Policy Settings**

Setting	Description
Restricted	This is the default setting. No PowerShell scripts will run at all, under any circumstances.
AllSigned	Only digitally signed scripts (including profile scripts, which I describe in the next section) will run; in addition, you are prompted to grant permission to run scripts signed by the specific certificate used.
RemoteSigned	Scripts (and profiles) that have been written locally will run. Scripts that have been downloaded from the Internet will not run unless they are signed and you have approved the signing certificate.
Unrestricted	All scripts will run, but you are warned about scripts that have been downloaded and must approve them before they'll run.
Bypass	Any script will run, regardless of its origin. This is a potentially very risky setting and should be used only in very specific circumstances, where some other security system is in place to prevent rogue scripts from running without your permission.
(Undefined)	If no policy setting is in place, PowerShell treats the setting as Restricted and no script will run.

I recommend the RemoteSigned setting. Scripts you write and store on your computer or retrieve across your local area network will run without any problem, but scripts that arrive via programs with Internet connectivity won't run unless they have a digital signature and you've confirmed that you trust the person or company that signed the script. This is a good security compromise.

To change the setting, open a privileged PowerShell window as described in the previous section. Then, type the command

```
set-executionpolicy remotesigned
```

You will have to confirm that you want to make this change by typing **y** and Enter. (You can disable that prompt by adding -force to the command line.)

Now, you can run PowerShell scripts and profiles. I talk more about scripting in the next two chapters.

There are few things you should know about this security setting:

- If your computer is part of a corporate domain network, this setting is probably under the control of your network manager via Group Policy. Type get-executionpolicy to see what your current setting is. You might not able to change it yourself.

- If you are forced into, or choose, the AllSigned policy setting, you'll have to digitally sign any script you want to run. It's a cumbersome process, but it's not too bad after you get used to it. I talked about digital signatures in Chapter 9, "Deploying Scripts for Computer and Network Management." For more information, see "Script Signing" on page 409.

- You might recall that files downloaded from the Internet are marked as "potentially risky" through information stored in a separate data stream associated with the downloaded file. To remove this marker from a downloaded script that you are *certain* is safe, use Windows Explorer to open the file's properties dialog box and click Unblock. It will now be considered a local file and will run under the RemoteSigned execution policy.

Finally, remember that if you have a local area network (LAN) but not a Windows domain network, and the scripting execution policy isn't set by Group Policy, you'll have to change this setting on every computer on your network that you want to manage using PowerShell.

PowerShell Profiles

As I showed in the previous sections, you can customize the PowerShell environment to suit your preferences by adding custom aliases, adding directories to the path, and so on. It would be a pain to have to retype these commands every time you started PowerShell—and you don't have to if you set up a PowerShell *profile*, which is a script of commands that PowerShell runs every time you start a new instance. You might want to put commands of this sort in a profile script:

```
new-alias -name "n" -val "notepad" -descr "Edit a file with Notepad"
$env:path += "c:\PSscripts"
```

so that your favorite, custom aliases will be available every time you use PowerShell.

Here's the skinny: Whenever you start Windows PowerShell in any of its various flavors (the regular command-line PowerShell, the GUI PowerShell ISE, or a PowerShell variant that's embedded inside another application), it looks for profile scripts in the following two locations, in this order:

```
%windir%\system32\WindowsPowerShell\v1.0
```

where `%windir%` is the folder in which Windows is installed, usually `c:\windows`, and

```
%userprofile%\[My] Documents\WindowsPowerShell
```

where `%userprofile%` is your account's profile folder, usually `c:\Users\`*username* on Windows 7 and Vista and `c:\Documents and Settings\`*username* on Windows XP.

Within these two folders, the different flavors of Windows PowerShell look for different profile filenames. Every PowerShell variant looks first for a script named `profile.ps1` and runs it if it's found. The command-line PowerShell then looks for a profile script named `Microsoft.Powershell_profile.ps1` and executes that one if it's found. The GUI PowerShell ISE program, on the other hand, looks first for `profile.ps1` and then `Microsoft.PowerShellISE_profile.ps1`.

Profile scripts in the `%windir%` folder affect all users on the computer, while profile scripts in your `%userprofile%` location affect only shells that you use. So, you can decide to make some customizations available to everyone and make some just for yourself by setting up separate profile scripts. Likewise, you adjust every PowerShell variant by putting commands in `profile.ps1`, or you can season the different PowerShells to taste by putting commands in the version-specific files.

PowerShell executes each of the scripts it finds, so the environment you end up with is the result of the cumulative changes made by all the script(s) that you've set up.

Creating a PowerShell Profile

PowerShell has a predefined variable named `$profile` that points to the version-specific profile file in your `%userprofile%` folder. For example, in my command-line PowerShell, `$profile` has the value `"c:\Users\bknittel\Documents\WindowsPowerShell\Microsoft.PowerShell_profile.ps1"`.

So, you can instantly create a PowerShell profile by typing the command `notepad $profile`. Notepad will ask whether you want to create a new file. Click Yes, and you're ready to go. You'll learn more about writing scripts in the next two chapters.

To create a profile for all users in folder `%windir%\system32\WindowsPowerShell\v1.0` on Windows 7 or Vista, remember that you'll need to use an elevated Command Prompt or PowerShell instance. This folder name is stored in variable `$PSHOME`, so from PowerShell you can use the command `notepad $pshome\profile.ps1` or `notepad $pshome\Microsoft.PowerShell_profile.ps1` to create or edit the file.

However, and this is a big *however*, profile scripts are still scripts and PowerShell will only run profile scripts that meet the security guidelines I described in the previous section. Remember that the default execution policy is Restricted, so profile scripts won't run at all (unless you're on a Windows domain network and your network manager has enabled script execution).

To take advantage of the profile feature to customize your PowerShell environment, you will need to change the execution policy and possibly digitally sign your scripts. The previous section tells you how to do this.

15

PowerShell Programming

IN THIS CHAPTER

- This chapter describes PowerShell as a programming language. In Chapter 16 "Using PowerShell," we'll put it to practical use.

- PowerShell has all the structures you'd expect in a modern programming language. (It should—it borrowed things from just about every language out there!)

- The PowerShell language has some really unusual tricks up its proverbial sleeve, especially in the ways it works with arrays. It also has built-in tools for matching, parsing, and substituting text using regular expression patterns.

- All PowerShell variables are .NET Framework objects, so there are methods and properties that you can manipulate on any variable. This chapter will get you started learning about many useful objects.

The Windows PowerShell Programming Language

This chapter describes PowerShell as a programming language. We'll go through almost all the language's features in a linear fashion, top to bottom, one item to the next. Whether you're a novice or experienced programmer, I think that this approach is a more helpful introduction than the fragmented PowerShell help files or the equally fragmented, web-based references and tutorials out there on the Internet.

I suggest you skim through this chapter quickly, so you see all of PowerShell's programming features. Then, you can go back and read through any parts you want to see in more detail.

After that, for more detailed information about individual language elements, you'll be better prepared to learn from PowerShell's online help pages. Just type `help` or `help topicname` at the PowerShell command prompt. (See "Getting Help" on p. 610. You'll probably find it easier to browse these same help pages online at technet.microsoft.com. At the top, select Library; then at the left, open Scripting,

Windows PowerShell, Windows PowerShell Core, and browse the entries titled "Windows PowerShell About Help Topics" and "Windows PowerShell Cmdlet Help Topics."

Windows PowerShell Syntax

Windows PowerShell is a command-line environment, and like the old Command Prompt shell, at the most basic level it lets you type commands one line at a time. It runs each command and displays the results. I discussed how it runs cmdlets and Windows commands and how to pipe and redirect output in the previous chapter. Now, we'll look at PowerShell as a scripting/programming language.

As you'll see, PowerShell is a new language. Although Windows Script Host's (WSH) VBScript is based on Visual Basic for Applications, which many people are familiar with as the macro and scripting language used in Microsoft Office, PowerShell was created from scratch. This has its good and bad points. Good because PowerShell's authors were free to incorporate some interesting new ideas into the language, and as a result you can do some very sophisticated things with it. But, they came up with a syntax that is in some places awkward and sometimes looks more like a Unix command shell from the 1970s than a programming language from the 2000s. This might be the most
charitable way of putting it: Its beauty is not superficial.

Nonetheless, it's very powerful (it *does* live up to is name), and it can be a very useful tool. Let's start by looking at the basics of the PowerShell language.

Comments

One of the first language constructs to learn in any programming language is the comment. In PowerShell, a # character begins a comment. You can put # at the beginning of a line so the whole line is a comment, or you can put it anywhere in a command line. Everything from # to the end of the line is ignored. Here is an example:

```
$cname = 'dualcore'          # set name of remote computer
```

If you want to write a large block of comment text, you can enclose the text between <# and #>, as follows:

```
<#
   this is a block of
   comment text
#>
```

This only works in Windows PowerShell V2.0 and later. V1 doesn't support the block comment markers.

Variables and Types

PowerShell variables begin with the $ character to distinguish variable names from cmdlets, commands, and other programming language keywords. You can see how it works by typing the following two commands at the PowerShell prompt:

```
$stone = 'opal'
$stone
```

The first command stores the string opal in a variable named $stone, and the second command prints the value of the variable.

> **Tip**
>
> A PowerShell command line that consists of just a value, a variable name, or an expression prints the resulting value in the command window. You don't *have* to use a special "output" command to print things, unless you want to do special formatting. I talk about formatting in Chapter 16.

Variable names always start with a dollar sign $ and can contain any mix of letters, numbers, spaces, or other symbols—any printing characters, in fact, except the curly bracket characters { and }, and the colon (:). If the name contains spaces or special symbols, enclose the name in curly brackets. Upper- and lowercase don't matter. Here are some examples:

```
$deli = 'Ba Le Vietnamese Sandwiches'
${my computer name} = 'dualcore'
${[weird]>variable|name I'd#never%really*use} = 'abc'
```

Now, things get interesting: *All* PowerShell variables are objects. Specifically, they're .NET Framework objects, and every .NET Framework object type is available. String values like 'abc' are stored as objects named System.String, and numeric values like 123 are stored, by default, as System.Int32 objects. All the properties and methods of these objects are available to variables. For example, with my sample variable $deli, the expression $deli.Length prints the length of the string, 27.

The variable types you'll encounter most frequently are listed in Table 15.1. Table 15.2 lists some additional types that can be useful if you have to manipulate bits or specific types of values and objects that occur in system programming and management.

Table 15.1   **Common PowerShell Variable Types**

Object Name	Cast Shortcut	Values Represented	Example
System.Boolean	[boolean] or [bool]	True and False	True
System.DateTime	[datetime]	Date and time	10/01/2010 11:30 AM

continues

Table 15.1 **Continued**

Object Name	Cast Shortcut	Values Represented	Example
System.TimeSpan	[timespan]	Time interval	1 day 2 hours
System.Double	[double]	Floating-point number with about 15 digits of precision	3.14159265358979
System.Int32	[int] or [int32]	Integer value from –2147483648 to +2147483647	559038736
System.String	[string]	Character strings	'abc'

Table 15.2 **Somewhat More Exotic Variable Types**

Object Name	Cast Shortcut	Values Represented	Example
System.Byte	[byte]	Unsigned integer value from 0 to 255	47
System.Char	[char]	A single Unicode character	'a'
System.Decimal	[decimal]	Floating-point number with about 28 digits of precision	12345678901234567
System.Int16	[int16]	Integer value from –32768 to +32767	4747
System.Int64	[long]	Integer value from –9223372036854775808 to +9223372036854775807	12345678901234567
System.SByte	[sbyte]	Integer value from –128 to +128	47
System.Single	[single]	Floating-point number with about 7 digits of precision	3.141593
System.UInt16	[uint16]	Unsigned integer value from 0 to 65535	4747
System.UInt32	[uint32]	Unsigned integer value from 0 to 4294967295	474747
System.UInt64	[uint64]	Unsigned integer value from 0 to 18446744073709551615	4747474747474747

Literal Values

Normally, PowerShell figures out an appropriate object type for any value you type. For example, if I type `$v = 3`, PowerShell recognizes that 3 is an integer value. By default, it creates a `System.Int32` object to represent this value and sets up variable `$v` to hold a reference to the object. On the other hand, `$v = 'abc'` clearly represents a string, so PowerShell uses `System.String`.

Table 15.3 shows the ways that you can key-in various types of values and how PowerShell interprets them.

Table 15.3 **Literal Value Formats**

Format	Value Type
`'xyz'`	`System.String`
`"xyz"`	`System.String`, with interpolation (discussed shortly)
`123` `0x12ab`	`System.Int32` (hexadecimal notation)
`1234L` `0x12abL`	`System.Int64` (hexadecimal notation)
`123.45` `4.321e-6`	`System.Double` (scientific notation)
`123.45D`	`System.Decimal`
`$true, $false`	`System.Boolean`

If you are working with numbers, you have to think about the appropriate object type to use to hold the values you are working with. If you're working with whole numbers no more than nine digits in length, the default `[int]` (`System.Int32`) type should be fine. If you expect to encounter numbers with 10 or more digits, though, you'll want to explicitly tell PowerShell to either use `[int64]` or `[uint64]` for integers or use `[decimal]`, which is a floating-point format that gives you 28 digits of precision, with a decimal point anywhere in those 28 digits. If you're going to work with floating-point (fractional) numbers that need to handle larger or smaller values, use `[double]` (`System.Double`). There's no reason to use `System.Single`.

Again, most of the time, PowerShell can figure out which object to use automatically. You can explicitly tell PowerShell which object types you want to use using a language structure called a *cast*, which I describe later in this chapter.

I should say here that by default, PowerShell variables are generic and hold objects of any type: string, number, array, WMI management, or whatever. You can explicitly restrict the type of object a variable can hold by putting the type name in square brackets *before* the variable name, on the *left* side of an equals sign, as in these two equivalent examples:

```
[int] $v = 3
[System.Int32] $v = 3
```

If you do this, the variable can *only* hold objects of this sort, and you get an error message if (a) you try to put a different type of value into the variable and (b) PowerShell can't figure out how to store the value as the declared object type. For example, after the previous commands, the first of these two commands work but the second generates an error:

```
$v = '21'
$v = 'xyz'
```

because PowerShell can convert the string '21' into its numeric value but it can't convert 'xyz' to a number. The object type casts that I describe later in this chapter force the value on the *right* side of the equals sign to be converted to a specified type, independently of whether the variable itself has been declared to hold only specific types or if it was left as a generic object holder.

Object Methods and Properties

All variables—and all values and expressions—in PowerShell are .NET Framework objects, either the simple value object types described in the previous section or more complex objects. All of these objects have methods and/or properties.

To retrieve the value of an object's property, type a reference to the object followed by a period and then the property name, as in this example:

```
$a = "my string"
$a.Length
```

which computes and prints the length of the string. Do likewise, with *fields*, which are read-only object properties that are constants; they don't depend on any particular data value.

To invoke one of an object's methods, you *must* put parentheses after the method name, as in this example:

```
$a.ToUpper()
```

With the parentheses, PowerShell prints a copy of the string converted to uppercase. If you omit the parentheses, you get a printout of not terribly useful information about the method itself. (Technically, without the parentheses, the value of *object.method* is a reference to the method but doesn't invoke the method.) If you've done a lot of work with Visual Basic languages or its variants, where parentheses can be omitted after method names, you're going to have to force yourself to remember this!

Tip

An object's properties, methods, and fields are collectively called *members*. You can look up information about .NET objects' members online at msdn.microsoft.com by selecting the Library tab and then searching for phrases like ".NET array object members.".

PowerShell can also print a lot of information about objects. To get a list of any object's properties and methods, type **gm -in *object***, where *object* is an object value or variable name. (gm is an alias for the get-member cmdlet, and -in is an abbreviation of -inputobject. The full command is get-member -inputobject, but who wants to type *that* 10 times a day?)

Try this yourself: Type **gm -in 'abc'** to see the methods and properties of the .NET string object. Then, type these commands:

```
$a = 1,2,3
gm -in $a
gm -in $a[0]
```

This creates an array. The first gm prints information about the array object itself. The second gm prints information about the object stored in the first element of the array.

Object Constructors

When you use a new object, you often immediately want it to hold a specific value. For example, the statement $v = 3 creates an [int] object that holds the value 3 right from the get-go. For more complex .NET objects that hold more complex values, such as the [datetime] object I discuss later in this chapter, you can use a constructor method. A *constructor* builds an object and stores data in it as it's created. Many .NET objects have several constructor variations, which accept differing numbers of arguments or different data types. The constructor options are listed in the online .NET Framework documentation I discussed in the previous section. .NET works out which version you're using based on the number of arguments and the types of values you specify. For instance, you can create a new [datetime] by providing a year, month, and day; a year, month, day, hour, minute, and second; or any of several other variations.

To use a constructor in PowerShell, you have to use the new-object cmdlet and pass the constructor's arguments in an array. For example, to create a DateTime for March 6, 2010 at 9:22:33 AM, you can use this statement: $dt = new-object System.DateTime 2010,3,6,9,22,33. This uses the constructor version that accepts six integer arguments: year, month, day, hour, minute, and second. You should use the full object name, for example, System.DateTime or System.Timespan.

> **Note**
>
> You won't often have to use constructors this explicitly. PowerShell can convert string values to several object types, including dates and times, and for these data types, the string method is easier. I show you how this works later in the chapter.

String Interpolation

PowerShell lets you specify strings by enclosing text between two single quote (') characters or two double quote (") characters. If you use the single quote, the text is interpreted exactly as you've typed it. If you use the double quote, any occurrences of *$name* inside the string are replaced by the value of the named variable. This can be handy, but don't let it catch you by surprise.

Here's what I mean: With the following script,

```
$name = 'Brian'
$nametag1 = 'Hello, my name is $name'
$nametag2 = "Hello, my name is $name"
```

variable $nametag1 is set to the string Hello, my name is $name, but $nametag2 is set to Hello, my name is Brian. In addition, inside double-quoted strings, whole expressions can be substituted into the string using the format $(*expression*), as in this example:

```
"You are $($current_year - $birth_year) years old."
```

That command line prints something like You are 32 years old. This is a really good use of string interpolation; use it to format output that includes literal text and the content of variables and expressions. But, in the middle of scripts where you're working with strings, you probably don't want string interpolation to occur, so you should use the single quote character.

Tip

For those of us used to working in C, C++, C#, VBScript, or most other languages, the double quote is a hard habit to break, but it's worth trying. You'd be safe using double quotes *most* of the time, but one day, they would bite you. In PowerShell, it's best to use double quotes *only* where you really do want to use interpolation.

To put the quote mark that surrounds a string *inside* the string, just use two of them. For example,

```
$b = 'John''s book'
v = '''name in quotes'''
```

puts the string John's book in variable $b, and 'name in quotes' in variable $v. In this second example, the first single quote starts the string. The adjacent second and third ones are interpreted as one quote character and put into the string. Alternatively, you can just use the "other" quote mark, like this:

```
$v = "'name in string'"
$v = '"name in string"'
```

to get a string containing single or double quotes, respectively. As I mentioned, though, with double quotes on the outside of the string, this might not work as expected if the string contains dollar signs.

Note

If you use double-quotes to enclose a string, you can prevent PowerShell from performing interpolation by putting the back-quote character (`) before a $ in the string. For example, the string "The variable name is `$a" prints The variable name is $a.

Special Characters

The back-quote character is also used to place special characters within a string. Between single or double quotes, the following strings are replaced with single characters:

String	Replacement
`0	ASCII NUL (0) character
`a	Bell (ASCII 7) character, produces a beep if printed to the command window
`b	Backspace (ASCII 8)
`f	Form feed (ASCII 12)
`n	Line feed (ASCII 10)
`r	Carriage return (ASCII 13)
`t	Horizontal tab (ASCII 9)
`v	Vertical tab (ASCII 11)

Here-Strings

You can create a string value that contains embedded carriage-return/line-feed characters using a construct called a *here-string*. It's a string that spans multiple lines. The format is

```
$variable = @'
these lines are copied
into the variable
'@
```

You can use either @' and '@ or @" and "@ as the begin and end markers. Blank lines in the block of text are ignored and don't appear in the resulting string variable. Within the block of text, quote characters have no special significance and are copied literally. If you use @" and "@ as the markers, variable name interpolation occurs.

Releasing Variables

You won't often need to remove a variable you've defined in a script, but it sometimes does come up when, for example, you have a script that has to run for a very long time and works with a lot of data. In this case, you might want to free up variables, particularly arrays or objects holding a large amount of data.

The easiest method is to assign a new value to the variable, replacing the old one. If a variable $a holds a huge array, the statement $a = $null has the effect of discarding the array. Alternatively, you can use the cmdlet statement remove-variable *variablename* to delete the variable name and its contents.

Note

After freeing variables, you won't necessarily see powershell.exe's memory usage go down in the Task Manager. The .NET Framework on which PowerShell is based frees up memory through a process called garbage collection only when it decides it wants to. You can force it to perform garbage collection with the statement [GC]::Collect(), but I don't recommend doing this except under extreme circumstances. Using it frequently can hurt performance.

Predefined Variables

Several variables are predefined by PowerShell, and some of them change while PowerShell is executing commands. PowerShell calls them *automatic* variables. I have listed some of them in Table 15.4. For the full list, see the PowerShell help topic about_automatic_variables.

Table 15.4   **Partial List of Automatic (Predefined) Variables**

Variable	Contains
$$	The last token in the last line read from the command window.
$?	True, if the previous operation succeeded; otherwise, it's False. You can test this to see whether an exception has occurred when $ErrorActionPreference is set to Continue (see "Exception Handling," p. 662 for more on this setting).
$^	The first token in the last line read from the command window.
$_	The current object, when used in a pipeline command or in a foreach () or switch () statement with an array or a command stream as the input.
$Args	Parameters passed to a script or function.
$PSCulture	The language and culture identifier for Windows (for example, en-US).

Variable	Contains
$Error	An array containing information about errors encountered by PowerShell. $Error[0] contains information about the most recent error, $Error[1] the next most recent, and so on. Up to $MaximumErrorCount errors are saved.
$False	The Boolean value False.
$ForEach	Inside a foreach loop, contains a reference to the enumerator that controls the loop. It's actually not terribly useful.
$Home	Path to the user's home directory.
$Host	An object that contains information about the executable program in which PowerShell is running.
$Input	The object currently in the pipeline in the process block of a function or all of the input to a function.
$LastExitCode	Exit code of the last external program executed.
$Matches	A hash table containing any string values matched by the previous -match operator.
$MyInvocation	An object containing information about the current PowerShell script, command line, or function. Can be helpful in printing debugging messages.
$NULL	The value Null.
$PID	The process identifier number of the PowerShell executable program.
$Profile	Full path to your PowerShell user profile.
$PSHome	Full path to the folder containing the PowerShell executable.
$PSScriptRoot	The path to the directory containing the currently executing script.
$PSVersionTable	Hash table containing version information about PowerShell.
$Pwd	The full path of the current directory.
$ShellID	The object name for the PowerShell instance.
$This	In script code that implements an object property or method, it represents the object itself.
$True	The Boolean value True.
$PSUICulture	The language and culture identifier for PowerShell.

There is also a set of Preference variables that control how PowerShell operates. Table 15.5 has a partial list.

Table 15.5 **Partial List of PowerShell Preference Variables**

Variable	Purpose
`$ConfirmPreference`	Controls how PowerShell cmdlets prompt the user before performing high-risk activities such as deleting Windows services. The settings are "None" (no confirmation required), "Low" (confirmation required even for low-risk actions), "Medium," and "High" (confirmation required only for high-risk actions).
`$DebugPreference`	Controls what PowerShell does with cmdlet debugging output and the output from the write-debug cmdlet. The options are "Stop" (PowerShell halts after any debug output), "Inquire," "Continue," and "SilentlyContinue".
`$ErrorActionPreference`	Controls what PowerShell does after a nonterminating (nonfatal) program error. The options are "Stop," "Inquire," "Continue," and "SilentlyContinue." Terminating (fatal) errors are always handled with the "Stop" action, unless they're caught with one of the exception handling mechanisms I describe later in the chapter.
`$Log`*xxx*`Event`	Several variables control which types of events are written to the Windows Event Log. See the help topic for details.
`$MaximumErrorCount`	Maximum number of errors to keep in `$Error` array.

For the full list, see the PowerShell help topic `about_preference_variables`.

Arrays

Arrays let one variable hold many independent values, and they are used frequently in programming, as when you need to do the same things to a list of similar items. PowerShell lets you create arrays several ways. You can create an array on-the-fly by typing several values separated by commas:

```
$powers = 8, 4, 2, 1
```

to create an array of integers or with strings,

```
$names = 'Alpha', 'Bravo', 'Charlie', 'Delta'
```

PowerShell also lets you type the list of values using parentheses and using an optional @ sign, as in these examples:

```
$powers = (8,4,2,1)
$names = @('Alpha', 'Bravo', 'Charlie', 'Delta')
```

You can print the whole list of names by just typing the array name:

```
$names
```

(which I discuss in more detail shortly). You can also access the individual entries: `$names[0]`, `$names[1]`, `$names[2]`, and `$names[3]`. In PowerShell, array indexes start with 0.

These examples both create simple arrays that hold four values by listing the individual values one by one. You can set up an array that contains a range of integer values using the `..` syntax:

```
$a = 1..5
```

In PowerShell, an expression in the form $n..m$ creates an array of integers from n to m, so `1..5` creates an array with five elements, containing the values 1, 2, 3, 4, and 5. To make an array with just one element, precede the one value with a comma, like this:

```
$a = ,1
```

The expression `@()` produces an empty array with no elements at all.

Extending Arrays

If you don't know in advance how many values you'll need, no fear. You can create an array with no elements, as I just showed, and then extend it one item at a time using the addition operator:

```
$a = @()
$a = $a + 100
```

or equivalently

```
$a += 100
```

This peculiar syntax looks like ordinary addition, but with arrays, the + sign adds a new element to an array. The example turns `$a` into an array containing now two elements: 1 and 100. You can also use the + operator to combine whole arrays. This example:

```
$a = 1, 2, 3
$b = 4, 5, 6
$c = $a + $b
```

makes `$c` an array with 6 elements: 1, 2, 3, 4, 5, and 6. In a similar manner, the multiplication operator (*) copies an array multiple times. For example, the value of `(1,2,3,4)*3` is an array with 12 elements: 1,2,3,4,1,2,3,4,1,2,3,4.

Tip

If you want to predefine an array with a specific number of entries without typing a list of values, you can use the * (multiply) operator to duplicate a single-item array, as in this example, which creates a 1000-element array:

```
$a = (,1)*1000
```

Determining an Array's Size

Remember that all PowerShell variables are objects. Arrays are no exception. An array is just another type of object called `System.Array`. It has a property named `.Count` that equals the number of elements in the array. You can access all the items in the array with a PowerShell loop like this:

```
for ($i = 0; $i -lt $a.Count; $i++) {
    write-output ("Element " + i +  " is " + $a[$i])
}
```

which executes the statement inside the curly brackets with indexes 0, 1, 2, and so on up to `$Count-1`, which is the last element. The language has an easier way to loop through arrays, though, using the `foreach` command:

```
foreach ($x in $a) {
    … some statements here…
}
```

which sets the variable `$x` to each of the values in array `$a` in turn. This is slightly easier to write and to understand, but inside this loop you won't know what the current index number is. If you need to know, use the previous method to loop through all values.

Multidimensional Arrays

When you create an array by typing a list of values, you can surround the list with parentheses:

```
$powers = (8, 4, 2, 1)
```

I recommend doing this as a general practice. It's a bit clearer to someone reading your script, and it lets you do some interesting things, like creating an array of arrays:

```
$a = ((1, 2, 3, 4, 5), (6, 7, 8, 9, 10))
```

A PowerShell array is just a list of objects, and those objects can be anything, including other arrays. This example creates an array containing two elements. Those two elements are themselves arrays of five elements each. The value of `$a[1][3]` is 9. (Can you see why? `$a[1]` is the second array because indexing starts with 0. If we stick `[3]` on that, we get its fourth value. Thus, `$a[1][3]` is 9.)

You can create three-dimensional arrays in a similar way, for example:

```
$a = (((1,2), (3,4)), ((5, 6), (7, 8))
```

Here, `$a[0][1][0]` is 3.

However, this method of creating and using multidimensional arrays is cumbersome. PowerShell can create multidimensional arrays directly using a different syntax:

```
$a = new-object 'object[,]' n,m
```

where *n* and *m* are the number of elements desired for the first array index, and m is the number of elements desired for the second. You access the elements of the array, as in `$a[3,2] = 104`. You can create a three-dimensional array with

```
$a = new-object 'object[,,]' n,m,p
```

where n, m, and p are the desired number of elements for the first, second, and third subscripts, respectively, and so on, up to a total of 17 dimensions.

Negative Index Values

PowerShell lets you extract elements from the end of an array by using negative index values. For example, with the array `$v = 1, 2, 3, 4, 5`, the expression `$v[-1]` gives you the value **5**.

Arrays with Pipelines and Cmdlets

PowerShell is designed entirely around working with objects. Cmdlets work with streams of objects, and in a PowerShell command line, an array is treated as a stream of objects. Here's what I mean.

If you type the name of a array variable, PowerShell emits its entire contents as a stream of objects. As you recall, when a stream of objects hits the console window, PowerShell formats and prints their values in a nice table. This is why these two statements:

```
$a = 1, 2, 3, 4, 5
$a
```

print a list of numbers. `$a` emits a stream of `System.Int32` objects, and PowerShell prints them:

```
1
2
3
4
5
```

You can use this to send objects from an array to a cmdlet. The statement

```
$a | get-member
```

pipes those `System.Int32` objects to `get-member`, which prints a table of the properties and methods of any object type it reads. Thus, this command prints information about the `System.Int32` objects that are stored in the array.

You can also store the output of a cmdlet in an array. For example:

```
$a = get-childitem
```

runs the `get-childitem` cmdlet, which in this case lists all the file and folder objects in the current directory and stores this list of objects in array `$a`. You can now use `$a` in a script to extract and work with the file and folder information it contains.

This very unusual behavior is one of the things that justifies the word *Power* in the program's name. PowerShell lets you easily switch back and forth between *declarative* or *functional programming*, where a command line sets up a flow of objects that does all the work, and *imperative programming*, where you use commands, loops, `if` statements, and the like to perform a task step-by-step.

One interesting thing to note is the pipeline character can be used in expressions, too, and a statement like this:

```
$v = command 1 | command 2 | command 3
```

stores the result of command 3 in variable `$v` because = has the lowest precedence. I discuss operator precedence later in the chapter.

Note

There is another way to store cmdlet output in a variable: Most cmdlets accept the command-line option **-OutVariable** *variablename*, which stores a copy of the cmdlet's output stream in the named variable as an array of objects. Don't type the $ before the variable name. You can optionally put a + sign in front of the variable name to add the cmdlet's output to whatever's already in the variable.

Besides being stored in the named variable, the cmdlet's output is also written to the standard output, so you can pipe the objects to another cmdlet or view them in the command window.

Extracting More than One Value from an Array

Another of PowerShell's unusual features lets you extract more than one item from an array at once. Most programming languages used in the last 50 years let you retrieve a value from an array using a syntax something like this: `$array[n]`, which pulls out the *n*th value from the array. n is called an *array index*. (About all that differs from one language to another is whether you use parentheses or square brackets and whether the first array slot is numbered 0 or 1. As I've mentioned, PowerShell indexing starts with 0.)

Here's an unusual twist: In PowerShell, you aren't limited to using a simple integer as an array index value. You can use an array as an index! What PowerShell does in this case is take all the values out of the inner, indexing array; uses those values as indexes; and returns all the referenced values from the outer array. Here's what I mean:

```
$array = 'a', 'b', 'c', 'd', 'e', 'f'
$array[1, 3, 5]
```

The second statement prints b, d, and f. What happens is this: 1, 3, 5 is an array containing these three numbers: 1, 3, and 5. These numbers are used to pull out the second, fourth, and sixth items from variable $array (since indexing starts with 0), and that gives us the strings 'b', 'd', and 'f'. Of course, the indexing array doesn't have to be typed literally; it can be a variable itself:

```
$x = 1, 3, 5
$array[$x]
```

that produces the same result. You can use PowerShell's range array and concatenation operators, too, as in this expression: $array[1..3 + $x + 3, 4, 5]. This one takes a moment to decipher. Inside the square brackets, we have an array with elements 1, 2, 3. We add (concatenate) the array $x, which has elements, 1, 3, and 5, and then tack on another array with elements 3, 4, and 5. The indexing array is thus 1, 2, 3, 1, 3, 5, 3, 4, 5. This extracts and prints strings b, c, d, b, d, f, d, e, and f. (Phew!)

Arrays are just one of a category of object types called *collections*, which contain one or more other objects. As you saw in earlier chapters of this book, you'll use collections to manage files, folders, Windows services, and so on. Later in this chapter. I mention another collection type used in PowerShell called the Hash Table.

Comparisons with Arrays

Here is one of PowerShell's more unusual features: If you use any of the comparison operators with an array, PowerShell performs the comparison on each element of the array and returns an array containing the *items that matched the comparison*. For example, this expression: (1,2,1,2,1,2) -eq 1 is equivalent to the array (1,1,1). I discuss this further later in the chapter in "Comparison Operators" on page 639.

Constants

You can define variables that can't be changed using this syntax:

```
set-variable -name variablename -value value -option constant
```

with no dollar sign in front of *variablename*. You can omit the —name and —value switch indicators and just type the variable name and its value. Here's an example: set-variable MaxItems 100 -option constant. It's sometimes helpful to define program values that never need to be changed this way, so a script can't inadvertently change them; it also signals someone who's reading your script that the value is something predetermined. This corresponds to the const *name = value* structure in VBScript.

Expressions

PowerShell lets you write expressions that perform computations with numbers and strings. The ideas are similar to what you saw in Chapter 2, "VBScript Tutorial." Table 15.6 lists the expression operators. All the operators work with numeric values. The + and * operators also work with strings, as noted. PowerShell's authors also borrowed a few additional operators that originally came from the C programming language, as you'll see.

Table 15.6   **PowerShell Expression Operators**

Operator	Computes	Example	Yields
+	With numbers: addition With strings and arrays: concatenation. If you add a numeric value and a string, PowerShell converts the number to a string and then concatenates the results.	3+4 'a' + 'b' '2' + 3	7 'ab' '23'
-	Subtraction.	5-2	3
*	With numbers: multiplication. With strings and arrays: duplication.	4*3 'ab' *3	12 'ababab'
/	Division. Dividing integers produces an integer result if there is no remainder, otherwise, produces a floating point result. This is unlike most other programming languages! You must cast the result to an integer type if you want a truncated result.	7/2 7./2. 7/[double]2	3.5 3.5 3.5
%	Modulus (remainder after dividing).	7%2	1
++	Autoincrement. Placed before a variable, PowerShell adds 1 to the variable and then uses this new value.	++a	a+1
	Placed after a variable, PowerShell uses the current value of the variable and then adds 1 to it afterward.	a++	a
--	Autodecrement. Placed before a variable, PowerShell subtracts 1 from the variable and then uses this new value.	--a	a-1
	Placed after a variable, PowerShell uses the current value of the variable and then subtracts 1 from it afterwards	a--	a
-and	Logical (boolean) AND.	$true -and $true	True

Operator	Computes	Example	Yields
-or	Logical OR.	`$true -or $false`	`True`
-xor	Logical Exclusive OR.	`$true -xor $true`	`False`
-not	Logical Not.	`-not $true`	`False`
!	(! is the same as `-not`.)	`! $true`	`False`
-bAND	Bitwise (binary) AND.	`7 -bAND 4`	`4`
-bOR	Bitwise (binary) OR.	`5 -bOR 3`	`7`
-bXOR	Bitwise (binary) Exclusive-OR.	`5 -bXOR 3`	`6`
-bNOT	Bitwise (binary) negation.	`-bNOT 4`	`-5` *

★ The result of `-bNOT 4` is negative because the default object type for integers is `[System.Int32]`, which is a signed 32-bit integer. 4 in binary is 0000...0100. The binary negation of this is 1111...1011. The result of `-bNOT` is always a signed integer type (even if its argument value is an unsigned type), so the result is interpreted as -5.

Comparisons use the operators listed in Table 15.7 and produce either `True` or `False` as their values.

Table 15.7 **Comparison Operators**

Operator	Computes	Example	Yields
-lt	Less than	`3 -lt 4`	`True`
-gt	Greater than	`3 -gt 4`	`False`
-le	Less than or equal to	`3 -le 4`	`True`
-ge	Greater than or equal to	`3 -ge 4`	`False`
-eq	Equal	`3 -eq 4`	`False`
-ne	Not equal	`3 -ne 4`	`True`
-like	Wildcard string match	`'file 2.doc' -like '*.doc'`	`True`
-notlike	Inverse of `-like`	`'file 2.doc' -notlike '*.xls'`	`True`
-match	Regular expression string match	`'abc' -match 'a[a-z]*'`	`True`
-notmatch	Inverse of `-match`	`'abc' -notmatch '.*c$'`	
-contains	Set membership	`(1,2,3) -contains 3`	`True`
-notcontains	Inverse of `-contains`	`(1,2,3) -notcontains 3`	`False`
-is [objname]	Object equivalence	`3 -is [System.Int32]`	`True`
-isnot [objname]	Inverse of `-is`	`3 -isnot [System.Char]`	`True`

Note

By default, all these operators are case-insensitive when comparing strings. To make them case-sensitive, put a c in front of the comparison name. These are the case-sensitive operators: -clt, -cgt, -cle, -cge, -ceq, -cne, -clike, -cnotlike, -cmatch, -cnotmatch, -ccontains, and -cnotcontains.

Comparisons with Arrays

One of PowerShell's more unusual properties is that you can do comparisons with arrays. The result of comparing an array to some value isn't a True/False answer as you might expect. What PowerShell does is perform the comparison test on each of the items in the array and produces an array result that contains just those items that pass the comparison test. For example:

```
(1,2,3,4,5) -ge 3
```

produces the array result (3,4,5) because these are the items whose values are greater than or equal to 3. (If no items pass the test, the result is an empty array, but it's still an array.)

All the comparison operators work this way with arrays. This is true for −like, −match, −eq, −ge, and so on.

If you want instead to just see if any of the elements of an array equals a specific value, use the -contains comparison operator. If you want to know how many items an array passed the comparison test, examine the .Count property on the resulting array, as in this example:

```
if (((('abc', 'def', 'ghi') -match 'abc').Count -eq 1) {'Just one abc found'}
```

For more information, see the PowerShell help page about_comparison_operators.

Wildcard Matching with -like and -clike

You can match strings that contain simple wildcard operators using −like and its several variants: -like and -ilike are identical and perform case-insensitive tests. −clike is case sensitive. In addition, the inverse tests (-notlike, -inotlike, and -cnotlike) simply return the opposite True/False values.

The wildcard characters are *, which matches 0 or more characters of any sort, and ?, that matches exactly one character. Here are some examples:

Test	Returns
`'abcd' -like 'a*'`	True
`'abcd' -like 'a???'`	True
`'abcd' -like '*abcd'`	True
`'abcd' -like 'ab?cd'`	False

In addition to * and ?, you can use the format [a-z], which matches any character in the specified range. For example, `'aqb' -like 'a[m-r]b'` is True.

One thing to be aware of is that these tests don't work exactly like the standard Windows command prompt's wildcards. The standard command prompt would match filename "test", with no extension, with the wildcard "test.*". In PowerShell, though, `'test' -like 'test.*'` is False.

Regular Expression Matching with `-match` and `-cmatch`

PowerShell has built-in support for regular expressions, which provides a powerful way for matching strings based on a pattern of characters. Regular expressions are used with `-match` and `-notmatch`, which are case-insensitive comparison operators, and `-cmatch` and `-cnotmatch`, which are case sensitive. The pattern can include literal characters that must be matched exactly and/or any of the special characters and patterns listed in Table 15.8.

Table 15.8 **Regular Expression Patterns**

Pattern	Matches
.	(Period) Any single character.
^	The beginning of the string being tested.
$	The end of the string being tested.
[set]	Any of the characters in the set. Between the square brackets you can list individual characters and/or ranges in the form m—q, which implies any character from m to q.
[^set]	Any character *not* in the set.
*	Zero or more occurrences of the previous item.
+	One or more occurrences of the previous item.
?	Zero or one occurrence of the previous item.
	As an additional modifier after *, +, ?, or {}, means "but match as few times as possible."
{n}	Exactly *n* occurrences of the previous item.
{n,}	*n* or more occurrences of the previous item.
{n,m}	*n* to *m* occurrences of the previous item.

continues

Table 15.8   **Continued**

Pattern	Matches
(*pattern*)	Groups one or more pattern items so that the *, +, ?, or { } items can be used, as in: ([a-z][0-9])+ which matches a1b2.
|	Within parentheses, functions as an "or" operator. For example, 'yes' -match '(yes|no)' is True.
\a	Bell character (ASCII 7).
\b	Backspace character (ASCII 8).
\t	Tab character (ASCII 9).
\n	Newline character (ASCII 10).
\v	Vertical tab character (ASCII 11).
\f	Form feed character (ASCII 12).
\r	Carriage return character (ASCII 13).
\e	ESC character (ASCII 27).
nnn	ASCII character by value. *nnn* is three octal (0–7) digits.
\x*nn*	ASCII character by value. *nn* is two hexadecimal digits.
\c*x*	Control-*x* character (ASCII 1–26), where *x* is a letter from A to Z in upper- or lowercase.
\u*nnnn*	Unicode character by value. *nnnn* is four hexadecimal digits.
\p{*xx*}	A character in the Unicode character class named *xx*.
\P{*xx*}	A character *not* in the Unicode class named *xx*.
\w	Any character normally found in a word. Often used with + to pick up a whole word: \w+.
\W	Any character *not* normally found in a word (whitespace, punctuation, and so on).
\s	Any whitespace character (space, tab, and so on).
\S	Any printing character.
\d	Any decimal digit, much like [0-9] but includes other Unicode digit characters.
\D	Any nondigit character.
n	Where *n* is a small number, matches whatever the *n*th parenthesized pattern group matched.
x	The character *x*, where *x* is not one of the characters listed previously, as a literal character. For example, use * to match the special character * literally.

▶ **Note**

I've abbreviated this list a bit. For the full list, go to msdn.microsoft.com and search for "Regular Expression Language Elements."

Here's an example:

```
if ($filename -match 'a[0-9]*.docx?') {
    …
```

The `if` statement would be executed for filenames `a.doc`, `a1.docx` and `a12345.doc`, but not `az.doc`.

I don't have room to describe regular expressions in more detail, but you can read the `about_regular_expressions` PowerShell help page for more information.

> **Note**
>
> If the match operator returns True, it also sets up a predefined variable name `$matches` as a side effect. `$matches[0]` contains the input text that was matched by the regular expression pattern. If you used parentheses in the pattern, `$matches[1]` contains the text matched by the first parentheses group, `$matches[2]` the text matched by the second, and so on.

String Operators

PowerShell has three operators that have the same format as comparisons: `-replace`, `-split`, and `-join`, but they are actual string manipulation tools returning string values, not True/False results. I describe these operators briefly.

> **Note**
>
> All the following string operators can operate on arrays as well as on individual string values. If you use them on an array, the result is an array containing the results of the operation performed on each element of the input array. For example, `('a','b','c')` `-replace` `'a'`, `'X'` produces the array `('X', 'b', 'c')`.

`-split` string

As a unary operator (with nothing to the left of `-split`), it splits the input *string* at whitespace (tabs, spaces, and so on). The result is an array of strings. For example, `-split 'now is the time'` returns the array `('now','is','the','time')`.

The *string* argument to `-split` can be a single string or array of strings, in which case the result is the collection of tokens extracted from all of the input strings.

string `-split` *delimiter* [, *maxstrings* [, *'options'*]]

As a binary operator, splits *string* into separate tokens separated by the *delimiter* pattern. The value of the expression is an array of strings. By default, the delimiter is interpreted using regular expression rules. The input string is broken into tokens wherever the delimiter pattern is matched. For more information about regular expressions, see "Regular Expression Matching with –match," p. 641. You can have –split search for a literal delimiter string by specifying the SimpleMatch option, as described shortly.

maxstrings is an optional maximum number of tokens to extract from each input string. If the input string is an array, the limit is applied to each of the input strings independently.

options is an optional string argument that can contain one or more of the following keywords separated by commas:

- **RegExMatch**—This is the default mode. The *delimiter* string is interpreted as a regular expression.

- **SimpleMatch**—Use straightforward character matching when looking for the delimiter characters within the input. Can't be used with RegExMatch.

- **IgnoreCase**—Use case-insensitive matching, even if you use the -csplit operator. This is the default with -split and -isplit.

  The remaining options are used only in RegExMatch mode and are not valid if you specify SimpleMatch.

- **CultureInvariant**—Ignores local language rules used by default to determine uppercase and lowercase character relationships.

- **Multiline**—If the input string contains multiple lines (that is, contains carriage return/line feed characters), this options makes ^ and $ match the beginning and end of a line, rather than the beginning and end of the input string.

- **SingleLine**—Makes the . character match carriage return and/or line feed characters as well as all other characters. By default, . doesn't match line-ending characters.

- **ExplicitCapture**—Stores only named parenthesized pattern groups in the $matched[] array. By default, all groups are stored.

-csplit and -isplit

-isplit is exactly the same as -split; it's case insensitive by default. -csplit is the same as -split except that it's case sensitive by default. The IgnoreCase option can override this, however.

-replace

The -replace operator matches text in a string using regular expressions and replaces the matches with something else. The syntax is

```
string -replace pattern, replacement
```

and the value of this, in an expression, is a string. The *pattern* is a regular expression, as discussed previously in "Regular Expression Matching with `-match` and `–cmatch`." As many times as the pattern can be matched in the input string, the text that is matched is replaced with the *replacement* string. Here's an example: `'abcdef'` `-replace '[a-c]+', 'X'` yields the string `Xdef`.

In the most simple usage, without any of the special regular expression characters, `-replace` performs simple string substitutions. For example, `'Hello Hello' -replace 'Hello', 'Goodbye'` prints `Goodbye Goodbye`.

In the replacement string, there are some special constructs you can use:

Pattern	Replaced with
$&	The entire matched text from the input string. So, `'abcd'` `—replace '.*', '$&$&'` produces `abcdabcd`.
$`	All of the input string prior to the part that matched.
$'	All of the input string after the part that matched.
$_	The entire input string.
$*n*	Text matched by the *n*th parenthesized group in the pattern. `$1` is replaced with the text matched by the first parentheses group, `$2` by the second, and so on.
$$	A single `$`.

If you use any of these items, be sure to enclose the replacement string with single quotes to prevent PowerShell from seeing them as variable names to interpolate (see "String Interpolation," in this chapter on p. 628, for details on that) or put the string in double quotes and precede these dollar signs with back quotes (`).

> **Note**
>
> As with regular expression patterns, I've abbreviated this list a bit. For the full list, go to msdn.microsoft.com and search for "Regular Expression Language Elements."

-join *array*

As a unary operator (with nothing to the left of `-join`), `-join` concatenates the contents of the array without any intervening whitespace. For example, `-join ('a','b','c')` produces the string `abc`.

array -join *delimiter*

As a binary operator, `-join` joins all the strings in the specified array into one string, inserting the specified delimiter string between each array element. For example, `('a','b','c') -join '/'` produces the string `a/b/c`.

string **-f** *expression*

Formats the *expression* according to the information in the *string* value. I discuss the format operator in Chapter 16.

The & (Execute) Operator

The & character operates on the string value after it and runs the value as a PowerShell command. For example,

```
$cmd = 'get-childitem'
&$cmd
```

runs the get-childitem cmdlet. This operator is useful when you want to run a command whose path contains spaces, and so must be enclosed in quotes.

Operator Precedence

An expression such as 3+2*4 tells PowerShell to do some math, but it could be interpreted two ways: add 3 and 2 and then multiply the result by 4 to get 20, or multiply 2 and 4 and then add that to 3 to get 11. PowerShell uses the second interpretation because it follows the rules of algebra which dictate that unless parentheses are used to indicate a different ordering, multiplication has a higher precedence than addition. The * multiplication operator binds tighter than the + sign, so the value of 2*4 is computed first.

The precedence of PowerShell's operators is listed here, from the highest precedence to the lowest. Items on the same line have equal precedence.

Operator	Description
( )	Parentheses
$( ) @( )	Subexpression operators
[*n*]	Array indexing
[*objtype*]	Casting
-split -join	Text operators used as unary operators
,	Array item separator
++ --	Autoincrement/autodecrement
! -not -bNOT	Negation
..	Array range
-f	Format operator (discussed in Chapter 16)
-	Unary negation (for example, –3)
* / %	Multiplication/division remainder
+ -	Addition/subtraction

Operator	Description

`-lt` `-gt` `-le` `-ge` `-eq`
`-ne` `-clt` `-cgt` `-cle` `-cge`
`-ceq` `-cne` `-is` `-isnot`
`-like`   `-notlike`   `-clike`
`-cnotlike`   `-match`   `-notmatch`
`-cmatch`   `-cnotmatch` `-contains`
`-notcontains` `-ccontains`
`-cnotcontains` `-replace`   `-creplace`
	Comparisons, other types of tests, binary string operators; all these have equal precedence

`-bAND` `-bOR` `-bXOR`	Binary and, or, exclusive or
`-and` `-or` `-xor`	Logical (boolean) and, or, exclusive or
`&(obj)`	Execute
<code>|</code>	Command pipeline
`>` `>>` `2>` `2>>` `2>&1`	Output redirection
`=` `+=` `-=` `*=` `/=` `%=`	Assignment

You can use parentheses to force expressions to be evaluated in a different order. For example, `(3+2)*4` does produce 20. When in doubt, use parentheses. They don't cost anything, but they do make it clear what you want.

> **Tip**
>
> Always use parentheses when you combine math and comparisons or when you use more than one comparison. The expression
>
> `(($a + 4) -lt $b) -bOR ($b -gt 5)`
>
> returns the value True if (`$a+4`) is less than `$b` or if `$b` is greater than 5. Without the parentheses:
>
> `$a + 4 -lt $b -bOR $b -gt 5`
>
> it actually would still work because the precedence rules happen to work in your favor in this instance, but it's much easier to understand with parentheses, and they eliminate any uncertainty about the rules.

For more information, see the PowerShell help page `about_Operator_Precedence`.

Assignment Operators

You can store the result of an expression in a variable using the = operator, as in most programming languages:

`$v = 5`

PowerShell also borrowed some assignment operators from the C language, which are listed in Table 15.9.

Table 15.9 **Assignment Operators**

Operator	Action
=	Stores value in variable.
+=	Adds value to variable. Note that this works with strings and arrays as well as numbers. += appends a new string to an existing string and adds the elements of a new array to the end of an existing array.
-=	Subtracts value from variable.
*=	Multiplies variable by value. For strings, duplicates the string by a specified quantity. For arrays, appends a number of additional copies of the array
/=	Divides variable by value.
%=	Divides variable by value and stores just the remainder.

For example, these two statements

```
$v = 3
$v += 5
```

have the exact same meaning as

```
$v = 3
$v = $v + 5
```

and both leave $v with holding the value 8.

Tip

The most commonly used of these is +=. You might use it inside a loop that adds up numbers—for example, this bit of code that adds up the numbers in an array:

```
$sum = 0
foreach ($v in $array) {$sum += $v}
```

Statement Values

All PowerShell structures have a value. That is, any PowerShell statement can be put on the right side of an equals sign. You might find this particularly useful with the if and switch statements because you can type things like this:

```
$inverse = if ($a -eq 0) {0} else {1./$a}   # if $a is 0, don't divide by 0, use 0
                                            #instead
```

and like this:

```
$size = switch ([int] $weight) {    # compute size of box to use based on weight
           0   {'small'}
           1   {'medium'}
           2   {'medium'}
           default {'large'}
       }
```

Casts

There are times when you will want to tell PowerShell to use a particular type of object to represent a value. You might recall from Chapter 2 that VBScript uses functions like cstr() and cint() to turn values into strings and integers, respectively. In PowerShell, you use *casts*. A cast is a language construct that lets you indicate the exact type of variable or object that you want an expression to be converted to. In PowerShell, to cast a value to a specific object type, put the name of the desired object in square brackets in front of the value, like this:

```
$v = [System.Int32] '3'
```

In effect this says, "Take the string value 3, turn it into a System.Int32 object, and assign that to variable $v."

In casts, you can specify the full .NET Framework object name, or you can use any of the handy shortcuts names listed in Table 15.1; for example, the previous example could just as well be written

```
$v = [int] '3'
```

Now, there are two ways that you can organize casts in Windows PowerShell. I just showed the first way, where you put the object name before a value. This method changes the values themselves. Here are two such casts:

```
$a = '3'
$v = [int] $a
$array = [int] '3', [int] '4', [int] '5'
```

The first cast turns the string value $a into an integer. The second shows casts turning each of three string values into integers, which are then packaged into an array.

The second way to use casts in PowerShell is to put the cast before the variable name on the *left* side of the equals sign. For example,

```
[int] $v = '3'
```

This version says, "Create a `System.Int32` object and assign the string value '3' to it." It's a subtle difference. The resulting variable can, from this point forward, only hold values of this type. This form of casting is most useful if you want to create an array of a specific object type. The `$array` example I just gave could also be written this way:

```
[int[]] $array = '3', '4', '5'
```

The outermost square brackets indicate that you are specifying a cast. The `int[]` inside them indicates the type of object you want to create—in this case, an array of `int`s.

Passing by Reference

By default, values are passed to methods, procedures, and user-defined functions by value. This means that a procedure call like this, `$dt.AddSeconds($n)`, gives `AddSeconds` the value of variable `$n`, but `$n` cannot be modified in the process. Some methods are intended to change argument values. In these cases, you must pass a *reference* to the variable, so that the method can assign a new value to it. To pass a reference, where required, cast the variable name to the `[ref]` type, as in this example:

```
$dt = 0
[datetime]::TryParse("11/20/2010 3:00 PM", [ref] $dt)
```

The variable you want to pass by reference must exist beforehand.

Hash Tables

The easiest way to think of a hash table is as an array whose slots are identified by names rather than by position numbers. That is, whereas an array's slots are identified by index numbers 0, 1, 2, 3, and so on, a hash table's slots are identified by, well, by any arbitrary type of value. It could be a string or a number. As such, hash tables don't have a specific "length," that is, a fixed range of slot numbers. Other than this, they work just like arrays.

Here's an example of a hash table created in PowerShell:

```
$table = @{'alpha' = 1; 'bravo' = 2; 'charlie' = 3; 'delta' = 4}
```

The difference between creating a hash table and an array is that you use curly brackets instead of parentheses after the @ sign and you separate the values with semicolons (;) instead of commas.

For this hash table, the expression `$table['abc']` returns the value 1. If you use an index value that doesn't exist in the table, the value returned is `null`.

The "index" values in this example are strings, but they could just as well be numbers. How would a hash table indexed with numbers differ from a regular array? With an array, the slot numbers have to be 0, 1, 2, 3, and so on, and PowerShell would have to reserve enough memory for every possible slot. If you use numbers as the indexes of a hash table, though, the slot numbers can be any arbitrary numbers. You could use indexes 101, –34, 5432, and 11453434. And, PowerShell only has to use memory to hold the items that are actually used.

Like arrays, the values stored in each slot of the hash table can be any sort of object, from numbers, to strings, to arrays, to WMI management objects, or whatever you need to store. If you only need to store a single value for each name, then a simple integer or string value is fine. If you need to store many values for each name, you can put arrays or objects into the hash table.

To create an empty hash table, use a command like this:

```
$table = @{}
```

The script can then add new items to it as necessary. You can add to a hash table by simply assigning to a new index value. This statement:

```
$table['echo'] = 5
```

adds a new element to the table I created previously. Equivalently, you can use the hash table's **Add** method this way:

```
$table.Add('echo', 5)
```

Both versions do the exact same thing. .NET hash table objects have several useful methods and properties, the most important of which are listed in Reference List 15.1. Some of them are new to hash tables, and others are common to all .NET collection objects.

Reference List 15.1—Important Properties and Methods of
`System.Collections.HashTable`

Properties:

Count

The number of items in the hash table.

Keys

Returns a collection containing all the keys (index values) for this hash table.

Values

Returns a collection containing all the values stored in the hash table.

Methods:

Clear()

Empties the hash table of all items.

ContainsKey(*key***)**

Returns True if the hash table contains an entry for the specified key (index value); returns False otherwise.

ContainsValue(*value***)**

Returns True is some item in the hash table contains the specified value; returns False otherwise.

Remove(*key***)**

Removes the key and its associated value from the hash table.

Usually, hash tables are used to look up the value associated with a known index value, but if you need to scan through all the items in a hash table, you can do it easily using the `Keys` property:

```
foreach ($k in $table.Keys) {
    # on each turn through this loop, $k contains a different key . You can
    # get the associated value with $table[$k]
}
```

But Why?

Why bother with hash tables? Are they really that useful when you're managing Windows computers or performing other practical tasks? Yes! For one thing, they're used to hold the arguments passed to a cmdlet, as I discuss later, so you'll need to use them if you write your own cmdlets. More importantly, they are really helpful when you have a job that involves counting things or when you have to manage arbitrary lists of items of any type. If you find yourself thinking about (a) using an array to hold names and some other information, and (b) using a loop to see whether a particular entry is already in the array before adding it, then you have a job that could probably be done more easily with a hash table. I give an example in Chapter 16.

Note

To be fair, a `Scripting.Dictionary` object is available in WSH that could let you do something similar in VBScript, but it's not very well-known. The hash table, on the other hand, is an integral part of PowerShell.

Other Types of Collections

PowerShell has access to all the types of collection objects that are part of the .NET Framework programming platform. Besides `System.Collections.HashTable` and `System.Array`, which is the object behind all .NET arrays, other collection objects include `System.Collections.Stack`, `System.Collections.Queue`, and `System.Collections.SortedList`. Each of these has special uses:

Collection	Behavior
Array	Lets you store and retrieve items at will using an integer index value.
Stack	Lets you store an arbitrary number of objects and retrieve them one at a time. When you remove an item from a stack, you get the most recently added first.
Queue	Similar to a stack, but when you remove an item from a queue, you get the oldest one in there.
HashTable	Works like an array, except the index values don't have to be integers, they can be any type of value.
SortedList	Works like a hash table, except when you scan the collection using the foreach command, the keys are enumerated in sorted order.

To read more about the .NET collections, visit msdn.microsoft.com and search for the phrase "System.Collections Namespace." There, you can read about each of the collection objects and see their methods and properties.

Flow of Control

As a programming language, PowerShell has all the usual flow-of-control commands that let you test values and perform different actions based on what you find. They are pretty much the same as the ones found in all modern programming languages, so I'll just go through them quickly here.

if

The if statement uses an expression that produces either the value True or False to determine whether to execute a group of other PowerShell statements. It can take any of the following forms:

```
if (expression) {          if (expression) {          if (expression) {
    statement(s)               statement(s)               statement(s)
    ⋮                          ⋮                          ⋮
}                          }                          }
                           else {                     elseif (expression) {
                               statement(s)               statement(s)
                               ⋮                          ⋮
                           }                          }
                                                      ⋮
```

If the first expression is True, PowerShell executes the first block of statements inside curly brackets. If the expression is False, it evaluates any following elseif expressions, and if no expression is True, it executes the final else group, if present. The elseif group can be repeated any number of times. The final else group is optional.

The *expression* should result in the value True or False. If the result is a number, it's considered to be False if the value is 0; otherwise, it's True. Any other type of result is considered to be True. Normally, you'll use comparisons as in this example:

```
$v = 100
if ($v -ge 100) { ' v is at least 100' }
```

which indeed prints v is at least 100.

while

The while loop has the following form:

```
while (expression) {
    statement(s)
      ⋮
}
```

The first time through, the expression is tested. If it's True, the statement(s) is executed, just as with the if statement. The difference here is that, after completing the statements, PowerShell goes back to the top. The expression is evaluated again, and if it's True again, the statements are executed again, and so on, until the expression is finally False. Then, the script continues with whatever comes after the while loop.

Inside a while loop, the break statement immediately exits the loop and the continue statement immediately starts the next iteration. break is discussed in more detail shortly.

do...while and do...until

The do loop is similar to the while loop, except that it performs the test at the end of the loop. The statement(s) is always executed at least once. There are two versions of the loop, with the following forms:

```
do {                          do {
    statement(s)                  statement(s)
      ⋮                             ⋮
} while (expression)          } until (expression)
```

do…while repeats the loop if the expression is True and exits if it's False. do…until repeats if the expression is False and exits if it's True.

Inside a do loop, the break statement immediately exits the loop and the continue statement immediately starts the next iteration. break is discussed in more detail shortly.

for

The PowerShell `for` loop was taken from the C and C++ programming languages, and it's a bit peculiar and a bit harder to explain. The form of the statement is

```
for (initializer; condition; incrementer) {
    statement(s)
        ⋮
}
```

where *initializer* and *incrementer* are statements that typically set and modify a variable, respectively, and *condition* is a Boolean expression that evaluates to either True or False. Inside the curly brackets are zero or more separate statements.

Here's what it does: The *initializer* statement sets up the loop for its first turn; the *condition* determines whether to repeat the statements; and the *incrementer* prepares the loop for the next iteration. The `for` statement is exactly the same as the following:

```
initializer
while (condition) {
    statement(s)
        ⋮
    incrementer
}
```

The `for` loop just provides a more concise way of doing the job. After you're used to it, it can make the loop easier to understand because all the stuff that controls the loop is in one place. Here is an example:

```
for ($i = 1; $i -le 10; $i++) {
    $i
}
```

This prints the numbers 1–10. The *initializer* statement sets `$i` to 1. The first time through `$i` is indeed less than or equal to 10, so the statement inside the curly brackets is executed, printing 1. The *incrementer* statement changes `$i` from 1 to 2. Then we go back to the top. The condition is still true, so the statement is executed again, printing 2. This repeats a total of 10 times. The tenth time through `$i` gets incremented to 11. The condition test now evaluates to False, so the loop is finished.

If your particular code doesn't require them, any of the three parts inside the parentheses, or even the statements inside the curly brackets, can be omitted. For example, if the variable you want to use to control the loop has already been set up, you can omit the *initializer* statement. If you omit both the *initializer* and *incrementer*, you have something that works exactly like a `while` loop. You have to keep the two semicolons between the parentheses no matter what. If you omit the *condition* expression, it's treated as True, and you'll have to use a `break` statement inside the loop to prevent it from running forever.

You might be scratching your head wondering how it could make sense to omit the statements inside the curly brackets—what would the loop do? Remember that the *incrementer* statement or even the *condition* expression (if it calls a function or uses the ++ or -- operators) can modify variables, and in some cases, this is enough. For example, the following loop leaves $i set to the index of the first value in $array that is less than or equal to 0:

```
$array = 5, 1, 7, 0, 11, 16
for ($i = 0; $array[$i] -gt 0; $i++) {}
write-output ("The index of the first zero value is: " + $i)
```

This sort of loop makes perfect sense to a C programmer, but I'm guessing that anyone used to a more modern language will find this at first confusing and then annoying.

Inside a for loop, the break statement immediately exits the loop and the continue statement immediately starts the next iteration. break is discussed in more detail shortly.

foreach

The foreach loop is a tamer animal than the plain for loop. It examines each of the items in an array, a hash table, or another collection object in turn. There are two forms of the statement. The first form is as follows:

```
foreach ($variable in collection) {
    statement(s)
    ⋮
}
```

Each time through the statement(s), the specified variable has the value of one of the items in the collection. Here's an example:

```
$array = 1,2,3,4
foreach ($v in $array) {
    write-output ("Array value: " + $v)
}
```

Inside a foreach loop, the break statement immediately exits the loop and the continue statement immediately starts the next iteration. break is discussed in more detail shortly.

Scanning the Results of a Cmdlet

The collection scanned by foreach doesn't have to be a variable. It could be a literally typed array—as in foreach ($v in 1,2,3,4,5) {…}—or it can be a PowerShell cmdlet that generates a stream of objects. This is an extremely powerful tool! You can generate a list of files and scan through it with a statement like this:

```
$docsize = 0
foreach ($file in get-childitem c:\* -include *.doc*  -recurse) {
    $docsize += $file.length
}
$docsize
```

This totals the amount of disk space used by all files named .doc, .docx, and so on in all folders on drive C: and prints the result.

Note

As I mentioned previously in "Determining an Array's Size," the foreach loop doesn't let you know the item number of the values you're seeing. If you need to know, say, the index number of an array's values as you scan it, you have to use a regular for loop as I showed in that section.

Tip

The % sign is a predefined alias for the foreach command. That is, you can type something like

```
get-childitem | % {$docsize += $_.Length}
```

I don't recommend using it in scripts; it's sort of cryptic and makes the script just a bit harder for a human to understand. But you can use it to save keystrokens when you're typing at the command prompt.

foreach in a Pipeline

The second form of the foreach statement can be used in PowerShell command lines with a stream of objects piped into it. You omit the parentheses section. The statement(s) is executed once for each object received through the pipeline. Inside the statements, the predefined variable $_ holds the current object. Here's an example:

```
$docsize = 0
get-childitem c:\* -include *.doc*  -recurse | foreach {
    $docsize += $_.length
}
$docsize
```

This does the same thing as the previous example, but notice that in this case the objects are piped to foreach.

switch

The switch statement lets you examine a value and do one of several things based on the value you find. It replaces this sequence of statements:

```
if (expression -eq value1) {
    first set of statements
}
```

```
else if (expression -eq value2) {
    second set of statements
}
else if (expression -eq value3) {
    ⋮
```

with the following:

```
switch (expression) {
    value1    {first set of statements}
    value2    {second set of statements}
    ⋮
    default    {final set of statements}
}
```

Inside the `switch` statement, the matching values before the statement blocks can be integers, strings, variables, or expressions.

What this does is evaluate the `switch` *expression*, and then it examines the *value*(s) listed inside the `switch` statement. If the expression matches one of the values, PowerShell executes the corresponding set of statements. Here are some details about the PowerShell version of `switch`, some of which differ strikingly from similar statements in other languages:

- The `switch` expression doesn't have to be a scalar (single value); it can be an array or command that generates a stream of objects. If the expression generates more than one value, the `switch` is evaluated once for each item. (That is, it acts like `foreach`. Perhaps the statement should have been named `switcheach`!) Here's an example:

  ```
  $a = (1,2,3,4,5)
  switch ($a) {
      2        {'The number is TWO'}
      default {"The number is $_"}
  }
  ```

- Inside the `switch`, you can use the predefined variable `$_` to retrieve the value being tested by the `switch`. This is especially useful if you're using the `switch` to test an expression, array or cmdlet output.

- If the expression doesn't match any of the listed values and there is an entry labeled with the keyword `default`, the default statement(s) is executed. If there is no `default` entry, no statements are executed.

- The values can be listed in any order; `default` doesn't have to be last.

- String matching is case insensitive by default. For example, `switch ('ABC')` matches the entry `'abc'`. You can make the comparisons case sensitive with the `-casesensitive` option, which I discuss shortly.

- The values don't have to be literal constants: They can be expressions, variable references, functions calls, and so on. Every expression is evaluated every time the `switch` statement is executed, so be sure that the expressions have no side effects (that is, don't call functions that cause permanent changes and don't use the `++` or `--` operators).

- The same *value* can appear more than once (either as a duplicate literal value or as a result of using expressions). If the `switch` expression matches a value that is listed more than once, each of the corresponding statement blocks are executed, in the order in which they appear in the `switch` statement. If necessary, you can prevent this from happening by ending a statement block with the `break` statement, which exits the `switch` statement immediately.

  The `default` block, if present, is not executed if any of the other blocks are matched and executed.

- Surprisingly, you can't use an array as a matching *value*. This is a disappointment. It would be terrific if you could type an expression like 1..5 to match any of the values 1, 2, 3, 4, or 5.

  There is, however, a way around this: You can use a matching expression of this form: (*array* `-eq` `$_`), for example, (`1..5` `-eq` `$_`). This has no value if the switch control value `$_` is not in the array `1..5`, so it doesn't match. But, if the control value is in the array, `-eq` extracts that value, and the switch statement matches it. It's not pretty, but it works. Just be sure that the *array* contains just one instance of each distinct value. If there are duplicates, the `-eq` result could be an array, and `switch` won't match it.

There are some variations on the `switch` statement. The full syntax description is as follows:

```
switch [-regex|-wildcard|-exact] [-casesensitive] (expression)|-file filename
{
    expression {statement(s)}
    …
    [ default     {statement{s}} ]
}
```

The options are as follows:

Option	Description
`-regex`	These first three options apply only to `switch` statements where the `switch` value and the values listed inside the statement are strings. With `-regex`, the listed values are interpreted as regular expressions. For example, `switch regex ('abcd')` would match the value entry `'a[bc]+d'`.

Option	Description
-wildcard	The listed values are interpreted with wildcards. For example, switch -wildcard ('abcd') would match the value entry 'ab*'.
-exact	The listed values are compared to the switch value exactly. This is the default.
-casesensitive	String comparisons are case sensitive. By default, they're case insensitive.
-file *filename*	This option can be used instead of the (*expression*) value after the word switch. Instead of testing an expression (or array or command), PowerShell reads text from the named file one line at a time and processes each line with the switch statement.

break

The simplest version of the break statement immediately exits a while, do, for, or foreach loop. You can use break to terminate a loop if, for example, some unexpected condition is detected. It's also useful when you need to have some instructions that are executed before the loop's condition test and some that are executed afterward. The while loop always performs the test at the beginning, and the do loop at the end, but sometimes you need the test in the middle, which you can do with break as follows:

```
while (True) {
    statement(s)
    ⋮
    if (condition)
        break;
    more statements
    ⋮
}
```

break also exits a switch statement, as I discussed previously. This can be useful in cases where something happens that makes you want to stop processing the statements for a given switch value or to stop processing after handling one value in situations where the same value might appear more than once.

PowerShell has a second variation of the break command that lets you exit more than one nested loop. Here's how it works: You can assign a name to any while, do, or for loop by preceding the while, do, or for keyword with a colon followed by a name. Then, you can use the name in a break statement to terminate the named loop and any loops nested within it. Here's an example:

```
:mainloop while (True) {
    $text = ReadLine()
    for ($token = GetToken($text); -not IsEmpty($token); $token = NextToken()) {
```

```
        if ($token -eq 'STOP') {break mainloop}
        process($token)
    }
}
```

If this code encounters the value 'STOP' in its input text, the break statement terminates both the inner for loop and the while loop, which is labeled with the name
mainloop.

continue

The continue statement works inside a do, while, for, or foreach loop. It jumps
immediately to the end of the loop and starts the next iteration. For example, this
loop:

```
for ($i = 1; $i -le 5; $i++) {
    if ($i -eq 3) {continue}
    $i
}
```

prints the numbers 1, 2, 4, and 5, skipping 3. Note that continue doesn't skip the for
loop's incrementer statement.

Program Blocks

Any place that a single PowerShell statement can appear, you can use a program block,
which consists of zero or more statements inside curly brackets. Inside a statement
block, you can use the break statement to exit the block immediately, without executing any of the remaining statements.

If you assign a value to a variable inside a program block, a new variable is created
locally within the block and is released when the block is exited. Previous versions of
the variable are unaffected. (This doesn't apply to the blocks that comprise an if statement, do statement, and so on—just blocks that you create separately). For example:

```
$a = 3
{
    $a = 2   # this is a different $a
    $a
}
$a
```

This prints 2 and then 3 because the original variable $a is unaffected by the new $a
that was created just for the program block.

I talk more about this in the section "Variable Scope," later in the chapter.

Exception Handling

It's a fact of life that scripts run into unexpected situations from time to time. A file your script needs to overwrite will be marked read-only, or a remote computer that you're connected to will get shut down while you're working with it, or…the list is endless. PowerShell has a mechanism that lets you anticipate and respond to problems like this. It lets you write code that is used only if an error, called an *exception*, interrupts the normal flow of your script. Where VBScript has only the very limited on error resume next mechanism, PowerShell has two exception handling mechanisms: the trap statement and the try/catch/finally statement.

trap

The format of the trap command is as follows:

```
trap [[ExceptionType]] {
    statement(s)
    ⋮
    break | continue | return value
}
```

It can appear in the main body of your script, inside the block of statements after if, while, for, and so on, or inside a user-defined function, and it can be placed before, after, or in the middle of other statements. Either way, the code in it is executed only if an error occurs.

Just about every error that PowerShell or a .NET object could encounter has a specifically named exception type associated with it. In the trap statement, you can optionally specify the *ExceptionType,* the name of the type of exception you want to capture, enclosed in square brackets. You can write several different trap statements to separately handle different exception types, or you can omit the *ExceptionType* entirely or specify the generic name [Exception], to capture all types of exceptions. If more than one trap statement is present in a program block, PowerShell invokes the one that is most specifically matches the error that occurred.

If an error occurs and a trap construct is present in the part of your script that is executing, PowerShell immediately runs the trap statement. Within the trap statement, the predefined variable $_ contains a text description of the error that occurred. The most recent exception is also described in more detail by the object in $Error[0]. The trap block should end with break, continue, or return. Here's what these do:

Statement	Action
break	Stops processing the `trap` handler code and passes the exception on to any `trap` handlers in code that contains the current block or in functions that called the current function, on up to the main script block. If no other `trap` block catches the exception, PowerShell handles it like a nonterminating (nonfatal) error and takes the action set by the `$ErrorActionPreference` variable, which was described in Table 15.5.
continue	Execution resumes with the statement after the one that caused the error.
return *value*	Like `break`, but exits the current function, returning the specified value. However, `return` might or might not work, depending on the value of `$ErrorActionPreference`, so you might not want to use this option in your scripts.

If you don't use any of these exit statements, the default action is `break`.

try/catch/finally

PowerShell 2.0 introduces the `try/catch/finally` statement that is somewhat more straightforward to use than `trap`. The format of the statement is as follows:

```
try {
    statement(s)
    ⋮
}                                               } required
catch [[ExceptionType] [, [ExceptionType] …] {
    statement(s)
    ⋮
}                                               } zero or more
finally {
    statement(s)
    ⋮
}                                               } optional
```

Here, the statements inside the `try` block are executed. If an exception occurs of a type listed in a `catch` section, the statements inside the `catch` are executed. (If there is more than one `catch` statement, the one that most specifically matches the `Exception` is the one that is used, as described previously for the `trap` statement.)

After that, whether an exception occurred or not, and whether a `catch` statement handled the exception or not, the statements in the `finally` group are executed.

As with `trap`, you can use `try` inside functions, program statements like `if` and `for`, and even inside other `try` statements. For more information about exception handling, see the PowerShell help topics `about_trap` and `about_try_catch_finally`. For more information on the types of exception you can catch, browse the Internet for information on .NET exceptions. One concise, useful list is at msdn.microsoft.com. Search for "Common Exception Types."

throw

The statement `throw` *value* generates an exception and invokes your script's `trap` or `try/catch/finally` handler. *value* can be any of the exception objects defined by .NET or any string or numeric value. If you use a string or number, it is made available to the exception handler in the `$_` variable.

You can use `throw` inside a catch block to give up and let PowerShell handle an exception. Or, in the case of nested `try/catch/finally` statements, to pass an exception from an inner statement to an outer statement. You can also use it to generate exceptions so that you can test your `catch` statements during debugging. I suggest another use for `throw` in Chapter 16 in "Exception Handling as an Exit Strategy," p. 702.

Defining Functions

Most programming languages let you define subroutines and functions, which are collectively known as *subprograms*. As a simple way to describe a subprogram, you could say that it's a portion of program code that is somewhat self-contained and which you can use (*invoke*) from other parts of your program or script without having to retype all its instructions. A function is a subprogram that returns some sort of result or answer to the part of the program that invoked it. You've seen many examples of these in the preceding chapters in this book. All PowerShell subprograms are technically functions, so that's the term we'll use from here on.

A simple function is shown here:

```
function simple {
    return 1
}
```

You can type this and then type `simple` on the command line, and PowerShell will prints the resulting value 1. Or type `$v = simple`, and then type `$v` to see that the value returned was 1. No parentheses are used unless the function takes parameters.

A function specifies the return value with a `return` statement. `return` can be used anywhere in a function. It causes the function to end immediately and passes the specified value back to the function's caller. If a function reaches the end of its statements without a `return` statement, it returns the value `$NULL`.

Function Parameters

User-defined functions in PowerShell can be given argument values, but the calling syntax is not, for example, `funcname(arg1, arg2)` as you might expect. No parentheses or commas are used. The calling syntax is instead `funcname arg1 arg2 …`, just as on a command line. By default, items on the function calling line are interpreted as literal values. Thus, `funcname abc def` is interpreted as a call to function `funcname` with two arguments, strings `abc` and `def`. If you want to pass a string that contains spaces, enclose it in quotes.

> ### Caution
> It's important to remember what parentheses mean in PowerShell; they define arrays. If you call a user-defined function like this:
>
> `funcname(arg1,arg2)`
>
> what you're doing is calling function `funcname` with *one* argument. It's an array of two elements.

When defining a function, technically, you don't have to specify whether it needs parameters. If called with parameters, even function `simple` works correctly; it just doesn't use the parameters. For example, `simple 1 2 3` still returns 1. Parameters passed to a function are available in the predefined `$args` array; in this example, `$args` would contain three elements—the values 1, 2, and 3.

Still, you can describe which parameters a function takes, so that PowerShell can do some helpful processing for you, such as copying parameter values to named variables and filling in default values for omitted parameters. There are two formats you can use: the `param` statement and the more traditional argument list placed right after the function name.

The `param` Statement

You can assign names to the parameters used by a function by placing a `param` statement as the first statement in the functions' block of statements. The format is somewhat complex:

```
param ([[objtype]]$paramname [= defaultvalue] [, …])
```

That is, the `param` statement has a list of variable names separated by commas. You can optionally put a `[objectname]` type specifications before a parameter name, and an optional = sign and value to set the parameter's default value if the user omits it when calling the function. The `param` statement copies items from the `$args` array into named variables, but it is more sophisticated than it looks at first.

You can also define a function parameter that doesn't require a value but simply has the value `$true` if it was present in the function call or `$false` if omitted using this format in the `param` statement `[switch] $paramname`.

Here's an example of a function that takes up to two arguments—an integer and an optional -verbose switch—and a third argument whose type is unspecified:

```
function printmsg
{
    param ([int]$level = 1, [switch] $verbose, $message)
    if ($level -gt $current_output_level) {
        if ($verbose) write-output 'THIS IS EXTRA INFORMATION...'
        write-output $message
    }
}
```

Equivalently, you can put the contents of the param statement within parentheses right after the function name:

```
function printmsg ([int]$level = 1, [switch]$verbose, $message)
{
    if ($level -gt $current_output_level) {
        write-output $message
    }
}
```

which looks more like what a function definition looks like in other languages. If this format is more comfortable for you, by all means use it!

Either way, this function prints the message argument if the value of level is greater than or equal to variable $output_level. If the user omits argument level, its value is assumed to be 1. The function doesn't return a value itself.

What's unusual about PowerShell is that when you call the function, you can specify the arguments by position:

```
printmsg 4 'This is the message'
```

or by name:

```
printmsg -level 4 -message 'This is the message'
```

or with a mixture. All of the following commands work exactly the same way:

```
printmsg -level 4 'this is the message'
printmsg 'This is the message' -level 4
printmsg -message 'this is the message' 4
```

The level argument can be omitted entirely because its default value was specified:

```
printmsg 'this is a level 1 message'
```

When you invoke a function, PowerShell first tries to assign -*name value* and named -*switch* arguments to the function's named parameters; then. it assigns whatever's left from the command line to any remaining parameters. (A switch argument is never inferred by position, so in all the preceding examples, the value of $verbose is False.) If you call the function with argument names that are not defined in the param statement, they're ignored. They still appear in the $args array, along with any others, but no error message is printed. For example, -unknown does nothing in the previous function.

In PowerShell version 2, you can define a function that has required parameters or that accepts switch-type arguments like –verbose that don't require a value after them by adding additional information to the param list. Before a variable name and before its [type] declaration, if any, you can add an optional set of specifications in the form

```
[parameter( option = value [, …] )]
```

with one or more options names. Some of the options are listed here:

Option	Value	Description
Mandatory	$true or $false	If $true, the parameter is mandatory. By default, parameters are optional.
ValueFromRemainingArguments	$true or $false	If $true, this parameter receives all remaining values on the calling command line, as an array.
HelpMessage	string	A brief description of the parameter's purpose.
Alias	string	An alternative (probably shorter) name the user can specify on the command line for this parameter.

For example, the following function takes an optional numeric parameter -npings and a required argument -ComputerName. More than one ComputerName value can be specified; all values after the -ComputerName argument will be used for this argument. The values are stored in an array of strings:

```
function pingtest (
    $npings = 3,
    [parameter(Mandatory=$true,Alias=CN,
        ValueFromRemainingArguments=$true)][String[]] $ComputerName
)
{
    foreach ($name in $Computername) {
       for ($test = 1; $test -le npings; $test++) {
            # Perform one ping test on computer $name and print results.
            # …
       }
    }
}
```

The following command tests four different computers two times each:

```
pingtest -npings 2-cn server1 server2 server3 server4
```

Additionally, you can specify the minimum and maximum number of values that can be specified for an argument, required numeric ranges or string length ranges for the values, and more. Parameter options can actually get quite complex. I don't have the room to discuss it further here, but for more information, you can see the PowerShell help topic about_functions_advanced_parameters.

Function Scope

By default, functions typed at the command prompt are available as long as the PowerShell window stays open. Functions defined inside a script file are available only in that script file. There are two ways you can make a function definition stick, so it's available at the command prompt and in other script files:

- Put `global:` before the function's name, as in the definition `function global:simple`. Put functions that you use frequently in your `profile` script so they will always be available. Be sure to put `global:` before their names. See "PowerShell Profiles" on page 617.

- Put the function in a script file and dot-source the script so that PowerShell treats definitions in it as if you'd typed them at the command prompt. I explain dot-sourcing in the next section.

A script that is used just to define global functions doesn't have to contain any other statements. If you do mix function definitions and script statements, the position of a function inside the script file is important. It must be defined before it's used by the main body of the script. You can intersperse functions throughout the main body of the script, but my habit is to put all functions at the start of the script and the main body of a script at the end.

Note

A function can refer to functions that appear after it in the script file as long it isn't called by the main script body before those other functions appear.

Note

A list of all user-defined functions is kept in a virtual drive named `function:`. You can list functions with the command `dir function:`, and you can delete a function using a statement like `rm function:functionname`.

The Dot-Source Operator

The period (.) by itself is a special operator that means "run the following script file as if it was being typed in at the command line." This is called *dot-sourcing* a script. The difference between running a script file named `myscript.ps1` by typing

```
myscript
```

and by typing

```
. myscript
```

at a PowerShell command prompt is that the first version runs the script in the normal way. Variables and functions defined in the script are deleted when the script is finished, unless you put the `global:` scope qualifier before their names. The second version dot-sources the script. The script runs at the command prompt's scope, so global scope is the default for all functions and variables. They persist after the script completes, unless you put `local:` or `script:` before their names.

> **Note**
>
> Recall from Chapter 14 that if you want to run a script that's in the current directory but not in the system PATH, you have to type the script's name as `.\scriptname.ps1`. This `.` is not the dot-source operator! It's part of the script file's path. To dot-source a script in the current directory, you have to type `.` followed by a space and then `.\scriptname.ps1`, like this:
>
> ```
> . .\myscript.ps1
> ```

Variable Scope

By default, variables and functions defined in a PowerShell script are actually visible in the script file, function, or program block (inside curly braces) that defines it and to any script, function, or program block that this script, function, or program block calls. Here's an example:

```
function sample_function {
    "2. Inside sample_function v = $v"
    $x = 1
    "3. Inside sample_function x = $x"
}
$v = 1
"1. In main script, v = $v"
sample_function
"4. In main script, x = $x"
```

Here is the output of the script:

```
1. In main script, v = 1
2. Inside sample_function v = 1
3. Inside sample_function x = 1
4. In main script, x =
```

Look at variable `$v` first. The main body of the script defines `$v` and prints its value. When `sample_function` is called, it can "see" `$v`, too, because `sample_function` is called from the main script. We say that it's at a deeper *nesting level*.

Now look at variable `$x`. It's defined for the first time inside `sample_function`. When `sample_function` returns, `$x` is deleted, so in the main script body, it's undefined. When the main body attempts to print `$x`, it has no value.

sample_function was able to see the variable $v defined in a parent scope, but something interesting happens if it tries to change the value of $v. By default, PowerShell creates a *new* variable with the same name. So, by default, changes made to a variable inside a function apply only inside the function. The net effect is that nested script code or functions effectively see *copies* of variables defined in parent scopes. Here's a modified version of the previous example:

```
function sample_function {
    "2. Inside sample_function v = $v"
    $v = 47
    "3. Inside sample_function v = $v"
}
$v = 1
"1. In main script, v = $v"
sample_function
"4. In main script, v = $v"
```

This script prints the following:

```
1. In main script, v = 1
2. Inside sample_function v = 1
3. Inside sample_function v = 47
4. In main script, v = 1
```

What happened is that sample_function created a new local copy of $v that temporarily hid the original. After the function returned, the main body of the script still has the original value for $vr.

You can change the default behavior by putting a scope qualifier before a variable name. If you put local: before a variable name the first time you use it, as in $local:v = 1, it will be visible in its own nesting level but not in deeper levels. If we assigned $v this way in the previous sample script, it would appear to be undefined in sample_function.

Conversely, if you put script: before a variable name, you will create or reference a copy of the variable that is visible at every nesting level in the script file or put global: before a name and create or reference a variable that is visible to all scripts and to the command line.

> **Note**
>
> When you're working within nested program blocks or inside functions, you need to use the script: or global: qualifier every time you reference the variable; otherwise, you'll simply create a new variable with this name at the current scope.

Pipeline Functions and Filters

You can call a PowerShell function in a statement that includes a pipeline operator, as in this command: `get-childitem | my_function`. The function has to be written in special way so that it can examine each of the objects passed through the pipeline.

The simplest method would be to write a function that examines each of the objects in the `$input` variable, using something like `foreach ($obj in $input)` to step each of the pipelined objects through variable `$obj`. However, this method can be slow, as the function isn't called until the previous cmdlet has finished writing objects into the pipeline and array `$input` is complete.

There is a more efficient and sophisticated way, using the `BEGIN`, `PROCESS`, and `END` statements. PowerShell lets you define three sections of code within a function that is to be used in a pipeline: `BEGIN` lets you initialize the function, `PROCESS` is called once for each object passed through the pipeline, and `END` lets you do any necessary clean-up or summary work. Using this method, PowerShell can run all the pipeline's cmdlets and functions simultaneously, with each cmdlet or function processing objects as soon as they're passed through by the previous item in the pipe. The basic structure looks like this:

```
function func_name
{
    param (parameter list)
    BEGIN {
        initialization statements
        ⋮
    }
    PROCESS {
        processing statements, where $_ holds the current object
        ⋮
    }
    END {
        finalizing statements
        ⋮
    }
}
```

The function is called just once, so you should process any command-line options (which are passed through the function's parameters list, as well as in array `$args`, as I have mentioned previously) in the `BEGIN` section. Then, the `PROCESS` section is executed once for each object passed through the pipeline. The variable `$_` holds the current object. Finally, when all objects have been processed, PowerShell executes the `END` section. Any of these sections might be omitted or might contain no statements between the curly brackets.

Note

If your BEGIN and END sections are blank, you instead can define the function using the keyword filter in place of function. In this case, omit the BEGIN and END blocks, and the function body takes the place of the PROCESS block. It looks like this:

```
filter filter_name
{
    statements
    ...
}
```

You can include a parameter list. With a filter, the function is called once per pipeline object, and the command-line arguments are passed every time.

Whether you use the function or filter format, if you want your function to be able to be used in the middle of a pipeline, it has to pass complete objects to the standard output. You can do this by running a cmdlet that emits objects within the process block. You can pass an input object straight through to the output using the statement $_ (which emits the input object.) You can also use the command write-output *object*, where *object* is any object you want to pass to the next cmdlet or function in the pipeline. As an example, here is a fairly useless filter that simply passes every other object through to the output and discards the rest:

```
function every_other {
    begin   { $count = 1}
    process { if (($count++ % 2) -eq 1) { write-output $_}}  # emit objects 1, 3,
}
```

We'll discuss pipeline functions in more detail in Chapter 16.

Splatting

If you run cmdlets from within a PowerShell script, you can keep the arguments you want to pass to a cmdlet in an array or a hash table. Then, when you run the cmdlet, you can put @ in front of the variable name. This is called the *splat* operator, and it has the effect of taking the contents of the hash table or array and putting each item onto a command line or function call as if it was a separately typed argument. The order of the items coming out of a hash table is essentially random, so hash tables should only be used to hold arguments whose order doesn't matter. Use arrays to hold options whose order matters.

This is actually easier to demonstrate than describe. In this script,

```
$options = @{'-flag'; '-option=value'}    # options in a hash table (random
                                          # order)
$files = 'file1', 'file2', 'file3'        # filenames in an array (fixed order)
cmdlet @$args @$files                     # pass these values to cmdlet
```

PowerShell takes the hash table and array and splat their contents onto the command line. The effect is the same as if you'd typed

```
cmdlet -flag -option-value file1 file2 file3
```

In general, you can put variables that contain text anywhere on a command line, but be aware that a single variable is always seen as a single command-line argument. Here's what I mean. Let's take a typical command:

```
dir -recurse c:\users
```

which lists the contents of folder `c:\users` and any subfolders it contains. The following commands:

```
$location = '-recurse c:\users'
dir $location
```

do not produce the same result. Instead of a directory listing, it produces an error message because there is no folder named `-recurse c:\users`. This is a significant difference between PowerShell and the old command prompt world. In cmd.exe, environment variables are expanded *before* a command is executed, so a single variable can be seen as more than one argument. In PowerShell, variables used as command-line arguments are seen as a single argument value.

Using the .NET API

So far in this chapter, I've covered just language elements that are built in to Windows PowerShell. As you can see, there's a lot there! And, we haven't even started looking at the .NET Platform objects and functions that you will use to work with data, let alone all the cmdlets that are provided with PowerShell that give you access to Windows itself. We'll start looking at the cmdlets in Chapter 16. Here, I want to give you a brief look at the data manipulation tools in the .NET API. They are an essential part of PowerShell programming, and they stand in for the functions that are built in to scripting tools like VBScript, so I think it makes sense to cover them as part of this survey of the PowerShell language.

Calling Static Member Functions

Whereas VBScript provides built-in functions such as `left()` and `mid()` to manipulate strings, dates, and so on, PowerShell gives you access to *static member functions*. These are methods of .NET objects that you can use without actually creating the objects themselves. The syntax is a bit strange:

```
[objectname]::methodname(arguments…)
```

For example, this computes the absolute value of –3:

```
$v = -3
$av = [System.Math]::abs($v)
```

Besides static methods, many objects have *static fields*. Fields are like properties, except they are constant and don't depend on any particular data values. An example of a field is `[math]::pi`, which holds the value of the mathematical constant π.

There are scads of .NET Framework objects that have useful static methods and fields. I list just a few of them here. For more detailed information, go to msdn.microsoft.com and select the Library tab. To get a good start, search for the following phrases:

- Convert Methods (System)
- Math Methods (System)
- Math Fields (System)
- Date Methods (System)
- String Methods (System)

You want to view the pages with these titles in the .NET Framework Class Library documentation. Items in the list that are marked with a fat red **S** in the left column are static methods that can be called as I've just described. Methods without the **S** can only be used on instances of the objects. For example, in the String class, `Compare(string1, string2)` is static and can be used like this: `[System.String]::Compare($x, $y)`. The `PadLeft` method can only be used with an instance of a string, as in `$x.PadLeft(32)`.

In the online documentation, you can click on any of the method names to get more detail on how the function works. However, this documentation is written for Visual Basic .NET, C#, C++, and F# programmers, not PowerShell programmers, so you'll have to sort of fill in some of the blanks yourself. In most cases, the C# information is closest to what you need for PowerShell.

Tip

If you're familiar with VBScript and are having trouble figuring out what .NET function to use for a given task, go to technet.microsoft.com and search for "VBScript-to-Windows PowerShell Conversion Guide." Under this topic are entries that describe the ".NET" alternatives for most VBScript functions and most of the WSH objects.

Working with Strings

The `[System.String]` class has static methods that operate on strings, but you don't actually need them because they are what's behind the PowerShell operators `-join`, `-split`, `-replace`, `-eq`, `-lt`, and so on. PowerShell lets you use `[string]` as shorthand for this class name, so that's what I use here. There are, however, many useful methods you can apply directly to `[string]` objects, such as string expressions or variables holding string values. Several of the most important are listed in Reference List 15.2.

Reference List 15.2—Methods and Properties of [System.String] (Partial List)

Properties:

Length

Returns the number of characters in the string.

Chars(n)

Returns a single character from the string. With n = 0, you get the first character; with n = 1, the second; and so on. You can also treat a string like an array. $s[0] also returns the first character.

Methods:

Contains(s [, t])

Returns True if the [string] contains the substring s within it. Argument t controls case sensitivity. Omit t entirely or specify [System.StringComparison]::Ordinal for a case-sensitive match or specify [System.StringComparison]::Ordinal IgnoreCase to make the test case insensitive.

EndsWith(s [, t])

Returns True if the [string] objects ends with the same letters as string s. Optional argument t is the same as with Contains.

IndexOf(s [,n [,m]][, t])

Returns the index (0-based) of the position of character or string s within the [string] or -1 if s is not found. If n is specified, the search starts at position n. If both n and m are specified, only m characters are searched before giving up. The search is case sensitive by default; optional argument t can be specified as with Contains to make the test case insensitive. You can specify t even if you omit n and m. Like InStr() in VBScript.

Insert(n, s)

Inserts string s into the [string] starting at position n.

LastIndexOf(s [,n [,m]][, t])

Like IndexOf, but returns the index of the last occurrence of string or character s.

PadLeft(n [, c])

Returns a [string] exactly n characters long by adding space characters to the left end of the string. Optional argument c can specify a string other than space to use for padding.

PadRight(n [, c])

Like PadLeft, but adds padding to the right side.

Remove(*n* [, *m*])

Trims off the end of the [string] from position *n* to the end. If optional argument *m* is specified, deletes only *m* characters.

StartsWith(*s* [, *t*])

Returns True if the [string] starts with string *s*. Optional argument *t* is as with Contains.

SubString(*n* [, *m*])

Extracts the substring from position *n* to the end; if optional argument *m* is specified, returns at most *m* characters. Like mid() in VBScript or with *n* = 0, like Left() in VBScript.

ToLower()

Turns all uppercase characters into lowercase.

ToUpper()

Turns all lowercase characters into uppercase.

Trim([*w*])

Removes whitespace (tabs and spaces) from the beginning and end of the [string]. Optional argument *w* is a string or an array of strings or characters; if specified, the specified characters are trimmed off instead of whitespace characters.

TrimEnd([*w*])

Like trim but only removes trailing whitespace.

TrimStart([*w*])

Like trim but only removes leading whitespace.

> **Note**
>
> None of these methods change the original string. They return a new string, a copy of the original with the desired changes. To really change the value of a string variable, assign the method's result to the variable, replacing the original value—for example, $v = $v.trim().

Working with Dates and Times

The .NET [System.DateTime] object stores and performs calculations with dates and times. PowerShell lets you substitute the abbreviation [datetime], so I use that name in the examples that follow. A [datetime] represents a specific time on a specific date.

It's an absolute time. When you subtract one [datetime] from another, you get a different object: a [System.TimeSpan] object, which is a relative amount of time. This object name can be abbreviated [timespan]. The basic unit of the [timespan] is the *tick*, which is 100 nanoseconds. This a terribly convenient quantity to use directly because there are 10,000,000 ticks per second. When you encounter a [timespan] object, you'll need to use its various properties and methods to convert it to more useful time units.

Reference List 15.3 lists some of the more useful static [datetime] methods and fields.

Reference List 15.3—Static Member Functions and Field of [System.DateTime] (Partial List)

Functions:

Compare(*a*,*b*)

With two date-time values as arguments, returns +1 if time *a* is later than time *b*, 0 if the times are identical, and –1 if *a* is earlier than *b*. (You can also compare [datetime] values with, for example, -lt and -gt.)

Format([*s*])

Formats the date as a string. You can optionally pass a string argument *s* that specifies the format. See "Formatting Output" in Chapter 16 for more information.

TryParse(*s*, *ref*)

Returns True if string *s* can be converted to a [datetime] and False if the string is uninterpretable. You must pass a variable by reference (see "Passing By Reference," in this chapter on page 650) to receive the [datetime] value.

Parse(*s*)

Converts string *s* to a [datetime]. *s* must to be formatted in a way that .NET can interpret. "10/3/2010 11:15 AM" is an example. The time is interpreted relative to the local time zone. Alternatively, you can simply cast a string, as in [datetime] "10/3/2010 11:15 AM".

Field:

Now

Returns the current date and time. This is a static field (property), not a method, so you reference it as follows: [datetime]::now.

The [datetime] object also has many methods and properties that you can use to operate directly on a [datetime] object, variable, or expression. Several of them are listed in Reference List 15.4.

Reference List 15.4—Methods of [System.DateTime] (Partial List)

Add(*ti*)

Returns the [datetime] object's value plus [timeinterval] value **ti**. It's easier, probably, to simply use the + operator to add a [datetime] and a [timespan] value. Note that if you use .Add or + with an integer value, it's interpreted in ticks (100 nsec). To add a specific amount of time, create the desired interval as a [timespan] value and add it or use one of the following methods:

AddDays(*n*)	**AddHours(*n*)**
AddMonths(*n*)	**AddMinutes(*n*)**
AddYears(*n*)	**AddSeconds(*n*)**
AddMonths(*n*)	**AddMilliseconds(*n*)**

Adds *n* days, months, and so on, to the [datetime]. *n* can be an integer (whole number) or a floating-point value.

As with the [string] methods I discussed previously, these methods don't modify the original [datetime] value. They return a new [datetime] value that you can use, display, or store in a variable.

[timespan] Values

[timespan] (System.TimeSpan) objects represent an interval of time or a difference between two times and can be positive or negative. Several of its more important properties and methods are listed in Reference List 15.5.

Reference List 15.5—Properties and Methods of [System.TimeSpan] (Partial List)

Properties:

Duration

Returns the "absolute value" of the time span, that is, a positive [timespan].

Days
Hours
Minutes
Seconds

Returns the days, hours, minutes, and seconds components of the [timespan] value. An interval of 1.5 days would yield .Days = 1 and .Hours = 12. These are all read-only properties.

TotalDays	**TotalMinutes**
TodayHours	**TotalSeconds**

Returns the whole time interval expressed in various units as a floating-point [double] value. An interval of 1.5 days would yield .Days = 1.5 and .Hours = 36. These are all read-only properties.

Methods:

Format([s])

Formats the timespan as a string. You can optionally pass a string argument *s* that specifies the format. See "Formatting Output" in Chapter 16 for more information.

TryParse(s, ref)

Returns True if string *s* can be converted to a [timespan] in this chapter on page 650) and False if the string is uninterpretable. You must pass a variable by reference (see "Passing By Reference", p. 650) to receive the converted value.

Creating [datetime] and [timespan] Values

You can't set a [datetime] or [timespan] object to a specific date and/or time by changing its properties, so if you need to create a specific value, you must use one of the following techniques:

- Represent the date or interval as a string and cast it, as in these examples: `$dt = [datetime] '3/6/2010 9:22:33 PM'` or `$ts = [timespan] '1.22:33:44.55'`, which represents 1 day, 22 hours, 33 minutes, and 44.55 seconds. Dates are interpreted according to your computer's localization setting, so for example, `'3/6/2010'` would be March 6, 2010 in the United States but June 3 in Europe. The system also recognizes dates in these formats: `2010-03-06`, `6-Mar-2010` and a few others.

- Use a constructor method. I discussed constructors earlier in this chapter. As an example, to create a [datetime] for March 6, 2010 at 9:22:33 a.m., you can use this statement: `$dt = new-object System.DateTime 2010,3,6,9,22,33`. This uses the constructor that accepts six integer arguments: year, month, day, hour, minute, and second. You must use the full object name, for example, `System.DateTime` or `System.Timespan`.

- For [timespan] values, you can use the static methods `FromDays`, `FromHours`, `FromSeconds`, and so on—for example, `$ts = [timespan]::FromDays(1.5)`.

> **Tip**
>
> I don't think you'll ever need to use the tick time unit directly, but if you do, don't write your script around the assumption that there are 10,000,000 ticks per second, in case a future version of Windows uses a different definition. Instead, use the static field value `[timespan]::tickspersecond` in your calculations.

Converting Values

The .NET [System.Convert] object has a slew of methods that let you convert values from one numeric format to another. Many of the conversions they perform can be done more simply using casts, as I described earlier in the chapter. It's easier to type `$i = [int] $v` than to type `$i = [System.Convert]::ToInt32($v)`, and the result is the same.

However, [System.Convert] does have useful functions that let you specify the base of the conversion you want to perform. You can use [System.Convert]::ToString (*value*, *base*) to convert an integer value to its representation in binary (base = 2), octal (base = 8), decimal (base = 10), or hexadecimal (base = 16), and similarly, [System.Convert]ToInt32(*string*, *base*) to convert a string to an integer, where the string has the number in binary, octal, decimal, or hexadecimal. (There are corresponding "To" functions for all of the integer formats.)

Mathematical Functions

The .NET [System.Math] object has a large number of static member functions you can use to perform calculations. Reference List 15.6 lists several of the more interesting ones. To use these values and functions in your scripts, precede the name by [System.Math]::.

Reference List 15.6—Static Member Functions and Fields of [System.Math] (Partial List)

Functions:

`Min(`*a*`,`*b*`)`

Returns the smaller of *a* and *b*.

`Max(`*a*`,`*b*`)`

Returns the larger of *a* and *b*.

`Abs(`*a*`)`

Returns the absolute value of *a*.

`Round(`*a*`)`

Returns *a* rounded to the nearest integer.

`Round(`*a*`,`*n*`)`

Returns *a* rounded to *n* decimal places. When doing financial calculations in the United States, for example, results can be rounded to the nearest cent with something like [System.Math]::Round($value,2).

sin(*a*)   sinh(*a*)
cos(*a*)   cosh(*a*)
tan(*a*)   tanh(*a*)

The standard trigonometric functions, with *a* expressed in radians. If *a* is in degrees, use, for example, `[System.Math]::sin(a/180.*[System.Math]::pi)`.

asin(*v*)   acos(*v*)
atan(*v*)   atan2(*y*,*x*)

Inverse trigonometric functions of *v* and *y*/*x*.

log(*v*)   log10(*v*)
log(*v*,*b*)

Natural, base-10 and base *b* logarithms of *v*.

sqrt(*v*)

Returns the square root of *v*.

Fields:

E

Returns *e*, 2.71828….

Pi

Returns π, 3.14159….

Many more functions of course are available. For more information, search the msdn.microsoft.com for ".NET System.Math Class."

16

Using PowerShell

Real-World PowerShell

In the previous two chapters, I described how to use the PowerShell command line and described the PowerShell programming language. In this chapter, we'll put this information to use with real-world examples, both interactive and scripted. Here's what I mean by *interactive* and *scripted*: As I mentioned in the previous chapter, there are two distinct ways that you can harness PowerShell's capabilities:

- You can construct command lines that use cmdlets. With command lines, you let the command statement itself do all the work; the command describes a flow of objects from one cmdlet to the next. The cmdlets select desired objects and perform the desired actions. To make an analogy to racing cars, using the command-line method is like setting up a racetrack on a hill and letting the cars roll down by themselves. All your work is in setting up the course's banks and turns so that the cars end up at the right place at the bottom.

- Alternatively, you can write script programs that use functions, .NET objects, loops, `if` statements, and so on. In the racecar analogy, this is like telling each piston when to move up and when to move down and giving detailed instructions to the driver that tell him how to react to each possible circumstance.

All in all, it's quite remarkable that the folks behind PowerShell came up with something that can work either way and that actually blurs the line between them—the `foreach` and `switch` statements, for example, operate as program statements but can also operate on a cmdlet pipeline.

There is no better or worse way to work. The scripting approach can do anything that the command-line approach can do, and more; it just takes more typing to get the job done. The cmdlet approach can do quite a bit in a very compact, elegant way, although you are limited by the selection of available cmdlets. And, for the most part, cmdlets can only make "do or don't" decisions. To some extent, you will probably find that you prefer one approach or the other based on how best your mind works: Scripting is very literal, left-brained work, while command-line constructs are more abstract and right-brained in origin. As I mentioned, you can actually use both techniques at once. You can use a string of cmdlets to generate a stream of objects and then use a custom function and `foreach` or `switch` statement to work with them.

In the examples that come later in this chapter, I show how you to perform a selection of tasks using both the cmdlet and scripting techniques.

Tip

Here's a great debugging tip you can use both when you're working interactively and when you're writing scripts. Most cmdlets that actually do something to your computer—that is, cmdlets that delete or modify files, change Registry entries or other Windows settings, and so on—accept the `-whatif` command-line option. With `-whatif` on the command line, a cmdlet prints text telling you what it *would* have done given the other input you fed it, but it won't actually make any permanent changes.

When you're constructing a command line, add `-whatif` so you can verify that your command line does what you want. When you're satisfied with the results, press the up-arrow key, edit out the `-whatif`, and then press Enter to issue the command for real.

When you're writing a script or cmdlet of your own, have it look for and handle `-whatif` as a command-line option. If `-whatif` is present, the script should print what it *would* do but shouldn't actually do anything that has permanent consequences.

If you're already experienced with Windows Script Host (WSH) and you find yourself in a jam writing a PowerShell script, here's a little secret: You can still use any of the objects you're used to using in WSH. It's not the "PowerShell way," but it can work in a pinch. In fact, you can use any COM object within PowerShell. Where you would have used the `CreateObject` function, use the `new-object` cmdlet with the `-comobject` command-line argument. Here's an example:

```
$fso = new-object -comobject Scripting.FileSystemObject
$tmp = $fso.GetFolder("c:\temp")
⋮
```

I recommend using this trick only if you're stuck, and I suggest that you go back as soon as you can and replace the old objects with their .NET or PowerShell equivalents.

One exception is if you need to pop up a message dialog box. You would have used the `MsgBox` function in WSH, but there is no simple PowerShell equivalent. It's fine to use the `WScript.Shell` popup method this way:

```
$wsh = new-object -comobject wscript.shell
$wsh.popup("This is the message text", 0, "This is the title text")
```

(You can omit the title text argument, but if you do, the dialog box's title will say "Windows Script Host," which can be somewhat confusing.) Look up Microsoft's online documention for the `Wscript.Shell` popup method if you want to choose which buttons appear on the dialog box.

Command–Line Techniques

The PowerShell command line gives you access to more than 200 built-in cmdlets that can manage files, folders, Windows services, printers, and so on. Here is a conceptual way to construct a PowerShell command pipeline:

```
generate-objects | pass-only-desired-objects | take-actions >output
```

These aren't real cmdlets, of course, but it shows the idea; to perform a given task, it's often useful to split the job into three smaller parts and worry about them separately.

In fact, the PowerShell command-line example I gave at the beginning of Chapter 14, "Windows PowerShell," is organized exactly this way. The command was

```
dir | where-object {$_.LastWriteTime -lt (get-date).addmonths(-6)} | remove-item
```

The first cmdlet (which is an alias for `Get-ChildItem`) generates a stream of file objects found in the current directory. The second cmdlet passes only those that haven't been modified in more than six months. The third cmdlet deletes these "old" files.

Generating Objects

PowerShell has a large number of cmdlets that can generate objects for a pipeline command. Many of them have names that start with the verb `Get`. Table 16.1 lists some of the more important ones.

Table 16.1   **Important** Get- **Cmdlets**

Cmdlet Name	Extracts
Get-ChildItem	Files and subfolders in a folder, subkeys in a Registry key, and so on. (Refer to Table 14.1 on page 614 to see how to specify paths in the Registry and other locations.)
Get-Content	Lines of text from a file.
Get-Counter	Performance counter information.
Get-EventLog	Event log entries.
Get-HotFix	Installed Windows Update packages.
Get-Item	A specific file, folder, Registry key, or such. Or, with wildcards, multiple files, or keys. (Refer to Table 14.1 on page 614 for information on specifying paths for items other than files and folders.)
Get-ItemProperty	Specific properties of an object or objects coming through the pipeline.
Get-Process	Active Windows processes.
Get-Services	Windows services.
Get-WinEvent	Windows Event log entries from the Event logs or from recorded event tracing log files.
Get-WmiObject	Windows Management Instrumentation (WMI) objects. (WMI was discussed in more detail in Chapter 7, "Windows Management Instrumentation").

Remember, to get information on any of these cmdlets, type `help` `cmdletname` or `help -examples` `cmdletname` at the PowerShell command prompt. Alternatively, use the graphical user interface (GUI) version of the documentation in the Integrated Scripting Envonment (discussed later in this chapter) or online at technet.microsoft.com.

Filtering

Some of the object-generating cmdlets listed in the preceding section have command-line options that can provide a certain amount of specificity to start with, so that your command pipeline starts with only the objects you're interested in. In most cases, you'll find that for real-world management tasks, you'll need to restrict the results to only objects with very specific property values—for example, only those files with timestamps before a specified date. This is where filtering comes in. PowerShell has cmdlets that let you precisely select which objects pass through the pipeline.

The easiest way to filter and organize a stream of objects is with the Where-Object cmdlet. `Where-Object` (you can type just `where`; it's a predefined alias) reads a stream of objects and passes along only those that meet a specified condition. The full syntax is

```
Where-Object {expression} [-InputObject object] [CommonParameters]
```

The *expression* must be enclosed in curly brackets, and it can be any valid PowerShell expression, function call, or statement that produces a True or False result. In the expression, the built-in variable $_ holds the object being tested at any given time. For example, the expression {$_.Length -ge 100} is True if an object's Length property is greater than or equal to 100.

By default, Where-Object reads a stream of objects from its standard input (that is, from the cmdlet that precedes it in a pipelined command), evaluates the PowerShell expression for each one, and passes along to its output only those objects for which the expression is True. Alternatively, you can have its input come from an array or a variable that contains objects, using the -InputObject argument. For example, if array $a contains objects, then

```
Where-Object {$_.Length -ge 100} -InputObject $a
```

passes through only those array objects whose Length property is greater than or equal to 100.

You can also define a function that has global or script scope (see "Function Scope," page 668 in Chapter 15, "PowerShell Programming") and use the function to perform the test. For example, if I defined this function:

```
function global:PassThisObject ($obj)
{
    return $obj.Length -ge 100
}
```

I could test objects this way:

```
Where-Object {PassThisObject $_}
```

This is a trivial example, but the function can be as complex as you need it to be; it could also do other things like keep a record of all the objects that it saw.

> **Tip**
>
> The trick to filtering is knowing which object properties to use for your testing expressions. I could fill this book trying to list all the .NET objects' properties for you! But, there's no need to. Just remember that PowerShell can self-document any object. Pass an object stream to cmdlet get-member, which prints a list of object properties and methods for each distinct object type it sees. It's also handy to remember that gm is an alias for Get-Member. For example, the command dir | gm shows you all the properties of file and folders as represented by the System.IO.FileInfo and System.IO.DirectoryInfo objects.

CommonParameters represents a list of optional command-line arguments that can be used with any standard cmdlet. They are described in Table 16.2.

Table 16.2 **Common Parameters**

Argument	Description
-Verbose	Enables output of descriptive diagnostic output, if the cmdlet is designed to emit any.
-Debug	Enables output of debugging output, if the cmdlet is designed to emit any.
-ErrorAction:*action*	Tells the cmdlet what it do if it encounters a situation that it considers an error. The valid *action*s are SilentlyContinue, Continue, Inquire, and Stop.
-ErrorVariable [+]*name*	Stores error messages in the variable specified by *name* (typed here without a $ sign). Precede the name with + to append error messages to an existing variable's contents. The variable is an array.
-WarningAction:*action*	Like -ErrorAction, but it tells the cmdlet what it do if it encounters what it considers to be a less serious but unusual "warning" situation.
-WarningVariable [+]*name*	Like –ErrorVariable, but it stores warning messages in the variable.
-OutBuffer *n*	Gathers *n* output objects before passing any on to the next cmdlet in the pipeline. (This isn't useful often.)
-OutVariable [+]*name*	Stores the cmdlet's output object stream in an array named *name*, as well as passing them to the standard output. Precede the name with a + sign to append to the variable's existing content.
-WhatIf	Prints messages describing what the cmdlet *would* do given its input but makes no permanent changes. (Used only with cmdlets that make real changes.)
-Confirm	Prompts the user to type Y or N to confirm making any permanent changes. (Used only with cmdlets that make real changes.)

Using sort-object

In addition to selecting objects, you can also organize the items in your cmdlet streams. With no arguments, sort-object sorts objects by their default properties. For example dir | sort-object lists files and folders in the current directory and sorts them by name because the Name field is these objects' default property.

You can specify sorting by a property value using the -property *propertyname* command-line argument, for example:

```
dir | sort-object -property Length
```

Other helpful arguments are -descending, which reverses the sort order, and -unique, which sorts the object stream and passes through just one item with any given value of the selected property.

> **Tip**
>
> You might want to read about the select-object cmdlet. You can use it to pass through just the first *n* or last *n* objects from its input stream. For example,
>
> dir | sort -property Length | select-object -last 10
>
> lists the 10 largest files in the current directory. select-object can also create "stripped-down" objects with only a few of the original objects' properties.

Filtering with Select-String

The Select-String cmdlet passes just strings that match a specified pattern. It's similar to findstr at the Windows command prompt or grep at the Unix command prompt.

If the objects passed to Select-String aren't string objects, be careful! You might not get what you expect. With file objects, for example, Select-String examines the contents of each file passed to it one line at a time and passes on any matching strings from within them.

For more information, you can type help select-string -detailed and help select-string -examples.

Taking Actions

The third step in our typical cmdlet command line does something with the objects that have been generated and filtered. This is a potentially huge topic, so I'll limit myself to just a few "action" options.

First of all, and the most important to remember, you can directly invoke any method of the objects passed through the pipeline using a foreach statement. Remember that in a foreach statement, variable $_ is set to the current item, so the statement

```
pipeline … | foreach {$_.Method()}
```

calls the specified *Method* on each object passed through the pipeline. Actually, the statement or statements inside foreach can be as simple or complex as you need them to be; you can have a simple pipeline end with a complex bit of PowerShell code that performs detailed calculations and takes complex actions.

Several cmdlets perform general-purpose actions: Remove-Item, Move-Item, Rename-Item, and Copy-Item. Several others can be used with file objects to delete, move, rename, and so on.

The `Invoke-Item` cmdlet calls the objects' default method, which sounds sort of hit-or-miss to me. I'd rather be explicit about the method I want to call.

Formatting Cmdlet Output

By default, objects that fall into the PowerShell command window or are redirected into a file are formatted as a table, with a row of property names at the top of the list. The formatting for this listing and the selection of properties that are listed are actually defined in an XML file stored on your computer, and you can customize it, although that's beyond the scope of this chapter.

You can use the `format-table` cmdlet to customize the list of properties that is listed and to select their formatting. For example,

```
dir | format-table -property mode, length, lastwritetime
```

lists the current directory and prints three selected properties for each listed file or folder. You can type `help format-table -detailed` and `help format-table -examples` for more information. The `-GroupBy` and `-Wrap` options are particularly useful.

For detailed formatting, you might find it easiest to end the command line with a `foreach` statement. Within that final statement, you can use the built-in variable `$_` to access each object that is fed through the command pipeline and use program code to compute one or more output strings for each object.

The `-f` Operator

The PowerShell language's `-f` operator formats one or more values into an output string. It's similar to the C language's `printf` statement. It's used this way: `"format-string" -f value` or `"formatstring" -f array`. It produces a string value. Characters within *formatstring* are copied literally, except that within the string, occurrences of `{0}`, `{1}`, `{2}`, and so on are replaced by the first, second, third, and subsequent values from the right side of `-f`. Here's an example. This string expression

```
'My name is {0} and I am {1} years old' -f $name, $age
```

might produce the string `My name is Tice Robert and I am 2 years old`.

Of course, you'd never do something like this because it produces incorrect English when the age is 1 year old. Instead, you'd do this:

```
'My name is {0} and I am {1} year{2} old' -f
    ➥ $name, $age, $(if ($age -eq 1) {''} else {'s'})
```

which displays `year` or `years` as appropriate.

If you want any of the formatted replacement items to have a minimum width in spaces, follow the item index number within the curly braces with a comma and then a number. Use a positive number to left-align the formatted item in the indicated number of spaces or a negative number to right-align the result. For example, `'{0,3}'` `-f 1` produces `'  1'`, while `'{0,-3}'` `-f 1` produces `'1  '`. If the replacement value takes more spaces than you've allotted, the result is simply made wider; characters are never cut off.

Finally, you can add a colon and additional formatting specifiers within each value's curly brackets. The specifiers are

`:d`	Decimal formatting (the default).
`:d`*n*	Decimal formatting with 0-padding to *n* digits, where *n* is a number. For example, `'{0:d3}'` `-f 1` prints `001`.
`:x`	Hexadecimal formatting with lowercase letters.
`:X`	Hexadecimal formatting with uppercase letters.
`:p`	Percentage (for example, `.1` prints as `10.00 %`).
`:c`	Currency (for example, `.1` prints as `$0.10`).
`:n`	Number with comma delimiters.
`:ddd...`	Date/time formatting, consisting of literal characters and any or all of the following items: `hh` (hours), `mm` (minutes), `ss` (seconds), `dd` (day), `MM` (numeric month), `yy` (two-digit year), `yyyy` (four-digit year), `MMM` (three-letter month abbreviation), `MMMM` (full month name), `dddd` (day of week), and `ddd` (three-letter day of week abbreviation). For example, `'{0:dddd, MMMM dd, yyyy}'` `-f (Get-Date)` prints `Thursday, August 26, 2010`.

There are additional formatting specifiers for floating-point numbers that I won't describe here. For more information about formatting, go to msdn.microsoft.com and search for "Composite Formatting." There is a page with this title in the .NET Framework documentation that does a decent job of explaining the formatting options with examples. At the bottom of the page, the "See Also" entries lead to descriptions of the numeric, string, and date formatting options.

Working with Files and Folders

You will encounter several basic object types when you use PowerShell to scout through files, folders, and even the Registry. The primary objects are `System.IO.DirectoryInfo` and `System.IO.FileInfo`, which represent folders and files, respectively. They have many methods and properties in common, so I list those in Reference List 16.1. The directory- and file-specific members follow in Reference Lists 16.2 and 16.3.

I don't have room to describe other .NET objects in this level of detail, but these file and folder objects are so important that it's useful. You'll probably be using them frequently in cmdlet pipelines and programmatically. I give examples of both types of usage after the reference lists.

> **Note**
>
> Be aware that you can create a System.IO.FileInfo or System.IO.DirectoryInfo object for a file or folder that does not exist. You can do this with the new-object cmdlet, for example. Just creating the object and assigning a name to it does *not* create the underlying item; you have to eventually use one of the Create methods if you want to really create the file or folder. The Exists property tells you whether the underlying item actually exists.
>
> If you obtain these objects with, for example, the get-item or get-childitem cmdlets, or with methods like GetDirectories or CreateSubdirectory, the underlying file system item already exists because these methods create objects based on what's in the file system.

Reference List 16.1—Properties and Methods Common to System.IO.DirectoryInfo and System.IO.FileInfo (Partial List)

Properties:

Attributes
An object that represents the object's read-only, archive, hidden, and other attribute bits.

CreationTime
The date/time the object was created, in the local time zone.

Exists
True if the underlying file, folder, or Registry key named by the object actually exists.

Extension
The object's file extension (for example, .txt).

FullName
The object's name including the drive and path.

LastAccessTime
The date/time the object was last opened for reading or writing, in the local time zone.

LastWriteTime
The date/time the object was last modified, in the local time zone.

Mode()
A string representing the object's Attributes as five characters, in this order: d if the object is a directory, a if the object has been altered since it was last backed up,

r if the object is read-only, h if the object is hidden, and s if the object is a system file. Each corresponding position is the character - if not.

(This property is added to `System.IO.FileInfo` and `System.IO.DirectoryInfo` objects by PowerShell and is not part of the .NET Framework version of these objects.)

Name
The object's name without the path.

Methods:

Delete([*recursive*]**)**

Deletes the object. For a directory, the directory must be empty, unless you pass the Boolean value `True` as an argument. In this case, the directory's files and subdirectories are recursively deleted.

GetAccessControl([*sections*]**)**

Returns an object representing the object's access control (security) settings. An optional argument limits the type of information retrieved.

MoveTo(path**)**
Moves the file or folder into another folder specified by the *path* argument. The name can be changed as well. The new location need not be on the same drive as the original.

Refresh()
Updates the object's properties to reflect the current file system status.

SetAccessControl(security_settings**)**
Sets an object's access control (security) settings as specified by a System.Security.AccessControl.FileSecurity object.

ToString()
Returns the path of the file or folder (*not* the file's contents) as a string.

Reference List 16.2 lists the methods and properties that `System.IO.DirectoryInfo` has in addition to those listed in Reference List 16.1.

Reference List 16.2—Properties and Methods Specific to `System.IO.DirectoryInfo` (Partial List)

Properties:

Parent
Returns a `System.IO.DirectoryInfo` object representing the directory's parent directory or NULL if the directory is a top-level (root) directory.

Root

Returns a System.IO.DirectoryInfo object representing the root directory on the drive containing the object's directory.

Methods:

Create([*security_settings*])

Creates the real directory that the object represents if it does not already exist.

CreateSubdirectory(*string* [, *security_settings*])

Creates a new subdirectory with the specified path name. If *path* is a relative path, the new directory is created relative to the directory represented by the object.

GetDirectories([*pattern*[, *searchoption*]])

Returns an array of System.IO.DirectoryInfo objects representing the directory's subdirectories. The optional string *pattern* specifies a wildcard pattern to match. The optional *searchoption* argument can be the value [System.IO.SearchOption]::TopDirectoryOnly to look for items only in the object's immediate subdirectories or [System.IO.SearchOption]::AllDirectories to search deeper within its subdirectories. The default is TopDirectoryOnly.

GetFiles([*pattern*[, *searchoption*]])

Returns an array of System.IO.FileInfo objects representing the directory's files. The optional string *pattern* specifies a wildcard pattern to match. The optional *searchoption* value works as with GetDirectories.

Reference List 16.3—Properties and Methods Specific to System.IO.FileInfo (Partial List)

Properties:

Directory
A System.IO.DirectoryInfo object representing the directory that contains the file.

DirectoryName
The path name of the containing directory.

IsReadOnly
True if the file is read-only; otherwise False. You can change the setting by assigning a new value to this property.

Length
The size of the file in bytes.

Methods:

`AppendText()`

Returns a `System.IO.StreamWriter` object that lets you append text data to the end of the file, if it already exists, or creates the file and lets you write text to if it does not already exist. Writing text is discussed in a following section.

`CopyTo(`*filename*`[, `*overwrite*`])`

Makes a copy of the file with the specified name. To overwrite an existing file, the optional Boolean *overwrite* value must be passed as `True`; otherwise, if the file already exists, an exception occurs. (Exceptions were discussed in Chapter 15.)

`Create([`*security_settings*`])`

Returns a `System.IO.FileStream` object that lets you write data to the file. The file's original contents are deleted. Writing to files is discussed in a following section.

`CreateText()`

Returns a `System.IO.StreamWriter` object that lets you write text to the file. The file's original contents are deleted. (See `AppendText`, listed previously, to add text to an existing file instead of replacing it.)

`Decrypt()`

Decrypts the file, if it was encrypted by the Windows Encrypting File System.

`Encrypt()`

Encrypts the file using the Windows Encrypting File System.

`Open(`*filemode* `[, `*access*`[, `*sharemode*`]])`

Returns a `System.IO.FileStream` object with which you can read from or write to the file. The *mode* value must be `[System.IO.FileMode]::`*xxx*, where *xxx* is one of the following:

FileMode	Description
`Append`	Opens the file for appending or creates it if it does not already exist.
`Create`	Creates an empty file. If the file already exists, its contents are deleted. (This mode is typically used when writing files.)
`CreateNew`	Creates a new, empty file. If the file already exists, an exception occurs.
`Open`	Opens an existing file. If the file does not already exist, an exception occurs. (This mode is typically used when reading files.)
`OpenOrCreate`	Opens an existing file or creates it if it does not already exist.
`Truncate`	Opens an existing file, deleting the existing content. If the file does not already exist, an exception occurs.

The optional *access* argument, if passed, must be [System.IO.FileAccess]::*xxx*, where *xxx* is one of Read, ReadWrite, or Write. If not specified, the default is Read.

The optional *sharemode* argument, if passed, determines how other people might access the file at the same time as your script. The value, if passed, must be [System.IO.ShareMode]:*xxx*, where *xxx* is one or more of the following values:

ShareMode	Description
None	No sharing permitted; that is, other programs can neither read nor write while the script is working with it. If another program already has the file open for reading or writing, your .Open attempt will fail with an exception.
Read	Permits other programs to read the file while you are working with it. Other programs cannot open the file for writing, however, and you cannot open the file if others are writing to it.
Write	Permits other programs to write to the file but not read it while you have it open.
ReadWrite	Permits both read and write sharing. Programs must take care to coordinate access to the file.
Delete	Allows another program to delete the file while you have it open. It won't actually go away until you close the file.

The default value is None. If you specify more than one value, combine them using the -bOR operator.

The following three methods are shortcut versions of the Open() method:

OpenRead()
Opens the file for reading and returns a System.IO.FileStream object.

OpenText()
Opens the file for reading UTF8-encoded text and returns a System.IO.StreamReader object.

OpenWrite()
Opens the file for writing and returns a System.IO.FileStream object.

Replace(*replfile, backupfile*[, *ignore_errors*])
Replaces *replfile* with the file represented by the object. A backup copy of the original file *replfile* is saved with the name *backupfile*. Both arguments are strings. Returns a new System.IO.FileInfo object that describes the new *replfile*. Specify the optional Boolean third argument as True to ignore errors during the replacement.

Now, let's look at some practical examples of using these objects.

Seeing Whether a File Exists

To see whether a file exists, you can create a `System.IO.FileInfo` object and test its `Exists` property, as in this example:

```
$fobj = new-object System.IO.FileInfo "c:\temp\testfile.txt"
if ($fobj.Exists) {'The file does exist'}
```

Note

This is an example of a case where you can have a `FileInfo` object that doesn't necessarily represent an actual file.

You can also use the cmdlet named `Test-Path` to do this job. You might find it easier to use in some cases. Here's an example of its use:

```
if (test-path 'c:\temp\testfile.txt') {'The file does exist'}
```

Reading Text from Files

You can read binary data from files using the .NET `System.IO.FileStream` object. If you're reading text data, it's more convenient to use the `System.IO.StreamReader` object. I don't have room to give you all the details on these objects. You can find the details at msdn.microsoft.com by searching for, for example, "System.IO.StreamReader members." Instead, I'll just how you a basic pattern for reading text strings from a file. This sample script simply numbers and prints the lines in the file, but you could anything you wanted to do inside the loop:

```
                                    # Example File script1601.ps1
$fobj = get-item '\path\filename.txt'  # get file object for desired text file
$strm = $fobj.OpenText()            # open for reading
$n = 0                              # initialize line counter
while (! $strm.EndOfStream) {        # read lines until end of file
    $txt = $strm.ReadLine()
    $n++                            # increment line counter
    "$n : $txt"                     # display line number and text from file
}
$strm.Dispose()                     # close the file
```

As you might expect, there is a way to do this same thing with a cmdlet. Here is the same script using a pipeline command:

```
$n = 0
get-content "\path\filename.txt" | foreach {
    $n++
    "$n : $_"
}
```

You might try to simplify this even further by using the ++ autoincrement operator and printing at the same time, like this:

```
$n = 0
get-content "\path\filename.txt" | foreach {"$(++$n) : $_"}
```

Recall that inside double quotes, $(...) prints the result of a statement or expression. So, this *should* work. But, ++$n by itself, as a statement, doesn't print anything. It's a commonly used programming statement, and if it printed anything, scripts would emit undesired output. So, you have to force PowerShell to treat ++$n as expression value by surrounding it with parentheses. This version does work:

```
get-content "\path\filename.txt" | foreach {"$((++$n)) : $_"}
```

Writing Text to Files

You can, of course, redirect cmdlet output to a file using the normal > operator; however, in many cases, you might want to more precisely build a file. The pattern for writing text to a file is shown here:

```
$fobj = new-item System.IO.FileInfo "c:\path\filename.txt"
$strm = $fobj.CreateText()
$strm.WriteLine('This is the first line')
for ($i = 1; $i -le 10; $i++) {
    $strm.Write("$i ")
}
$strm.WriteLine()
$strm.Dispose()
```

This creates file "c:\path\filename.txt" with two lines of text inside:

```
This is the first line
1 2 3 4 5 6 7 8 9 10
```

> **Tip**
>
> To write a tab character (which is helpful in creating tab-delimited files that you can later open with, for example, Excel), create a variable named $tab this way:
>
> ```
> $tab = [char] 9
> ```
>
> Then, write output lines like this:
>
> ```
> $strm.WriteLine "abc" + $tab + "def"
> ```

Identifying Files by Size

A practical example of working with files is a script to delete all files in a folder that are over a designated size. You might use this as part of a cleanup script that deletes unwanted temporary files.

You've probably noticed in the preceding sections that the `System.IO.FileInfo` object has a `Length` property that indicates the file's size. As we discussed earlier, our strategy for cmdlet pipelines is to generate files, filter, and then act. This file cleanup task is a perfect example of this. A single command line can do the job easily:

- The `Get-Item` cmdlet can generate a list of all the files in the folder using a wildcard pattern.
- The `Where-Object` cmdlet can pass through just the large files by examining the `Length` property.

Using just these two cmdlets lists the big files to the output window:

```
get-item 'c:\temp\*.*' | where-object {$_.Length -ge 10000}
```

To actually get rid of the bulky files, you have choices. One approach would be to use a `foreach` statement to call the `Delete` method on each object:

```
get-item 'c:\temp\*.*' | where-object {$_.Length -ge 10000} | foreach
{$_.Delete()}
```

This works. Alternatively, you could use the `Remove-Item` cmdlet:

```
get-item 'c:\temp\*.*' | where-object {$_.Length -ge 10000} | Remove-Item
```

`Remove-Item`, with no arguments, deletes the physical items behind file, Registry, and other object types streamed to it. (Normally, you use this cmdlet as a command by itself; it's a lot like the regular command prompt's `del` command.)

Creating Useful Scripts

To make really useful scripts that will help you in the long run, it's not enough to work out how to make a script do its job. The script should also address the following concerns:

- It should contain comments that describe how it works.
- If you are writing a module script that extends PowerShell by defining functions or new cmdlets, it should contain documentation for end users, so that the PowerShell help file knows about your extensions.
- If appropriate, the script should process command-line arguments that tell it what to do, where to look for things, whether to enable or disable options, and so on.

I talk briefly about these points in this section.

Comment Your Work!

Put comments in any script you write, no matter how trivial, so that later you can understand just what you did and why. It's important to write comments that describe *why* something is done—the code itself already describes *what* it's doing. This type of comment isn't very helpful:

```
$v = $v  + 10   # add 10 to variable v
```

We can already see that the script is adding 10. The question the comment should answer is why 10? Good comments will make it easier to come back at a later date and modify the script, or at least, will remind you how you solved one problem so you can apply what you learned to the next problem.

If you are writing new cmdlet modules, which I discuss shortly, you should know about comment-based help. You can put comment text in your file that the PowerShell help system can read and integrate into its online help system. For more information, you can type about_comment_based_help.

Command-Line Processing

You can often make your scripts more useful by having them take direction from the command line instead of wiring in things like filenames and file locations. The command-line arguments specified when a PowerShell script was run are available in array $args[]. For example, if you have a script named myscript.ps1 in the search path, the PowerShell command line

```
myscript a b c
```

runs your script and the array args[] will have three values: 'a', 'b', and 'c'. If you have a script that processes a file, you can make it more general-purpose by putting the "working" part in a function and calling the function once for every command-line argument:

```
# do_work filename - do something useful with file 'filename'
function do_work
{
    param ($filename)

    … work with file $filename
}

# main script - call function do_work for every file named on command line

if ($a.Length -eq 0) {
    'Usage: myscript filename ...'
}
else {
    foreach ($a in $args) {do_work $a}
}
```

This script processes every file named on the command line; if no files are named, it prints a message indicating how it is to be used.

In PowerShell you can easily construct scripts that accept much more complex command-line syntax. You don't need to manipulate the argument items directly. The param statement becomes complex, but PowerShell does all the heavy lifting for you. For information about using the param statement to specify command-line options, see "The param Statement" on page 665.

Writing Modules

You can write your own PowerShell functions that act just like built-in cmdlets. To do this, package the function in a module file that will be loaded every time PowerShell starts and use the following PowerShell language features:

- Define the cmdlet as a PowerShell function, using the BEGIN, PROCESS, and END statements. I discussed these in the section "Pipeline Functions and Filters" on page 671.

  I don't have room to describe this in detail, but you can find more information in the PowerShell help topic about_functions_advanced.

- Put the cmdlet function in a file with the extension .psm1. If you will be using only the module, it can be saved as %userprofile%\[my]documents \windowspowershell\modules*mymodule**mymodule*.psm1. Note that no matter what name you use for the script file, it should be placed in a folder of the same name. To make it available to all users, the file should be saved as \windows \system32\windowspowershell\V1.0\modules*mymodule**mymodule*.psm1. Then, to make it active in your current PowerShell session, type the command **import-module -name *mymodule*** or put this command in your PowerShell profile script.

  For more information about how to register a module with PowerShell, go to msdn.microsoft.com and search for "Windows PowerShell Module Concepts".

- Use the param method of handling command-line arguments in the cmdlet function, as discussed in "The param Statement" on page xxx (Chapter 15.)

- Write descriptive text that will help other users understand how to use your new cmdlet. The help information goes into the script file inside <# #> comment blocks and will be made available through the regular PowerShell help command. For information about formatting this help information, type **help about_comment_based_help**.

> **Tip**
> The PowerShell documentation says that when a script file is running, variable $PSScriptRoot contains the name of the directory in which the script file is located. This is useful information to have because, if your script needs additional data files to do its job, it's handy to just put them in the same

folder as the script and compute the path to the script to find the extra file. However, `$PSScriptRoot` works only for `.psm1` module files, not regular `.ps1` script files. To get the path to the running script's folder in a regular `.ps1` script, use this expression:

```
$ScriptDir = Split-Path $MyInvocation.MyCommand.Path -Parent
```

Now you can construct the path to the extra file with, for example,

```
$filename = $ScriptDir + "\script_setup_file.txt".
```

Exception Handling as an Exit Strategy

The Exception Handling mechanism in PowerShell lets your scripts gracefully exit or resolve unexpected errors. (I described Exception Handling on p. 702.)

You can also use Exception Handling as a tool to simplify scripts that perform a long series of steps. Here's what I mean: Before performing a task, you might need to perform a long, complex series of checks to be sure that it's okay to proceed. The usual method of handling complex tests is to set a variable named something like `ok_to_proceed` to `True` at the top, set it to `False` if any of the tests in the middle fail, and finally perform the action if it's still `True` at the end, like this:

```
ok_to_proceed = True

if (something_is_true) {
    if (check_one_thing) {
        if (-not check_this_other_thing)
            ok_to_proceed = False

        if (it_is_Tuesday) {
            if (-not check_something_else)
                ok_to_proceed = False
        }
    }
    else {
        ok_to_proceed = False
    }
}
else
    ok_to_proceed = False

if (ok_to_proceed)                # finally, see if all our tests succeeded
    do something important
```

What a mess! In many cases, if one of the tests fails, you don't want to continue with other tests. For example, if one test finds that a network host can't be reached, you don't want to try to ask it about its current configuration.

Exception Handling lets you avoid nasty, convoluted code like this by letting you create your own exceptions using the `throw` keyword. An exception immediately bails out of a sequence of statements. You can simply perform a series of tests one after another. If any test fails, use throw to stop testing. If you reach the end of the tests, you know all of them succeeded. Here's how the previous example can be reworked:

```
try {
    if (-not something_is_true) throw "Problem 1"

    if (-not check_one_thing) throw "Problem 2"

    if (-not check_this_other_thing) throw "Problem 3"

    if (it_is_Tuesday)
        if (-not check_something_else) throw "Problem 4"

    do something important
)
catch (exception) {
    "Unable to proceed:", exception      # explain which test failed
}
```

The sequence of steps here is much easier to read, and as a bonus, if any of the statements generates a real exception, the catch statement handles it as well. For more information on using try and catch, see "Exception Handling," p. 662.

Using Hash Tables

As I mentioned in Chapter 15, hash tables are a type of array where the index value doesn't have to be a number (it can be, though). Items are indexable by numbers or strings. And, they can be useful in scripting, after you see how they can be used.

Here's an example: Suppose I have an error log file that lists server names, one name per line, and I want to count the number of times that each name appears in the log file. Using VBScript, I would have to use code like the following example:

```
set fso = CreateObject("Scripting.FileSystemObject")
dim errcount()                          ' set up dynamically-sized array
max_names = 20                          ' make room for 20 names initially
redim errcount(2, max_names)
n_names = 0                             ' no names in list yet
set strm = fso.OpenTextFile("c:\logs\server.names")
do while not strm.AtEndOfStream         ' loop through all entries in log
    servername = strm.ReadLine()        ' get server name from log entry
                                        ' increment its error count
    for i = 1 to n_names                ' is name already in the list?
        if errcount(1,i) = servername then   ' yes, just
            errcount(2,i) = errcount(2,i)+1  ' increment its error count
            exit for
        end if
```

```
        next
        if i > n_names then                        ' not found, add it
            if n_names = max_names then            ' list is full, so increase size
                max_names = max_names+20
                redim preserve errcount(2,max_names)
            end if
            n_names = n_names+1                    ' add new name to list
            errcount(1, n_names) = servername
            errcount(2, n_names) = 1               ' set error count to 1
        end if
    loop
    strm.Close
                                                   ' now print out list counts
    wscript.echo "Server" & vbTab & "# of errors"
    for i = 1 to n_names
        wscript.echo errcount(1,i) & vbTab & cstr(errcount(2,i))
    next
```

Now, here's how to do the same thing in PowerShell:

```
    $errcount = @{}                         # create empty hash table
    $fobj = get-item '\logs\server.names'   # get file object for desired text file
    $strm = $fobj.OpenText()                # open for reading
    while (! $strm.EndOfStream) {           # read lines until end of file
        $servername = $strm.ReadLine()
        $errcount[$servername]++            # increment count. (If name is new,
                                            # default value
    }                                       # is null, and null+1 = 1, so it works)
    $errcount                               # finally, print out list of names and
    errors
```

How about that? And by using the `get-content` cmdlet that I discussed earlier in this chapter in "Reading Text from Files," you can shorten this further:

```
    $errcount = @{}                         # create empty hash table
                                            # get lines from file, and count
    get-content '\logs\server.names' | foreach {$errcount[$_]++}
    $errcount
```

This does the same job with just three statements! To be fair, VBScript has access to a `Dictionary` object that can simplify the job in the same way; however, it's not well-known, whereas hash tables are an integral part of the PowerShell language.

The PowerShell Integrated Scripting Environment

Windows PowerShell 2.0 comes with a script editing and debugging tool called the Integrated Scripting Environment (ISE) that lets you develop and test scripts in a GUI-based editor. It beats Notepad hands down because it lets you step through a script line-by-line, view variables and intermediate results, and even interact with PowerShell while the script is running. I show you how to use it in this section.

→ PowerShell ISE is installed by default on Windows 7. For information about installing PowerShell 2.0 on earlier versions of Windows, see "Windows Vista and Windows XP," p. 598.

Starting the PowerShell ISE

There are several easy ways to open the ISE:

- In a Command Prompt or PowerShell window, type **powershell_ise**.
- On Windows 7, click Start, All Programs, Accessories, Windows PowerShell, Windows PowerShell ISE.
- On Windows Vista or XP, after downloading and installing PowerShell 2.0, click Start, All Programs, Windows PowerShell 2.0, Windows PowerShell ISE.

Whichever way you start it, the default screen is shown in Figure 16.1.

Figure 16.1 The PowerShell ISE screen is divided into sections that let you edit a script file, view script output, and type interactive PowerShell commands.

By default, the window is divided into three panes: a script editor, an output window, and an input window. The editor pane has one or more tabs, corresponding to the script file(s) you have open for editing. The output pane is initially blank and will contains any text printed to the standard output or standard error output streams. The input pane displays a PowerShell prompt, and you can type PowerShell commands and input into this window.

The Help menu displays a complete PowerShell reference with information about all built-in cmdlets and language features.

Configuring the ISE

The View menu has options that position the Script pane across the top of the ISE window or down the right side of the window. You can also hide the script editor pane entirely by unchecking View, Show Script Pane.

The font size in the ISE is controlled by View/Zoom In and Zoom Out or, equivalently, by moving the slider at the bottom-right corner of the ISE window. I find that I prefer 12-point type.

Beyond these options, however, you'll find that the ISE menu has no options for customizing the interface. For example, there is no way to change the font used in the ISE window from the menu. You probably won't be surprised to hear that you can further customize the interface from the PowerShell command prompt. (On your first reading of this chapter, you might want to skip this section, but what I'm about to describe is pretty cool, so do come back to it!)

The ISE program itself is described by PowerShell objects that have methods and properties you can change. For example, the property `$psISE.Options.FontName` controls the font, and if you type `$psISE.Options.FontName = "Lucida Console"`, the font changes in the editor pane and subsequent text in the input and output panes appears in the new font.

You can also add items to the ISE menu. The method

```
$psISE.CurrentPowerShellTab.AddOnsMenu.SubMenus.Add("text",{command},"shortcutkey")
```

displays a new menu selection named Add-ons, and each call to this method adds a new item to the Add-ons list. *text* is the name of the item to display in the menu, *command* is a PowerShell cmdlet or function that the menu item is to invoke, and *shortcutkey* is an optional string that assigns a keyboard shortcut to the menu item. Here's an example:

```
$psISE.CurrentPowerShellTab.AddOnsMenu.SubMenus.Add("_Processes",
⮑{get-process}},"Alt+P")
```

(In the text argument, the underscore character (_) causes the following character P to be underlined to give the user the hint that Alt+P is the corresponding keyboard shortcut.)

You can put your favorite display and menu customizations in a profile script so that they take effect every time you start the ISE. For information on profile scripts, see "PowerShell Profiles" on page xxx (Chapter 14).

> **Tip**
>
> If you use the `AddOnsMenu` method I just described, you'll need to assign the method's result to a variable; otherwise, it prints junk in the output window. Type the command like this:
>
> ```
> $v = $psISE.CurrentPowerShellTab.AddOnsMenu.SubMenus.Add(arguments)
> ```

For more information about the customizations you can make by altering the ISE's objects, click Help, Windows PowerShell Help; open the section "Windows PowerShell Integrated Scripting Environment (ISE) Help"; and see "The Windows PowerShell ISE Scripting Object Model."

Creating and Editing Scripts

To create a new script, click File, New and start typing in the "Untitled" editing pane that opens. You can save your work at any time using the usual File, Save As or File, Save menu items. For most scripts, save the script file with the extension `.ps1`. Use `.psm1` for Module files that contain cmdlet you've written, as discussed earlier in this chapter.

To make it easy to run scripts from the PowerShell command line, save your scripts in a folder that's in the Windows search path.

➔ For instructions on setting up a pathed script folder, see "Adding Scripts to the Path", p. 37.

Editing

The editing window is fairly primitive compared to that provided by full-scale development programs like Microsoft Visual Studio, but it's still much better than what Notepad offers. Figure 16.1, shown earlier, shows a script in the upper pane of the editor. PowerShell keywords and variable names are color-coded and distinct.

Open the Edit menu and note that it has Find Next and Find Previous (shortcuts F3 and Shift+F3, respectively), which search forward or backward from the cursor's location. The Find dialog box has check boxes that let you match case, search for text as a whole word, or use Regular Expression wildcards to match desired text.

Note

One terrific benefit of the ISE is its autocomplete function. Just as at the PowerShell command prompt, if you start to type a cmdlet, function, or variable name; filename; or Registry path, you can press Tab and the ISE attempts to finish typing the name for you. If it selects the wrong name, keep pressing Tab to cycle through all names that start with whatever you typed before pressing Tab. This works in both the Input and Editor panes. For example, if you type `get-co` and then press Tab, the ISE expands it to `get-command`. Another Tab gets you `Get-ComputerRestorePoint`, and so on.

Running Scripts in the ISE

You can type any PowerShell command in the lower PowerShell prompt pane at any time. The command's output appears in the middle output window. This isn't any different from running commands and scripts in the regular PowerShell window.

The real power of the ISE is its capability to debug scripts and run them step-by-step. If you have a script that isn't working as you expect, you can run it in the ISE and watch what it does at every step to understand where it's going wrong.

To step through a script, put the cursor in the first line and press the F9 key (or click Debug, Toggle Breakpoint). The script line will be highlighted in red by default. This indicates that when PowerShell reaches this step in the script, it will stop and wait for you before proceeding. To try this, open the sample script `script1602.ps1` that you can download from www.helpwin7.com/scripting or type it in by hand:

```
                                            # example file script1602.vbs
"The script is starting now"
$v = 1
for ($i = 0; $i -le 5; $i++) {
    $v *= 2                            # double the value v
    "In loop, i = $i, v = $v"
}
```

Then, press F5 to run the script. The script's output should appear in the middle pane, as shown in Figure 16.2.

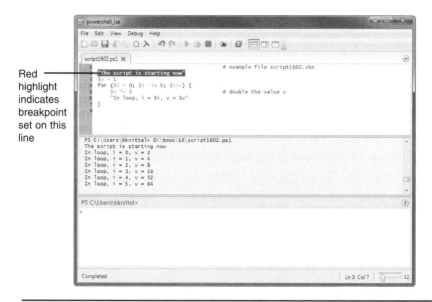

Red highlight indicates breakpoint set on this line

Figure 16.2 Breakpoints let you stop the script at any selected statements.

Setting Breakpoints and Single-Stepping

To set a breakpoint in a script, put the cursor in the script that you want to see run. Press F9 or click Debug, Toggle Breakpoint. The line will be highlighted in red, as seen in Figure 16.2. (If the line that you mark has no executable statements, the breakpoint will appear in the next actual PowerShell statement below this point in the file.)

Now, when you run the script in the ISE, PowerShell stops *before* it executes the marked statement. You can try it with the sample script I discussed in the previous section. Put the cursor in the first line of the script and press F9. Then, press F5 to run the script.

PowerShell starts the script and highlights the marked line in yellow. This means it's the next statement to execute. Press F11 to execute the first statement and notice that after it has run, the text The script is starting now appears in the output window, but no more. PowerShell is now waiting at the second statement.

You can step through a script using these keys:

Key	Action
F10	Runs just the next statement. If the statement is a call to a user-defined PowerShell function, PowerShell runs the function and doesn't stop again until it returns to the current script location. This is called "Step Over."
F11	Runs just the next statement. If the statement is a call to a function, PowerShell steps to the first statement in the function and stops there. This is called "Step Into."
Shift+F11	If you are debugging inside a function, runs continuously until the function returns to whatever script command called it and then stops. This is called "Step Out."
F5	Runs until the script ends. This is called "Run/Continue."

Note that even if you press a key that potentially runs many instructions (F10, Shift+F11, or F5), PowerShell stops if it hits a statement that is marked with a breakpoint.

You can place as many breakpoints in the file as you want. For a smaller script, you can place just one at the beginning and step through the entire script using F11. For larger scripts, it's often helpful to place breakpoints just at trouble spots, after loops, and so on because it can be tedious to go one step at a time. Press F5 to run to the next breakpoint.

At any point, you can press Shift+F5 to stop running the script in the debugger. PowerShell cancels the script at whatever step it happened to be at.

Interactively Examining and Changing Variables

Whenever PowerShell has stopped a script, either because you've run just one step or because it has hit a breakpoint step, you can type commands in the lower command window to examine or change variables.

Try this with the sample script. You can press F11 several times to walk through the script. Each time you have executed the $v *= 2 statement, type **$v** in the lower command window and press Enter. PowerShell displays the current value of $v.

With larger scripts, it can take a long time to get through all the statements and to work through any errors in the script, especially a newly written script. It can be really tedious to find a bug, cancel the script, fix the bug, step through until you find the next bug, cancel and start over, and so on. After a script command has made a mistake, if possible, I manually type a command to compute the correct result and then continue running the script. I just make a note to go back and fix the error later. For example, if you had mistyped a new-object command halfway through a large script:

```
$fso = create-object -comobject Scriptingg.FileSystemObject
```

it might be faster to simply type the command into the command window (without the extra g in Scripting), which sets $v to the correct object, and let the script continue than to cancel the script and start over.

Conditional Breakpoints

Sometimes a problem occurs only occasionally in a section of code that is executed over and over. This can be the case inside a loop or a function, for example. If you set a breakpoint in this code, you'll have to press F5 repeatedly to get to the point where the error finally occurs—perhaps thousands of times. That's no good! In this case, what you need is a breakpoint that stops the script only when it's really time. This is called a *conditional breakpoint*. The ISE doesn't have them as a built-in feature, but you can fake it. Just add an if statement that triggers only when you want the breakpoint to trigger and set a breakpoint inside the if statement's code block.

For example, suppose I have a for loop that runs 500 times and something's going wrong inside that loop:

```
for ($i = 0; $i < 500; $i++) {
    loop statements here…
}
```

To find out where the script is crashing, I would add a statement that prints the value of $i inside the loop:

```
for ($i = 0; $i < 500; $i++) {
    "Loop iteration $i"
    loop statements here…
}
```

The last number printed before the script fails tells me when the problem occurs. Let's say it's when $i is 47. Now, I can add an if statement to test for this:

```
for ($i = 0; $i < 500; $i++) {
    "Loop iteration $i"
    if ($i -eq 47) {
        "breakpoint here"
    }
    loop statements here…
}
```

If I put a breakpoint on the line "breakpoint here" and run the script again, it halts when $i is 47, and I can single-step through the loop's remaining statements to diagnose the problem.

Remote and Background PowerShell

You can run PowerShell scripts on remote computers (that is, other computers on your network), provided that you have the required security permissions. This can be a great tool for managing networked computers. You can, for instance, write a script that runs through a list of Windows workstations or servers and run a management script on each of them in turn. I don't have room to describe this in detail here, but you can find information in the PowerShell help topics `about_remote` and `about_remote_faq`. You can run scripts remotely only if you are an administrator on a domain network or if you significantly relax Windows security settings on a non-domain network (I personally don't recommend doing this), as described in the `about_remote_faq` help file.

You can also run scripts on your own computer or other computers unhooked from the command prompt, that is as background or batch jobs. They run without interfering with your work, and you can use PowerShell commands and scripts to retrieve their results after they finish. For information on this technique, see the PowerShell help topics `about_jobs` and `about_remote_jobs`.

Where to Go from Here

In three PowerShell chapters, I've just given you an introduction to what it can do. I tried to use the available pages to explain what is going on inside PowerShell, to show you how it works, rather than to show you how to solve a laundry list of management tasks with it because there are already myriad websites that do just that. With this background in how PowerShell operates, I think you'll be in a good position to understand what all those sample scripts out there do and how they work, and then you'll be able to create your own.

I've found the following resources to be useful:

- The `powershell_ise` program's Help menu has all of PowerShell's help files available in an easy-to-navigate, readable format.

- The Scripting Center at technet.microsoft.com has extensive sample scripts and documentation. The "Hey, Scripting Guy" column is very informative. There are also online forums for TechNet members where you can ask questions of other PowerShell users. You can become a TechNet member for free.

  After you understand the basics of the PowerShell language, reading the real-life scripts shown on these sites will probably teach you more than any other source could.

- There are several books devoted entirely to PowerShell. I found the following to be useful: *Windows PowerShell Unleashed, 2nd Edition* (Que) and *Windows PowerShell 2.0 Administrator's Pocket Consultant* (Microsoft Press).

A

VBScript Reference

VBScript 5.6 Language Features

This appendix provides a quick summary of VBScript syntax. This reference covers only the features of VBScript used with Windows Script Host (WSH). For detailed documentation of VBScript language features, I recommend you download the most recent Microsoft VBScript reference manual from microsoft.com/downloads. Search for "Windows Script Documentation" and download the most current version listed. At the time this was written, this was version 5.6. You might find it handiest if you save this file to your Desktop.

Tip

If Windows won't display the contents of the `script56.chm` file after you download it, right-click its icon, select Properties, click Unblock, and then click OK. This removes its status as a potentially dangerous downloaded file.

If you are familiar with Visual Basic (VB) or Visual Basic for Applications (VBA), you will note that some VB and VBA language features are not provided in VBScript. The specific differences between these versions are listed in Table A.6 and are described in more detail in the Microsoft downloaded reference under VBScript, VBScript Language Reference, Feature Information (VBScript).

Syntax

In this reference, the following conventions are used:

- Parts of program statements that must be typed literally are shown in **boldface**.
- Items that represent something that must be replaced with your own choice of variable names or expressions are shown in *italics*.
- Optional parts are placed in square brackets ([ ]).
- Items that might be repeated arbitrarily are followed with ellipses (...).
- Items from which you must choose one alternative are listed in curly brackets ({ }) and separated by vertical lines (|), as in {**this** | **that**}.

General Structure of a VBScript Program

A VBScript program is a plain text file, such as one you'd edit with Notepad. Whitespace (spaces, tabs, and blank lines) is permitted to improve readability. Case is not significant.

There is no limit to the length of source code lines. However, to improve readability, you can break long program lines into two or more shorter lines. You must end broken-up lines with the underscore (_) character and continue them on the subsequent line (or lines). Here's an example:

```
wscript.echo "This is a long " & _
    "input line, isn't it?"
```

The main program body consists of all input lines outside `Class`, `Sub`, or `Function` groups. Generally, global variable definitions should be entered first; followed by the main script program; and then followed by class, subroutine, and function definitions.

VBScript ignores anything after a single quote (') character, treating it as a comment.

Data Types and Variables

VBScript variable names can have up to 255 characters; must begin with a letter; must not contain blanks, periods, or punctuation characters; and must not be one of the reserved language keywords, such as `public` or `while`.

In VBScript, all variables are of type Variant. A Variant can hold integers, floating-point numbers, dates, times, date-times, strings, Boolean values, and object references. When Variants are combined in expressions, VBScript attempts to interpret them in such a way as to make the expression sensible. To force VBScript to use a particular conversion or interpretation in expressions, use the conversion functions `CStr()`, `CInt()`, `CDbl()`, and so on.

Table A.1 lists the Variant types and examples of constant expressions that can be used in programs.

Table A.1   **VBScript Variant Types and Constants**

Variant Type	Constant Example	Remarks
Integer, Short	123 &H12AB (hex) &0177777 (octal)	Range: −32768 to 32767.
Integer, Long	1234567 &H47DFE123 &0123456712	Range: −2147483648 to 2147483647.
Floating-point, single precision	3.1416	Range: $\pm 3.4 \times 10^{38}$, seven digits accuracy.
Floating-point, double precision	3.14159265359	Range: $\pm 1.8 \times 10^{308}$, 15 digits accuracy.
Currency	100.47	Range: $\pm 922,337,203,685,$ 477.5808. Currency values retain only four decimal places.
String	"abc"	A quotation mark can be embedded in the string by doubling it (for example, "a "" quote" represents a " quote).
Date	#03/02/2002# #March 2, 2002#	The short date form is interpreted according to the Windows Locale setting.
Time	#14:30:15# #2:30:15 PM#	—
Date-Time	#03/02/2002 14:30:15# #March 2, 2002 2:30:15 PM #	You might force a specific output conversion format with FormatDateTime. Date-times are stored as floating-point numbers.
Boolean	True False	—
Object	Nothing	Nothing is a predefined null object reference.
Empty	Empty	Uninitialized.
Null	Null	Defined as invalid. Using a Null value has various results: In Boolean expressions, it's treated as False. In numeric expressions, the result is always Null. In most other cases, an error is generated.

Note on Dates and Times

Variants of type Date, Time, and Date-Time (combinations of a date and a time of day) are encoded as floating-point numbers. Dates are stored as the number of days since January 1, 1900. Dates prior to that epoch are allowed and are stored as negative numbers. Times are stored as fractions of a day, with one second equaling 0.0000115741. For example, the representation of `#March 2, 2002 2:30:15 PM#` is `37317.6043402778`.

This is important to know if you want to use date, time, or date-time values in mathematical operations. Care must be taken in the interpretation of the sums and differences of dates and times with numeric or other date-time values. It's best to use the functions `DateAdd` and `DateDiff` to perform computations on dates and times.

Variable Scope

By default, when a variable is declared or created in the main body of a script file, it has public (global) scope and is accessible in the main script and in all procedures (subs and functions) called in the script. Variables defined within procedures, by default, have private (local) scope and are accessible only within the procedure in which they're declared. When the defining procedure terminates, the variable is destroyed.

The keywords `Public` and `Private` can be used to override the default behavior. In the main script program, `Private` variables will not be visible to called procedures. In a procedure, a variable declared `Public` will be visible to any other procedures it calls. (However, the variable will still be destroyed when the defining procedure ends.)

A variable can also be set without having first been declared with `Dim`, `Private`, or `Public`. In the main script program, this creates a public variable. If a procedure references a variable name previously defined as `Public`, the public copy is used. Otherwise, a private variable is created.

Procedures might define private variables with the same names as public variables defined elsewhere. In this case, the procedure creates a local, private variable and cannot see the public version.

Expressions and Operators

The following precedence order is used when evaluating expressions:

1. Subexpressions in parentheses
2. Arithmetic operators
3. Comparison operators
4. Logical operators

Note

VBScript always evaluates the entire expression, even when it's not necessary. Therefore, the following type of test will not protect a program from an argument value error:

```
a = -3
if a > 0 and sqr(a) > 2 then ...
```

Arithmetic Operators

Listed in order of precedence from highest to lowest, the arithmetic operators are as follows:

Operator	Meaning
^	Exponentiation
-	Unary negation
*	Multiplication
/	Division
\	Integer division
mod	Modulus (integer remainder)
+	Addition
-	Subtraction
&	String concatenation

Comparison Operators

Comparison operators have equal precedence and are evaluated in left-to-right order, as shown here:

Operator	Meaning
=	Equal to
<>	Not equal to
<	Less than
>	Greater than
<=	Less than or equal to
>=	Greater than or equal to
is	Object equivalence

Logical Operators

Logical operators perform logical operations on Boolean values and bitwise operations on numeric values. Listed in order of precedence from highest to lowest, the logical operators are as follows:

Operator	Meaning
not	Negation
and	Conjunction
or	Disjunction
xor	Exclusion (different)
eqv	Equivalence (same)
imp	Implication (same or second value true)

Program Statements

The general structure of a VBScript program is as follows:

```
[global variable declarations]

main procedure VBScript statements

[subs and functions]
```

Program statements can be split onto multiple lines to improve readability. When a line ends with the underscore character (_), the next line is considered to be part of the same statement.

VBScript program statements are listed in Table A.2. For details on each statement, see the Microsoft VBScript documentation described at the beginning of this appendix.

Note

In Table A.2, *condition* refers primarily to an expression or a variable with a Boolean (True or False) value. However, VBScript also accepts a string or numeric value where a Boolean value is expected. For numeric values, zero is treated as False and any nonzero value as True. The strings values "True" and "False" are also accepted, as are strings that can be interpreted as numbers.

Table A.2 **VBScript Statements**

[**Call**] *name* [(*argumentlist*)]	[*name = expression*]
Class *name*	[**Exit Function**]
statements...	[*statements...*]
End Class	**End Function**
[{**public**|**private**}] **Const** *name_*	*arguments:*
= *expression* [, ...]	[{**ByVal**|**ByRef**}] *argname* [, ...]
Dim *name*[([*subscripts*])] [,...]	**If** *condition* **Then** *statement_*
Do [{**While** | **Until**} *condition*]	[**Else** *statement*]
[*statements...*]	**If** *condition* **Then**
[**Exit Do**]	*statements...*
[*statements...*]	[**ElseIf** *condition* **Then**
Loop	*statements...*]
or	[**Else**
Do	*statements...*]
[*statements...*]	**End If**
[**Exit Do**]	**On Error Resume Next**
[*statements...*]	**On Error Goto 0**
Loop [{**While** | **Until**}_	**Option Explicit**
condition]	**Private** *name*[(*subscripts*)][, ...]
Erase *arrayname*	**Public** *name*[(*subscripts*)][, ...]
Execute *string*	**Randomize** [*number*]
ExecuteGlobal *string*	**Redim** [**Preserve**]_
Exit Do	*name*(*subcripts*)[, ...]
Exit For	**Rem** *text*
Exit Function	**Select Case** *expression*
Exit Property	**Case** *expression* [, ...]
Exit Sub	*statements...*
For Each *element* **in** *group*	[**Case** *expression* [, ...]
[*statements...*]	*statements...*]
[**Exit For**]	[**Case Else**
[*statements...*]	*statements...*]
Next [*element*]	**End Select**
For *counter* = *startval* **to_**	**Set** *var* = *objectexpr*
endval [, *increment*]	**Set** *var* = **New** *classname*
[*statements...*]	**Set** *var* = **Nothing**
[**Exit For**]	**Stop**
[*statements...*]	[{**Public** [**Default**] | **Private**}]_
Next [*counter*]	**Sub** *name* [(*arguments*)]
[{**Public** [**Default**] | **Private**}]_	[*statements...*]
Function *name* [(*arguments*)]	[**Exit Sub**]
[*statements...*]	[*statements...*]
	End Sub

continues

Table A.2   **Continued**

While *condition*	**With** *object*
statements...	*statements...*
Wend	**End With**

Functions

The built-in functions shown in Table A.3 are provided with VBScript.

Table A.3   **VBScript Functions**

Function	
Abs(*value*)	**DateValue**(*date*)
Array(*arglist*)	**Day**(*date*)
Asc(*string*)	**Eval**(*expression*)
Ascb(*string*)	**Exp**(*value*)
Ascw(*string*)	**Filter**(*InputStrings, Value* [,_
Atn(*number*)	*Include* [, *Compare*]])
CBool(*expr*)	**Fix**(*value*)
CByte(*expr*)	**FormatCurrency**(*value* [,_
CCur(*expr*)	*NumDigitsAfterDecimal* [,_
CDate(*expr*)	*IncludeLeadingDigit* [,_
CDbl(*expr*)	*UseParensForNegativeNumbers* [,_
Chr(*value*)	*GroupDigits*]]]])
CInt(*value*)	
CLng(*value*)	**FormatDateTime**(*DateVal*[, *Format*])
Cos(*number*)	**FormatNumber**(*value* [,_
CreateObject(*servername*	*NumDigitsAfterDecimal* [,_
typename [, *location*])	*IncludeLeadingDigit* [,_
CSng(*value*)	*UseParensForNegativeNumbers* [,_
CStr(*value*)	*GroupDigits*]]]])
Date	**FormatPercent**(*value* [,_
DateAdd(*interval, number, date*)	*NumDigitsAfterDecimal* [,_
DateDiff(*interval, date1,_*	*IncludeLeadingDigit* [,_
date2 [, *firstdayofweek* [,_	*UseParensForNegativeNumbers* [,_
firstweekofyear]])	*GroupDigits*]]]])
DatePart(*interval, date* [,_	**GetLocale**()
firstdayofweek [,_	**GetObject**([*filename*] [, *class*])
firstweekofyear]])	**GetRef**(*procname*)
DateSerial(*year, month, day*)	**Hex**(*value*)
	Hour(*time*)

InputBox(*prompt* [, *title* [,_
  default][, *xpos*, *ypos*] [,_
  helpfile, *context*])

InStr([*start*,] *string1*, *string2* [,_
  compare])

InStrRev([*start*,] *string1*,_
  string2 [, *compare*])

Int(*value*)

IsArray(*varname*)

IsDate(*expr*)

IsEmpty(*expr*)

IsNull(*expr*)

IsNumeric(*expr*)

IsObject(*varname*)

Join(*array* [, *delimiter*])

LBound(*arrayname* [, *dimension*])

LCase(*string*)

Left(*string*, *length*)

Len(*string*)

LoadPicture(*picturename*)

Log(*value*)

LTrim(*string*)

Mid(*string*, *start*[, *length*])

Minute(*time*)

Month(*date*)

Monthname(*month*, [*abbrev*])

MsgBox(*prompt* [, *buttons* [,_
  title [, *helpfile*,_
 context]]])

Now()

Oct(*value*)

Replace(*expr*, *find*,_
  replacewith [, *start* [,_
  count [, *compare*]]])

RGB(*red*, *green*, *blue*)

Right(*string*, *length*)

Rnd[(*value*)]

Round(*value* [, *nplaces*])

RTrim(*string*)

ScriptEngine

ScriptEngineBuildVersion

ScriptEngineMajorVersion

ScriptEngineMinorVersion

Second(*time*)

SetLocale(*localeid*)

Sgn(*value*)

Sin(*value*)

Space(*number*)

Split(*string* [, *delimiter* [,_
  count [, *compare*]]])

Sqr(*value*)

StrComp(*string1* [, *string2* [,_
  compare]])

String(*number*, *char*)

StrReverse(*string*)

Tan(*value*)

Time

Timer

TimeSerial(*hour*, *minute*, *second*)

TimeValue(*expr*)

Trim(*string*)

TypeName(*varname*)

UBound(*arrayname* [, *dimension*])

UCase(*string*)

VarType(*varname*)

Weekday(*date* [, *firstday*])

WeekdayName(*number*, *abbrev*,_
  firstday)

Year(*date*)

Date Function Intervals

Date functions such as `DateAdd`, `DateDiff`, and `DatePart` take an interval argument, which is a string with one of the values listed in Table A.4.

Table A.4 **Intervals Used with `DateAdd`, `DateDiff`, and `DatePart`**

Value	Meaning
`"YYYY"`	Year
`"q"`	Quarter
`"m"`	Month
`"y"`	Day of year (a number from 1 to 365)
`"d"`	Day
`"w"`	Weekday
`"ww"`	Week of year (a number from 1 to 52)
`"h"`	Hour
`"n"`	Minute
`"s"`	Second

Predefined Special Values

The constants listed in Table A.5 define the Boolean values `True` and `False` as well as special constant values.

Table A.5 **Special Constants**

Constant	Description
`Empty`	The value of a declared but uninitialized variable.
`False`	The Boolean **False** value. Numerically equivalent to **0**.
`Nothing`	Assigning `Nothing` to a variable disconnects the variable from the object, and if no other references exist, the object is released (destroyed).
`Null`	The `Null` value is used to indicate invalid data. `Null` is not the same as `Empty`.
`True`	The Boolean `True` value. Numerically equivalent to `-1` (all bits set).

You can test for the values `Empty` and `Null` with the functions `IsEmpty()` and `IsNull()`. Attempting to use a `Null` value in any other expression results in an error.

Several other constants are defined for colors, dates, times, special characters, and so on. These are described in the downloadable reference under the heading "Constants". See the beginning of this appendix for download instructions.

VBA Features Omitted from VBScript

VBScript is a scaled-down version of VBA, which is itself a scaled-down version of Microsoft VB. Programmers familiar with VBA through its use as the Word/Excel macro language should be aware that some familiar language features are not available in VBScript.

Table A.6 summarizes the features omitted from and added to VBScript. The differences are described in more detail in the downloadable VBScript documentation under the headings VBScript, VBScript Language Reference, Feature Information (VBScript).

Table A.6   **Differences Between VBScript and Visual Basic**

Statement or Function	Remarks
!	*object*!*keyname* cannot be used to access an item in a collection. Use *object*.item(*keyname*) instead.
#Const	Compile-time constants are not supported. Use Const instead.
#If...Then, #Else	Conditional compilation is not supported.
Clipboard	The Clipboard object is not provided.
Collection	Ad hoc Collection objects cannot be created. Some predefined objects return collections, however.
CVar CVDate	Unnecessary. All variables are of type Variant already.
Date	All variables are of type Variant.
Debug.Print	Use Wscript.Echo instead.
Declare	External DLLs are not accessible.
DefBool and so on	All variables are of type Variant.
DoEvents	Use Wscript.Sleep instead.
End	Not supported. You can, however, place your script's main code in a Sub and use Exit Sub. Here's an example: `myscript` `sub myscript` `...` `exit sub` `...` `end sub`
Erl	The Erl function (which indicates the line number of the last error) is not available.
Error	Not available. Use err.Raise instead.
FV, IRR, PV, and so on	Financial functions are not provided.

continues

Table A.6   **Continued**

Statement or Function	Remarks
Gosub...Return	Gosub and labels are not supported.
GoTo	Goto and labels are not supported.
Integer	All variables are of type Variant.
Is (in Select Case)	Object typing with Is isn't supported in Select Case.
Like	Pattern matching is not directly supported. Use the RegExp object.
Link*xxx*	DDE is not supported.
Long	All variables are of type Variant.
LSet and Rset	Not supported.
Mid statement	The Mid assignment statement (mid on the left side of =) is not supported.
On...GoSub On...GoTo	Event and error handling are not supported.
Open, Read, Write, Close, and so on	Basic file I/O is not supported. Use FileSystemObject instead.
Option Base	In VBScript, all array indexing starts at 0.
Option Compare Option Private Module	These option settings are not applicable.
Optional	Arguments may not be specified as optional. You can indicate unspecified arguments by passing the value Null and testing with IsNull() in the procedure.
ParamArray	ParamArray arguments are not supported.
Resume Resume Next	Error trapping is not supported.
SendKeys	Not a built-in statement. Use Wscript.Sendkeys instead.
Static	Static (persistent) variables are not supported.
Str	Use CStr().
StrConv	The StrConv() function is not supplied. Use UCase() or LCase() if possible.
Time	All variables are of type Variant.
To (in Select Case)	Expression ranges with To are not supported in Select Case.
TypeOf	If TypeOf and Select Case TypeOf are not supported. Use VarType() or TypeName() instead.
Val	Use CDbl(), CInt(), or possibly Eval().

B

CMD and Batch File Language Reference

The format of the CMD command line is

cmd [/**a** | /**u**] [/**q**] [/**d**] [/**t:***bf*] [/**e:on**|**off**] [/**f:on**|**off**] [/**v:on**|**off**] [[/**s**]
  [/**c** | /**k**] *command*]

Table B.1 lists the options.

Table B.1 **CMD Command-Line Options**

Option	Description
/**a**	Causes standard output to use ANSI encoding.
/**u**	Causes standard output to use Unicode encoding.
/**q**	Turns batch file echo default to off.
/**d**	Disables execution of AutoRun commands defined in the Registry.
/**t:***bf*	Two digits set the background (window) and foreground (text) colors for the window. For example, /**t:1e** specifies yellow text on a blue background. Table 10.1 on page 439 lists the color values.
/**e**	Enables or disables the command extensions.
/**f**	Enables or disables the file and directory name completion feature.
/**v**	Enables or disables delayed environment variable expansion of !varname! items, as discussed in Chapter 11, "Batch Files for Fun and Profit."
/**x**	Same as /**e:on**.

continues

Table B.1   **Continued**

Option	Description
/y	Same as `/e:off`.
/s	Modifies the treatment of quotation marks on the command line, as discussed in Chapter 11.
/c	Executes the command(s) in *command* and then quits.
/r	Same as `/c`.
/k	Executes the command(s) in *command* and then reads further commands from the standard input until end of file or until the `exit` command is received.

Batch File Argument and **for** Variable Replacement

The expressions listed in Table B.2 expand into batch file command-line arguments and for command variables. In the expressions, *n* is an argument number or the letter corresponding to a for command variable.

Table B.2   **Argument and for Variable Replacement and Editing**

Expression	Result
%*n*	Argument or variable *n*.
%~*n*	Removes surrounding quotes (").
%~f*n*	Fully qualified path name.
%~d*n*	Drive letter only.
%~p*n*	Path only.
%~n*n*	File name only.
%~x*n*	File extension only.
%~s*n*	Short DOS 8.3 file and path.
%~a*n*	File attributes.
%~t*n*	Modification date/time of file.
%~z*n*	Length of file in bytes.
%~$PATH:*n*	Fully qualified name of first matching file when searching the **PATH**. If no file is found, the result is a zero-length string. The filename must include the proper extension; **PATHEXT** is not used.

The filename modifiers can be used in combination. For example, "%~dp*n*" returns the combined drive and path. Visit the Windows Help and Support Center for more examples (search for "for").

Environment Variable Expansion

The expressions listed in Table B.3 expand into environment variable values. In the expressions, *name* is the name of an environment variable.

Table B.3   **Environment Variable Replacement and Editing**

Expression	Result
%*name*%	Value of environment variable *name*.
%*name*:~*n*%	Skips the first *n* letters and returns the rest.
%*name*:~*n*,*m*%	Skips the first *n* letters and returns the next *m*.
%*name*:~,*m*%	First (leftmost) *m* letters.
%*name*:~ – *m*%	Last (rightmost) *m* letters.
%*name*:~, – *m*%	All but the last *m* letters.
%*name*:*str1*=*str2*%	Replaces every occurrence of *str1* with *str2*. *Str2* can be blank to delete all occurrences of *str1*. *Str1* can start with * to match any string characters ending with *str1*.
!*name*!	When Delayed Expansion is enabled with /v:on or setlocal ENABLEDELAYEDEXPANSION, this expression is replaced with the value of variable *name* just before the command is executed.

Predefined Environment Variables

Table B.4 lists the default environment variables defined automatically by Windows. Table B.5 lists dynamic variables that automatically reflect current system properties. The values shown are typical for Windows 7 and similar to Windows Vista. Windows XP values for user profile locations, however, are different. Use the environment variables to construct folder paths in your batch files, so you don't have to make assumptions about how user profile folders are organized.

Table B.4   **Predefined Environment Variables**

Variable Name	Typical Value
ALLUSERSPROFILE	C:\ProgramData
APPDATA	C:\Users*username*\AppData\Roaming
CommonProgramFiles	C:\Program Files\Common Files
COMPUTERNAME	*computername*
ComSpec	C:\WINDOWS\system32\cmd.exe
HOMEDRIVE	C:
HOMEPATH	\Users*username*

continues

Table B.4   **Continued**

Variable Name	Typical Value
LOCALAPPDATA*	C:\Users*username*\AppData\Local
LOGONSERVER	(Varies)
NUMBER_OF_PROCESSORS	(Varies)
OS	Windows_NT
Path	C:\WINDOWS\system32;C:\WINDOWS; C:\WINDOWS\System32\Wbem; C:\Windows\System32\WindowsPowerShell\v1.0 (varies depending on the location of Windows and add-on programs)
PATHEXT	.COM;.EXE;.BAT;.CMD;.VBS;.VBE;.JS ;.JSE;.WSF;.WSH;.MSC
PROCESSOR_ARCHITECTURE	(Varies)
PROCESSOR_IDENTIFIER	(Varies)
PROCESSOR_LEVEL	(Varies)
PROCESSOR_REVISION	(Varies)
ProgramData*	C:\ProgramData
ProgramFiles	C:\Program Files
PROMPT	PG
PUBLIC*	C:\Users\Public
SESSIONNAME	(Varies)
SystemDrive	C:
SystemRoot	C:\WINDOWS
TEMP	C:\users*username*\AppData\Local\Temp
TMP	C:\users*username*\AppData\Local\Temp
USERDOMAIN	*computername* or *domainname*
USERNAME	*username*
USERPROFILE	C:\Users*username*
windir	C:\WINDOWS

Not defined on Windows XP.

Table B.5 lists additional dynamic environment variables that are available when command extensions are enabled. If variables with these names are defined using the SET command or in the System Properties dialog box, these fixed definitions take precedence, and the dynamic values are not available.

Table B.5 **Dynamic Environment Variables**

Variable Name	Dynamic Value
CD	Current directory drive and path.
DATE	Current date, formatted by the DATE command.
TIME	Current time, formatted by the TIME command.
RANDOM	Random number between 0 and 32,767.
ERRORLEVEL	Exit status of previous program.
CMDEXTVERSION	Version number of command extensions.
CMDCMDLINE	Command line used to start CMD itself.

Command Formatting

Table B.6 lists the input/output redirection options. Multiple redirection options can be used on one command.

Table B.6 **Redirection and Multiple Command Formats**

Format	Result
command >filename	Directs output to file filename.
command >>filename	Appends output to filename.
command <filename	Command reads input from filename.
command 1>filename	Redirects standard output (same as >).
command 1>>filename	Appends standard output.
command 2>filename	Redirects standard error.
command 2>>filename	Appends standard error.
command 2>&1	Sends standard error to the same destination as standard output. Then, standard output can be redirected or piped.
command1 | command2	Standard output of command1 is piped to the standard input of command2.
command1 & command2	Multiple commands run sequentially.
command1 && command2	Like &, but command2 is run only if command1 is successful (exits with error status 0).
command1 || command2	Opposite of &&; command2 is run only if command1 fails.
(command)	Nests commands for if and for.
^x	Escapes special character x. For example, ^> is interpreted as the character ">" rather than a redirection operator.

Built-in Commands

Table B.7 lists the built-in commands implemented by CMD.

Table B.7 **Built-in Commands**

Command	Purpose
@*command*	Executes *command* without echoing it to the console.
:*label*	Identifies the target of goto *label* or call :*label*.
assoc	Associates file extensions with file types.
break	Causes a breakpoint in debugger; otherwise, it has no effect.
call *batchfile* [*arguments*...] **call** :*label* [*arguments*...]	Performs a "subroutine" call.
cd [[*drive:*]*directory*]	Changes the current working directory.
chdir [[*drive:*]*directory*]	Same as **cd**.
cls	Clears the screen (window).
color *bf*	Changes the screen color to **b** and the text color to **f** using the codes listed in Table 11.5.
copy [/**d**][/**v**][/**n**][/**y**|/**-y**] [/**z**][/**a**|/**b**] *source* [/**a**|/**b**] [+*source* [/**a**|/**b**]]... [*destination* [/**a**|/**b**]]	Copies files or folders from *source* to *destination*. The options are: /**d**—Decrypt files /**v**—Verify file integrity /**y**—Don't confirm overwrite /**z**—Network file copy /**a**—Use eASCII interpretation /**b**—Use binary interpretation
date [/**t**	*mm-dd-yyyy*]	Displays or sets the date. Option /**t** means don't prompt for a new date.
del *filename*... [/**p**|/**q**|/**f**][/**s**] [/**a**[:*attributes*]]	Deletes files, bypassing the Recycle Bin. The options are: /**p**—Prompt to confirm /**f**—Delete read-only files /**s**—Delete files in all subdirectories /**q**—Do not confirm /**a**—Delete files with specified attributes The attribute codes are: [-]R—Read-Only [-]S—System [-]H—Hidden [-]A—Archive Note that - before R, S, H, or A means "Select the file if the attribute is not set."

Command	Purpose
dir *pathname* ... [**/p**][**/q**] [**/w**|**/d**|**/b**|**/n**|**/x**][**/s**] [**/l**][**/c**][**/4**] [**/a**[[**:**]*attributes*]] [**/o**[[**:**]*sortfields*]] [**/t**[[**:**]*timefield*]]	Displays lists of files and/or folders in directories. The options are: /p—Pause every screenful /q—Display file owners' names /w—Multicolumn wide listing /d—Like /w but sorts columns /n—Long list format /x—Display 8.3 names /b—Brief listing: names only /s—Recurse into subfolders /l—Display names in lowercase /c—Use 1000's separators /4—Use four-digit year format /a—Select by attributes /o—Set sort order /t—Choose time field for sort or time to display
echo on|**off**	Enables or disables echo.
echo *text*	Types *text*.
echo.	Types a blank line.
endlocal	Restores variables and settings to pre-**setlocal** values.
erase	Same as **del**.
exit [**/b**] [*exitcode*]	Terminates the command or batch file. Option /b means terminate batch execution, not **CMD** itself.
for [*modifier*] **%**variable **in** (*list*) **do** command [*arguments*]	Executes *command* for each item in *list*. *List* can contain wildcards to match filenames. *Variable* is a single, case-sensitive letter that can be substituted anywhere in *command* or *arguments* using the replacement options listed in Table B.3. See Table B.7 for the *modifier* options. Use **%%** in batch files.
ftype *filetype*[=[*OpenCommand*]]	Displays or sets associations from file types to the "file open" command.
goto *label*	Jumps to *label*.
goto :EOF	Jumps to end of file.

continues

Table B.7 **Continued**

Command	Purpose

if *condition command*
if *condition* (*command*) **else**
   command
if *condition* (
   commands
) else (
   commands
)
Conditions:
  [**not**] *strng1* == *strng2*
  [**not**] **errorlevel** *number*
  [**not**] **exist** *filename*
  [**/i**] *strng1 compareop strng2*
  cmdextversion *number*
  defined *variable*
	Executes *command* if the condition is true. The optional *else* command is executed if the condition is not true. *Commands* can span more than one line if enclosed in parentheses. Option /I means ignore case in comparisons. *Compareops* are as follows:
	EQU—Equal to
	NEQ—Not equal to
	LSS—Less than
	LEQ—Less than or equal to
	GTR—Greater than
	GEQ—Greater than or equal to

md *pathname*	Creates directory path.
mkdir *pathname*	Same as md.
move [**/y**|**/-y**] *frompath topath*	Moves files or folders. Here's the one option: /y—Don't confirm overwrite.
path [*folder*[;*folder*...]]	Sets the search path and **path** environment variable.
pause	Prints "Press any key to continue" and waits.
popd	Restores the previous current directory saved by pushd.
prompt *TextAndCodes*	Sets the command prompt string and the prompt environment variable.
pushd *path*	Changes the directory and can also map a network drive.
rd [**/s**] [**/q**] *path*	Removes the directory named by *path*. With /s, it recursively deletes all subdirectories. Option /q suppresses the confirmation prompt.
rem *text*	Remark text.
rename *oldname newname*	Renames files or folders.
rmdir [**/s**] [**/q**] *path*	Same as rd.
set [*name*[=[*value*]]]	Sets or displays an environment variable.
set /a *expression*	Calculates an arithmetic expression. See Table B.2.
set /p *name=promptstring*	Prompts for input.

Command	Purpose
setlocal [**enableextensions**| **disableextensions**] [**enabledelayedexpansion**| **disabledelayedexpansion**]	Saves environment variables, the working directory, and option settings.
shift [/*n*]	Shifts batch arguments by deleting the first argument or the argument number specified by optopn /*n*.
start "*title*" [/**d***path*] [/**i**] [/**min** | /**max**] [/**separate** | /**shared**] [/**low** | /**belownormal** | /**normal** | /**abovenormal** | /**high** | /**realtime**] [/**wait**] [/**b**] *command* [*arguments*]	Starts a command in a new window. The options are /d—Set default directory /i—Use initial environment /min—Start minimized /max—Start maximized /separate—Use separate Win16 process★ /shared—Use common Win16 process★ /low.../realtime—Set priority /wait—Wait for exit /b—Use same window
time [/**t** | *hh*:*mm*:**ss**]	Displays or sets the time. Option /t means don't prompt for new time.
title [*string*]	Sets the window title.
type *filename*	Writes a file's contents to the standard output.
ver	Displays the Windows version.
vol [*drive*:]	Displays the disk volume label.

★*32-bit versions of Windows only. 64-bit versions cannot run 16-bit Windows applications.*

For Command Modifiers

Table B.8 lists the modifiers that might precede the (*list*) entry in a `for` command when command extensions are enabled.

Table B.8 *For* **Command Modifiers**

Modifier	Effect
/**D**	Wildcards in *set* match directories only.
/**R** [*path*]	Executes the `for` statement in the specified directory and all its subdirectories.

continues

Table B.8 **Continued**

Modifier	Effect
/L	Steps *variable* through a range of numeric values. *Set* must be in the form *start#,step#,end#*.
/F ["*keywords*"]	Reads the contents of the file(s) named in *list* and parses them for text strings. The results are used as the set of values for the **for** variable. The output of a command can be used as the text source by specifying ('*command*') as the (*list*) entry. The hideous syntax for this option is discussed in the Windows Help and Support Center (search for "for").

set /a Expression Operators

Table B.9 lists operators that might be used in arithmetic expressions in the **set** /a command. The operators are listed in decreasing order of precedence.

Table B.9 *set* /a **Expression Operators**

Operators	Functions
( )	Expression grouping.
! ~ -	Unary operators: boolean NOT, bitwise invert, arithmetic negative.
* / %	Multiply, divide, remainder.
+ -	Add, subtract.
<< >>	Bitwise shift left, shift right.
&	Bitwise AND.
| ^	Bitwise OR and exclusive OR.
=	Assignment.
*= /= %= += -= &= ^= |= <<= >>=	Combined math and assignment operators borrowed from the C programming language: A += 3 is the same as A = A + 3.
,	Separates multiple expressions.

Any alphanumeric tokens are taken to indicate environment variables. In an expression, if a named environment variable is undefined or does not contain a number, it is treated as the value **0**. Variables are treated as decimal numbers, except that numbers starting with **0x** are interpreted as hexadecimal (base 16), and numbers starting with **0** are treated as octal (base 8).

C

Command Line Program Reference

This appendix lists all the executable programs provided with Windows 7, Vista, and XP that can be used from the command line. Graphical user interface (GUI) programs, executable programs that operate only as system services, and programs that are otherwise not directly usable from the command prompt are (for the most part) not listed.

In the following sections, in the OS column,

X means the programs is available in Windows XP Professional.

V means the program is available in Windows Vista Ultimate edition.

7 means the program is available in Windows 7 Ultimate edition.

Lower-level editions of Windows might not include all these programs.

In addition, some Windows installations include extra programs not listed here, and some do not include all of these standard programs. Variations occur due to differing hardware configurations (Windows tends not to install software when there is no installed hardware that can use it) and due to corporate licensing and policy decisions.

Administrative Tools

The following programs can be used to configure and manage Windows.

Program	OS	Purpose
appcmd	V7	IIS Application Server configuration tool
asr_fmt	X	Automated System Recovery backup and restore
asr_ldm	X	Automated System Recovery Logical Disk manager
at	XV7	Add/manage scheduled tasks
auditpol	V7	Configures audit policy
auditusr	X	Configures audit policy
bcdedit	V7	Configures "new" Windows boot manager
bdehdcfg	V7	Bitlocker Drive Preparation tool
bitsadmin	V7	Windows Update downloader config tool
bootcfg	XV7	Modifies the "old" BOOT.INI configuration file
certreq	V7	Certificate request tool
certutil	V7	Certificate management tool
cmdkey	V7	Manages stored credentials (passwords)
cscript	XV7	Windows Script Host (command-line version)
diskperf	XV7	Starts the physical disk performance counters
dispdiag	V7	Extracts graphic adapter diagnostic information
driverquery	XV7	Lists the installed device drivers
esentutl	XV7	MS database utility
eventcreate	XV7	Adds an event to the event log
eventquery	X	Lists events from the event log★
eventtriggers	X	Displays and configures event triggers
fsutil	XV7	Manages the Windows file system
gpresult	XV7	Computes and displays Group Policy Resultant Set of Policy
gpupdate	XV7	Forces the update of Local and Group Policy settings
grpconv	XV7	Program Manager Group converter
iexpress	XV7	Creates simple Installer applications
ktmutil	V7	Kernel transaction manager utility
lodctr	XV7	Installs, backs up, or restores performance-counter definitions
logman	XV7	Schedules the automatic collection of performance information
msg	XV7	Sends a message to another user
odbcconf	XV7	Configures ODBC database drivers and data sources
openfiles	XV7	Displays files in use by local processes or network users
pagefileconfig	X	Manages the virtual memory page file★
printui	V7	Installs and configures printers

★*VBScript program*

Program	**OS**	**Purpose**
prncnfg	XV7	Configures printers★°
prndrvr	XV7	Installs and lists print drivers★°
prnjobs	XV7	Manages print jobs★°
prnmngr	XV7	Manages local and network printer connections★°
prnqctl	XV7	Prints test pages as well as starts and stops the printer queue★°
qprocess	XV7	Displays information about processes (local or remote)
qwinsta	XV7	Displays information about Terminal Services sessions
reg	XV7	Edits or displays Registry data
regedit	XV7	Edits the Registry
regini	XV7	Creates Registry entries and sets permissions
relog	XV7	Changes the format or rate for performance log files
reset	XV7	Deletes a Terminal Services session
rsm	XV7	Manages removable storage media pools
runas	XV7	Runs a program with another user's credentials
rundll32	XV7	Launches a 32-bit DLL program
rwinsta	XV7	Resets the session subsystem hardware and software to their known initial values
sc	XV7	Displays and manages installed services
schtasks	XV7	Displays and manages scheduled tasks
sdbinst	XV7	Application compatibility database installer
setx	V7	Sets default or system-wide environment variables
sfc	XV7	Verifies system file integrity
shadow	XV7	Monitors or controls a Terminal Services session
shutdown	XV7	Shuts down, logs off, or restarts a computer
sxstrace	V7	Side-By-Side (SXS) debugging tool
syskey	XV7	Encrypts and secures the system database
systeminfo	XV7	Displays a system hardware and software summary
taskkill	XV7	Terminates a process
tasklist	XV7	Lists active processes
tracerpt	XV7	Gathers or summarizes event trace information
tsdiscon	XV7	Disconnects a Windows/Terminal Services session
tskill	XV7	Terminates a process in a Terminal Services session
tsshutdn	X	Shuts down or restarts a Terminal Services server
typeperf	XV7	Displays performance data
unlodctr	XV7	Removes performance-counter definitions
vssadmin	XV7	Displays shadow copy backups and providers
wecutil	V7	Manages subscription to remote management event notifications

★*VBScript program*

°*On Windows 7 and Vista, these are located in \windows\system32\Printing_Admin_Scripts\xx-xx, where xx-xx is the local language code.*

Program	OS	Purpose
wevtutil	V7	Extracts information from the Event Logs
whoami	V7	Prints name of logged-on user
winmsd	X	Displays system-configuration information
wmic	XV7	Queries and manages Windows XP via Windows Management Instrumentation
wusa	V7	Installs Windows Update packages manually
wscript	XV7	Windows Script Host (windowed version)

Built-in and Batch File Commands

The following commands are implemented by CMD.EXE and perform basic file and console window management functions as well as provide the basis for the batch file programming language. These built-in commands are available in every edition of Windows 7, Vista, and XP.

Program	Purpose
assoc	Associates filename extensions with file types
break	Does nothing
call	Calls subroutines (batch files)
cd	Changes the current working directory (same as chdir)
chcp	Changes the console code page
chdir	Changes the current working directory (same as cd)
cls	Clears the command prompt window
cmd	Command shell
color	Changes the Command Prompt window color
copy	Copies files and/or folders
date	Displays or sets the date
del	Deletes files (same as erase)
dir	Displays a file directory
echo	Displays text
endlocal	Restores environment variables
erase	Deletes files (same as del)
exit	Ends a program or subroutine
for	Repeat command (many options)
ftype	Associates file types to "open" commands
goto	Goes to the label in a batch file
help	Displays command-line program usage information
if	Executes a command conditionally
md	Creates a directory (same as mkdir)
mkdir	Creates a directory (same as md)
move	Moves files or folders

Program	Purpose
path	Sets the command search path
pause	Stops a batch file until the user presses Enter
popd	Restores the current directory
prompt	Sets the command-line prompt
pushd	Saves the current directory
rd	Removes a directory (same as `rmdir`)
rem	Remarks or comments text
ren	Renames files or folders (same as `rename`)
rename	Renames files or folders (same as `ren`)
rmdir	Removes a directory (same as `rd`)
set	Sets environment variables
setlocal	Saves the current environment
shift	Deletes and moves command-line arguments
start	Runs a command or opens a document in a new window
time	Displays and sets the time of day
title	Sets the window title
type	Copies a text file to the console window
ver	Displays the operating system version
verify	Controls automatic verify-after-write
vol	Displays disk volume label

DOS Commands

The following programs are provided for compatibility with MS-DOS programs and legacy DOS batch files. These commands are available on all 32-bit editions of Windows 7, Vista, and XP, except as noted. On 64-bit editions, only the commands with asterisks (★) are available (because they are Windows console applications, which is not true MS-DOS applications).

Program	Purpose
append	Makes directories appear "local" (archaic)
command	MS-DOS command shell
debug	Debugs programs (archaic)
diskcomp	Compares two floppy disks ★
diskcopy	Copies a floppy disk ★
doskey	Command-line aliases and editing extensions ★
dosx	DOS Extender, loaded in `AUTOEXEC.NT`
edit	Edits text files
edlin	Edits text files (primeval)
exe2bin	Converts EXE files to COM files (archaic)
fastopen	Does nothing

★Available on 64-bit Windows

Program	Purpose
forcedos	Runs a program in the MS-DOS environment (XP only)
graftabl	Enables the display of graphics characters in the MS-DOS environment
graphics	Loads the graphics printer driver (obsolete)
loadfix	Runs a program above the first 64KB of memory
loadhigh	Loads an MS-DOS Terminate-and-Stay-Resident (TSR) program into high memory
mem	Displays free memory in the MS-DOS subsystem
mode	Configures port, display, and keyboard settings ★
mscdexnt	MS CD Extensions, loaded in AUTOEXEC.NT
nlsfunc	Loads country/region information
ntvdm	MS-DOS virtual machine environment
nw16	NetWare 16-bit redirector, loaded in AUTOEXEC.NT (XP only)
print	Copies a file to a local LPT-port printer ★
redir	Networking redirector, loaded in AUTOEXEC.NT
setver	Lies about the MS-DOS version to old applications
share	Does nothing on Windows XP
subst	Maps a drive letter to a local folder ★
vwipxspx	NetWare protocol stack, loaded in AUTOEXEC.NT (XP only)

★Available on 64-bit Windows

File-Management Commands

Most GUI disk-management programs and tools have command-line counterparts. The following commands manage files, disks, and directories.

Program	OS	Purpose
attrib	XV7	Displays and sets file/folder attributes
cacls	XV7	Displays and modifies NTFS permissions
chkdsk	XV7	Checks and repairs file system integrity
chkntfs	XV7	Schedules automatic chkdsk at boot time
cipher	XV7	Encrypts and decrypts files and folders
clip	V7	Copies data to or from clipboard
comp	XV7	Compares files
compact	XV7	Enables and disables file and folder compression
convert	XV7	Schedules the conversion of a volume from FAT to NTFS
defrag	XV7	Defragments a disk volume
diantz	XV7	Compress files into a CAB file (same as makecab)
diskpart	XV7	Manages disk partitions
diskraid	V7	Manages RAID disk configuration
expand	XV7	Expands a file from a CAB file

★VBScript program

Program	OS	Purpose
fc	XV7	Compares files
find	XV7	Finds text in files
findstr	XV7	Finds text in files using regular expressions
forfiles	V7	Executes a command on each of several files
format	XV7	Formats a fixed or removable disk
icacls	V7	Saves, edits, and restores NTFS permissions
label	XV7	Sets the volume label on a disk or mount point
makecab	XV7	Compresses files into a CAB file
mountvol	XV7	Creates, deletes, and lists volume mount points
recover	XV7	Extracts data from a damaged disk
replace	XV7	Replaces files
takeown	V7	Takes ownership of a file
tree	XV7	Displays the directory structure
wbadmin	V7	Configures Windows Backup
where	V7	Searches for files by name
xcopy	XV7	Copies multiple files

Handy Programs

Several useful, general-purpose programs are somewhat difficult to categorize.

Program	OS	Purpose
choice	V7	Batch file tool: prompts for user input
logoff	XV7	Logs off from Windows
more	XV7	Displays text a page at a time
sort	XV7	Sorts text files alphabetically (filter)
timeout	V7	Pauses batch file for specified time period
waitfor	V7	Coordinates activity between multiple computers

Networking Tools

Windows comes with a large set of programs that lets you manage, configure, and use Windows networking functions.

Program	OS	Purpose
atmadm	X	Manages ATM network connections
change	XV7	Manages Terminal Services (remote desktop)
getmac	XV7	Displays network adapter MAC addresses
ipsec6	X	Configures IPSec over IPv6 security
ipv6	X	Installs and configures IPv6
ipxroute	X	Displays and edits the TCP/IP routing table
mrinfo	XV7	Queries multicast router configuration using SNMP
nbtstat	XV7	Displays NetBIOS-over-TCP/IP statistics and name tables
net	XV7	Networking management utility
netcfg	V7	Network component installation/config tool
netsh	XV7	Network-configuration utility (very powerful!)
pubprn	XV7	Publishes printers to Active Directory*°
qappsrv	XV7	Displays the available application terminal servers on the network
rasautou	XV7	Creates a dial-up or VPN connection
rasdial	XV7	Starts and ends Dial-up Networking connections
rasphone	XV7	Pop-up Dial-up Networking manager
rpcping	V7	Remote Procedure Call diagnostic tool
tscon	XV7	Manages terminal server (remote desktop) connections

*VBScript program

°On Windows 7 and Vista, this is located in \windows\system32\Printing_Admin_Scripts\xx-xx, where xx-xx is the local language code.

Software Development Aids

Several programs are used to configure Windows program exception handling and to configure system services used in the development of Windows applications.

Program	OS	Purpose
clspack	X	Lists Java system packages
drwatson	XV7	Dr. Watson for Win16 programs (not on 64-bit editions)
drwtsn32	X	Configures Dr. Watson for Win32 programs
iexpress	XV7	Creates simple Installer applications
mqbkup	X	MS Message Queue backup and restore utility
ntsd	X	System-level debugger
regsvr32	XC7	Registers a DLL file as a COM component

TCP/IP Utilities

Windows includes a complement of TCP/IP utilities that provides cross-platform compatibility with Unix systems as well as general-purpose TCP/IP diagnostic and configuration tools. The commands with asterisks (*) are not installed by default on all versions of Windows; you might need to install optional Windows components ("Turn Windows Features On and Off"). On Windows 7 and Vista, the Unix "r" commands are only available as part of the Subsystem for Unix Based Applications, and then—only on Enterprise—Professional/Business and Ultimate editions.

Program	OS	Purpose
arp	XV7	Displays and edits the ARP cache
finger	XV7	Displays information about a user (Unix)
ftp	XV7	File Transfer Protocol
hostname	XV7	Displays the local computer's TCP/IP hostname
ipconfig	XV7	Displays the TCP/IP configuration and manages DHCP leases
lpq	XV7	Displays the printer queue (Unix)*
lpr	XV7	Prints a file (Unix)*
netstat	XV7	Displays the current TCP/IP connections and open sockets
nslookup	XV7	Queries DNS servers
pathping	XV7	Tests TCP/IP connectivity
ping	XV7	Tests TCP/IP connectivity
ping6	X	IPv6 Ping (use ping -6 on Windows 7 and Vista)
prnport	X	Manages TCP/IP printers*
proxycfg	X	Sets the HTTP Proxy server
rcp	X	Copies files to another computer (Unix)*
rexec	X	Unix remote execute*
route	XV7	Displays or edits the current routing tables
rsh	X	Remote shell (Unix) *
telnet	XV7	Establishes a command-line session on another computer*
tftp	XV7	Trivial File Transfer Protocol
tlntadmn	XV7	Telnet Server Administrator*
tlntsess	X	Displays the current Telnet server sessions*
tracert	XV7	Checks TCP/IP connectivity
tracert6	X	IPv6 trace route (use tracert -6 on Windows 7 and Vista)

*Installed with various optional Windows features

Windows GUI Programs

I said that this appendix would not list GUI programs. I lied. Some GUI programs are actually useful, and if you know them by name, you can easily run them from the command line or the Start menu's Search or Run box. You can run them from scripts or batch files as well. Remember that if you run a GUI program from a batch file, the batch file will not proceed until the GUI program exits, unless you precede the GUI command with the `start` command.

Items marked with an asterisk are Microsoft Management Console plug-ins. To run them on XP, precede the name with `start`, and add `.msc` to the end of the program name

Program	OS	Purpose
calc	XV7	Windows calculator
cleanmgr	XV7	Disk-cleanup program
cliconfg	XV7	SQL Server client network utility
clipbrd	X	Clipboard viewer (multiuser)
control	XV7	Opens the Control Panel
colorcpl	V7	Opens Color Manangement
compmgmt	XV7	Opens Computer Management★
dcomcnfg	XV7	Displays and manages DCOM configuration
dxdiag	XV7	Direct-X diagnostics
eudcedit	XV7	Private character editor
eventvwr	XV7	Event Viewer
explorer	XV7	Windows Explorer
fontview	XV7	Displays fonts in a font file
fxsclnt	X	Fax console
fxscover	XV7	Fax cover page editor
fxssend	X	Send Fax Wizard
hh	XV7	HTML Help
mmc	XV7	Microsoft Management Console
mobsync	XV7	Synchronization Manager/Wizard
mplay32	X	MS Media Player
mspaint	XV7	Microsoft Paint
mstsc	XV7	Terminal Services client (remote desktop)
netsetup	X	Network Setup Wizard
notepad	XV7	Notepad accessory
ntbackup	X	Backs up and restores files
optionalfeatures	V7	Turn Windows Features On or Off control panel
osk	XV7	Onscreen keyboard
perfmon	XV7	Performance console with a Windows NT 4 settings file
regedt32	XV7	Registry editor (old version)
rtcshare	X	NetMeeting Desktop Sharing
sdclt	V7	Windows Backup

Program	OS	Purpose
secedit	XV7	Manages and analyzes system security policies
shrpubw	XV7	Create and Share Folders Wizard
sigverif	XV7	Signature verifier for system files
sndrec32	X	Sound Recorder
sndvol32	X	Volume control
sysedit	XV	Edits obsolete Windows configuration files
taskmgr	XV7	Starts the Task Manager (same as Ctrl+Alt+Del)
tcmsetup	XV7	Manages the TAPI Telephony client
verifier	XV7	Driver Verifier Manager
wfs	V7	Windows Fax and Scan
wiaacmgr	XV7	Scanner and Camera Wizard
winchat	X	Windows Chat
winhelp	XV7	Windows Help (HLP file) viewer (not on 64-bit Windows)
winhlp32	X	Windows Help file viewer
winmine	X	Minesweeper game
winver	XV7	Displays the current version of Windows
wuapp	V7	Windows Update
write	XV7	WordPad accessory
wupdmgr	X	Windows Update (launches Internet Explorer)

Finally, while these were listed more completely in Table 13.1 (page 546), let me remind you of some quick commands to launch frequently used control panel applets.

Command	Control Panel
start appwiz.cpl	Add/Remove Programs
start firewall.cpl	Windows Firewall
start ncpa.cpl	Network Connections
start sysdm.cpl	System Properties

D
Index of Patterns and Sample Scripts

Index of Patterns

Index of Sample Scripts and Batch Files

Index

B

X-Y-Z

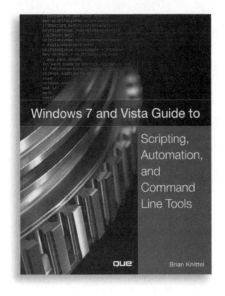

FREE Online Edition

Your purchase of **Windows 7 and Vista Guide to Scripting, Automation, and Command Line Tools** includes access to a free online edition for 45 days through the Safari Books Online subscription service. Nearly every Que book is available online through Safari Books Online, along with more than 5,000 other technical books and videos from publishers such as Addison-Wesley Professional, Cisco Press, Exam Cram, IBM Press, O'Reilly, Prentice Hall, and Sams.

SAFARI BOOKS ONLINE allows you to search for a specific answer, cut and paste code, download chapters, and stay current with emerging technologies.

Activate your FREE Online Edition at www.informit.com/safarifree

> **STEP 1:** Enter the coupon code: PJLKYFA.

> **STEP 2:** New Safari users, complete the brief registration form.
> Safari subscribers, just log in.

If you have difficulty registering on Safari or accessing the online edition, please e-mail customer-service@safaribooksonline.com